How This Book Will Make You a More Successful Writer

By applying rhetorical reading techniques to your writing, you will learn

- To shape your own texts to accomplish your specific purposes in relation to varying situations and audiences

- To use the composing processes of skilled academic writers

- To practice the three ways that writers typically use readings in academic settings: as models to adapt, as objects to analyze, and as voices to respond to in a conversation

- To communicate your understanding of a text through effective summaries and paraphrases

- To expand your repertoire of writing strategies so that you can adopt and use methods you encounter in a wide variety of texts

- To write successful analyses and critiques of a text's argument and rhetorical strategies

- To write successful college-level research papers that address significant questions and make important points within a larger conversation

- To follow appropriate conventions for incorporating excerpts from source materials into your own writing without letting them take over your paper

How This Book Will Make You
a More Successful Writer

Reading Rhetorically

A Reader for Writers

JOHN C. BEAN
Seattle University

VIRGINIA A. CHAPPELL
Marquette University

ALICE M. GILLAM
University of Wisconsin–Milwaukee

New York • San Francisco • Boston
London • Toronto • Sydney • Tokyo • Singapore • Madrid
Mexico City • Munich • Paris • Cape Town • Hong Kong • Montreal

Vice President/Publisher: Eben W. Ludlow
Executive Marketing Manager: Carlise Paulson
Supplements Editor: Donna Campion
Production Manager: Charles Annis
Project Coordination, Text Design, and Electronic Page Makeup: Pre-Press Company, Inc.
Cover Design Manager: Wendy Fredericks
Manufacturing Buyer: Al Dorsey
Printer and Binder: RR Donnelley and Sons, Co.
Cover Printer: The Lehigh Press, Inc.

Library of Congress Cataloging-in-Publication Data

Bean, John C.
   Reading rhetorically: a reader for writers / John C. Bean, Virginia A. Chappell, Alice M. Gillam.
      p. cm.
   Includes bibliographical references and index.
   ISBN 0-205-30885-6 (alk. paper)
   1. College readers. 2. English language—Rhetoric—Problems, exercises, etc. 3. Report writing—Problems, exercises, etc. I. Chappell, Virginia A. II. Gillam, Alice M. III. Title.

PE1417 .B393 2001
808'.0427—dc21   2001041414

ISBN 0-205-30885-6

DOH—04 03 02

10 9 8 7 6 5 4 3 2

Contents

———— • ————

3   *Strategies for Reading Rhetorically*   27

Part Two: Reading and Responding to Texts

4   *Listening to a Text*   45

Part Four: An Anthology of Readings

9   *Expressing and Reflecting*   147

10 *Inquiring and Exploring*   *209*

11 *Informing and Explaining*   255

15 *Proposing Solutions*   491

16 *Seeking Common Ground*   *531*

Thematic Contents

———— • ————

Preface

———— • ————

Reading Rhetorically grows out of our belief that academic reading, writing, and inquiry are inextricably linked and that all three are best learned within a rhetorical framework. Increasingly, many first-year writing courses emphasize reading as well as writing, not because students have reading problems but because college writing assignments require the ability to read analytically. Despite this increased emphasis on reading, few textbooks explicitly address reading as a process and those that do seldom treat reading as a rhetorical act. *Reading Rhetorically* does both.

Reading Rhetorically is an aims-based reader that teaches students to read rhetorically and to write about what they have read with rhetorical insight. Two important features distinguish it from other first-year readers: (1) its emphasis on reading as an interactive process of composing meaning, and (2) its emphasis on academic writing as a process in which writers engage with other texts. *Reading Rhetorically* teaches students how to see texts as positioned in a conversation with other texts, how to recognize the bias or perspective of a given text, and how to analyze texts for both content and rhetorical method. The book defines "reading rhetorically" as attending to a writer's purposes within a rhetorical situation by examining both what the author says and how he or she says it. Specifically, this book teaches students how to analyze other texts by reading them with and against the grain, how to imitate other texts by learning their rhetorical strategies and genre conventions, and how to use other texts for their own purposes in conducting research. Many composition readers offer readings that provide either topics or models for student writing. In contrast, this collection organizes its selections by rhetorical aims. Our goal is to offer readings for rhetorical analysis so that students can learn about and then apply various rhetorical strategies in their own writing.

Distinctive Features

Reading Rhetorically is distinguished by the following features:

- The anthology contains high-interest readings that vary widely by aim, genre, length, subject matter, and rhetorical situation. These readings span a range of textual types that students will encounter in college.
- Explanations of rhetorical concepts provide an analytical framework for both reading and writing.

- Discussion of reading processes shows students how skilled academic readers construct a text's meaning.
- Presentation of writing processes emphasizes strategies for writing about reading.
- Three strands of writing assignments invite students to engage with the readings in the anthology chapters by (1) writing to match the rhetorical aim of the chapter's readings, (2) writing to examine rhetorical strategies, and (3) writing to conduct inquiry and synthesize multiple readings.
- Research is treated as a process of rhetorical reading in which students learn to develop research questions and evaluate sources within a rhetorical context.
- Citation conventions are presented as integral to rhetorical effectiveness.
- Through an extended example, the text follows the evolution of one student's writing project through several phases as the student moves from summary to rhetorical analysis to researched critique of a reading.
- Extensive discussion of argument introduces important concepts for rhetorical analysis such as categories of claims and ethical, logical, and audience-based appeals. In addition, the discussion of argument recognizes distinct forms of argument—position statements, evaluative arguments, proposals, and Rogerian arguments.
- All eight anthology chapters include a sample of student writing, three of them with MLA internal citations and a works cited list.
- The anthology features individual chapters on two important but often ignored aims: writing to explore and writing to seek common ground.
- Each reading selection is accompanied by prompts for (1) preview, (2) rhetorical analysis, and (3) application of techniques to one's own writing.
- The appendix integrates citation formats for print and electronic materials (including periodicals databases) in an extensive list of model MLA style citations.

Structure

The opening instructional portion of the text (Chapters 1 through 8) is organized into three parts that explain the demands of college reading and writing and offer conceptual frameworks and practical strategies for meeting these demands. Part One (Chapters 1 through 3) begins by asking students to reflect on *what* they read and *why*. Chapters 2 and 3 describe the special demands of academic reading and introduce students to the rhetorical reading strategies used by experts: building a context for reading and matching reading strategies to a text's genre and purpose. Part Two (Chapters 4 and 5) teaches students *how* to read rhetorically, first by "listening" to what a text is saying and doing, and second by "questioning" what a text is saying and doing. Chapter 4 offers practice in listening through annotating, mapping idea structure, summarizing, descriptive outlining, and writing a rhetorical précis, while Chapter 5 provides practice in questioning through analysis of a text's rhetorical appeals, language, and ideology.

Part Three (Chapters 6 through 8) focuses on writing about reading. Chapter 6 begins with an overview of typical reading-based writing assignments across the curriculum and then advises students on how to maintain writerly authority and manage their writing process as they write about what they have read. Chapter 7 teaches students how to use rhetorical reading as a research strategy as they formulate research questions and then choose readings by evaluating their relevance and reliability. Chapter 8 instructs students in the conventions of source based writing—summary, paraphrase, direct quotation, citation formats—by placing these practices in a rhetorical framework.

Part Four (Chapters 9 through 16) offers an anthology of readings organized by aim. Each chapter in the anthology begins by examining distinctive features of each rhetorical aim: expressing and reflecting; inquiring and exploring; informing and explaining; analyzing and interpreting; taking a stand; evaluating and judging; proposing solutions; and seeking common ground. Readings are accompanied by a contextualizing headnote, preview questions for reading logs, and questions that help students analyze rhetorical methods and recognize techniques they might adopt in their own writing. Chapters end with a set of three writing assignments based on ways in which academic writers use readings: as models, objects for analysis, and voices in a conversation.

Three Strands of Writing Assignments

The three writing assignments that appear at the end of each chapter in Part Four invite students to engage with the chapter's readings in ways that parallel common academic ways of writing about reading:

- *As models:* Options in this strand ask students to write in a particular aims-based genre, using their own topic and purpose. This book's emphasis on rhetorical reading takes students beyond the usual imitation assignments found in other aims-based readers. Before trying their hand at a given type of writing, students learn to examine how context and genre affect writers' rhetorical choices.
- *As objects of analysis:* Options in this strand ask students to analyze rhetorically one or more of the texts in the chapter. Because many academic writers take as their field of study the texts produced by others (for example, historians analyze primary source documents, cultural critics analyze song lyrics or advertisements, lawyers examine the laws and statutes produced by legislators or the decisions of appellate courts), this strand prepares students for a type of writing assignment frequently encountered across the curriculum. In producing their own rhetorical analyses, students are aided by the questions that begin each chapter and those that accompany each reading. These questions help students identify and evaluate the effects of authors' rhetorical choices and offer beginning points for analytical essays.
- *As voices in a conversation:* Options in this strand ask students to place texts in conversation with one another and to join that conversation by

forwarding their own argument. These assignments invite students to use the readings in the chapter as a springboard for inquiry and discovery. Nearly all call for further research based on carefully formulated research questions and rhetorically based strategies for assessment and selection of sources. This strand of assignments prepares students to write the kind of multisource research papers frequently required in college courses across the curriculum.

Together, these strands offer instructors flexibility in the design and sequencing of assignments and give students guided practice in the three main ways that academic readers use texts in their writing.

Apparatus

The apparatus for the readings in the anthology section, Part Four, builds on the rhetorical reading concepts introduced in the first three parts. Specifically, Chapters 9 through 16 each begin with a discussion of the ways in which a particular rhetorical aim shapes a text and influences reader response. Following this discussion students will find a series of generic questions designed to facilitate their rhetorical reading of the chapter's texts. Because the questions are based on rhetorical features common to texts within a particular aim, these questions encourage focused rhetorical reading.

To enable students to read each text through a rhetorical lens, *Reading Rhetorically* provides contextualizing headnotes and pre- and post-reading questions. Headnotes provide not only biographical information about the author or authors but also information about the original context of the text's publication. Each reading selection is preceded by "For Your Reading Log" questions that ask students to consider their background knowledge and attitudes toward the text's topic and make predictions about the text. The "Thinking Critically" questions that follow each reading are of two types: "Responding as a Reader" and "Responding as a Writer." Generally, the first set of questions asks students to reflect on their experience of reading a given text and helps them analyze the ways it works rhetorically, both internally and in relationship to various external contexts. The second set of questions is designed to help students identify writing strategies that they might transfer to their own writing.

Strategies for Using **Reading Rhetorically**

The text's organizational structure facilitates easy syllabus design. The introductory chapters (Chapters 1 through 8) provide conceptual frameworks and practical strategies for reading and writing about the texts that appear in Part Four. Because the first three parts provide numerous opportunities for practicing the strategies being presented, students can work their way through these first eight chapters before proceeding to the anthology chapters, or they can move back and forth between parts, trying out the reading and writing strategies on the selections in the anthology chapters.

Organized by aim, the anthology section offers high-interest reading selections that vary widely by aim, genre, length, and subject matter. There are many ways to use the chapters in the anthology section; instructors can select the aims-based chapters that best fit their course goals. For those instructors who wish to select readings by theme, we provide a thematic table of contents.

Reading Rhetorically is accompanied by an *Instructor's Resource Manual* and *Companion Website* <www.ablongman.com/bean> that offer teaching suggestions to assist both experienced and new instructors, including suggested syllabi, chapter-by-chapter teaching ideas, and additional resources for student reading and research. In addition, the manual suggests activities that will help students meet the outcomes identified in the Council of Writing Program Administrators' *Outcomes Statement:* (1) rhetorical knowledge; (2) the ability to connect critical thinking, reading, and writing; (3) acquisition of writing process strategies; and (4) knowledge of academic writing conventions and genres.

Acknowledgments

We begin by thanking colleagues at each of our universities who have assisted us in preparing this text: Jami Carlacio, Shelley Circle, and Crystal Grotberg at the University of Wisconsin–Milwaukee and Colin Irvine, Meg Jaskolski, Dan Knauss, Robert McGuire, and Julie O'Keefe at Marquette University. John Bean also thanks June Johnson, his colleague at Seattle University, for her insights into teaching rhetorical reading.

Deep appreciation goes to our editor, Eben Ludlow, vice president of Longman Publishers. His enthusiastic support and wise counsel were a central inspiration for our work. In addition, our sincere thanks go to Marcy Lunetta of Page-to-Page and the able staff at Allyn & Bacon/Longman, especially Doug Day and Greg Bell, who assisted us at various stages of this book's creation and production.

To the colleagues from other universities who reviewed *Reading Rhetorically* in its various stages of development, we owe special thanks: Larry Beason, University of South Alabama; Carol A. Lowe, McLennan Community College; James C. McDonald, University of Louisiana at Lafayette; Kathy Overhulse Smith, Indiana University Bloomington; James Wallace, University of Akron.

Finally, we would like to thank our students. Truly, the insights that inform this book largely come from what we have learned from them. For these learning opportunities we are profoundly grateful.

Reading Rhetorically

CHAPTER

1

Your Life as a Reader

Reading is food for the mind and soul. It is counsel. It is calm.
It is. It is a constant reminder of the story yet to be told.

—Isoke Titilayo Nia

Beginning college students are often overwhelmed by the heavy reading they are assigned in college, intimidated by its complexity, and bewildered by their teachers' expectations. For the most part, students adapt to these new demands, gradually learn what academic reading entails, and—by the time they are juniors and seniors within their major fields—learn how to do the reading and writing demanded in their disciplines and future professions. But the process is often slow and frustrating, marked by trial and error and the panicky feeling that reading this way is like hacking through a jungle when there might be a path nearby that could make the journey easier.

This book is designed to help you find that path and thus accelerate your growth as a strong academic reader and writer. It aims to describe the special demands and pleasures of academic reading, teach you the reading strategies used by experts, and show you the interconnections between reading and writing in almost all college courses. As you can see from the table of contents, the last and largest section of this book (Part Four, comprising Chapters 9–16) is an anthology of readings, arranged along a spectrum of writers' purposes, chosen to illustrate the wide range of styles, subject matter, and formats (or "genres") that you are likely to encounter in college or the world of work. Preceding the anthology are three parts (Chapters 1–8) that explain strategies for handling the demands of college reading assignments and of writing assignments based on readings. Part One, "Reading Rhetorically," invites you to explore your changing purposes for reading and teaches you how to *read rhetorically*—that is, to pay attention both to what authors say and to how they say it. Reading this way enables you to discern how well your purposes for reading match the author's purposes for writing. Part Two, "Reading and Responding to Texts," addresses the nuts and bolts of reading by presenting a compendium of reading strategies used by experts—strategies that you can employ to become a more effective reader and writer. Part Three, "The Rhetorical Reader as Writer," focuses on the connections between reading and writing processes. Because most of your college writing assignments will probably involve readings that you are asked to imitate, analyze, or use as source material in pursuing your own inquiry, these chapters show you how to apply rhetorical reading strategies to your own writing.

Throughout these instructional chapters and the anthology itself, we stress the value of rhetorical reading's double focus on "what" and "how." The "how" is particularly important because writers try to change their readers' view of a subject, and you have to be aware of the persuasive strategies they are using. As a strong reader, you decide whether to assent to an author's views, to modify those views and build upon them, or to resist them. In a nutshell, that's what rhetorical reading is all about.

Exploring Your Reading Life

Given this overview of the whole book, let's turn directly to this opening chapter, where we ask you to explore the role that reading has played in your own life up until now. Because awareness of your own purposes as well as an author's purposes is so important to reading rhetorically, we'll start by asking you to identify a couple of things you have read lately and then to consider your motivation. Why did you do this reading? Were you reading for relaxation and pleasure? For guidance or information? For keeping in touch with friends or family? For deeper understanding of something that interested you? For a school assignment? (That's probably why you're reading this page right now.) Chances are that you have read something recently for several of the above reasons.

Of course, people read for many different reasons. We gather facts by reading sports scores, menus, schedules, price lists. We find out what we're supposed to do, and how to do it, by reading recipes, safety warnings, course syllabi, laboratory protocols, computer help screens. Reading makes it possible for us to explore new worlds, sometimes with serious goals in mind, sometimes just for fun, as when we pick up (or click into) song lyrics, catalog copy, chat rooms, magazines, novels, even poetry. In each of these very different cases, reading is ultimately an important way of making contact with another person's mind. Written texts create ongoing conversations and document the exploration of ideas across time and space. If nobody's reading, the flow of ideas stops.

Most of us take our ability to read for granted, but anyone who has ever watched a young child learning to read knows the adventure of making meaning out of letters. Once we acquire the ability to construe meaning from written texts, we find texts everywhere—on paper, on computer screens, on TV, and out in urban and suburban landscapes. People tend to think of reading as a deliberate act, but we frequently take in texts without paying attention. Indeed, advertisers are counting on us to read and absorb their messages without thinking much about them. It is quite likely that among the materials you have read lately are texts that just happened to be in front of you, perhaps a sidewalk chalked to advertise a new band, a bus sign promoting a soft drink, or clever marketing material on a cereal box. How many texts like those do you suppose your eyes have encountered and read in just the last twenty-four hours? What lasting impressions did they make?

As you reflect in this chapter upon your reading life, we invite you to reflect also on the thinking processes you use as you read. Our goal is to help you strengthen these processes so that you can meet the reading and writing challenges that fill a busy college student's life—and a busy college graduate's career. After all, in our information age, reading is at the center of our civic and work lives as well as school life. Whether you read to relax, to become better informed, to solve problems, to keep in contact with friends, to make informed civic or business decisions, or simply to skim a text you've encountered by chance, reading is a lifelong activity.

Taking Stock of Why You Read

We become more aware of our reading processes and our motivation for reading when we are challenged by a text. Inevitably, we adjust our reading strategies to fit our purposes. Consider the intricacies of bus and train schedules, the baffling documentation for a new word processing program, or the densely packed explanations in your college textbooks. How you read these texts will be governed by your purpose. If you need to know when the next train to Richmond leaves or how to import a pie chart into your marketing proposal, you can skip over lots of difficult but irrelevant material. On the other hand, if you are preparing to give a workshop on the essential features of a new computer program or trying to grasp the essential concepts of macroeconomics, you must look beyond specific details and attend to overall patterns and meanings.

The beginning of a college writing course is a good time to examine your individual reading processes. In the following exercise we invite you to take an inventory of your recent reading experiences.

• *For Writing and Discussion*

This exercise asks you to list your recent reading experiences and then to reflect on your motives and strategies, which probably varied with the occasion. The first part asks you to jot down answers on paper; the second part asks you to use these notes in class to compare your responses with those of your classmates. In Chapter 3, we will invite you to extend this exploration of *why* you read into an exploration of *how* you read.

ON YOUR OWN

1. What have you read so far today? Divide a sheet of paper into two columns labeled "What?" and "Why?" In the left column, jot down as many items and occasions for reading as you can remember from the past twenty-four hours. Try to make this list as long as you can. Have fun!

2. In the right column, note what prompted you to read each item—a school or work assignment? A discussion with a friend? A desire to find out something specific, such as tomorrow's weather or the score in yesterday's game? A desire for relaxation, as when you thumb through a magazine? Or was it chance—the item was "just there" (such as a cereal box, a poster in a elevator, or lyrics in a CD case)?

3. Were the last twenty-four hours of reading typical for you? If not, draw a horizontal line at the bottom of the "what" and "why" columns and add any other items that you would typically read on a given day when school is in session but didn't happen to read in the last twenty-four hours, such as a novel in progress or a favorite magazine. Perhaps you ordinarily would have read the textbook for a particular course. Perhaps you usually visit a chat room or turn on the TV to check the sports scores scrolling across the screen, but you didn't for some reason yesterday or today. Because this exercise is meant to help you explore your own reading processes, add whatever you think gives a full picture of your reading activities.

4. Draw another horizontal line across the page. Extending your view to the past month, note something that you have read in each of the following categories:
   a. Something you found particularly enjoyable
   b. Something you thought particularly important
   c. Something you struggled to understand
   d. Something you were eager to talk about with your family or friends

5. Now, as you look back over your notes, consider what they say about you as a reader, as a college student, and as a person. Freewrite for several minutes about the proportion of time you spend reading "on assignment" as opposed to just following your own inclinations, how you feel about that discovery, and about reading in general. (By "freewrite" we mean writing rapidly nonstop in order to brainstorm on paper—without worrying about spelling, punctuation, or structure. Your goal is to discover new insights by using nonstop writing to stimulate thinking.)

6. What are your strengths as a reader? Where could you be stronger?

7. To sum up this taking stock exercise, draw one last horizontal line across the page and address this question: *Why* do you read? Freewrite for several minutes, trying to sum up all you have discovered in this exercise.

WITH YOUR CLASSMATES

In small groups or as a whole class, compare responses to the reading inventory. As the discussion unfolds, listen carefully so that you can jot down notes about these questions:

1. What patterns of common experience emerged during the discussion?
2. In what ways are your typical reasons for reading different from those of your classmates?

ONCE MORE ON YOUR OWN

Take a few minutes after the discussion to reflect in writing about what you've become aware of through your writing and class discussion. Consider these questions:

1. How was your description of your reading habits similar to and different from what your classmates described?
2. If others seem to enjoy reading more or less than you, how do you explain that difference?
3. What would you like to change about your typical approach to reading? How can you gain greater strength as a reader?

Summary

In this chapter, we have provided a brief overview of the book and explained how it will help you build a repertoire of reading strategies to meet the challenges of academic reading and writing assignments. We explained that rhetorical reading means paying attention to both the content of a text ("what") and the author's method of presenting that content ("how"). As a foundation for your work in this book, we invited you to take stock of your typical reasons for reading.

Scenes of Reading

• A Brief Writing Project

We conclude this chapter with a short writing project that offers three options that will enable you to reflect on the role of reading in your own life or in our culture: (1) the role reading has played for you (based on your childhood memories or your later intellectual or personal development); (2) observations of the reading of others; and (3) the potential role of reading in your future career, learned through interviews and observations. The assignment asks you to write a brief description or narrative based on "scenes of reading" from your own experience or observation. The goal of this assignment is to extend your responses to the previous "Taking Stock" inventory and prompt some additional exploration of why people read. As a jumping off point, we provide three brief readings that might help stimulate ideas. For the length of this essay, use the selection by novelist Gloria Naylor as a guide. Her reflection was originally a three-minute speech. Aim for something you could read aloud in about the same amount of time.

OPTION 1: MEMORIES

What do you remember from your childhood about books and reading? For example, was having a story read aloud to you an important bedtime ritual? Do you remember, or have you been told stories about, your early efforts to read? Naylor recalls a particularly memorable trip to the library. You may have similar memories of a library or a special reading place or a good or bad experience with reading. Sketch one or more "scenes of reading" from your childhood, or, if you prefer, from a memorable reading experience later in your intellectual or personal development.

OPTION 2: OBSERVATIONS

We tend to think of reading as a solitary activity, but many people read in public places while ordinary life swirls around them. You can spot readers on airplanes and buses, on beaches and park benches, and in restaurants, coffee shops, and maybe your own residence. You probably read in some of these places yourself. Spend some time in one of these public "scenes of reading" and write about what you observe. What can you tell about what the readers are reading? What can you tell about their involvement with the reading? Sketch a "scene of reading" based on this observation.

OPTION 3: INTERVIEWS

Consider the role that reading currently plays for you on the job or that you expect it will play in your future career. Through observation at your current work situation or by interviewing someone whose career you might like to have, describe a workplace "scene of reading." As you learn *why* someone reads on the job, take particular note of what kind of reading is directly involved in the work tasks (such as instructions and correspondence) and what kind of reading plays a background role (such as the design magazines mentioned in Chappell's essay or the company newsletters described by Martinie). Sketch an imagined or observed "scene of reading" in a workplace setting.

Three Samples to Read

Gloria Naylor

The Writing Life

This essay by Gloria Naylor, a prize-winning African American novelist and essay-ist, began as a speech at a gala reading event in 1989 at the Folger Shakespeare Li-brary in Washington, D.C., sponsored by the PEN/Faulkner Foundation, a prestigious international writers' organization. Naylor was one of twenty well-known writers invited to speak for three minutes on the theme of "Beginnings." The text ap-peared in the *Washington Post* Sunday book review section in February 2000 and was published later that year in a collection from Bloomsbury Press entitled *Three Min-utes or Less: America's Greatest Writers on the Universal Themes of Life.* For another es-say by Naylor about her childhood, see "Mommy, What Does 'Nigger' Mean?" in Chapter 10 of this book.

─────────── ● ───────────

This is going to be short, okay? While I am by birth a native New Yorker, I've of-ten mentioned publicly that I was conceived in Robinsville, Miss., because, for me, that conception was the beginning of my writing career. It was through my mother's genes that I inherited my passionate love of books. But since she was from a sharecropping family, who could not afford the luxury of buying books, and the public libraries in the South were closed to black Americans, she would take her spare Saturday afternoons and hire herself out in someone else's fields to earn the money to send away to book clubs. And she made a vow to herself that all of her children would be born in a place where you could be poor and still read.

She kept that promise and my earliest pre-school memories are of being taken to a low brick building in the Bronx with dark walnut shelves that stretched high over my head, shelves that seemed to a 4-year-old to almost stretch into eternity. And she told me that once I could write my name, all of those books would be mine. She would repeat this ritual with her second daughter and then the third. My sisters were average readers; I became an avid one. I was the shyest of the three, painfully shy, and fortunately I was taught early to revere a place that would become the repository of all my unspoken fears and my unspoken needs. And today, with my own writing, that's basi-cally what I'm giving back. Words that attempt to make some order out of the inarticulate chaos I have within. But writing for me is also about dreaming, and I grew up being encouraged to dream by a woman who, in spite of her very limited personal circumstances, somehow managed to find a way to hold onto a fierce belief in the limitless possibilities of the human spirit.

Virginia Chappell

Reading on the Fourth of July

Virginia Chappell, one of the authors of this book, wrote the following essay as part of designing this assignment.

_____ • _____

1 It rained off and on all day last year at Crab Lake on the Fourth of July. After breakfast, all the interesting pieces of the *New York Times* that I still wanted to look at had been claimed by someone else, so I decided I might as well start reading one of the books I was going to assign for my class in the fall. (I'd brought it all the way to northern Wisconsin just to soothe my conscience, choosing it because it was small and didn't weigh much. I hadn't expected to actually *read* it.) Four of us were gathered on chairs and a couch by the fireplace, reading. Kate, a junior in college, looked up, scowled at the yellow highlighter in my hand, and teased me about not being able to take time off from "work." It occurred to me that our fireside scene was something like a social studies diorama (the ones that show a train and a truck on a highway by a river with an airplane overhead), only this one was devoted to reading. Kate was looking through a book about loons, and her high school age brother was engrossed in a sci-fi novel.

2 "OK," I said. "I'll admit I'm reading for work right now. In fact, I'm reading about reading. So let me ask, why are you reading?" I addressed the room at large, not sure who would be willing to stop reading and talk. "What leads you to read, in general?"

3 Kate shrugged that mostly she reads because she has to, for school. Her brother Ed, prodded to answer, scowled in a friendly way from the couch and held up his novel. Wasn't it obvious? Our hostess, Janet, piped up from the dining table, where she'd been reading excerpts from the *Times* to us about interesting political and foreign affairs developments, to say that she reads to stay informed. "I'm a news junkie." Her husband was over on that side of the room reading a book about China in preparation for a trip they were planning later in the summer. Kate and Ed's mother and grandfather couldn't hear my informal survey because they were poring over the latest *Guide to Wisconsin Hook and Line Fishing Regulations* to determine exactly what size and type of fish they could keep and what they would have to throw back. We knew why they were reading.

4 Reading for analysis and teaching, reading for entertainment, reading for information, practical and abstract. That left Tom, sitting across from me, who had stopped flipping through a magazine to listen. He's Kate and Ed's dad, a finish carpenter. I waited for an answer. "How about reading as stalling?" he

offered. "When I come home at night, if one of my design magazines has come in the mail, I'll sit right down and read for as long as I can get away with before it's time to fix dinner or drive somebody someplace." The reading diorama was complete.

My dog signaled that it had stopped raining, so we all headed outside. I   5
had read two pages of my scholarly book; I think that highlighter pen is still hiding somewhere in the chair cushions up north.

Melissa Martinie (Student)

A Lawyer and His Reading

Melissa Martinie, a student at Virginia Tech, is considering a number of career possibilities, including law and engineering.

———————   •   ———————

1   When you first begin to read, you do it to have fun and entertain yourself, but as you grow up, reading quickly becomes a useful tool. That's what happened to my dad, Steve Martinie, a lawyer at a large financial corporation. He started his reading career at age five for the purpose of enjoyment and has developed it to the point that reading is more than half of his job.

2   He uses this skill to help decide whether his employer should sign legal documents or insist upon revision prior to signing. My dad deals with real estate purchases and sales, mortgage loans, contracts, and some very complex investments. Information about these transactions comes to him in the form of legal documents, business memos, and simpler forms like periodicals and e-mails. Each of these different forms he reads for a different purpose. For instance, he must read legal documents very carefully because small terms can have a big impact on a multimillion dollar investment. In order to not miss any of these important details, he often finds it useful to read a document several times with different purposes in mind—for example, to catch clerical errors or get a general understanding. He says that through experience he's found that no matter how many times he reads a document there are always more improvements that he can find with one more reading. What limits the number of times that he rereads a document is time and the fact that the more he reads the less critical the improvements are that he can make. Eventually, the minuscule errors are no longer worth the time.

3   When my dad reads business memos, he reads them to gather factual information on transactions rather than to revise the documents. He can use this information to learn about a particular business transaction such as a real estate investment. These business memos are his primary source for learning about a topic, but there is always someone he can call in order to clarify the information.

4   In addition to reading legal documents and business memos, he also reads e-mails and periodicals. For example, his daily routine consists of reading the *Legal Times* and the *Daily Tax Reporter.* When he's reading these, he focuses on just getting the important information as quickly as possible without taking too much time from his other work. Nobody ever trained him to read all these different ways—he learned it from experience.

CHAPTER

2

The Special Demands of Academic Reading

*The process of reading is not just the interpretation of a text
but the interpretation of another person's worldview as
presented by a text.*

—Doug Brent

In Chapter 1 you explored the role that reading has played in your life so far. In this chapter, the focus shifts to reading in college. Once you get immersed in the academic life—caught up in the challenge of doing your own questioning, critical thinking, analysis, and research—you'll discover that academic reading has unique pleasures and demands. If you ask an experienced academic reader engaged in a research project why she reads, her answer may be something like this: "I'm investigating a problem, and much of my research requires extensive reading. As part of my investigation, I am doing a close analysis of several primary sources. Also I read to see what other researchers are saying about my problem and to position myself in that conversation."

This may seem a curious answer—one that you won't fully understand until you have had more experience writing papers requiring analysis or research. To help you appreciate this answer—and to see how it applies to you—consider that most college courses have two underlying goals. The first is for you to learn the body of information presented in the course—to master the course's key concepts and ideas, to understand its theories, to see how the theories try to explain certain data and observations, to learn key definitions or formulas, and to memorize important facts. Cognitive psychologists sometimes call this kind of learning *conceptual knowledge*—that is, knowledge of the course's subject matter. Transmitting conceptual knowledge is the primary aim of most college textbooks.

But a second goal of most college courses is for you to learn the discipline's characteristic ways of thinking about the world by applying your conceptual knowledge to new problems. What questions does the discipline ask? What are its methods of analysis or research? What counts as evidence? What are the discipline's shared or disputed assumptions? How do you write arguments in this discipline, and what makes them convincing (say in literature, sociology, engineering, or accounting)? Thus in addition to learning the basic concepts of a course, you need to learn how experts in the discipline pose problems and conduct inquiry.

Once you realize that each academic discipline is a contested field full of uncertainties, disagreements, and debate—rather than an inert body of knowledge—you will see why college professors want you to *do* their discipline rather than simply to study it. They want you not just to study history or chemistry or sociology, but to *think like a historian or a chemist or a sociologist*. Cognitive psychologists call this kind of learning *procedural knowledge*—the ability to apply conceptual knowledge to new problems using the discipline's characteristic methods of thinking. Teachers focus on procedural knowledge when they assign readings beyond the typical textbook—newspaper or magazine articles, scholarly articles, or primary sources such as historical documents or literary texts—and ask you to analyze these readings or use them in other discipline-specific ways. Procedural knowledge is also at the heart of most out-of-class writing assignments or essay exams, especially those that ask you to address challenging problems using disciplinary methods of analysis and argument.

If we return now to how our experienced researcher answered the question "Why do you read?" we see that she is immersed in *doing* her discipline: She has formulated a problem and is conducting research. She obviously sees reading as central to her work. But how does she read? What is she looking for? How does she know what to use and not use? What does she do when she analyzes an important source? What does she mean by positioning herself in a conversation? These are the kinds of questions we will address in this and subsequent chapters.

Reading as Conversation

Let's begin with the notion of reading as conversation. Writers talk to readers, who often talk back. Consider again our researcher mentioned in the previous section. If her investigation leads to new insights, she will write an article (if she is a professor) or a research paper (if she is an undergraduate). She will aim her writing at readers interested in the same problem, explaining the results of her research and trying to persuade readers to accept her argument and claims. She writes because she thinks she has produced something new or challenging or otherwise useful to add to the conversation—something that is different from, or that extends or improves upon, the work of others who have investigated the same problem.

Whenever you write, therefore, it is helpful to think of yourself as conversing with readers who share your interest in the problem you are addressing. You are joining a conversation. Similarly, when you read, you have to understand not only the text you are reading but also the conversation that it joins. (One of the reasons that an assigned reading might seem difficult to you—say a journal article on urban violence in a sociology course—is that you are unfamiliar with the conversation it is part of.) To take a broad view, then, we can extend the metaphor of "conversation" to say that texts themselves are in a conversation with previously published texts. Each text acts in relationship to other texts. It asserts a claim on a reader's attention by invoking certain interests and understandings, reminding readers of what has been written about the subject before. For example, articles in scientific journals typically include a summary of important research already conducted on the problem (this section is called a *literature review*). Similarly, political commentators will summarize the views of others so that they can affirm, extend, or take issue with those views. Music, film, and book reviewers are likely to refer not just to the item under review but to the given artist's reputation, which, of course, was established not just by word of mouth but by other texts, texts with which the current reader may or may not be familiar.

The reasons any of us engage in conversation, oral or written, will vary widely according to the occasion and our individual needs. In general, we read because we want—perhaps need—to find out what others are saying about a given matter. Sometimes we may have purely personal reasons for reading, with no intention of extending the conversation further through writing of our own. Ultimately though, in school and workplace writing, we read so that we can make informed contributions to a conversation that is already in progress. Indeed, we are expected to join in.

Entering an oral conversation can sometimes be a simple process of responding to a question. ("Have you seen the new film at the Ridgemont?") But if a conversation is already well underway, finding an opening can sometimes be a complex process of getting people's attention and staking claim to authority on a subject. ("Um, you know, I've seen all of John Woo's films, and I think....") The challenge is even greater if the goal is to redirect the conversation or contradict the prevailing opinion. ("Yes, but, listen! The reading I've done for my cinematography class tells me that his action films are not as innovative as the ads claim.") When we take up writing as a way of entering the conversation, we don't have to worry about interrupting, but we do have to review the conversation for the reader by laying out introductory background.

To explore the similarities between your motives for joining a conversation and your motives for reading, consider how the influential rhetorician and philosopher Kenneth Burke uses conversation as a metaphor for reading and writing.

Imagine you enter a parlor. You come late. When you arrive, others have long preceded you, and they are engaged in a heated discussion, a discussion too heated for them to pause and tell you exactly what it is about. In fact, the discussion had already begun long before any of them got there, so that no one present is qualified to retrace for you all the steps that had gone before. You listen for a while, until you decide that you have caught the tenor of the argument; then you put in your oar. Someone answers; you answer him; another comes to your defense; another aligns himself against you, to either the embarrassment or gratification of your opponent, depending upon the quality of your ally's assistance. However, the discussion is interminable. The hour grows late, you must depart. And you do depart, with the discussion still vigorously in progress.

• *For Writing and Discussion*

The following exercise will help you explore the implications of Burke's parlor metaphor for your own reading processes. Write your answers to the questions in a notebook, or as your teacher directs, so that you can compare your responses with those of your classmates.

ON YOUR OWN

1. In what ways does Burke's parlor metaphor fit your experience? Freewrite for a few minutes about an oral conversation in which you managed to assert your voice—or "put in your oar," as Burke says—after listening for a while.
2. Then consider how the metaphor applies to your experience as a reader. Freewrite for another few minutes about a time when reading helped you gather a sense of the general flow of ideas so that you could have something to say about a topic.
3. Not all the "parlors" we enter are filled with unfamiliar conversations. Sometimes we engage in heated discussions on subjects that are very familiar to us. Make a list of one or more communities that you belong to where you feel that you can quickly catch the drift of an in-progress oral conversation. What are some "hot topics" of conversation in these communities? For example, in summer 2000, when we were writing this chapter, a hot cultural topic was the lawsuit between Metallica and Napster over the "pirating" of music on the Internet. Most of our students—who were familiar with popular music, knew how to download songs, and understood the Internet pirating issue—could join this conversation immediately. Many faculty members, however, especially the older generation, didn't have a clue. How much background information about the music industry, e-commerce, the electronic transfer of digital information, and the music-listening habits of rock and postrock culture would you have to provide to bring oldsters up to speed?
4. Now let's reverse the situation. Have you ever listened to a conversation in which you were a baffled outsider rather than an insider? (Think of the plight of those oldsters suffering through a conversation about

Metallica versus Napster.) Describe such an experience. How might that experience be an appropriate analogy for your frustration trying to read a book or article addressed to an insider audience rather than to someone with your background?

WITH YOUR CLASSMATES

Share your notebook entries with other members of your class. See if others have had experiences similar to yours. Help each other appreciate the concepts of insider and outsider audiences and of reading as joining a conversation.

Challenges Presented by Academic Reading

As we have seen, reading is at the center of the work you will do in almost every college course. Through reading you will learn the information and concepts that define the course (what we have called *conceptual knowledge*). Reading will also help you learn how each discipline explores the world—how it asks questions, constructs hypotheses, gathers and analyzes data, and makes arguments (what we have called *procedural knowledge*). Reading, in short, introduces you to the conversations you will join as a writer.

College-level reading, as we have already acknowledged, can be difficult and challenging. A textbook for a new course, for example, can be daunting because each new paragraph challenges you with new concepts, vocabulary, and dense information. Each new sentence seems just as important as the one before. With so much unfamiliar material, it is difficult to separate key concepts from supporting details, leaving you with the overwhelming feeling "I've got to know all of this."

When you switch from textbooks to scholarly articles and primary sources, your problems increase because you need to figure out the conversation the text is joining and focus simultaneously on both content and the author's persuasive strategies. By observing different authors' purposes and methods, you will begin to recognize the ways that claims are typically asserted and supported within a given discipline. You will learn what "counts" as evidence in a variety of fields. For example, historians value primary sources such as letters and diaries, government records, legal documents, and other manuscripts written during the times being investigated. Psychologists gather different kinds of research data such as observations of the learning behavior of pigeons, "think aloud" transcripts of the problem-solving processes of persons with certain kinds of brain damage, or statistics about the reduction of anxiety symptoms following different kinds of therapy. You will also discover how different disciplines use different *genres*—that is, particular styles and formats—for reporting and discussing research, such as experimental reports, book reviews, philosophical arguments, or literary analyses. Your accumulating knowledge about disciplinary discourses will in turn teach you new ways of thinking and writing.

The greatest challenge of your college reading may be the expectation that you do more than just understand what you have read. You will often be expected to write about your reading in a way that shows that you are "doing" the discipline. Reporting about what you have read will be just a beginning point. You will be asked to find meaning, not merely information, in books and articles. You will be asked to respond to that meaning—to explain it, to analyze it, to critique it, to compare it to alternative meanings that you or others create. To fulfill such assignments, you will need to analyze not just *what* texts say, but *how* they say it. We call reading with this double awareness *reading rhetorically*. By analyzing both the content and technique of a given text, a rhetorical reader critically considers the extent to which he or she will accept or challenge that text's apparent intentions.

Rhetorical Reading as an Academic Strategy

In most cases, a writer's goal is to change a reader's understanding of a topic in some way. Occasionally, the change might simply involve a stronger confirmation of what the reader thought beforehand. Sometimes the change might involve an increase in knowledge or in clarity of understanding (an article explains how bluenose dolphins use whistling sounds to converse with each other; for you, this new knowledge increases your awe of sea mammals). Sometimes the change might radically reconstruct your whole view of a subject (an article convinces you to reverse your position on legalization of hard drugs). How much change occurs? The reader decides.

The concept of rhetorical reading recognizes an inevitable tension between writers' purposes for writing and readers' purposes for reading. By *rhetorical* we mean "related to an intended effect." Invoking the term *rhetoric* always draws attention to a writer's relationship to and intentions toward an audience. Aristotle defined *rhetoric* as the art of discovering the available means of persuasion in a given situation. In accordance with modern approaches to reading and writing, we use the term in a broader sense that includes not just direct persuasion but the entire range of aims and techniques that a writer/speaker might draw upon to influence readers/listeners and modify their understanding of a subject.

Writers want to change readers' perceptions and thinking, and their efforts to do so involve both direct and indirect means. Readers decide not only the extent to which they accept the ideas and information put forth in a text, but how they will act in response. They determine—sometimes unconsciously, sometimes deliberately—whether the information they read is reliable, the ideas significant, the presentation convincing. Because writers try to persuade their intended audiences to adopt their perspective, they select and arrange evidence, choose examples, include or omit material, and select words and images to best support their perspective. As a rhetorical reader, you have to be aware of how a text is constructed to persuade its intended audience (and you may not be part of its intended audience at all). In short, no text tells the whole story. You have to be aware of the perspectives that the text makes invisible.

As an illustration, suppose you are researching the problem of the melting Arctic ice cap. You become interested in this problem when you read an online article explaining that scientists are divided on how to interpret recent data about the melting of polar ice, whether it is part of a natural cycle that will reverse itself or part of long-term, irreversible, global warming caused by humans. As you research this issue, you will need to realize how different writers, in trying to persuade their intended audiences toward their position on the issue, use rhetorical strategies that best support their own cases. You need to be wary. Some research may be biased by economic or political entanglements—for example, many people charge that global warming research funded by petroleum companies should be discounted. Some research may provide what seems like frightening data and yet draw's only a few cautious conclusions. For example, an article in the July 2000 issue of the highly specialized journal *Science* reported that eleven cubic miles of ice are disappearing from the Greenland ice sheet annually, but left it up to the article's intended audience of experts to ponder what kinds of conclusions to draw. However, when the findings of the *Science* article were reported in the popular press, many articles downplayed the scientists' caution and highlighted imagined details of a world fifty years from now with no ice caps—an approach swaying readers to accept uncritically the assumption that the melting ice is an irreversible trend, presumably resulting from human-caused global warming. Once political commentators got hold of the *Science* article, they put a spin on it that reflected their own values and beliefs. Environmentalists used the melting ice cap data to support their case for international regulations to slow or eventually to reverse global warming. Pro-business writers in turn emphasized the original study's cautious call for more research. A more balanced and neutral approach was demonstrated by a *Chronicle of Higher Education* article, also in July 2000, that was headlined, "The Great Melt: Is It Normal, or the Result of Global Warming? Scientists Are Having Difficulty Pinpointing the Causes of Glacial and Sea-Ice Decline." This article provided a background overview for curious academic readers who accept the tentativeness of scientific findings and want to learn about the conflicting interpretations in this controversy. For student writer-researchers, such articles can be gold mines because they provide balanced explanations without attempting to draw the reader to a specific set of conclusions. Our point here is that your ability to recognize the persuasive strategies built into a text grants you considerable power in deciding how you will respond to an author's views.

Questions That Rhetorical Readers Ask

In the language of the epigraph to this chapter, rhetorical readers have learned to recognize and interpret the worldview that a text sets forth. We will discuss *worldview* in more detail later, but for now consider "worldview" to mean a writer's underlying beliefs, values, and assumptions. You probably already do this without much effort when you are reading material on familiar subjects. What you already know about a close friend's values makes it relatively easy to recognize whether that friend's e-mail is serious or teasing. Similarly, you can quickly tell whether a review of your favorite musician's latest CD reflects your own musical values and assumptions. In academic settings, though, unfamiliar subject matter and contexts can make analyzing a writer's underlying values and assumptions more problematic. With difficult new material, readers' natural tendency is to concentrate on getting what information and meaning they can from a text without paying attention to its rhetorical strategies. Rhetorical readers, however, analyze rhetorical strategies as a way of understanding a writer's purpose and worldview. This analysis involves five key questions about the how the text works:

1. What questions does the text address? (Why are these significant questions? What community cares about them?)
2. Who is the intended audience? (Am I part of this audience or an outsider?)
3. How does the author support his or her thesis with reasons and evidence? (Do I find this argument convincing? What views and counterarguments are omitted from the text? What counterevidence is ignored?)
4. How does the author hook the intended reader's interest and keep the reader reading? (Do these appeals work for me?)
5. How does the author make himself or herself seem credible to the intended audience? (Is the author credible for me?)

Chapter 5 will show in detail how these questions about rhetorical features can reveal a writer's basic values and assumptions. By critically considering these "how" questions, you will understand a text more fully and be ready to respond to it by considering three additional sets of questions:

6. Are this writer's basic values, beliefs, and assumptions similar to or different from my own? (How does this writer's worldview accord with mine?)
7. How do I respond to this text? (Will I go along with or challenge what this text is presenting? How has it changed my thinking?)
8. How do this author's evident purposes for writing fit with my purposes for reading? (How will I be able to use what I have learned from the text?)

Writers' Purposes Versus Readers' Purposes

As you read various selections in this textbook, you will often be asked to consider the fit between your purposes and the writer's purposes. This is an important question, one that is particularly pertinent when you are assigned research projects that require you to select sources from among what may be hundreds of possibilities. These potential sources will pose reading challenges different from those of your course textbooks because, like the articles on polar ice melt just referred to, they will be written for many different audiences and purposes. On any given topic, it's likely your research will turn up books, scholarly articles, popular magazine articles, news reports, and so forth written originally for readers with a range of different concerns—for experts and nonexperts, theorists and practitioners, policymakers and ordinary citizens. As a reader who is planning to write, you will need to determine what among all this material suits *your* needs and purposes.

What do we mean then when we refer to *your purposes* as a reader? To understand the answer to this question, consider our earlier explanation that you as a reader decide whether you will assent to a writer's views, resist them, use them in a new context, or in some other manner respond to them in ways that the writer might not have envisioned. Suppose, for example, that you read an article forecasting a dangerous level of global warming. If you are a pro-business advocate who believes that the threat of global warming is an environmentalist scare tactic, your goal might be to figure out a way to refute the article. However, if you are undecided on the issue, you might examine the author's argument carefully and compare it to other articles with somewhat different points of view. If you are already convinced that global warming is underway, you might read it without any skepticism whatsoever.

To fulfill your own purposes, you often have to overcome the difficulty of not being part of the text's intended audience. For one thing, such texts often omit background information that you need. When you encounter such materials, you will have to skim carefully to decide whether to move on to something easier or to keep reading to see what you can learn. Eventually you will read enough material to be able to fill in the background—and thus begin to read with an expert's understanding. Until you are thoroughly familiar with the conversation a text is joining, you may also have to overcome the difficulty of determining whether a text suppresses opposing perspectives. How can you tell whether a text is trying to give you the whole picture in a fair and reliable way or is simply another one-sided argument in a hotly contested debate? By learning to read rhetorically.

A Further Look at Writers' Purposes

As a reader, then, you need to appreciate how your purpose for reading may or may not match the writer's purpose for writing. We turn next to *writers' purposes*—the aims writers typically set for themselves when they compose. This section will focus on a scheme developed by rhetoricians to categorize various kinds of writing on the basis of the writer's aim or purpose. For rhetorical readers, this scheme is particularly powerful because it helps them understand the writer's relationship to subject matter and audience. The scheme identifies a spectrum of eight purposes or aims: (1) expressing and reflecting, (2) inquiring and exploring, (3) informing and explaining, (4) analyzing and interpreting, (5) taking a stand, (6) evaluating and judging, (7) proposing solutions, and (8) seeking common ground. (The chapters in the anthology section of this book are organized according to the same scheme.) The following brief overview of these aims, illustrated with examples from environmental issues, will help you understand the scheme.

EXPRESSING AND REFLECTING

Writers whose aim is to express or reflect focus on their own lives and experiences. They often write personal stories or narratives, often using literary techniques such as plot, character, setting, evocative language, and even symbolism. They hope to reproduce for their readers their own experiences and emotional or intellectual life in connection with a subject. An environmental writer might tell the story of her visit to the canopy of a tropical rain forest or detail her experiences kayaking to a fog-hidden island. Or she might write reflectively by looking back on what nature has meant to her over the years, perhaps showing how her relationship to the natural world has evolved. Reflective writing is often characterized by a look backward at a particular incident or time from a new perspective, sometimes with the goal of clarifying events or meaning. In all these cases, the writer's own life and experiences are at the heart of the text.

INQUIRING AND EXPLORING

Writers seeking to inquire or explore often don't have thesis statements, or if they do, the statements don't appear until the very end. Such writers are wrestling with a question or problem. They hook us with that problem early in the text and then let us watch them wrestle with it, narrating the progression of their thinking, which may or may not find closure. As in expressive and reflective writing, these texts implicitly invite readers to share the writer's experience of sorting through an issue's complexity, but now the focus is on phenomena outside the writer. Consider, for example, an environmental writer surprised by news reports that radical environmentalists had destroyed valuable trees at a U.S. Forest Service research nursery in the Midwest. The writer might ask several questions: Why did environmentalists destroy trees? What collusion of issues led to this strange incident? In an exploratory essay, this writer could begin by laying out the significance of his question and then trace his efforts to find answers among the multiple viewpoints on the matter. Foregrounded throughout would be the writer's own intellectual process of struggling with the problem—the writer's turns of thought, quandaries, discoveries, rephrasings and refocusings of the problem, and new understandings.

INFORMING AND EXPLAINING

When writers are trying to inform or explain, their own personality, reflections, and questioning take a back seat to the subject matter. Such writing is also called *expository writing*. Texts with this aim often, but not always, state a main point about their subject matter and purpose, typically near the beginning. Because a reader is likely to stop reading if the information is already known or seems irrelevant, oversimplified, or overly difficult, effective expository writers must hook the reader's interest in the new information, establish its significance, and explain the material in a way that fits the reader's knowledge level. To engage readers' interest, writers often present the information in a surprising way so that its new or unexpected elements are foregrounded. As an illustration, let's consider several examples of explanatory texts prompted by the tree vandalism incident. The initial news reports simply explained what happened—who, what, when, where, how, why. Later, the sheriff's department, FBI, and Forest Service sought to explain why and how security efforts had failed to prevent the incident. Still later, writers for a variety of periodicals sought to explain the conflict between the underground group and the researchers, sometimes as part of a larger discussion about environmental or forestry issues. These texts provided information about who the activists were, what they stood for, and what they hoped to accomplish. Each of the different texts—aimed at different audiences ranging from expert botanists to taxpaying tourists—focused on different facts, definitions, and examples.

ANALYZING AND INTERPRETING

Writers who seek to analyze and interpret typically focus on phenomena that are difficult to understand or explain. This purpose dominates academic prose. For example, a literary critic might analyze puzzling imagery patterns in a modern poem; an anthropologist might analyze the meaning of bone and artifact arrangements in a gravesite; a marine biologist might analyze recorded whistles from bottlenose dolphins in an attempt to discover meaningful patterns. Unlike the writer's role in expository prose—where writers confidently explain concepts they already understand or convey information they already know—the writer's role in analytical prose is more tentative. The writer must assert a thesis that sums up his or her interpretation of the puzzling phenomenon and then support that thesis with evidence and arguments. Readers, meanwhile, need to be persuaded. Neither writer nor reader assumes that the evidence speaks for itself. In cases where a new interpretation might go against common understanding or even be unsettling to readers, the burden of proof lies on the writer to provide a convincing argument.

Environmental writers frequently adopt the purpose of analyzing and interpreting. During the summer of 2000, for example, an unusual number of whales were dying at sea and washing up on the shores of Oregon and Washington. Could this phenomenon be interpreted as part of a natural cycle in a healthy whale population or could it indicate a serious environmental problem? Scientists debated this issue through prose that attempted to analyze and interpret the available data.

TAKING A STAND

When writing to take a stand, authors seek to persuade audiences to accept a particular position on a controversial issue. What initiates this aim is an *issue question*—that is, a question that divides the community and that can be answered reasonably in two or more different ways. Because issues frequently involve competing values or beliefs and entail significant consequences, the stakes can be high and the questions complex: Should hard drugs be legalized? Should the

United States adopt socialized medicine? Should gasoline taxes be raised to help curb global warming?

Although writers sometimes take a stand to rally support among sympathetic readers, the real challenge of persuasive writing is to convince neutral, skeptical, or opposing readers to adopt a specific point of view. The success of a written argument depends in large part upon a writer's ability to present clear reasons and evidence to support a position and to anticipate and counter opposing views without alienating readers. Because an issue question presupposes no one "right" answer, a persuasive argument must build its case by connecting with some aspect of readers' existing beliefs. Examples of environmental issues dividing American citizens are numerous. Here is a sampling derived from a quick perusal of daily newspapers: Should four federal dams on Idaho's Snake River be breached to promote recovery of salmon? Should the Macah Indians be allowed to hunt whales? Should federal controls on pesticides be tightened or relaxed? Should the United States trade with countries that violate international agreements on pollution control? What actions should be taken to stop the spread of Africanized honey bees?

EVALUATING AND JUDGING

Writers whose work involves evaluating and judging must try to persuade readers to accept a particular view of something's worth or value. Whereas writing "to take a stand" is a broad category comprising all types of persuasive writing, writing "to evaluate and judge" is a subcategory of persuasion focusing on disputes about the worth or value of a person, object, idea, or other phenomenon. Was Bill Clinton a good president? What is the most effective approach for treating prostate cancer? What is the best solution to the problem of balancing our need for wood products with our desire to preserve forests? Writers of evaluation arguments generally proceed systematically by specifying the criteria for "good" in the specific case and then matching those criteria to the object being evaluated. For example, criteria for an effective approach to treating prostate cancer might include mortality rates, quality of life, risk of unwanted side effects, and cost. Evaluation arguments are particularly common in the workplace, where criteria must routinely be established for hiring, retaining, and promoting personnel or for making decisions about investments, production, and marketing. Evaluation arguments are also crucial in the sphere of public policy.

When their intention is to evaluate and judge, writers have to decide whether the intended audience already accepts their criteria. For example, suppose an environmentalist supports candidate Greentree for the U.S. Senate on the basis of her strong environmental record. If he writes an editorial for the Sierra Club newsletter, he can be sure his readers already accept "strong environmental record" as an essential criterion for the office. He can therefore argue directly that Greentree's voting record on the environment is better than that of her opponents. But if he writes for a local newspaper, where many readers might place other issues above the environment, he must first argue that the environment is a priority concern.

PROPOSING SOLUTIONS

A writer who is proposing solutions is calling for action. This aim or purpose is another subcategory of persuasion. The writer's goal is to persuade readers that a problem exists and then to offer a solution to that problem, showing how the proposed solution will solve the problem, how it will work better than alternative solutions, and how its benefits will outweigh its costs. Proposal arguments are common in both the workplace and public sphere, where people must constantly identify problems, figure out alternative ways to solve them, and argue for the best solutions.

Environmental writers frequently compose proposal arguments. A controversial environmental issue in the Pacific Northwest focuses on the problem of declining salmon runs. Concerned scientists have proposed dozens of possible solutions such as changing water flow over the dams, trucking salmon smolts downstream, building different kinds of fish ladders, legislating new kinds of logging practices to improve stream banks, and even breaching dams on the Snake River. All of these solutions are costly and require complexly interwoven arguments to be persuasive. When environmentalists write to persons already concerned with declining salmon runs (that is, people who acknowledge the problem in advance), they can concentrate on arguing for the feasibility of their proposed solutions. When they write to audiences that do not place a high priority on the salmon problem (for example, persons who believe the benefits of dams outweigh the loss of salmon), they must argue first for the worth of keeping the salmon. In other words, if readers do not acknowledge that a problem exists and that action is needed, the significance of the problem itself must first be addressed.

SEEKING COMMON GROUND

This aim or purpose is still another subcategory of persuasion—one in which a writer aims to calm the intensity of much persuasive discourse and to seek solutions that benefit the largest number of persons. Traditional argument is often cast as a pro-con debate with a clear winner and a clear loser; holders of alternative views are often seen as "opponents" who must be refuted and rejected. In contrast, writers who seek a common ground try to find solutions to problems that respect the values of all stakeholders. Texts written with this aim try to resolve conflicts through mediation and negotiation rather than a winner-take-all victory. Often texts in this category don't propose solutions at all. Rather, they lay out the values and goals of the various stakeholders so that potential solutions can be built upon whatever common ground is discovered. The success of their methods depends upon persuading stakeholders to listen carefully to each other, inquire into multiple solutions, and deliberate together persuasively, but gently and fairly, in pursuit of mutual understanding. Together they may find solutions that synthesize or at least accommodate alternative views.

An environmental writer might undertake a common ground project by interviewing people on all sides of a local land use conflict in order to describe fairly the concerns and values of stakeholders and to uncover and highlight points of agreement. The results might not immediately resolve the conflict, but the discovery of mutual interests could lead eventually to a cooperative resolution.

Summary

Throughout these first two chapters, we have shown how academic writers must read rhetorically, how they must engage in inquiry and argument. We explained how reading entails joining a conversation in which a given text responds to other texts as one voice in a conversation. We then discussed the special challenges of academic reading, which often requires you to read texts addressed to unfamiliar audiences. The heart of this chapter is our explanation of rhetorical reading, in which a reader must attend both to the content of a text and to its persuasive strategies in order to decide how to respond—whether to assent to the writer's ideas, to modify them, or to resist them. Part of rhetorical reading, as we also explained, is to see how writers' purposes and readers' purposes are often at odds. Finally, to help you understand writers' purposes more fully, we described the spectrum of purposes or aims that writers typically employ.

3

Strategies for Reading Rhetorically

It is like the rubbing of two sticks together to make a fire, the act of reading, an improbable pedestrian task that leads to heat and light.

—Anna Quindlen

In the preceding chapter we saw that academic readers read because they are captivated by questions and are challenged to find new or better answers. They also read to pursue their research projects, to see what other researchers are saying, and to position themselves in a scholarly conversation. To read effectively, they have to read rhetorically by attending to both the content and the persuasive strategies in a text. In this chapter, we focus specifically on introducing the rhetorical reading strategies used by experts. We begin by explaining two pieces of background knowledge you will need to read rhetorically: (1) that reading is an active rather than passive process (we say that both reading and writing are acts of composing) and (2) that the choices skilled writers make about content, structure, and style depend on their rhetorical context. Understanding these concepts will help you employ the rhetorical strategies we describe in the last half of the chapter.

Reading and Writing As Acts of Composing

As part of their background knowledge, rhetorical readers know that reading, like writing, is an active process of composing. The idea that writing is an act of composing is probably familiar to you from your high school English classes. Indeed, the terms *writing* and *composing* are often used interchangeably. Originally associated with fine arts such as painting, music, or literary writing, the term *composing* still carries with it the idea of originality or creativity even though it has come to mean the production of any kind of written text from a memo to a Pulitzer-prize-winning novel. Unlike the term *writing, composing* suggests more than just the transcription of a preexisting meaning or idea; it suggests a creative putting together of words and ideas to make a new whole. Except for literally recopying what someone else has written, all writing, even memo writing, is a matter of selecting and arranging language to accomplish a purpose that is unique to a particular situation and audience.

The idea that reading is an act of composing, however, may be less familiar. The ancients thought of reading as a passive activity in which the author via the text deposited meaning in a reader; the text was metaphorically (or even literally) "consumed." The Old Testament prophet Ezekiel, for example, has a vision in which he is instructed by the Lord to open his mouth and literally consume a book that gives him the knowledge he needs to speak to the rebellious Israelites. Commenting on the consumption metaphors associated with reading, Alberto Manguel in *A History of Reading* notes the parallels between the cooking metaphors associated with writing—the author "cooks up" a plot or "spices" up her introduction—and the eating metaphors associated with reading—the reader "devours" a book, finds "nourishment" in it, then "regurgitates" what he has read.

While the image of Ezekiel's eating a text seems fantastic, the mistaken idea persists that reading is a one-way transaction: author → text → reader. To illustrate the flaws in this model of the reading process, let's try a simple experiment described by reading researcher Kathleen McCormick. Read the following passage and jot down your interpretation of its meaning:

> Tony slowly got up from the mat, planning his escape. He hesitated a moment and thought. Things were not going well. What bothered him most was being held, especially since the charge against him had been weak. He considered his present situation. The lock that held him was strong but he thought he could break it. . . . He was being ridden unmercifully. . . . He felt that he was ready to make his move.

There are two common interpretations: readers assume that Tony is either in jail or in a wrestling match. Unless you are familiar with wrestling, you probably thought Tony was a prisoner planning a jailbreak. However, if this paragraph appeared in a short story about a wrestler, you would immediately assume that "mat," "escape," "charge," "being held," and "lock" referred to wrestling even if you knew very little about the sport. This experiment demonstrates two important aspects of the reading process: (1) readers use their previous experiences and knowledge to create meaning from what they read; and (2) context influences meaning.

Research such as McCormick's shows that readers make sense of a text not by passively receiving meaning from it but by actively composing a reading of it. This composing process links the reader's existing knowledge and ideas with the new information encountered in the text. What the reader brings to the text is as important as the text itself. In other words, reading is not a process in which an author simply transfers information to the reader. Rather it is a dynamic process in which the reader's worldview interacts with the writer's worldview; the reader constructs meaning from the text, in effect creating a new "text" in the reader's mind—that reader's active reading or interpretation of the text.

This view of reading as a transaction between text and reader is captured evocatively in the poem "The Voice You Hear When You Read Silently" by Thomas Lux. Take a moment at this time to read Lux's poem and then to do the exercises that follow it.

The Voice You Hear When You Read Silently

is not silent, it is a speaking-out-loud voice in your head: it is *spoken,*
a voice is saying it as you read.
It's the writer's words, of course, in a literary sense his or her "voice"
but the sound of that voice is the sound of *your* voice.
Not the sound your friends know or the sound of a tape played back
but your voice
caught in the dark cathedral of your skull, your voice heard by an internal
ear informed by internal abstracts
and what you know by feeling, having felt.
It is your voice saying, for example, the word "barn" that the writer wrote
but the "barn" you say is a barn you know or knew.
The voice in your head, speaking as you read, never says anything
neutrally — some people hated the barn they knew,
some people love the barn they know
so you hear the word loaded and a sensory constellation is lit:
horse-gnawed stalls, hayloft, black heat tape wrapping a water pipe,
a slippery spilled *chirrr* of oats from a split sack,
the bony, filthy haunches of cows . . .
And "barn" is only a noun — no verb or subject has entered into the
sentence yet! The voice you hear when you read to yourself
is the clearest voice: you speak it
speaking to you.

—Thomas Lux

- ### *For Writing and Discussion*

ON YOUR OWN

1. When you hear the word *barn*, what barn or barns from your own life do you first see? What feelings and associations do you have with this word? How do you think the barn in your head is different from the barns in your classmates' heads?

2. When you hear the word *cathedral*, what images and associations from your own life come into your head? Once again, how might your class-mates' internal images and associations with the word *cathedral* dif-fer from yours?

3. Now reread the poem and consider the lines "Not the sound your friends know or the sound of a tape played back / but your voice / caught in the dark cathedral of your skull." What do you think Lux means by the metaphor "dark cathedral of your skull"? What seems important about his choice of the word *cathedral* (rather than, say, *house* or *cave* or *gymnasium* or *mansion*)? How does *skull* work (rather than *mind* or *brain* or *head*)? Freewriting for several minutes, create your interpretation of "dark cathedral of the skull."

4. Finally, think for a moment about your thinking processes in trying to interpret "cathedral of the skull." Did you go back and reread the poem, looking for how this line fits other lines of the poem? Did you explore further your own ideas about cathedrals and skull? Our goal is to see if you can catch yourself in the act of interacting with the text—of actively constructing meaning.

WITH YOUR CLASSMATES

5. Compare your responses to questions 1 and 2 with those of your class-mates. How do images of and associations with barns and cathedrals vary?

6. Compare your interpretations of "dark cathedral of the skull." Are there any interpretations that become purely private—that is, that range so far from the text that they can't be supported by evidence in the rest of the poem? (For example, it would be difficult to argue that this metaphor means that the poem is secretly about religion because it uses the term *cathedral*.) Which interpretations make the most sense of the text?

What we have tried to show in the preceding exercise is that a reader's read-ing or interpretation of the text results from a dynamic *two-way interaction*. On the one hand, the text shapes and limits the range of possible meanings: "The Voice You Hear When You Read Silently" cannot be plausibly interpreted as be-ing about racing in the Indianapolis 500, or about the schizophrenic experience of hearing strange voices in your head. On the other hand, each reader will have a slightly different interpretation or set of associations with the text based on her or his experiences, knowledge, and attitudes.

Frequently college writing assignments ask you to explain and support your reading of a text. In these cases, it is important to distinguish between *private* as-sociations that are only loosely related to a text and interpretations that are *pub-licly* defensible in terms of textual evidence. Private associations are one-way responses in which a certain word, image, or idea in a text sends you off into your own world, causing you to lose track of the network of cues in the text as a whole. While such private responses are natural, and indeed one of the pleasures of reading, if you are to offer a public interpretation, you must engage in a two-way interaction with a text, attending both to the text's network of cues and to your personal responses and associations with the text. Thus a good interpretation of "dark cathedral of the skull" must connect to the whole of the poem and illuminate its meaning in a way that makes sense to other readers.

Texts and Their Rhetorical Contexts

A second piece of background knowledge used by rhetorical readers is their awareness that authors base their choices about content, structure, and style on their *rhetorical context*—what we define as the combined factors of audience, genre, and purpose.* Recognizing the influence of context helps rhetorical readers understand a writer's intentions regarding the subject matter and the intended audience and thus to reconstruct the strategy behind the author's choices.

For example, suppose a writer wants to persuade legislators to raise gasoline taxes in order to reduce fossil fuel consumption. His strategy is to persuade different groups of voters to pressure their congressional representatives. If he writes for a scientific audience, his article can include technical data and detailed statistical analyses. If he addresses the general public, however, the style will have to be less technical and more lively, with storylike anecdotes rather than tabular data. If he writes for an environmental publication, he can assume an audience already supportive of his pro-environment values. However, if he writes for a business publication such as the *Wall Street Journal,* he will have to be sensitive to his audience's pro-business values—perhaps by arguing that what's good for the environment is in the long run good for business. Besides adapting content and style to different audiences, writers also adapt their work to the genre in which they publish. A newspaper op-ed piece has different conventions than a hypertext piece in an advocacy Website. A *Popular Science* article has a structure and style different from a *Scientific American* article or an article in a scholarly journal. Finally, suppose the author's purpose changes from persuasion (trying to get voters to support strict environmental laws) to exposition (simply trying to explain to an audience how fossil fuels contribute to global warming). Once again, the content, structure, and style of the article would shift to meet this new purpose.

When you recognize how a text is shaped according to the writer's purpose, audience, and genre, you can decide how to use the text for your own purposes. Let's turn to a more specific example.

AN EXTENDED EXAMPLE: ARTICLES ABOUT TEENAGERS' SLEEP HABITS

In this section we provide specific examples of how purpose, audience, and genre affect the way texts are presented. Consider how differently scientific findings are presented in specialized journals versus the popular press. An original scientific study usually appears first as a technical report in a scientific journal. Such articles

---

Genre is the term rhetoricians use to refer to the conventions of a particular category of writing such as a popular book review versus a research article, a newspaper editorial versus a Webzine opinion piece, or an article in *Seventeen* versus an article in *Rolling Stone* or *Newsweek* or *Scientific American*.

are written for highly specialized experts and are accepted for publication only after being extensively scrutinized for methodology and integrity by expert peer reviewers (also called referees). When a published scientific article contains news-worthy findings, science writers for general circulation newspapers and magazines or for specialized professional organizations "translate" the original technical ma-terial into a form and style appropriate for their targeted audiences. The actual con-tent varies also since the "translators" focus on some parts of the original article and omit other parts. In the original scientific article, the authors carefully review pre-vious literature, describe their methodology in great detail, and usually express their findings cautiously. In the popular press articles, in contrast, the writer usu-ally lavishes attention upon the findings, speculates on their potential usefulness to the public, downplays the original scientists' caution, and says little about meth-ods. Writers for specialized professional publications focus only on aspects of the article relevant to a particular professional field. For example, a scientific study about the effectiveness of a new chicken pox vaccine might be discussed in the *Jour-nal of Community Health Nursing* in terms of patient care and in the *Journal of Health Politics, Policy and Law* in terms of government regulations.

To illustrate the different forms that the information from a scientific study can take, we traced the work of sleep researchers Amy Wolfson and Mary Carskadon through several types of publications whose readers differ in their in-terests and purposes for reading.* Because these articles represent the variety of texts you are likely to encounter when you do research for college papers, the fol-lowing exercise will be good preparation for your work as a rhetorical reader.

• *For Writing and Discussion*

In this exercise we provide the opening paragraph(s) of five articles con-cerning a "Sleep Habits Survey" that Wolfson and Carskadon administered to high school students in 1994. They reported their findings at a scholarly meeting in June 1996, and the study itself was published in 1998. The excerpts are from articles printed in five different periodicals that target five different audiences. Each introduction signals the kinds of interests the writers expect their readers will bring to the articles. Read the excerpts *rhetorically* to see what you can discern about the intended readers for each (their interests, their val-ues, their purposes for reading) and then try to match each introduction to its place of original publication on the list that follows the excerpts.

To guide your analysis, consider the following questions:

1. What implicit question or problem does each introduction address?
2. Who, in particular, does each article seem to be targeting as readers? Educators? Parents? Doctors? Teenagers?

---

*Our approach builds on Arthur Walzer's study, "Articles from the 'California Divorce Project': A Case Study of the Concept of Audience," *College Composition and Communication* 36 (1985): 150–59.

3. How does the introduction draw the reader in? What shared understanding or value between writer and reader is used as a starting point?
4. What beneficial knowledge does each suggest that the reader will gain from the article?
5. How do the format, style, and tone of each introduction give clues about its genre and about the author's methods for establishing credibility with the intended audience?

Article 1

An epidemic of sleeplessness is taking a heavy toll on the nation's children and their ability to learn. A majority of kids say they are sleepy during the day and 15 percent admit to falling asleep in school, a survey reveals.

The problem, which hits teenagers especially hard, is of such looming concern that parents and school districts across the country are considering starting high school hours later, so students will not only rise but shine.

"School is starting at a time when their brains are still on their pillows," said Mary Carskadon, an expert on adolescent sleep and a professor at Brown University. "They're just not there."

Article 2

Our understanding of the development of sleep patterns in adolescents has advanced considerably in the last 20 years. Along the way, theoretical models of the processes underlying the biological regulation of sleep have improved, and certain assumptions and dogmas have been examined and found wanting. Although the full characterization of teen sleep regulation remains to be accomplished, our current understanding poses a number of challenges for the education system.

Article 3

Adolescence is a time of important physical, cognitive, emotional, and social change when the behaviors in one developmental stage are constantly challenged by new abilities, insights, and expectations of the next stage. Sleep is a primary aspect of adolescent development. The way adolescents sleep critically influences their ability to think, behave, and feel during daytime hours. Likewise, daytime activities, changes in the environment, and individual factors can have significant effects on adolescents' sleeping patterns. Over the last two decades, researchers, teachers, parents, and adolescents themselves, have consistently reported that they are not getting enough sleep (Carskadon, 1990a; Carskadon, Harvey, Duke, Anders, & Dement, 1980; Price, Coates, Thoresen, & Grinstead, 1978; Strauch & Meier, 1988).

Article 4

High school will open at 8:30 AM this fall, 65 minutes later than last year, in Edina, Minn, a Minneapolis suburb. School officials hope the 1300 students in grades 9 through 12 will get more sleep and, as a result, be sharper in class.

Area physicians lobbied for the new hours. The Minnesota Medical Association (MMA) wrote the state's 450 school district superintendents in 1994, noting that puberty resets the internal biological clock, prompting teenagers to go to bed later and to need to sleep later than younger children. The MMA cited studies linking inadequate sleep with lower grades and more frequent car crashes. It urged high schools to open at 8 AM or later.

"When the medical community speaks out on an issue of health," said Kenneth Dragseth, Edina superintendent of schools, "it carries a lot of clout."

Article 5

Tired all the time? It's not your fault! Three reasons why:

1. Teens naturally fall asleep later than adults or young children. "People assumed this was because teens wanted independence or had more going on socially," says Mary Carskadon, Ph.D., professor of psychiatry and human behavior at Brown University School of Medicine. Recent studies show that teens secrete melatonin, the hormone that induces sleep, about an hour later than children and adults.

The five introductions you have just read appeared in the publications listed below. Which article introduction goes with which periodical? Briefly freewrite your reasons for linking each piece to its appropriate source. What evidence supports your choice?

- *JAMA: The Journal of the American Medical Association*
- *YM: Young and Modern*
- *Child Development* (published by the Society for Research in Child Development)
- *The Arizona Republic* (daily newspaper in Phoenix)
- *Phi Delta Kappan* (published by the educators' honor society, Phi Delta Kappa)

Additional hint: The *JAMA* article was published under the "Medical News and Perspectives" section.

For the correct answers, see the full article citations at the end of this chapter (but don't look until after you have made your own arguments!).

Learning from the Practices of Experienced Readers

When we ask students to describe the behaviors of good readers, many initially say "speed" or "the ability to understand a text in a single reading." Surprisingly, most experienced readers don't aim for speed reading, nor do they report that reading is an easy, one-step process. On the contrary, experienced readers put considerable effort into reading and rereading a text, adapting their strategies and speed to the demands of the text at hand and to their purpose for reading. Studies of experienced readers show that they consistently do the following:

- Build a context for reading by attending to textual cues as well to their own purpose and knowledge
- Match their reading strategies with the text's genre
- Vary their reading strategies according to their purpose for reading

Let's look at each in turn.

BUILDING A CONTEXT FOR READING

Experienced readers understand that a text is more than just content or information; it is the work of a real person writing on a specific occasion in order to have real effects on real readers. They understand that the text is a part of a larger conversation about a particular topic, and they use textual cues and their own background knowledge to speculate about the context that produced the writing and to formulate questions and make predictions about the text.

These strategies for actively building a context for reading are illustrated in Ann Feldman's report of interviews with expert readers reading texts in their own field. For example, Professor Lynn Weiner, a social historian, had this to say about a chapter from Philippe Aries' *Centuries of Childhood: A Social History of Family Life* entitled "From the Medieval Family to the Modern Family," written in 1962:

> This work isn't precisely in my field and it is a difficult text. I also know it by its reputation. But, like any student, I need to create a context in which to understand this work. When the book was written, the idea of studying the family was relatively new. Before this time historians often studied kings, presidents, and military leaders. That's why this new type of social history encouraged us to ask, "How did ordinary people live?" Not the kings, but the families in the middle ages. Then we have to ask: "Which families is [Aries] talking about? What causes the change that he sees? . . . For whom is the change significant?" . . . I'll want to be careful not . . . to assume the old family is bad and the new family is good. The title suggests a transition so I'll be looking for signs of it.

As Professor Weiner reads, she continues to elaborate this context, confirming and revising predictions, asking new questions, evaluating what Aries has to say in light of the evidence he can provide, and assessing the value of his ideas to her work as a social historian. She concludes by saying, "A path-breaking book, it was credited with advancing the idea that childhood as a stage of life is historically constructed and not the same in every culture and every time. In my own work I might refer to Aries as I think and write about families as they exist today."

Professor Weiner's description of creating a context for understanding Aries suggests that the ability to recognize what you do not know and to raise questions about a text is as important as identifying what you do know and understand. Even experts encounter texts that they find "difficult." As a college student, you will often be asked to read texts in disciplines that are new to you. Although it may seem challenging to build a context for reading in these situations, it is on these very occasions that it is particularly important to do so. By using textual cues to speculate about the situation that produced the text, you will be in a much better position (1) to identify *what you do understand* about the text and (2) to identify *what you do not yet understand* about the text (terms, concepts, references to other texts). Equipped with this kind of information, you can make better predictions about the text's meaning and decide what you need to know and ask in order to accomplish your purposes for reading.

• *For Writing and Discussion*

Even when a text is about an unfamiliar or difficult subject, you can use textual cues to uncover a surprising amount of information that will help you build a context for reading. Imagine that you are enrolled in an introductory philosophy course and have been asked to read philosopher Anthony Weston's *Toward Better Problems: New Perspectives on Abortion, Animal Rights, the Environment, and Justice*. The passage below excerpts key sentences from the opening of Chapter 1, "Practical Ethics in a New Key." In it, find textual cues that might help you build a context for reading. After you have read the passage, answer the questions below.

> Many other "practical ethics" books take up the same topics as this one: abortion, other animals, the environment, justice. Peter Singer covers much the same ground in a book called simply *Practical Ethics*.
>
> The actual practicality of the usual brand of practical ethics, however, is somewhat partial. What we are usually offered is the systematic application of some ethical theory to practice. Singer's book represents an admirably lucid application of utilitarianism. Others apply theories of rights to the same set of issues. . . .
>
> In these well-known kinds of practical ethics, moreover, there is a natural tendency toward a certain kind of closure. The project is to sort out the practical questions at stake in a way that finally allows one or a few facts—one or a few kinds of issues, one or a few aspects of value—to determine the answer. . . .
>
> It is possible, however, to take up practical problems in a radically different spirit, a spirit associated in particular with the work of the American pragmatist John Dewey. This book is an attempt to do so.

ON YOUR OWN

Jot down brief answers to the following questions.

1. What, if any, background knowledge do you bring to this text?
2. Given your level of background knowledge, how would you go about reading the chapter?

3. What seems to be Weston's purpose for writing? How will his text be different from other texts?
4. What questions can you pose for getting as much as possible from your first reading?
5. What terms or references are unfamiliar to you? Where might you find out more about these terms and references?
6. What do you understand so far about the text's meaning? What don't you understand? What do you predict that Weston will say next?

WITH YOUR CLASSMATES

Compare your answers with those of your classmates.

1. What strategies for reading did people offer? Can you agree on a recommended strategy?
2. List the various questions that people formulated for getting as much as possible from the reading. How are they similar and different?
3. List the various predictions your group has made about what will follow in this text. What are various points of agreement and disagreement based upon? Can you clarify any confusion by sharing perspectives?

MATCHING STRATEGIES WITH A TEXT'S GENRE

Besides creating a context for reading, experienced readers use their knowledge of a text's genre conventions to guide their reading process. They know that different genres invite different ways of reading. As we explained earlier, genres are distinguished by recurring patterns in form, style, and use of evidence. Familiarity with a particular genre, such as news stories, can guide your reading of that genre, sometimes unconsciously. Knowing from experience that news reports begin with the key facts of the story and then broaden out to offer background information and additional details (what journalists call the *pyramid structure*), you may just read the first paragraph of the report and skip the details if you're in a hurry or not particularly interested in them.

The same predictability permits expert readers to use genre conventions quite consciously to make their reading more strategic and efficient. Illustration comes from the work of researchers who studied the way that physicists read articles in physics journals. They found that the physicists seldom read the article from beginning to end but instead used their knowledge of the typical structure of scientific articles to find the information most relevant to their interests. Scientific articles typically begin with an abstract or summary of their contents. The main body of the article includes a five-part structure: (1) an introduction that describes the research problem, (2) a review of other studies related to this problem, (3) a description of the methodology used in the research, (4) a report of the results, and (5) the conclusions drawn from the results. The physicists in the study began by reading the abstracts first to see if an article was relevant to their own research. If it was, the experimental physicists went to the methodology section to see if the article reported any new methods while the theoretical physicists went to the results section to see if the article reported any significant new results. These experts, in other words, were guided both by their purpose for reading (based on their own research interests) and by their familiarity with the genre conventions of the scientific research report (which they used to select the portions of the text most relevant to their purpose).

In your college education, you will encounter a wide range of genres, many of which will be initially unfamiliar. Learning the conventions of new genres is one of the ways you gain expertise in the subjects you are studying. When you major in a subject, you need to learn to read and write in the genres valued by that discipline—for example, business majors learn to read and write business proposals and reports; philosophy majors learn to read and write philosophical arguments; anthropology majors learn to read and write ethnographic narratives, and so forth.

MATCHING STRATEGIES WITH PURPOSE FOR READING

Although all readers change their approach to reading according to their purpose, the situation, and the text at hand, most do so unconsciously, relying on a limited set of strategies. By contrast, experienced readers vary their reading process self-consciously and strategically. Here's how one accomplished undergraduate, Sheri, contrasts her "school" reading process with her "reading-for-fun" process:

> When I am reading for class, for starters I make sure that I have all of
> my reading supplies. These include my glasses, a highlighter, pencil, blue pen,
> notebook paper, dictionary, and a quiet place to read, which has a desk or
> table. (It also has to be cold!) Before I read for class or for research purposes I
> always look over chapter headings or bold print words and then formulate
> questions based on these. When I do this it helps me to become more
> interested in the text I am reading because I am now looking for answers.
>
> Also, if there are study guide questions, I will look them over so that I have
> a basic idea of what to look for. I will then read the text all the way through,
> find the answers to my questions, and underline all of the study guide answers
> in pencil.
>
> When I read for fun, it's a whole other story! I always take off my shoes
> and sit on the floor/ground or in a very comfortable chair. I always prefer to
> read in natural light and preferably fresh air. I just read and relax and totally
> immerse myself in the story or article or whatever!

You'll notice, no doubt, that Sheri's reading strategies combine idiosyncratic habits (the blue pen and cold room) with sound, widely used academic reading habits (looking over chapter headings, checking for study guide questions, and so on). Your own reading process is probably a similar combination of personal habits or rituals and more general types of reading behaviors.

As we noted in Chapter 2 when we introduced rhetorical reading as an academic strategy, your purposes for reading academic assignments will vary considerably. So must your academic reading strategies. You will read much differently, for example, if your task is to interpret or analyze a text than if you are simply skimming it for its potential usefulness in a research project. Experienced readers pace themselves according to their purpose, taking advantage of four basic reading speeds.

- *Very fast:* Readers scan a text very quickly if they are looking only for a specific piece of information.
- *Fast:* Readers skim a text rapidly if they are trying to get just the general gist without worrying about details.
- *Slow to moderate:* Readers read carefully in order to get complete understanding of an article. The more difficult the text, the slower they read. Often difficult texts require rereading.
- *Very slow:* Experienced readers read very slowly if their purpose is to analyze a text. They take elaborate marginal notes and often pause to ponder over the construction of a paragraph or the meaning of an image or metaphor. Sometimes they reread the text dozens of times.

As you grow in expertise within the fields you study, you will undoubtedly learn to vary your reading speed and strategies according to your purposes, even to the point of considering "efficient" reading to be a matter of rereading certain texts multiple times.

TAKING STOCK OF HOW YOU READ

The first step in self-consciously managing your reading process is to become aware of what you already do when you read. In the following exercise, we invite you to think about how you read and how you read differently according to situation and purpose.

- ## For Writing and Discussion

  ON YOUR OWN

  Choose two different reading situations that will occur in the next day or two. When you actually do the reading, record all the details you can about these two activities. Use the following questions to guide your two accounts:

  1. List your reasons or purposes for undertaking each reading.
  2. Describe the setting as fully as possible—the place where you are reading, the surroundings, the level of noise or other distractions, the presence or absence of other materials besides the text (pens, laptop, coffee, etc.).

3. Notice what you do to get started—what do you say to yourself, what do you actually do first, what "rituals," if any, do you have for this kind of reading?

4. What were your initial feelings or expectations regarding this reading? If it was an assignment for class, what did you understand about how the specific text fit into the course?

5. List all of the strategies you use as you read—glancing ahead; pausing to reread; reading word-for-word, scanning, or skimming; taking notes. How do you "manage" this particular reading experience? That is, what do you do to keep yourself moving along?

6. Note how often you stop, and think about why you stop. What do you do when you stop? How do you get restarted?

7. How long does it take you to complete this reading?

8. What are the results of this reading? Did the text meet your expectations? What criteria are you using to judge whether the reading experience was successful or satisfying in this case?

After you have completed your two accounts, compare the various aspects of the way you read the two texts and note differences and similarities, then answer these two additional questions:

9. To what extent did your purposes for reading and the reading situations account for these differences or similarities?

10. What most surprised you about your reading processes?

WITH YOUR CLASSMATES

In small groups or as a whole class, share passages from your two accounts and the results of your comparison. What range of reading situations emerges? How did these differences in situation affect reading processes? What common reading practices emerge? What idiosyncratic reading practices are reported?

Summary

This chapter has focused on general strategies for rhetorical reading. It began by explaining two essential pieces of knowledge that you need in order to read rhetorically. First, reading and writing are acts of composing. Reading is an active process in which readers construe a text's meaning by bringing their own values and experiences to the text. Second, authors vary their texts according to their rhetorical context—audience, genre, and purpose. This background knowledge prepared you for the second half of the chapter, which focused on three general strategies used by experienced readers: (1) they build a context for reading; (2) they match their reading strategy with the text's genre; and (3) they match their reading strategy with their own purpose for reading.

SOURCES OF THE ARTICLE EXCERPTS
ABOUT TEENAGERS' SLEEP PATTERNS

This list of sources is presented in the same order as the excerpts used in the For Writing and Discussion exercise on page 32. The citations follow Modern Language Association (MLA) format. (Sample MLA formats for other types of sources are presented in the appendix at the end of this book.)

Article 1
McFarling, Usha Lee. "Kids Clobbered by Sleeplessness; Schools Try Later Starting Times." *Arizona Republic* 27 Mar. 1999, final chaser ed.: A9.

Article 2
Carskadon, Mary A. "When Worlds Collide: Adolescent Need for Sleep Versus Societal Demands." *Phi Delta Kappan* Jan. 1999: 348–53.

Article 3
*Wolfson, Amy R., and Mary A. Carskadon. "Sleep Schedules and Daytime Functioning in Adolescents." *Child Development* 69 (1998): 875–87.

Article 4
Lamberg, Lynne. "Some Schools Agree to Let Sleeping Teens Lie." *JAMA* 276 (1996): 859.

Article 5
Rapoport, Jennifer. "The ZZZ-Files." *YM: Young and Modern* Sept. 1998: 48–49.

---

* This article is reprinted in full in Chapter 11.

Reading and
Responding to Texts

CHAPTER

4

Listening to a Text

Read as though it made sense and perhaps it will.

—I. A. Richards

In Part One we explained what it means to read rhetorically, highlighted the value of rhetorical reading as an academic skill, and provided an overview of the strategies experienced readers use when they encounter academic texts. In Part Two we focus specifically on the nuts and bolts of reading the kinds of texts you will be assigned in college. You will learn to make the strategies used by experienced readers part of your own reading repertoire. These strategies will make you both a better reader and a shrewder writer. Indeed, rhetorical reading strategies overlap with the process of writing by providing you lots of grist for your writing mill.

Our discussion in Part Two extends the metaphor of reading as conversation by using the terms "listening" and "questioning" to describe specific reading techniques. In this chapter we show how listening to a text involves preparation strategies as well as careful reading. As you apply these various techniques for rhetorical reading, your goal is to understand what an author is trying to say by encountering the text empathically, without judgment. *Listening strategies* help you attend closely to a text and thus give it the fairest hearing possible. When you listen attentively to a text, you are reading with the grain, trying to understand it in the way the author intended. In Chapter 5, we explain *questioning strategies*, which will take you back to the text with a different purpose and approach: to read against the grain in order to compose a deeper, critical reading of the text. Your goal then is to apply your own critical thinking so that you can "speak back" to texts with authority and insight.

Let's turn now to the present chapter on listening strategies. We begin by explaining how rhetorical readers read with pen in hand in order to interact with the text and record their ideas-in-progress. We then offer specific *preparing strategies* to help you build an initial context for reading. These include identifying your purpose, recalling background knowledge, reconstructing the text's rhetorical context, and spot reading, all of which encourage you to keep a sense of control and authority as you read. Next we suggest strategies to use while you are in the process of reading: noting organizational signals, marking unfamiliar terms and references, identifying points of difficulty, and annotating. Finally we show you ways to review and deepen your understanding of a text by idea-mapping or diagramming, writing descriptive outlines, summarizing, and writing a rhetorical précis.

Writing as You Read

Skilled rhetorical readers write as they read. Often they write in the margins of the text (unless it is a library book) or they keep a reading log or journal in which they record notes. Sometimes they stop reading in the middle of a passage and freewrite their ideas-in-progress. The text stimulates them to think; writing down their ideas captures their thinking for future reference and stimulates further thought. To put it another way, rhetorical reading strategies focus on both *comprehension* (a reader's understanding of a text) and *invention* (the ideas generated in response to a text). Thus writing while you read helps you generate ideas as well as interact more deeply with the text.

For these reasons, most of the rhetorical reading strategies that we present require you to write. To foster the reading-writing connection, we recommend that you keep a reading log (a notebook or journal) in which you practice the strategies described in this chapter. Keeping a reading log will help you develop advanced reading skills as well as generate a wealth of ideas for essay topics. (Reading log questions accompany all the readings in Part Four, the anthology.)

Depending on your goals for reading a given text, some of the strategies described in this chapter will probably seem more appropriate than others. Some are used consciously by experienced readers on a regular basis; others are designed to help you acquire the mental habits that have become second nature to experienced readers. Experienced readers, for example, almost always take notes as they read, and they frequently write summaries of what they have read. However, experienced readers would be less likely to write a descriptive outline with *says* and *does* statements (see p. 58)—not because the exercise isn't valuable but because they have already internalized the mental habit of attending to both the content and function of paragraphs as they read. By practicing descriptive out-lines on a couple of readings, you too will internalize this dual focus of rhetori-cal reading.

To illustrate the strategies in the rest of this chapter and in Chapter 5, we will use excerpts from philosopher Anthony Weston's *Toward Better Problems* (a por-tion of which was examined in Chapter 3), and the full text of Larissa MacFar-quhar's "Who Cares If Johnny Can't Read?", which you will find at the end of this chapter (p. 65). We use Weston's text to illustrate the difficult kind of read-ing you are likely to be assigned in courses across the curriculum. We use Mac-Farquhar's text as an example of the lively popular pieces you are likely to encounter when doing research on a contemporary culture topic.

Preparing to Read

In completing the "Taking Stock of How You Read" exercise in Chapter 3 (p. 39) you probably discovered that you already have various rituals for reading—a place where you typically read, a favorite snack or beverage that you like to have on hand, and various tricks to keep yourself reading. But did the exercise reveal any time spent preparing to read, such as previewing the text for its gist, scope, and level of difficulty? Taking some time to plan your reading enables you to work efficiently and get the most out of your reading experience from the start. Furthermore, thinking about your purpose will help you maintain a sense of your own authority as you read. The strategies we present encourage you to pre-pare to read as though you were about to join the text in a multivoiced conver-sation. The text you are reading is one voice; a second voice (actually a set of voices) is the network of texts the writer refers to—previous participants in the conversation. The third voice is yours. Articulating your purpose and recalling your background knowledge about the subject (or lack of it) will alert you to what you bring to a text and what you want to get out of reading it. Recon-structing the text's rhetorical context will alert you to the writer's purpose, au-dience, and occasion for writing and thus enable you to make predictions about the text's content, methods, scope, and level of difficulty. Finally, spot reading will enable you to flesh out the context for reading by assessing the fit between your aims for reading and the writer's aims for writing.

IDENTIFYING YOUR PURPOSE

Identifying your purpose at the outset helps you set goals and plan your read-ing accordingly. Your purpose for reading may seem like a self-evident matter—"I'm reading this sociology chapter because it was assigned by my professor." That may be, but what we have in mind is a more strategic consideration of your purpose. How does the reading assignment tie in with themes established in class? How does it fit with concepts laid out on the course syllabus? Is this your first course in sociology? If so, then your purpose might be "to note the types of topics, questions, and special vocabulary used by sociologists." This basic but strategically stated goal might lead you to allow extra time for the slowed down reading that is usually necessary at the beginning of introductory courses.

Let's assume you are skimming articles to select some to read more closely for possible use in a researched argument on gun control. As we discuss in detail in Chapter 7, if you've identified a clear and compelling research question, you will know what you're looking for, and your reading will be more purposeful and productive. At times, your purpose may be at odds with a particular author's purpose in writing the text. Suppose, for example, that you oppose gun control and are reading pro–gun control articles in order to summarize and rebut their arguments. In such a case, you are intentionally reading against the purposes of those authors. Setting goals ahead of time helps you know what to look for. At the same time, you should leave open the possibility that your purposes might change as you read. Reading pro–gun control articles might cause you to moderate your anti–gun control stance a bit. Sometimes you might even discover a new and unexpected purpose. For example, in doing gun control research, you might encounter discussions about conflicts between the right to privacy and background checks and decide that this subissue could become the focus of your paper. Our point, then, is that articulating your purpose for reading will make your reading more efficient and productive.

RECALLING BACKGROUND KNOWLEDGE

Another preparation strategy is to recall your prior knowledge, experience, and opinions regarding the text's subject. What experiences, for example, led to your opposition to gun control? What do you need to learn from your research to write a persuasive argument? A brief review of your background will give you benchmarks for recognizing gaps in your knowledge that you hope to fill through reading and for assessing a given text's effect on your current views or beliefs. Considering your background knowledge will help you determine whether a text has taught you something new, made you consider something you hadn't thought of before, changed your mind, or confirmed your prior knowledge and beliefs. A journal or reading log is the perfect place to brainstorm what you already know or feel about a subject. If you have little knowledge about the subject, jot down some questions about it that will enable you to engage more interactively with what you read.

RECONSTRUCTING RHETORICAL CONTEXT

In Chapter 3 we showed how a text's content, organization, and style are influenced by a writer's rhetorical context—that is, by the writer's intended audience, genre, and purpose. Reconstructing that context before or as you read is a powerful reading strategy. What prompted the author to produce this text? To whom was she writing? What was she trying to accomplish? Sometimes readers can reconstruct context from external clues: a text's title, background notes on the author, date and place of publication, table of contents, graphics or cover design, headings, introduction, and conclusion. But readers often have to rely on internal evidence to get a full picture. A text's context and purpose may become evident through some quick spot reading (described below), especially of the introduction. Sometimes, however, context can be reconstructed only through a great deal of puzzling as you read. It's not unusual that a whole first reading is needed. Once context becomes clear, the text is easier to comprehend upon rereading.

To establish a sense of the text's original rhetorical context, use the available sources of information to formulate at least tentative answers to the following questions:

1. What question(s) is the text addressing?
2. What is the writer's purpose?
3. Who is the intended audience(s)?
4. What situational factors (biographical, historical, political, or cultural) apparently caused the author to write this text?

To explore how external clues reveal context, suppose you are enrolled in a philosophy class and have been assigned to read the Anthony Weston book first mentioned in Chapter 3 (p. 36), *Toward Better Problems: New Perspectives on Abortion, Animal Rights, the Environment, and Justice*. The title and subtitle suggest that the book will address the following question: "How can we find better ways to define difficult social problems such as abortion, animal rights, the environment, and justice?" The words "better" and "new" in the title also imply that this book is a response to other books on the subject and that the author's purpose is to propose a change in outlook. The phrase "better problems" is intriguing— is there such a thing as a "good" or "better" problem? This strange notion, along with the promise of "new" perspectives on thorny social issues, seems designed to pique readers' curiosity.

To place the book in a larger context, however, and to identify the intended audience, we need further information. A quick perusal of the back cover tells us the publisher, Temple University Press, has categorized the text as "Philosophy/Applied Ethics," so we might predict that the book was written for an academic audience, or at least a well-educated one, and that Weston will deal with ethical issues from a philosophical perspective (as opposed to a theological, sociological, or political one). This conclusion is further confirmed by information on the cover that Weston teaches philosophy at the State University of New York–Stony Brook, a note that establishes his academic credentials for writing about this subject. If you don't have a strong background in philosophy, this information may further lead you to conclude that this text may be difficult to read—all the more reason to devote time to investigating its context and purpose, which we explore further in the next section. After all, by virtue of enrolling in the philosophy course, you have become part of Weston's intended audience.

SPOT READING

Spot reading is a process that gives you a quick overview of a text's content and structure, thus accomplishing two purposes: (1) determining the fit between the text's purpose and your own purposes for reading; and (2) giving you an initial framework for predicting content and formulating questions. For example, when your purpose for reading is to acquaint yourself with the vocabulary and concepts of a new field, then spot reading will help you to determine whether a book or article is written at an introductory level. If it is, then you can expect textual cues to point to important new vocabulary and concepts. If it is not, then you may decide to find a more introductory text to read first, or you may decide to allot extra time to reread and look up unfamiliar terms.

If the text that interests you has an abstract or introduction, you might begin spot reading there. Other places for productive spot reading are the opening and concluding paragraphs or sections of a text. The opening usually introduces the subject and announces the purpose, and the conclusion often sums up the text's major ideas. If the text is short, you might try reading the opening sentences of each paragraph. If the text is longer, note chapter titles in the table of contents. Sometimes tables of contents, particularly in textbooks, provide chapter contents and subdivisions. If you are working with a text that provides summaries and study questions, read through these before beginning to read the section they describe. Spot reading a table of contents can help you determine what content will be covered and whether a text will help you address a research question. The organizational strategy revealed through a table of contents also provides important information about an author's method, perhaps guiding you to choose certain sections as essential reading.

As illustration, let's return to Weston's *Toward Better Problems* to consider what the chapter titles in his table of contents reveal about his purpose and method:

Chapter 1: Practical Ethics in a New Key

Chapter 2: Pragmatic Attitudes

Chapter 3: Rethinking the Abortion Debate

Chapter 4: Other Animals

Chapter 5: The Environment*

Chapter 6: Justice

Chapter 7: Conclusion

These titles suggest that the first two chapters spell out his theory for constructing "better problems" and "new perspectives" while each of the next four chapters is devoted to one of the topics listed in the book's subtitle. If you were reading this book independently for background on just one of these topics,

---

*An excerpt from this chapter appears in Chapter 15.

perhaps environmental ethics, you might read only the first two chapters and then the one on the environment.

This particular table of contents lists major subtopics within all but the first chapter (which is only five pages long). The list of subtopics for Chapter 2 gives further indication not only of Weston's purpose and method but of the chapter's crucial value for understanding his approach in the problem-focused chapters that follow:

CHAPTER 2: PRAGMATIC ATTITUDES

From Puzzles to Problematic Situations

Reconstructive Strategies

Integrative Strategies

Given the book title's forecast of "better problems" and "new perspectives," it seems reasonable to predict that in this chapter Weston contrasts two ways of viewing ethical problems: as "puzzles" and as "problematic situations," and that he favors the latter. From these basic clues you can begin to articulate your own purpose for reading and to formulate questions that will help you understand the text: What's the main difference between thinking of ethical problems as puzzles and thinking of them as problematic situations? Why is the latter approach better than the former?

The framework that spot reading provides for making predictions and posing questions about content will help you make sense of ideas and information as you read. It can also help you anticipate and tolerate difficult-to-understand passages, confident that even though you don't understand every bit of the text on the first reading you nevertheless have some sense of its overall meaning. In short, spot reading helps you to stay in control of your reading process by helping you confirm and revise your predictions and look for answers to your questions. It takes little time and offers a worthwhile payoff in increased understanding.

• *For Writing and Discussion*

To demonstrate the value of the various preparation strategies we have described, we invite you to try them out on Larissa MacFarquhar's "Who Cares If Johnny Can't Read?" (p. 65). Later in the chapter we will ask you to read this article carefully. For now, set yourself 10 minutes of preparation time (look at your watch) and try to accomplish the following.

ON YOUR OWN

1. Do some initial spot reading of the text and headnote to get a sense of what the article is about.
2. Based on what you discover about its content, write down a possible purpose you might have for reading it (other than for an assignment).

3. Freewrite briefly about your background on this topic and your feelings about it.
4. Reconstruct the text's rhetorical context: What question(s) does this text address? Who is the intended audience? What seems to be MacFarquhar's main purpose? What historical or cultural factors cause her to write?
5. Continue to spot read to help you answer the above questions.

WITH YOUR CLASSMATES

Share what you each accomplished in 10 minutes.

1. Compare various purposes proposed by group members.
2. What different backgrounds and feelings emerged?
3. What agreement was there about the text's rhetorical context?

ON YOUR OWN AGAIN

Our goal in presenting this exercise is to show you the value of taking a short time to prepare to read, as opposed to simply plunging into a text. What did you learn from the experience? How successful have we been in convincing you to use these strategies?

Listening as You Read Initially

"Listening" to a text means trying to understand the author's ideas, intentions, and worldview—that is, reading *with the grain* of the text, trying to understand it on its own terms. Just as good listeners attend carefully to what their conversational partners say, trying to give them a fair hearing, so too do good readers attend carefully to what a text says, trying to consider the ideas fairly and accurately before rushing to judgment. In particular, college reading requires you to give an impartial hearing to ideas and positions that are new and sometimes radically different from your own. Moreover, in class discussions, examinations, and paper assignments, you will frequently be asked to demonstrate that you have listened well to your assigned texts. Professors want to know that you have comprehended these texts with reasonable accuracy before you proceed to analyze, apply, or critique the ideas in them. In the language of Kenneth Burke's metaphor of the conversational parlor introduced in Chapter 2, you might think of this listening phase of the reading process as the phase where you try to catch the drift of the conversation and give it the fullest and fairest hearing before "putting in your oar."

Listening strategies help you to understand what to listen for, how to hear it, and how to track your evolving understanding of what the text is saying. We have divided this section into two sets of strategies because you need to listen differently the first time you are reading a text than when you are rereading. The first time through, you are trying to understand a text's overall gist and compose a "rough-draft interpretation" of its meaning. The second time through, after you have a sense of the gist, you are aiming to confirm, revise if necessary, and deepen your understanding.

We opened this chapter by urging you to read with a pen or pencil in hand, to adopt experienced readers' practice of marking passages, drawing arrows, and making notes. The following four strategies will guide you through your first reading of a text. These techniques enable you to use textual cues as a road map and your own annotations as trail markers. By marking and annotating a text in this fashion, you will have a record of your reading to use when you are rereading it, writing about it, or reviewing it for a test.

NOTING ORGANIZATIONAL SIGNALS

Organizational signals help you to anticipate and then track the text's overall structure of ideas. Experienced readers use these signals to identify the text's central ideas, to distinguish major ideas from minor ones, to anticipate what is coming next, and to determine the relationship among the text's major ideas. Organizational signals and forecasting statements (which directly tell you what to expect) function like road signs, giving you information about direction, upcoming turns, and the distance yet to go. For example, experienced readers note words such as *however, in contrast,* or *on the other hand* that signal a change in the direction of thought. Likewise, they note words such as *first, second,* and *third* that signal a series of parallel points or ideas; words such as *therefore, consequently,* or *as a result* that signal cause/effect or logical relationships; and words such as *similarly, also,* or *likewise* that signal additional evidence or examples in support of the current point. In addition to transition words and phrases, experienced readers also note a text's use of headings, white space, and other document design elements that signal or emphasize key ideas or relationships among ideas. They often circle or otherwise mark these terms so that a quick glance back will remind them of the structure of ideas.

MARKING UNFAMILIAR TERMS AND REFERENCES

As you read, it is important to mark unfamiliar terms and references because they offer contextual clues about the intended audience and the conversation of which this text is a part. Their very unfamiliarity may tell you that the text is written for an insider audience whose members share a particular kind of knowledge and set of concerns. We suggest that you mark such terms with a question mark or write them in the margins and return to them after you finish your initial reading. Stopping to look them up as you read will break your concentration. By looking them up later, after you have a sense of the text's overall purpose, you will gain insight into how key terms function and how they represent major concerns of a particular field or area of study.

IDENTIFYING POINTS OF DIFFICULTY

Perhaps one of the most important traits of experienced readers is their tolerance for ambiguity and initial confusion. They have learned to read through points of difficulty, trusting in I. A. Richards's advice in the epigraph to this chapter,

"Read as though it made sense and perhaps it will." When you are reading about new and difficult subject matter, you will inevitably encounter passages that you simply do not understand. As we suggested in our advice about building a context for your reading, explicitly identifying what you don't understand is an important reading strategy. We recommend that you bracket puzzling passages and keep reading. Later you can come back to them and try to translate them into your own words or to frame questions about them to ask your classmates and professor.

ANNOTATING

When you annotate a text, you underline, highlight, draw arrows, and make marginal comments. Annotating is a way of making the text your own, of literally putting your mark on it—noting its key passages and ideas. Experienced readers rely on this common but powerful strategy to note reactions and questions, thereby recording their in-process understanding of a text. By using their pen or pencil to mark the page, they are able to monitor their evolving construction of a text's meaning.

Annotations also serve a useful purpose when you return to a text to reread or review it. They can not only remind you of your first impressions of the text's meaning but also help you identify main points and come to new levels of understanding—clearer answers to earlier questions, new insights, and new questions. Indeed, we recommend that you annotate each time you read a text, perhaps using a different colored pen so that you have a record of the new layers of meaning you discover each time you read. Of course, annotating can become counterproductive if you underline or highlight too enthusiastically: a completely underlined paragraph tells you nothing about its key point. To be useful, underlining must be selective, based both on your own purposes for reading and on what you think the writer's main points are. In general, when it is time to review the text and recall its main ideas, notes in the margin about main ideas, questions or objections, and connections among ideas will be far more useful to you than underlining or highlighting.

To illustrate these listening strategies, we have annotated a passage from Weston's *Toward Better Problems*. The annotations were made from the perspective of a student enrolled in an introductory philosophy class who is trying (1) to uncover Weston's purpose in writing, especially the distinctions he makes between other ethicists and himself, and (2) to understand his use of key terms such as "practical," "problem," and "puzzle." The annotated paragraphs come from Chapter 1, "Practical Ethics in a New Key," and immediately follow the passage we presented in Chapter 3's discussion of building a context for reading (p. 36).

> 1 In this book I do *not* propose new "solutions" to the old problems to put alongside the two or five plausible principle-based solutions already debated in the literature. Nor do I propose a

new set of ethical principles to put alongside the familiar utilitarianisms and theories of rights. I am not concerned with rearranging the contours of the familiar problems so that somewhat different dimensions determine a somewhat new set of answers. Instead, I have pursued two rather different general strategies.

First, in engaging practical issues I aim to draw out their complexity, to view them from multiple sides and on many levels. I will *resist* taking one or a few dimensions of a problem to alone determine an ethical response. I will insist that ethical problems are seldom "puzzles," allowing specific and conclusive "solutions." Instead I will treat them as larger and vaguer regions of tension, requiring very different strategies in response. In addition I will regularly ask how we ended up in a situation where these particular kinds of difficulties emerge as problems in the first place. "The" problems as first presented are not taken as sacrosanct, and they may end up still more complex once viewed in social and historical perspective.

This may hardly seem practical. One may certainly wonder how making a problem still more complex contributes to solving it. Part of my answer will be that "solutions" in the contemporary sense are not exactly what we should seek. We *are* concerned, in the pragmatic spirit, with effective and intelligent action in the present and with progressive change in the future. But viewing problems in a more complex and multi-sided way, I will argue, is actually a means to those ends. By keeping our conception of a problem many-sided and flexible, we begin to make ethical thinking a process of engagement rather than a more episodic kind of problem solving. In such an ongoing process there is more room for inventiveness, experiment, and imagination. It will be understood that the problem allows many different approaches and that their promise cannot be known a priori. Moreover, by inquiring into the social and historical roots of ethical problems, we open the possibility of transforming "the" problem itself into something more manageable. This project Dewey called "reconstruction," and it will be a central theme in this book.

Second, in engaging the values at stake in such problems, the approach in this book will be "integrative." Rather than trying to define certain dimensions of value as determinative, overriding others, the project here is to engage and sort out a complex and conflicting set of values from *within:* to try to clarify their dynamics without simplifying them, and to suggest ways to rearrange and better integrate some of the less clear values while still honoring their place within the whole.

Marginal annotations:

2

Not familiar to me! Need to check these terms. Assumes audience knows terms.

First way his approach differs from other approaches. Ethical problems not puzzles with neat solutions but "regions of tension." What does he mean?

3

Anticipates objections.

Claims his approach will lead to more long-term action and change.

What does this term mean?

4

Second new approach— integrating complex and conflicting values. How? Examples?

• *For Writing and Discussion*

Earlier in this chapter you tried out some "preparing to read" strategies on Larissa MacFarquhar's "Who Cares If Johnny Can't Read?" (p. 65). It is now time for you to read that essay carefully, listening to MacFarquhar's argument.

ON YOUR OWN

As you read the essay the first time, try your hand at marking and annotating.

1. Note organizational signals, unfamiliar terms, and difficult passages.
2. Annotate what you believe to be her key ideas and the most important passages.
3. Record your reactions and questions in the margins.

WITH YOUR CLASSMATES

Compare your markings and annotations of this essay.

1. What differences and similarities were there in different people's underlining, marking, and marginal notes? What do you conclude will be an efficient strategy for you?
2. As a group, make a brief list of MacFarquhar's key points and ideas. Compare your group's list with those of other groups and try to arrive at a consensus.

Listening as You Reread

Rhetorical reading, as we have been suggesting, is not a one-step process but requires careful reading and rereading to confirm and deepen your understanding of a text. All four of the following strategies aim to extend your interaction with texts. They will help you acquire the mental habits of strong readers and will give you practice with the types of writing you will use frequently as part of college-level analysis and research.

MAPPING THE IDEA STRUCTURE

One of the goals of rereading is to get a sense of how the text works as a whole—how its ideas connect and relate to one another. Idea maps provide a visual representation of the ways that a text's ideas relate to each other, enabling you to distinguish main ideas from subordinate ones and to understand relationships among the writer's points. You might think of idea maps as X-rays of the text's idea structure.

To create a map, draw a circle in the center of a page and write the text's main idea inside the circle. Then record the text's supporting ideas on branches and subbranches that extend from the center circle. In Figure 4.1 we offer a sample idea map of the Weston passage annotated on page 55. Creating a map is not an

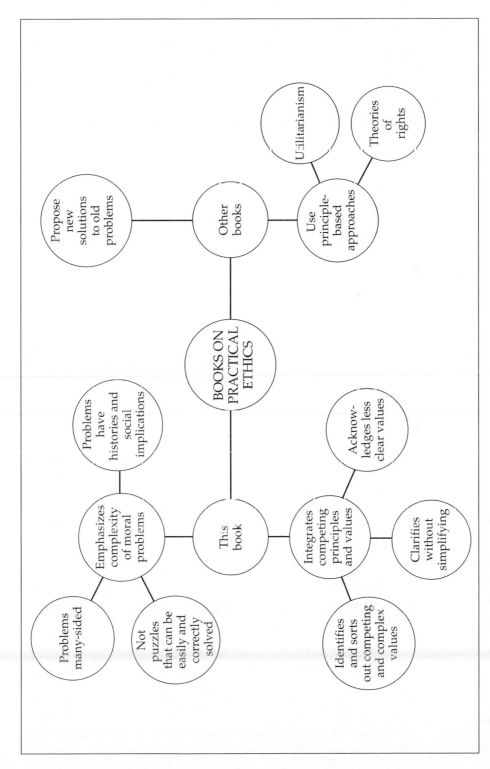

FIGURE 4.1 An Idea Map for the Weston Passage

easy task because it forces you to think about the text's main ideas in a new way. You may even find that creating a map reveals inconsistencies in the text's organizational structure or puzzling relationships among ideas. This, too, is important information and may be an issue you should bring up in class discussion or in your written responses to the text. In any case, creating idea maps is a way to understand a text at a deeper level and thus to evaluate its importance in relation to course content or in relation to a writing project of your own.

DESCRIPTIVE OUTLINING

Making a descriptive outline is a particularly powerful technique for examining how a text is constructed in terms of what discrete parts of it *do* and *say*.* The technique calls for brief statements about the function and content of each paragraph or cluster of related paragraphs in a text. The *does* statement identifies a paragraph's or section's function or purpose, while the *says* statement summarizes the content of the same stretch of text. *Does* statements should not repeat the content but focus instead on the purpose or function of the content in relation to the overall argument. Sample *does* statements might be, "offers an anecdote to illustrate previous point," "introduces a new reason in support of main argument," "provides statistical evidence to support the claim," or "summarizes the previous section."

Does and *says* statements help you to see how the text works at the microlevel, paragraph by paragraph, section by section. These statements are particularly useful if you intend later to write an analysis or critique of the author's rhetorical methods. Here are *does* and *says* statements for the Weston passage that we annotated and mapped above:

- Par. 1: *Does:* Distinguishes the author's approach to practical ethics from other authors' approaches. *Says*: This book will not offer new solutions nor apply new principles to "old" ethical problems, but it will introduce two new ways of thinking about ethical problems.
- Par. 2: *Does:* Describes aim and effect of author's first new approach to ethical problems. *Says:* This approach complicates ethical issues, viewing them as multisided and without simple solutions.
- Par. 3: *Does:* Anticipates objections to the author's first approach and explains it further. *Says:* Although complicating ethical issues seems "impractical," it actually can enable us to transform ethical problems into more manageable issues—that is, Dewey's idea of "reconstruction," which will be a major theme of the book.
- Par. 4: *Does:* Describes aim and effect of author's second new approach to ethical problems. *Says:* His approach is "integrative" because it seeks to sort out and integrate the multiple and competing values entailed in ethical problems without defining any as determinative.

---

*For our discussion of descriptive outlining, we are indebted to Kenneth Bruffee, *A Short Course in Writing*, 3rd ed. (Boston: Little Brown, 1985) 103.

• *For Writing and Discussion*

ON YOUR OWN

Make an idea map of Larissa MacFarquhar's essay (p. 65). Now make a descriptive outline of the essay, paragraph by paragraph. At first you will find both tasks difficult, and you will probably be forced to reread the article slowly, part by part. (That's one of our points—the need to reread.) Soon, however, your puzzlement will evolve into a much clearer understanding of her argument. Trust us. You may find that it is easier to do the descriptive outline first and then the idea map. To help you get started, here is a descriptive outline of the first three paragraphs of MacFarquhar's essay. This outline was written by a student named Jenny, whose work we will follow closely in this and later chapters.

> Par. 1: *Does:* Introduces subject of article and presents three common beliefs about the subject. *Says:* Many believe America is in a state of cultural decline because Americans read less than they used to, because they don't read the "classics," and because new media threaten to make the book obsolete.

> Par. 2: *Does:* Rebuts all three of these common beliefs with facts. *Says:* The claims that Americans read less and know nothing about the classics are false as is the idea that books are becoming obsolete.

> Par. 3: *Does:* Continues to rebut opposing claims with facts and figures. *Says:* Americans are buying and reading more books than they did in the past.

WITH YOUR CLASSMATES

Working in small groups, compare your idea maps and descriptive outlines. Each group can then draw a revised idea map and put it on the board or an overhead for comparison with those of other groups.

COMPOSING A SUMMARY

Probably the best way to demonstrate your understanding of what a writer has said is to compose a *summary*—a condensed version of a text's points written in your own words, conveying the author's main ideas but eliminating all the supporting details. In academic and professional work, summaries take many forms and fulfill a variety of functions. In research papers you will often present brief summaries of sources to give readers an overview of another writer's perspective or argument, thus bringing another voice into the conversation. Such summaries are particularly useful to set the context for a quotation. If the source is particularly important, you might write a longer summary—perhaps even a full paragraph. Many academic writing assignments call for a *review of the literature,* a section in which you summarize how previous researchers have addressed your research problem. In a persuasive "take a stand" paper, you'll likely use summaries to provide evidence that supports your view as well as to present fully and accurately any arguments that oppose your view (after which you will try to counter these arguments). If you are writing a paper in the social or physical sciences, you will often be expected to write an *abstract* (another type of summary) of your paper, since it is conventional in the sciences to begin published work with a highly condensed overview in case busy readers don't have time to read the whole paper. In business and professional life, the equivalent of an abstract is the *executive summary,* a section that appears at the front of any major business report or proposal. Summary writing, in other words, is not simply a strategy for rhetorical reading; it is one of the most frequent types of writing you will do in your academic and professional life.

Depending upon their purpose, summaries can vary in length. At times, you may summarize a text in a single sentence as a way of invoking the authority of another voice (probably an expert) to support your points. For example, suppose you wanted to use Weston's approach to ethical issues in a paper exploring whether the Makah people of the Pacific Northwest should be allowed to hunt whales. In part this is an ethical issue pitting the rights of whales against the rights of native peoples to follow their ancient traditions. You might begin a section by summarizing Weston as follows: "In *Toward Better Problems,* Anthony Weston argues that complex ethical problems like environmental issues cannot be viewed as simple puzzles to be solved." After this brief summary, which helps you make your point that environmental issues are many-sided without right answers, you would proceed to explain how the puzzle concept has been wrongly applied in this controversy. Perhaps you would later use ideas Weston develops in his chapters "Other Animals" and "The Environment" as frames for presenting an alternative way of understanding the Makah whaling controversy.

At other times, summaries may be one of your main purposes for writing. A typical college assignment might ask you to summarize the arguments of two writers and then analyze the differences in their views. In the summary part of this assignment, your professor is asking you to demonstrate your understanding of what may be quite complex arguments.

Writing a fair and accurate summary requires that you identify a text's main ideas, state them in your own words, and omit supporting details. The best first step for writing a summary is to create a descriptive outline of the text, where the *says* statements summarize the main point of each paragraph. (A first draft of your summary could be simply your sequencing of all your *says* statements.) Writing descriptive outlines also helps you see how almost all texts—even very short ones—can be divided into a sequence of sections, parts, or stages. In other words, groups of paragraphs often chunk together to form distinctive sections of the argument. Identifying these parts or chunks is particularly helpful because you can then write a summary of each chunk and then combine the chunks. Here then is a general procedure you can use:

- Step 1: Read the text first for its main points.
- Step 2: Reread carefully and make a descriptive outline.
- Step 3: Write out the text's thesis or main point. (Suppose you had to summarize the whole argument in one sentence.)
- Step 4: Identify the text's major divisions or chunks. Each division develops one of the stages needed to make the whole main point. Typically these stages or parts might function as background, review of the conversation, summary of opposing views, or subpoints in support of the thesis.
- Step 5: Try summarizing each part in one or two sentences.
- Step 6: Now combine your summaries of the parts into a coherent whole, creating a condensed version of the text's main ideas in your own words.

To illustrate this process, let's look at the notes Jenny took while following these steps, and then examine her summary of MacFarquhar's essay. (The beginning of Jenny's descriptive outline appears on page 59; these notes begin at Step 3 of the summary procedure.)

Jenny's Process Notes for Writing a Summary

Step 3—Text's main idea:

MacFarquhar disagrees with the popular idea that reading is good and TV watching is bad and asks us to think more deeply about what kinds of reading and what kinds of TV watching might be good.

Steps 4 and 5—Text's major chunks and main points of each chunk:

Par. 1-2: Introduces debate about literacy. Main point: Common claim that reading is declining is wrong.

Par. 3-8: Compares old and new reading habits. Main points: Differences between present and past reading habits are exaggerated. Certain genres of reading are very popular today, although not the classics.

Par. 9-14: Discusses two related questions: Does it matter what one reads? Or is reading valuable in and of itself? Main point: It is too simple to say that reading is good and TV watching is bad.

Par. 15: Concludes with new question. Main point: We are asking the wrong question. We should be asking why certain kinds of reading and television matter in terms of cultural health.

Jenny's Summary

In "Who Cares If Johnny Can't Read?" published in the online journal *Slate* on April 16, 1997, Larissa MacFarquhar informs readers that those who think that Americans no longer read books are mistaken. According to MacFarquhar, Americans are reading more than ever, although they are reading genre fiction and self-help books instead of the classics. This preference for "popular" books leads MacFarquhar to raise two related questions: Does it matter what people read or only if they read? Many persons today, says MacFarquhar, believe that reading in and of itself matters because reading is considered more intellectually stimulating and culturally valuable than watching television. MacFarquhar opposes this view by suggesting that both questions are "beside the point," for in her opinion, the key question should be "why certain kinds of reading and certain kinds of television might matter in the first place" (par. 16).*

CHECKLIST FOR EVALUATING SUMMARIES

Good summaries must be fair, balanced, accurate, and complete. This checklist of questions will help you evaluate drafts of a summary.

- Is the summary economical and precise?
- Is the summary neutral in its representation of the original author's ideas, omitting the writer's own opinions?
- Does the summary reflect the proportionate coverage given various points in the original text?
- Are the original author's ideas expressed in the summary writer's own words?
- Does the summary use attributive tags (such as "Weston argues") to remind readers whose ideas are being presented?
- Does the summary quote sparingly (usually only key ideas or phrases that cannot be said precisely except in the original author's own words)?
- Will the summary stand alone as a unified and coherent piece of writing?
- Is the original source cited so that readers can locate it?

WRITING A RHETORICAL PRÉCIS

A *rhetorical précis* differs from a summary in that it is a less neutral, more analytical condensation of both the content and method of the original text. ("Précis" means "concise summary.") If you think of a summary as primarily a brief representation of what a text says, then you might think of the rhetorical précis as a brief representation of what a text both says and does. Although less common than summary, a rhetorical précis is a particularly useful way to sum up your understanding of how a text works rhetorically.

---

*Because MacFarquhar's essay was published in an online magazine without page or paragraph numbers, page references for quotes cannot be provided. (Guidelines for such situations are discussed in Chapter 8.) Here, Jenny is following her teacher's request for in-text references to the paragraph numbers provided in the reprint at the end of this chapter.

Part summary and part analysis, the rhetorical précis is a powerful skill-building exercise often assigned as a highly structured four-sentence paragraph.* These sentences provide a condensed statement of a text's main point (the summary part), followed by brief statements about the text's essential rhetorical elements: the author's purpose, methods, and intended audience (the analysis part). Here are specific directions for what to include in a four-sentence rhetorical précis:

Structure of a Rhetorical Précis

- **Sentence 1:** Name of author, genre, and title of work, date in parentheses; a rhetorically accurate verb (such as "claims," "argues," "asserts," "suggests"); and a THAT clause containing the major assertion or thesis statement in the work.
- **Sentence 2:** An explanation of how the author develops and supports the thesis, usually in chronological order.
- **Sentence 3:** A statement of the author's apparent purpose, followed by an "in order to" phrase.
- **Sentence 4:** A description of the intended audience and/or the relationship the author establishes with the audience.

Jenny's Rhetorical Précis

In her online article "Who Cares If Johnny Can't Read" (1997), Larissa MacFarquhar asserts that Americans are reading more than ever despite claims to the contrary and that it is time to reconsider why we value reading so much, especially certain kinds of "high culture" reading. MacFarquhar supports her claims about American reading habits with facts and statistics that compare past and present reading practices, and she challenges common assumptions by raising questions about reading's intrinsic value. Her purpose is to dispel certain myths about reading in order to raise new and more important questions about the value of reading and other media in our culture. She seems to have a young, hip, somewhat irreverent audience in mind because her tone is sarcastic, and she suggests that the ideas she opposes are old-fashioned positions.

---

*For the rhetorical précis assignment, we are indebted to Margaret K. Woodworth, "The Rhetorical Précis," *Rhetoric Review* 7 (1988): 156–65.

Summary

This chapter focused on the nuts and bolts of preparing to read and listening to a text. First we pointed out that effective readers read with pen in hand, interacting with texts by making annotations as they read. Before reading, skilled readers practice preparatory strategies such as identifying their purpose for reading, recalling background knowledge, reconstructing the text's rhetorical context, and spot reading. While reading, they note organizational signals, mark unfamiliar terms and references, identify points of difficulty, and annotate the text with marginal comments and queries. When they reread and prepare to write about a text, skilled readers employ various strategies for deepening their understanding: idea mapping, writing descriptive outlines, summarizing, and writing a rhetorical précis.

In the next chapter we show how rhetorical readers "speak back" to a text through questioning.

● *A Brief Writing Project*

Your instructor will identify a text for you to read carefully and annotate using the rhetorical reading strategies suggested in this chapter. Then submit to your instructor the following three pieces of writing:

1. A descriptive outline of the text
2. A 150- to 200-word summary of the text
3. A four-sentence rhetorical précis of the text

Larissa MacFarquhar

Who Cares If Johnny Can't Read?
The Value of Books Is Overstated.

This essay was published on April 16, 1997, in *Slate,* Microsoft's online magazine about politics and culture. Larissa MacFarquhar, a widely published book reviewer and magazine writer, was then a frequent contributor to that magazine as well as a contributing editor of *Lingua Franca,* a magazine about higher education, and an advisory editor at the *Paris Review,* a prestigious literary journal. The title of the following selection alludes to Rudolf Flesch's 1955 *Why Johnny Can't Read,* one of the first books to declare a national literacy crisis. To find out more about *Slate* and read other articles by MacFarquhar, go to its Website at http://slate.msn.com.

———————　●　———————

Among the truisms that make up the eschatology of American cultural decline, 1 one of the most banal is the assumption that Americans don't read. Once, the story goes—in the 1950s, say—we read much more than we do now, and read the good stuff, the classics. Now, we don't care about reading anymore, we're barely literate, and television and computers are rendering books obsolete.

None of this is true. We read much more now than we did in the '50s. In 1957, 2 17 percent of people surveyed in a Gallup poll said they were currently reading a book; in 1990, over twice as many did. In 1953, 40 percent of people polled by Gallup could name the author of *Huckleberry Finn;* in 1990, 51 percent could. In 1950, 8,600 new titles were published; in 1981, almost five times as many.

In fact, Americans are buying more books now than ever before—over 2 3 billion in 1992. Between the early '70s and the early '80s, the number of bookstores in this country nearly doubled—and that was before the Barnes & Noble superstore and Amazon.com. People aren't just buying books as status objects, either. A 1992 survey found that the average adult American reads 11.2 books per year, which means that the country as a whole reads about 2 billion— the number bought. There are more than 250,000 reading groups in the country at the moment, which means that something like 2 million people regularly read books and meet to discuss them.

In his book about Jewish immigrants in America at the turn of the century, 4 *World of Our Fathers,* Irving Howe describes a time that sounds impossibly antiquated, when minimally educated laborers extended their workdays to attend lectures and language classes. Howe quotes an immigrant worker remembering his adolescence in Russia: "How can I describe to you . . . the excitement we shared when we would discuss Dostoyevsky? . . . Here in America young people can choose from movies and music and art and dancing and God alone knows what. But we—all we had was books, and not so many of them, either."

Hearing so much about the philistinism of Americans, we think such sen- 5 timents fossils of a bygone age. But they're not. People still write like that about books. Of course, most aren't reading Dostoyevsky. The authors who attract thousands and thousands of readers who read everything they write and send letters to them begging for more seem to be the authors of genre fiction—romances, science fiction, and mysteries.

6   Romance readers are especially devoted. The average romance reader spends $1,200 a year on books, and often comes to think of her favorite authors as close friends. Romance writer Debbie Macomber, for instance, gets thousands of letters a year, and when her daughter had a baby, readers sent her a baby blanket and a homemade Christmas stocking with the baby's name embroidered on it. It's writers like Macomber who account for the book boom. In 1994, a full 50 percent of books purchased fell into the category of "popular fiction." (Business and self-help books were the next biggest group at 12 percent, followed by "cooking/crafts" at 11 percent, "religion" at 7 percent, and "art/literature/poetry" at 5 percent.)

7   These reading habits are not new. Genre fiction and self-help books have constituted the bulk of the American book market for at least 200 years. A survey conducted in 1930 found that the No. 1 topic people wanted to read about was personal hygiene. And you just have to glance through a list of best sellers through the ages to realize how little we've changed: *Daily Strength for Daily Needs* (1895); *Think and Grow Rich* (1937); *Games People Play: The Psychology of Human Relationships* (1964); *Harlow: An Intimate Biography* (1964).

8   Romance writers tend to be clear-eyed about what it is they're doing. They don't think they're creating subversive feminine versions of Proust. They're producing mass-market entertainment that appeals to its consumers for much the same reason as McDonald's and Burger King appeal to theirs: It's easy, it makes you feel good, and it's the same every time. The point of a romance novel is not to dazzle its reader with originality, but to stimulate predictable emotions by means of familiar cultural symbols. As romance writer Kathleen Gilles Seidel puts it: "My reader comes to my book when she is tired. . . . Reading may be the only way she knows how to relax. If I am able to give her a few delicious, relaxing hours, that is a noble enough purpose for me."

9   But then, if romance novels are just another way to relax, what, if anything, makes them different from movies or beer? Why should the activity "reading romances" be grouped together with "reading philosophy" rather than with "going for a massage"? The Center for the Book in the Library of Congress spends lots of time and money coming up with slogans like "Books Make a Difference." But is the mere fact of reading something—*anything*—a cultural achievement worth celebrating?

10   We haven't always thought so. When the novel first became popular in America in the latter half of the 18th century, it was denounced as a sapper of brain cells and a threat to high culture in much the same way that television is denounced today. In the 1940s, Edmund Wilson declared that "detective stories [are] simply a kind of vice that, for silliness and minor harmfulness, ranks somewhere between smoking and crossword puzzles." You almost never hear this kind of talk anymore in discussions of American reading habits: *Not all reading is worth doing. Some books are just a waste of time.*

As fears of cultural apocalypse have been transferred away from novels 11
onto a series of high-tech successors (radio, movies, television, and now computers), books have acquired a reputation for educational and even moral worthiness. Books are special: You can send them through the mail for lower rates,
and there are no customs duties imposed on books imported into this country.
There have, of course, been endless culture wars fought over what kind of
books should be read in school, but in discussions of adult reading habits these
distinctions tend to evaporate.

The sentimentalization of books gets especially ripe when reading is com- 12
pared with its supposed rivals: television and cyberspace. Valorization of reading over television, for instance, is often based on the vague and groundless
notion that reading is somehow "active" and television "passive." Why it is
that the imaginative work done by a reader is more strenuous or worthwhile
than that done by a viewer—or why watching television is more passive than,
say, watching a play—is never explained. Sven Birkerts' maudlin 1994 paean
to books, *The Gutenberg Elegies: The Fate of Reading in an Electronic Age*, is a classic example of this genre. *Time* art critic Robert Hughes made a similarly sentimental and mysterious argument recently in the *New York Review of Books:*

> Reading is a collaborative act, in which your imagination goes halfway to meet
> the author's; you visualize the book as you read it, you participate in mak-
> ing up the characters and rounding them out. . . . The effort of bringing some-
> thing vivid out of the neutral array of black print is quite different, and in
> my experience far better for the imagination, than passive submission to the
> bright icons of television, which come complete and overwhelming, and tend
> to burn out the tender wiring of a child's imagination because they allow no
> re-working.

I cannot remember ever visualizing a book's characters, but everyone who 13
writes about reading seems to do this, so perhaps I'm in the minority. Still, you
could equally well say that you participate in making up TV characters because
you have to imagine what they're thinking, where in a novel, you're often provided with this information.

Another reason why books are supposed to be better than television is that 14
books are quirky and individualistic and real, whereas television is mass-
produced corporate schlock. But of course popular books can be, and usually
are, every bit as formulaic and "corporatized" as television. The best books
might be better than the best television, but further down the pile the difference gets murkier. Most of the time the choice between books and television is
not between Virgil and Geraldo but between *The Celestine Prophecy* and
Roseanne. Who wouldn't pick *Roseanne*?

If the fertility of our culture is what we're concerned about, then 15
McLuhanesque musing on the intrinsic nature of reading (as if it had any such
thing) is beside the point. Reading *per se* is not the issue. The point is to figure
out why certain kinds of reading and certain kinds of television might matter
in the first place.

CHAPTER

5

Questioning a Text

*A good question is never answered. It is not a bolt to be tight-
ened into place but a seed to be planted and to bear more seed toward the hope of greening the landscape of idea.*

—John Ciardi

Whereas the previous chapter focused on listening to a text *with the grain* in order to understand it as fully as possible, in this chapter we focus on questioning a text, which involves reading it analytically and skeptically, *against the grain*. If you think of listening to a text as the author's turn in a conversation, then you might think of questioning the text as your opportunity to respond to the text by interrogating it, raising points of agreement and disagreement, thinking critically about its argument and methods, and then talking back.

What It Means to Question a Text

Learning to question a text is central to your academic success in college. Your professors will ask you to engage with texts in ways that you may not be used to. They expect you to do more than just "bank" the knowledge you glean from reading; they expect you to use this knowledge to do various kinds of intellectual work—to offer your own interpretations or evaluations, to launch a research project of your own, to synthesize the ideas among readings and draw independent conclusions.

However, questioning does not necessarily mean just fault-finding, and it certainly doesn't mean dismissing an author's ideas wholesale. Rather, it entails carefully interrogating a text's claims and evidence and its subtle forms of persuasion so that you can make sound judgments and offer thoughtful responses. Your job in critiquing a text is to be "critical." However, the term *critical* means "characterized by careful and exact evaluation and judgment," not simply by "disagreement" or "harsh judgment." In questioning a text, you bring your critical faculties as well as your experience, knowledge, and opinion to bear on it, but you do so in a way that treats the author's ideas fairly and makes judgments that can be supported by textual evidence.

This chapter offers you a repertoire of useful strategies to help you question a text and explore your responses to it. At the end of the chapter, we show you an analytical paper that student writer Jenny (whose work you followed in Chapter 4) wrote in response to an assignment calling for a rhetorical analysis of Larissa MacFarquhar's article, "Who Cares If Johnny Can't Read?" In that paper, Jenny uses the questioning strategies described in this chapter to analyze MacFarquhar's argument and methods. Our purpose is to demonstrate how such strategies can enable you to write critical analyses valued by college professors.

Strategies for Questioning a Text

The five questioning strategies in this section offer powerful ways to question a text's argument, assumptions, and methods by examining a writer's credibility, appeals to reason, strategies for engaging readers, and language as well as the text's ideology. The first three strategies examine an author's use of the three classical rhetorical appeals identified by Aristotle: *ethos* (the persuasive power of the author's credibility or character); *logos* (the persuasive power of the author's reasons, evidence, and logic); and *pathos* (the persuasive power of the author's appeal to the interests, emotions, and imagination of the audience). Although these three appeals interconnect and sometimes overlap—for example, a writer may use a touching anecdote both to establish credibility as an empathic person and to play on the reader's emotions—we introduce them separately in order to emphasize their distinct functions as means of persuasion. The last two questioning strategies that we present focus on language and ideology. Though not persuasive appeals themselves, language and ideology are the materials with which appeals are made. They merit separate treatment because they can reveal additional ways that texts attempt to influence readers.

EXAMINING A WRITER'S CREDIBILITY

To change readers' minds about something, writers must make themselves credible by creating an image of themselves that will gain their readers' confidence. In most cases, writers want to project themselves as knowledgeable, fair-minded, and trustworthy. To examine a writer's credibility, ask yourself, "Do I find this author believable and trustworthy? Why or why not?" Experienced readers always try to find out as much as possible about an author's background, interests, political leanings, and general worldview. Sometimes they have independent knowledge of the writer, either because the writer is well known or because the reading has a headnote or footnote describing the writer's credentials. Often, though, readers must discern the writer's personality and views from the text itself by examining content, tone, word choice, figurative language, organization, and other cues that help create an image of the writer in the reader's mind. Explicit questions to ask might include these: Does this writer seem knowledgeable? What does the writer like and dislike? What are this writer's biases and values? What seems to be the writer's mood? (Is he or she angry? Questioning? Meditative? Upset? Jovial?) What is the writer's approach to the topic? (Formal or informal? Logical or emotional? Scientific or personal?) What would it be like to spend time in this writer's company?

• *For Writing and Discussion*

ON YOUR OWN

1. To help you consider an author's image and credibility, try these activities the next time you are assigned a reading. Describe in words your image of this author as a person (or draw a sketch of this person). Then try to figure out what cues in the text produced this image for you. Finally, consider how this image of the writer leads you to ask more questions about the text. You might ask, for example, Why is this writer angry? Why does this writer use emotionally laden anecdotes rather than statistics to support his or her case? What is this writer afraid of?
2. Try these activities with Larissa MacFarquhar's article on page 65. What kind of an image does she create for herself in this text? How would you describe her in words or portray her in a drawing? Take a few minutes to find and jot down the cues in the text that create this image for you.

WITH YOUR CLASSMATES

Compare your impressions of MacFarquhar with those of your classmates. Do any contradictory traits come up? That is, do some people in the group interpret the textual cues differently? Some people, for example, might see a comment as "forthright" and "frank" while others might see it as "rude." What aspects of her character (as represented in the text) do you as a group agree on? What aspects do you disagree about?

EXAMINING A WRITER'S APPEALS TO REASON

Perhaps the most direct way that writers try to persuade readers is through logic or reason. To convince readers that their perspective is reasonable, skilled writers work to anticipate what their intended readers already believe and then use those beliefs as a bridge to the writer's way of thinking. They support their claims through a combination of reasons and evidence.

For example, imagine a writer arguing for stricter gun control laws. This writer wants to root his argument in a belief or value that he and his readers already share, so he focuses on concerns for the safety of schoolchildren. The line of reasoning might go something like this: Because the ready availability of guns makes children no longer safe at school, we must pass strict gun control laws to limit access to guns. Of course, readers may or may not go along with this argument. Some readers, although they share the writer's concern for the safety of schoolchildren, might disagree at several points with the writer's logic: Is the availability of guns the main cause of gun violence at schools or are there other more compelling causes? Will stricter gun control laws really limit the availability of guns? If this same writer wished to use evidence to strengthen this argument, he might use statistics showing a correlation between the rise in the availability of guns and the rise in gun violence in schools. Here, the writer would be operating on the assumption that readers believe in facts and can be persuaded by these statistics that increased gun violence in schools is linked to the availability of firearms.

Experienced readers are alert to the logical strategies used by authors, and they have learned not to take what may appear as a "reasonable" argument at face value. In other words, they have learned to question or test this reasoning before assenting to the position the author wants them to take. To examine a writer's reasoning, think about two questions: (1) What perspective or position does the writer want me to take toward the topic? and (2) Do the writer's claims, reasons, and evidence convince me to take this perspective or position? Answering these questions requires you to examine the argument carefully. In Chapter 13, "Taking a Stand," we discuss the four elements of an argument—claims, reasons, evidence, and assumptions—in relation to the specific case of texts whose main purpose is persuasion. Here we briefly explain these four key elements as they generally apply to writers' use of reasoning for a range of rhetorical purposes.

Claims

The key points that a writer wants readers to accept are referred to as *claims*. For example, Anthony Weston's main claim in the passage on page 55 is this: "Ethical problems are seldom 'puzzles,' allowing specific and conclusive 'solutions.'" Or take another example. Early in her essay on page 65, MacFarquhar claims that "None of this [a series of beliefs about reading] is true." Once you have identified various claims in a text, then you can raise questions about them, especially about their wording and scope. Is the meaning of key words in the claim clear? Can particular words be interpreted in more than one way? Is the claim overstated? For example, one might ask of Weston's claim, "Aren't there some ethical problems that really *are* puzzles that have conclusive solutions?" Similarly, one could ask of MacFarquhar, "Are none of these beliefs true in any sense?"

Reasons

Reasons are subclaims that writers use to support a main claim. A reason can usually be linked to a claim with the subordinate conjunction "because." Consider the gun control argument mentioned earlier, which we can now restate as a claim with reason: "We must pass gun control laws that limit access to guns [claim] because doing so will make children safer at school [reason]." This argument has initial appeal because it ties into the audience's belief that it is good to make children safe at school, but as we have discussed earlier, the causal links in the argument are open to question. To take another example, Weston offers readers the following reasons for accepting his approach to ethical problems:

It is better to treat ethical issues as multifaceted problems rather than as puzzles with correct answers [claim]

- because doing so allows more options for action in the present and change in the future
- because doing so will allow for more inventiveness and experimentation
- because doing so can make problems seem more manageable.

Certainly action, change, creativity, and manageability will be valued by many readers when it comes to solving difficult problems. However, without further proof or evidence, how do we know that Weston's approach will result in these positive outcomes? Moreover, some readers might not consider these outcomes positive at all: They might distrust such flexibility and prefer more precise moral guidelines.

As these examples illustrate, once you've identified the reasons that the author offers for various claims, then you can proceed to examine the adequacy of these reasons. Do they really support the claim? Do they tie into values, assumptions, and beliefs that the audience shares?

Evidence

The facts, examples, statistics, personal experience, and expert testimony that an author offers to support his or her view of the topic are referred to as *evidence*. To examine the author's use of evidence, consider whether the evidence is reliable, timely, and adequate to make the case. Or ask whether there is more than one way the evidence can be interpreted. When MacFarquhar argues that none of the "truisms" many people believe about reading are true, she relies heavily on evidence. She offers facts, statistics, expert testimony, example, and so forth throughout the essay mainly to refute positions with which she disagrees. Readers skeptical of MacFarquhar's argument might question her interpretations of some facts and statistics: Couldn't people just be saying that they are reading a book because they're embarrassed to admit they're not? Couldn't people have learned the name of the author of *Huckleberry Finn* from television and not from reading? Similarly, in our gun control example, skeptics could question whether the statistical correlation between rising availability of guns and rising gun violence in schools is in fact a causal relationship. The fact that A and B happened at the same time does not mean that A caused B.

Assumptions

In an argument, the often unstated values or beliefs that the writer expects readers to accept without question are referred to as *assumptions*. You can interrogate an argument by casting doubt on those assumptions. For example, when Weston argues that many issues don't have single right answers, he assumes the audience will value the flexibility of his approach. But many readers may fear that Weston's approach will lead to cultural relativism and the loss of absolute moral values. Similarly, part of the gun control argument is based on an assumption that gun control legislation will in fact limit the availability of guns. You can question this assumption by pointing to the existence of black markets.

EXAMINING A WRITER'S STRATEGIES FOR ENGAGING READERS

The third of the classical rhetorical appeals is to an audience's interests and emotions—the process of engaging readers. How does a writer hook and keep your interest? How does a writer make you care about the subject? How does a writer tweak your emotions or connect an argument with ideas or beliefs that you value?

Rhetoricians have identified four basic ways that writers engage readers at an emotional or imaginative level: by urging the reader (1) to identify with the writer, (2) to identify with the topic or issue, (3) to identify with a certain group of fellow readers, or (4) to identify with certain interests, values, beliefs, and emotions. Let's look at each in turn.

In the first approach, writers wanting readers to identify with them might use an informal conversational tone to make a reader feel like the writer's buddy. Writers wanting to inspire respect and admiration might adopt a formal scholarly tone, choose intellectual words, or avoid "I" altogether by using the passive voice—"it was discovered that. . . ." In the second approach, writers wanting readers to identify with the topic or issue might explain the importance of the issue or try to engage readers' emotions. In urging community action against homelessness, for example, an author might present a wrenching anecdote about a homeless child. Other methods might be the use of vivid details, striking facts, emotion-laden terms and examples, or analogies that explain the unfamiliar in terms of the familiar. In the third approach, writers try to get readers to identify with a certain in-group of people—fellow environmentalists or feminists or Republicans or even fellow intellectuals. Some writers seek to engage readers by creating a role for the reader to play in the text. For example, Weston invites readers to think of themselves as serious and intelligent, interested in tough ethical issues. In the fourth approach, writers appeal to readers' interests by getting them to identify with certain values and beliefs. For example, a politician arguing for changes in the way social security is funded might appeal to voters' desires to invest in high-yield stocks. If workers could pay lower social security taxes, they could invest the difference in the stock market. If you are aware of how these appeals work, you will be able to distance yourself from the argument in order to examine it more critically.

• *For Writing and Discussion*

Consider all of the ways in which Larissa MacFarquhar tries to engage readers of her text. What kind of a relationship does she try to establish with readers? How does she try to make you care about her topic? How does she try to engage and keep your interest? What interests and values does she assume her audience shares? Do you consider yourself part of her intended audience? Why or why not?

EXAMINING A WRITER'S LANGUAGE

Besides looking at a text's classical appeals, you can question a text by paying careful attention to its language and style. Diction (which includes tone, word choice, and level of formality), figurative language, sentence structure and length, and even punctuation are all techniques through which a writer tries to influence readers' view of a subject. Consider, for example, the connotation of words. It makes a difference whether a writer calls a person "decisive" rather than "bossy," or an act "bold" rather than "rash." Words like "decisive" and "rash" are not facts; rather they present the writer's interpretation of a phenomenon. You can question a text by recognizing how the writer makes interpretive words seem like facts.

At times, you might overlook features of the writer's language because they seem natural rather than chosen. You probably seldom stop to think about the significance of, say, the use of italics or a series of short sentences or a particular metaphor. Readers rarely ask what's gained or lost by a writer saying something one way rather than another—for example, calling clear-cut logging in the Northwest a "rape" rather than a "timber extraction process."

Take, for example, the first paragraph of the passage from Weston's *Toward Better Problems* (p. 55). He uses a form of the negative three times, the first time placing *not* in italics. Through this typographical cue as well as repetition, he emphasizes the distinction between what he is suggesting and the usual proposals of practical ethicists. If he were speaking this line, his tone of voice would emphasize the word "not." Or consider the last two sentences in the first paragraph of MacFarquhar's essay: "Once, the story goes—in the 1950s, say—we read much more than we do now, and read the good stuff, the classics. Now, we don't care about reading anymore, we're barely literate, and television and computers are rendering books obsolete." Try reading those sentences aloud, paying particular attention to the punctuation. It's hard to say them out loud in anything but a mock serious, singsong, sarcastic tone of voice. Her tone tells us that these are not her own sentiments but rather sentiments she is ascribing to others. To signal her distance from and disdain for these views, she makes the claims sound vague and baseless ("once . . . in the 1950s, say"), exaggerated ("we're barely literate"), and trite (classics are "the good stuff"). By contrast, the voice in the next paragraph is very businesslike—the sentences are short and clipped; the information is presented in listlike fashion. We know it is this voice we are supposed to listen to. Through language that creates particular tones of voice, MacFarquhar tries to get readers to think about the subject—commonplace beliefs about reading—in the same way she does.

Experienced readers have developed antennae for recognizing these subtle uses of language to manipulate responses. One way to develop this sensitivity is to ask why a writer made certain choices rather than others. For example, if you were examining paragraph 9 of MacFarquhar's essay, you might note her striking comparison of reading romance novels to drinking beer and getting a massage. What effect does she achieve through these specific comparisons? What would be different if she'd compared reading romances to going dancing or floating down a river?

• *For Writing and Discussion*

BACKGROUND

What follows below is the introduction to an article by freelance writer Bruce Barcott entitled "Blow-Up," which appeared in the February 1999 issue of *Outside,* a magazine described by its editors as "driven by the search for innovative ways to connect people to the world outdoors." After you have read the introduction, consider the following questions: What do you think is the author's persuasive intention in the whole article? How does the use of language in this introduction help contribute to the author's persuasive intentions? Pay attention to word choice, tone, sentence patterns, punctuation, figurative language, levels of diction, and other language features.

ON YOUR OWN

Write out your own analysis of the use of language in this passage.

WITH YOUR CLASSMATES

Share your analyses. See if you can reach consensus on the ways that this writer uses language for persuasive intent.

——————— • ———————

Introduction to "Blow-Up"

1   By God we built some dams!

2   We backed up the Kennebec in Maine and the Neuse in North Carolina and a hundred creeks and streams that once ran free but don't anymore. We stopped the Colorado with the Hoover, high as 35 houses, and because it pleased us we kept damming and diverting the Colorado until the river no longer reached the sea. We dammed our way out of the Great Depression with the Columbia's Grand Coulee, a dam so immense you had to borrow another fellow's mind because yours alone wasn't big enough to wrap around it. The Coulee concrete was not even hardened by the time we finished building a bigger one still, cleaving the Missouri with Fort Peck Dam, a structure second only to the Great Wall of China, a jaw-dropper so outsized they put it on the cover of the first issue of *Life,* and wasn't that a hell of a thing? We turned the Tennessee, the Colorado, the Columbia, and the Snake from continental arteries into still bathtubs. We dammed the Clearwater, the Boise, the Santiam, the Deschutes, the Skagit, the Willamette, and the McKenzie. We dammed the North Platte and the North Yuba, the South Platte and the South Yuba. We dammed the Blue, the Green, and the White as

well. We dammed Basher Kill and Schuylkill; we dammed Salt River and we dammed Sugar Creek. We dammed Crystal River and Muddy Creek, the Little River and the Rio Grande. We dammed the Minnewawa and the Minnesota, and we dammed the Kalamazoo. We dammed the Swift and we dammed the Dead.

One day we looked up and saw 75,000 dams impounding more than half 3 a million miles of river. We looked down and saw rivers scrubbed free of salmon and sturgeon and shad. Cold rivers ran warm, warm rivers ran cold, and fertile muddy banks turned barren.

And that's when we stopped talking about dams as instruments of holy 4 progress and started talking about blowing them out of the water.

EXAMINING A TEXT'S IDEOLOGY

Another approach to questioning a text is to identify its *ideology,* a more technical term for the word *worldview,* which we introduced in the epigraph to Chapter 2. An ideology is a belief system—a coherent set of values and concepts through which we interpret the world. We sometimes think that ideology applies only to other people's worldviews, perhaps those of zealots blinded by a certain rigid set of beliefs. In fact, the term *ideology* applies to all of us. Each of us has our own beliefs, values, and particular ways of looking at the world. Our perspectives are inevitably shaped by family background, religion, personal experience, race, class, gender, sexual orientation, and so on. Moreover, it is true, each of us is to some extent "blinded" by our worldviews, by our way of seeing. For instance, middle-class persons in the United States, by and large, share a variety of common beliefs: "Hard work leads to success." "Owning your own home is an important good." "Punctuality, cleanliness, and respect for the privacy of others are important values." "All persons are created equal." If we are among the privileged in this country, we literally may not be able to see existing inequities and barriers to success faced by less privileged Americans.

If we are to become astute readers, we must look for signals that reveal the ideology informing a text. One way to begin doing so is to look for patterns of opposites or contrasts in a text (sometimes called binaries) and see which of the opposing terms the writer values more. We generally understand things through contrast with their opposites. We would have no concept of the term *masculine,* for example, without the contrasting term *feminine.* To understand light, we have to understand dark (or heavy). Our concept of liberal depends on its contrast with conservative. We could list hundreds of these opposites or binaries: civilized is that which is not primitive; free is that which is not enslaved; abnormal is that which is not normal; people of color are those who are not Caucasian. When these binaries occur as patterns in a text, one term is generally valued above the other. When you examine the pattern of those values, you begin to uncover the text's ideology. Sometimes the opposite or devalued terms are only implied, not even appearing in the text. Their absence helps mark the text's ideology.

Words, Concepts, and Ideas Valued by This Text	Words, Concepts, and Ideas Not Valued by This Text
2nd Amendment: the right to keep and bear arms	Bureaucratic bungling that will result in infringements on the right to keep and bear arms
Reliance on individual self to oppose an assailant	Reliance on police to oppose an assailant; administration of waiting periods would drain police resources
Conservatives	Liberals
Limited government	Active government
Examples of well-known shootings where waiting period would have been irrelevant—no statistical evidence of effectiveness	Examples of mentally ill persons with guns harming or killing people
Examples of criminals thwarted by individual citizens with guns	Examples of children killed by accidental shootings (excluded from text)
Hard time for hard crime, victim's rights	Plea bargaining, lax enforcement of existing gun control laws

FIGURE 5.1   Binary Patterns in Anti-Waiting Period Article

For example, suppose you are reading an article that opposes a proposed five-day waiting period for the purchase of handguns. If you make a list of valued words, concepts, or ideas and then match them against their nonvalued opposites, you might produce the two-column pattern shown in Figure 5.1. Lists such as these can help you clarify a text's ideology—in this case, conservative, individualistic, and supportive of the rights of individuals against the state.

Sometimes it is not immediately evident which terms are valued by a text and which ones are devalued. In such cases you can often identify a major contrast or binary in the text—for example, loggers versus tree huggers, school vouchers versus neighborhood schools, old ways versus new ways, scientific medicine versus alternative medicine. You can then determine which of the

Valued Terms and Ideas	Less Valued Terms and Ideas
New problems	New solutions to old problems
Complexity	Simplicity
Problems based on large and often vague regions of tension	Puzzles with correct answers
Problem solving as process	Episodic problem solving
Integrative values	Isolated values

FIGURE 5.2   Binary Patterns in Weston Excerpt

opposed terms is more valued. Once you can identify the main controlling binary, you can often line up other opposites or contrasts in the appropriate columns.

If you were to make a chart of the binaries in the excerpt from Weston's *Toward Better Problems* in Chapter 4 (p. 55) for example, it might look something like the pattern shown in Figure 5.2. If you were to use these oppositions to draw conclusions about the ideology informing Weston's text, you might say something like the following: "Weston's text seems informed by liberal values because he wants people to approach ethical problems such as abortion from many perspectives. He opposes the idea that there are black-and-white solutions to controversial ethical problems and that there are absolute principles or moral truths that can guide us in solving these problems."

• *For Writing and Discussion*

ON YOUR OWN

Return to the introduction to "Blow-Up" (p. 76). Make a two-column list of the binaries you find in that passage. Put the words, concepts, or ideas that the author values in the left column; place the opposing words, concepts, or ideas that the author doesn't value in the right column. (Remember, the nonvalued terms may only be implied and not actually appear in the text.) Then write a short analysis of the author's ideology, following the models we provided based on the anti-waiting period argument and Weston's text.

WITH YOUR CLASSMATES

Share your list of binaries and your analysis of Barcott's ideology. Try to reach consensus on both.

Exploring Your Responses to a Text

The previous section has explained five questioning strategies based on examining the details of a text. In this section we explain a different approach to interrogating a text, one that asks you simply to explore your own reactions to something you've read. This approach encourages you to record on paper your first gut reactions to a text and then, after reflection, your more sustained and considered responses. We describe in this section three easy-to-use strategies for helping you explore and articulate your own reaction to a text: (1) before/after reflections, (2) the believing and doubting game, and (3) interviewing the author.

BEFORE/AFTER REFLECTIONS

To consider how much a text has influenced your thinking, try writing out some before and after reflections by freewriting your responses to the following statements:

1. What effect is this text trying to have on me? What kind of change does the writer hope to make in my view of the subject?

Here is how Jenny answered this question after she first read Larissa Mac-Farquhar's article:

> MacFarquhar wants me to reject certain commonplaces about reading—that Americans don't read much any more, for example—and to question other common assumptions such as the assumption that reading is always a more worthwhile activity than watching TV or that reading the classics is better than reading romance fiction.

2. Before reading this text, I believed this about the topic: _____ _____. But after reading the text, my view has changed in these ways: _____ _____.
3. Although the text has persuaded me that _____, I still have the following doubts: _____.
4. The most significant questions this text raises for me are these: _____ _____.
5. The most important insights I have gotten from reading this text are these: _____.

- ### *For Writing and Discussion*

    We gave you an example of Jenny's before/after reflection responding to the question "What kind of change does the writer hope to make in my view of the subject?" Based on your own reading of the MacFarquhar article, write out your own before/after reflections for Exercises 2 through 5. Share your responses with classmates.

THE BELIEVING AND DOUBTING GAME

Playing the believing and doubting game with a text is a powerful strategy both for recording your reaction to a text and for stimulating further thinking. Developed by writing theorist Peter Elbow, the believing and doubting game will stretch your thinking in surprising ways. You begin the game by freewriting all the reasons why you believe the writer's argument. Then you freewrite all the reasons why you doubt the same argument. In the "believe" portion, you try to look at the world through the text's perspective, adopting its ideology, actively supporting its ideas and values. You search your mind for any life experiences or memories of reading and research that help you sympathize with and support the author's point of view or ideas. If you find the author's ideas upsetting, dangerous, or threatening, the believing game may challenge—even disturb—you. It takes courage to try to believe views that you feel are dead wrong or contrary to your most deeply held beliefs. Nevertheless, to be a strong rhetorical reader, you need to look at the world through perspectives different from your own.

According to Elbow, the believing game helps you grow intellectually by letting you take in new and challenging ideas. In contrast, the doubting game helps you solidify your present identity by protecting you from outside ideas. Like an antiballistic missile, the doubting game lets you shoot down ideas that you don't like. The "doubt" portion of this game thus reverses the believing process. Here you try to think of all of the problems, limitations, or weaknesses in the author's argument. You brainstorm for personal experiences or memories from reading and research that refute or call into question the author's view. (Of course, the doubting game can be threatening if you already agree with the author's views. In such a case, doubting causes you to take a stand against your own beliefs.)

In the following example, student writer Jenny plays the believing and doubting game with MacFarquhar's article. Note how this exercise promotes critical thinking that goes beyond just expressing her subjective opinions. The results of playing the believing and doubting game are nearly always a bit surprising.

Jenny's Believing-Doubting Game Freewrite

Believe

It's easy for me to believe what MacFarquhar has to say about how Americans are not reading less than they used to but actually more, especially books like romance fiction. I used to read every Sweet Valley High book I could get my hands on. As a kid, I also loved the Judy Blume books. It irritates me when people think that the only reading that counts is Shakespeare or something. I've learned a lot about life from reading Judy Blume's books. For example, Hey, God, It's Me Margaret is about a girl whose parents get divorced just like mine did. It really meant a lot to me to read about a character who had some of the same experiences and feelings I had. If reading is not about helping you get through life, then what is it about? Like MacFarquhar says, book clubs are a big thing nowadays and that proves that reading is as popular as ever. I heard that a professor here offered a literature course called "Oprah's Books," and so many students enrolled that they had to open up another section of the course. My next door neighbor and her middle-school-aged daughter even belong to a mother/daughter book club. MacFarquhar also presents a lot of facts about reading that are hard to argue with. Also, it has always irked me that people think you are an idiot if you like to watch a lot of TV. I think many shows today are as good as many books. Even though some people call it just "fluff," I love Friends and try not to miss it. Plus, I know that many educated adults (including some of my profs!) watch shows like the West Wing and NYPD Blue even though some people call them nighttime soap operas. I agree with MacFarquhar that TV and video games are not destroying people's love of reading and that Americans are reading more than ever!

Doubt

It's harder for me to doubt what MacFarquhar is saying because I generally agree with everything she has to say. I suppose some people might call into question her statistics. How reliable are the responses people give to Gallup polls? MacFarquhar seems to think facts and statistics absolutely prove that people read a lot—but can't facts and statistics be manipulated? I know a lot of my teachers feel that students' reading abilities and knowledge of the classics are not what they were in the past. I must admit that I did get a lot out of the "classics" that I have had to read in high school and college even though I wouldn't have read them on my own. I particularly remember reading Heart of Darkness in high school, and just recently reading The Great Gatsby. Recently, I was watching a television report on the famine in Africa, and the news report quoted a line from The Heart of Darkness—"The horror

of it all"—and it really made me feel good that I knew what the reporter was
referring to. I also guess I can see why people are concerned that television
and video games are replacing reading. My younger brother is just addicted to
video games, and he never reads. I know, even for myself, sometimes I sit
down to watch just one favorite program and end up watching the next show
even though I'm not that interested in it and it isn't even that good. So I
realize that TV can be addictive and a lot of it does feel more passive
than reading.

INTERVIEWING THE AUTHOR

Another strategy for exploring your reactions to a text is to imagine interviewing
the author and brainstorm the questions you might ask. This strategy urges you to
identify the text's hot spots for you. These might be places where you want the author to clarify something, expand on something, or respond to your own objections
or counterviews. Here are some questions Jenny developed to ask MacFarquhar.

Jenny's Interview Questions

Are Gallup polls really conclusive evidence that more Americans are
reading? Couldn't people just be saying that they are reading a book out of
embarrassment? You offer convincing evidence that the books that are the
most popular in contemporary America are genre fiction and self-help books,
but what do you think of this? Do you think it's a loss or problem that not
many Americans read the classics? You seem to think that watching TV can
be as valuable as reading. Why do you think that? What would you say to the
accusation that you spend most of your time attacking others' positions
without really offering your own opinions?

Applying Rhetorical Reading Strategies:
An Example

In Chapter 4, we looked at the summary and rhetorical précis of Larissa Mac-
Farquhar's "Who Cares If Johnny Can't Read" written by Jenny, the first-year
writing student whose work we have been following. We now present the paper Jenny wrote about MacFarquhar's essay in response to the assignment below. We have annotated Jenny's paper to highlight the questioning strategies that
she uses to analyze the article as well as the rhetorical writing strategies she uses
to support her analysis.

JENNY'S ASSIGNMENT TO EXAMINE RHETORICAL STRATEGIES

Write an essay of approximately 500 to 600 words in which you examine a key rhetorical strategy (or several related ones) used by Larissa MacFarquhar to engage readers with her point of view regarding reading and its value. Your purpose is to offer your readers a new perspective on how the text works rhetorically, a perspective gleaned from your analysis of the text. Your essay should include the following: a brief summary that sets a context for the reader, a reason to be concerned about what the author says and how she says it, a thesis or conclusion that you've drawn from your analysis, and textual evidence that develops and supports your thesis.

JENNY'S PAPER

Who Cares If the Value of Books Is Overstated?

1   As a future elementary school teacher, interested particularly in language arts, I am always interested in stories about electronic books and the supposed decline in reading due to television and the Internet. Therefore, I was curious to see what Larissa MacFarquhar had to say about the subject in her essay, "Who Cares If Johnny Can't Read," published in the online magazine Slate in 1997. As the attention-getting title of her essay suggests, MacFarquhar's essay calls into question some common assumptions regarding reading, specifically that reading books is important for everyone and that reading books is better and more intellectually challenging than watching TV or surfing the Internet. But what is her opinion about the importance of reading? A one-line subtitle suggests that she doesn't think reading is very important: "The value of books is overstated." However, a close examination of MacFarquhar's essay reveals that she focuses more on disproving the ideas of others than she does on stating her own position clearly and supporting it convincingly.

2   Perhaps an editor at Slate, not MacFarquhar, wrote this subtitle, but in any case, its bold claim made me expect an explanation of what she meant, proof that it is true, and discussion of why we should care if it is true. The more I tried to understand the connection between this claim and

States topic's relevance to her.

Offers one-sentence summary of LM article.

Identifies what appears to be LM's main claim.

States thesis.

Notes audience expectations set up by LM's subtitle.

the ideas in the essay, the more confused I became until I realized what she was doing. For much of the essay, she is actually trying to prove that Americans do value books and to refute those who believe they don't. It is not until towards the end of the essay that she gets around to explaining the kind of valuing of books that she thinks is overstated.

MacFarquhar begins her essay by disputing those 3 who claim that "we don't care about reading anymore." If judged by book sales and people's reading habits, Americans actually value books more than they used to, according to MacFarquhar. She says Americans bought over 2 billion books in 1992 and that a 1992 survey "found that the average adult American reads 11.2 books a year" (par. 3).* She goes on to say that currently there are more than 250,000 reading groups. This kind of valuing is proven by facts and statistics and is not, according to MacFarquhar, even open to dispute. Now, of course, some people might question the faith she puts in statistics. Perhaps people lied to the survey takers about how many books they read in a year. But for MacFarquhar, the fact that Americans do still care about books is a closed case.

MacFarquhar offers further evidence that Americans still 4 care about reading and books by comparing people's past love of reading with the current devotion of many readers, particularly readers of romance fiction. She quotes Irving Howe, who remembers the excitement about books that he witnessed as a child in Russia: "How can I describe to you . . . the excitement we shared when we would discuss Dostoyevsky?" (par. 4). According to MacFarquhar, people still feel this same excitement; it's just that they feel it for different sorts of books: "People still write like that about books. Of course, most aren't reading Dostoyevsky. The authors who attract thousands and thousands of readers who read everything they write and send letters to them begging

Margin notes:
- Notes LM's use of facts and statistics.
- Questions LM's faith in facts and statistics.
- Identifies LM's use of comparison to refute idea that people no longer love to read.
- Summarizes LM's point about change in readers' tastes.

---

*As in her summary in the previous chapter, Jenny's in-text citations refer to the paragraph numbers on the reprint of "Who Cares If Johnny Can't Read?" at the end of Chapter 4 (p. 65). The original online publication does not include either page or paragraph numbers.

Observes that LM belittles both past and current book lovers.

for more seem to be the authors of genre fictions—romances, science fiction, and mysteries" (par. 5). Although she is openly sarcastic about what Howe has to say, calling his ideas "fossils of a bygone age," and she seems to make fun of the romance readers who sent their favorite romance writer, Debbie Macomber, baby blankets and a homemade Christmas stocking for her granddaughter, the fact that they and others love and value books can't be overstated. Her own statistics show that it's a matter of fact, proven by romance book sale statistics and reader testimony.

Identifies LM's main claim.

5   Toward the end of the essay, MacFarquhar finally gets around to discussing the kind of valuing that she thinks is overstated. Those who claim that reading in and of itself offers unique intellectual and cultural benefits are the ones who she believes overvalue reading. In explaining the fears of many that television and computers will make books obsolete, MacFarquhar writes, "books have acquired a reputation for education and even moral worthiness" (par.

Identifies examples that LM uses to back up claim.

3). To illustrate this particular view of books, she offers two examples. First, she refers to Sven Birkerts's <u>The Gutenberg Elegies: The Fate of Reading in an Electronic Age</u>, published in 1994, as "a classic example of this genre" (par. 12). Second, she quotes at length <u>Time</u> critic Robert Hughes, who describes reading as a "collaborative act, in which your imagination goes halfway to meet the author's" (par. 12). He argues that reading is "far better for the imagination" than television (par. 12). Referring to these claims about the value of books as "sentimental" and "mysterious," she challenges Hughes's contention that books stimulate the imagination by citing her own experience: "I cannot remember ever visualizing a book's characters, but . . . perhaps I'm in the

Criticizes LM's reliance on personal experience.

minority" (par. 13). Her own experience is actually the only evidence she offers to disprove Hughes's claims in favor of reading. While she claims that people like Hughes and Birkerts offer no proof for their claims, the same could be said of her.

In conclusion, MacFarquhar spends the majority of her essay contradicting the mistaken idea that Americans don't value books and does not get to what appears to be her main claim until toward the end of the essay. Even at this point, she offers little in the way of proof that these claims are "overstated." So, while it is clear that MacFarquhar cares about what she considers some people's overstatements about the benefits of reading, it is not clear that others share her view or that we, as readers, should care about whether the value of books is overstated.

6 *Concludes that LM's argument is insufficiently developed and unconvincing.*

Work Cited

MacFarquhar, Larissa. "Who Cares If Johnny Can't Read?" Slate 16 Apr. 1997. Rpt. in Reading Rhetorically. Ed. John C. Bean, Virginia A. Chappell, and Alice M. Gillam. New York: Longman, 2002. 65–67.

- ### *For Writing and Discussion*

ON YOUR OWN

In your reading log, write a response to Jenny's paper. How does her reading of MacFarquhar compare with yours? What issues or ideas does she leave out? Is hers a fair criticism of the essay? Does she back up her analysis with adequate and convincing evidence? If you had been given the same assignment, what rhetorical aspects of the text would you have written about?

WITH YOUR CLASSMATES

Share your responses with classmates. Working as a whole class or in small groups, list some additional ideas or insights that Jenny might have incorporated into her paper.

Summary

This chapter has explained strategies for questioning a text, which involves carefully interrogating a text's argument and methods in order to critique it and join its conversation. We presented questioning strategies for examining (1) the writer's credibility, (2) the argument's reasoning and logic, (3) the writer's appeals to the audience's interests and emotions, (4) the text's language, and (5) the text's ideology. We then explained three easy-to-use methods for exploring your own reactions to a text: writing out before/after responses, playing the believing and doubting game, and imagining an interview with the author. Finally we presented Jenny's rhetorical analysis of MacFarquhar's article. This essay showed how the questioning strategies described in this chapter can help you write a college-level analysis of a text.

The Rhetorical Reader as Writer

6

Writing About Reading: The Special Demands of Academic Writing

Academic writing, reading, and inquiry are inseparably linked; and all three are learned by not doing any one alone, but by doing them all at the same time.

—James Reither

As our epigraph suggests, academic tasks often require you to read, write, and inquire simultaneously. To read, as we have been suggesting all along, is an act of inquiry—a process in which you both listen to and question a text. Similarly, writing is an inquiry process that usually involves reading. The next three chapters focus on helping you do the kind of writing most frequently required by college professors: writing that grows out of reading. However, it is not just college or the academic life that requires writing based on reading. To dramatize the practical value of rhetorical reading as an integral part of effective writing well beyond academic study, we invite you to consider the following scenarios.

- A public relations intern at a regional theater company is asked to report on how comparable theaters around the country are presenting themselves on the World Wide Web. Her supervisor expects detailed information about the visual and verbal content of the other Web pages along with an overview of their various advertising strategies. The intern also wants to communicate her own marketing and design expertise because she hopes to do such a good job that she'll be hired to revamp this theater's Web page.

- A management trainee at an electric utility is assigned to research the cost and competitive features of microform readers and printers that the company might purchase as part of its overhaul of document-handling procedures. As he works, he discovers that he not only has to boil down extensive technical data in the stacks of sales material he's collected but must also decipher marketing lingo that makes it difficult to compare the equipment directly. He knows that his own boss wants a report that will enable a speedy purchasing decision by a management committee. He also knows that a good report will speed up his own promotion out of "trainee" status.

- A law clerk assisting a judge with an important legal opinion must summarize reams of government documents and position papers about a controversial new environmental policy. He knows that the judge expects his report to provide legal, not political, criteria for analyzing and evaluating the opposing arguments in the case.

- The judge, who chairs the board of a nonprofit women and children's shelter, sits down to write an annual report for volunteers and donors. She must distill a year's worth of dry monthly reports into a short, readable text that will thank these supporters for past effort and inspire them to further generosity.

All these writers must read and synthesize multiple texts so that they can create a new document with an audience and purpose quite different from that of the original materials. The workplace and community contexts we have described may be unfamiliar to you, but the rhetorical problems facing these reader/writers are parallel to those that you will need to solve when you are asked to incorporate material from outside sources into your own academic writing. These writers may have never heard the term "rhetorical reading," but the effectiveness of the texts they write will depend upon how well they analyze both content and technique in their sources and then, on the basis of this analysis, select material that will serve their purposes for influencing the thinking of the next set of readers.

Overview of Part Three

In Parts One and Two of this book, we introduced you to the whys and hows of rhetorical reading, arguing for its value in deepening your understanding of what you read and in generating ideas for writing. Now, in Part Three, we turn our attention to the special demands of using the ideas gleaned from reading to create new texts. In Chapter 6, we begin by describing typical types of reading-based writing assignments that you are apt to receive in classes across the curriculum. Then we turn to the problem of how to assert your authority when you use readings—that is, how you make an argument in your own voice rather than patch together quotes and paraphrases from your sources. Finally, we offer tips on how to manage your writing process—how to produce effective texts that assert your authority as a writer and meet the expectations of college professors.

Chapter 7 guides you through the task of searching for and selecting readings to use in your research-based writing. It explains how to formulate and then use strategic questions to find and evaluate readings that fit your purposes for writing. Chapter 8 covers the nuts and bolts of incorporating the ideas and words of others into your own text. It discusses the rhetorical choices involved when you decide to summarize, paraphrase, or quote a source and explains the conventions for doing so ethically and effectively.

Typical Reading-Based Writing Assignments Across the Curriculum

In college, a reading assignment is often only the first step in a complex series of activities that lead toward writing something that will be graded. What you write will naturally vary from situation to situation and can range from a quick answer on an essay exam to an extensive source-based paper. In this section, we discuss five common college writing assignments in which reading plays a major role:

1. Writing to understand course content more fully
2. Writing to report your understanding of what a text says
3. Writing to practice the conventions of a particular type of text
4. Writing to make claims about a text
5. Writing to extend the conversation

These roles can be placed along a continuum, starting with writing tasks in which the ideas in the readings predominate and moving to assignments in which the readings are subordinated to your own ideas and aims. The first two assignment types focus primarily on using writing to learn course subject matter and to practice careful listening to texts. The last three focus primarily on writing your own analyses and arguments for academic audiences. Writing teachers sometimes distinguish these two categories of assignment goals by the terms "writing to learn" versus "learning to write."

WRITING TO UNDERSTAND COURSE CONTENT MORE FULLY

One common type of college writing assignment is intended to help you understand more fully the material you have read. These "writing-to-learn" assignments aim to deepen your understanding of the reading material by asking you to put the author's ideas into your own words or to identify points of confusion for yourself. The primary audience for these types of writing is often yourself even though teachers sometimes ask you to turn in these writings so that they can check on your understanding and progress. The style is informal and conversational. Organization and grammatical correctness are less important than the quality of your engagement with the content of the reading. These assignments typically take one of the following forms.

In-Class Freewriting

The point of freewriting is to think rapidly without censoring your thoughts. Freewriting is often done in class as a way to stimulate thinking about the day's subject. A typical in-class freewrite assignment might be this:

> Choose what for you personally is the single most important word in the text we read for today. You need not speculate about which word the author or your instructor or any other classmate would choose. Just choose the word that seems most important to you. This word may occur only once, a few times, or perhaps it appears frequently. Then explore in writing why you chose the word as the most important word in the essay.*

Reading or Learning Logs

Reading or learning logs are informal assignments that ask you to record your understanding, questions, and responses to a reading. Some teachers give specific prompts to guide your entries while others just ask that you write entries with a certain regularity and/or of a certain length. A typical question about the Larissa MacFarquhar essay might be "How would you describe the author's voice in this essay?" If a teacher asks you simply to write your own reflections in a log, you might use some of the questions rhetorical readers ask presented in Chapter 2 about the text's method and your response to it (p. 20).

Double-Entry Notebooks

Double-entry notebooks are a special kind of reading log in which you conduct an ongoing dialogue with your interpretations and reactions to the text. Here's how they work: divide a notebook page with a line down the middle. On the right side of the page record reading notes—direct quotations, observations, comments, questions, objections. On the left side, record your later reflections about those notes—second thoughts, responses to quotations, reactions to earlier comments, answers to questions or new questions. Rhetorician Ann Berthoff, who popularized this approach, says that the double-entry notebook provides readers with a means of conducting a "continuing audit of meaning." In keeping a double-entry journal, you carry on a conversation with yourself about a text.

One-Page Response Papers or Thought Pieces

Written for an instructor, one-page response papers or "thought" pieces are somewhat more formal than the previous writing-to-learn assignments but still a great deal more informal than essay assignments. They call for a fuller response than the previous types of writing-to-learn assignments, but the purpose will be similar—to articulate an understanding of a text and to respond to it, often within the context of major themes or concepts being addressed in a particular course. Usually, a teacher will give students a specific question as a prompt for these papers. Here is a sample thought piece written in response to a prompt

---

*We thank Joan Ruffino, an instructor at the University of Wisconsin–Milwaukee, for this freewriting assignment.

from a freshman seminar in psychology. The teacher asked the students to write about the insights they gleaned about obsessive-compulsive disorder (OCD) from reading Lauren Slater's "Black Swans" (found in Chapter 9).

Reading Lauren Slater's "Black Swans" taught me some basic information about OCD, but more importantly, it taught me how terrifying this disease can be. It begins with a single obsessive thought that leads to a cycle of anxiety, repetitive behaviors such as repeatedly washing one's hands, and avoidance of situations that produce the obsessive thoughts. In severe cases, like Slater's, the person completely avoids life because the obsessive thought invades every aspect of one's life. The essay also makes it clear that experts understand very little about the causes for this disease or about how to treat it.

What impressed me most about this essay, however, was Slater's ability to put me in her shoes and make me feel some of the terror she felt. She vividly describes her experience at being stricken with this condition without warning. A single thought—"I can't concentrate"—suddenly blocked out all other thoughts. Ordinary surroundings like the blue floor of her room appeared strange and frightening. Even her own body seemed foreign to her and grotesque: "the phrase 'I can't concentrate on my hand' blocked out my hand, so all I saw was a blur of flesh giving way to the bones beneath, and inside the bones the grimy marrow, and in the grimy marrow the individual cells, all disconnected. Shattered skin." To me, this was the most frightening description in the essay. I can't imagine being disconnected from my own body. I think the most terrifying aspect of this disease is the sense of being completely out of control of your mind. Slater describes it as, "My mind was devouring my mind." While one can never really know what the disease feels like without actually experiencing it, this essay gives us a disturbing glimpse of what it might be like.

Effective response papers or thought pieces, like the one above, identify significant points in the reading and offer a personal response or interpretation of those significant points. In this book, there are numerous places where we give short writing-to-learn tasks designed to help you learn and apply key concepts of rhetorical reading.

WRITING TO REPORT YOUR UNDERSTANDING OF WHAT A TEXT SAYS

Another common reading-based assignment asks you to report your understanding of what a text says. For example, you will frequently need to summarize readings in a paper and to explain an author's ideas as part of an essay exam. You may also be asked to write an annotated bibliography that provides brief summaries of sources related to a particular topic or question. In Chapter 4, we discussed how to write summaries and the various purposes they serve in college reading and writing assignments. In your own writing, a summary of an article might be short; for example, you might write a one-sentence summary in order to contextualize a quotation you are going to use in your research paper. Or it might be fairly detailed; for example, you might want to summarize the complete argument of an important article on a controversial issue. Sometimes an entire paper can be a sequence of summaries, as when you write a *review of literature* about a particular topic—for example, about new treatments for obsessive-compulsive disorder in a psychology course or about scientific studies of the relationship between pesticides and cancer in a biochemistry course. Although summaries or reports of your understanding of a text will vary in length and purpose, they are all expected to be accurate, fair, and balanced. In short, they require you to listen carefully to the text.

WRITING TO PRACTICE THE CONVENTIONS
OF A PARTICULAR TYPE OF TEXT

Assignments that ask you to analyze and practice the conventions of a particular type of writing—its organizational format, style, ways of presenting evidence, and so on—use readings as models. Such assignments are common in college courses. In a journalism class, for example, you would learn to write a news report using the inverted pyramid structure; in a science course you might be asked to write up results of experiments in the form of a laboratory report. Similarly, in courses using this textbook, you might be asked to write aims-based essays modeled after some of the readings in the anthology—that is, to write your own reflective essay, informative essay, exploratory essay, or proposal argument.

For each chapter in the anthology section of this book, one of the formal assignment options asks you to use the chapter's readings as models. This assignment asks you to write your own aims-based essay, on a subject matter of your choosing, using the chapter's essays as examples or guides for creative imitation or adaptation. Generally, using readings as models involves the following activities:

- Identifying the features that characterize a particular type of text
- Noting the ways in which rhetorical situation affects the features identified in model texts
- Coming up with your own topic and reason for writing this particular type of text
- Using the features of the model text (or texts) and your own rhetorical situation to guide your writing

Let's say, for example, that you've been asked to write a proposal argument. Chapter 15 identifies three features of proposal writing: description of the problem, proposal of a solution, and justification of that solution. As you read through this chapter, you will find that various authors deal with these features differently depending upon their audience and purpose. In some cases, for example, there is a great deal of description of the problem because the intended audience is unfamiliar with it; in other cases, there is very little description because it is presumed that the intended reading audience already knows a lot about the problem. The key is to adapt the model's characteristic structure and style to your own rhetorical purpose, not to follow the model slavishly.

In courses across the curriculum, your ability to analyze and adopt the conventions particular to a given discipline's ways of writing will help you write successful papers. For example, when you are asked in a philosophy class to write an argument in response to Immanuel Kant's *Critique of Pure Reason,* you are primarily being asked to engage with the ideas in the text. But secondarily you are also being asked to practice the conventions of writing a philosophical argument in which counterexamples and counterarguments are expected. It pays, then, to be alert to the structure and style of material you are assigned to read in any field of study as well as to the ideas.

WRITING TO MAKE CLAIMS ABOUT A TEXT

Assignments in this category ask you to analyze or critique readings. Many academic writers take as their field of study the texts produced by others. Literary critics study novels, poems, and plays; cultural critics analyze song lyrics, advertisements, cereal box covers, and television scripts; historians analyze primary source documents from the past; theologians scrutinize the sacred texts of different religions; lawyers analyze the documents entered into court proceedings, the exact wording of laws and statutes produced by legislators, or the decisions of appellate court judges.

Because this kind of assignment is so common in college courses, another of the assignment options in each of the anthology chapters in this book asks you to analyze a specific text. These assignments ask you to analyze one or more readings by identifying specific rhetorical methods and strategies used by the author, showing how these rhetorical choices contribute to the text's impact, and evaluating the choices in light of the author's evident purpose. Your claims must go beyond what a text says to make judgments and draw conclusions. In these types of assignments, the text and your ideas about the text are of equal importance. Assignments asking for analysis or critique are not invitations for you to refer briefly to the text and then take off on your own opinions about the topic, nor are they invitations merely to summarize or rehearse what the text has said. Rather, these assignments expect you to engage critically with a specific text. On the one hand, you will be expected to represent what the text said accurately and fairly. On the other hand, you will be expected to offer your own analysis, interpretation, or critique, one that enables readers to see the text differently. Jenny's rhetorical analysis of Larissa MacFarquhar's article at the end of Chapter 5 demonstrates writing for this kind of assignment.

WRITING TO EXTEND THE CONVERSATION

These assignments treat texts as voices in a conversation about ideas. They typically call for you to read and synthesize material from several sources. Here, your own ideas and aims take center stage; your source texts play important but less prominent backup roles. The most familiar form this assignment takes is the research or seminar paper. What distinguishes such college work from high school research paper assignments is the expectation that the paper will present your own argument, not the arguments provided by the sources. In other words, you are expected to articulate a significant question or problem, investigate relevant data, research what published authors have said about it, and then formulate your own argument. To write these multisource papers successfully, you should use other texts primarily to position yourself in the conversation and to supply supporting data, information, or testimony. The argument—your main points—must come from you.

To help you understand the importance of research writing in college, each of the anthology chapters in this book offers an assignment that asks you to treat texts you have read as springboards for further research and discovery. These assignments treat the chapter's readings as voices in a conversation. They ask you to write an essay that joins the conversation introduced by one or more of the readings in the chapter or by other texts you have read on your own. Frequently they ask you to seek out other voices—often through library, Web, or field research—and then to enter the conversation with your own position and argument. By giving you the opportunity to define your own purposes for writing in dialogue with other texts, this category of assignments will prepare you for the research assignments typical of many college courses, where your goal is to synthesize material from a number of sources and then produce your own paper, inserting another voice—your own— into the ongoing conversation. To illustrate this kind of research writing, we include at the end of Chapter 8 Jenny's researched argument on romance novels, a paper that grew out of her initial reading of Larissa MacFarquhar's essay.

Asserting Your Authority As a Reader and Writer

"I have nothing to say! It's all been said!" This complaint is a familiar one. In the midst of a complicated reading and writing project, it's not unusual for any of us—students, teachers, or professional writers—to lose sight of our original goals and thus lose our confidence that we have ideas worth writing about.

Throughout this book, we have argued that reading is an active, constructive process. We don't need to convince you that writing, too, is an active process; after all, to write, one must actually make words appear on a page or screen. Nevertheless, as we turn to the subject of connecting reading and writing, we do want to warn you against *passive writing,* writing that just translates what's on someone else's page onto your page. Passive writing is packed full of summaries, paraphrases, and quotes (sometimes very lengthy quotes) but contains very little content from the writer. Some teachers refer to such writing as "patch-writing"—patches from source materials stitched together by a few sentences of the student's own. Such papers don't make their own arguments. They just cut and paste their sources' writing in order to fill the page. Passive writing of this sort doesn't assert its author's reason for writing and so it doesn't give its audience a reason for reading.

Passive writing occurs because many people (not just students!), when confronted with already published materials, find it difficult to maintain their own sense of purpose as authors: they lose track of their *author-ity*. Perhaps uncertain about the source text's content or purposes, they begin to insert quotations or paraphrases into their own texts without clear purpose. Perhaps awed by the rush of facts and abstractions in materials they are reading, they yield their authority as readers/writers to previously published texts. They begin to copy rather than compose, to cut and paste rather than argue. In effect, they let themselves be silenced by the experts. When they simply must put words on a page (because the assignment is due), the resulting product resembles a pasted-together collage of quotes and paraphrases. By letting their source materials take over the paper, writers not only fail to gain their readers' confidence but lose the opportunity to make their own contribution to the discussion.

As you work with the advice in this chapter, you will begin to discover a powerful truth: rhetorical reading leads to rhetorically powerful writing. Just as rhetorical reading involves analyzing and critiquing an author's method as well as content, rhetorically effective writing asserts its purpose and method along with its content. Strong writers use the knowledge and understanding gained from their reading to build their own authority so that they can, in turn, *author* their own texts. These strong texts will engage readers because they not only "say" clearly what they mean but "do" what they intend: extend the conversation by providing new information and asserting new ideas that will alter their readers' view of the subject.

Seeing Writing As a Process of "Putting in Your Oar"

To assert your authority as a writer, you need to think of writing as an active process of making new meaning, of adding your voice to an ongoing conversation about a subject. As you may recall from Chapter 2, Kenneth Burke describes the unique contribution each speaker or writer makes to a conversation as "putting in your oar." It is not a matter of just retrieving something that is fully formed in your head or finding other voices to cobble together; rather, it is a matter of finding a compelling reason to write and then actively constructing a text that accomplishes that purpose. Recognizing that the process of creating a text will vary from writer to writer and from situation to situation, we offer in this section a variety of strategies that will help you claim your own authority as a writer. You should think of the processes we describe as *recursive*; in other words, you don't go lockstep through the strategies in a strictly linear fashion but frequently circle back to repeat earlier strategies because you have discovered a new angle or refined your main idea or purpose for writing.

STRATEGIES FOR GETTING STARTED

As a college writer, you are more likely to succeed when you can make an assignment your own. Rather than writing just to fulfill an assignment, you need to construct your own "take" on the subject by imagining yourself writing to a real audience for a real purpose. You assert your own authority by creating your own *exigence*—a useful term from rhetorical theory that means a circumstance that is other than it should be, a situation in need of attention. To resolve the situation, you write to bring about some kind of change in your audience—to correct a misunderstanding, to talk back to something someone else has said, to propose a solution to a problem, to explore and shed new light on an issue, to change your audience's thinking or attitudes, to make your audience appreciate something or value it differently, to call for action.

In writing projects that involve reading, the exigence or reason for writing grows either out of your analysis and response to a single text (you have something new to say about the text that is surprising or challenging to your audience) or out of your own research question, which then leads to a search for texts that will expand and complicate your understanding of your subject. Your increased understanding, in turn, provides you with insights and information you need to develop an argument that brings about a desired change in your audience's view of a subject. When your writing project involves reading, here are some strategies for getting started:

- For assignments that ask you to analyze and respond to a text, the questioning strategies explained in Chapter 5 should generate responses that can serve as points of departure. As you consider various starting points for writing about a text, consider what kind of change you want to make in *your* readers' thinking about this text and why this change is important. For example, do you want readers to see an inconsistency or contradiction they might otherwise miss? Do you want them not to be taken in by a particular persuasive ploy or faulty reasoning? Do you want to impress upon them the broad significance of what the text has to say?

- For assignments that ask you to begin with your own question, issue, or stance and to conduct research, you might begin by brainstorming a list of questions or problems that intrigue you. What are the points of disagreement? Why does this question or problem matter? To whom is this question or issue important and why? These questions can help you refine your starting point or stance and thus help guide your research. In Chapter 7 we discuss question analysis, a technique for formulating strategic questions to guide you through the process of finding, evaluating, and selecting sources.

Whatever kind of writing assignment you are given, the starting point of the writing process should be a problematic question or a risky claim. Although it might be tempting to start with ideas that are familiar or safe, that you are already firmly committed to or that are already settled in your mind, this approach usually leads to flat, perfunctory writing that fails to engage readers. The better approach is instead to start with a question that is genuinely puzzling to you or with a tentative claim that provokes multiple perspectives and invites audience resistance or skepticism.

STRATEGIES FOR GENERATING IDEAS

Once you have identified a starting point, you'll need to develop your ideas by analyzing more fully the single text you are writing about or by finding additional texts that can expand, deepen, and challenge your understanding of your research question. In either case, the rhetorical reading strategies in Chapters 4 and 5 should help you generate ideas for your writing project. Here are a few additional suggestions:

- A useful place to begin is to consider your rhetorical situation: Whose minds are you trying to change about what, and why? What kind of information do you need to establish your credibility? How can you make your readers concerned about your topic? What kind of supporting evidence will be persuasive to them? What values or interests do you share with your readers? What differences in opinions or values might you need to try to overcome?
- If you are writing to make a claim about a particular text, reread the text with your starting point in mind and note all the textual details you might use to support your claim. Likewise, look for counterevidence that you will have to account for in some way. Perhaps this counterevidence will cause you to modify your claim.
- If you are assigned to do library or Internet research, consider how a given source will advance your purpose for writing. (Chapter 7 offers extensive advice on both finding and evaluating sources.) As you take notes from the texts you plan to use as sources, consider how you might use each source in your paper. Does this source provide background information? Support for your claims? An alternative perspective? A compelling example or illustration of a point? With answers to these questions in mind, try out various organizational plans by making an informal outline or drawing an idea map of how the materials you've read connect with each other. This kind of preliminary planning can help you see the "big picture" of your evolving ideas.
- Conferencing with your teacher, peer group, or a writing center tutor is another good way to generate ideas for writing. When you try to explain your rough or tentative ideas to someone else, it's likely you will discover new ideas and connections that you didn't see before. Moreover, your conferencing partners will also ask you questions that will trigger new lines of thinking or enable you to see gaps in your current thinking that may require further analysis or research.

STRATEGIES FOR WRITING A FIRST DRAFT

Good first drafts are usually messy, confusing, and imperfect. Fear of this messi-
ness, or fear of the blank screen or page, often prevents writers from producing
idea-generating early drafts and thus reduces the time available for multiple revisions. To get past such fears, it can be helpful to think of first drafts as *discovery drafts.* Their purpose, in other words, is to extend the process of figuring out
what you have to say and how to say it. A writer's most original ideas often appear in final paragraphs, at the point where the writer discovered them. This is
not a problem at the rough draft stage because your goal is simply to start working out ideas. During revision you can reshape these ideas to meet your readers'
needs. What follows are some strategies for getting your ideas onto screen or paper so that you can work with them, learn from them, and use them to guide your
next steps in writing:

- Try to produce a complete first draft without worrying about perfection
  or even clarity for readers. When you get stuck, make notes to yourself in
  caps about ideas that might go in a particular section—a transition, an example, another point in support of your claim, or even just your doubts.
  If you have a vague idea but can't figure out how to say it, freewrite, again
  in caps, "WHAT I REALLY WANT TO SAY IS. . . ."
- Another strategy for overcoming the fear of getting started is to "blind
  write": Turn off the monitor on your computer so that you can't see what
  you're writing, and write for a while. The idea of blind writing is to silence
  your internal critic that finds fault with every sentence you write. What
  you want to do is get the words flowing so that you can determine how
  the ideas you have generated so far work, where the gaps are, what is still
  not clear to you.
- If you have trouble with introductions, try starting in the middle or with
  a particularly strong or well-formulated point. When you have most of the
  paper drafted and know what it will say, you can come back and write a
  focused opening.
- If your paper assignment calls for a particular organizational format—
  such as a classical argument, a technical report, an evaluative review of
  literature—use that format as an idea-generating template for producing
  various parts of your text. For example, a classical argument includes an
  introduction that explains the significance of the issue, provides background information, and gives the writer's thesis or claim; a section that
  supports the claim through a sequence of reasons and evidence; a section
  that summarizes and responds to opposing views; and a concluding section that calls for action or relates the argument to larger issues. Structures
  like this can help you build your first draft section by section. The specific requirements for each section will provide you with implicit questions to address in it. When you write out the answers, you'll have a
  discovery draft.

- Try talking out your draft by having a conversational partner (classmate, writing center tutor, teacher, or friend) listen to your ideas and take notes, or try talking directly into a tape recorder and then transcribing what you said. Since we're often more accustomed to talking than we are to writing, we can often discover what we have to say orally better than we can in writing.

STRATEGIES FOR EVALUATING YOUR DRAFT FOR REVISION

Producing an initial draft is only the first step in producing a final polished product. For most college assignments, success requires substantial revision through multiple drafts. Effective revision is not just minor repair or sentence correction but literally reseeing a draft's ideas. As you gain experience as a writer, you will find that the urge to revise begins when, in reading a draft, you discover confusing passages, points that need support and development, contradictions or flaws in thinking, gaps in your argument, places where the text fails to anticipate audience questions or objections, and so forth. Sometimes you will even decide to change your thesis and reorganize. To see these sorts of things requires a critical distance that is not easy to achieve. Therefore, you will benefit from specific techniques that enable you to adopt a reader's perspective toward your own text. Here are some suggestions:

- Try to "listen" to your own text in some of the ways outlined in Chapter 4. Write a descriptive outline of your draft, draw an idea map, or write a rhetorical précis. Because these strategies ask you to take your draft apart in various ways, they will inevitably provide you with a new, more "objective" view of your text and in the process reveal various problems— missing connections among ideas, digressions, gaps, vagueness, and so on.
- Most of us compose on screen these days, but reviewing your draft screen by screen can make you lose sight of the big picture. Instead, we recommend that you print up your draft periodically and read from hard copy, annotating it for problems and ideas for revision.

STRATEGIES FOR PEER RESPONSE AND REVISION

One of the best ways to see your text differently is through another reader's eyes. Because you know what you meant to write, it is often difficult to see any gaps or confusing points in what you actually wrote. Other readers, not privy to your inner thoughts, can spot these problems much more readily. A common technique for getting this kind of perspective on your draft is through peer response. Peer response groups allow you to receive feedback from a "live" audience, whether this feedback comes in the form of written comments by a peer or face-to-face response to your draft. The benefits of working in a peer response group go beyond the insights you gain about your own draft; you also benefit from the experience of offering feedback to others. For one thing, you learn to recognize and understand various kinds of writing problems better by seeing them in someone else's writing. This understanding, with practice, helps you to detect them in your own writing. In addition, offering constructive feedback helps you to develop a language for talking about what's working and what's not working in writing. This language, in turn, helps you to analyze your own writing. Put simply, receiving and giving peer response enables you to achieve the kind of critical distance on your own writing that is so crucial to revision.

Tips for Offering Feedback to Others

- Get a sense of the whole before formulating your responses. If the peer is reading a draft aloud, listen to the whole draft before jotting down a few notes. Ideally, you should make your notes while listening to the paper being read aloud a second time so that you can confirm or rethink your first impressions. For convenience, you might record your responses in three columns: positive comments, negative comments, and questions. If you are reading the draft and will write out your response, read the paper through completely, marking passages that you want to look at again or comment on with wavy lines or marginal notes such as question marks. A second reading will then help you to fill out a peer response form or decide upon the most constructive feedback you might offer the writer. If you are not given explicit guidelines for responding, be sure to be selective in your comments. Although you may mark various passages with a question mark or underline a number of confusing sentences, select only two or three major concerns to comment on in detail. When there are too many comments, writers are not sure where to start with their revision. They feel overwhelmed and discouraged rather than motivated to revise.
- Respond honestly and productively. Perhaps the most frequent complaint we hear from student writers about peer response groups is that the responders didn't offer any real feedback but instead offered vague, polite comments.
- Offer your comments from a reader's perspective, not an evaluator's. Instead of saying—"This is illogical"—say "I don't follow your reasoning here. After you offered example X, I was expecting you to come to conclusion Y." Or if the paper seems disorganized, explain where as a reader you get lost.
- Make sure that your comments are text-specific, not general. Rather than praising a paper by saying, "I liked your introduction," say "The personal anecdote you started with really captured my attention and made me want to read on." Or rather than saying that "Some points are unclear," identify those specific points that were unclear to you as a reader and try to explain what was unclear about them, the questions that were raised in your mind.
- Ask questions to help the writer generate ideas for clarification and support and to help the writer extend and complicate his or her thinking

about the topic. Depending upon the paper's aim, you may want to play the devil's advocate and introduce objections or other points of view to help the writer make a more convincing argument.

Tips for Using Feedback to Revise

- When possible, ask for feedback in terms of your rhetorical aim and your own assessment of your draft's rhetorical effectiveness. That is, think about the change you hope to make in your reader's attitude, understanding, or opinion about your subject matter and ask your peer responders whether your text accomplished this purpose. Ask specific questions about passages that you have already identified as potentially problematic. For example, you might ask readers if you need further evidence to support a particular point or if you need to explain an unfamiliar term more fully. Or you might ask if you come on too strong in a given passage or if your tone is appropriate in light of your purpose.

- Try to keep an open mind as you listen to or read through peer responses. That is, try to resee your paper from the reader's perspective. Let go of the urge to defend what you've written. Remember that the feedback from response groups is meant to help you improve your writing and should not be viewed as a personal attack. Experienced writers regularly seek feedback on their writing and understand that it enables them to see their writing in a way they can't on their own.

- Expect to get some mixed or contradictory feedback from peers. Try on these varied and conflicting perspectives to determine what in the text is causing these mixed responses or confusion. If several readers identify the same problem, you should probably try to fix it even if you don't fully agree with the feedback. Ultimately, however, it is up to you to weigh the feedback you receive and decide which responses you will attend to in your revising process.

- Use the peer feedback to develop a revision plan. Two considerations should guide your revision plan: (1) what the feedback tells you about this draft's successes and failures, and (2) your sense of which responses are the most important to address first. Generally, you should attend to higher-order concerns (focus, organization, development of ideas, logic) before lower-order concerns (sentence-level and grammatical and mechanical problems). You might find that problem sentences disappear once you focus on higher-order concerns. By revising for clearer ideas, you may create clearer sentences without grammatical tangles.

STRATEGIES FOR EDITING AND POLISHING
YOUR FINAL DRAFT

College professors expect final drafts that are carefully edited and proofread. Editing can be difficult, however, because most of us have trouble seeing the surface errors in our own writing—omitted words, spelling and punctuation errors, wrong or repeated words. We literally fail to see what's on the page, substituting instead what we intended to write for what's there. Consequently, you must train yourself to detect and correct errors in sentence structure, word choice, spelling, punctuation, citation conventions, and grammar or usage. We suggest the following strategies for producing a polished final draft:

- As simple as it may sound, reading your text aloud to yourself or someone else (classmate, friend, tutor) is one of the most effective ways to catch missing words, wrong words, and other kinds of errors. Conversely, sometimes it's helpful to have someone else read your paper back to you. Although there are many errors that you cannot detect through just hearing your paper, you can often recognize snarled or unclear sentences and awkward wording when you hear someone else's voice reading it.

- Another effective strategy is to read through your paper line by line, using another sheet of paper to cover the part of the text you have not yet read. Such a practice slows down your reading and forces you to look at each word and sentence, making it more likely you'll see what's really on the page, not what you hope is there.

- Computer programs now provide a number of editing aids—spelling and grammar checkers. You may want to turn these checkers off while you are drafting because they can intrude on your composing process. But once you are ready to proofread, take advantage of them, particularly the spell checker. But do not rely on them solely to detect the errors in your paper. Spell checkers, for example, do not detect homonym errors—*its* when you need *it's*—and they don't flag misspellings that turn out to be correctly spelled words that are not what you meant—*cant* for *want*. Similarly, grammar checkers mechanically mark things like passive voice or repeated words that may actually be appropriate in a particular writing context. For example, the computer highlighted the second *that* in the following sentence: "I believe that that is wrong." But this sentence might be perfectly appropriate in a context where what the second *that* refers to is perfectly clear. As a rule of thumb, use such computerized aids as only *one* of several steps in your editing process. Many experienced writers have an intense dislike for grammar checkers, which can only perform countable calculations and do not actually understand language.

- You may find that having a friend or classmate read over your final paper is a necessary step in your editing process because no matter how careful you are, there are errors that you miss.

- To improve your editing skills, try to keep track of the kinds of errors you habitually make, and try to be on the lookout for these errors as you proofread.

- To check on word choices, punctuation, grammar, and usage rules as well as citation conventions, keep nearby a recently published handbook and dictionary or a CD-ROM reference guide.

Summary

In this chapter, we began with an overview of five typical types of reading-based writing assignments: writing (1) to understand course content more fully, (2) to report your understanding of what a text says, (3) to practice the conventions of a particular type of text, (4) to make claims about a text, and (5) to extend the conversation. We then discussed the importance of asserting your own authority when you use readings—that is, of making an argument in your own voice rather than patching together quotes and paraphrases from your sources. Further, we offered advice about how to claim and maintain your authority as you work through several drafts of a paper, and we suggested that you read your own drafts rhetorically, analyzing them the same way you would analyze a published text—as a document aimed at changing readers' minds or attitudes in some way. This approach will help you attend to both your content ("what") and your methods ("how") as you revise through multiple drafts.

CHAPTER

7

Using Rhetorical Reading to Conduct Research

The only way in which a human being can make some approach to knowing the whole of a subject is by hearing what can be said about it by persons of every variety of opinion and studying all modes in which it can be looked at by every character of mind. No wise [person] ever acquired wisdom in any mode but this; nor is it in the nature of human intellect to become wise in any other manner.

—John Stuart Mill

As the opening epigraph suggests, wisdom emerges only through careful examination of many differing perspectives. John Stuart Mill's admonition to hear "every variety of opinion" on a subject, although probably not literally possible to follow, serves as an important reminder that new knowledge is made only through our interaction with the thinking and writing of others, including—perhaps, especially—those with whom we do not expect to agree. In this chapter we address the difficult challenge of finding and selecting materials that will provide you with reliable and diverse perspectives on the questions and issues you investigate for college writing assignments. As our chapter title suggests, our intent is to demonstrate the value of reading rhetorically as an efficient and revealing method of inquiry.

Writing assignments that expect you to synthesize material from outside readings pose a threefold set of challenges: (1) finding sources that speak directly to the questions your paper seeks to address, (2) evaluating their reliability, and (3) incorporating material from them into your own writing. We devote this chapter to the first two matters, finding and evaluating sources, and the next chapter to incorporating source materials into your own writing. Chapter 7 will introduce question analysis, a method that will help you explore the questions you seek to address and predict where you will find good sources. The final section of this chapter provides a list of questions to use for evaluating potential sources in terms of their reliability and their relevance for your purposes as a writer. In Chapter 8 we will describe specific, practical techniques for incorporating material from your reading into your own writing so that your papers make new knowledge out of your diverse sources.

Choosing Readings

You may be familiar with what we'll call "pseudo-research," assignments that expect the writer to do little more than report on a topic by providing extensive paraphrases or quotes from an assigned number of sources. The expectations and standards of your college teachers who assign papers with research components will be quite different. These professors will expect you to do more than merely gather information and funnel it into your paper. In the language of our service economy, they expect you to provide "value-added" content that demonstrates your own thinking about the subject of your paper. The information you need for your paper is "out there" in publications and on Websites. But it is either unanalyzed information or information selected and analyzed by writers whose purpose, audience, and context are very different from your own. Your task, like that of the writers in the workplace scenarios in Chapter 6, is to survey the raw data of the information you collect, discover patterns of meaning within it, select relevant material from it, and then explain that material's significance to your readers. The value you add comes from the analysis and organization you provide to help your readers make sense out of the disconnected array of available information.

This multilayered researching/reading/writing process involves rhetorical reading at its most challenging. In our electronic information age, where thousands, even millions, of research sources are available within seconds of a mouse click, locating information is only a small step in the research process. Some new college students make the mistake of thinking there is so much information available now that researching a paper is a quick, easy matter. It's true that computers make it easy to obtain potential source materials. With the full text of many magazine and journal articles available through library databases such as EBSCOhost, Lexis-Nexis, or ProQuest, it's possible to collect many sources without even looking up a call number and going to the stacks. But making sense of the information in all those potential sources presents a wholly different challenge. What if those full text articles in the database only skim the surface of your subject? Where will you find fuller discussions? What if they are out of date? How can you tell if they are written by knowledgeable researchers or published by reputable organizations? How can you tell if they are one-sided and limited? How can you know what they have left out?

Now that so many potential sources are readily available, choosing *reliable* sources that are *relevant* to your research purposes is actually more difficult than it used to be. We are awash in information. We need to figure out what it means. To be effective, student writer-researchers must think of themselves as *question formulators, resource evaluators,* and *knowledge makers.*

This chapter presents strategies you can use to sharpen your skills for both reading and writing as you undertake the work necessary in each of these roles. We will illustrate our discussion by following the work of Jenny, the composition student working on Larissa MacFarquhar's "Who Cares If Johnny Can't Read?", as she responds to the evaluative writing assignment in the next section. Her final essay—a researched argument entitled "Romance Fiction: Brain Candy or Culturally Nutritious?"—appears at the end of Chapter 8.

JENNY'S ASSIGNMENT TO EXTEND THE CONVERSATION

Here is the writing assignment Jenny received in her first-year composition class to evaluate a particular genre of reading or television. Note that by asking students to "extend the conversation," the assignment invites them to contribute their own ideas to an ongoing conversation initiated by other writers. (For additional discussion of evaluative writing, see the introduction to Chapter 14.)

> In the last paragraph of "Who Cares If Johnny Can't Read?" Larissa MacFarquhar poses the following challenge to readers: "Reading *per se* is not the issue. The point is to figure out why certain kinds of reading and certain kinds of television might matter in the first place." Write a paper in which you extend the conversation introduced by MacFarquhar's challenge. Choose a particular kind of reading with which you are familiar—romance fiction, science fiction, detective fiction, inspirational books—or a kind of television program—the Nature channel, police dramas, reality TV—and ask these questions: Is this kind of reading or television culturally valuable? If so, how? If not, why not?
>
> Your paper should include the following: a working definition of "cultural value" and criteria for judging it; your own experience with this kind of print or media text; and the published opinion of others regarding its cultural value. It should be 4 to 6 pages in length and include MLA in-text citations and a works cited list.

FORMULATING QUESTIONS: KNOW WHAT YOU'RE LOOKING FOR

Whether you are fulfilling an assignment for a first-year writing course or for a capstone seminar in your major, you need to begin not by searching for information on the Internet or in a periodicals database but by articulating your purpose: What is it that you want to investigate and write about? The first step of a research project is to become familiar with the published conversation relevant to the question you seek to answer. The best way to do that is to determine in advance what you will be "listening" for once you begin looking at sources. Experienced researchers go to the library (perhaps via their Internet browser) with more than a generalized "topic" in mind. They begin with a carefully worked out question and a set of expectations about how they will recognize relevant answers. You need to do the same. As your research progresses, you will probably revise your original question, narrowing or broadening it as you catch the drift of the ongoing conversation about it. (Most researchers—not only students—find that they must narrow their initial questions significantly just to make their project feasible for the amount of time available and the number of pages allotted for the assignment.) Although your question will undoubtedly change somewhat as your project unfolds, it will eventually become part of your paper's introduction. Combined with the answers you find, it will lead into your thesis statement to signal your paper's purpose to your readers.

But first you need the question. How else will you recognize answers?

Think of research-based writing assignments this way: Your job is to conduct an inquiry, not to shop around for sources. We offer a cautionary tale. Consider what went wrong when a student we'll call Stacey treated a research assignment as a hunt for bargains instead of an inquiry. Her assignment was an explanatory paper that would examine the potentially negative consequences of something that interested her. She had heard that Barbie dolls were being redesigned to have more natural proportions, so she thought Barbies would be an interesting "topic." She skipped the assigned step of writing out an initial question because, as she wrote in a later reflection, she thought that since Barbie was in the news, it would be faster just to do some computer searches and see "what there was to say." She felt overwhelmed at first by all the sources she found in just one periodicals database, but she chose three articles for which full text was available online. She used them for a paper that amounted to the "patch-writing" we caution against in Chapter 6. It interspersed engaging descriptions of her own favorite Barbies between three long paragraphs that summarized a feminist's reflections about her childhood dolls, a psychological study about gender stereotypes and eating disorders, and a commentary about the negative impact of Teen Talk Barbie's dislike for math class. There was nothing about Barbie's new figure. The descriptions of her dolls were fun to read and showed that Stacey was a fluent writer with a good vocabulary. But other than that, the paper was three long, loosely connected summaries. It lacked purpose. Stacey had not defined a purpose for her reading and research, and so she did not have one for her paper.

QUESTION ANALYSIS

What could Stacey have done instead? We recommend a technique called *question analysis* (QA), a systematic examination of your initial research question in terms of what you already know about your subject matter and what you hope to find out in your research.* Through QA you can make a preliminary map of the terrain you'll need to cover so that you can plan your research and consider in advance what kind of sources are going to be most useful for you to retrieve, read, and eventually integrate into your paper. The QA process will help you begin your actual searching with a focused sense of purpose so that you can use your rhetorical reading skills efficiently to select sources most relevant to your purposes. The QA process takes you out of a passive role like Stacey's, waiting to see what you can find, and puts you in charge of your research.

Clarifying Your Purpose

In a nutshell, the goal of a research process is to find source readings that will support your writing project in two basic ways: (1) by helping you uncover and understand the ongoing conversation about the subject, and (2) by providing information and concepts you can use to develop your paper. The following list of QA prompts will help you with both the overview and the specific information because the questions are designed to focus your thinking about the kind of sources that are likely to meet both needs.

Prompts for Question Analysis

Jot down answers to these questions *before* you begin searching for sources.

1. What question do you plan to investigate in this paper?
2. What makes this question worth pursuing?
3. What kind of expert would be able to provide good answers, or the current best thinking about finding answers? (Perhaps a physician? Wildlife biologist? Water resource engineer? CPA? Social worker?)
4. Where do you expect to find particularly good information about the matter? General interest publications? Specialized publications? Are you aware of a specific source with material relevant to your needs?
5. How recent must materials be to be relevant? What factors might make information outdated (such as a congressional election or the announcement of important medical findings)? Do you need information recorded *before* a particular event? For situations that change rapidly, such as AIDS research or foreign policy, even a few months could make a difference in the relevance of some material to your project. Defining a particular calendar period will help you search more efficiently.
6. What individuals or interest groups have a major stake in answering your question in a particular way? For example, players' unions and sports team owners look at salary caps from different perspectives; lumber companies and environmental activists evaluate the effectiveness of the Endangered Species Act differently.

---

*The term *question analysis* comes from the work of academic librarian Cerise Oberman, who first broached it in "Question Analysis and the Learning Cycle," *Research Strategies* 1 (Winter 1983): 22–30.

7. What kinds of bias do you need to be especially alert for on this particular question? Neutral sources are valuable, but bias of some kind is unavoidable, so it's important to recognize how it is operating in your sources.

8. Finally, jot down some words or phrases that you might use to begin searching.

QA is preliminary to your active search for sources, just as note-taking and freewriting during planning stages of the writing process are preliminary to active drafting. Students who use QA for the first time are often surprised to discover how much they already know about where they are likely to find relevant material and what issues those sources will raise. Like pounding out a first draft, searching for sources is a messy process that involves a lot of false starts, rethinking, and a certain amount of trial and error. But both types of work are more productive if you have thought in advance about your purpose and method. The notes you scratch out as part of your "pre-researching" through QA will help you maintain your focus and sense of purpose during the research process itself. Careful advance thinking about your research process will also help you choose among the many potential sources you find and avoid Stacey's problem of being distracted by intriguing but not directly relevant materials.

The QA prompts begin by asking you to jot down not only the question that you will address in your paper, but also your reasons for pursuing that question. Thinking carefully about the importance of your question will help you negotiate complexities you may find in your sources. For an academic project, a question with an obvious or simple answer is probably not worth investigating. You'll want to choose a question without clear-cut answers. Perhaps experts have been unable to discover an answer or are at odds with each other because of different values, political perspectives, or research approaches. Ask yourself also why pursuing the question is important. What benefits will come from answering the question? What readers are interested in the question? Why are you yourself interested in the question? Whatever your purpose, if you clarify it for yourself in advance, you will greatly reduce the risk of losing sight of your purpose once you dive into the search process. To illustrate the QA process, we invite you to examine the following excerpts from Jenny's answers to the QA prompts.

Excerpts from Jenny's Research Log

Question Analysis

1. <u>My question</u>: How do people defend romance novels? (I'm assuming some people do!) What do they say is the value of them? What criteria do they use? Maybe I have to set up criteria, but I'd like some experts to base my ideas on and use for support!

2. <u>Why it's worth pursuing</u>: Because (1) MacFarquhar uses romance novels as an example, so they'll fit the "extending the conversation"

idea, (2) lots of people read them—including me, sometimes, (3) I need to understand what my future students might be reading. . . .

3. Experts I need: teachers, librarians, maybe that Center for the Book that LM mentions

4. Sources I think will work: I hope there will be good material in regular newsstand magazines, possibly women's magazines, maybe magazines/journals for teachers & librarians.

5. Dates? They have to be pretty current, from 1997 (LM's article) to now.

6. People with a stake in this: teachers, except I don't know which way they'd lean. Some of my teachers thought they were OK!

7. Bias to watch for: Publishers and bookstores—they want to sell books, no matter what kind. I have to watch out for material that's just hyping romance writing. Would data about bestsellers prove cultural value? Probably not. Need to find serious discussion, not just somebody arguing back at MacFarquhar.

8. Words for searching: "romance novels" (obviously), "reading" ?? (possibly too broad) "readers" ?? Maybe look for reviews of books by specific authors—Nora Roberts, Amanda Quick—and see how reviewers talk about them for evidence of cultural value. Look for author names on bestseller list? Ask at bookstore?

Discerning Purpose in Potential Sources

Notice that the QA prompts about experts, publication type, controversy, and bias all draw attention to matters that are important for rhetorical reading: the credibility, intended audience, and evident purpose of the texts being considered as possible sources for a paper. Since these matters are a function of a text's context of publication, the same bibliographic information that can help you locate materials will also help you quickly assess the reliability of a potential source and its relevance to the question(s) you are researching. That assessment will in turn help you make good decisions about how far you want to pursue a given source. The next section of this chapter provides detailed guidance about making those decisions.

In the meantime, for the QA questions about what kinds of material to look for and where you might find it, we offer some brief background points about the publication processes behind basic categories of print texts.

- In general, print publications undergo a more rigorous editorial process than most Internet sources do. This editing work involves multiple readers, fact-checking, quote-checking, and even background checking of the people quoted. With so many people staking their own professional reputations on the quality and credibility of the material in them, print sources should be your preferred sources, especially during the early stages of your research, when your main goal is to catch the drift of the published conversation relevant to your question. (You should not, of course, exclude Internet material as potential sources. Rigorous editorial processes stand behind many Web materials, and print periodicals often publish material on the Web. We offer tips for evaluating these matters in the next section.)

- Librarians usually recommend that you begin a research project by look-ing for relevant magazine and journal articles. These materials are efficient to use, and are usually more current than books, which take a long time to produce.

- Since your ability to understand the sources you find will be crucial to the success of your project, it is important that you determine whether dis-cussion of your question will be available at a suitable level of expertise. You can count on being able to read general interest publications comfort-ably, but if they don't provide the depth of information you are looking for, you will need specialized periodicals, where readers expect in-depth cov-erage. Newsstand periodicals aimed at members of the general public who share specialized interests (such as *Sports Illustrated, American Health, Rolling Stone,* or *Money*) are good places for a student researcher to find ex-tended but easily understood discussions of a given subject. If the publi-cation targets readers with a high level of expertise, however, you may not be able to understand the material. The more specialized the publication, the greater the likelihood that you will find it difficult to understand, ei-ther because the material is too technical or because the author assumes readers are more familiar with the subject than you are. If your question has been addressed only at these high levels of scholarship, you will prob-ably need to revise it.

- In the academic world, the most highly regarded periodicals are peer-reviewed journals, also known as *refereed journals.* Articles published in them have been approved by several experts as meeting high scholarly standards and contributing to new knowledge. These high levels of cred-ibility make these journals excellent sources for college papers. The drawback is that material written for experts and scholars may be diffi-cult for readers outside the field to understand. However, the abstracts and literature reviews that are standard in this genre can often provide helpful background. Furthermore, even if you cannot understand all the details in material from scientific journals such as the *New England Journal of Medicine* or *JAMA,* reading the abstract, background, and con-clusions sections of a study may provide you with better insights than a newspaper report of that same study.

- Avoid searching for information on the World Wide Web until after you've done initial research through print sources. Immediate access to infor-mation—the great wonder of the Internet—is also its great disadvantage, especially if you are new to a field. The Web contains garbage as well as gold. It can be difficult to assess the credibility of Web authors or the motives of a site sponsor. Furthermore, the Web's global reach and the vastness of its contents make finding reliable and relevant overview discussions difficult. For example, when Jenny did a Web search for "romance novels," she turned up 147,000 "hits," which a quick sampling suggested were mostly book lists and fan mail.

• *For Writing and Discussion*

Working individually or in small groups, use the question analysis method to develop a more productive approach than Stacey's for researching a paper about the potential negative effects of Barbie dolls.

1. Start by brainstorming a few possible research questions. Then choose one that you consider significant to use for practicing all eight steps of the QA method.
2. Compare notes with other classmates or groups to see how many different approaches to the subject your class can come up with.

Evaluating Potential Sources

In this section we offer specific guidelines for evaluating the reliability of texts you might use as sources for a research project. These evaluation tips suggest ways to apply your rhetorical reading skills to infer the context and purpose of potential sources. Your understanding of a source's context and purpose will give you a basis for deciding *whether it helps answer your research question* and *how you might use it in your own writing*. To illustrate how one student applied these guidelines to her work, we include at the end of this chapter more excerpts from Jenny's research log (p. 121). As you look over this material, note that she continues to use questions to sift through potential sources and define her purpose.

LIBRARY DATABASES AND WEB SEARCH ENGINES

Rhetorical readers make their first evaluative decisions when they start their search. They know, for example, that materials retrieved via their computer will differ depending on whether they search library periodicals databases (sometimes called *subscription services*) or search the World Wide Web via a search engine such as Yahoo! or Google. Library databases and the World Wide Web both offer important research resources, but the type of material found through them differs significantly. You can readily access both from a desktop computer, but they search entirely different parts of the Internet. Library database services give you access to computerized indexes of material that has appeared in print periodicals, such as magazines and scholarly journals—indexes for which the library must pay substantial fees. In contrast, World Wide Web search engines search the free access part of the Internet. You can use these engines without charge because their revenue comes from advertisers. When you enter keywords in the search box of one of these engines and click "search," the engine software scours computers around the globe—all the computers linked to the free access portion of the Web—to find postings that include your word or phrase. Every item or "hit" on your results list will link your computer to another computer where the words appear on a Web page. This can amount to an overwhelming amount of information, much of it worthless.

In contrast, searching a periodicals or reference database to which your library subscribes will restrict your search to indexes of material that has appeared in print sources such as magazines and scholarly journals, the starting place recommended by experienced researchers. These same print articles will appear on World Wide Web searches only if the material happens to have been published both on paper and on the Web. Thus, when you are looking for magazine, journal, or newspaper articles originally published on paper, you need to use one of the periodicals databases available through your library such as EBSCOhost, ProQuest, or Lexis-Nexis. Although some specialized databases are available only on CD-ROM in the library itself, the extensive general interest databases are stored on computers that may be miles away from the library. When you use them from campus, access appears to be as free of cost as it is with a Web search engine; however, libraries pay substantial subscription fees to the database companies and often restrict access from off campus by requiring a PIN number.

These periodicals databases are indexed according to traditional bibliographic categories (author, article title, publication title, etc.) as well as a set of specialized search terms connected to their subject matter. When you enter search terms, the computer checks these index categories as well as the text of an abstract or the article itself. The results, usually a much smaller and more manageable list than from the Web, will give you a list of bibliographic citations with brief abstracts of the articles. As we'll show you in the next section, rhetorical readers can pick up additional important evaluative cues from material in these citations. When it is available, you can link directly to the full text of an article from its citation. A bonus of database searches is that most citations will include all the article's official subject terms, which sometimes provide valuable clues about a better way to find what you need. It's worth paying attention to the subject terms listed in a citation, especially if you aren't finding good materials, because different databases use different wording (for example, "death penalty" versus "capital punishment" and "secondary school" versus "high school"). However, manipulating subject terms can be a complex and frustrating business. (If you aren't getting the results you expect, *ask a librarian for help*!)

QUESTIONS ABOUT RELEVANCE

You can determine many basic relevance issues from the bibliographic information you will find in library catalogs and databases. (For World Wide Web sources, however, we recommend that you examine the actual source, not just the link supplied by the search engine.)

To evaluate a potential source's relevance to your project, you need to ask three basic questions about its purpose and method.

1. *What ideas and information does this text offer?* For answers about a print publication, examine the title, subtitle, and abstract in the bibliographic citation. Also note carefully the title of the magazine or journal the article appeared in, or, if the publication is a book, note the publisher. What you already know or can discern about the intended audience of the periodical or the book publisher will indicate the article's approach.
2. *Can I trust the source of information?* Consider what you know or can gather about the author's and the publisher's/Web sponsor's credentials and reputation. For Web sources, if there's no evidence of a reputable sponsor, don't use the source. (Material from an individual's home page isn't usually acceptable for academic papers, no matter how impressive it may appear.)
3. *Will I be able to understand what the source says—was it written for someone at my level of expertise?* Draw inferences about the intended readers from the title, publisher's reputation, and abstract, then spot read as needed. If the article is full of technical diagrams, concentrate on making sense of the abstract, the literature review, and the conclusions sections.

QUESTIONS ABOUT CURRENCY AND SCOPE

Take your evaluation further by using bibliographic information about date of publication and length to determine how usable the material is for your purposes. Abstracts, if supplied, will frequently help you catch a publication's tone and scope, but in many instances you may have to find paper copy that you can skim to see if you want to read the source in detail. Use the following questions as a guide.

1. *How current is the source?* You will usually want the most recent information available, but if you are researching a historical phenomenon, "current" doesn't necessarily mean "recent."
2. *How extensive is the source? How much detail is present? What kind of evidence is used?* A twenty-page article contrasting American and Japanese management styles might be just what you need, or it might be far too detailed for your purposes. A cheery three-paragraph piece in *Glamour* or *GQ* about the value of regular dental checkups might enable you to make a point about dental education in popular magazines, but it probably won't tell you much about how well people take care of their teeth or the quality of available dental care.

QUESTIONS ABOUT AUTHORS AND EXPERTS

Your background knowledge about subject matter and sources will often help you answer questions about the trustworthiness of an author or expert. When you need more information, look for quick answers within the bibliographical data about the source, then try other available search tools as explained below. Once you have selected certain materials to read in depth, use those texts to consider again the following questions about credibility.

1. *What are the author's credentials and qualifications regarding the subject?* If you recognize the name, it will tell you a lot. But if you don't, see what you can tell about this person's professional expertise. An abstract or a note at the end of a full text article may supply biographical information. Is the writer an expert in the field? A journalist who writes about the subject frequently? A quick search by author (perhaps via a click on the name) will show you what else this person has written recently. You might discover, for example, that the author of a piece on rap music regularly writes about the business side of the entertainment industry. This discovery may signal that the article is not likely to help you if you plan to write about rap's roots in the African American folk tradition, but if you are interested in how rap has been marketed or how it fits into the larger entertainment market, looking for additional articles by this author may lead to just what you need.

2. *What are the credentials and qualifications of experts who are cited?* In journalistic pieces, the writer's expertise is probably less important than that of the sources interviewed. Gathering information about the people quoted usually requires skimming to see what background information is supplied. Looking for material written by those experts can lead to more in-depth sources.

3. *What can you tell about the writer's or expert's political views or affiliations that might affect their credibility?* You are more likely to uncover this information in the text than in the citation. (Much of the time you have to use your rhetorical reading skills to infer the writer's ideology—see Chapter 5, p. 77.) If the purpose of your paper dictates that you find out more about a writer's ideological biases, a quick search in *Books in Print,* in a biography database, or on the World Wide Web itself will probably tell you what you need to know. You might learn, for example, that a particular writer recently received an award from the American Civil Liberties Union or that a medical expert interviewed about the dangers of plastic surgery is a well-known celebrity doctor. It will be up to you to determine the extent to which this information adds or detracts from the person's credibility in relation to your research project's purposes.

QUESTIONS ABOUT PUBLISHERS AND SPONSORS

Crucial information for evaluating a source can become apparent when you examine the purposes and motives of its publisher. Whether you are considering a paper or online source, it is important to consider how and why the material has become available in the first place. These questions about audience, review process, and reputation will help you round out the process of evaluating your sources.

1. *What is the periodical's target audience? Is this a well-known general interest magazine or is it a little-known journal for a specialized audience? Is it known for providing good information about the subject that interests you?* If you are researching antidepressants, for example, articles in popular magazines

are often upbeat about their value. You'll probably find more reliable information about the potential side effects of drugs in medically oriented journals.

2. *How extensive a review process did the article have to undergo before the text was published? Is it from a scholarly journal?* Most Internet materials have not undergone any editorial screening. But not everything on the Web is posted by individuals. As increasing numbers of print periodicals, particularly newspapers, post material on the Web, you will be able to rely on their editorial processes. Nevertheless, it's important to remember that most general circulation publications are driven by marketplace concerns. Their editors choose articles that will help sell copies (or draw eyeballs) because circulation increases advertising revenue. Be alert for overstatement.

3. *Is the publisher or site sponsor known to have a viewpoint that might influence its coverage of material relevant to your question?* Pay attention to liberal and conservative political biases, for example, not because you can avoid bias but because you may want to be sure to consult sources with different leanings. A wide variety of nonprofit, public service, and governmental entities have extensive and useful Websites. You must determine how the organization's mission may influence its Web presentations. If you use material from an organization known for supporting certain causes or positions, scrutinize it carefully and be sure to let your own readers know any relevant but nonobvious information about the source's reputation.

More Excerpts from Jenny's Research Log

To illustrate how a student might apply the above evaluation strategies to her own research project, we conclude this chapter with more excerpts from Jenny's research log.

Evaluating Sources

My Searches

"Romance novels" and "Romance + reading" led me to lots of articles in Publishers Weekly about publishing trends (more emphasis on romance novels from a multicultural point of view, for example) and specific authors. But I don't want to write about the commercial side of this.

Most Relevant Article So Far

TIME, 3/20/2000, "Passion on the Pages" – Paul Gray and Andrea Sachs. (EBSCOhost) Abstract suggests it's much more factual and analytical than the catchy title, but that's TIME. Definitely trustworthy and written for the general reader. It includes reports from a survey. I emailed full text to myself.

<u>Currency and Scope</u>? Yes, well-known magazine, fairly recent (more recent than LM, so it's an update!).

<u>Author and experts quoted</u>? Yes. Stats from the Romance Writers Association (self-interested?) and interview of a famous author, Nora Roberts (!). Paul Gray, author of article, writes book reviews for almost every issue of TIME. This is solid.

* * *

Still to Do

- I want to check out the Web page I saw mentioned in an <u>Entertainment Weekly</u> article: theromancereader.com.
- Find book reviews. Where? Do newspapers review romance novels? Seems like a good place to get an everyday view. Check.
- I saw a <u>Library Journal</u> article that reviewed TWO reference books about romance novels. Didn't print it out because I'm not sure how relevant it is. Depends. How could these reference books add to my points about cultural value?
- Most of all, I need to find something related to teaching and education!! Nothing's working on the databases. These books are so popular with teenagers, people MUST have written about whether to use them in schools. <u>Ask a librarian where I should look</u>.

Summary

This chapter has described the role of student researchers as that of question formulators and resource evaluators. College teachers expect students to write papers in which the writer's claims and commentary are more prominent than their sources so that the paper demonstrates the student's own thinking about the research question. To assist this process, we presented a series of question analysis (QA) prompts to use before your active searching for sources begins. Next, we offered background tips about the publication of Web and print material, and we explained differences between searching for sources through library databases and Web search engines. Finally, we presented a list of questions for evaluating potential sources in terms of the relevance of a text's purpose and method, its currency and scope, the background of its author, the reputations of experts who are cited, and the biases and credibility of publishers and Web page sponsors. To illustrate these processes, we provided excerpts from Jenny's research log.

8

Making Knowledge: Incorporating Reading into Writing

The mind in action selects and orders, matches and balances, sorting and generating as it shapes meanings and controls their interdependencies.

—Ann E. Berthoff

I n this chapter we address one of the biggest challenges in college writing: incorporating other texts into your own without having them take over. The techniques we present here will help you foreground your sense of purpose in your writing and thus to author strong, rhetorically effective texts. As we have stressed in the preceding chapters, composing a text is an opportunity to add your voice to the ongoing conversation about a particular topic. Your readers, whether your peers or your professors, want to read what *you* have to say, not a rehash of what others have said. Our warning against "passive writing" in Chapter 6 urged you to take an active role in analyzing how the goals and methods of your source materials fit with your purpose for writing. In Chapter 7, we provided guidelines and evaluation questions for selecting source materials directly relevant to the questions that shape your research inquiries. We now turn to specific techniques for using these materials to extend and develop your points and for making the distinctions between your ideas (and words) and your sources' ideas (and words) absolutely clear to your readers. We will illustrate our discussion with sample passages from Jenny's "Extending the Conversation" paper, "Romance Fiction: Brain Candy or Culturally Nutritious?", which appears at the end of this chapter.

Summary, Paraphrase, and Direct Quotation

The effective use of sources in your papers will enable you to position your ideas in relation to those of others and will establish your credibility as an informed writer. Success in this aspect of your writing will be measured by your ability to incorporate the words and ideas of others judiciously (keeping readers' attention on *your* points), smoothly (using clear, grammatically correct sentences), and correctly (representing the points and language of your sources without distortion). In the next few pages, we will discuss in detail three techniques for accomplishing these goals: summary, paraphrase, and direct quotation. Because each serves a useful and distinct purpose, you should become expert at all three so that you can choose the one that best suits your purpose. Why and how you use sources in your texts should be a careful rhetorical choice.

USING SUMMARY

Summary is probably the most common way of incorporating a source in your own writing. As we described in Chapter 4, when you summarize all or part of another writer's text, you present in your own words a condensed version of that writer's points. The original material that you summarize must, of course, be cited through an attributive tag and an in-text citation, both of which are discussed in detail later in this chapter.

Summarizing is an especially effective rhetorical strategy in the following situations:

- When the source directly supports your thesis, or alternatively, when the source offers a position you wish to argue against or analyze
- When the source offers important background information for your ideas
- When you need to provide readers with an overview of a source's whole argument before analyzing particular ideas from it

In using summary to accomplish these purposes, you may find that you need to summarize the whole of a text or only the portion that is relevant to the point you are making. Similarly, the length of the summary will depend on its location and function in your paper.

Let's examine two different uses of summaries in Jenny's two papers about Larissa MacFarquhar's article, "Who Cares If Johnny Can't Read?" The first comes from the opening paragraph of Jenny's rhetorical analysis paper at the end of Chapter 5, "Who Cares If the Value of Books Is Overstated?" (p. 84). Notice how the summary gives readers a context for the analysis that will follow. Jenny's one-sentence summary nutshells MacFarquhar's whole argument.

Summary Example 1

As the attention-getting title of her essay suggests, MacFarquhar's essay calls into question some common assumptions regarding reading, specifically that reading books is important for everyone and that reading books is better and more intellectually challenging than watching TV and surfing the Internet.

Our second example is from paragraph six of Jenny's paper at the end of this chapter, "Romance Fiction: Brain Candy or Culturally Nutritious?" (p. 140). In this example, Jenny summarizes the views of Carol Ricker-Wilson, a high school teacher who finds value in romance novels.

Summary Example 2

Although not a romance fiction reader herself, Carol Ricker-Wilson, a high school English teacher, offers an interesting perspective on the potential educational value of romance novels in "Busting Textual Bodices: Gender, Reading, and the Popular Romance." Writing in the English Journal for teachers who think of romance fiction as "escapist trash" (58), Ricker-Wilson argues that this widespread belief blinds teachers from seeing its personal value to their students and its possibilities for classroom use.

This longer summary sets up a series of paragraphs that will discuss in more detail the article by Ricker-Wilson, one of several experts Jenny uses in the paper to support her claim that romance fiction has cultural value. The summary's opening sentence introduces Ricker-Wilson's credentials, which are of key interest here because she is an English teacher, someone whom readers would probably expect to condemn romance fiction. Ricker-Wilson's authority adds authority to Jenny's paper. The summary's second sentence articulates Ricker-Wilson's core point, which Jenny goes on to develop through additional summary as well as paraphrase and a few brief quotations.

We offer two cautions about writing summaries to include in your texts. First, even though the length of summaries may vary, be sure that you condense the source to only the ideas that are essential to your purpose. If only part of a source is relevant to your purpose, summarize only that part. Second, make sure that your summary fairly and accurately represents the original text's meaning. Be on guard against distorting the original to make it fit your argument. Ask yourself whether the original author would consider the summary points to be fair and accurate.

USING PARAPHRASE

Paraphrase involves a more detailed presentation of the ideas from a source. Because paraphrases follow the original wording closely, you must include the page number, if one is available, when you cite the source.* Unlike summaries,

---

*MacFarquhar's online article, for example, was published without page numbers, so none are available for citation. See the discussion of citation conventions later in this chapter.

in which you condense the original text's ideas, paraphrases restate in your words all of the original passage's points. Often, they are as long as or even longer than the original, so it is best to paraphrase only short passages.

Paraphrase is a particularly valuable rhetorical strategy in the following situations:

- When you want to emphasize especially significant ideas by retaining all of the points or details from the original
- When you want to clarify ideas that are complex or language that is dense, technical, or hard to understand

Because paraphrase involves closely re-presenting the original text, you must take care not to give the impression that these are your ideas. Putting someone else's ideas into your own words does not make these ideas your own. To paraphrase effectively and ethically, you must translate the writer's wording entirely into your own words and acknowledge the source with an attributive tag and a citation.

Here are some suggestions for how to transform a passage into your own words:

- Avoid mirroring the sentence structure or organization of the original.
- Simplify complex ideas by pulling them apart and explaining each smaller component of the larger idea.
- Use synonyms for key words in the original and replace unfamiliar or technical vocabulary with more familiar terms.
- As a check, try paraphrasing the passage twice, the second time paraphrasing your own paraphrase; then compare your second paraphrase with the original to make sure that you have sufficiently recast it into your own language.

To illustrate the process and rhetorical effects of paraphrasing, we invite you to consider the parallels and variations between a passage from the Ricker-Wilson article on romance fiction and a paraphrase of it from Jenny's paper about romance fiction.

Ricker-Wilson's Original Passage

But while a number of researchers such as Radway and Christian-Smith have maintained that romance reading operates primarily as an unfortunate but justifiable effort to escape from the adversities of real heterosexual relations, it may also offer an escape from what its readers construe to be even less favorable depictions of women in other genres. Fundamentally, I would argue, romance readers *really like to read,* they like to read about women, and they don't want to read about their unmitigated despoliation and dispatch. But once readers venture out of the formulaic romance genre, fiction is a wild card and identification with female protagonists an emotional risk.

Jenny's Paraphrase

Ricker-Wilson acknowledges that some researchers claim that romance fiction provides women readers with escape from their difficult relationships with the men in their lives. She counters this negative view by proposing that romance fiction permits readers to escape something even worse: the negative images of women in other literature. She argues that readers who enjoy romance novels do so because they enjoy reading about women but do not like to read about women who are victimized or killed off, as they often are in other forms of fiction (58).

Jenny's paragraph accomplishes the two important goals of paraphrase. It elaborates and thereby emphasizes two significant and surprising ideas from Ricker-Wilson: that reading romance fiction to escape might actually be a positive thing and that reading other types of fiction might actually be a bad thing for young women. Furthermore, her paraphrase recasts the scholarly language of the *English Journal* article into more everyday terms.

As with summary, our advice must include words of caution. First, using paraphrase as a way to present difficult ideas or dense passages raises the potential problem of inadequate or inaccurate presentation. Be sure you fully understand the passage you are transforming. If you can't move beyond the words of the original, it's likely that you need to obtain a better understanding of it before you use the ideas in your paper. Second, the close ties between a paraphrase and the original raise not only the danger of committing plagiarism, but the possibility of the paraphrase taking over your paper. Just as a summary can, a lengthy paraphrase can draw so much attention to itself that it takes the reader's focus away from your own argument. Paraphrase from the original only what you need to develop your points.

USING DIRECT QUOTATION

Direct quotation inserts the words of someone else into your own text. Whenever you use another writer's exact wording, you must mark the beginning and end of the passage with quotation marks and provide as precise a reference to the original source as possible. Used selectively and sparingly, quotations strengthen your credibility by showing that you have consulted appropriate authorities on a particular subject. However, quoting too frequently or using unnecessarily long quotations in your text can actually have the opposite effect on your credibility. Overreliance on direct quotations weakens your authority and suggests that you have no ideas of your own to contribute to the conversation.

Direct quotations are most effective in enhancing your credibility in the following situations:

- When the language of the source is vivid, distinctive, or memorable
- When the quotation directly supports a key point in your paper
- When the person quoted is such a well-known authority on the matter that even a few well-chosen words carry considerable weight

To demonstrate the importance of these guidelines, we present two versions of a passage from Jenny's paper on romance fiction. When she first composed the paper, Jenny included in the fourth paragraph the following long quotation from MacFarquhar to illustrate derogatory views of romance fiction.

Ineffective Long Quotation from Jenny's First Draft

She says that romance writers are "producing mass-market entertainment that appeals to its consumers for much the same reason as McDonald's and Burger King appeal to theirs: It's easy, it makes you feel good, and it's the same every time. The point of a romance novel is not to dazzle its reader with originality, but to stimulate predictable emotions by means of familiar cultural symbols."

MacFarquhar's vivid comparison to McDonald's and Burger King led Jenny to include this quote in her first draft. But later, when she read over the whole paper to consider revisions, she realized that the quotation was too long for what she wanted to accomplish at that point in her text (the end of paragraph 4). She had already introduced her own claim about the positive aspects of romance fiction and was using the MacFarquhar quote to indicate typical criticisms of romance fiction that the paper would counter. But the long quotation unduly shifted the reader's focus to negative opinions about romance novels. Furthermore, the colorful language from MacFarquhar detracted from Jenny's own important phrase at the end of the paragraph: "brain candy." She decided to pare down her use of MacFarquhar by using paraphrase with a few direct quotations, a decision that shifts the focus to her own argument:

Jenny's Revised Use of Quotation

She describes romance fiction as "mass-market entertainment" that appeals to people because "it's easy, it makes you feel good, and it's the same every time." Its purpose, she says, is not to stimulate thinking and the imagination, "but to stimulate predictable emotions by means of familiar cultural symbols."

The quotations that Jenny has woven into her own prose are now serving her purposes instead of competing with them. By using more of her own language, Jenny is able to keep the focus on her own argument. In addition, Jenny's version achieves greater coherence because her words "stimulate thinking and imagination" echo concepts she develops earlier in the essay as criteria for judging something's cultural worth. By replacing MacFarquhar's vivid phrase "not to dazzle its readers with originality" with her own less vivid phrase "not to stimulate thinking and imagination," Jenny links this paragraph back to the criteria.

The following general guidelines will help you use direct quotations to good rhetorical effect:

- Prefer short quotations. Use long quotations only rarely because they will distract from the focus of your own discussion.
- Whenever possible, instead of quoting whole sentences, work quotations of key phrases into your own sentences.
- Make sure you are absolutely accurate in the wording of direct quotations.
- Punctuate your quotations exactly as in the original.
- When you must include a quotation that extends longer than four typed lines of your paper, separate the quotation from your text by indenting the quote a full inch; then type the quotation double-spaced without quotation marks.
- Make sure your use of quotations fairly and accurately represents the original source.
- Make sure you fully understand the ideas that you quote directly. While the words in a quotation may sound impressive, if you cannot explain them and relate them to your own ideas, incorporating the quotation will detract from your credibility instead of enhancing it.
- As part of your proofreading routine, compare all quoted material to the original passage and make any needed adjustments, no matter how small.

These guidelines carry implicit notes of caution. Not only is absolute accuracy important ethically, but any inaccuracies will undermine your credibility. The credibility you gain by quoting an important authority is quickly lost if your reader checks the original source and finds that you have misquoted or misrepresented that source. A related problem comes from quoting someone out of context. For example, if you quoted one of the statements that Larissa MacFarquhar sarcastically makes in her opening paragraph—"Now, we don't care about reading anymore"—as though it were her opinion and not one of the opinions she is trying to discredit, you would misrepresent her. It is always important to make sure that you are using a quotation in a way that does not misconstrue or misinterpret its original meaning.

• *For Writing and Discussion*

One way to develop skill at incorporating the ideas of others into your own papers is to see how other writers do it. To try this out, track the use of direct quotations in Jenny's paper at the end of this chapter.

ON YOUR OWN

List all of the sources directly quoted, noting the paragraph in which the quotation appears, and then describe how the quotation is used. Find places, for example, where she uses sources to support or illustrate one of her points, to represent an opinion she opposes, to increase her credibility, or to capture vivid or distinctive language from a source. Some of her direct quotations may serve more than one function.

WITH YOUR CLASSMATES

Compare your lists and descriptions. Are there differences or disagreements about how a particular direct quotation is being used? How effectively does she use quotations? Are there any quotations that might have been eliminated or shortened? Are there any places where you think her paper might have been strengthened by the use of a direct quotation where there isn't one?

Avoiding Plagiarism

Whether you are summarizing, paraphrasing, or quoting, using sources ethically requires that you always give credit to others' words and ideas through footnotes or in-text citations that refer to a full bibliography or works cited list. (We explain the Modern Language Association system of in-text citations that refer to a works cited list later in this chapter.) It is absolutely essential that you put all directly quoted language in quotation marks, even if you quote only a short phrase from the original source. Omission of either the quotation marks or the reference information has the effect of creating a text that presents someone else's words or ideas as if they were your own. In that case, you are committing *plagiarism,* a serious form of academic misconduct in which a writer takes material from someone else's work and fraudulently presents it as if it were the writer's own ideas and wording.

The three most common forms of plagiarism are the following:

- Failure to use quotation marks to indicate borrowed language
- Failure to acknowledge borrowed ideas and information
- Failure to change the language of the source text sufficiently in a paraphrase

Student writers sometimes have problems managing the details of quotations because they neglect to take careful notes that clearly mark all directly quoted material. During their revision processes, inexperienced writers sometimes lose track of which sentences and phrases are directly quoted. To avoid such problems and symptoms of potential plagiarism, make sure you take scrupulous care to mark all directly quoted language and its source in your notes. *Write down all relevant bibliographic information even before you begin reading and taking notes.* In drafting papers, some writers use color highlighting or put directly quoted language in a different font so that, as they move passages around during revision, they can keep track of which words are directly quoted. Other writers keep full original quotations at the end of their paper file or in a separate electronic file so that they can check for accuracy and proper citation as part of their final preparations before submission.

You must also acknowledge borrowed ideas and information, as well as borrowed language. That is, all ideas and information that are not your own require citation through attributive tags, internal citation, and acknowledgment on the works cited list. The only exception is "common knowledge." Common knowledge, as the phrase suggests, refers to information and knowledge that is widely known. (For example: George Washington was the first president or Toni Morrison won a Nobel Prize.) You can verify that certain information is common knowledge by consulting general information sources such as encyclopedias. If you are in doubt about whether something is common knowledge, or if you are concerned that your readers might credit an idea to you that is not yours, cite your source.

Perhaps the most difficult aspect of incorporating sources in a way that avoids plagiarism is sufficiently rewording the language of a source when you paraphrase. (This is why we recommend paraphrasing source material twice.) As we noted in the section on paraphrase, using the same sentence pattern as the original source and changing only a few words does not create an acceptable paraphrase, even if the writer includes a reference to the source. In the following examples, compare the acceptable and unacceptable paraphrases with the original passage from Paul Gray and Andrea Sachs's "Passion on the Pages," one of the sources on romance fiction that Jenny used for her paper.

Original

Other genres—mystery, thriller, horror, sci-fi—attract no cultural stigma, but those categories also appeal heavily to male readers. Romances do not, and therein, some of the genre's champions argue, lies the problem.

Plagiarism

According to Gray and Sachs, other types of books—horror, mystery, sci-fi—experience no cultural stigma, but these types of books are those that appeal mainly to male readers. Romances, by contrast, do not, and that, some of its champions argue, is the problem (76).

Acceptable Paraphrase

According to Gray and Sachs, popular books that attract mostly male readers, such as science fiction and thriller novels, do not suffer the same public condemnation as romance novels. Some fans of romance fiction believe that this is no coincidence and that condemnation of it is due to the fact most of its readers are female (76).

By following the guidelines we present for quoting and paraphrasing, you can incorporate the ideas of others while avoiding plagiarism. We close this section by passing along a final bit of advice: when incorporating materials from outside sources, write with your eyes on your own text, not on your source.* Your unfolding text should come from your mind, not someone else's text.

---

*This advice comes from *The Craft of Research* by Wayne Booth, Gregory Colomb, and Joseph Williams, who say "If your eyes are on your source at the same moment your fingers are flying across the keyboard, you risk doing something that weeks, months, even years later could result in your public humiliation" (Chicago: U Chicago P, 1995) 170.

Attributive Tags

The recurrent theme in this chapter has been that the success of your academic writing will frequently depend upon how well you integrate outside sources into your papers. To make your points most effectively, you need to show your readers how your source materials fit your points and serve the overall purpose of your paper. In order to do this smoothly, we recommend that you use short phrases called *attributive tags*. These phrases not only signal that you are borrowing outside material but also indicate the source of that material. These tags commonly contain just a few words: "Stephen Jones says" or "According to Stephen Jones." But if your readers need background information about who Jones is or why Jones should be taken seriously, the tag can be longer: "Stephen Jones, an independent pollster, says. . . ."*

Smooth, clear attributive tags will make your paper easier to read as well as add to your own credibility. Good tags will assert the authority of your well-chosen sources and clarify for readers where they can find out more about the subject. Furthermore, good tags let your readers know that you, not the sources, are in charge of the paper.

Your first attributive tag about a source is likely to be longer than subsequent ones, as illustrated by these contrasting examples from Jenny's paper:

> Although not a romance fiction reader herself, Carol Ricker-Wilson, a high school English teacher, offers . . .
>
> According to Ricker-Wilson . . .
>
> Ricker-Wilson argues . . .

In some instances, an author's name may not be as interesting or important to your readers as the place where an article appeared. For example, Jenny's reference to *Time* at the start of the following sentence from the second paragraph of her paper tells readers much more than the authors' names would have; the parenthetical citation with the authors' names provides the necessary reference information.

Periodical Title Used as Attributive Tag

A *Time* magazine article published in July 2000 verifies this claim and reports that over 50% of all paperbacks sold in the U.S. each year are romance novels (Gray and Sachs 76).

The absence of attributive tags in a paper is often a symptom of the passive patch-writing we warn against. Consider the difference between two versions of a sentence from Jenny's paper.

---

*We are grateful to freelance writer Robert McGuire, formerly a writing instructor at Marquette University, for his valuable insights and advice about attributive tags.

Confusion Caused by Lack of Attributive Tag

Romance readers insist on formulaic plots of "childlike restrictions and simplicity," and as a result, these books lack "moral ambiguity" (Gray and Sachs 76).

Sentence Revised with Attributive Tag

The *Time* article mentioned earlier claims that romance readers insist on formulaic plots of "childlike restrictions and simplicity," and says that as a result, these books lack "moral ambiguity" (Gray and Sachs 76).

As the first sentence begins, a reader has every reason to think that it states Jenny's ideas. Matters become confusing when the quotation marks signal that another voice has entered the text, but we don't know its source and the authors' names in the citation are not particularly informative. Readers would have to go to the works cited list to get the contextualizing information that the second sentence provides. In contrast, the attributive tag in the revised sentence not only makes clear the source of the idea, but specifically refers back to earlier discussion of material from the same source.

Attributive tags can appear at any natural break within a sentence. Here are some examples of attributive tags from Jenny's paper:

> Published in 1997 in the online journal *Slate,* MacFarquhar's essay offers . . .
>
> At the end of her essay, MacFarquhar challenges readers . . .
>
> Its purpose, she says, is not to stimulate thinking and the imagination, but . . .
>
> Predictable plots, so the argument goes, offer escape . . .

As the examples we have used illustrate, attributive tags can offer a variety of information, depending upon a writer's purpose and sense of the intended audience's background knowledge of the subject. Possible elements, which can be used alone or in combination, include

- Author's name
- Title of the work
- Publisher of the work
- Author's or expert's credentials or relevant specialty (e.g., "a high school teacher," "an avid fan of romance novels," "a lawyer who has defended spies in the past," "the Justice Department's main espionage prosecutor for over 20 years")
- A quick statement of the work's purpose or reputation (e.g., "a review of Victoria M. Johnson's book," "an article detailing the study's results," "King's well-known speech at the 1963 march on Washington")
- An indication of the work's context and the conversation it is part of (e.g., "Birkerts's essays praising books" or "a scathing letter to the editor published online")

Of course, if you used all this information in one tag, the sentence would have hardly any room left for your own ideas. It is up to you to decide what kind of information, and how much, readers need at a given point in a text. If you decide readers need a lot of background, you may want to provide it in a separate sentence, as Jenny does at the beginning of her extended discussion of the Ricker-Wilson article: "Although not a romance fiction reader herself, Carol Ricker-Wilson, a high school English teacher, offers an interesting perspective on the potential educational value of romance novels in 'Busting Textual Bodices: Gender, Reading and the Popular Romance.'"

The following guidelines will help you use attributive tags effectively.

- Make the tag part of your own sentence.
- The first time you bring in a particular source, put the tag before the quotation or summary so that readers will have the background they need when they reach the borrowed source material.
- Vary the format and vocabulary of your tags. You want to avoid a long string of phrases that repeat "according to" or "he says."
- Provide just enough background to help readers understand the significance of the material you are bringing in, not everything there is to say about the source.
- Base your decisions about attributive tags on what you are confident readers will recognize and what will help them recognize the relevance of the source you are using. For example, *Time* is a well-known magazine and the *Journal of Urban History* has a self-explanatory title, so using those titles in a tag would probably provide more context than an author's name would. However, stating that an article appeared in a journal with an ambiguous title—for example, we are aware of at least three periodicals named *Dialogue*—would probably be pointless without further explanation. In such cases, you would have to decide whether to supply details about the journal's purpose and audience or to substitute other, more readily understandable information, such as the author's background ("a Canadian philosopher") or a quick statement about how the article fits into the larger published conversation ("Arguing against this point, Smith contends . . .").

Citation Conventions

It is always important to give credit where credit is due, but even more important when you are writing a text that must place itself within a published conversation. Whenever writers of academic papers use any material that is neither common knowledge nor their own original idea, they are expected to include a *citation* that provides full publication information about the source of the material. Citations include page numbers, publication information, and/or Internet addresses that will help readers find source materials if they want to; their most important function, however, is to tell readers about the quality of the sources used.

The formats used for citing sources, known as *citation conventions,* vary across different academic fields, but all disciplines require that you cite the source of all statistics, quotations, paraphrases, and summaries of other writers' work and ideas. The variety of citation convention systems across disciplines is evident among the reading selections included in this book from refereed journals. Compare, for example, the numbered endnotes used by historian Kirk Savage in "The Past in the Present: The Life of Memorials" (p. 340) with the in-text author-date citatons used by psychology professors Amy Wolfson and Mary Carskadon in "Sleep Schedules and Daytime Functioning in Adolescents" (p. 275). Besides using different methods to refer readers to information about source material, these different citation styles present publication details in somewhat different order and use different punctuation. Each style follows conventions established by the discipline in which the authors are publishing.

Citation conventions are not something that writers memorize; rather, scholars use handbooks and model citations such as those in this book as guides. You should do the same, for citations, like attributive tags, add to a writer's authority and enhance a text's readability. Because following a particular citation format necessitates attention to many small details of form, students sometimes overlook the rhetorical value of carefully prepared citations. Clear, accurate, stylistically consistent citations not only give credit where credit is due, but present the author as knowledgeable and responsible. Furthermore, since the publication information contained in them gives readers information about the context and purpose of sources, citations demonstrate the reliability and authority of the material being presented.

The citation format that we explain and use in this book follows the recommendations of the Modern Language Association (MLA). Usually referred to as "MLA style," this system is widely used in the humanities. MLA style has two basic components: (1) short parenthetical references in the text, also called *internal* or *in-text* citations, which refer the reader to an alphabetized works cited list; and (2) the alphabetized works cited list itself. Unlike a full bibliography, this list includes only citations of works referred to, or cited, in the text itself. (Some instructors may ask for a works consulted list as well.) In MLA style, footnotes are reserved for supplementary comments, such as the one for this sentence.*

It is worth noting that although we recommend and use MLA style in this book, you will find readings in Part Four that use not only different types of citation formats but different punctuation conventions. We present the readings in a format as close to the original as possible, other than changes in page lay out. As a result, you will find that pieces originally published in newspapers, for instance, typically use quotation marks rather than italics or underlining on

---

*Social science classes may require the somewhat different author-date style for in-text citations recommended by the American Psychological Association (APA) system. In other disciplines, instructors may want you to use footnotes in the manner of the *Chicago Manual of Style.* Natural science and technical classes may call for a citation-sequence system such as that laid out by *The CBE Manual,* published by the Council of Biology Editors. These and other systems are frequently described in composition handbooks; guides are readily available on line or at library reference desks.

book titles. Another commonly noticed difference is that writers who follow the "AP style" of the Associated Press do not use a series comma before *and* in phrases such as "magazines, newspapers and Web pages." But in the MLA style of this book, we use that "final series comma" in our own text and would punctuate that same phrase this way: "magazines, newspapers, and Web pages." While these and other conventions may vary from text to text, genre to genre, *within* a given text, consistency is of paramount importance.

Always check with your instructor about what citation format to use in a paper. The remainder of this chapter explains the basics of using reader-friendly in-text citations according to MLA conventions. In addition to the examples we discuss from Jenny's paper at the end of this chapter, you will find details of MLA style illustrated in three student-written papers in Part Four: Thomas Roepsch's informative paper, "America's Love Affair with Pizza" (p. 322), Heather Wendtland's analytical paper, "Rebellion Through Music" (p. 385), and Jenny Trinitapoli's common ground analysis, "Public Libraries and Internet Filters" (p. 570). The appendix at the end of this book, entitled "Building a Citation," provides model MLA style citation formats to use in works cited lists for the types of print and electronic sources most commonly used in college papers.

FORMATS FOR IN-TEXT CITATIONS

- The basic shell for an MLA style in-text citation is simple, a pair of parentheses inserted between the last word of a sentence and its period:

      . . . these books lack "moral ambiguity" (Gray and Sachs 76).

We want to point out two often overlooked details of this format: (1) a space is left between the last word of the sentence and the first parenthesis, and (2) the final punctuation mark *follows* the citation.

- Within the parentheses, this basic format provides readers with two crucial bits of information: (1) the author of the source and (2) the page number of the material referred to, summarized, paraphrased, or quoted. Note that in MLA format there is no comma between the name and the page number:

      (Ricker-Wilson 58)

The brief information inside the parentheses permits a reader to locate complete bibliographic details on the works cited list, where entries are arranged alphabetically by the authors' last names.

Placement Guidelines

An in-text citation usually comes at the end of the sentence in which you are using material from your source. When you use several sentences in a row for a summary, the citation may come at the end of the summary. (An attributive tag at the beginning of the summary will alert readers to expect a citation.) However, even within a multisentence summary, all quoted material should be cited immediately at the end of the phrase or sentence in which it appears. Note, for example, where Jenny cites page numbers for the quotes within the following summary from her "Romance Fiction" paper. (As we explain later in this chapter, the attributive tag referring to Ricker-Wilson makes it unnecessary for the in-text citations to repeat the author's name.)

> Writing in the *English Journal* for teachers who think of romance fiction as "escapist trash" (58), Ricker-Wilson argues that this widespread belief blinds teachers from seeing its personal value to their students and its possibilities for classroom use. By allowing a group of young women in her lower track English class to read the novels of Danielle Steele for extra credit, she learned about the many benefits romance fiction offered her students. Among the benefits were camaraderie and escape in a positive sense. According to Ricker-Wilson, these five women students became an "authentic community" of readers, regularly exchanging books and eagerly sharing their ideas about them (62).

Page Number Guidelines

As a rule, you should plan to include page numbers in every in-text citation you use; however, page numbers may not always be necessary or available in the following situations.

- If the complete work being cited appears on just one page, that page number needs to appear only in the full citation on the works cited list. Note, for example, that in paragraph 5 of her paper, Jenny does not need a page number citation even when she quotes from Wikoff's book review, which we can tell from the works cited list appeared on just one page.
- If you retrieve a print source through an online periodicals database, it may be difficult to ascertain specific pages for quotes and paraphrases. In such cases, you may omit the page number in the in-text citation, but the full citation in the works cited list must nevertheless include the exact page numbers from the original paper publication. As illustration, compare Jenny's in-text citation of Rosen in paragraph 9 with the entry for Rosen's article on her works cited list. Some instructors insist that students work with a paper copy of print sources so that they can specify the page numbers for all quotes. Be sure you know what your instructor expects.
- If you are citing Web documents, give page or paragraph numbers only if the original source provides them. Do not include numbers from your own printout or from your browser screen because these will vary on other machines. If you provide the correct Web address, your reader will be able to use a search function to find the specific quote or material.

Author and Title Guidelines

The phrasing of your sentences and paragraphs will sometimes give you a reason for deviating from the basic last name-page format for in-text citations, especially in sentences with attributive tags. Reading efficiency dictates several rules of thumb about how much information to include.

Rule of Thumb 1.   Always be guided by your knowledge that the purpose of an in-text citation is to help your reader quickly find the full citation in the works cited list. Because the works cited list is arranged alphabetically, the in-text citation should always match the first word of the full citation. Then all your reader has to do to find the information is scan down the left margin of the alphabetized list.

- If a work has two or more authors, list their last names in the order that they appear in the source and in the works cited list:

    (Gray and Sachs 76)

- If your list has two authors with the same last name, add the first initial to the in-text citation:

    (B. Jones 17)

- If the reader will find two entries beginning with the same author's name, include in the parenthetical reference a short version of the specific title:

    (Naylor, "Writing")
    (Naylor, "Mommy")

    Note that a comma is used between the author's name and the title and that correct title punctuation (quotation marks or underlining) is required. The sample citations refer to articles that were complete on one page. Both are reprinted in this book.

- If the source doesn't list an author, as is the case for many Web pages and many short articles, the citation in the works cited list will begin with the source's title. For the in-text citation, create a *short title* from the first one or two words of that title so that readers can readily find the right source in the alphabetized works cited list. For example, material from the second page of an article cited this way in the works cited list

    "Can Antioxidants Save Your Life?" *UC Berkeley Wellness Letter* July 1998: 4–5.

    would be referred to this way in an in-text citation

    ("Can Antioxidants" 5)

    Note: Don't use "anonymous" in place of an author's name even though some databases cite articles without bylines this way. Use a short title instead.

Rule of Thumb 2.   Avoid repetition between attributive tags and in-text citations.

- If the author's name already appears in an attributive tag, include in parentheses only the specific page number of the original material:

According to Ricker-Wilson, these five women students became an "authentic community" of readers, regularly exchanging books and eagerly sharing their ideas about them (62).

- You may also omit the author's name if it appears in an immediately preceding sentence and there is no chance of confusion:

Finally, Ricker-Wilson argues for the educational benefits of romance novels if they are treated seriously. Her one requirement for reading these books was that students write about them in response to her romance questionnaire, which asked about the depiction of women, romantic relationships, and other aspects of the novels (58).

- Similarly, when you are working with material that has no listed author and the title is already mentioned in a tag, you may include only the page number in the parenthetical citation:

In an article entitled "Can Antioxidants Save Your Life?" two years later, the newsletter reported . . . (5).

Note, however, that if the wording of the attributive tag doesn't match the full citation exactly, the in-text citation must include a short title so that readers can find the full citation in the alphabetical works cited list:

As a 1998 *Wellness Letter* report explained, . . . ("Can Antioxidants" 5).

- In situations where the words that begin the full citation are included in an attributive tag and no page numbers are available or needed, a parenthetical citation is not needed, even for an exact quote:

In "The Writing Life," Naylor describes library shelves "that stretched high over my head, shelves that seemed to a 4-year-old to almost stretch into eternity."

This sentence provides all the information a reader needs to locate this full citation on a works cited list:

Naylor, Gloria. "The Writing Life." *Washington Post* 27 Feb. 2000: X8.

Rule of Thumb 3.   If you are not sure how to handle a citation, err on the side of providing too much information, not too little.

The preceding guidelines are meant to illustrate only a few of the basic principles of MLA style in-text citations. For more complicated citation problems, you should check the handbook assigned for your course, the latest edition of the *MLA Handbook for Writers of Research Papers* (designed for undergraduates), or the *MLA Style Manual and Guide to Scholarly Publishing* (for graduate students and scholars). Whenever you aren't sure what is required, *check with your instructor.*

Summary

In this chapter we showed how skillful incorporation of source texts into your own argument enhances your credibility as a writer and clarifies how your ideas fit into the overall conversation about the subject matter. We began by presenting guidelines for including brief summaries, paraphrases, and direct quotations of source material and explained the importance of acknowledging these sources fully so that you avoid plagiarism. We then explained the basics of the MLA citation system and showed you specific techniques for acknowledging the sources of such material through attributive tags and parenthetical in-text citations.

In the sample student paper that follows, you will find numerous examples of these techniques. The appendix to this book offers models of full citations for other types of materials you will be likely to use in your own papers.

Incorporating Reading into Writing: An Example

Here is Jenny's researched argument in response to the "Extending the Conversation" assignment at the beginning of Chapter 7 (p. 111).

Romance Fiction: Brain Candy or Culturally Nutritious?

1   In junior high school, I was a big fan of Sweet Valley High novels. I read every one I could get my hands on, and my friends and I passed them around and talked about the characters as though they were a part of our group of friends. Even then, I could see that there was a formula: heroine pines for popular boy who doesn't know she's alive; things look hopeless for a long time; then something happens and he notices her; and in the end they walk off into the sunset. Actually, knowing that there would be a happy ending was part of the fun. The interesting thing was how it would work out. My parents, who are both teachers, considered these books a waste of time, but I loved them anyway.

2   I haven't read novels like this since junior high, but reading Larissa MacFarquhar's "Who Cares Why Johnny Can't Read?" reminded me of this early fondness for romance fiction and the widespread idea that these books lack cultural value. Published in 1997 in the online journal Slate,

MacFarquhar's essay offers extensive evidence that Americans are reading more than ever, especially "popular fiction" like romance novels. A _Time_ magazine article published in July 2000 verifies this claim and reports that over 50% of all paperbacks sold in the U.S. each year are romance novels (Gray and Sachs 76). At the end of her essay, MacFarquhar challenges readers to consider whether or not it is reading in and of itself that has cultural value or whether it is what people read (or watch on TV) that contributes to "the fertility of our culture." Since romance fiction is so popular, it seems to me that we ought to ask this question about romance fiction. Does it have cultural value and contribute to "the fertility of our culture"? Is it only brain candy or does it have some cultural nutrition?

But how do we determine what contributes to cultural growth or nutrition? 3 Although it is unclear how MacFarquhar herself might define and judge cultural value, she refers disapprovingly to the "reputation for educational and even moral worthiness" that books have acquired. According to MacFarquhar, book advocates claim that books activate the imagination and encourage original thinking because they are "quirky and individualistic and real." Despite MacFarquhar's sarcasm about these claims for books, it seems to me that educational and moral worth as well as stimulation of the imagination and intellect are all legitimate bases for judging cultural value. However, research and the memory of my early reading experiences have convinced me that these criteria, though valid, are too limited. Other factors such as emotional sustenance and community building also contribute to our cultural welfare. In this essay, I review briefly the arguments of those who believe romance fiction is without cultural value, then offer arguments for why romance fiction does have cultural value, even in terms of traditional criteria, and certainly in terms of other, equally important, criteria.

The key reason that many people believe that romance fiction has no 4 cultural value is its lack of originality. Predictable plots, so the argument goes, offer escape but not intellectual stimulation. The _Time_ article mentioned earlier claims that romance readers insist on formulaic plots of "childlike restrictions and simplicity," and says that as a result, these books lack "moral ambiguity" (Gray and Sachs 76). Although MacFarquhar makes no direct judgment about the cultural value of romance fiction, her description of this genre echoes the criticism of Gray and Sachs. She describes romance fiction as "mass-market entertainment" that appeals to people because "it's easy, it makes you feel good, and it's the same every time." Its purpose, she says, is not to stimulate thinking and the imagination, "but to stimulate predictable emotions by means of familiar cultural symbols." As my friends would put it, MacFarquhar describes romance fiction as brain candy.

5   There are many intelligent fans of romance fiction, however, who would disagree and who, in fact, describe romance fiction as having some of the characteristics that people traditionally associate with cultural value. Katherine Hennessey Wikoff, an English professor at Milwaukee School of Engineering and a self-described "lifelong romance reader," for example, says that "Years of romance fiction amply reinforced my own character growth." In her review of Victoria M. Johnson's book, All I Need to Know in Life I Learned from Romance Novels, Wikoff says that she "cut her romance novel teeth" at age twelve on Gone with the Wind, from which she learned both positive and negative lessons: to be resourceful like Scarlett but not to be so proud like Scarlett, who lost Rhett because she wouldn't risk telling him she loved him for fear of rejection. Wikoff goes on to list the life lessons she, like Johnson, claims to have learned from romance fiction. A few examples are these: "Communication is the key to a healthy relationship"; "Attitude makes all the difference"; and "Love changes everything." In Wikoff's opinion, and apparently Victoria Johnson's, reading romance fiction can be morally uplifting and contribute to character growth, surely important cultural values.

6   Although not a romance fiction reader herself, Carol Ricker-Wilson, a high school English teacher, offers an interesting perspective on the potential educational value of romance novels in "Busting Textual Bodices: Gender, Reading, and the Popular Romance." Writing in the English Journal for teachers who think of romance fiction as "escapist trash" (58), Ricker-Wilson argues that this widespread belief blinds teachers from seeing its personal value to their students and its possibilities for classroom use. By allowing a group of young women in her English class to read the novels of Danielle Steele for extra credit, she learned about the many benefits that romance fiction offered her students. Among the benefits were camaraderie and escape in a positive sense. According to Ricker-Wilson, these five women students became an "authentic community" of readers, regularly exchanging books and eagerly sharing their ideas about them (62).

7   Ricker-Wilson acknowledges that some researchers claim that romance fiction provides women readers with escape from their difficult relationships with the men in their lives. She counters this negative view by proposing that romance fiction permits readers to escape something even worse: the negative images of

women in other literature. She argues that readers who enjoy romance novels do so because they enjoy reading about women but do not like to read about women who are victimized or killed off, as they often are in other forms of fiction (58).

Finally, Ricker-Wilson argues for the educational benefits of romance novels if they are treated seriously. Her one requirement for reading these books was that students write about them in response to her romance questionnaire, which asked about the depiction of women, romantic relationships, and other aspects of the novels (58). What Ricker-Wilson discovered was that her students were quite capable of criticizing these books and seeing the mixed messages they give to women. Despite Ricker-Wilson's reservations about some of the "troubling" messages sent by these books, she concludes that "popular romance offers one of the richest imaginable repositories for exploring conflicting understandings of gender and sexuality" (63).

Ricker-Wilson's point about the potential of shared reading experiences to build community is something that the publishers of romance novels seem to understand. A November 1999 Publishers Weekly article describes the trend of targeting new romance books to "niche markets," particularly African Americans, Latinos, and readers looking for a spiritual dimension in their romance reading (Rosen). Another aspect of community is evident at The Romance Reader (TRR) Website (located at www.theromancereader.com), where many fans of romance novels post reviews and comments. In an article for the TRR Forum, Linda Mowery tells of the pleasure of rereading favorite books and the personal benefits offered by these novels. She calls the romance books that she rereads "comfort reads" and "emotional safety nets." She writes, "Rereading favorite books is being with old friends, friends who understand us and accept us." Tina Engler, one of the TRR reviewers who posted comments in response, adds "To me, rereading a favorite book is like crawling under the covers with a cup of hot cocoa on a rainy day . . . it's relaxing, invigorating, and acts as an emotional security blanket in that I already know everything that's going to happen."

Comments such as these remind me of all the good times my friends and I had talking about Sweet Valley High novels. These books gave us a way to talk indirectly about our own insecurities about being popular and liking boys who often didn't notice us. If romance novels can create bonds among people, honor their ethnic or spiritual identity, and help them cope with difficult times by escaping into a book from time to time, aren't these important cultural values?

Like comfort food, romance novels may not provide the same nutrition that the literary equivalents of granola and tofu do, but apparently, they provide a kind of nutrition that many people in our culture need.

Works Cited

Engler, Tina. The Romance Reader Forum. D. N. Anderson. 11 July 2000. 8 Aug. 2000 <http://www.theromancereader.com/forum21.html>.

Gray, Paul, and Andrea Sachs. "Passion on the Pages." Time 20 March 2000: 76–78. Academic Search Elite. EBSCO Publishing. Memorial Lib., Marquette Univ. 31 July 2000 <http://www.epnet.com/>.

MacFarquhar, Larissa. "Who Cares If Johnny Can't Read?" Slate 16 April 1997. 23 May 2000 <http://slate.msn.com/Concept/97-04-16/Concept.asp>.

Mowery, Linda. "The Second Time Around: The Magic of Rereading." The Romance Reader Forum. D. N. Anderson. 11 July 2000. 8 Aug. 2000 <http://www.theromancereader.com/forum21.html>.

Ricker-Wilson, Carol. "Busting Textual Bodices: Gender, Reading, and the Popular Romance." English Journal 88.3 (1999): 57–64.

Rosen, Judith. "Love Is All Around You." Publishers Weekly 8 Nov. 1999: 37–43. Proquest Research Library. Bell & Howell. Memorial Lib., Marquette Univ. 31 July 2000 <http://proquest.umi.com/>.

Wikoff, Katherine Hennessey. "Romance Novels More Than Heaving Bosoms." Rev. of All I Need to Know in Life I Learned from Romance Novels by Victoria M. Johnson. Milwaukee Journal Sentinel 4 Feb. 1999: E2.

PART

IV

An Anthology of Readings

CHAPTER

9

Expressing and Reflecting

eadings that express and reflect grow out of writers' desires to tell their stories—to share experiences or ideas with others and in the process, to articulate for themselves what those experiences or ideas mean. To one degree or another, this double purpose characterizes all writing that expresses and reflects. In her essay "Why I Write," Joan Didion comments on both motivations. On the one hand, she says, "writing is the act of saying *I*, of imposing oneself upon other people, of saying *listen to me, see it my way, change your mind*"; on the other hand, she says, "I write to remember what it was like to be me." Both in sharing their experiences with others and in reflecting upon these experiences for themselves, writers of expressive essays focus on the self. However, it is important to remember that the "self" or "I" created in the text is not identical with the writer composing the text nor is the experience a "factual" account of what happened. As you are probably well aware, no two people remember an event in quite the same way nor do people see themselves quite as others see them. Therefore, experiences put into words and representations of oneself in language are inevitably shaped by the speaker/writer's subjective perceptions, intentions, and communicative situation.

While expressive or reflective writing may address issues beyond the writer's experience—writers may, for example, reflect on public events or include information about a subject—personal experience is nevertheless at the heart of the essay, forming the lens for reflecting on the topic at hand. To *reflect* is to turn or look back, to reconsider something thought or done in the past from the perspective of the present. The term comes from the Latin word meaning to bend *(flectere)* back *(re)*. Etymologically, then, the term means "to throw or bend back (light, for example) from a surface," the phenomenon by which a mirror throws back images. When we contemplate our image in a mirror, we have a double perspective, the self who is viewing and the self being viewed. Similarly, reflective writers consider their experiences from the double perspective of the past and present, from the self who was and the self who is. And just as the purpose of self-contemplation before a mirror is often to assess, study, or interpret one's appearance, so, too, the purpose of reflective writing is to evaluate, analyze, or interpret the meaning of one's experiences.

Barbara Kingsolver, for example, uses the occasion of a trip to her small Kentucky hometown to recount with wry amusement her awkward adolescence as seen from her current perspective as a successful author returning home for a book signing. On a much more somber note, Lauren Slater painstakingly describes her lifelong struggle with obsessive-compulsive disorder (OCD)—from its bewildering and terrifying onset to her present intimate acquaintance with it, from her various attempts to overcome it to her present ways of coping and living with the disorder. Other writers in this section use personal observations and experience to illuminate and comment on larger social, cultural, and political issues. In each case, personal experience is viewed from multiple perspectives created by time, cultural difference, different aspects of the self, or the perspectives of others.

Not only does reflective writing include a dual or multiple authorial perspective but also it often includes a dual sense of audience and purpose as suggested in the comments of Joan Didion cited earlier. Some reflective writers seem to be writing for themselves as much as they are for the reader; therefore, readers of self-expressive prose sometimes feel as if they are eavesdropping on an inner dialogue, privy to the unfolding of meaning as it occurs to the writer. In such inner-directed reflections, the tone may be contemplative and intimate, even lyrical and poetic. At other times, reflective writing seems primarily directed to others. In these cases, the primary aim of self-expression and reflection may be coupled with other aims, such as explanation or even argument.

But whether the purpose is self- or other-directed, exploratory or didactic, expressive writing always has some sort of design upon its readers although that design may be much less obvious than in writing to inform or persuade. Indeed, expressive writing that blatantly uses the writer's experience to teach or preach usually leaves readers cold. Often the intended effect is a subtle one. The writer is trying to enable readers to apprehend vicariously something they have never experienced before or to consider familiar experiences from a new perspective. Effective expressive writing is more interested in using the author's experience and perspective to defamiliarize the familiar, uncover contradictions, and challenge commonplace ideas than it is in using personal experience to arrive at moralistic lessons or conventional truths.

To accomplish this aim of offering readers a new perspective, effective expressive writing must re-create or render the writer's experience in a compelling manner—through carefully selected and telling details and through the use of various literary devices, such as plot, setting, character, and evocative or figurative language. The verb *to express* comes from Latin and literally means "to press out," to take inward ideas, feelings, and perceptions and give them external form. The famous dictum "show rather than tell" is thus particularly applicable to expressive and reflective writing. Expressive writing is most effective in communicating new insights and perspectives when readers feel as if they have come to this new realization on their own. Rather than telling readers, for example, that witnessing an execution is a horrifying experience that should cause them to pause and reconsider their views on capital punishment, the writer tries to render her experience of this event in a way that evokes horror in readers and prompts them to change their attitude toward capital punishment even if they don't change their position on the subject.

As a college student, you may read academic texts that include personal experience as well as scholarly analysis. For example, anthropologist Clifford Geertz uses both personal experience and analysis to understand the social function of cockfighting in Bali. Additionally, you may be asked to write reflectively about your own experiences in order to make connections between the concepts you are learning in a course and your prior experience, knowledge, and beliefs. For example, you might be asked by a writing teacher to write a literacy narrative—that is, a story of a significant reading or writing experience. The aim of this assignment is to make you aware of the hidden assumptions you may have toward reading and writing and to connect your past literacy learning with the new academic ways of reading and writing you are learning in college. Or perhaps a social psychology professor will ask you to write about a time when you were an outsider as a backdrop for studying various theories regarding the nature of social belonging.

Yet another kind of reflective writing that is increasingly required in college courses is self-evaluative reflections in which you are asked to describe or evaluate your process of writing a paper, solving a problem, conducting an experiment, or learning a new concept. According to learning theorists, self-reflective evaluations such as these enhance learning because the activity of identifying and assessing your own intellectual work enables you to control such activities more consciously in the future. You gain a certain "know-how" or process knowledge from retracing your steps in learning or performing a particular academic task. Moreover, such writing prepares you for the workplace—where you will quite likely be asked to write self-reflective performance reviews on a regular basis. Whether the context for reading and writing expressive/reflective prose is personal, academic, or professional, such activities nurture a certain habit of mind and create self-awareness.

Questions to Help You Read Expression and Reflection Rhetorically

The reading selections in this chapter present a range of expressive and reflective purposes and strategies. Use your knowledge of rhetorical strategies to identify and connect these writers' aims with their strategies, particularly their use of literary devices to engage readers in relating to their experiences and the meaning they make of these experiences.

1. What seems to be the author's intention(s) in writing this reflection? What new perspective or insight is the author offering the reader?

2. How does the "story" of the author's experience—that is, the presentation of plot, setting, and characters—contribute to this purpose or purposes? How does the author's use of details contribute to this purpose or purposes?

3. How would you describe the speaker or the "I" in this text? Is there more than one version of the "self" presented? That is, does the speaker offer double or even multiple perspectives? Does the speaker's character change in the course of the essay? What in the text accounts for your impressions of the speaker's character?

4. What is the speaker's attitude(s) toward the event(s) or issues represented? How does the speaker's language reveal his or her feelings, attitudes, or stances toward the experience? (See Chapter 5, p. 75, for tips on examining a writer's use of language.) Does the author's attitude toward the experience change? If so, what accounts for the change?

5. Are points of view or perspectives other than the author's introduced? If so, how do these perspectives affect the author's account of his or her experience and your interpretation of it as a reader?

6. Does the primary audience seem to be the writer himself or herself or other readers? What leads you to this conclusion? That is, what in the text seems directed to the writer? To readers?

7. How is the occasion or experience(s) about which the author writes related to other, more general issues?

Barbara Kingsolver

In Case You Ever Want to Go Home Again

Barbara Kingsolver (b. 1955), an author of best-selling novels as well as short fiction, poetry, and essays, grew up in rural Kentucky. Trained as a biologist, she worked as a science writer and journalist before turning mainly to fiction. Her first novel, *The Bean Trees* (1988), is about a young Kentucky woman who travels west to resettle and along the way finds herself the unofficial adoptive mother of a withdrawn two-year-old Cherokee girl. Now living in Tucson, Kingsolver says that she sees her writing "as a form of social action." Her most recent novels are the critically acclaimed *The Poisonwood Bible* (1998) and *The Prodigal Summer* (2000). In this selection, taken from *High Tide in Tucson*, a collection of essays published in 1995, the author reflects on her trip back to her hometown in Kentucky, where she had been invited to appear for a book signing for *The Bean Trees*.

● *For Your Reading Log*

1. Recall a time when you revisited a house where you used to live, school you used to attend, or town you used to live in. What was this experience like? What surprised you? How did this experience make you feel? What were the differences between your memory of the place and your perceptions on your return visit? Take a few minutes to freewrite about this experience.
2. Since the author is recalling her experiences and feelings of being in high school, you will no doubt find passages that resonate with your own experiences and feelings, whether you felt like the misfit that she did in high school or not. As you read, note the passages that remind you of your feelings about high school.

———————   ●   ———————

I have been gone from Kentucky a long time. Twenty years have done to my hill   1
accent what the washing machine does to my jeans: taken out the color and starch, so gradually that I never marked the loss. Something like that has happened to my memories, too, particularly of the places and people I can't go back and visit because they are gone. The ancient brick building that was my grade school, for example, and both my grandfathers. They're snapshots of memory for me now, of equivocal focus, loaded with emotion, undisturbed by anyone else's idea of the truth. The schoolhouse's plaster ceilings are charted with craters like maps of the moon and likely to crash down without warning. The windows are watery, bubbly glass reinforced with chicken wire. The weary wooden staircases, worn shiny smooth in a path up their middles, wind up to an unknown place overhead where

the heavy-footed eighth graders changing classes were called "the mules" by my first-grade teacher, and believing her, I pictured their sharp hooves on the linoleum.

2   My Grandfather Henry I remember in his sleeveless undershirt, home after a day's hard work on the farm at Fox Creek. His hide is tough and burnished wherever it has met the world—hands, face, forearms—but vulnerably white at the shoulders and throat. He is snapping his false teeth in and out of place, to provoke his grandchildren to hysterics.

3   As far as I know, no such snapshots exist in the authentic world. The citizens of my hometown ripped down the old school and quickly put to rest its picturesque decay. My grandfather always cemented his teeth in his head, and put on good clothes, before submitting himself to photography. Who wouldn't? When a camera takes aim at my daughter, I reach out and scrape the peanut butter off her chin. "I can't help it," I tell her, "it's one of those mother things." It's more than that. It's human, to want the world to see us as we think we ought to be seen.

4   You can fool history sometimes, but you can't fool the memory of your intimates. And thank heavens, because in the broad valley between real life and propriety whole herds of important truths can steal away into the underbrush. I hold that valley to be my home territory as a writer. Little girls wear food on their chins, school days are lit by ghostlight, and respectable men wear their undershirts at home. Sometimes there are fits of laughter and sometimes there is despair, and neither one looks a thing like its formal portrait.

5   For many, many years I wrote my stories furtively in spiral-bound notebooks, for no greater purpose than my own private salvation. But on April 1, 1987, two earthquakes hit my psyche on the same day. First, I brought home my own newborn baby girl from the hospital. Then, a few hours later, I got a call from New York announcing that a large chunk of my writing—which I'd tentatively pronounced a novel—was going to be published. This was a spectacular April Fool's Day. My life has not, since, returned to normal.

6   For days I nursed my baby and basked in hormonal euphoria, musing occasionally: all this—and I'm a novelist, too! *That*, though, seemed a slim accomplishment compared with laboring twenty-four hours to render up the most beautiful new human the earth had yet seen. The book business seemed a terrestrial affair of ink and trees and I didn't give it much thought.

7   In time my head cleared, and I settled into panic. What had I done? The baby was premeditated, but the book I'd conceived recklessly, in a closet late at night, when the restlessness of my insomniac pregnancy drove me to compulsive verbal intercourse with my own soul. The pages that grew in a stack were somewhat incidental to the process. They contained my highest hopes and keenest pains, and I didn't think anyone but me would ever see them. I'd bundled the thing up and sent it off to New York in a mad fit of housekeeping, to be done with it. Now it was going to be laid smack out for my mother, my postal clerk, my high school English teacher, anybody in the world who was willing to plunk down $16.95 and walk away with it. To find oneself suddenly published is thrilling—that is a given. But how appalling it also felt I find hard to describe. Imagine singing at the top of your lungs in the shower as you always do, then one day turning off the water and throwing back the curtain to see there in your bathroom a crowd of people, rapt, with videotape. I wanted to throw a towel over my head.

There was nothing in the novel to incriminate my mother or the postal clerk. 8
I like my mother, plus her record is perfect. My postal clerk I couldn't vouch for;
he has tattoos. But in any event I never put real people into my fiction—I can't
see the slightest point of that, when I have the alternative of inventing utterly
subservient slave-people, whose every detail of appearance and behavior I can
bend to serve my theme and plot.

Even so, I worried that someone I loved would find in what I'd written a rea- 9
son to despise me. In fact, I was sure of it. My fiction is not in any way about my
life, regardless of what others might assume, but certainly it is set in the sort of
places I know pretty well. The protagonist of my novel, titled *The Bean Trees*,
launched her adventures from a place called "Pittman, Kentucky," which does
resemble a town in Kentucky where I'm known to have grown up. I had written: "Pittman was twenty years behind the nation in practically every way you
can think of except the rate of teenage pregnancies. . . . We were the last place in
the country to get the dial system. Up until 1973 you just picked up the receiver
and said, Marge, get me my Uncle Roscoe. The telephone office was on the third
floor of the Courthouse, and the operator could see everything around Main
Street square. She would tell you if his car was there or not."

I don't have an Uncle Roscoe. But if I *did* have one, the phone operator in my 10
hometown, prior to the mid-seventies, could have spotted him from her second-
floor office on Main Street square.

I cherish the oddball charm of that town. Time and again I find myself writ- 11
ing love letters to my rural origins. Growing up in small-town Kentucky taught
me respect for the astounding resources people can drum up from their backyards,
when they want to, to pull each other through. I tend to be at home with modesty,
and suspicious of anything slick or new. But naturally, when I was growing up
there, I yearned for the slick and the new. A lot of us did, I think. We craved shopping malls and a swimming pool. We wanted the world to know we had once won
the title "All Kentucky City," even though with sixteen-hundred souls we no more
constituted a "city" than New Jersey is a Garden State, and we advertised this glorious prevarication for years and years on one of the town's few billboards.

Homely charm is a relative matter. Now that I live in a western city where 12
shopping malls and swimming pools congest the landscape like cedar blight, I
think back fondly on my hometown. But the people who live there now might
rather smile about the quaintness of a *smaller* town, like nearby Morning Glory
or Barefoot. At any rate, they would not want to discover themselves in my
novel. I can never go home again, as long as I live, I reasoned. Somehow this
will be reckoned as betrayal. I've photographed my hometown in its undershirt.

During the year I awaited publication, I decided to calm down. There were 13
other ways to think about this problem:

    1. If people really didn't want to see themselves in my book, they 14
wouldn't. They would think to themselves, "She is writing about Morning Glory,
and those underdogs are from farther on down Scrubgrass Road."

    2. There's no bookstore in my hometown. No one will know.   15

In November 1988, bookstoreless though it was, my hometown hosted a big 16
event. Paper banners announced it, and stores closed in honor of it. A crowd

assembled in the town's largest public space—the railroad depot. The line
went out the door and away down the tracks. At the front of the line they were
plunking down $16.95 for signed copies of a certain book.

17   My family was there. The county's elected officials were there. My first-grade
teacher, Miss Louella, was there, exclaiming to one and all: "I taught her to write!"

18   My old schoolmates were there. The handsome boys who'd spurned me at
every homecoming dance were there.

19   It's relevant and slightly vengeful to confess here that I was not a hit in
school, socially speaking. I was a bookworm who never quite fit her clothes.
I managed to look fine in my school pictures, but as usual the truth lay elsewhere. In sixth grade I hit my present height of five feet almost nine, struck it
like a gong, in fact, leaving behind self-confidence and any genuine need of a
training bra. Elderly relatives used the term "fill out" when they spoke of me,
as though they held out some hope I might eventually have some market
value, like an underfed calf, if the hay crop was good. In my classroom I came
to dread a game called Cooties, wherein one boy would brush against my
shoulder and then chase the others around, threatening to pass on my apparently communicable lack of charisma. The other main victim of this game was
a girl named Sandra, whose family subscribed to an unusual religion that
mandated a Victorian dress code. In retrospect I can't say exactly what Sandra
and I had in common that made us outcasts, except for extreme shyness, flat
chests, and families who had their eyes on horizons pretty far beyond the hills
of Nicholas County. Mine were not Latter-day Saints, but we read Thoreau and
Robert Burns at home, and had lived for a while in Africa. My parents did not
flinch from relocating us to a village beyond the reach of electricity, running
water, or modern medicine (also, to my delight, conventional schooling) when
they had a chance to do useful work there. They thought it was shameful to
ignore a fellow human in need, or to waste money on trendy, frivolous things;
they did not, on the other hand, think it was shameful to wear perfectly good
hand-me-down dresses to school in Nicholas County. Ephemeral idols exalted
by my peers, such as Batman, the Beatles, and the Hula Hoop, were not an issue at our house. And even if it took no more than a faint pulse to pass the fifth
grade, my parents expected me to set my own academic goals, and then ex-
ceed them.

20   Possibly my parents were trying to make sure I didn't get pregnant in the
eighth grade, as some of my classmates would shortly begin to do. If so, their
efforts were a whale of a success. In my first three years of high school, the number of times I got asked out on a date was zero. This is not an approximate number. I'd caught up to other girls in social skills by that time, so I knew how to
pretend I was dumber than I was, and make my own clothes. But these things
helped only marginally. Popularity remained a frustrating mystery to me.

21   Nowadays, some of my city-bred friends muse about moving to a small
town for the sake of their children. What's missing from their romantic picture
of Grover's Corners is the frightening impact of insulation upon a child who's
not dead center in the mainstream. In a place such as my hometown, you file
in and sit down to day one of kindergarten with the exact pool of boys who

will be your potential dates for the prom. If you wet your pants a lot, your social life ten years later will be—as they say in government reports—impacted. I was sterling on bladder control, but somehow could never shake my sixth-grade stigma.

At age seventeen, I was free at last to hightail it for new social pastures, and 22 you'd better believe I did. I attended summer classes at the University of Kentucky and landed a boyfriend before I knew what had hit me, or what on earth one did with the likes of such. When I went on to college in Indiana I was astonished to find a fresh set of peers who found me, by and large, likable and cootie-free.

I've never gotten over high school, to the extent that I'm still a little surprised 23 that my friends want to hang out with me. But it made me what I am, for better and for worse. From living in a town that listened in on party lines, I learned both the price and value of community. And I gained things from my rocky school years: A fierce wish to look inside of people. An aptitude for listening. The habit of my own company. The companionship of keeping a diary, in which I gossiped, fantasized, and invented myself. From the vantage point of invisibility I explored the psychology of the underdog, the one who can't be what others desire but who might still learn to chart her own hopes. Her story was my private treasure; when I wrote *The Bean Trees* I called her Lou Ann. I knew for sure that my classmates, all of them cool as Camaros back then, would not relate to the dreadful insecurities of Lou Ann. But I liked her anyway.

And now, look. The boys who'd once fled howling from her cooties were 24 lined up for my autograph. Football captains, cheerleaders, homecoming queens were all there. The athlete who'd inspired in me a near-fatal crush for three years, during which time he never looked in the vicinity of my person, was there. The great wits who gave me the names Kingfish and Queen Sliver were there.

I took liberties with history. I wrote long, florid inscriptions referring to our 25 great friendship of days gone by. I wrote slowly. I made those guys wait in line *a long time.*

I can recall every sight, sound, minute of that day. Every open, generous face. 26 The way the afternoon light fell through the windows onto the shoes of the people in line. In my inventory of mental snapshots these images hold the place most people reserve for the wedding album. I don't know whether other people get to have Great Life Moments like this, but I was lucky enough to realize I was having mine, right while it happened. My identity was turning backward on its own axis. Never before or since have I felt all at the same time so cherished, so aware of old anguish, and so ready to let go of the past. My past had let go of *me*, so I could be something new: Poet Laureate and Queen for a Day in hometown Kentucky. The people who'd watched me grow up were proud of me, and exuberant over an event that put our little dot on the map, particularly since it wasn't an airline disaster or a child falling down a well. They didn't appear to mind that my novel discussed small-town life frankly, without gloss.

In fact, most people showed unsurpassed creativity in finding themselves, 27 literally, on the printed page. "That's my car isn't it?" they would ask. "My service station!" Nobody presented himself as my Uncle Roscoe, but if he had, I happily would have claimed him.

28 It's a curious risk, fiction. Some writers choose fantasy as an approach to truth, a way of burrowing under newsprint and formal portraits to find the despair that can stow away in a happy childhood, or the affluent grace of a grandfather in his undershirt. In the final accounting, a hundred different truths are likely to reside at any given address. The part of my soul that is driven to make stories is a fierce thing, like a ferret: long, sleek, incapable of sleep, it digs and bites through all I know of the world. Given that I cannot look away from the painful things, it seems better to invent allegory than to point a straight, bony finger like Scrooge's mute Ghost of Christmas Yet to Come, declaring, "Here you will end, if you don't clean up your act." By inventing character and circumstance, I like to think I can be a kinder sort of ghost, saying, "I don't mean *you*, exactly, but just give it some thought, anyway."

29   Nice try, but nobody's really fooled. Because fiction works, if it does, only when we the readers believe every word of it. Grover's Corners is Our Town, and so is Cannery Row, and Lilliput, and Gotham City, and Winesburg, Ohio, and the dreadful metropolis of *1984.* We have all been as canny as Huck Finn, as fractious as Scarlett O'Hara, as fatally flawed as Captain Ahab and Anna Karenina. I, personally, am Jo March, and if her author Louisa May Alcott had a whole new life to live for the sole pursuit of talking me out of it, she could not. A pen may or may not be mightier than the sword, but it is brassier than the telephone. When the writer converses privately with her soul in the long dark night, a thousand neighbors are listening in on the party line, taking it personally.

30   Nevertheless, I came to decide, on my one big afternoon as Homecoming Queen, that I would go on taking the risk of writing books. Miss Louella and all those football players gave me the rash courage to think I might be forgiven again and again the sin of revelation. I love my hometown as I love the elemental stuff of my own teeth and bones, and that seems to have come through to my hometown, even if I didn't write it up in its Sunday best.

31   I used to ask my grandfather how he could pull fish out of a lake all afternoon, one after another, while my line and bobber lay dazed and inert. This was not my Grandfather Henry, but my other grandfather, whose face I connected in childhood with the one that appears on the flip side of a buffalo nickel. Without cracking that face an iota, he was prone to uttering the funniest things I've about ever heard. In response to my question regarding the fishing, he would answer gravely, "You have to hold your mouth right."

32   I think that is also the secret of writing: attitude. Hope, unyielding faith in the enterprise. If only I hold my mouth right, keep a clear fix on what I believe is true while I make up my stories, surely I will end up saying what I mean. Then, if I offend someone, it won't be an accidental casualty. More likely, it will be because we actually disagree. I can live with that. The memory of my buffalo-nickel grandfather advises me still, in lonely moments: "If you never stepped on anybody's toes, you never been for a *walk.*"

I learned something else, that November day, that shook down all I thought 33
I knew about my personal, insufferable, nobody's-blues-can-touch-mine isolation of high school. Before the book signing was over, more than one of my old schoolmates had sidled up and whispered: "That Lou Ann character, the insecure one? I know you based her on me."

● *Thinking Critically About "In Case You Ever Want to Go Home Again"*

RESPONDING AS A READER

1. The title of this essay seems to address the reader directly. In the last two sentences of paragraph 7, the speaker again addresses the reader directly. What effect does this use of direct address have on you as a reader? What other techniques does Kingsolver use to engage readers' interest and enable identification with the experiences she is describing? What is your response to these techniques? At what points in the essay were you most engaged?

2. Most readers find Kingsolver's essay humorous even though she is clearly writing about some very painful experiences. Find various passages in which she communicates a painful experience with humor. What effect does her use of humor have on your attitude toward the image(s) that Kingsolver constructs of herself in the essay?

3. Like many reflective texts, this essay relies on figurative language to recreate experience and communicate emotions and ideas. Several metaphors recur—for example, the snapshot, telephone party line, and pregnancy/birth. Choose one of these repeated metaphors or another one that appeals to you and track the references to it throughout the essay. How is this metaphor helpful in enabling you to understand the writer's experiences, emotions, or ideas?

RESPONDING AS A WRITER

1. Kingsolver's essay has three parts, which are signaled by a break in the text. What's the thematic focus of each part? How do these themes connect with one another? How does she make these connections apparent to readers? Are there passages that you find difficult to connect to the other themes? Write a paragraph in which you explain your understanding of the connections among Kingsolver's themes, raising questions about any passages that don't seem to you to fit with other themes.

2. In the opening four paragraphs, Kingsolver reflects on different kinds of memories and the roles memory plays in our lives. She uses specific memories to illustrate the ideas she wants to suggest about memory. Choose two or three of these specific memories, and list them on a sheet of paper. Beside each example, write a few sentences, explaining

your understanding of this example's meaning and your response in terms of your own memories.

3. Describe the image that Kingsolver creates of her adolescent "self." How did she feel about various high school experiences at the time? Now describe her adult attitude toward this adolescent self and her adult attitude toward these same high school experiences. What are some differences in the adolescent and adult point of view toward these high school experiences? Think of a memorable grade school or high school experience, and write for about ten minutes about how you perceived and felt about the experience at the time, how you perceive and feel about it now, and the differences between your two points of view.

Kyoko Mori

Language

A Japanese-born naturalized American citizen, Kyoko Mori (b. 1957) writes about her experiences growing up in one culture and living her adult life in another. Her books include *Shizuko's Daughter* (1993), a young adult novel, and *The Dream of Water* (1995), a memoir. "Language" is taken from a collection of essays entitled *Polite Lies: On Being a Woman Caught Between Two Cultures* (1997). Except for one chapter, "Women's Place," each of the twelve essays in *Polite Lies* uses a single word as its title: "Family," "Secrets," "Rituals," "School," "Bodies," "Home," and so on. As the subtitle of the book suggests, each chapter explores a particular aspect of being "a woman caught between two cultures."

● **For Your Reading Log**

1. What does the phrase "polite lies" mean to you? Think of a time when you felt you had to choose your words carefully to avoid causing someone else pain or yourself embarrassment. Take a few minutes to describe the situation, the words you used, and the consequences of the polite lie.

2. Think of the contact you have had either with languages other than your native one or dialects other than the one you speak. How would you characterize some of the differences between your native language and this other language or dialect? What is your attitude toward these language differences?

———————   ●   ———————

When my third grade teacher told us that the universe was infinite and endless, 1 I wrote down her words in my notebook, but I did not believe her. An endless universe was too scary to be true—a pitch-black room in which we were lost forever, unable to find the way out. It worried me just as much, though, to think of the universe having an end. What was on the other side? I pictured a big cement wall floating in outer space, light-years away. At night, I dreamed that I was alone on a spaceship that orbited the earth in gradually widening circles. I didn't know how to turn the ship around or steer it out of its orbit. Outside the window the black sky stretched all around me, and the Earth looked like an old tennis ball, faded and fuzzy. Unable to go back home or to land on another planet, I circled around endlessly.

Now, thirty years later, I think of that dream when I fly to Japan from the 2 American Midwest. On the twelve-hour flight between Detroit and Tokyo or Osaka, I imagine myself traveling in outer space for eternity, always getting farther and farther away from home.

3   Japan has not been my home for a long time. Though I was born in Kobe, I have not lived there as an adult. I left at twenty to go to college in Illinois, knowing that I would never return. I now live in Green Bay, Wisconsin. I am an American citizen. My life can be divided right down the middle: the first twenty years in Japan, the last twenty years in the American Midwest. I'm not sure if I consider Green Bay to be my "home," exactly. Having grown up in a big city, I am more comfortable in Chicago or Milwaukee. But even the small towns in the Midwest are more like my home than Japan, a country I know only from a child's perspective. I don't understand Japan the way I have come to understand the Midwest—a place I learned gradually as an adult so that I can't remember when I didn't know the things I know now and take for granted. I recall Japan with the bold colors and truncated shapes of a child's perception. My memory seems vivid and yet unreliable.

4 Since I left, I have made only five short trips to Japan, all of them in the last seven years, all for business, not pleasure. Japan is a country where I was unhappy: my mother killed herself when I was twelve, leaving me to spend my teenage years with my father and stepmother. I usually think of those years as a distant bad memory, but a trip to Japan is like a sudden trip back in time. The minute I board the plane, I become afraid: the past is a black hole waiting to suck me up. When I was in kindergarten, I worried at night that my room was full of invisible holes. If I got out of my bed and started walking, I might fall into one of the holes and be dragged through a big black space; eventually, I would come out into the wrong century or on another planet where no one would know me. I feel the same anxiety as I sit on the plane to Japan, my elbows and knees cramped against the narrow seat: one wrong move and I will be sucked back into the past.

5   As soon as everyone is seated on the plane, the Japanese announcement welcoming us to the flight reminds me of the polite language I was taught as a child: always speak as though everything in the world were your fault. The bilingual announcements on the plane take twice as long in Japanese as in English because every Japanese announcement begins with a lengthy apology: "We apologize about how long it's taken to seat everyone and thank you for being so patient," "We are so sorry that this has been such a long flight and we very much appreciate the fact that you have been so very cooperative with us," "We apologize for the inconvenience you will no doubt experience in having to fill out the forms we are about to hand out."

6   Every fourth or fifth sentence has the words *sumimasenga* (I am sorry but) or *osoremasuga* (I fear offending you but) or *yoroshikereba* (if it's all right with you). In the crowded cabin, the polite apologies float toward us like a pleasant mist or gentle spring rain. But actually this politeness is a steel net hauling us into the country where nothing means what it says. Already, before the plane has left American airspace, I have landed in a galaxy of the past, where I can never say what I feel or ask what I want to know.

7 In my family, proper language has always been an obstacle to understanding. When my brother called me from Japan in 1993, after our father's death, and asked me to come to Japan for a week, he never said or hinted at what he wanted

me to do once I got there. I could not arrive in time for the funeral even if I were to leave within the hour. He didn't tell me whether he wanted me to come all the same to show moral support or to discuss financial arrangements. In a businesslike manner, he said, "I was wondering if you could spare a week to come here. I know you're busy with school, but maybe you could make the time if it's not too inconvenient." When I agreed, he added, "It'll be good to see you," as if I were coming to visit him for fun. And I replied, "I'll call my travel agent right away and then call you back," businesslike myself, asking no questions, because we were speaking in Japanese and I didn't know how to ask him what he really wanted.

Our conversation wasn't unusual at all. In Japanese, it's rude to tell people 8 exactly what you need or to ask them what they want. The listener is supposed to guess what the speaker wants from almost nonexistent hints. Someone could talk about the cold weather when she actually wants you to help her pick up some groceries at the store. She won't make an obvious connection between the long talk about the cold weather and the one sentence she might say about going to the store later in the afternoon, the way an English speaker would. A Japanese speaker won't mention these two things in the same conversation. Her talk about the cold weather would not be full of complaints—she might even emphasize how the cold weather is wonderful for her brother, who likes to ski. She won't tell you how she hates the winter or how slippery and dangerous the sidewalks are. But if you don't offer her a ride, you have failed her. My Japanese friends often complain about people who didn't offer to help them at the right time. "But how could these people have known what to do?" I ask. "You didn't tell them." My friends insist, "They should have done it without being asked. It's no good if I have to spell things out to them. They should have been more sensitive."

Having a conversation in Japanese is like driving in the dark without a 9 headlight: every moment, I am on the verge of hitting something and hurting myself or someone else, but I have no way of guessing where the dangers are. Listening to people speak to me in Japanese, over the phone or face to face, I try to figure out what they really mean. I know it's different from what they say, but I have no idea what it is. In my frustration, I turn to the familiar: I begin to analyze the conversation by the Midwestern standard of politeness. Sometimes the comparison helps me because Midwesterners are almost as polite and indirect as Japanese people.

Just like Japanese people, Midwesterners don't like to say no. When they are 10 asked to do something they don't want to do, my Midwestern friends answer, "I'll think about it," or "I'll try." When people say these things in Japanese, everyone knows the real meaning is no. When people in Wisconsin say that they will "think about" attending a party or "try to" be there, there is a good chance that they will actually show up. "I'll think about it" or "I'll try" means that they have not absolutely committed themselves, so if they don't come, people should not be offended. In Japan or in the Midwest, when people don't say yes, I know I should back off and offer, "Don't worry if you can't. It isn't important."

In both cultures, the taboo against saying no applies to anything negative. 11 Once, in Japan, I was speaking with my aunt, Akiko, and my brother. My aunt was about to criticize my stepmother, whom she disliked. Because she was with my brother, who feels differently, Akiko began her conversation by saying, "Now,

I know, of course, that your stepmother is a very good person in her own way. She means well and she is so generous."

12   I could tell that my aunt didn't mean a word of what she said because my Midwestern friends do the exact same thing. They, too, say, "I like So-and-so. We get along just fine, but" before mentioning anything negative about almost anyone. They might then tell a long story about how that person is arrogant, manipulative, or even dishonest, only to conclude the way they started out: "Of course, he is basically a nice person, and we get along fine." They'll nod slightly, as if to say, "We all understand each other." And we do. "I like So-and-so" is simply a disclaimer meant to soften the tone. I expect to hear some version of the disclaimer; I notice when it is omitted. If a friend does not say "So-and-So is a nice person" before and after her long, angry story, I know that she truly dislikes the person she is talking about—so much that the only disclaimer she can make is "I don't like to be so negative, but," making a reference to herself but not to the other person. The omission implies that, as far as she is concerned, the other person no longer deserves her courtesy.

13   When I go to Japan and encounter the code of Never Say No and Always Use a Disclaimer, I understand what is really meant, because I have come to understand the same things in the Midwest. But sometimes, the similarities between the two forms of politeness are deceptive.

14   Shortly after my father's death, my uncle, Kenichi—my mother's brother—wanted to pay respects to my father's spirit at the Buddhist altar. I accompanied him and his wife, Mariko, to my stepmother's house, where the alter was kept. Michiko served us lunch and tried to give Kenichi my father's old clothing. She embarrassed me by bragging about the food she was serving and the clothes she was trying to give away, laughing and chattering in her thin, false voice.

15   As we were getting ready to leave, Michiko invited Kenichi and Mariko to visit her again. She asked them to write down their address and phone number. Squinting at the address Mariko was writing down, my stepmother said, "Hirohatacho. Is that near the Itami train station?"

16   "Yes," Mariko replied. "About ten minutes north, on foot." Then, smiling and bowing slightly, she said, "Please come and visit us. I am home every afternoon, except on Wednesdays. If you would call me from the station, I would be very happy to come and meet you there."

17   "You are welcome to visit here any time, too," Michiko returned, beaming. "You already know where I live, but here is my address anyway." She wrote it down and handed it to Mariko.

18   Putting the piece of paper in her purse, Mariko bowed and said, "I will look forward to seeing you."

19   As I walked away from the house with Mariko and Kenichi, I couldn't get over how my stepmother had wangled an invitation out of them. The thought of her coming to their house made me sick, so I asked point-blank, "Are you really going to have Michiko over to your house?"

20   They looked surprised. Kenichi said, "We didn't mean to be insincere, but we don't really expect her to come to our house."

21   "So you were just being polite?" I asked.

22   "Of course," Kenichi replied.

I would never have guessed the mere formality of their invitation even 23
though polite-but-not-really-meant invitations are nothing new to me. People in
Wisconsin often say, "We should get together sometime," or "You should come
and have dinner with us soon." When I hear these remarks, I always know
which are meant and which are not. When people really mean their invitations,
they give a lot of details—where their house is, what is a good time for a visit,
how we can get in touch with each other—precisely the kind of details Mariko
was giving Michiko. When the invitations are merely polite gestures, they remain
timeless and vague. The empty invitations annoy me, especially when they are
repeated. They are meant to express good will, but it's silly to keep talking about
dinners we will never have. Still, the symbolic invitations in the Midwest don't
confuse me; I can always tell them apart from the real thing.

In Japan, there are no clear-cut signs to tell me which invitations are real and 24
which are not. People can give all kinds of details and still not expect me to show
up at their door or call them from the train station. I cannot tell when I am about
to make a fool of myself or hurt someone's feelings by taking them at their word
or by failing to do so.

I don't like to go to Japan because I find it exhausting to speak Japanese all day, 25
every day. What I am afraid of is the language, not the place. Even in Green Bay,
when someone insists on speaking to me in Japanese, I clam up after a few
words of general greetings, unable to go on.

I can only fall silent because thirty seconds into the conversation, I have al- 26
ready failed at an important task: while I was bowing and saying hello, I was
supposed to have been calculating the other person's age, rank, and position in
order to determine how polite I should be for the rest of the conversation. In
Japanese conversations, the two speakers are almost never on an equal footing:
one is senior to the other in age, experience, or rank. Various levels of politeness
and formality are required according to these differences: it is rude to be too familiar, but people are equally offended if you are too formal, sounding snobbish
and untrusting. Gender is as important as rank. Men and women practically
speak different languages; women's language is much more indirect and formal
than men's. There are words and phrases that women are never supposed to say,
even though they are not crude or obscene. Only a man can say *damare* (shut up).
No matter how angry she is, a woman must say, *shizukani* (quiet).

Until you can find the correct level of politeness, you can't go on with the 27
conversation: you won't even be able to address the other person properly.
There are so many Japanese words for the pronoun *you*. *Anata* is a polite but intimate *you* a woman would use to address her husband, lover, or a very close
woman friend, while a man would say *kimi*, which is informal, or *omae*, which
is so informal that a man would say this word only to a family member; *otaku*
is informal but impersonal, so it should be used with friends rather than family. Though there are these various forms of *you*, most people address each
other in the third person—it is offensive to call someone *you* directly. To a
woman named Hanako Maeda, you don't say, "Would you like to go out for
lunch?" You say, "Would Maeda-san (Miss Maeda) like to go out for lunch?" But
if you had known Hanako for a while, maybe you should call her Hanako-san

instead of Maeda-san, especially if you are also a woman and not too much younger than she. Otherwise, she might think that you are too formal and un-friendly. The word for *lunch* also varies: *hirumeshi* is another casual word only a man is allowed to say, *hirugohan* is informal but polite enough for friends, *ohirugohan* is a little more polite, *chushoku* is formal and businesslike, and *gochushoku* is the most formal and businesslike.

28   All these rules mean that before you can get on with any conversation be-yond the initial greetings, you have to agree on your relationship—which one of you is superior, how close you expect to be, who makes the decisions and who defers. So why even talk, I always wonder. The conversation that follows the mu-tual sizing-up can only be an empty ritual, a careful enactment of our differences rather than a chance to get to know each other or to exchange ideas.

29   Talking seems especially futile when I have to address a man in Japanese. Every word I say forces me to be elaborately polite, indirect, submissive, and unassertive. There is no way I can sound intelligent, clearheaded, or decisive. But if I did not speak a "proper" feminine language, I would sound stupid in another way—like someone who is uneducated, insensitive, and rude, and therefore cannot be taken seriously. I never speak Japanese with the Japanese man who teaches physics at the college where I teach English. We are colleagues, meant to be equals. The language I use should not automatically define me as second best.

30 Meeting Japanese-speaking people in the States makes me nervous for another reason. I have nothing in common with these people except that we speak Japan-ese. Our meeting seems random and artificial, and I can't get over the oddness of addressing a total stranger in Japanese. In the twenty years I lived in Japan, I rarely had a conversation with someone I didn't already know. The only excep-tion was the first day of school in seventh grade, when none of us knew one an-other, or when I was introduced to my friends' parents. Talking to clerks at stores scarcely counts. I never chatted with people I was doing business with. This is not to say that I led a particularly sheltered life. My experience was typ-ical of anyone—male or female—growing up in Japan.

31   In Japan, whether you are a child or an adult, ninety-five percent of the peo-ple you talk to are your family, relatives, old friends, neighbors, and people you work or go to school with every day. The only new people you meet are con-nected to these people you already know—friends of friends, new spouses of your relatives—and you are introduced to them formally. You don't all of a sud-den meet someone new. My friends and I were taught that no "nice" girl would talk to strangers on trains or at public places. It was bad manners to gab with shopkeepers or with repair people, being too familiar and keeping them from work. While American children are cautioned not to speak with strangers for rea-sons of safety, we were taught not to do so because it wasn't "nice." Even the most rebellious of us obeyed. We had no language in which we could address a stranger even if we had wanted to.

32   Traveling in Japan or simply taking the commuter train in Kobe now, I no-tice the silence around me. It seems oppressive that you cannot talk to someone who is looking at your favorite painting at a museum or sitting next to you on the train, reading a book that you finished only last week. In Japan, you can't

even stop strangers and ask for simple directions when you are lost. If you get lost, you look for a policeman, who will help you because that is part of his job.

A Japanese friend and I got lost in Yokohama one night after we came out 33 of a restaurant. We were looking for the train station and had no idea where it was, but my friend said, "Well, we must be heading in the right direction, since most people seem to be walking that way. It's late now. They must be going back to the station, too." After about ten minutes—with no train station in sight yet— my friend said that if she had been lost in New York or Paris, she would have asked one of the people we were following. But in her own country, in her own language, it was unthinkable to approach a stranger.

For her, asking was not an option. That's different from when people in the 34 Midwest choose not to stop at a gas station for directions or flag down a store clerk to locate some item on the shelves. Midwestern people don't like to ask because they don't want to call attention to themselves by appearing stupid and helpless. Refusing to ask is a matter of pride and self-reliance—a matter of choice. Even the people who pride themselves on never asking know that help is readily available. In Japan, approaching a stranger means breaking an unspoken rule of public conduct.

The Japanese code of silence in public places does offer a certain kind of pro- 35 tection. In Japan, everyone is shielded from unwanted intrusion or attention, and that isn't entirely bad. In public places in the States, we all wish, from time to time, that people would go about their business in silence and leave us alone. Just the other day in the weight room of the YMCA, a young man I had never met before told me that he had been working out for the last two months and gained fifteen pounds. "I've always been too thin," he explained. "I want to gain twenty more pounds, and I'm going to put it all up here." We were sitting side by side on different machines. He indicated his shoulders and chest by patting them with his hand. "That's nice," I said, noncommittal but polite. "Of course," he continued, "I couldn't help putting some of the new weight around my waist, too." To my embarrassment, he lifted his shirt and pointed at his stomach. "Listen," I told him. "You don't have to show it to me or anything." I got up from my machine even though I wasn't finished. Still, I felt obligated to say, "Have a nice workout," as I walked away.

I don't appreciate discussing a complete stranger's weight gain and being 36 shown his stomach, and it's true that bizarre conversations like that would never happen in a Japanese gym. Maybe there is comfort in knowing that you will never have to talk to strangers—that you can live your whole life surrounded by friends and family who will understand what you mean without your saying it. Silence can be a sign of harmony among close friends or family, but silent harmony doesn't help people who disagree or don't fit in. On crowded trains in Kobe or Tokyo, where people won't even make eye contact with strangers, much less talk to them, I feel as though each one of us were sealed inside an invisible capsule, unable to breathe or speak out. It is just like my old dream of being stuck inside a spaceship orbiting the earth. I am alarmed by how lonely I feel—and by how quietly content everyone else seems to be.

In Japanese, I don't have a voice for speaking my mind. When a Japanese flight 37 attendant walks down the aisle in her traditional kimono, repeating the endlessly apologetic announcements in the high, squeaky voice a nice woman is expected to use in public, my heart sinks because hers is the voice I am supposed to mimic. All my childhood friends answer their telephones in this same voice, as do the young women store clerks welcoming people and thanking them for their business or TV anchor women reading the news. It doesn't matter who we are or what we are saying. A woman's voice is always the same: a childish squeak piped from the throat.

38   The first time I heard that voice coming out of my own mouth, about three years ago, I was lost at a subway station in Osaka. Though there were plenty of people gathered around the wall map I was trying to read, I did not stop any of them. I flagged down a station attendant, identifiable by his blue uniform. "*Ano, sumimasen,*" I started immediately with an apology ("Well, I'm so sorry to be bothering you"). Then I asked where I could catch the right train. Halfway through my inquiry, I realized that I was squeezing the air through my tightly constricted throat, making my voice thin and wavering. *I have to get out of here,* I thought. *It's a good thing I'm leaving in just a few days.*

39   I was afraid of being stuck in Japan, unable to speak except in that little-bird voice. I'm afraid of the same thing every time I go there.

40   People often tell me that I am lucky to be bilingual, but I am not so sure. Language is like a radio. I have to choose a specific station, English or Japanese, and tune in. I can't listen to both at the same time. In between, there is nothing but static. These days, though, I find myself listening to static because I am afraid to turn my dial to the Japanese station and hear that bird-woman voice. Trying to speak Japanese in Japan, I'm still thinking in English. I can't turn off what I really want to say and concentrate on what is appropriate. Flustered, I try to work out a quick translation, but my feelings are untranslatable and my voice is the voice of a foreigner. The whole experience reminds me of studying French in college and being unable to say or write what I thought.

41   In my second-year French class, I had to keep a journal. I could only say stupid things: "I got up at six. I ate breakfast. It's cold. I'm tired." I was reduced to making these idiotic statements because I didn't have the language to explain, "It's cold for September and I feel sad that summer is over. But I try to cheer myself up by thinking of how beautiful the trees will be in a month." In my French, it was either cold or not cold. Nothing in between, no discussion of what the weather meant. After finishing my entry every day, I felt depressed: my life sounded bleak when it was reduced to bad weather and meal schedules, but I wasn't fluent enough in French to talk about anything else. Now, my Japanese feels thin in the same way.

42   In any language, it is hard to talk about feelings, and there are things that are almost unsayable because they sound too harsh, painful, or intimate. When we are fluent, though, we can weave and dodge our way through the obstacles and get to the difficult thing we want to say; each of us weaves and dodges in slightly different ways, using our individual style or voice. In the way we say the almost unsayable, we can hear the subtle modulations and shifts that make each of our voices unique.

43   When I studied the poetry of Maxine Kumin, Anne Sexton, and Sylvia Plath in college, I was immediately drawn to their voices. I still love the eloquence with

which these poets talk about daily life and declare their feelings, balancing grace-
fully between matter-of-fact observations and powerful emotions. After a particularly emotional statement, the poets often step back and resume describing
the garden, the yew trees and blackberries, before returning to the feelings again.
They say the almost unsayable by balancing on the edge of saying too much and
then pulling back, only to push their way toward that edge again. Reading them
in college, I wanted to learn to speak with a voice like theirs.

My whole schooling has been a process of acquiring a voice. In college and 44
graduate school, I learned to speak, write, and think like my favorite writers—
through imitation and emulation, the way anyone learns any language. I have
not had the same experience in Japanese. The only voice I was taught was the
one that squeezed my throat shut every time I wanted to say, *Help me. This is what
I want. Let me tell you how I feel.*

On my trips to Japan, I am nervous and awake the whole way. Sitting stiffly up- 45
right in the cone of orange light, I read my favorite novelists in English: Margaret
Atwood, Amy Tan, Anne Tyler. I cannot shed my fear of the Japanese language.
When the plane begins its descent toward Tokyo or Osaka and the final sets of
announcements are made in the two languages, I don't try to switch from the
English station of my mind to the Japanese. I turn the dial a little closer to the
Japanese station without turning off the English, even though my mind will fill
with static and the Japanese I speak will be awkward and inarticulate. I am willing to compromise my proficiency in Japanese so that I can continue to think the
thoughts I have come to value in English.

Yet as the plane tips to the right and then to the left, I feel the pull of the 46
ground. Gravity and nostalgia seem one and the same. Poised over the land of
my childhood, I recognize the coastline. The sea shines and glitters just like the
one in the old songs we sang in grade school. The mountains are a dark green
and densely textured. It comes to me, like a surprise, that I love this scenery. *How
could I have spent my adult life away from here?* I wonder. *This is where I should have
been all along.* I remember the low, gray hills of the Midwest and wonder how I
could have found them beautiful, when I grew up surrounded by real mountains.
But even as part of me feels nostalgic, another part of me remains guarded, and
my adult voice talks in the back of my mind like a twenty-four-hour broadcast.
Remember who you were, it warns, *but don't forget who you are now.*

• *Thinking Critically About "Language"*

RESPONDING AS A READER

1. In the first paragraph of the essay, Mori tells the story of a childhood fear.
   What kind of tone is set by this opening anecdote? Do you think this
   story is an effective opening to her essay? How is this opening story related to other themes in the essay?
2. Throughout the essay, Mori offers a number of anecdotes to illustrate particular Japanese or American language practices. What do you see as the

function of these examples? Select two or three that you found particularly engaging, and be prepared to discuss your response to these examples.

3. How is language tied to self-image or identity in this essay? How many different images of Mori's self can you identify (for example, her Japanese-speaking self, her Midwestern-American-speaking self, her childhood self)? What characterizes these various selves and how does she connect language use to each?

RESPONDING AS A WRITER

1. "Language" is divided into seven short sections, with each one indicated by extra spacing between paragraphs. Using the instructions in Chapter 4 for descriptive outlining (p. 58), write *does* and *says* statements for each of these sections. What new insights does this exercise give you about the essay's meaning?

2. In Chapter 5, we explain how a text's value system or ideology is often revealed through the use of opposing terms in which one set of terms is clearly valued by the author and another set of terms is not. Make a list of valued terms and concepts in this essay and match them with terms and concepts not valued. (Remember that valued and not-valued terms or concepts may be implied rather than directly stated.) For example, the concept "voice for speaking my mind" is clearly a positive term in this text, and its opposite—the "high, squeaky voice a nice [Japanese] woman is expected to use in public"—is not (par. 37). After you have compiled a list, write a paragraph in which you draw some conclusions about the beliefs or values that inform this text.

3. "My whole schooling," writes Mori, "has been a process of acquiring a voice. In college and graduate school, I learned to speak, write, and think like my favorite writers—through imitation and emulation, the way anyone learns any language" (par. 44). How would you describe this "voice" and "language" she has worked to acquire as they are evident here? What are their characteristics? Find passages in this essay that are examples of this voice and language.

Lauren Slater

Black Swans

A practicing psychologist, Lauren Slater (b. 1962) has written extensively about mental illness, both her own and that of her clients. Her books include *Welcome to My Country: A Therapist's Memoir of Madness* (1996) and *Lying, A Metaphorical Memoir* (2000). While some have criticized "illness memoirs" like hers as self-absorbed, Slater defends their value. After reading an unfavorable review of *Lying,* for example, she published an article in *Salon,* the online magazine, arguing that the best illness narratives deserve admiration for "tussling with the great human themes in an utterly contemporary context." "Black Swans," originally published in 1996 in the *Missouri Review,* narrates the onset of and her ongoing battle with obsessive-compulsive disorder (OCD).

● *For Your Reading Log*

1. What do you know about OCD or Prozac, the drug used to treat OCD and other mental conditions such as depression? How knowledgeable do you think people are generally about anxiety disorders and various kinds of mental illness? What attitudes have you heard your friends or family express toward mental disorders and illnesses?

2. Stop after you read the first two paragraphs of the essay, and respond to the following questions in your reading log: What details in this passage suggest that this is not an ordinary childhood memory of making snow angels? What expectations do these opening paragraphs set up for what is to follow?

There is something satisfying and scary about making an angel, lowering your 1 bulky body into the drowning fluff, stray flakes landing on your face. I am seven or eight and the sky looms above me, gray and dead. I move my arms and legs—expanding, contracting—sculpting snow before it can swallow me up. I feel the cold filter into my head, seep through the wool of my mittens. I swish wider, faster, then roll out of my mold to inspect its form. There is the imprint of my head, my arms which have swelled into white wings. I step back, step forward, pause and peer. Am I dead or alive down there? Is this a picture of heaven or hell? I am worried about where I will go when I die, that each time I swallow, an invisible stone will get caught in my throat. I worry that when I eat a plum, a tree will grow in my belly, its branches twining around my bones, choking. When I walk through a door I must tap the frame three times. Between each nighttime prayer to Yahweh I close my eyes and count to ten and a half.

And now I look down at myself sketched in the snow. A familiar anxiety 2 chews at the edges of my heart, even while I notice the beauty of the white fur on all the trees, the reverent silence of this season. I register a mistake on my angel, what looks like a thumb-print on its left wing. I reach down to erase it, but unable to smooth the snow perfectly, I start again on another angel, lowering myself, swishing and sweeping, rolling over—no. Yet another mistake, this time the symmetry in the wingspan wrong. A compulsion comes over me. I do it again, and again. In my memory hours go by. My fingers inside my mittens get wrinkled and raw. My breath comes heavily and the snow begins to blue. A moon rises, a perfect crescent pearl whose precise shape I will never be able to re-create. I ache for something I cannot name. Someone calls me, a mother or a father. *Come in now, come in now.* Very early the next morning I awaken, look out my bedroom window, and see the yard covered with my frantic forms—hundreds of angels, none of them quite right. The forms twist and strain, the wings seeming to struggle up in the winter sun, as if each angel were longing for escape, for a free flight that might crack the crystal and ice of her still, stiff world.

3   Looking back on it now, I think maybe those moments in the snow were when my OCD began, although it didn't come to me full-fledged until my mid-twenties. OCD stands for obsessive-compulsive disorder, and some studies say more than three million Americans suffer from it. The "it" is not the commonplace rituals that weave throughout so many of our lives—the woman who checks the stove a few times before she leaves for work, or the man who combs his bangs back, and then again, seeking symmetry. Obsessive-compulsive disorder is pervasive and extreme, inundating the person's life to the point where normal functioning becomes difficult, maybe even impossible.

4   For a long time my life was difficult but not impossible. Both in my childhood and my adulthood I'd suffered from various psychiatric ailments—depressions especially—but none of these were as surreal and absurd as the obsessive-compulsive disorder that one day presented itself. Until I was twenty-five or so, I don't think I could have been really diagnosed with OCD, although my memory of the angels indicates I had tendencies in that direction. I was a child at once nervous and bold, a child who loved trees that trickled sap, the Vermont fields where grass grew the color of deep-throated rust. I was a child who gathered earthworms, the surprising pulse of pink on my fingers, and yet these same fingers, later in the evening, came to prayer points, searching for safety in the folds of my sheets, in the quick counting rituals.

5   Some mental health professionals claim that the onset of obsession is a response to an underlying fear, a recent trauma, say, or a loss. I don't believe that is always true because, no matter how hard I think about it, I remember nothing unusual or disorienting before my first attack, three years out of college. I don't know exactly why at two o'clock one Saturday afternoon what felt like a seizure shook me. I recall lying in my apartment in Cambridge. The floors were painted blue, the curtains a sleepy white. They bellied in and out with the breezes. I was immersed in a book, *The Seven Storey Mountain,* walking my way through the tale's church, dabbing holy water on my forehead. A priest was crooning. A monk moaned. And suddenly this: a thought careening across my cortex. I CAN'T CONCENTRATE. Of course the thought disturbed my concentration, and the monk's moan turned into a whisper, disappeared.

I blinked, looked up. I was back in Cambridge on a blue floor. The blue floor 6 suddenly frightened me; between the planks I could see lines of dark dirt and the sway of a spider crawling. Let me get back, I thought, into the world of the book. I lowered my eyes to the page, but instead of being able to see the print, there was the thought blocking out all else: I CAN'T CONCENTRATE.

Now I started to panic. Each time I tried to get back to the book the words 7 crumbled, lost their sensible shapes. I said to myself, *I must not allow that thought about concentration to come into my mind anymore,* but, of course, the more I tried to suppress it, the louder it jangled. I looked at my hand. I ached for its familiar skin, the paleness of its palm and the three threaded lines that had been with me since birth, but as I held it out before my eyes, the phrase I CAN'T CONCENTRATE ON MY HAND blocked out my hand, so all I saw was a blur of flesh giving way to the bones beneath, and inside the bones the grimy marrow, and in the grimy marrow the individual cells, all disconnected. Shattered skin.

My throat closed up with terror. For surely if I'd lost the book, lost language, 8 lost flesh, I was well on my way to losing the rest of the world. And all because of a tiny phrase that forced me into a searing self-consciousness, that plucked me from the moment into the meta-moment, so I was doomed to think about thinking instead of thinking other thoughts. My mind devouring my mind.

I tried to force my brain onto other topics, but with each mental dodge I be- 9 came aware that I was dodging, and each time I itched I became aware that I was itching, and with each inhalation I became aware that I was inhaling, and I thought, *If I think too much about breathing, will I forget how to breathe?*

I ran into the bathroom. There was a strange pounding in my head, and then 10 a sensation I can only describe as a hiccup of the brain. My brain seemed to be seizing as the phrase about concentration jerked across it. I delved into the medicine cabinet, found a bottle of aspirin, took three, stood by the sink for five minutes. No go. Delved again, pulled out another bottle—Ativan, a Valium-like medication belonging to my housemate, Adam. Another five minutes, my brain still squirting. One more Ativan, a tiny white triangle that would put me to sleep. I would sleep this strange spell off, wake up me again, sane again. I went back to my bed. The day darkened. The Ativan spread through my system. Lights in a neighboring window seemed lonely and sweet. I saw the shadow of a bird in a tree, and it had angel wings, and it soared me someplace else, its call a pure cry.

"What's wrong with you?" he said, shaking my shoulder. Adam stood over 11 me, his face a blur. Through cracked eyelids I saw a wavering world, none of its outlines resolved: the latticed shadow of a tree on a white wall, my friend's face a streak of pink. I am O.K., I thought, for this was what waking up was always like, the gentle resurfacing. I sat up, looked around.

"You've been sleeping for hours and hours," he said. "You slept from yes- 12 terday afternoon until now."

I reached up, gently touched a temple. I felt the faraway nip of my pulse. My 13 pulse was there. I was here.

"Weird day yesterday," I said. I spoke slowly, listening to my words, testing 14 them on my tongue. So far so good.

15   I stood up. "You look weird," he said, "unsteady."

16   "I'm O.K.," I said, and then, in that instant, a surge of anxiety. I had lied. I had not been O.K. *Say "God I'm sorry" fourteen times,* I ordered myself. *This is crazy,* I said to myself. *Fifteen times,* a voice from somewhere else seemed to command. "You really all right?" Adam asked. I closed my eyes, counted, blinked back open.

17   "O.K.," I said. "I'm going to shower."

18   But it wasn't O.K. As soon as I was awake, obsessive thoughts returned. What before had been inconsequential behaviors, such as counting to three before I went through a doorway or checking the stove several times before bed, now became imperatives. There were a thousand and one of them to follow: rules about how to step, what it meant to touch my mouth, a hot consuming urge to fix the crooked angles of the universe. It was constant, a cruel nattering. *There, that tilted picture on the wall. Scratch your head with your left hand only.* It was noise, the beak of a woodpecker in the soft bark of my brain. But the worst by far were the dread thoughts about concentrating. I picked up a book but couldn't read, so aware was I of myself reading, and the fear of that awareness, for it meant a cold disconnection from this world.

19   I began to avoid written language because of the anxiety associated with words. I stopped reading. Every sentence I wrote came out only half coherent. I became afraid of pens and paper, the red felt tip bleeding into white, a wound. What was it? What was I? I could not recognize myself spending hours counting, checking, avoiding. Gods seemed to hover in their air, inhabit me, blowing me full of their strange stellar breaths. I wanted my body back. Instead, I pulsed and stuttered and sparked with a glow not my own.

20   I spent the next several weeks mostly in my bedroom, door closed, shades drawn. I didn't want to go out because any movement might set off a cycle of obsessions. I sat hunched and lost weight. My friend Adam, who had some anxiety problems of his own and was a real pooh-pooher of "talk therapy," found me a behaviorist at McLean.

21   "These sorts of conditions," the behavioral psychologist, Dr. Lipman, told me as I sat one day in his office, "are associated with people who have depressive temperaments, but unlike depression, they do not yield particularly well to more traditional modes of psychotherapy. We have, however, had some real success with cognitive/behavioral treatments."

22   Outside it was a shining summer day. His office was dim, though, his blinds adjusted so only tiny gold chinks of light sprinkled through, illuminating him in patches. He was older, maybe fifty, and pudgy, and had tufts of hair in all the wrong places, in the whorls of his ears and his nostrils. I had a bad feeling about him.

23   Nevertheless, he was all I had right now. "What is this sort of condition exactly?" I asked. My voice, whenever I spoke these days, seemed slowed, stuck, words caught in my throat. I had to keep touching my throat, four times, five times, six times, or I would be punished by losing the power of speech altogether.

24   "Obsessive-compulsive disorder," he announced. "Only you," he said, and lifted his chin a little proudly, "have an especially difficult case of it."

25   This, of course, was not what I wanted to hear. "What's so especially difficult about my case?" I asked.

He tapped his chin with the eraser end of his pencil. He sat back in his leather 26 seat. When the wind outside blew, the gold chinks scattered across his face and desk. Suddenly the world cleared a bit. The papers on his desk seemed animated, rustling, sheaves full of wings, books full of birds. I felt creepy, despondent, and excited all at once. Maybe he could help me. Maybe he had some special knowledge.

He then went on to explain to me how most people with obsessive 27 thoughts—*my hands are filthy*, for instance—always follow those thoughts with a compulsive behavior, like hand washing. And while I did have some compulsive behaviors, Dr. Lipman explained, I had also reported that my most distressing obsession had to do with concentration, and that the concentration obsession had no clear-cut compulsion following in its wake.

"Therefore," he said. His eyes sparkled as he spoke. He seemed excited by 28 my case. He seemed so sure of himself that for a moment I was back with language again, only this time it was his language, his words forming me. "Therefore, you are what we call a primary ruminator!"

A cow, I thought, chewing and chewing on the floppy scum of its cud. I low- 29 ered my head.

He went on to tell me about treatment obstacles. Supposedly, primary ru- 30 minators are especially challenging because, while you can train people to cease compulsive behaviors, you can't train them nearly as easily to tether their thoughts. His method, he told me, would be to use a certain instrument to desensitize me to the obsessive thought, to teach me not to be afraid of it, so when it entered my mind, I wouldn't panic and thereby set off a whole cycle of anxiety and its partner, avoidance.

"How will we do it?" I asked. 31

And that is when he pulled "the instrument" from his desk drawer, a Walk- 32 man with a tiny tape in it. He told me he'd used it with people who were similar to me. He told me I was to record my voice saying "I can't concentrate I can't concentrate" and then wear the Walkman playing my own voice back to me for at least two hours a day. Soon, he said, I'd become so used to the thought it would no longer bother me.

He looked over at the clock. About half the session had gone by. "We still have 33 twenty more minutes," he said, pressing the red Record button, holding the miniature microphone up to my mouth. "Why don't you start speaking now."

I paid Dr. Lipman for the session, borrowed the Walkman and the tape, and left, 34 stepping into the summer light. McLean is a huge, stately hospital, buildings with pillars, yawning lawns. The world outside looked lazy in the sweet heat of June. Tulips in the garden lapped at the pollen-rich air with black tongues. A squirrel chirped high in the tuft of a tree. For a moment the world seemed lovely. Then, from far across the lawn, I saw a shadow in a window. Drawn to it for a reason I could not articulate, I stepped closer, and closer still. The shadow resolved itself into lines—two dark brows, a nose. A girl, pressed against glass on a top-floor ward. Her hands were fisted on either side of her face, her curls in a ratty tangle. Her mouth was open, and though I could not hear her, I saw the red splash of her scream.

Behavior therapy is in some ways the antithesis of psychoanalysis. Psycho- 35 analysis focuses on cause, behavior therapy on consequence. Although I've always been a critic of old-style psychoanalysis with its fetish for the past, I don't completely discount the importance of origins. And I have always believed in the mind as an entity that at once subsumes the body and radiates beyond it, and therefore in need of interventions surpassing the mere technical—interventions that whisper to mystery, stroke the soul.

36   The Walkman, however, was a purely technical intervention. It had little red studs for buttons. The tape whirred efficiently in its center like a slick dark heart. My own voice echoed back to me, all blips and snaky static. I wondered what the obsession with concentration meant. Surely it had some significance beyond the quirks in my neuronal wiring. Surely the neuron itself—that tiny pulse of life embedded in the brain's lush banks—was a God-given charge. When I was a girl, I had seen stalks of wheat filled with a strange red light. When I was a girl, I once peeled back the corn's green clasps to find yellow pearls. With the Walkman on, I closed my eyes, saw again the prongs of corn, the wide world, and myself floating out of that world, in a place above all planets, severed even from my own mind. And I knew the obsession had something to do with deep disconnection and too much awe.

37   "There may be no real reasons," Dr. Lipman repeated to me during my next visit. "OCD could well be the result of a nervous system that's too sensitive. If the right medication is ever developed, we would use that."

38   Because the right medication had not yet been found, I wore the Walkman. The earplugs felt spongy. Sometimes I wore it to bed, listening to my own voice repeat the obsessive fear. When I took the earphones off, the silence was complete. My sheets were damp from sweat. I waited. Shadows whirled around. Planets sent down their lights, laying them across the blue floor. Blue. Silver. Space. *I can't concentrate.*

39   I did very little for the next year. Dr. Lipman kept insisting I wear the Walkman, turning up the volume, keeping it on for three, now four hours at a time. Fear and grief prevented me from eating much. When I was too terrified to get out of bed, Dr. Lipman checked me into the local hospital, where I lay amidst IV drips, bags of blood, murmuring heart machines that let me know someone somewhere near was still alive.

40   It was in the hospital that I was first introduced to psychiatric medications, which the doctors tried out on me, to no avail. The medications had poetic names and frequently rhymed with one another—nortriptyline, desipramine, amitriptyline. Nurses brought me capsules in miniature paper cups or oblong shapes of white that left a salty tingle on my tongue. None of them worked, except to make me drowsy and dull.

41   And then one day Dr. Lipman said to me, "There's a new medication called Prozac, still in its trial period, but it's seventy percent effective with OCD. I want to send you to a Dr. Stanley, here at McLean. He's one of the physicians doing trial runs."

42   I shrugged, willing to try. I'd tried so much, surely this couldn't hurt. I didn't expect much though. I certainly didn't expect what I finally got.

43 In my memory, Stanley is the Prozac Doctor. He has an office high in the eaves of McLean. His desk gleams. His children smile out from frames lined up behind

him. In the corner is a computer with a screen saver of hypnotic swirling stars. I watch the stars die and swell. I watch the simple gold band on Stanley's hand. For a moment I think that maybe in here I'll finally be able to escape the infected repetitions of my own mind. And then I hear a clock tick-tick-ticking. The sound begins to bother me; I cannot tune it out. *The clock is ruining my concentration,* I think, and turn toward it. The numbers on its face are not numbers but tiny painted pills, green and white. A chime hangs down, with another capsule, probably a plastic replica, swinging from the end of it. Back. Forth. Back. Back.

The pads of paper on Stanley's desk are all edged in green and white, with 44 the word "Prozac" scripted across the bottom. The pen has "Prozac" embossed in tiny letters. He asks me about my symptoms for a few minutes, and then uses the Prozac pen to write out a prescription.

"What about side effects?" I ask. 45

"Very few," the Prozac Doctor answers. He smiles. "Maybe some queasiness. 46 A headache in the beginning. Some short-term insomnia. All in all it's a very good medication. The safest we have."

"Behavior therapy hasn't helped," I say. I feel I'm speaking slowly, for the 47 sound of that clock is consuming me. I put my hands over my ears.

"What is it?" he asks. 48

"Your—clock." 49

He looks toward it. 50

"Would you mind putting it away?" 51

"Then I would be colluding with your disease," he says. "If I put the clock 52 away, you'll just fixate on something else."

"Disease," I repeat. "I have a disease." 53

"Without doubt," he says. "OCD can be a crippling disease, but now, for the 54 first time, we have the drugs to combat it."

I take the prescription and leave. I will see him in one month for a follow- 55 up. Disease. Combat. Collusions. My mind, it seems, is my enemy, my illness an absurdity that has to be exterminated. I believe this. The treatment I'm receiving, with its insistence upon cure—which means the abolition of hurt instead of its transformation—helps me to believe this. I have, indeed, been invaded by a virus, a germ I need to rid myself of.

Looking back on it now, I see this belief only added to my panic, shrunk my 56 world still smaller.

On the first day of Prozac I felt nothing, on the second and third I felt nauseated, 57 and for the rest of that week I had headaches so intense I wanted to groan and lower my face into a bowl of crushed ice. I had never had migraines before. In their own way they are beautiful, all pulsing suns and squooging colors. When I closed my eyes, pink shapes flapped and angels' halos spun. I was a girl again, lying in the snow. Slowly, one by one, the frozen forms lifted toward the light.

And then there really was an angel over me, pressing a cool cloth to my fore- 58 head. He held two snowy tablets out to me and in a haze of pain I took them.

"You'll be all right," Adam said to me. When I cried it was a creek coming 59 from my eyes.

I rubbed my eyes. The headache ebbed. 60

61   "How are you?" he asked.

62   "O.K.," I said. And waited for a command. *Touch your nose, blink twelve times, try not to think about think about concentrating.*

63   The imperatives came—I could hear them—but from far far away, like birds beyond a mountain, a sound nearly silent and easy to ignore.

64   "I'm . . . O.K.," I repeated. I went out into the kitchen. The clock on the stove ticked. I pressed my ear against it and heard, this time, a steady, almost soothing pulse.

65   Most things, I think, diminish over time, rock and mountain, glacier and bone. But this wasn't the nature of Prozac, or me on Prozac. One day I was ill, cramped up with fears, and the next day the ghosts were gone. Imagine having for years a raging fever, and then one day someone hands you a new kind of pill, and within a matter of hours sweat dries, the scarlet swellings go down, your eyes no longer burn. The grass appears green again, the sky a gentle blue. *Hello hello. Remember me?* the planet whispers.

66   But to say I returned to the world is even a bit misleading, for all my life the world has seemed off-kilter. On Prozac, not only did the acute obsessions dissolve; so too did the blander depression that had been with me since my earliest memories. A sense of immense calm flooded me. Colors came out, yellow leaping from the light where it had long lain trapped, greens unwinding from the grass, dusk letting loose its lavender.

67   By the fourth day I still felt so shockingly fine that I called the Prozac Doctor. I pictured him in his office, high in the eaves of McLean. I believed he had saved me. He loomed large.

68   "I'm well," I told him.

69   "Not yet. It takes at least a month to build up a therapeutic blood level."

70   "No," I said. "It doesn't." I felt a rushing joy. "The medicine you gave me has made me well. I've—I've actually never felt better."

71   A pause on the line. "I suppose it could be possible."

72   "Yes," I said. "It's happened."

73   I became a "happening" kind of person. Peter Kramer, the author of *Listening to Prozac*, has written extensively on the drug's ability to galvanize personality changes as well as to soothe fears or elevate mood. Kramer calls Prozac a cosmetic medication, for it seems to reshape the psyche, lift the face of the soul.

74   One night, soon after the medication had kicked in, I sat at the kitchen table with Adam. He was stuck in the muck of his master's thesis, fearful of failure.

75   "It's easy," I said. "Break the project down into bits. A page a day. Six days, one chapter. Twelve days, two. One month, presto." I snapped my fingers. "You're finished."

76   Adam looked at me, said nothing. The kitchen grew quiet, a deliberate sort of silence he seemed to be purposefully manufacturing so I could hear the echo of my own voice. Bugs thumped on the screen. I heard the high happy pitch of a cheerleader, the sensible voice of a vocational counselor. In a matter of moments I had gone from a fumbling, unsure person to this—all pragmatism, all sure solutions. For the first time on Prozac I felt afraid.

I lay in bed that night. From the next room I heard the patter of Adam's 77
typewriter keys. He was stuck in the mire, inching forward and falling back.
Where was I? Who was I? I lifted my hand to my face, the same motion as before, when the full force of obsession had struck me. The hand was still unfamiliar, but wonderfully so now, the three threaded lines seams of silver, the
lights from passing cars rotating on my walls like the swish of a spaceship
softly landing.

In space I was then, wondering. How could a drug change my mind so 78
abruptly? How could it bring forth buried or new parts of my personality? The
oldest questions, I know. My brain wasn't wet clay and paste, as all good brains
should be, but a glinting thing crossed with wires. I wasn't human but machine.
No, I wasn't machine but animal, linked to my electrified biology more completely than I could have imagined. We have lately come to think of machines
and animals, of machines and nature, as occupying opposite sides of the spectrum—there is IBM and then there's the lake—but really they are so similar. A
computer goes on when you push its button. A gazelle goes on when it sees a
lynx. Only humans are supposedly different, above the pure cause and effect of
the hard-wired primitive world. Free will and all.

But no, maybe not. For I had swallowed a pill designed through technology, 79
and in doing so, I was discovering myself embedded in an animal world. I was
a purely chemical being, mood and personality seeping through serotonin. We
are all taught to believe it's true, but how strange to feel that supposed truth bub-
bling right in your own tweaked brainpan. Who was I, all skin and worm, all
herd? For the next few weeks, amidst feelings of joy and deep relief, these
thoughts accompanied me, these slow, simmering misgivings. In dreams, beasts
roamed the rafters of my bones, and my bones were twined with wire, teeth tiny
silicon chips.

I went to Drumlin Farm one afternoon to see the animals. A goose ate grass 80
in an imperturbable rhythm. Sheep brayed robotically, their noses pointing toward the sky. I reached out to touch their fur. Simmering misgivings, yes, but my
fingers alive, feeling clumps of cream, of wool.

Every noon I took my pill. Instead of just placing it on my tongue and swal- 81
lowing with water, I unscrewed the capsule. White powder poured into my
hands. I tossed the plastic husk away, cradled the healing talc. I tasted it, a burst
of bitterness, a gagging. I took it that way every day, the silky slide of Prozac
powder, the harshness in my mouth.

Mornings now, I got up early to jog, showered efficiently, then strode off to 82
the library. I was able to go back to work, cutting deli part-time at Formaggio
while I prepared myself for divinity school the next year by reading. I read with
an appetite, hungry from all the time I'd lost to illness. The pages of the books
seemed very white; the words were easy, black beads shining, ebony in my quieted mind.

I found a book in the library's medical section about obsessive-compulsive 83
disorder. I sat in a corner, on a corduroy cushion, to read it. And there, surrounded by pages and pages on the nature of God and mystery, on Job who
cried out at his unfathomable pain, I read about my disorder from a medical

perspective, followed the charts and graphs and correlation coefficients. The author proposed that OCD was solely physical in origin, and had the same neurological etiology as Tourette's. Obsessive symptoms, the author suggested, are atavistic responses left over from primitive grooming behaviors. We still have the ape in us; a bird flies in our blood. The obsessive person, linked to her reptilian roots, her mammalian ancestors, cannot stop picking parasites off her brother's back, combing her hair with her tongue, or doing the human equivalent of nest building, picking up stick after stick, leaf after leaf, until her bloated home sits ridiculously unstable in the crotch of an old oak tree.

84   *Keel keel,* the crow in me cries. The pig grunts. The screen of myself blinks on. Blinks off. Darkens.

85   Still, I was mostly peaceful, wonderfully organized. My mind felt lubed, thoughts slipping through so easily, words bursting into bloom. I was reminded of being a girl on the island of Barbados, where we once vacationed. My father took me to a banquet beneath a tropical sky. Greased black men slithered under low poles, their liquid bodies bending to meet the world. Torches flared, and on a long table before me steamed food of every variety. *A feast,* my father said, *all the good things in life.* Yes, that was what Prozac was first like for me, all the good things in life: roasted ham, delicate grilled fish, lemon halves wrapped in yellow waxed paper, fat plums floating in jars.

86   I could, I thought, do anything in this state of mind. I put my misgivings aside—how fast they would soon come back! how hard they would hit!—and ate into my days, a long banquet. I did things I'd never done before: swimming at dawn in Walden Pond, writing poetry I knew was bad and loving it anyway.

87   I applied for and was awarded a three-month grant to go to Appalachia, where I wanted to collect oral histories of mountain women. I could swagger anywhere on the Zack, on Vitamin P. Never mind that even before I'd ever come down with OCD I'd been the anxious, tentative sort. Never mind that unnamed trepidations, for all of my life, had prevented me from taking a trip to New Hampshire for more than a few days. Now that I'd taken the cure, I really could go anywhere, even off to the rippling blue mountains of poverty, far from a phone or a friend.

88   A gun hung over the door. In the oven I saw a roasted bird covered with flies. In the bathroom, a fat girl stooped over herself, without bothering to shut the door, and pulled a red rag from between her legs.

89   Her name was Kim, her sister's name was Bridget, and their mother and father were Kat and Lonny. All the females were huge and doughy, while Lonny was a single strand of muscle tanned to the color of tobacco. He said very little, and the mother and daughters chattered on, offering me Cokes and Cheerios, showing me to my room, where I sat on a lumpy mattress and stared at the white walls.

90   And then a moon rose. A storm of hurricane force plowed through fields and sky. I didn't feel myself here. The sound of the storm, battering just above my head, seemed far far away. There was a whispering in my mind, a noise like silk

being split. Next to me, on the night table, my sturdy bottle of Prozac. I was fine. So long as I had that, I would be fine.

I pretended I was fine for the next couple of days, racing around with 91 manic intensity. I sat heavy Kat in one of her oversized chairs and insisted she tell me everything about her life in the Blue Ridge Mountains, scribbling madly as she talked. *I am happy happy happy,* I sang to myself. I tried to ignore the strange sounds building in my brain, kindling that crackles, a flame getting hot.

And then I was taking a break out in the sandy yard. It was near one hundred degrees. The sun was tiny in a bleary sky. Chickens screamed and pecked. 92

In one swift and seamless move, Lonny reached down to grab a bird. His fist 93 closed in on its throat while all the crows cawed and the beasts in my bones brayed away. He laid the chicken down on a stump, raised an ax, and cut. The body did its dance. I watched the severing, how swiftly connections melt, how deep and black is space. Blood spilled.

I ran inside. I was far from a phone or a friend. Maybe I was reminded of 94 some pre-verbal terror: the surgeon's knife, the violet umbilical cord. Or maybe the mountain altitudes had thrown my chemistry off. I don't really know why, or how. But as though I'd never swallowed a Prozac pill, my mind seized and clamped and the obsessions were back.

I took a step forward and then said to myself, *Don't take another step until you* 95 *count to twenty-five.* After I'd satisfied that imperative, I had to count to twenty-five again, and then halve twenty-five, and then quarter it, before I felt safe enough to walk out the door. By the end of the day, each step took over ten minutes to complete. I stopped taking steps. I sat on my bed.

"What's wrong with you?" Kat said. "Come out here and talk with us." 96

I tried, but I got stuck in the doorway. There was a point above the doorway 97 I just had to see, and then see again, and inside of me something screamed *back again back again,* and the grief was very large.

For I had experienced the world free and taken in colors and tasted grilled 98 fish and moon. I had left one illness like a too tight snakeskin, and here I was, thrust back. What's worse than illness is to think you're cured—partake of cure in almost complete belief—and then with no warning to be dashed on a dock, moored.

Here's what they don't tell you about Prozac. The drug, for many obsessives 99 who take it, is known to have wonderfully powerful effects in the first few months when it's new to the body. When I called the Prozac Doctor from Kentucky that evening, he explained to me how the drug, when used to treat OCD as opposed to depression, peaks at about six months and then loses some of its oomph. "Someday we'll develop a more robust pill," Dr. Stanley said. "In the meantime, up your dose."

I upped my dose. No relief. Why not? Please. Over the months I had come 100 to need Prozac in a complicated way, had come to see it as my savior, half hating it, half loving it. I unscrewed the capsules and poured their contents over my fingers. Healing talc, gone. Dead sand. I fingered the empty husks.

101   "You'll feel better if you come to church with us," Kat said to me that Sunday morning. She peered into my face, which must have been white and drawn. "Are you suffering from some city sickness?"

102   I shrugged. My eyes hurt from crying. I couldn't read or write; I could only add, subtract, divide, divide again.

103   "Come to church," Kat said. "We can ask the preacher to pray for you."

104   But I didn't believe in prayers where my illness was concerned. I had come to think, through my reading and the words of doctors, and especially through my brain's rapid response to a drug, that whatever was wrong with me had a simplistic chemical cause. Such a belief can be devastating to sick people, for on top of their illness they must struggle with the sense that illness lacks any creative possibilities.

105   I think these beliefs, so common in today's high-tech biomedical era in which the focus is relentlessly reductionistic, rob illness of its potential dignity. Illness can be dignified; we can conceive of pain as a kind of complex answer from an elegant system, an arrow pointing inward, a message from soil or sky.

106   Not so for me. I wouldn't go to church or temple. I wouldn't talk or ask or wonder, for these are distinctly human activities, and I'd come to view myself as less than human.

107   An anger rose up in me then, a rage. I woke late one night, hands fisted. It took me an hour to get out of bed, so many numbers I had to do, but I was determined.

108   And then I was walking outside, pushing past the need to count before every step. The night air was muggy, and insects raised a chorus.

109   I passed midnight fields, a single shack with lighted windows. Cows slept in a pasture.

110   I rounded the pasture, walked up a hill. And then, before me, spreading out in moonglow, a lake. I stood by its lip. My mind was buzzing and jerking. I don't know at what point the swans appeared—white swans, they must have been, but in silhouette they looked black. They seemed to materialize straight out of the slumbering water. They rose to the surface of the water as memories rise to the surface of consciousness. Hundreds of black swans suddenly, floating absolutely silent, and as I stood there the counting ceased, my mind became silent, and I watched. The swans drifted until it seemed, for a few moments, that they were inside of me, seven dark, silent birds, fourteen princesses, a single self swimming in a tepid sea.

111   I don't know how long I stood there, or when, exactly, I left. The swans disappeared eventually. The counting ticking talking of my mind resumed.

112   Still, even in chattering illness I had been quieted for a bit; doors in me had opened; elegance had entered.

113   This thought calmed me. I was not completely claimed by illness, nor a prisoner of Prozac, entirely dependent on the medication to function. Part of me was still free, a private space not absolutely permeated by pain. A space I could learn to cultivate.

114   Over the next few days, I noticed that even in the thicket of obsessions my mind sometimes swam into the world, if only for brief forays. There, while I

struggled to take a step, was the sun on a green plate. *Remember that*, I said to my-self. And here, while I stood fixated in a doorway, was a beetle with a purplish shell, like eggplants growing in wet soil. *Appreciate this*, I told myself, and I can say I did, those slivers of seconds when I returned to the world. I loved the bee-tle, ached for the eggplant, paddled in a lake with black swans.

And so a part of me began to learn about living outside the disease, culti- 115 vating appreciation for a few free moments. It was nothing I would have wished for myself, nothing to noisily celebrate. But it was something, and I could choose it, even while mourning the paralyzed parts of me, the pill that had failed me.

A long time ago, Freud coined the term "superego." A direct translation 116 from German is "over I." Maybe what Freud meant, or should have meant, was not a punitive voice but the angel in the self who rises above an ego under siege, or a medicated mind, to experience the world from a narrow but occasionally gratifying ledge.

I am thirty-one now, and I know that ledge well. It is a smaller space than I 117 would have wished for myself—I who would like to possess a mind free and flexible. I don't. Even after I raised my dose, the Prozac never worked as well as it once had, and years later I am sometimes sad about that, other times strangely relieved, even though my brain is hounded. I must check my keys, the stove; I must pause many times as I write this and do a ritual count to thirty. It's dis-tracting, to say the least, but still I write this. I can walk and talk and play. I've come to live my life in those brief stretches of silence that arrive throughout the day, working at what I know is an admirable speed, accomplishing all I can in clear pauses, knowing those pauses may be short-lived. I am learning something about the single moment, how rife with potential it is, how truly loud its tick. I have heard clocks and clocks. Time shines, sad and good.

And what of the unclear, mind-cluttered stretches? These, as well, I have 118 bent to. I read books now, even when my brain has real difficulty taking in words. Half a word, or a word blurred by static, is better than nothing at all. There is also a kind of stance I've developed, detaching my mind from my mind, letting the static sizzle on while I walk, talk, read, while the obsessive cy-cles continue and I, stepping aside, try to link my life to something else. It is a meditative exercise of a high order, and one I'm getting better at. Compensations can be gritty gifts.

Is this adaptation a spiritual thing? When I'm living in moments of clarity, 119 have I transcended disease, or has disease transformed me, taught me how to live in secret niches? I don't know.

A few nights ago, a man at a party, a psychologist, talked about the brain. 120 "The amazing thing," he said, "is that if you cut the corpus callosum of small chil-dren, they learn without the aid of medication or reparative surgery how to transfer information from the left to the right hemisphere. And because we know cerebral neurons never rejuvenate, that's evidence," he said, "for a mind that lives beyond the brain, a mind outside of our biologies."

Perhaps. Or perhaps our biologies are broader than we ever thought. Per- 121 haps the brain, because of its wound, has been forced into some kink of creativity we can neither see nor explain. This is what the doctors didn't tell me about ill-ness: that an answer to illness is not necessarily cure, but an ambivalent com-pensation. Disease, for sure, is disorganization, but cure is not necessarily the synthetic, pill-swallowing righting of the mess. To believe this is to define brain function in rigid terms of "normal" and "abnormal," a devastating definition for many. And to believe this, especially where the psyche is concerned, may also mean dependence on psychotropic drugs, and the risk of grave disappointment if the drugs stop working.

122   I think of those children, their heads on white sheets, their corpus callosa exposed and cut. I wonder who did that to them, and why. I'm sure there is some compelling medical explanation—wracking seizures that need to be stopped—but still, the image disturbs me. I think more, though, of the chil-dren's brains once sewn back inside the bony pockets of skull. There, in the se-cret dark, between wrenched hemispheres, I imagine tiny tendrils growing, so small and so deep not even the strongest machines can see them. They are real but not real, biological but spiritual. They wind in and out, joining left to right, building webbed wings and rickety bridges, sending out messengers with crit-ical information, like the earliest angels who descended from the sky with news and challenge, wrestling with us in nighttime deserts, straining our thighs, stretching our bodies in pain, no doubt, until our skin took on new shapes.

● *Thinking Critically About "Black Swans"*

RESPONDING AS A READER

1. What kind of reader does Slater seem to have in mind—a reader who has experienced OCD or one who has not? What evidence do you have for this answer?

2. What purpose or purposes do you think Slater wishes to accomplish in writing this essay? Which do you consider her main purpose and why? How successful is she in accomplishing this purpose? Cite passages that support your answer.

3. What was your first response to the title "Black Swans"? In the context of the essay, what do black swans represent? How is this image con-nected to other themes and ideas in the essay?

RESPONDING AS A WRITER

1. If you were to think of this essay as a drama, what role do the following scenes play in moving the plot forward: (1) the scene of making snow angels, (2) the scene of suddenly being unable to read, (3) the scenes of being on Prozac, (4) the scenes in Appalachia? Choose a scene and ex-plain its role and effect.

2. The narrator draws three portraits of herself besides the childhood im-ages she creates in the opening paragraphs—the self first afflicted with

full-blown OCD, the self that is temporarily "cured" with Prozac, and the self that has adapted to living with OCD. Describe each of these selves and the narrator's attitude toward each. What evidence can you find to back up your claims about the narrator's attitudes?

3. In paragraph 78, Slater says, "We have lately come to think of machines and animals, of machines and nature, as occupying opposite sides of the spectrum . . . but really they are so similar." How does she use animal imagery and machine imagery to explain her disease and the human condition generally? How successful is she in changing your perspective on mental illness and treatments such as Prozac?

bell hooks

keeping close to home: class and education

Writer Gloria Watkins (b. 1952) writes under the name of her "sharp-tongued" grand-mother, bell hooks, whom she "discovered, claimed, and invented" as her "ally." Feminist, scholar, essayist, poet, and public intellectual, bell hooks is known for her incisive critiques of white feminism, classicism, and patriarchy. hooks has taught at Oberlin College, City College of New York, and Yale University. The first book to bring hooks national recognition was *Ain't I a Woman: black women and feminism* (1981); since then, she has written twelve books of nonfiction, several books of po-etry, and numerous essays. "keeping close to home: class and education" is taken from *Talking Back: thinking feminist, thinking black* (1988), which was published by South End Press, a nonprofit collectively run book publisher "committed to radical social change." *Talking Back* includes twenty-five essays by hooks; other essay titles include "on being black at yale: education as the practice of freedom" and "'when i was a young soldier for the revolution': coming to voice."

• *For Your Reading Log*

1. Given the above background information about hooks and the title of the collection, *Talking Back,* make some predications about what she will have to say about "home," "education," and "class."

2. When hooks left her small town home of Hopkinsville, Kentucky, and her working-class black family to attend Stanford University, she expe-rienced something of a culture shock. Many students experience some kind of culture shock when they first enter college though often it is not as dramatic as that experienced by hooks. Think about whether you have experienced any culture shock upon entering college. If so, describe this experience and your feelings about it in your reading log. If not, speculate about why not. What accounts for your ease or difficulty in ad-justing to college?

————————   •   ————————

1 We are both awake in the almost dark of 5 a.m. Everyone else is sound asleep. Mama asks the usual questions. Telling me to look around, make sure I have everything, scolding me because I am uncertain about the actual time the bus ar-rives. By 5:30 we are waiting outside the closed station. Alone together, we have a chance to really talk. Mama begins. Angry with her children, especially the ones who whisper behind her back, she says bitterly, "Your childhood could not have been that bad. You were fed and clothed. You did not have to do without—that's

more than a lot of folks have and I just can't stand the way y'all go on." The hurt in her voice saddens me. I have always wanted to protect mama from hurt, to ease her burdens. Now I am part of what troubles. Confronting me, she says accusingly, "It's not just the other children. You talk too much about the past. You don't just listen." And I do talk. Worse, I write about it.

Mama has always come to each of her children seeking different responses. 2 With me she expresses the disappointment, hurt, and anger of betrayal: anger that her children are so critical, that we can't even have the sense to like the presents she sends. She says, "From now on there will be no presents. I'll just stick some money in a little envelope the way the rest of you do. Nobody wants criticism. Everybody can criticize me but I am supposed to say nothing." When I try to talk, my voice sounds like a twelve year old. When I try to talk, she speaks louder, interrupting me, even though she has said repeatedly, "Explain it to me, this talk about the past." I struggle to return to my thirty-five year old self so that she will know by the sound of my voice that we are two women talking together. It is only when I state firmly in my very adult voice, "Mama, you are not listening," that she becomes quiet. She waits. Now that I have her attention, I fear that my explanations will be lame, inadequate. "Mama," I begin, "people usually go to therapy because they feel hurt inside, because they have pain that will not stop, like a wound that continually breaks open, that does not heal. And often these hurts, that pain has to do with things that have happened in the past, sometimes in childhood, often in childhood, or things that we believe happened." She wants to know, "What hurts, what hurts are you talking about?" "Mom, I can't answer that. I can't speak for all of us, the hurts are different for everybody. But the point is you try to make the hurt better, to heal it, by understanding how it came to be. And I know you feel mad when we say something happened or hurt that you don't remember being that way, but the past isn't like that, we don't have the same memory of it. We remember things differently. You know that. And sometimes folk feel hurt about stuff and you just don't know or didn't realize it, and they need to talk about it. Surely you understand the need to talk about it."

Our conversation is interrupted by the sight of my uncle walking across the 3 park toward us. We stop to watch him. He is on his way to work dressed in a familiar blue suit. They look alike, these two who rarely discuss the past. This interruption makes me think about life in a small town. You always see someone you know. Interruptions, intrusions are part of daily life. Privacy is difficult to maintain. We leave our private space in the car to greet him. After the hug and kiss he has given me every year since I was born, they talk about the day's funerals. In the distance the bus approaches. He walks away knowing that they will see each other later. Just before I board the bus I turn, staring into my mother's face. I am momentarily back in time, seeing myself eighteen years ago, at this same bus stop, staring into my mother's face, continually turning back, waving farewell as I returned to college—that experience which first took me away from our town, from family. Departing was as painful then as it is now. Each movement away makes return harder. Each separation intensifies distance, both physical and emotional.

4   To a southern black girl from a working-class background who had never been on a city bus, who had never stepped on an escalator, who had never travelled by plane, leaving the comfortable confines of a small town Kentucky life to attend Stanford University was not just frightening; it was utterly painful. My parents had not been delighted that I had been accepted and adamantly opposed my going so far from home. At the time, I did not see their opposition as an expression of their fear that they would lose me forever. Like many working-class folks, they feared what college education might do to their children's minds even as they unenthusiastically acknowledged its importance. They did not understand why I could not attend a college nearby, an all-black college. To them, any college would do. I would graduate, become a school teacher, make a decent living and a good marriage. And even though they reluctantly and skeptically supported my educational endeavors, they also subjected them to constant harsh and bitter critique. It is difficult for me to talk about my parents and their impact on me because they have always felt wary, ambivalent, mistrusting of my intellectual aspirations even as they have been caring and supportive. I want to speak about these contradictions because sorting through them, seeking resolution and reconciliation has been important to me both as it affects my development as a writer, my effort to be fully self-realized, and my longing to remain close to the family and community that provided the groundwork for much of my thinking, writing, and being.

5   Studying at Stanford, I began to think seriously about class differences. To be materially underprivileged at a university where most folks (with the exception of workers) are materially privileged provokes such thought. Class differences were boundaries no one wanted to face or talk about. It was easier to downplay them, to act as though we were all from privileged backgrounds, to work around them, to confront them privately in the solitude of one's room, or to pretend that just being chosen to study at such an institution meant that those of us who did not come from privilege were already in transition toward privilege. To not long for such transition marked one as rebellious, as unlikely to succeed. It was a kind of treason not to believe that it was better to be identified with the world of material privilege than with the world of the working class, the poor. No wonder our working-class parents from poor backgrounds feared our entry into such a world, intuiting perhaps that we might learn to be ashamed of where we had come from, that we might never return home, or come back only to lord it over them.

6   Though I hung with students who were supposedly radical and chic, we did not discuss class. I talked to no one about the sources of my shame, how it hurt me to witness the contempt shown the brown-skinned Filipina maids who cleaned our rooms, or later my concern about the $100 a month I paid for a room off-campus which was more than half of what my parents paid for rent. I talked to no one about my efforts to save money, to send a little something home. Yet these class realities separated me from fellow students. We were moving in different directions. I did not intend to forget my class background or alter my class allegiance. And even though I received an education designed to provide me with a bourgeois sensibility, passive acquiescence was not my only option. I

knew that I could resist. I could rebel. I could shape the direction and focus of the various forms of knowledge available to me. Even though I sometimes envied and longed for greater material advantages (particularly at vacation times when I would be one of few if any students remaining in the dormitory because there was no money for travel), I did not share the sensibility and values of my peers. That was important—class was not just about money; it was about values which showed and determined behavior. While I often needed more money, I never needed a new set of beliefs and values. For example, I was profoundly shocked and disturbed when peers would talk about their parents without respect, or would even say that they hated their parents. This was especially troubling to me when it seemed that these parents were caring and concerned. It was often explained to me that such hatred was "healthy and normal." To my white, middle-class California roommate, I explained the way we were taught to value our parents and their care, to understand that they were not obligated to give us care. She would always shake her head, laughing all the while, and say, "Missy, you will learn that it's different here, that we think differently." She was right. Soon, I lived alone, like the one Mormon student who kept to himself as he made a concentrated effort to remain true to his religious beliefs and values. Later in graduate school I found that classmates believed "lower class" people had no beliefs and values. I was silent in such discussions, disgusted by their ignorance.

Carol Stack's anthropological study, *All Our Kin,* was one of the first books   7
I read which confirmed my experiential understanding that within black culture (especially among the working class and poor, particularly in southern states), a value system emerged that was counter-hegemonic, that challenged notions of individualism and private property so important to the maintenance of white-supremacist, capitalist patriarchy. Black folk created in marginal spaces a world of community and collectivity where resources were shared. In the preface to *Feminist Theory: from margin to center,* I talked about how the point of difference, this marginality can be the space for the formation of an oppositional world view. That world view must be articulated, named if it is to provide a sustained blueprint for change. Unfortunately, there has existed no consistent framework for such naming. Consequently both the experience of this difference and documentation of it (when it occurs) gradually loses presence and meaning.

Much of what Stack documented about the "culture of poverty," for example, would not describe interactions among most black poor today irrespective   8
of geographical setting. Since the black people she described did not acknowledge (if they recognized it in theoretical terms) the oppositional value of their world view, apparently seeing it more as a survival strategy determined less by conscious efforts to oppose oppressive race and class biases than by circumstance, they did not attempt to establish a framework to transmit their beliefs and values from generation to generation. When circumstances changed, values altered. Efforts to assimilate the values and beliefs of privileged white people, presented through media like television, undermine and destroy potential structures of opposition.

Increasingly, young black people are encouraged by the dominant culture   9
(and by those black people who internalize the values of this hegemony) to believe

that assimilation is the only possible way to survive, to succeed. Without the framework of an organized civil rights or black resistance struggle, individual and collective efforts at black liberation that focus on the primacy of self-definition and self-determination often go unrecognized. It is crucial that those among us who resist and rebel, who survive and succeed, speak openly and honestly about our lives and the nature of our personal struggles, the means by which we resolve and reconcile contradictions. This is no easy task. Within the educational institutions where we learn to develop and strengthen our writing and analytical skills, we also learn to think, write, and talk in a manner that shifts attention away from personal experience. Yet if we are to reach our people and all people, if we are to remain connected (especially those of us whose familial backgrounds are poor and working-class), we must understand that the telling of one's personal story provides a meaningful example, a way for folks to identify and connect.

10   Combining personal with critical analysis and theoretical perspectives can engage listeners who might otherwise feel estranged, alienated. To speak simply with language that is accessible to as many folks as possible is also important. Speaking about one's personal experience or speaking with simple language is often considered by academics and/or intellectuals (irrespective of their political inclinations) to be a sign of intellectual weakness or even anti-intellectualism. Lately, when I speak, I do not stand in place—reading my paper, making little or no eye contact with audiences—but instead make eye contact, talk extemporaneously, digress, and address the audience directly. I have been told that people assume I am not prepared, that I am anti-intellectual, unprofessional (a concept that has everything to do with class as it determines actions and behavior), or that I am reinforcing the stereotype of black people as non-theoretical and gutsy.

11   Such criticism was raised recently by fellow feminist scholars after a talk I gave at Northwestern University at a conference on "Gender, Culture, Politics" to an audience that was mainly students and academics. I deliberately chose to speak in a very basic way, thinking especially about the few community folks who had come to hear me. Weeks later, Kum-Kum Sangari, a fellow participant who shared with me what was said when I was no longer present, and I engaged in quite rigorous critical dialogue about the way my presentation had been perceived primarily by privileged white female academics. She was concerned that I not mask my knowledge of theory, that I not appear anti-intellectual. Her critique compelled me to articulate concerns that I am often silent about with colleagues. I spoke about class allegiance and revolutionary commitments, explaining that it was disturbing to me that intellectual radicals who speak about transforming society, ending the domination of race, sex, class, cannot break with behavior patterns that reinforce and perpetuate domination, or continue to use as their sole reference point how we might be or are perceived by those who dominate, whether or not we gain their acceptance and approval.

12   This is a primary contradiction which raises the issue of whether or not the academic setting is a place where one can be truly radical or subversive. Concurrently, the use of a language and style of presentation that alienates most folks who are not also academically trained reinforces the notion that the academic world is separate from real life, that everyday world where we constantly adjust

our language and behavior to meet diverse needs. The academic setting is separate only when we work to make it so. It is a false dichotomy which suggests that academics and/or intellectuals can only speak to one another, that we cannot hope to speak with the masses. What is true is that we make choices, that we choose our audiences, that we choose voices to hear and voices to silence. If I do not speak in a language that can be understood, then there is little chance for dialogue. This issue of language and behavior is a central contradiction all radical intellectuals, particularly those who are members of oppressed groups, must continually confront and work to resolve. One of the clear and present dangers that exists when we move outside our class of origin, our collective ethnic experience, and enter hierarchical institutions which daily reinforce domination by race, sex, and class, is that we gradually assume a mindset similar to those who dominate and oppress, that we lose critical consciousness because it is not reinforced or affirmed by the environment. We must be ever vigilant. It is important that we know who we are speaking to, who we most want to hear us, who we most long to move, motivate, and touch with our words.

When I first came to New Haven to teach at Yale, I was truly surprised by   13
the marked class divisions between black folks—students and professors—who identify with Yale and those black folks who work at Yale or in surrounding communities. Style of dress and self-presentation are most often the central markers of one's position. I soon learned that the black folks who spoke on the street were likely to be part of the black community and those who carefully shifted their glance were likely to be associated with Yale. Walking with a black female colleague one day, I spoke to practically every black person in sight (a gesture which reflects my upbringing), an action which disturbed my companion. Since I addressed black folk who were clearly not associated with Yale, she wanted to know whether or not I knew them. That was funny to me. "Of course not," I answered. Yet when I thought about it seriously, I realized that in a deep way, I knew them for they, and not my companion or most of my colleagues at Yale, resemble my family. Later that year, in a black women's support group I started for undergraduates, students from poor backgrounds spoke about the shame they sometimes feel when faced with the reality of their connection to working-class and poor black people. One student confessed that her father is a street person, addicted to drugs, someone who begs from passersby. She, like other Yale students, turns away from street people often, sometimes showing anger or contempt; she hasn't wanted anyone to know that she was related to this kind of person. She struggles with this, wanting to find a way to acknowledge and affirm this reality, to claim this connection. The group asked me and one another what we do to remain connected, to honor the bonds we have with working-class and poor people even as our class experience alters.

Maintaining connections with family and community across class bound-   14
aries demands more than just summary recall of where one's roots are, where one comes from. It requires knowing, naming, and being ever-mindful of those aspects of one's past that have enabled and do enable one's self-development in the present, that sustain and support, that enrich. One must also honestly confront barriers that do exist, aspects of that past that do diminish. My parents'

ambivalence about my love for reading led to intense conflict. They (especially my mother) would work to ensure that I had access to books, but would threaten to burn the books or throw them away if I did not conform to other expectations. Or they would insist that reading too much would drive me insane. Their ambivalence nurtured in me a like uncertainty about the value and significance of intellectual endeavor which took years for me to unlearn. While this aspect of our class reality was one that wounded and diminished, their vigilant insistence that being smart did not make me a "better" or "superior" person (which often got on my nerves because I think I wanted to have that sense that it did indeed set me apart, make me better) made a profound impression. From them I learned to value and respect various skills and talents folk might have, not just to value people who read books and talk about ideas. They and my grandparents might say about somebody, "Now he don't read nor write a lick, but he can tell a story," or as my grandmother would say, "call out the hell in words."

15   Empty romanticization of poor or working-class backgrounds undermines the possibility of true connection. Such connection is based on understanding difference in experience and perspective and working to mediate and negotiate these terrains. Language is a crucial issue for folk whose movement outside the boundaries of poor and working-class backgrounds changes the nature and direction of their speech. Coming to Stanford with my own version of a Kentucky accent, which I think of always as a strong sound quite different from Tennessee or Georgia speech, I learned to speak differently while maintaining the speech of my region, the sound of my family and community. This was of course much easier to keep up when I returned home to stay often. In recent years, I have endeavored to use various speaking styles in the classroom as a teacher and find it disconcerts those who feel that the use of a particular patois excludes them as listeners, even if there is translation into the usual, acceptable mode of speech. Learning to listen to different voices, hearing different speech challenges the notion that we must all assimilate—share a single, similar talk—in educational institutions. Language reflects the culture from which we emerge. To deny ourselves daily use of speech patterns that are common and familiar, that embody the unique and distinctive aspect of our self is one of the ways we become estranged and alienated from our past. It is important for us to have as many languages on hand as we can know or learn. It is important for those of us who are black, who speak in particular patois as well as standard English to express ourselves in both ways.

16   Often I tell students from poor and working-class backgrounds that if you believe what you have learned and are learning in schools and universities separates you from your past, this is precisely what will happen. It is important to stand firm in the conviction that nothing can truly separate us from our pasts when we nurture and cherish that connection. An important strategy for maintaining contact is ongoing acknowledgement of the primacy of one's past, of one's background, affirming the reality that such bonds are not severed automatically solely because one enters a new environment or moves toward a different class experience.

Again, I do not wish to romanticize this effort, to dismiss the reality of con- 17
flict and contradiction. During my time at Stanford, I did go through a period of
more than a year when I did not return home. That period was one where I felt
that it was simply too difficult to mesh my profoundly disparate realities. Critical
reflection about the choice I was making, particularly about why I felt a choice had
to be made, pulled me through this difficult time. Luckily I recognized that the insistence on choosing between the world of family and community and the new
world of privileged white people and privileged ways of knowing was imposed
upon me by the outside. It is as though a mythical contract had been signed somewhere which demanded of us black folks that once we entered these spheres we
would immediately give up all vestiges of our underprivileged past. It was my responsibility to formulate a way of being that would allow me to participate fully
in my new environment while integrating and maintaining aspects of the old.

One of the most tragic manifestations of the pressure black people feel to as- 18
similate is expressed in the internalization of racist perspectives. I was shocked
and saddened when I first heard black professors at Stanford downgrade and express contempt for black students, expecting us to do poorly, refusing to establish nurturing bonds. At every university I have attended as a student or worked
at as a teacher, I have heard similar attitudes expressed with little or no understanding of factors that might prevent brilliant black students from performing
to their full capability. Within universities, there are few educational and social
spaces where students who wish to affirm positive ties to ethnicity—to blackness,
to working-class backgrounds—can receive affirmation and support. Ideologi-
cally, the message is clear—assimilation is the way to gain acceptance and approval from those in power.

Many white people enthusiastically supported Richard Rodriguez's vehe- 19
ment contention in his autobiography, *Hunger of Memory*, that attempts to maintain ties with his Chicano background impeded his progress, that he had to
sever ties with community and kin to succeed at Stanford and in the larger
world, that family language, in his case Spanish, had to be made secondary or
discarded. If the terms of success as defined by the standards of ruling groups
within white-supremacist, capitalist patriarchy are the only standards that exist,
then assimilation is indeed necessary. But they are not. Even in the face of powerful structures of domination, it remains possible for each of us, especially those
of us who are members of oppressed and/or exploited groups as well as those
radical visionaries who may have race, class, and sex privilege, to define and determine alternative standards, to decide on the nature and extent of compromise.
Standards by which one's success is measured, whether student or professor, are
quite different for those of us who wish to resist reinforcing the domination of
race, sex, and class, who work to maintain and strengthen our ties with the oppressed, with those who lack material privilege, with our families who are poor
and working-class.

When I wrote my first book, *Ain't I A Woman: black women and feminism*, the 20
issue of class and its relationship to who one's reading audience might be came
up for me around my decision not to use footnotes, for which I have been sharply
criticized. I told people that my concern was that footnotes set class boundaries

for readers, determining who a book is for. I was shocked that many academic folks scoffed at this idea. I shared that I went into working-class black communities as well as talked with family and friends to survey whether or not they ever read books with footnotes and found that they did not. A few did not know what they were, but most folks saw them as indicating that a book was for college-educated people. These responses influenced my decision. When some of my more radical, college-educated friends freaked out about the absence of footnotes, I seriously questioned how we could ever imagine revolutionary transformation of society if such a small shift in direction could be viewed as threatening. Of course, many folks warned that the absence of footnotes would make the work less credible in academic circles. This information also highlighted the way in which class informs our choices. Certainly I did feel that choosing to use simple language, absence of footnotes, etc. would mean I was jeopardizing the possibility of being taken seriously in academic circles but then this was a political matter and a political decision. It utterly delights me that this has proven not to be the case and that the book is read by many academics as well as by people who are not college-educated.

21   Always our first response when we are motivated to conform or compromise within structures that reinforce domination must be to engage in critical reflection. Only by challenging ourselves to push against oppressive boundaries do we make the radical alternative possible, expanding the realm and scope of critical inquiry. Unless we share radical strategies, ways of rethinking and revisioning with students, with kin and community, with a larger audience, we risk perpetuating the stereotype that we succeed because we are the exception, different from the rest of our people. Since I left home and entered college, I am often asked, usually by white people, if my sisters and brothers are also high achievers. At the root of this question is the longing for reinforcement of the belief in "the exception" which enables race, sex, and class biases to remain intact. I am careful to separate what it means to be exceptional from a notion of "the exception."

22   Frequently I hear smart black folks, from poor and working-class backgrounds, stressing their frustration that at times family and community do not recognize that they are exceptional. Absence of positive affirmation clearly diminishes the longing to excel in academic endeavors. Yet it is important to distinguish between the absence of basic positive affirmation and the longing for continued reinforcement that we are special. Usually liberal white folks will willingly offer continual reinforcement of us as exceptions—as special. This can be both patronizing and very seductive. Since we often work in situations where we are isolated from other black folks, we can easily begin to feel that encouragement from white people is the primary or only source of support and recognition. Given the internalization of racism, it is easy to view this support as more validating and legitimizing than similar support from black people. Still, nothing takes the place of being valued and appreciated by one's own, by one's family and community. We share a mutual and reciprocal responsibility for affirming one another's successes. Sometimes we have to talk to our folks about the fact that we need their ongoing support and affirmation, that it is unique and special to us. In some cases we may never receive desired recognition and ac-

knowledgement of specific achievements from kin. Rather than seeing this as a basis for estrangement, for severing connection, it is useful to explore other sources of nourishment and support.

I do not know that my mother's mother ever acknowledged my college ed- 23 ucation except to ask me once, "How can you live so far away from your people?" Yet she gave me sources of affirmation and nourishment, sharing the legacy of her quilt-making, of family history, of her incredible way with words. Recently, when our father retired after more than thirty years of work as a janitor, I wanted to pay tribute to this experience, to identify links between his work and my own as writer and teacher. Reflecting on our family past, I recalled ways he had been an impressive example of diligence and hard work, approaching tasks with a seriousness of concentration I work to mirror and develop, with a discipline I struggle to maintain. Sharing these thoughts with him keeps us connected, nurtures our respect for each other, maintaining a space, however large or small, where we can talk.

Open, honest communication is the most important way we maintain rela- 24 tionships with kin and community as our class experience and backgrounds change. It is as vital as the sharing of resources. Often financial assistance is given in circumstances where there is no meaningful contact. However helpful, this can also be an expression of estrangement and alienation. Communication between black folks from various experiences of material privilege was much easier when we were all in segregated communities sharing common experiences in relation to social institutions. Without this grounding, we must work to maintain ties, connection. We must assume greater responsibility for making and maintaining contact, connections that can shape our intellectual visions and inform our radical commitments.

The most powerful resource any of us can have as we study and teach in uni- 25 versity settings is full understanding and appreciation of the richness, beauty, and primacy of our familial and community backgrounds. Maintaining awareness of class differences, nurturing ties with the poor and working-class people who are our most intimate kin, our comrades in struggle, transforms and enriches our intellectual experience. Education as the practice of freedom becomes not a force which fragments or separates, but one that brings us closer, expanding our definitions of home and community.

● *Thinking Critically About "keeping close to home: class and education"*

RESPONDING AS A READER

1. What differing images does hooks create of herself in this essay? Are some more likable or approachable than others? At what points did you respond positively or sympathetically to the self being described? At what points, if any, did you respond negatively or with resistance? How does she anticipate and attempt to forestall the resistance of readers positioned differently from herself in terms of race and class?

2. Who is her intended audience or audiences? What evidence can you point to in the text to support your answer? Do you feel part of that audience? Why or why not?

3. What do you think was the author's purpose(s) in writing this essay? What new perspective does she want readers to come away with? Did you come away with the new perspective you think she intended? Why or why not?

RESPONDING AS A WRITER

1. Reread the first three paragraphs of this essay, where hooks describes her attempt to communicate with her mother across the generation gap. What similar experiences have you had in trying to communicate with parents or other older relatives across the generation gap? Briefly describe one of these experiences.

2. In paragraph 12, hooks writes, "If I do not speak in a language that can be understood, then there is little chance for dialogue." To what extent do you think she is successful in speaking in a language that you, as a college student, can understand? To what extent does she persuade you that she is interested in establishing a dialogue with you about intersections of race, class, and education? Write out your answer to these questions, citing particular passages to support your answer.

3. To identify the ideology revealed in this essay, make a two-column list of the binaries you find. Put the words, concepts, or ideas that hooks values in the left column; place the words, concepts, or ideas that she doesn't value in the right column. Remember that some of the nonvalued or even the valued terms may only be implied and not stated directly. After you have created this list, write a paragraph discussing hooks's ideology as revealed in this text. (See Chapter 5 for examples of ideological mapping.)

David Updike

A Word with the Boy

David Updike (b. 1957) is the author of several children's books—*A Winter's Journey* (1985), *An Autumn Tale* (1988), and *Out on the Marsh* (1989). He teaches English at Roxbury Community College in Boston, Massachusetts. He is also coauthor of a volume of poems *A Helpful Alphabet of Family Objects: Poems* (1998) with his father, American author John Updike. This essay, "A Word with the Boy," was published in the Spring 2000 issue of *Doubletake*, a magazine about photography, the arts, and culture. Emphasizing the connections among the arts, *Doubletake* regularly includes photo essays as well as literary essays, "lookmarks" (paintings and other visual arts) as well as "bookmarks" (poetry and fiction).

● *For Your Reading Log*

1. What meanings do you associate with the word "doubletake"? Based on the brief description of this publication, speculate about who the readers of this magazine might be. That is, speculate about their values, interests, educational backgrounds, and income levels.
2. As you read through this essay, mark passages that you find particularly vivid or moving.

———————   ●   ———————

My son and I arrived in London in the morning, after an all-night flight from America. My wife, Wambui, met us at the airport and led us through the throngs of summer travelers to the underground, which would take us into the city, to the dormitory room where she had been staying. "You're dressed alike," she said, smiling, and it was true. We were both wearing khaki pants and button-down cotton shirts. At the last minute back at the house, as I made a final check of our luggage, Wesley had run upstairs to change his shirt to one like mine. He had been happy all day in anticipation of the journey, of seeing his mother after nearly a month apart.

On the train ride in from Heathrow he and I kept falling asleep, nodding off and blinking awake as the early-morning sunlight flashed through the car. Across the aisle a young woman was watching us, vaguely smiling as she worked out the simple genetic equation: light-skinned man + brown woman = light brown boy. But Wesley, as we are often told, looks more like me than like his mother. His face is shaped like mine, and his hair is straight, not curly. He looks more Indian or Latino than African. He is a handsome boy, and a sensitive one. We have been assured he will be a "heartbreaker" when he gets older, but it is his own heart I worry about—the hurts he may suffer at the hands of precocious girls.

Even now, at age eight, he spends hours by the stereo at home, listening to mellifluous love songs from the wounded hearts of teenage singers.

3   The day before, we had had to take three different subway trains and then a shuttle bus to the airport terminal. Wesley had insisted on carrying his own bags—his blue knapsack on his back, the sleeping bag I had bought him for his birthday hoisted at his side. He slept for much of the flight, his head resting on my shoulder as we drifted along through the strange intercontinental twilight; an edge of summer brightness never quite left the curve of the northern horizon. I had been taking care of Wesley by myself for the month, while Wambui attended classes on postcolonial literature at a summer institute in London, and our time together had been easier than I had expected. Wesley had surprised me by seldom mentioning his mother, but he had hugged me more than usual. Sometimes when walking down the street, if no one was around to see, he had held my hand, letting go only if someone his own age appeared. I noticed that he rarely cries anymore, and when he does, it is usually for reasons of physical rather than emotional pain; he squeezes back the tears as soon as he is able.

4   Yet on our subway ride into London it was Wambui's shoulder he slept on, not mine, and I suspected that it would be to her again that he would gravitate in moments of need, leaving me to return to the more recessed roles of fatherhood.

5   We changed trains once, at Green Park, lugged our bags up and down a maze of stairways and escalators, and emerged into the daylight. Soon we were in Wambui's dormitory room, where we shed our clothes. I climbed in under the bed covers while Wesley slid into his sleeping bag, and we both immediately fell into a deep, jet-lagged sleep.

6   I had lived in London once, for a year, when I turned twelve, and part of my hope for this visit was to show Wesley something of my own childhood haunts—the house where my family had lived; the vast, green reaches of Regents Park; the paths I followed on my way to school. I was only eleven when we arrived, but I quickly learned how to catch the bus and ride it by myself into central London, where I would wander through the cold and the crowds of Oxford Street. I would spend hours drifting through department stores, and then, toward evening, I would buy a bag of hot chestnuts from a grizzled man with blackened fingers and smuggle it up to the top of the bus, warming my hands on the ride home. It was 1968. The Vietnam War was in full swing, and anti-American sentiment was palpable, even to a boy my age. I felt unpopular on those streets, and I was always reluctant to open my mouth and reveal my nationality. But I fell in love with soccer on the open fields of Regents Park, and then with a pretty freckled girl from Texas in the American school that I attended with my brother and two sisters.

7   Ever since, my visits to London have given rise to nostalgia and a vague sense of entitlement, like that of an honorary citizen. Compared to American cities, with our hot summer streets and our guns and our simmering history of violence and racial tensions, London has always seemed a safe, benign place, where even the occasional horrific crime can take on a certain quaintness. But I

have recently noticed that the English television shows aired here now have a darker edge—creepy urban hoodlums and corrupt policemen converging in gritty "estates" that are anything but quaint. And often in these programs run the undercurrents of racial disharmony and cultural conflict that we Americans have seemed to claim as our own special province.

When I wake, Wesley is already up, nattering happily around the room, and 8 Wambui is preparing to go out to an afternoon seminar. Wesley and I will be on our own again.

We step outside and see that the morning sun has given way to low gray 9 clouds. The sidewalks are mottled from a rain that must have fallen while we slept. Everything is busier than I remember. The red buses of my childhood have been plastered with garish billboards, and some of the taxis have been painted improbable shades of purple and red. The cars don't stop, or slow, for pedestrians, and I hold Wesley's arm tightly as we try to get across the street. Half the people on the sidewalks, it seems, are talking into tiny portable telephones— "mobiles," they call them here.

As we drift down Tottenham Court Road, I try to remember what it is famous 10 for. The insides of phone booths are covered with pictures of nearly naked women and numbers to call. We pause in front of a store window featuring hundreds of Swiss Army knives, all opened to reveal their manifold functions. "How much do they cost?" Wesley asks, but I plead ignorance and prod us farther along. Soon there is an arcade full of bleeping, blaring machines and small boys steering tumbling, skidding race cars across video screens. This, too, I resist, and we wander down as far as a handsome "American" church that I vaguely remember from a previous visit, and then we head back. At the window display of knives, the gleaming blades draw our attention again, and we stand gazing at them for a minute.

"Let's go," I say then, and turn, and that's when I notice two hatted men 11 walking slowly toward us: policemen of some sort, though they're not bobbies with the jolly, comical hats. They are wearing hats of a more modern style that I recognize from English detective shows. I keep expecting the two men to veer off toward some more worthy target, but they don't; they keep stepping inexorably toward us, and then they stop and one of them is talking to us in not unkindly tones—something about how they noticed us "walking about." He asks where we are from and where we are staying, and, finally, what my relationship is to "the boy." He noticed that we are "different colors," he says.

"I'm his father," I say. I point around the corner toward the dorm where we 12 are staying, but, taken aback and suddenly nervous, I can't remember the name of the building. I explain that we are here to visit Wesley's mother—my wife— who has been studying at a six-week institute at the university, and add, "We just arrived this morning."

He explains that there are a lot of runaway boys in the neighborhood, "beg- 13 ging and the like," and sometimes they fall in with the wrong men. Would I mind if they had a word with the boy? "Separately," he says, nodding to the side.

I don't have the presence of mind to refuse, to say "Yes, I do mind." The 14 other policeman takes Wesley a few feet away, and the one who has been doing the talking asks me a few questions—what's my first name, what street do we live on back in the States. As I answer I can hear the other one asking Wesley the same questions, and I can make out Wesley's quiet, resolute answers. And then, in a moment, it is all over: one of them says "Thank you," and they turn and walk away, leaving us in an eerie, unsettling silence, uncertain of what has just happened.

15   "Come on," I say to Wesley, wanting to get away from this street, which now seems unclean. "Let's go over to that park we saw." But Wesley does not answer, and we walk without talking. I don't want to speak again until I can figure out what he has made of it all, or what I have made of it myself. I wonder how much of it he has picked up on—the part about being "different colors," for example. Couldn't they see that we are dressed alike, that we look alike—and that we are both American? The whole thing evolved so quietly, so peaceably, that I wasn't prepared to put a stop to it, to refuse to have Wesley separated from me, taken aside for questioning.

16   We walk a few more blocks and come upon a small cement soccer field. "I want to go home," Wesley says at last. There is a sternness in his voice that I am not familiar with.

17   "Back to the dorm?" I ask.

18   "No. Back to America. I don't like it here."

19   "The policemen, you mean?"

20   "Exactly."

21   "Ah, don't worry about them," I say.

22   We walk some more and find another park, this one with grass and a few people on their lunch hours, eating and talking. We sit on a small hill, and I find a white feather on the grass which has, I discover, a magical property: when dropped from a certain height, it turns sideways against the air and helicopters to the ground like a maple seed.

23   "Hey, let me see that," Wesley says, brightening. He plays with the feather for a while, throwing it up in the air and watching it spin down, trying to catch it before it lands. But across the park he notices two men, Indians in turbans, who seem to be watching us intently. "Why are those two men staring at us?" he asks.

24   "They like watching us play," I say, though unconvinced. He plays some more with the feather, and I hope it will rid us of the aftertaste of our encounter and re-store his good humor. We decide to keep the feather, for good luck, but on our way out of the park and back to the empty room, Wesley's gloom descends again.

25   "I want to go home," he repeats.

26   "Why?"

27   "I don't like it here. People aren't nice."

28   "Wesley, you can't let two silly policemen ruin your whole day. They're just trying to protect—" But I can't finish the sentence. Protect whom? Boys from their own fathers? "There are a lot of runaway boys around here," I start, aping the policeman. But what about my son looks like a runaway? At the back of my mind is the suspicion that I, too, am culpable—that I should have shown a little out-rage or defiance, should have made the policemen talk to us together, father and

son, indivisible. But it was such a gentle act of violence (yes, that is the right word) that I didn't know what was happening until it was over. "They're just trying to protect children," people will explain to me and Wambui later, an explanation that we will try to pass on to Wesley. But this is of no use now.

"I want to go home," he says again as we enter the dorm room, and our month   29 alone together seems like ancient history. He collapses onto the bed, and I start to unpack my bag. He's exhausted from our night of flying, that's all; after a little nap he'll be himself again. I hang my clothes in the closet and unpack his into two drawers beneath the bed. I put our bags in the closet and look over to see if he has fallen asleep. He is still in his rumpled travel clothes, and he has turned his face away from me and pulled the collar of his shirt over his eyes—to block out the light, I'd like to think. I sit down on the bed beside him and put my hand on his back. I can tell that he is not asleep. He has pulled his shirt up to hide his tears.

"What's the matter?" I ask, panicking now. "What is it?" I rub his small,   30 strong back, but he does not—or cannot—answer: there are no words for what the matter is, for what has hurt him, and I, too, give up on words, on explanation. I lie down on the bed beside him, drape my arm around him, and he turns and pulls me fiercely to him. And then, for the first time in our summer month together, he cries in earnest, his hurt released in short, breathless sobs, tears flowing freely now as he weeps, at last, in my arms.

● *Thinking Critically About "A Word with the Boy"*

RESPONDING AS A READER

1. In paragraphs 6 and 7 Updike recalls time he spent in London as a child. How do these paragraphs contribute to the essay? What does this memory have to do with the events that follow?

2. Reread paragraphs 8 through 10 slowly, noting the details as Updike and his son set out on their walk. What kind of mood do these details create for you? How does this mood affect your response to the encounter with the police that follows in paragraphs 11 through 14? How would you describe your reaction to the description of the encounter itself?

3. Now that you have read the story, think of the various meanings the title might have. Try to think of other possible titles that express for you the central point of the essay.

RESPONDING AS A WRITER

1. This essay turns on several types of irony—an ordinary day proves extraordinary, the encounter is a "gentle act of violence," the actions of the police are motivated by their wish to "protect children." Choose one of these ironies or another irony you find in the essay and briefly discuss how it works to communicate the essay's ideas or emotional content.

2. The incident itself is told from the father's perspective, but we also get hints of the boy's view of the event as well as the police's. Write a short

paragraph in which you narrate the event from the point of view of either Wesley or the police officers.

3. At several different points, even as early as paragraph 14, Updike considers how he might have acted differently and tries to make sense of what has happened, to assess his responsibility for allowing it to happen, and to find words to comfort his son. What do you make of the event? Who is responsible? Why do you think the father "give[s] up on words, on explanations" (par. 30)? What explanations can you offer?

Heidi Steenberg (Student)

Reflection as Knowledge

Heidi Steenberg (b. 1974) is a recent graduate of Marquette University, where she was a Writing-Intensive English major. Currently, she works as an agent and account executive for a Milwaukee insurance company. In the future, she hopes to return to school to earn a master's degree and a Ph.D. in English. "Reflection as Knowledge," which was written for a writing workshop she took in her junior year, reflects both on the meaning of her volunteer experience at Casa Maria, a homeless shelter for women and children in Milwaukee, Wisconsin, and on the act of writing about this experience.

• *For Your Reading Log*

1. Have you ever been involved in either a volunteer or service learning project where you encountered people whose experience was quite different from your own due to age, illness, ableness, or economic circumstance? If so, take a few minutes and jot down how it felt to encounter people different from yourself. What did you learn about yourself from this encounter? If not, try to imagine your concerns and expectations upon entering a shelter for homeless people, a home for the elderly, or some other facility as a volunteer.

2. Think of a time when you found it difficult to communicate an important experience to others. Take ten minutes to freewrite about this experience. What caused this difficulty? What ultimately happened? Did the experience remain a private one, unarticulated to others, or did you eventually find the words or perhaps a particularly receptive person to whom you could explain the experience? What do you see as the advantages and disadvantages of trying to communicate important experiences to others?

——————— • ———————

Last winter break I went to Casa Maria, which is a homeless shelter for women 1
and children here in Milwaukee. I was on a volunteer program through Marquette University called the Marquette Action Program (MAP) with four other women. The purpose of the MAP trip is to immerse students in areas of the country that need service, such as building houses for Habitat for Humanity in Georgia, helping immigrants in Texas, or in my case, helping the homeless in the inner city. Therefore, I lived at Casa Maria, I ate there, and I worked there for an entire week. It was this strange, wonderful, fascinating, crazy, heart-wrenching week. When I returned back to school, I was in a complete daze. I was overcome with emotions and thoughts about my experience. I was exhausted both physically and mentally. I couldn't unpack my bag or prepare for my classes that

started the next day. I listened to my friends tell me about their Christmas vacations, the brand new Trek bicycle, grandmother's famous homemade stuffing, and sitting on the couch in front of the television every day all day. They asked me how my week was at Casa Maria. I could not answer. I could not find the words or the energy to express what had happened to me there, how I had changed, and why it was so special. So I was silent.

2   As I began attending classes again, I was still thinking about my service trip. I kept remembering everything that I had seen and done that week. I could not stop thinking about what it was like to hand out bread at the welfare office or to know, really know, become friends with, a family who fled from an abusive father in Missouri with only a few of their most treasured possessions. The boy clings to his Sony Walkman.

3   Thoughts. Thoughts of the children without toothbrushes and coats. Thoughts of the mothers without homes, without food, without jobs, without money. Thoughts of the innocent faces of children dressed in clothes that were donated that day, trying to do math problems without notebooks or pencils. Thoughts of people so unlike me . . . and so like me. I could not stop thinking of Casa Maria. I could concentrate on little else. I needed to find a way to tell the story, to tell what happened to the homeless people, to tell what happened to me. I had already discovered that I could not communicate these thoughts to my friends in conversations. They were just too powerful, too emotional. So I wrote, recording my thoughts in my journal and writing about the experience for class assignments.

4   For Advanced Composition, I wrote an essay that I entitled "Breaking Down the Walls." The assignment was very broad, calling for a reflective essay. I could not even think of writing about anything but my service trip. It was as though I had to write about my experiences at Casa Maria before I could write any other words. Until I could understand this trip, I could not write another essay. In order to make sense of the experience, I needed to articulate and make sense of it in the framework of a formed essay. The journal entries I wrote while I was at Casa Maria were full of disbelief and confusion. For example, "Wow, Bambie found a winter coat today." This selection from my journal is descriptive, it tells something. However, it does not frame the experience. It does not tell why it was so special that Bambie received a coat, that his family's home was destroyed and all their possessions stolen by Southside gang members.

5   I wrote and I reflected. I reflected and I wrote. I was not worried about making any sense at first. I wrote about everything in one entire night. I closed my eyes and allowed myself to concentrate only on the service trip. I thought about everything that happened that week at Casa Maria. I began to resee things again and again, and I wrote about the suffering, wondering, yet still cheerful children staying at the shelter. Here is an excerpt from the final draft of my essay:

> A little boy tells me about his father's strong hands, under which the boy and his mother would suffer each day. A little girl explains to me, as if it were a natural occurrence in everyone's life, that she hears gunfire outside of her apartment each night as she plays with her brothers and sisters. A boy of nearly fourteen tells me he has no friends at school because, in order to have friends, he would

have to join a gang. Another child begs me to read her a story every time I walk into the room. Her mother never reads to her because, I learn from the child, her mother cannot read.

The confusion about my service at Casa Maria finally began to disappear. 6 The trip suddenly became real again. Writing became my means of speaking. It opened up a new understanding, knowledge of what I had discovered through my service. The random reflections began to take shape and form, and suddenly my word processor had a five page essay. I found a million different ideas in my reflection and writing about Casa Maria, yet I kept coming back to how it related to my experiences at Marquette, why I was unable to tell my friends about one of the most thought-provoking weeks of my life. I reflected on this central question and suddenly it became a title, "Breaking Down the Wall." Suddenly I had a self-discovery, a world-discovery, and a reflective essay that showed me what I had been wanting to say, needing to say, since the day I came back from my service trip to a homeless shelter:

> When I return to Marquette and walk to and from classes, I will see a community of people walking with me through the streets. I will see the Marquette students, and I will see the people beyond them, waiting at bus stops, doing laundry at the Laundromat, eating at Dairy Queen, and sipping coffee at Stone Creek Coffee Shop. . . . As I pull away from Casa Maria, I am not quite sure where this trip has taken me. I see the children and the mothers cry and, at the same time, I feel the warm trickle of my own tears as I leave Casa Maria only a week after I arrive. The children run after the car as I head back the few blocks, around the shattered remains of the wall, to the Marquette community where I have another home. In not even a few minutes, I arrive at my destination. It feels strange now, as I stare out the window of my apartment. It seems I can see so much farther . . . now that the walls have been torn down.

My journals had given wonderful detail, showing the chaos of the trip, but only through writing a complete essay was I able to answer the essential questions. Who really were the people at Casa Maria, why had the experience changed me, how could I show others the value in the trip?

I took the first draft of my paper, which I had written entirely in one night, into 7 the writing group of my Advanced Composition class. It was extremely difficult to make this move, to take criticism, and even praise, from a group of three complete strangers about a piece of writing that was so highly personal. The members of the writing group agreed on the places in my essay that were weak, which were the parts of the essay where I told and did not show. For example, I said that the homeless mothers in the shelter made me laugh. I know inside how the women made me laugh, by giving me advice about my relationships and making fun of me for the awful food I cooked, but I did not articulate these things in the essay. So in the revision I showed more. I wrote, "Laughter permeates the house during these late night talks about the day's events. I do not think I will ever hear the end of the casserole I accidentally burned to a crisp for dinner that night, or how ridiculously funny the black hair extensions would look in my blonde hair."

8   Because the essay was so personal, I was somewhat hesitant to change any of it. All the words, sentences, and paragraphs meant so much to me. But I soon realized that this essay was not part of the journal I kept during my stay at Casa. I had already done that, and the journal would always be mine. However, this was an essay for class. I felt the need now to show the importance of my experience to others. I had to show the audience why they should care. I framed the essay according to the trip's chronology—leaving Marquette to begin the experience, describing what happened during the week, and ending with what happened to me as I left Casa Maria. In the first draft of the essay, I would sometimes tell things later that actually happened earlier than others, which is okay as long as the chronology doesn't confuse readers. I knew the experience at Casa so well, but my audience did not. I needed to be clearer for them. I really didn't want to do this at first. It was my essay after all. But I found that as I clarified the organization of the paper, I also clarified the experience at Casa Maria. Confusing sentences, I learned, show confusing ideas and feelings. So I fixed the sentences, and the essay became even more mine, and more importantly, it became an essay for other people as well.

9   By writing an essay about the service I had done at Casa Maria, I found a way to subdue the confusion of this exhausting, yet gratifying week, into some kind of coherence. I used the form of a reflective essay for self-discovery, for sharing information about the neighborhoods beyond a given campus, and for perhaps even convincing others to become active in helping their own communities. I saw beyond the invisible barriers between my campus "home" and the shelter a few blocks away. I wanted to share that with others, so I wrote an essay that I shared with an Advanced Composition writing group, a class magazine, a writing contest, and later at a roundtable discussion attended by professors from other colleges. Now, in reflecting on both the experience itself and the experience of writing about my time at Casa Maria, I think I understand my experience even better, though I still get a little nervous sharing such personal reflections with others. Recording my private thoughts in a journal and writing a reflective essay for others to read helped me clarify my thoughts and feelings about my time at Casa Maria. In both cases, I used reflection as a means to knowledge, but every time I talk or write about the service trip again, I continue to learn new things. I say to you "Here, look what I did on my service trip to Casa Maria" . . . but sometimes I still am not sure what it is I have actually done.

• *Thinking Critically About "Reflection as Knowledge"*

RESPONDING AS A READER

1. In the first few paragraphs of this essay, Steenberg tries to re-create her state of mind and feelings after she returned to campus after a week at Casa Maria. How successful is she in doing this? Which sentences or passages are most effective in helping you, as a reader, identify with her thoughts and feelings?

2. Does the audience for this essay seem to be primarily the writer herself, her readers, or both? What assumptions does she make about her audience's ability to comprehend her experience? Explain your answers by referring to particular passages.
3. How would you describe Steenberg's tone and style in this essay? What kind of an image of the writer is created through these stylistic choices? How do you respond to this image?

RESPONDING AS A WRITER

1. Revisit your reading log entries and choose one of the two experiences about which you wrote. How do Steenberg's experiences compare to the experiences you reflected upon in your reading log entry? Did Steenberg's essay make you see your own experience in any new way?
2. If you were a member of a peer group reading and responding to this essay, what would you point out as its greatest strengths and weaknesses? What questions, if any, do you have after reading the essay? What suggestions for revision would you make to this writer?
3. There have been various proposals that young people be required to engage in two years of public or volunteer service just as young people in the past had to fulfill their civic obligation through military service. Would you support or be opposed to such a proposal? Why or why not? Write a letter to the editor in which you argue for or against this proposal. You may or may not wish to use evidence from Steenberg's essay to support your position.

Writing to Express and Reflect

The texts in this section communicate the writers' reflections on various kinds of experiences. In most cases, the writers reflect on a past experience in the present to explore its meaning for themselves and others. The assignment prompts below offer several kinds of invitations for you to engage further with expressive and reflective writing: (1) by writing an essay in which you reflect on your own experience; (2) by writing an essay that looks more closely at the strategies employed by a particular writer; or (3) by writing a reflective essay that extends the conversation introduced by one of the writers.

REFLECTING ON EXPERIENCE

Think of an experience that challenged your beliefs or attitudes or that perplexed, disturbed, or produced mixed feelings in you. Write an essay about this experience in which you look back, reconsider, question, and interpret this experience from your present perspective. How has your perspective on this experience changed over time? How has this experience affected your beliefs, attitudes, or values? What new perspective do you want your readers to come away with? Like Lauren Slater and Heidi Steenberg, you may wish to use this assignment to understand an experience better or more deeply, or like bell hooks, you may wish to examine this experience for insights into larger social or cultural issues. It will be important to describe your experience with enough detail so that the reader can understand the experience's significance to you.

As you plan and revise your essay, consider carefully the ways in which you hope to change your readers' perspectives. Then make organizational and stylistic decisions to support that purpose.

EXAMINING RHETORICAL STRATEGIES

Choose one of the reflective essays in this section and offer a rhetorical analysis of it, considering this author's rhetorical choices in light of what you believe to be the author's purpose or purposes. What seems to be the author's main purpose (or purposes) in writing this reflection? What makes you say so? How is this purpose reflected in the author's choice of narrative detail, tone, and style? What do tone and style reveal about the writer's point of view? Note the oppositions or tensions that you find in the text. What do these reveal about the writer's ideology? What is the main thing you take away from this reflection? That is, to what extent is your image of the subject or issue altered or "reconstructed" by this essay?

EXTENDING THE CONVERSATION

Some of the essays in this section use personal experience as a springboard to reflect on larger social or cultural issues such as race and class, language difference, or mental illness. Undoubtedly, at least one of the essays in this chapter raises an issue about which you have some concern, experience, or knowledge. Choose a reading (or two thematically related readings), and write an essay that "talks back" to or responds directly to that reading (or readings). In a way, this assignment asks you to reflect upon your experience in reading the essay. What questions did the author's treatment of the subject raise for you? At what points were you reminded of similar experiences? At what points did you identify or think of contrary experiences? You may wish to raise issues related to the topic that were not raised by the author or other ways of looking at the topic. Do you have explanations other than what the author offered?

C H A P T E R

10

Inquiring and Exploring

exts that inquire and explore may at first seem strange to some readers. We are so used to reading for information and new knowledge that students and teachers alike can overlook exploratory writing's subtlety and power. Yet exploration is at the heart of the academic enterprise because it is only through asking good questions that we can build new knowledge.

When their purpose is to inquire and explore, writers typically take the approach of explicitly posing questions and examining multiple ways of answering them. Some emphasize the process of exploration; others emphasize the multiplicity of answers. An exploratory piece may celebrate complexity by taking the reader on a journey through varying perspectives and experiences, as the Annie Dillard essay in this chapter does. Or an exploratory piece may undertake a deliberate investigation of a more public matter, looking for explanations and solutions, and finding many, some that are partially satisfactory but none that fully satisfy. We see this approach in Robert McGuire's article on family violence, which presents a collage of personal anecdotes and journalistic interviews. Some exploratory pieces ultimately offer the reader a fairly clear picture of the author's conclusions about the topic under discussion; others do not. Sometimes an exploratory approach is dictated by the fact that a phenomenon is so new that answers are still unfolding, as in Barbara Crossette's article on the limits of cultural tolerance. Other times the writer's questioning stance in relation to the material is a means of making a point, explicitly or implicitly, or of keeping alternative approaches in balance so that one need not choose among them.

209

The exploratory form has deep roots in the very idea of an "essay," a term from the French, *essayer*, "to try." In an exploratory essay, a writer tries on perspectives, tries out ideas, and invites a reader to do the same. As the texts in this chapter show, writers' presentations of their explorations can vary considerably. Like the expressive and reflective texts in Chapter 9, exploration allows for considerable personal expression and reflection, but external subject matter rather than personal expression receives the primary emphasis. Whatever the subject matter, exploratory pieces are driven by the questions they raise. Some are answered, some are not.

If you have been trained to "underline the main idea" when reading school assignments, you may be uncomfortable with the inherent ambiguity of many exploratory texts. Many readers aren't sure how to work with the open-ended structure and explicit uncertainty of exploratory texts. Students who have been taught that "good writing" means highly structured, thesis-driven papers may distrust essays that invite them to explore a topic and end without drawing a conclusion. Yet the very purpose of such texts (and writing assignments) is to help readers discover complexity, to get beyond simple explanations and customary perspectives. Only by disrupting our usual way of viewing things can we discover new ideas. Only by considering problems and experiences from multiple angles can we appreciate the viewpoints of people who express opinions that seem outlandish to us.

The emphasis on questioning and complexity in exploratory texts has made them increasingly popular as assignments for both reading and writing in a variety of college courses, not just writing courses. Why? Because moving beyond a simple answer to wrestle with new ideas fosters intellectual development. You probably already have experience with some forms of informal, exploratory writing in journals and reading logs. You will probably encounter other forms of exploratory assignments in your college classes. Faculty across the curriculum have found that when students take courses in a discipline that is new to them they tend to stop too soon in their efforts to address subject matter questions. To help students get beyond these roadblocks, or mind blocks, instructors assign readings that refuse to articulate a conclusion, readings that come to a conclusion only by a circuitous route, or readings that demonstrate that a unitary conclusion isn't justified. Similarly, your professors may ask you to write an exploratory paper to help you articulate your current understanding of a complex subject, perhaps as an informal assignment in advance of formal study about the subject. Exploratory writings may also serve as preliminary work that leads to a major research project. Whether formal or informal, assignments that stipulate an exploratory form will give you an opportunity to develop your ability to articulate questions, assert their significance, and gather multiple perspectives.

Questions to Help You Read
Explorations Rhetorically

As you read and work with the exploratory selections in this chapter, consider carefully how the writers' exploratory stances affect your understanding of their subject. The following questions will help you with your exploration and analysis.

1. What are the central questions posed in the piece, and what prompts the author to pose them? What makes them problematic? Why are they difficult to answer? What conflicts of evidence, values, or beliefs are involved?
2. On what basis does the author assert the significance of the question(s) that the text will explore? Did you need to be persuaded of the significance of the issue? Do you agree with that significance by the end of the essay?
3. Where does the author turn for answers? What kinds of authority and reasoning connect the answers with the author's question(s)? Do you find those connections credible?
4. How does the text engage you? What role does it construct for you as reader? What does the author assume about the audience's knowledge, beliefs, and values? Where do you find yourself doubting the author or having trouble following the train of thought?
5. How do questions change as the piece develops? Does the initial question, for example, develop into narrower, more specific subquestions? Does it build into broader, more general overarching questions? What organizational patterns are apparent in the search for answers (such as chronology or division into parallel parts)?
6. As the piece closes, to what extent does the *author* seem to consider the answers he or she has found to be satisfactory? From *your* point of view, which answers are more and less satisfactory?
7. What ambiguities remain? Where/when might additional views and more satisfactory answers be found?
8. What is your sense of how the author wanted to change your view of the questions and/or phenomena explored? To what extent was the author successful? Perhaps the subject is something that you'd never thought about before. Where do you predict your thinking about it might go from here?

Annie Dillard

Singing with the Fundamentalists

Annie Dillard (b. 1945), one of America's most popular nonfiction writers, is known particularly for her meditative observations of nature. Much of her work has spiritual dimensions. Her first nonfiction book, *Pilgrim at Tinker Creek* (1974), was awarded a Pulitzer Prize. This essay, first published in the *Yale Review* in 1985, is rooted in her experiences while a scholar-in-residence at Western Washington University in Bellingham, Washington.

•   *For Your Reading Log*

1. What images does the term *religious fundamentalism* bring to your mind? Before you start reading, freewrite for about five minutes about the sources of those images and what they lead you to predict about the content of this essay.
2. As you read, notice the effect that the extra white space between certain paragraphs has on your experience of the essay (for example, before paragraph 16 and after paragraph 17).

———————   •   ———————

1   It is early spring. I have a temporary office at a state university on the West Coast. The office is on the third floor. It looks down on the Square, the enormous open courtyard at the center of campus. From my desk I see hundreds of people moving between classes. There is a large circular fountain in the Square's center.

2   Early one morning, on the first day of spring quarter, I hear singing. A pack of students has gathered at the fountain. They are singing something which, at this distance, and through the heavy window, sounds good.

3   I know who these singing students are: they are the Fundamentalists. This campus has a lot of them. Mornings they sing on the Square; it is their only perceptible activity. What are they singing? Whatever it is, I want to join them, for I like to sing; whatever it is, I want to take my stand with them, for I am drawn to their very absurdity, their innocent indifference to what people think. My colleagues and students here, and my friends everywhere, dislike and fear Christian fundamentalists. You may never have met such people, but you've heard what they do: they pile up money, vote in blocs, and elect right-wing crazies; they censor books; they carry handguns; they fight fluoride in the drinking water and evolution in the schools; probably they would lynch people if they could get away with it. I'm not sure my friends are correct. I close my pen and join the singers on the Square.

4   There is a clapping song in progress. I have to concentrate to follow it:

Come on, rejoice,
And let your heart sing,

Come on, rejoice,
Give praise to the king.
Singing alleluia—
He is the king of kings;
Singing alleluia—
He is the king of kings.

Two song leaders are standing on the broad rim of the fountain; the water is splashing just behind them. The boy is short, hard-faced, with a moustache. He bangs his guitar with the backs of his fingers. The blonde girl, who leads the clapping, is bouncy; she wears a bit of make-up. Both are wearing blue jeans.

The students beside me are wearing blue jeans, too—and athletic jerseys, 5 parkas, football jackets, turtlenecks, and hiking shoes or jogging shoes. They all have canvas or nylon book bags. They look like any random batch of seventy or eighty students at this university. They are grubby or scrubbed, mostly scrubbed; they are tall, fair, or red-headed in large proportions. Their parents are white-collar workers, blue-collar workers, farmers, loggers, orchardists, merchants, fishermen; their names are, I'll bet, Olsen, Jensen, Seversen, Hansen, Klokker, Sigurdsen.

Despite the vigor of the clapping song, no one seems to be giving it much 6 effort. And no one looks at anyone else; there are no sentimental glances and smiles, no glances even of recognition. These kids don't seem to know each other. We stand at the fountain's side, out on the broad, bricked Square in front of the science building, and sing the clapping song through three times.

It is quarter to nine in the morning. Hundreds of people are crossing the 7 Square. These passersby—faculty, staff, students—pay very little attention to us; this morning singing has gone on for years. Most of them look at us directly, then ignore us, for there is nothing to see: no animal sacrifices, no lynchings, no collection plate for Jesse Helms, no seizures, snake handling, healing, or glossolalia. There is barely anything to hear. I suspect the people glance at us to learn if we are really singing: how could so many people make so little sound? My fellow singers, who ignore each other, certainly ignore passersby as well. Within a week, most of them will have their eyes closed anyway.

We move directly to another song, a slower one.   8

He is my peace
Who has broken down every wall;
He is my peace,
He is my peace.

Cast all your cares on him,
For he careth for you—oo—oo
He is my peace,
He is my peace.

I am paying strict attention to the song leaders, for I am singing at the top 9 of my lungs and I've never heard any of these songs before. They are not the old

American low-church Protestant hymns; they are not the old European high-church Protestant hymns. These hymns seem to have been written just yesterday, apparently by the same people who put out lyrical Christian greeting cards and bookmarks.

10   "Where do these songs come from?" I ask a girl standing next to me. She seems appalled to be addressed at all, and startled by the question. "They're from the praise albums!" she explains, and moves away.

11   The songs' melodies run dominant, subdominant, dominant, tonic, dominant. The pace is slow, about the pace of "Tell Laura I Love Her," and with that song's quavering, long notes. The lyrics are simple and repetitive; there are very few of them to which a devout Jew or Mohammedan could not give whole-hearted assent. These songs are similar to the things Catholics sing in church these days. I don't know if any studies have been done to correlate the introduction of contemporary songs into Catholic churches with those churches' decline in membership, or with the phenomenon of Catholic converts' applying to enter cloistered monasteries directly, without passing through parish churches.

> I'm set free to worship,
> I'm set free to praise him,
> I'm set free to dance before the Lord . . .

12   At nine o'clock sharp we quit and scatter. I hear a few quiet "see you's." Mostly the students leave quickly, as if they didn't want to be seen. The Square empties.

13 The next day we show up again, at twenty to nine. The same two leaders stand on the fountain's rim; the fountain is pouring down behind them.

14   After the first song, the boy with the moustache hollers, "Move on up! Some of you guys aren't paying attention back there! You're talking to each other. I want you to concentrate!" The students laugh, embarrassed for him. He sounds like a teacher. No one moves. The girl breaks into the next song, which we join at once:

> In my life, Lord,
> Be glorified, be glorified, be glorified;
> In my life, Lord,
> Be glorified, be glorified, today.

At the end of this singularly monotonous verse, which is straining my tolerance for singing virtually anything, the boy with the moustache startles me by shouting, "Classes!"

15   At once, without skipping a beat, we sing, "In my classes, Lord, be glorified, be glorified . . ." I give fleet thought to the class I'm teaching this afternoon. We're reading a little "Talk of the Town" piece called "Eggbag," about a cat in a magic store on Eighth Avenue. "Relationships!" the boy calls. The students seem to sing "In my relationships, Lord," more easily than they sang "classes." They seemed embarrassed by "classes." In fact, to my fascination, they seem embarrassed by almost everything. Why are they here? I will sing with the Fundamentalists

every weekday morning all spring; I will decide, tentatively, that they come pretty much for the same reasons I do: each has a private relationship with "the Lord" and will put up with a lot of junk for it.

I have taught some Fundamentalist students here, and know a bit of what they 16 think. They are college students above all, worried about their love lives, their grades, and finding jobs. Some support moderate Democrats; some support moderate Republicans. Like their classmates, most support nuclear freeze, ERA, and an end to the draft. I believe they are divided on abortion and busing. They are not particularly political. They read *Christianity Today* and *Campus Life* and *Eternity*—moderate, sensible magazines, I think; they read a lot of C. S. Lewis. (One such student, who seemed perfectly tolerant of me and my shoddy Christianity, introduced me to C. S. Lewis's critical book on Charles Williams.) They read the Bible. I think they all "believe in" organic evolution. The main thing about them is this: there isn't any "them." Their views vary. They don't know each other.

Their common Christianity puts them, if anywhere, to the left of their class- 17 mates. I believe they also tend to be more able than their classmates to think well in the abstract, and also to recognize the complexity of moral issues. But I may be wrong.

In 1980, the media were certainly wrong about television evangelists. Printed es- 18 timates of Jerry Falwell's television audience ranged from 18 million to 30 million people. In fact, according to Arbitron's actual counts, fewer than 1.5 million people were watching Falwell. And, according to an Emory University study, those who did watch television evangelists didn't necessarily vote with them. Emory University sociologist G. Melton Mobley reports, "When that message turns political, they cut it off." Analysis of the 1982 off-year elections turned up no Fundamentalist bloc voting. The media were wrong, but no one printed retractions.

The media were wrong, too, in a tendency to identify all fundamentalist 19 Christians with Falwell and his ilk, and to attribute to them, across the board, conservative views.

Someone has sent me two recent issues of *Eternity: The Evangelical Monthly*. 20 One lead article criticizes a television preacher for saying that the United States had never used military might to take land from another nation. The same article censures Newspeak, saying that government rhetoric would have us believe in a "clean bomb," would have us believe that we "defend" America by invading foreign soil, and would have us believe that the dictatorships we support are "democracies." "When the President of the United States says that one reason to support defense spending is because it creates jobs," this lead article says, "a little bit of *1984* begins to surface." Another article criticizes a "heavy-handed" opinion of Jerry Falwell Ministries—in this case a broadside attack on artificial insemination, surrogate motherhood, and lesbian motherhood. Browsing through *Eternity,* I find a double crosstic. I find an intelligent, analytical, and enthusiastic review of the new London Philharmonic recording of Mahler's second symphony—a review which stresses the "glorious truth" of the Jewish composer's

magnificent work, and cites its recent performance in Jerusalem to celebrate the
recapture of the Western Wall following the Six Day War. Surely, the evangelical
Christians who read this magazine are not book-burners. If by chance they vote
with the magazine's editors, then it looks to me as if they vote with the American Civil Liberties Union and Americans for Democratic Action.

21   Every few years some bold and sincere Christian student at this university
disagrees with a professor in class—usually about the professor's out-of-hand
dismissal of Christianity. Members of the faculty, outraged, repeat the stories of
these rare and uneven encounters for years on end, as if to prove that the crazies
are everywhere, and gaining ground. The notion is, apparently, that these kids
can't think for themselves. Or they wouldn't disagree.

22 Now again the moustached leader asks us to move up. There is no harangue, so
we move up. (This will be a theme all spring. The leaders want us closer together.
Our instinct is to stand alone.) From behind the tall fountain comes a wind; on
several gusts we get sprayed. No one seems to notice.

23   We have time for one more song. The leader, perhaps sensing that no one
likes him, blunders on. "I want you to pray this one through," he says. "We have
a lot of people here from a lot of different fellowships, but we're all one body.
Amen?" They don't like it. He gets a few polite Amens. We sing:

Bind us together, Lord,
With a bond that can't be broken;
Bind us together, Lord,
With love.

Everyone seems to be in a remarkably foul mood today. We don't like this song.
There is no one here under seventeen, and, I think, no one here who believes that
love is a bond that can't be broken. We sing the song through three times; then
it is time to go.

24   The leader calls after our retreating backs, "Hey, have a good day! Praise Him
all day!" The kids around me roll up their eyes privately. Some groan; all flee.

25 The next morning is very cold. I am here early. Two girls are talking on the fountain's rim; one is part Indian. She says, "I've got all the Old Testament, but I can't
get the New. I screw up the New." She takes a breath and rattles off a long list,
ending with "Jonah, Micah, Nahum, Habakkuk, Zephaniah, Haggai, Zechariah,
Malachi." The other girl produces a slow, sarcastic applause. I ask one of the girls
to help me with the words to a song. She is agreeable, but says, "I'm sorry, I can't.
I just became a Christian this year, so I don't know all the words yet."

26   The others are coming; we stand and separate. The boy with the moustache
is gone, replaced by a big, serious fellow in a green down jacket. The bouncy girl
is back with her guitar; she's wearing a skirt and wool knee socks. We begin,
without any preamble, by singing a song that has so few words that we actually
stretch one syllable over eleven separate notes. Then we sing a song in which the
men sing one phrase and the women echo it. Everyone seems to know just what
to do. In the context of our vapid songs, the lyrics of this one are extraordinary:

I was nothing before you found me.
Heartache! Broken people! Ruined lives
Is why you died on Calvary.

The last line rises in a regular series of half-notes. Now at last some people are actually singing; they throw some breath into the business. There is a seriousness and urgency to it: "Heartache! Broken people! Ruined lives . . . I was nothing."

We don't look like nothing. We look like a bunch of students of every stripe, 27 ill-shaven or well-shaven, dressed up or down, but dressed warmly against the cold: jeans and parkas, jeans and heavy sweaters, jeans and scarves and blow-dried hair. We look ordinary. But I think, quite on my own, that we are here because we know this business of nothingness, brokenness, and ruination. We sing this song over and over.

Something catches my eye. Behind us, up in the science building, professors 28 are standing alone at opened windows.

The long brick science building has three upper floors of faculty offices, 29 thirty-two windows. At one window stands a bearded man, about forty; his opening his window is what caught my eye. He stands full in the open window, his hands on his hips, his head cocked down toward the fountain. He is drawn to look, as I was drawn to come. Up on the building's top floor, at the far right window, there is another: an Asian-American professor, wearing a white shirt, is sitting with one hip on his desk, looking out and down. In the middle of the row of windows, another one, an old professor in a checked shirt, stands sideways to the opened window, stands stock-still, his long, old ear to the air. Now another window cranks open, another professor—or maybe a graduate student—leans out, his hands on the sill.

We are all singing, and I am watching these five still men, my colleagues, 30 whose office doors are surely shut—for that is the custom here: five of them alone in their offices in the science building who have opened their windows on this very cold morning, who motionless hear the Fundamentalists sing, utterly unknown to each other.

We sing another four songs, including the clapping song, and one which re- 31 peats, "This is the day which the Lord hath made; rejoice and be glad in it." All the professors but one stay still by their opened windows, figures in a frieze. When after ten minutes we break off and scatter, each cranks his window shut. Maybe they have nine o'clock classes too.

I miss a few sessions. One morning of the following week, I rejoin the Funda- 32 mentalists on the Square. The wind is blowing from the north; it is sunny and cold. There are several new developments.

Someone has blown up rubber gloves and floated them in the fountain. I saw 33 them yesterday afternoon from my high office window, and couldn't quite make them out: I seemed to see hands in the fountain waving from side to side, like those hands wagging on springs which people stick in the back windows of their cars. I saw these many years ago in Quito and Guayaquil, where they were a great fad long before they showed up here. The cardboard hands said, on their palms, HOLA GENTE, hello people. Some of them just said HOLA, hello, with a little wave to the universe at large, in case anybody happened to be looking. It is like our sending radio signals to planets in other galaxies: HOLA, if anyone is listening. Jolly folk, these Ecuadorians, I thought.

34   Now, waiting by the fountain for the singing, I see that these particular hands are long surgical gloves, yellow and white, ten of them, tied off at the cuff. They float upright and they wave, *hola, hola, hola;* they mill around like a crowd, bobbing under the fountain's spray and back again to the pool's rim, *hola.* It is a good prank. It is far too cold for the university's maintenance crew to retrieve them without turning off the fountain and putting on rubber boots.

35   From all around the Square, people are gathering for the singing. There is no way I can guess which kids, from among the masses crossing the Square, will veer off to the fountain. When they get here, I never recognize anybody except the leaders.

36   The singing begins without ado as usual, but there is something different about it. The students are growing prayerful, and they show it this morning with a peculiar gesture. I'm glad they weren't like this when I first joined them, or I never would have stayed.

37   Last night there was an educational television special, part of "Middletown." It was a segment called "Community of Praise," and I watched it because it was about Fundamentalists. It showed a Jesus-loving family in the Midwest; the treatment was good and complex. This family attended the prayer meetings, healing sessions, and church services of an unnamed sect—a very low-church sect, whose doctrine and culture were much more low-church than those of the kids I sing with. When the members of this sect prayed, they held their arms over their heads and raised their palms, as if to feel or receive a blessing or energy from above.

38   Now today on the Square there is a new serious mood. The leaders are singing with their eyes shut. I am impressed that they can bang their guitars, keep their balance, and not fall into the pool. It is the same bouncy girl and earnest boy. Their eyeballs are rolled back a bit. I look around and see that almost everyone in this crowd of eighty or so has his eyes shut and is apparently praying the words of this song or praying some other prayer.

39   Now as the chorus rises, as it gets louder and higher and simpler in melody—

I exalt thee,
I exalt thee,
I exalt thee,
Thou art the Lord—

then, at this moment, hands start rising. All around me, hands are going up— that tall girl, that blond boy with his head back, the redheaded boy up front, the girl with the McDonald's jacket. Their arms rise as if pulled on strings. Some few of them have raised their arms very high over their heads and are tilting back their palms. Many, many more of them, as inconspicuously as possible, have raised their hands to the level of their chins.

40   What is going on? Why are these students today raising their palms in this gesture, when nobody did it last week? Is it because the leaders have set a prayerful tone this morning? Is it because this gesture always accompanies this

song, just as clapping accompanies other songs? Or is it, as I suspect, that these kids watched the widely publicized documentary last night just as I did, and are adopting, or trying out, the gesture?

It is a sunny morning, and the sun is rising behind the leaders and the foun- 41 tain, so those students have their heads tilted, eyes closed, and palms upraised toward the sun. I glance up at the science building and think my own prayer: thank God no one is watching this.

The leaders cannot move around much on the fountain's rim. The girl has 42 her eyes shut, the boy opens his eyes from time to time, glances at the neck of his guitar, and closes his eyes again.

When the song is over, the hands go down, and there is some desultory chat- 43 ting in the crowd, as usual: can I borrow your library card? And, as usual, nobody looks at anybody.

All our songs today are serious. There is a feudal theme to them, or a feudal 44 analogue:

I will eat from abundance of your household.
I will dream beside your streams of righteousness
You are my king.

Enter his gates
with thanksgiving in your heart;
come before his courts with praise.

He is the king of kings.

Thou art the Lord.

All around me, eyes are closed and hands are raised. There is no social pres- 45 sure to do this, or anything else. I've never known any group to be less cohesive, imposing fewer controls. Since no one looks at anyone, and since passersby no longer look, everyone out here is inconspicuous and free. Perhaps the palm-raising has begun because the kids realize by now that they are not on display; they're praying in their closets, right out here on the Square. Over the course of the next weeks, I will learn that the palm-raising is here to stay.

The sun is rising higher. We are singing our last song. We are praying. We 46 are alone together.

He is my peace
Who has broken down every wall . . .

When the song is over, the hands go down. The heads lower, the eyes open 47 and blink. We stay still a second before we break up. We have been standing in a broad current; now we have stepped aside. We have dismantled the radar cups; we have closed the telescope's vault. Students gather their book bags and go. The two leaders step down from the fountain's rim and pack away their guitars. Everyone scatters. I am in no hurry, so I stay after everyone is gone. It is after nine o'clock, and the Square is deserted. The fountain is playing to an empty house. In the pool the cheerful hands are waving over the water, bobbing under the fountain's veil and out again in the current, *hola*.

• *Thinking Critically About "Singing with the Fundamentalists"*

RESPONDING AS A READER

1. Dillard's essay explores many implicit and explicit questions, some of which she answers (for example, see paragraph 16), and some of which she doesn't. Which of these questions do you judge to be more and less important to the essay as a whole? How do her questions, implicit and explicit, change as the essay develops? As you track the pattern of questions, what do you understand to be her overall purpose for writing the essay?

2. The portrait of the singing students evolves slowly. To identify the key moments in Dillard's presentation of them, look closely at the details she chooses to include. What values are implicit in her descriptive language? How do your attitudes toward the singers and toward religious expression develop and/or change in response to these details?

3. Something changes in the last scene of the essay. What do you make of Dillard's remark in paragraph 36, "I'm glad they weren't like this when I first joined them or I never would have stayed"?

RESPONDING AS A WRITER

1. Dillard uses a collage technique that moves back and forth between her direct experience with the singers to commentary about them and about Christian fundamentalism within the national political context. The only signal of these shifts is the extra white space between some paragraphs. What did you notice about the effect of these breaks on your reading experience? When might you use them effectively in your own writing? (For comparison, examine Robert McGuire's use of collage techniques in the essay that begins on p. 225.)

2. "Singing with the Fundamentalists" is a classic example of the tentative, questioning ethos of exploratory writing. How would the same material be different if presented as a thesis-driven essay? What would be lost and what would be gained? Can you and your classmates agree on what the thesis would be for this essay?

3. This essay was published several decades ago. The public image of Christian fundamentalism has changed considerably since then. If you had the opportunity to talk with Dillard about her approach to writing this essay and her views now of the experiences she describes here, what would you want to ask her? Working with a partner, outline questions for an interview and speculate about what Dillard's answers might be.

Barbara Crossette

Testing the Limits of Tolerance as Cultures Mix

Barbara Crossette (b. 1939) was United Nations bureau chief for the *New York Times* when this article was published in the Arts and Ideas section of that paper on March 6, 1999. Her more than twenty-five years of work as a foreign correspondent for the *Times* have led to extensive travel in India and the Middle East. She has published books on India and on vanishing Buddhist culture in the Himalayas.

• *For Your Reading Log*

1. When have you encountered a cultural practice that seemed shocking to you?
2. As you read, notice the origins of the questions that Crossette explores and the kinds of evidence she examines in response.

——————— • ———————

In Maine, a refugee from Afghanistan was seen kissing the penis of his baby boy, 1 a traditional expression of love by this father. To his neighbors and the police, it was child abuse, and his son was taken away. In Seattle, a hospital tried to invent a harmless female circumcision procedure to satisfy conservative Somali parents wanting to keep an African practice alive in their community. The idea got buried in criticism from an outraged public.

How do democratic, pluralistic societies like the United States, based on reli- 2 gious and cultural tolerance, respond to customs and rituals that may be repellent to the majority? As new groups of immigrants from Asia and Africa are added to the demographic mix in the United States, Canada and Europe, balancing cultural variety with mainstream values is becoming more and more tricky.

Many Americans confront the issue of whether any branch of government 3 should have the power to intervene in the most intimate details of family life.

"I think we are torn," said Richard A. Shweder, an anthropologist at the Uni- 4 versity of Chicago and a leading advocate of the broadest tolerance for cultural differences. "It's a great dilemma right now that's coming up again about how we're going to deal with diversity in the United States and what it means to be an American."

Anthropologists have waded deeply into this debate, which is increasingly 5 engaging scholars across academia, as well as social workers, lawyers and judges who deal with new cultural dimensions in immigration and asylum. Some, like Mr. Shweder, argue for fundamental changes in American laws, if necessary, to accommodate almost any practice accepted as valid in a radically different society if it can be demonstrated to have some social or cultural good.

6   For example, although Mr. Shweder and others would strongly oppose importing such practices as India's immolation of widows, they defend other controversial practices, including the common African ritual that opponents call female genital mutilation, which usually involves removing the clitoris at a minimum. They say that it is no more harmful than male circumcision and should be accommodated, not deemed criminal, as it now is in the United States and several European countries. At the Harvard Law School, Martha Minow, a professor who specializes in family and school issues, said that intolerance often arises when the behavior of immigrants seems to be "nonmodern, nonscientific and nonrational." She cites as an example the practice of "coining" among Cambodians, where hot objects may be pressed on a child's forehead or back as cures for various maladies, leaving alarming welts that for teachers and social workers set off warnings of child abuse.

7   Americans are more than happy to accept new immigrants when their traditions seem to reinforce mainstream ideals. There are few cultural critics of the family values, work ethic or dedication to education found among many East Asians, for example.

8   But going more than halfway to tolerate what look like disturbing cultural practices unsettles some historians, aid experts, economists and others with experience in developing societies. Such relativism, they say, undermines the very notion of progress. What's more, it raises the question of how far acceptance can go before there is no core American culture, no shared values, left.

9   Many years of living in a variety of cultures, said Urban Jonsson, a Swede who directs the United Nations Children's Fund, UNICEF, in sub-Saharan Africa, has led him to conclude that there is "a global moral minimum," which he has heard articulated by Asian Buddhists and African thinkers as well as by Western human rights advocates.

10   "There is a nonethnocentric global morality," he said, and scholars would be better occupied looking for it rather than denying it. "I am upset by the anthropological interest in mystifying what we have already demystified. All cultures have their bad and good things."

11   Murder was a legitimate form of expression in Europe centuries ago when honor was involved, Mr. Jonsson points out. Those days may be gone in most places, but in Afghanistan, a wronged family may demand the death penalty and carry it out themselves with official blessing. Does that restore it to respectability in the 21st century?

12   Scholars like Mr. Shweder are wary of attempts to catalogue "good" and "bad" societies or practices. Working with the Social Science Research Council in New York and supported by the Russell Sage Foundation, he helped form a group of about 15 legal and cultural experts to investigate how American law affects ethnic customs among African, Asian, Caribbean and Latin American immigrants.

13   A statement of purpose written by the working group, headed by Mr. Shweder and Ms. Minow, says that it intends to explore how to react to "official attempts to force compliance with the cultural and legal norms of American middle class life."

"Despite our pluralistic ideals, something very much like a cultural un- 14
American activities list seems to have begun circulating among powerful representatives and enforcers of mainstream culture," the group says in its statement.
"Among the ethnic minority activities at risk of being dubbed 'un-American' are
the use of disciplinary techniques such as shaming and physical punishment,
parent/child co-sleeping arrangements, rituals of group identity and ceremonies
of initiation involving scarification, piercing and genital alterations, arranged
marriage, polygamy, the segregation of gender roles, bilingualism and foreign
language use and many more."

Some sociologists and anthropologists on this behavioral frontier argue that 15
American laws and welfare services have often left immigrants terrified of the
intrusive power of government. The Afghan father in Maine who lost his son to
the social services, backed by a lower court, did not prevail until the matter
reached the state Supreme Court, which researched the family's cultural heritage
and decided in its favor—while making clear that this was an exceptional case,
not a precedent.

Spanking, puberty rites, animal sacrifices, enforced dress codes, leaving chil- 16
dren unattended at home and sometimes the use of narcotics have all been portrayed as acceptable cultural practices. But who can claim to be culturally beyond
the prevailing laws and why?

Ms. Minow said that issues of cultural practice were appearing in more law 17
school curriculums as Americans experience the largest wave of immigration
since the 1880–1920 era. "Immigration is now becoming a mainstream subject,"
she said. "There is also definitely a revival of interest in law schools in religion,"
including a study of the relation of beliefs to social practices and legal constraints.

Some of the leading thinkers in this debate will discuss the issue at a con- 18
ference at Harvard in April on the relationship between culture and progress. "If
you believe that there is such a thing as a successful society and an unsuccess-
ful society," said Lawrence Harrison, a conference panelist, "then you have to
draw some conclusions about what makes for a better society."

Mr. Harrison, who wrote "Underdevelopment as a State of Mind" (Har- 19
vard) and "Who Prospers?" (Basic Books), said he believed there were universal yearnings for "progress" and that to refrain from judging every practice out
there ignored those aspirations.

Paradoxically, while some Americans want judgment-free considerations of 20
immigrants' practices and traditional rituals in the countries they come from,
asylum seekers from those same countries are turning up at American airports
begging to escape from tribal rites in the name of human rights. Immigration
lawyers and judges are thus drawn into a debate that is less and less theoretical.

Mr. Jonsson of UNICEF, whose wife is from Tanzania, says he has had to con- 21
front cultural relativism every day for years in the third world. He is outraged
by suggestions that the industrial nations should be asked to bend their laws and
social norms, especially on the genital cutting of girls, which UNICEF opposes.

He labels those who would condemn many in the third world to practices they 22
may desperately want to avoid as "immoral and unscientific." In their academic
towers, Mr. Jonsson said, cultural relativists become "partners of the tormentors."

23   Jessica Neuwirth, an international lawyer who is director of Equality Now, a New York–based organization aiding women's groups in the developing world and immigrant women in this country, asks why the practices that cultural relativists want to condone so often involve women: how they dress, what they own, where they go, how their bodies can be used.

24   "Culture is male-patrolled in the way that it is created and transmitted," she said. "People who control culture tend to be the people in power, and who constitutes that group is important. Until we can break through that, we can't take the measure of what is really representative."

25   Other voices are often not being heard or are silenced. "People forget that inside every culture, there is a whole spectrum of ideas and values," she said. "There may be women in another culture who defend the practice of female genital mutilation, but in the same culture there will be women who oppose the practice. And men, too."

• *Thinking Critically About "Testing the Limits of Tolerance as Cultures Mix"*

RESPONDING AS A READER

1. Crossette's approach to her subject matter here contrasts with that of the several more personal essays in this section. How personally involved is Crossette with this subject matter? What effect does her approach have on your appreciation of the significance of the questions she explores? Refer to specific passages in the article as evidence that supports your answers.
2. The cultural practices described in this article as "testing the limits of tolerance" can be seen as quite shocking. Where did you find surprises? In what ways did the presentation test your tolerance? How did your views evolve as you read?
3. How do you think Crossette hoped readers would respond to this article? How can you tell? Was she successful in your case? Why or why not?

RESPONDING AS A WRITER

1. Do you feel that the question(s) presented in this piece were adequately explored in it? How do you think more satisfactory answers might be found?
2. Look carefully at the way Crossette identifies her sources and incorporates material from them. If this same discussion were presented as a formal academic paper, how would its format have to be different? What do you think would be the differences in how readers would respond to an academic article about this subject in contrast to Crossette's journalistic approach?
3. What questions does this article raise for you about the role of government in relationship to cultural practice? What questions does it raise about the nature of "tolerance" itself? If you were to undertake your own exploratory essay on one or more of the cultural practices discussed here, what questions would you focus on?

Robert McGuire

Witness to Rage

Robert McGuire (b. 1970), who now resides and writes in southwestern Connecticut, worked as a college writing teacher and freelance writer in Milwaukee during the late 1990s. This article, which combines emotionally intense personal narrative with journalistic interviews and fact-finding, was the cover story in *Milwaukee Magazine* in July 1999. Its first page had only the title, printed on a full page close-up of a man's angry face. On the next page, the first sentence was set in type .75 inches high. Large, boldface quotes from the narrative were interspersed throughout the text. The story won local and state prizes for excellence in nonfiction as well as a National Council on Crime and Delinquency award established to recognize "responsible and factual coverage that explores the root causes of crime."

● *For Your Reading Log*

1. What has been (or might be) your response to learning that a friend of yours, someone your own age, experienced domestic abuse as a child?
2. As soon you as you finish reading, while the experience is still fresh, take a few minutes to jot down your emotional response to the essay as a whole.

———————   ●   ———————

I boil inside.   1

There have been times when I have fled the house in fear of the tremor in   2
my arms, the pictures in my head of what might come next.

I have panted, short of breath, furious, stuttering. I have let a look come over   3
me, a tone come into my voice that has made my wife afraid of me.

I have punched holes in doors and walls. Once, I put my hands on my wife's   4
arms and shook her as I shouted during an argument—my greatest regret in life.

There is a regular kind of anger that comes in the arguments all couples have.   5
And then there is this irrational, out-of-the-blue rage that sometimes turns the
air in our home to poison.

My father was a wife beater. I am not. I've beaten the odds that say children   6
of violent homes will become violent. Still, during that out-of-the-blue anger, I
see the spittle flying from my lips and the fearful expression on my wife's face
and realize how much I must look like my father—sweat high on my forehead,
my Adam's apple bobbing.

There is a sense in which I am a violent man. When I feel put upon or mis-   7
understood, I feel that satisfaction would be mine if I would clench my fist and
swing, if I would demolish whatever is near me.

I have a happy life, work I enjoy, a terrific marriage—a true companion. I   8
have interests that I throw myself into with enthusiasm.

9   And I have spent afternoons pondering warm baths and sharp kitchen knives, high bridges, five-day waiting periods.

10   I am academically successful, cultured, a teacher, a person of authority and responsibility.

11   And I drift from one job to another, squandering the opportunities that come from sticking with one employer. At 28, I have yet to choose a career.

12   I've been wondering lately what happens when children witness domestic violence, when they see someone they love beaten, humiliated and degraded by another person they love.

13   At the Milwaukee Women's Center's shelter for battered women, where I have volunteered for three and a half years, children arrive in the playroom dazed and bashful. I play checkers with them and help them put together puzzles. They ask for their mothers, who are busy downstairs dealing with the crisis in their lives. Sometimes they squabble and hit each other and I tell them it's wrong to hit, that we don't allow hitting here.

14   Sometimes they're protective older brothers standing like sentinels behind their sisters, glowering at anyone who comes near them. When they play, their anxieties are transparent: They call police on plastic telephones, and spank and scold dolls. Some become angels after a little attention is paid to them. Others remain belligerent or withdrawn. Some seem fine and then burst into tears over a missing puzzle piece. Others appear normal.

15   When kids arrive, I am glad to see them out of harm's way, but I know they have a long road ahead. Witnessing violence has long-term effects. Young criminal offenders are four times more likely to have come from abusive homes, according to studies by the American Psychological Association. Boys from violent homes may end up batterers themselves and girls may later find themselves in relationships with men who beat them, reports the APA. Whether or not they repeat the violence, many children will suffer and participate in a host of emotional and social problems—from bedwetting to drug addiction.

16   Where I grew up, there is a long strip of diners, truck stops and cheap motels— squat cinder block buildings fronted by neon signs like "The Tropicana" or "The Thunderbird Inn." I passed these places every day of my childhood.

17   They were our domestic violence shelters. At the height of my father's drunken rages, when my mother feared for our lives, these are the places she took us, though both of my parents had family in town.

18   Many nights, I would lie in bed listening to the storm at the other end of the house, my mother begging my father to stop beating her. The walls rattled with the commotion and the air pulsed with antagonism. Finally, it would stop. My father would bang out of the house or simply go to bed, leaving my mother sobbing.

19   A few of these nights each year, though, my mother would suddenly appear beside my bed, whispering fiercely, "Robert. Get up. Get your shoes on." The urgency in her voice alarmed me. And then we would go fleeing into the night to these motels.

In the morning, my mother would drive us kids to school. We would stop 20
at a gas station and buy packaged cinnamon rolls for our breakfast. We would
take the bus home from school as usual and my parents would be there, apparently having taken the day off from work. My father would be contrite and
would keep his voice down for a few days.

Social workers now call this the cycle of violence—honeymoon, tension, 21
battering, honeymoon. The abuser will be on his best behavior, courting his
partner, reminding her of why she fell in love with him in the first place. As he
becomes more comfortable, he returns to his domineering and antagonistic behavior, building tension until there is a blowup, followed by another round of
apologies and courting.

Children under 12 live in more than half of the homes affected by domestic vi- 22
olence, according to a 1998 U.S. Department of Justice report. Seventy-five percent of the homes to which police are called on domestic violence cases have
children, according to an APA study, which included Milwaukee in its sample.
That adds up to an estimated 3.3 million children per year who are witnessing
fathers or boyfriends beating their mothers.

Because it is rarely reported, there's no accurate estimate of domestic violence 23
cases in the Milwaukee area, but in 1996, police in Milwaukee County, with its
population of 963,900, reported 12,364 incidents. Waukesha County, with a population of 334,077, reported 1,313 incidents. Across Wisconsin, which has more
than 5.1 million people, there were 30,479 cases of domestic violence that year.

It wasn't the night my father tried to kill us that made the biggest impression on 24
me but the next day. Coming through the door that afternoon, I saw it—the
brown plastic handle of a steak knife sticking out of the wall, its dull serrated
blade planted deep in the paneling about as high as my father's shoulder. He had
apparently plunged it there sometime during his raging the night before.

My mother and father were standing in the kitchen when I got home. They 25
had spent the day in their routine of cleaning up and making up. But they missed
the knife, the brown handle camouflaged against brown paneling.

That's when the significance of the previous 24 hours really hit me. The gun 26
in the night had made me limp with terror, but it was that steak knife the next
afternoon that wounded me. I had always wished things were different, but at
that moment, I stopped wishing. I started thinking in terms of what my life was
instead of what it should be.

As a society, we know little about what happens to children who witness do- 27
mestic violence. In fact, we know more about the effects violent television shows
have on children. The few dozen studies on the subject have been mostly limited to families that go to shelters or call the police. Social stigma, the unpredictable behavior of police called to the scene, fear of the abuser and fear of
government agencies all undermine accurate reporting. My mother, for example,
was beaten several times a year for about 13 years, but I only saw a cop once in
all that time. And I never saw a social worker. We weren't on the radar.

28   Most of the effort in domestic violence cases is placed upon impending threats or treating wounds. According to Mary Lauby, executive director of the Wisconsin Coalition Against Domestic Violence, child protection agencies and shelters for battered women have their hands full with these crises. When child protection agencies do take the issue of children witnessing violence seriously, they tend to blame mothers for not protecting their children. That puts them at odds with the shelters, which worry that mothers have enough difficulty leaving violent homes without worrying that their children will be taken away.

29   Meanwhile, according to Nancy Worcester, founder of the Wisconsin Domestic Violence Training Project, researchers suspect that when it comes to long-term consequences for children, there's not much difference between experiencing violence at home and witnessing it.

30   "In fact, they're very similar," she says. "They have the same warning signs."

31   When I was in fifth grade, my teacher called my mother and told her I had so many nervous habits that she wanted me to see the school psychologist. My grandmother was dying then from lung cancer, which upset me. So that's the official reason for my nervous habits. I still have them. I twitch and fidget a lot. I don't spend more than 15 minutes on any single task.

32   I talked to the psychologist about my grandmother and then played a game of checkers. She let me win, and I still resent her for it. I didn't know how to accept a favor or a compliment—and still don't. In my family, being nice to people and giving gifts aren't done out of genuine feeling but to discharge a social duty.

33   It's the cover-your-ass theory of relationships. I'm convinced my friends are kind to me because they have an obligation to be. If you knew me and told me you liked this article, I'd figure you were only saying what politeness demands. If you neglected to mention it at all, I'd stay up late worrying about what you thought of me.

34   "Survivors tend to isolate themselves, drawing only on their own strengths, intelligence, information-gathering skills and intuition. Since the outside world has proved to be very dangerous and unpredictable, it is safer not to interact, trust, depend or count on anyone other than oneself. Such behavior denies the survivor the experience of caring and being cared for that is the foundation of all social interaction."—Christina Crawford in *No Safe Place: The Legacy of Family Violence.*

35   What I most remember about growing up is not specific violent events but the atmosphere in our home the weeks before a major row. I can still feel the hostility and tension.

36   Watching television, we held our breath, hoping that tonight my father wouldn't snap at my brother or me because we were watching in a way he didn't like, laughing at the wrong time, fidgeting. My father would sigh heavily or curse under his breath at some private torment. At the commercial, he would stomp into the kitchen, slamming cabinets, looking for something not to be there so he could want it. He would come back to the living room and, star-

ing fiercely at the television, say softly to my mother: "Why can't we ever have the goddamn chips I asked you for?"

Menacing is the word. Everything we said or did was objectionable. We 37 moved, he shook his head in disgust. We spoke, he snorted. If we stopped speaking, he baited us: "What are you thinking? Why don't you say something?" The simple question, "What did you do today?" was deadly, especially when directed at my mother. There was something objectionable in every possible answer.

At our house, we learned early that if my mother hadn't bought the chips 38 my father wanted, it was because she was too busy screwing every man she knew (my father's language). Imperfect shopping made my mother a whore. I heard her called that as often as I heard her name. I heard her accused of the vilest treacheries as often as I heard her thanked for cooking dinner.

Witnessing domestic violence causes a variety of cognitive, emotional and be- 39 havioral effects, according to the only definitive, book-length source on the effects of children witnessing violence, *Children of Battered Women* (by Peter Jaffe, David Wolfe and Susan Wilson). The text is a summary of the smattering of surveys that appeared in academic journals in the 1980s.

These studies conclude that children who live in homes where violence oc- 40 curs have reduced intellectual competency and language delays, often misdiagnosed as attention deficit disorder. They also face emotional difficulties, including fear of abandonment and powerlessness, inability to set limits or follow directions, lethargy, loneliness, moodiness and anxiety.

This leads to social and behavioral problems such as delinquency, eating dis- 41 orders, excessive attention-seeking, poor impulse control, running away from home, early and risky sexual activity, suicide—and more violence. According to the APA, boys from violent homes are four times more likely than other boys to be violent with their dates, 25 times more likely to rape and 1,000 times more likely to be violent with their adult partners or children.

One night, when I was 13 years old, we ran off as usual. This time, my mother 42 was more fearful that my father would search for us so she settled on a motel that was just over the city limits. There was one bed that my brother and sister and I shared and no phone.

I woke up to the booming sound of the steel door rattling in its frame. 43 Crouched on the floor, my mother was begging my father to go away. "Just go home," she whispered into the crack at the door. "Just leave us alone. We'll see you in the morning."

The noise was terrific. When he finally went away, my mother took up a post 44 peeking out from behind the drapes, alert for his return. I fell asleep again.

A little later, I woke to the sound of more shouting. My mother was kneel- 45 ing on the floor, gagging from fear. Snot and tears streaming from her face, her voice hoarse, she was pleading with my father who demanded that my mother hand over my little sister—an infant at the time. "You're drunk. You can see her in the morning. Go home. We'll come home in the morning."

46   I heard the sound of the small engine on my father's import pickup wind up. My mother was gasping for breath. Then the sound of the truck returned. My mother was peeking through the drapes at the parking lot. "I'm really scared, kids," she said. And then a moment later, she croaked, "Oh my God, kids, I think he has a gun."

47   This is what terror is. The sound of fear in my mother's voice had completely incapacitated me. Next to me, my brother was whimpering like a puppy. I went cold. I felt like a puddle of ice water lying in bed. I'd never been so cold. My head was swimming and I couldn't get enough air, but I couldn't even gasp. It was as if the spark of life had been stolen from my body. I couldn't move or think or reflect. I couldn't even panic.

48   I don't remember anything else. I don't remember how it ended.

49   My mother tells me now that what I do remember isn't entirely accurate. He didn't leave and come back a few times; it all happened in just a couple of minutes. I didn't fall asleep during part of it. I didn't lie frozen in panic, she says, but threw my body over my brother as if to protect him.

50   She didn't actually see a gun, but he told her through the motel room door that he had one in the truck he would use. He had pointed his loaded deer rifle at her twice in the past, so she didn't doubt it.

51   She bargained that we were more likely to survive if she let him in than if he broke down the door. She was too afraid of him to keep him locked out. She let him in. He took my baby sister and drove away with her.

52   I've always suspected this, but I didn't know until now. I knew my sister was in that motel room and I couldn't remember her being there in any of the aftermath. But I couldn't make it add up in my head. I blocked it out. I suspect now that my memory of me falling asleep as he came and went was really me blacking out in fear.

53   The next thing I remember, my mother was ordering me to action: to cross the parking lot to the motel office and ask them to call the police. And to hurry.

54   I don't know how I walked across that asphalt in the middle of the night wearing my pajamas. I burned with shame to ask the motel clerk to call the police. He was one of the sons of a family of immigrants who lived in an apartment behind the office. I had to wake him up. I still remember the look of disgust he gave me. My mother tells me now what I had forgotten—that they refused to call the police and that I had to go back and explain to my mother that I hadn't done the job. I then went back to the office to use a pay phone.

55   Much of the night, we sat at a steel desk in the back of a small-town police station. Eventually, my grandparents came to get us—my father's parents. My mother was too humiliated to call her own father. My father's parents blamed her for their son's behavior, but she called them anyway.

56   The next morning, my mother and father left us at my grandparents' house. I played basketball a little with my uncle, still a teenager himself, and he told me Jesus is my savior. When I arrived home that afternoon, I saw the knife in the wall.

People often ask why women like my mother don't leave. Asking a question like   57
that is accusing a woman, making her responsible for the violence. It's impossible to see the shelter's bruised women too jumpy to look me in the eye and conclude that their injuries are their fault.

It's the kind of question that's usually asked after a woman is murdered, like   58
Milwaukeean Virginia Hansen, whose husband killed her last December. She *had*
left him. She had a restraining order and was cooperating with prosecutors on
a battery charge against him. She had even given neighbors flyers describing him
and his car and asking them to call 911 if they saw him. Still, the post-mortem
news reports were mostly about what else she should have done.

Leaving is often more dangerous than staying. A 1997 State of Florida review   59
of its homicides found that 65 percent of the women killed by husbands or
boyfriends were murdered *after* they left the relationship.

There are other, less tangible ways that make it difficult to leave. It was em-   60
barrassing for my mother to go into those motel offices, her eyes rimmed red
from sobbing, to ask for a room, to send us to school in the same clothes we wore
the day before, our homework unfinished.

Oftentimes, women simply don't have the resources—financial, emotional   61
or social—to leave. The time my mother came closest to leaving, we spent a few
days driving around looking at houses in terrible neighborhoods. Every once in
awhile, she would weep with frustration.

When women do leave, their children ask all kinds of heartbreaking ques-   62
tions. Is my pet okay? Will I get my Rollerblades back? Why can't I be on my soccer team anymore? Does my daddy know I still love him? It can't be easy to have
your children feel those anxieties when you can prevent it by just staying.

That question—"Why didn't she leave?"—is also hard for me because the   63
honest truth is that I sometimes resent my mother. "Why, why, why didn't you
protect us," I ask myself. I heard my father threaten to kill her many times and
I saw her knocked to the ground, a fistful of her hair in his hand. I saw, and I understand, but making sense of it is still hard.

That's the real effect of witnessing domestic violence—the effect researchers   64
haven't documented. It confuses you. It makes you ambivalent. It makes you angry at the people you love. It makes you identify with victim and abuser, makes
you hate in yourself what resembles both of them.

But who is to say if staying was the wrong decision? Surviving is the im-   65
portant thing, and we all did that. In my family, some of us are recovering ad-
dicts. Some of us are on Zoloft. Some of us have sleep disorders. We rarely speak
to each other much about anything of substance. But we're all alive.

Something about seeing that steak knife in the wall made me realize that things   66
weren't going to change. In fact, two years after the gun incident, my mother was
still waking us to flee to motel rooms. But that day was the beginning of a long period of giving in, of giving up the hard work of feeling anything in particular.

After these dustups, there would always be a little talk, always with my   67
mother, about how I shouldn't get stressed out about this. I waited this time for
her to come.

68   She would tell me how much my father loved us, how sorry and how sick with alcoholism he was. As I grew into an insolent teen, I grew less interested in these talks. She would say a few words along those lines and then fall silent, frustrated by my unwillingness to join in. She would weep and I would hold as still as I could, facing away from her. She would stare at me awhile, sometimes rubbing my back through my shirt.

69   Finally, she would say something conclusive like, "Dinner will be ready soon" or "Are you going to watch 'The Cosby Show' tonight?" She would start to slide off of the bed and then pause and say, "I love you, Robert." I would wait a few beats, and when I realized she had paused for a response, I would say, quietly, "I love you, too." The tone in my voice seemed to add, "I guess."

70   Nothing in this routine ever gave me the idea that what I had seen was wrong, that my outrage at it was justified.

71 My father left my mother when I was 16. The violence stopped. Shortly before they split up, I lay in my bed one night listening to him beat her up, and I felt so weary. I'm ashamed now of how unsympathetic I felt. The power I had to predict it all was my strength and my emotional defense.

72   Again my mother appeared at my bedside, whispering to get up and grab my clothes and books. I told her to go, that I would drive myself to school, that I would see her when she got home tomorrow. She was hurt. We argued about it for a minute, and she left with my brother and sister. I lay there trying to go to sleep with my dad prowling around the house. I don't think my mother and I have had a truly intimate conversation since.

73 So what?

74   You don't know me. You've got troubles of your own. There is already enough heartache in the world. Why should you care?

75   Author Christina Crawford says domestic violence, child abuse and the increasing violence of our culture generally cost all of us: "Family violence has directly or indirectly left its black mark on almost every aspect of our world civilization. . . . Family violence inevitably spills out onto the streets and into the next generation in some form or another. Billions of taxpayer dollars are poured into institutions such as foster care, hospital emergency rooms, prisons, police, social services, courts, etc. to deal with violence after the fact."

76   Consider the students in your child's classroom who are bullies or are completely withdrawn, who are more preoccupied with the crisis in their lives than with what school is trying to teach them.

77   Says Mary Lauby of the Wisconsin Coalition Against Domestic Violence: "It's our future. Children who are witnessing violence today are going to school with our children and, though we may not know it, are socializing with our children and are going to grow up to date and marry our children and have children with our children. They certainly affect our classrooms. Their happiness, their ability to fully participate is marginalized by living in a violent home."

78   Or consider the world all of us will live in a generation from now. Says Nancy Worcester of the Wisconsin Domestic Violence Training Project: "Children

who witness violence get more and more tolerant of violence. Every time we let it pass, we let it multiply."

Sometimes I worry that I'm like my father, but I understand that in the most im- 79 portant way, I am different. The most significant research statistic on this subject— 60 percent of the boys from homes like mine end up being batterers—doesn't apply to me.

How do some sons break the pattern? And what will keep my sister from 80 choosing a violent man as her partner, as many from violent homes do? There are no clear answers from professionals, only hunches and vague theories about "psychological hardiness."

Most social workers and therapists with whom I have spoken believe a link 81 to the world outside the family is what makes the difference: meaningful hobbies or another adult who cares about the child and helps give a sense of self-worth.

My own hunch is that talking is a big part of it—telling family secrets, telling 82 the stories of how we came to be the adults we are, making room for someone to say what is right and wrong. What if somebody had started talking after my father planted that steak knife in the wall? What if I had gotten the idea that somebody else believed that what I was seeing was wrong?

My father's younger brother was stabbed to death during a drunken fight 83 with kitchen knives. His killer was a roommate he lived with after his wife left him because he was violent. Another brother chased his ex-wife and their children into hiding last year. What did these three brothers see and not talk about? What if someone had talked?

My little brother is getting married next fall and I wonder what kind of fam- 84 ily he will create. Is his fiancée about to make the kind of mistake my mother did? Did he escape that cycle? Does he remember that motel? The steel desk in the back of the police station? Was he as scared as I was? I don't know. We never talk.

I'm not sure how to end this story—half-empty or half-full. 85

Worcester pleads with me to emphasize that things can turn out okay: "We 86 don't want any young man reading this to think, 'Oh, I've witnessed violence. It's inevitable that I'll be violent.' Anyone who's willing to take responsibility can beat it."

As a teenager, I was very active in Boy Scouts. I was on a lot of committees 87 and in charge of some of them. I earned the Eagle award. I worked at the camp swimming pool, teaching younger boys how to swim and save each other from drowning. I even planned a career in scouting.

I had a very close relationship with my scoutmaster. I saw him every Thurs- 88 day night at meetings and on 10 weekend camping trips a year. On those Friday and Saturday nights, we stayed up late gossiping and sipping Pepsi. We sat around the fire and I slowly learned over the years how to encourage younger boys instead of belittling them. He told me about his work and asked me about school.

Sunday afternoons, he would drop off all of the other boys first and take me 89 to a drive-in for a milkshake. He'd let me tune the radio station in his truck to the Top 40 stations he didn't like. He'd tell me not to play so much with the reclining passenger seat. He would explain grown-up concerns to me, how to keep focused on what's important, how to choose a good pickup truck, which choices in life will result in pride, which in regret.

90   He kept me afloat. Just slow, gentle talk, a little bit at a time, listening, gently correcting, taking me seriously. I came out barely all right. I feel like a man on the lake in a boat with a slow leak and a big pail. I'd rather be on dry land. I'd rather the boat didn't have a leak. But bailing out is manageable work.

91   It took a lot of campouts and a few hours every Thursday night for eight years, but I was saved.

92   I spend a few hours every Thursday night at the shelter that saw 360 children last year—almost one a day. They're gone in a couple of weeks. I don't remember the names of the ones I met last week.

93   Recently, I helped a talented girl write a story. She looked for ways to make it better, revised it, cut what didn't work. She read it to the other children, and they laughed spontaneously at her jokes. She showed it to all of her teachers.

94   When I look at individuals, I see cause for hope. But when I look at an entire community, I see a big boat with a very fast leak. And the only thing on board is a very small pail.

• *Thinking Critically About "Witness to Rage"*

RESPONDING AS A READER

1. Where were you drawn into this text? Where did you resist it? Focus on those specific passages and describe the impact on you of specific words and phrasings.
2. In the section that begins "So what?" (paragraph 73), McGuire makes clear how he hopes readers will respond to his essay. To what extent was he successful in your case? In what ways has your image of domestic abuse and its effect on the children who witness it changed? In what ways has your understanding of community responses to domestic abuse changed?
3. McGuire says that he isn't sure how to end the story—"half-empty or half-full." Does the final section satisfy you as a reader? Why or why not? In your experience of reading the article, which way does his story tip, positively, toward the glass half full, or negatively, half empty?

RESPONDING AS A WRITER

1. McGuire's collage organization here, a technique used by many writers of creative nonfiction, interrupts chronological order by juxtaposing narrative sections from his childhood with interview and analysis sections from the present. For insight into the roles that the different sections play in relation to the essay as a whole, do a descriptive outline with *does* and *says* statements (described in Chapter 4, p. 58) for the major sections. How does each section contribute to the article's overall effect? How does the mix of personal narrative and journalistic reporting contribute to that effect?

2. Readers have to fill in the gaps created by the collage organization. If McGuire had written this as a closed-form academic essay, he would have needed to write out transitions between the sections. To examine the differences this would make in the essay's effect, choose two or three gaps that interest you and try writing a transition sentence for them. Then compare notes with your classmates to see if you were composing similar or different readings to cover the gaps.

3. McGuire hoped that his article would inspire some readers to act in support of women and children hiding from domestic violence. He received many supportive letters in response to the article, but none mentioned that the writer felt called to take any action. As you understand the article, what actions might be appropriate? Try your hand at a simple, direct, one-paragraph letter to the editor of *Milwaukee Magazine* that seeks to motivate readers to take a specific action.

Beverly Gross

Bitch

Beverly Gross (b. 1938), an English professor at Queens College of the City University of New York, draws upon her teaching experience and her expertise as a literary scholar to explore meanings and uses of the loaded term "bitch." The combination of historical sources with references to pop culture is not unusual in the journal where this essay was originally published in the summer of 1994, *Salmagundi*, which bills itself as "a quarterly of the humanities and social sciences" and is known for publishing material on provocative topics.

• **For Your Reading Log**

1. How do you usually react to the word "bitch"? Before diving into Gross's discussion of other people's definitions and reactions, take a few minutes to freewrite about what the word means, how you might use it, and how you might feel if somebody used it, or one of its derivatives, to describe you.
2. Many of the words Gross encounters in her exploration of "bitch" are even less acceptable in polite society. Pay attention to your responses to this language so that you can fully appreciate Gross's carefully developed points.

———————   •   ———————

1   We were discussing Mary McCarthy's *The Group* in a course called Women Writers and Literary Tradition. McCarthy's biographer Carol Gelderman, I told the class, had been intrigued by how often critics called Mary McCarthy a bitch. I read a few citations. "Her novels are crammed with cerebration and bitchiness" (John Aldridge). "Her approach to writing [is] reflective of the modern American bitch" (Paul Schlueter). Why McCarthy? a student asked. Her unrelenting standards, I ventured, her tough-minded critical estimates—there was no self-censoring, appeasing Angel in the House of Mary McCarthy's brain. Her combativeness (her marital battles with Edmund Wilson became the stuff of academic legend). Maybe there were other factors. But the discussion opened up to the more inclusive issue of the word bitch itself. What effect does that appellation have on women? What effect might it have had on McCarthy? No one ever called Edmund Wilson a bitch. Do we excuse, even pay respect when a man is critical, combative, assertive? What is the male equivalent of the word bitch, I asked the class.

2   "Boss," said Sabrina Sims.

3   This was an evening class at a branch of the City University of New York. Most of the students are older adults trying to fit a college education into otherwise busy lives. Most of them have fulltime jobs during the day. Sabrina Sims works on Wall Street, is a single mother raising a ten-year-old daughter, is black,

and had to take an Incomplete in the course because she underwent a kidney transplant in December.

Her answer gave us all a good laugh. I haven't been able to get it out of my 4 mind. I've been thinking about bitch, watching how it is used by writers and in conversation, and have explored its lexical history. "A name of reproach for a woman" is how Doctor Johnson's Dictionary dealt with the word in the eighteenth century, as though anticipating the great adaptability of this particular execration, a class of words that tends toward early obsolescence. Not bitch, however, which has been around for a millennium, outlasting a succession of definitions. Its longevity is perhaps attributable to its satisfying misogyny. Its meaning matters less than its power to denounce and subjugate. Francis Grose in *A Classical Dictionary of the Vulgar Tongue* (1785) considered bitch "the most offensive appellation that can be given to an English woman, even more provoking than that of whore." He offered as evidence "a low London woman's reply on being called a bitch" in the late eighteenth century: "I may be a whore but can't be a bitch!" The meaning of bitch has changed over the centuries but it remains the word that comes immediately to the tongue, still "the most offensive appellation" the English language provides to hurl at a woman.

The *Oxford English Dictionary* records two main meanings for the noun bitch 5 up through the nineteenth century:

1. The female of the dog
2. Applied opprobriously to a woman; strictly a lewd or sensual woman. Not now in decent use.

It was not until the twentieth century that bitch acquired its opprobrious application in realms irrespective of sensuality. The Supplement to the *OED* (1972) adds:

2a: "In mod. use, esp. a malicious or treacherous woman."

Every current desk dictionary supplies some such meaning:

A spiteful, ill-tempered woman [*World Book Dictionary*]

A malicious, unpleasant, selfish woman, esp. one who stops at nothing to reach her goal. [*Random House Dictionary*]

But malice and treachery only begin to tell the story. The informal questionnaire that I administered to my students and a number of acquaintances elicited ample demonstration of the slippery adaptability of bitch as it might be used these days:

a conceited person, a snob

a self-absorbed woman

a complainer

a competitive woman

a woman who is annoying, pushy, possibly underhanded (in short, a man in a woman's body)

someone rich, thin and free!

7   "A word used by men who are threatened by women" was one astute response. Threat lurks everywhere: for women the threat is in being called a bitch. "Someone whiny, threatening, crabby, pestering" is what one woman offered as her definition. "Everything I try hard not to be," she added, "though it seeps through." I offer as a preliminary conclusion that bitch means to men whatever they find threatening in a woman and it means to women whatever they particularly dislike about themselves. In either case the word functions as a misogynistic club. I will add that the woman who defined bitch as everything she tries hard not to be when asked to free associate about the word came up immediately with "mother." That woman happens to be my sister. We share the same mother, who was often whiny and crabby, though I would never have applied the word bitch to her; but then again, I don't consider whiny, crabby and pestering to be prominent among my own numerous flaws.

8   Dictionaries of slang are informative sources, in touch as they are with nascent language and the emotive coloration of words, especially words of abuse. A relatively restrained definition is offered by the only female lexicographer I consulted for whom bitch is "a nasty woman" or "a difficult task" (Anita Pearl, *Dictionary of Popular Slang*). The delineations of bitch by the male lexicographers abound with such cascading hostility that the compilers sometimes seem to be reveling in their task. For example, Howard Wentworth and Stuart Berg Flexner in *Dictionary of American Slang:*

> A woman, usu., but not necessarily, a mean, selfish, malicious, deceiving, cruel, or promiscuous woman.

9   Eugene E. Landy's *The Underground Dictionary* (1971) offers:

> 1. Female who is mean, selfish, cruel, malicious, deceiving. a.k.a. cunt.
> 2. Female. See Female.

I looked up the entry for "Female" (Landy, by the way, provides no parallel entry for "Male"):

> beaver, bird, bitch, broad, bush, cat, chick, crack, cunt, douche, fish, fox, frail, garbage can, heffer, pussy, quail, ruca, scag, snatch, stallion, slave, sweet meat, tail, trick, tuna. See GIRL FRIEND; WIFE.

Richard A. Spears's *Slang and Euphemism* comments on the derivative adjective:

> bitchy 1. pertaining to a mood wherein one complains incessantly about anything. Although this applies to men or women, it is usually associated with women, especially when they are menstruating. Cf. DOG DAYS

Robert L. Chapman's definition in *Thesaurus of American Slang* starts off like 10 a feminist analysis:

bitch. 1 n. A woman one dislikes or disapproves of.

Followed, however, by a sobering string of synonyms: "broad, cunt, witch." And then this most interesting note:

Female equivalents of the contemptuous terms for men, listed in this book under "asshole," are relatively rare. Contempt for females, in slang, stresses their putative sexual promiscuity and weakness rather than their moral vileness and general odiousness. Some terms under "asshole," though, are increasingly used of women.

"See ball-buster," Chapman suggests under his second definition for bitch 11 ("anything arduous or very disagreeable"). I looked up "ball-buster":

n. Someone who saps or destroys masculinity.
ball-wacker
bitch
nut-cruncher.

Some*thing* has become some*one*. The ball-buster is not a disagreeable thing 12 but a disagreeable (disagreeing?) person. A female person. "A woman one dislikes or disapproves of." For someone so sensitive to the nuances of hostility and verbal putdown, Chapman certainly takes a circuitous route to get to the underlying idea that no other dictionary even touches: Bitch means ball-buster.

What one learns from the dictionaries: there is no classifiable thing as a 13 bitch, only a label produced by the act of name-calling. The person named is almost always a female. The name-calling refers to alleged faults of ill-temper, self-ishness, malice, cruelty, spite, all of them faults in the realm of interpersonal relating—women's faults: it is hard to think of a put-down word encompassing these faults in a man. "Bastard" and even "son of a bitch" have bigger fish to fry. And an asshole is an asshole in and of himself. A bitch is a woman who makes the name caller feel uncomfortable. Presumably that name-caller is a man whose ideas about how a woman should behave toward him are being violated.

"Women," wrote Virginia Woolf, "have served all these centuries as looking- 14 glasses possessing the magic and delicious power of reflecting the figure of man at twice its natural size." The woman who withholds that mirror is a bitch. Bitchiness is the perversion of womanly sweetness, compliance, pleasantness, ego-building. (Male ego-building, of course, though that is a virtual tautology; women have egos but who builds them?) If a woman is not building ego she is busting balls.

Ball-buster? The word is a nice synecdoche (like asshole) with great powers of 15 revelation. A ball-buster, one gathers, is a demanding bitch who insists on overexertion from a man to satisfy her sexual or material voraciousness. The bitch is probably his wife. But balls also bust when a disagreeable woman undermines a guy's ego and "saps or destroys masculinity." The bitch could be his wife, but also his boss, Gloria Steinem, the woman at the post office, the woman who spurns his advances. The familiar Freudian delineation of the male-female nexus depicts male sexuality as requiring the admiration, submission and subordination of the female. The ultimate threat of (and to) the back-talking woman is male impotence.

16   Bitch, the curse and concept, exists to insure male potency and female submissiveness. Men have deployed it to defend their power by attacking and neutralizing the upstart. "Bitch" is admonitory, like "whore," like "dyke." Borrowing something from both words, "bitch" is one of those verbal missiles with the power of shackling women's actions and impulses.

17   The metamorphosis of bitch from the context of sexuality (a carnal woman, a promiscuous woman) to temperament (an angry woman, a malicious woman) to power (a domineering woman, a competitive woman) is a touchstone to the changing position of women through this century. As women have become more liberated, individually and collectively, the word has taken on connotations of aggressive, hostile, selfish. In the old days a bitch was a harlot; nowadays she is likely to be a woman who won't put out. Female sensuality, even carnality, even infidelity, have been supplanted as what men primarily fear and despise in women. Judging by the contemporary colorations of the word bitch, what men primarily fear and despise in women is power.

Some anecdotes:

18   (1) Barbara Bush's name-calling of Geraldine Ferraro during the 1984 presidential election: "I can't say it but it rhymes with 'rich.' "

19   How ladylike of the future First Lady to avoid uttering the unmentionable. The slur did its dirty work, particularly among those voters disturbed by the sudden elevation of a woman to such unprecedented political heights. In what possible sense did Barbara Bush mean that Geraldine Ferraro is a bitch? A loose woman? Hardly. A nasty woman? Not likely. A pushy woman? Almost certainly. The unspoken syllable was offered as a response to Ferraro's lofty ambitions, potential power, possibly her widespread support among feminists. Imagine a woman seeking to be vice-president instead of vice-husband.

20   The ascription of bitchery seems to have nothing to do with Ferraro's bearing and behavior. Certainly not the Ferraro who wrote about the event in her autobiography:

> Barbara Bush realized what a gaffe she had made . . .
> "I just want to apologize to you for what I said," she told me over the phone while I was in the middle of another debate rehearsal. "I certainly didn't mean anything by it."
> "Don't worry about it," I said to her. "We all say things at times we don't mean. It's all right."
> "Oh," she said breathlessly. "You're such a lady."
> All I could think of when I hung up was: Thank God for my convent school training.

(2) Lady Ashley at the end of *The Sun Also Rises:* "It makes one feel rather good, 21 deciding not to be a bitch." The context here is something like this: a bitch is a woman who ruins young heroic bullfighters. A woman who is propelled by her sexual drive, desires and vanity. The fascination of Brett Ashley is that she lives and loves like a man: her sexuality is unrepressed and she doesn't care much for monogamy. (Literary critics until the 1960s commonly called her a nympho-maniac.) She turns her male admirers into women—Mike becomes a self-destructive alcoholic, Robert a moony romantic, Pedro a sacrificial virgin, and Jake a frustrated eunuch. At her entrance in the novel she is surrounded by an entourage of twittering fairies. Lady Ashley is a bitch not because she is nasty, bossy or ill-tempered (she has lovely manners and a terrific personality). And perhaps not even because of her freewheeling, strident sexuality. She is a bitch because she overturns the male/female nexus. What could be a more threat-ening infraction in a Hemingway novel?

(2a) Speaking of Hemingway: After his falling out with Gertrude Stein who had 22 made unflattering comments about his writing in *The Authobiography of Alice B. Toklas,* Hemingway dropped her off a copy of his newly published *Death in the Afternoon* with the handwritten inscription, "A bitch is a bitch is a bitch."
    [Q.] Why was Gertrude Stein a bitch?
    [A.] For no longer admiring Hemingway. A bitch is a woman who criticizes.

(3) "Ladies and gentlemen, I don't believe Mrs. Helmsley is charged in the in- 23 dictment with being a tough bitch" is how her defense lawyer Gerald A. Feffer addressed the jury in Leona Helmsley's trial for tax fraud and extortion. He ac-knowledged that she was "sometimes rude and abrasive," and that she "may have overcompensated for being a woman in a hard-edged men's business world." Recognizing the difficulty of defending what the New York *Post* called "the woman that everyone loves to hate," his tactic was to preempt the prose-cution by getting there first with "tough bitch." He lost.

(4) *Esquire* awarded a Dubious Achievement of 1990 to Victor Kiam, owner of the 24 New England Patriots football team, for saying "he could never have called Boston *Herald* reporter Lisa Olson 'a classic bitch' because he doesn't use the word classic." Some background on what had been one of that year's most dis-cussed controversies: Olson aroused the ire of the Patriots for showing up in their locker room with the male reporters after a game. Members of the Patriots, as *Es-quire* states, surrounded her, "thrusting their genitals in her face and daring her to touch them."
    Why is Lisa Olson a bitch? For invading the male domain of sports reportage 25 and the male territory of the locker room? For telling the world, instead of swal-lowing her degradation, pain and anger? The club owner's use of "bitch" seems meant to conjure up the lurking idea of castrating female. Seen in that light the Patriots' act of "thrusting their genitals in her face" transforms an act of loutish-ness into a position of innocent vulnerability.

26 (5) Bumper sticker observed on back of pickup truck:

> Impeach Jane Fonda, American Traitor Bitch

The bumper sticker seemed relatively new and fresh. I observed it a full two decades after Jane Fonda's journey to North Vietnam which is the event that surely inspired this call to impeachment (from what? aerobics class?). Bitch here is an expletive. It originates in and sustains anger. Calling Jane Fonda a "traitor" sounds a bit dated in the 1990s, but adding "bitch" gives the accusation time-lessness and does the job of rekindling old indignation.

27 (6) Claude Brown's account in *Manchild in the Promised Land* of how he learned about women from a street-smart older friend:

> Johnny was always telling us about bitches. To Johnny, every chick was a bitch. Even mothers were bitches. Of course there were some nice bitches, but they were still bitches. And a man had to be a dog in order to handle a bitch.
> Johnny said once, "If a bitch ever tells you she's only got a penny to buy the baby some milk, take it. You take it, 'cause she's gon git some more. Bitches can always git some money." He really knew about bitches. Cats would say, "I saw your sister today, and she is a fine bitch." Nobody was offended by it. That's just the way things were. It was easy to see all women as bitches.

28   Bitch in black male street parlance seems closer to its original meaning of a female breeder—not a nasty woman and not a powerful woman, but the biological bearer of litters. The word is likely to be used in courting as well as in anger by males seeking the sexual favor of a female, and a black female addressed as bitch by an admirer is expected to feel not insulted but honored by the attention. (Bitch signifies something different when black women use it competitively about other black women.) But even as an endearment, from male to female, there is no mistaking the lurking contempt.

29   *A Dictionary of Afro-American Slang* compiled by Clarence Major (under the imprint of the leftist International Publishers) provides only that bitch in black parlance is "a mean, flaunting homosexual," entirely omitting any reference to its rampant use in black street language as the substitute word for woman. A puzzling omission. Perhaps the word is so taken for granted that its primary meaning is not even recognized as black vernacular.

30   Bitch, mama, motherfucker—how frequently motherhood figures in street language. Mothers are the object of insults when playing the dozens. The ubiquitous motherfucker simultaneously strikes out at one's immediate foe as well as the sanctity of motherhood. Mama, which Clarence Major defines as "a pretty black girl," is an endearment that a man might address to a sexy contemporary. "Hey mama" is tinged with a certain sweetness. "Hey bitch" has more of an edge, more likely to be addressed to a woman the man no longer needs to sweet-talk. It is hard to think of white males coming on by evoking motherhood or of white women going for it. A white male addressing a woman as bitch is not likely to

be expecting a sexual reward. She will be a bitch behind her back and after the relationship is over or didn't happen.

The widespread use of bitch by black men talking to black women, its cur- 31 rency in courting, and its routine acceptance by women are suggestive of some powerful alienation in male-female relations and in black self-identity. Although there may be the possibility of ironic inversion, as in calling a loved one nigger, a black man calling a loved one bitch is expressing contempt for the object of his desire with the gratuitous fillip of associative contempt for the woman who gave him life. Bitch, like motherfucker, bespeaks something threatening to the male sense of himself, a furious counter to emasculation in a world where, as the young Claude Brown figured out, mothers have all the power. It is not hard to see that the problem of black men is much more with white racism than it is with black women. Whatever the cause, however, the language sure doesn't benefit the women. Here is still one more saddening instance of the victim finding someone even more hapless to take things out on. (Does this process explain why Clarence Major's only reference for bitch is to the "mean, flaunting homosexual"?)

(7) "Do you enjoy playing that role of castrating bitch" is a question put to 32 Madonna by an interviewer for *The Advocate.* Madonna's answer: "I enjoy expressing myself. . . ."

A response to another question about the public's reaction to her movie 33 *Truth or Dare:* "They already think I'm a cunt bitch, they already think I'm Attila the Hun. They already compare me to Adolf Hitler and Saddam Hussein."

Bitch has lost its power to muzzle Madonna. Unlike other female celebrities 34 who have cringed from accusations of bitchiness (Joan Rivers, Imelda Marcos, Margaret Thatcher, Nancy Reagan), Madonna has made her fortune by exploiting criticism. Her career has skyrocketed with the media's charges of obscenity and sacrilege; she seems to embrace the bitch label with the same eager opportunism.

"I enjoy expressing myself" is not merely the explanation for why Madonna 35 gets called bitch; "I enjoy expressing myself" is the key to defusing the power of bitch to fetter and subdue. Madonna has appropriated the word and turned the intended insult to her advantage. This act of appropriation, I predict, will embolden others with what consequences and effects it is impossible to foresee.

● *Thinking Critically About "Bitch"*

RESPONDING AS A READER

1. What is the importance of the opening anecdote to the essay as a whole? What expectations does it establish regarding both *what* the reader can expect in the essay and *why* the writer considers that to be important?

2. Gross builds her essay around the authority of numerous research sources and then a sequence of anecdotes. How do these materials enhance her credibility? How would you describe her personal engagement with the subject? In what ways does it change from the beginning of the essay to the end? What about it remains constant?

3. What do you understand to be Gross's purpose for writing this essay? How does she seem to want to influence readers' thinking about the word "bitch," its meanings and uses? How successful was she in your case?

RESPONDING AS A WRITER

1. Given your personal experience with the word "bitch" and that of people you know, male and female, would you say that its use has changed significantly since this essay was published? What examples from your own experience and from your observation of popular culture support your view?

2. This essay demonstrates how changeable language can be. Words develop new meanings over time, and slang expressions develop from wordplay that inverts the commonly understood meanings of words. What similar examples can you point to in the language of your peers or in current pop culture? Choose a particular word that interests you because of its varying meanings and sketch a brief anecdote that might serve to introduce an exploratory essay on the subject.

3. With your classmates, develop a list of slang words that have multiple meanings, either within slang itself (as "bitch" does) or between common and slang usage (such as the well-known examples of "cool" and "bad"). Use the reference works Gross cites as well as the most current dictionaries of slang that you can find to investigate the changing meanings of the words.

Gloria Naylor

"Mommy, What Does 'Nigger' Mean?"

A prominent African American author, Gloria Naylor (b. 1950) was raised in New York City. This article, which has been republished frequently, originally appeared February 20, 1986 as a *New York Times* "Hers" column, a place where noted women published commentaries on their experience. At the time, Naylor was acclaimed for her first novel, *The Women of Brewster Place*, which won the 1983 National Book Award. Since then, she has published numerous essays, articles, and books, including *Mama Day* and *Bailey's Café*, which were adapted for film and stage.

• *For Your Reading Log*

1. "Nigger"—often referred to as "the N word"—is very difficult for most Americans to deal with, regardless of their racial background. Before reading Naylor's description of her discovery of it, and its complex uses, freewrite for several minutes about your own encounters with the word up until now.
2. What (other) derogatory words are used to refer to people of your particular race and ethnicity? Are they always negative in their meaning and use?

Language is the subject. It is the written form with which I've managed to keep 1 the wolf away from the door and, in diaries, to keep my sanity. In spite of this, I consider the written word inferior to the spoken, and much of the frustration experienced by novelists is the awareness that whatever we manage to capture in even the most transcendent passages falls far short of the richness of life. Dialogue achieves its power in the dynamics of a fleeting moment of sight, sound, smell and touch.

I'm not going to enter the debate here about whether it is language that 2 shapes reality or vice versa. That battle is doomed to be waged whenever we seek intermittent reprieve from the chicken and egg dispute. I will simply take the position that the spoken word, like the written word, amounts to a nonsensical arrangement of sounds or letters without a consensus that assigns "meaning." And building from the meanings of what we hear, we order reality. Words themselves are innocuous; it is the consensus that gives them true power.

I remember the first time I heard the word nigger. In my third-grade class, our 3 math tests were being passed down the rows, and as I handed the papers to a little boy in back of me, I remarked that once again he had received a much lower mark than I did. He snatched his test from me and spit out that word. Had he called me a nymphomaniac or a necrophiliac, I couldn't have been more puzzled. I didn't know what a nigger was, but I knew that whatever it meant, it was something he shouldn't have called me. This was verified when I raised my hand, and in a loud voice repeated what he had said and watched the teacher scold him for using a "bad" word. I was later to go home and ask the inevitable question that every black parent must face—"Mommy, what does 'nigger' mean?"

4   And what exactly did it mean? Thinking back, I realize that this could not have been the first time the word was used in my presence. I was part of a large extended family that had migrated from the rural South after World War II and formed a close-knit network that gravitated around my maternal grandparents. Their ground-floor apartment in one of the buildings they owned in Harlem was a weekend mecca for my immediate family, along with countless aunts, uncles and cousins who brought along assorted friends. It was a bustling and open house with assorted neighbors and tenants popping in and out to exchange bits of gossip, pick up an old quarrel or referee the ongoing checkers game in which my grandmother cheated shamelessly. They were all there to let down their hair and put up their feet after a week of labor in the factories, laundries and shipyards of New York.

5   Amid the clamor, which could reach deafening proportions—two or three conversations going on simultaneously, punctuated by the sound of a baby's crying somewhere in the back rooms or out on the street—there was still a rigid set of rules about what was said and how. Older children were sent out of the living room when it was time to get into the juicy details about "you-know-who" up on the third floor who had gone and gotten herself "p-r-e-g-n-a-n-t!" But my parents, knowing that I could spell well beyond my years, always demanded that I follow the others out to play. Beyond sexual misconduct and death, everything else was considered harmless for our young ears. And so among the anecdotes of the triumphs and disappointments in the various workings of their lives, the word nigger was used in my presence, but it was set within contexts and inflections that caused it to register in my mind as something else.

6   In the singular, the word was always applied to a man who had distinguished himself in some situation that brought their approval for his strength, intelligence or drive:

7   "Did Johnny really do that?"

8   "I'm telling you, that nigger pulled in $6,000 of overtime last year. Said he got enough for a down payment on a house."

9   When used with a possessive adjective by a woman—"my nigger"—it became a term of endearment for husband or boyfriend. But it could be more than just a term applied to a man. In their mouths it became the pure essence of manhood—a disembodied force that channeled their past history of struggle and present survival against the odds into a victorious statement of being: "Yeah, that old foreman found out quick enough—you don't mess with a nigger."

10   In the plural, it became a description of some group within the community that had overstepped the bounds of decency as my family defined it: Parents who neglected their children, a drunken couple who fought in public, people who simply refused to look for work, those with excessively dirty mouths or unkempt

households were all "trifling niggers." This particular circle could forgive hard times, unemployment, the occasional bout of depression—they had gone through all of that themselves—but the unforgivable sin was lack of self-respect.

A woman could never be a "nigger" in the singular, with its connotation of 11 confirming worth. The noun "girl" was its closest equivalent in that sense, but only when used in direct address and regardless of the gender doing the addressing. "Girl" was a token of respect for a woman. The one-syllable word was drawn out to sound like three in recognition of the extra ounce of wit, nerve or daring that the woman had shown in the situation under discussion.

"G-i-r-l, stop. You mean you said that to his face?"   12

But if the word was used in a third-person reference or shortened so that it 13 almost snapped out of the mouth, it always involved some element of communal disapproval. And age became an important factor in these exchanges. It was only between individuals of the same generation, or from an older person to a younger (but never the other way around), that "girl" would be considered a compliment.

I don't agree with the argument that use of the word nigger at this social stra- 14 tum of the black community was an internalization of racism. The dynamics were the exact opposite: the people in my grandmother's living room took a word that whites used to signify worthlessness or degradation and rendered it impotent. Gathering there together, they transformed "nigger" to signify the varied and complex human beings they knew themselves to be. If the word was to disappear totally from the mouths of even the most liberal of white society, no one in that room was naïve enough to believe it would disappear from white minds. Meeting the word head-on, they proved it had absolutely nothing to do with the way they were determined to live their lives.

So there must have been dozens of times that the word "nigger" was spoken 15 in front of me before I reached the third grade. But I didn't "hear" it until it was said by a small pair of lips that had already learned it could be a way to humiliate me. That was the word I went home and asked my mother about. And since she knew that I had to grow up in America, she took me in her lap and explained.

• Thinking Critically About "Mommy, What Does 'Nigger' Mean?"

RESPONDING AS A READER

1. "Language is the subject," Naylor begins. How so? Look closely at the questions posed and answered by her exploration. To what extent is this essay about the ways that language functions interpersonally, and to what extent is it about African Americans' experience with the explosive word "nigger"? Point to specific passages to back up your answers.

2. How would you describe the personality that Naylor portrays for herself in this essay? What specific details contribute to that impression? How does this ethos contribute to your appreciation of her experience and its significance?

3. The *New York Times* has a multicultural, indeed, multinational audience. The vast majority of these readers would never have themselves been called a nigger in any sense of the term. What specific strategies do you see Naylor using to engage non–African American readers in her story?

RESPONDING AS A WRITER

1. To examine the cultural values that inform the uses of "nigger" that Naylor discusses, divide a piece of paper into two columns. Put a plus sign at the top of the left column and list in it the examples Naylor gives of positive uses for the word "nigger." Be sure to note what Naylor says about *who* says it and *how* it is said as well as *what* it means in that instance. In the right column, list the examples Naylor gives of negative uses of the word, again noting situational factors. As you look at both lists together, what pattern do you see in the positive and negative uses of the word? When you consider the implied opposite of each use of the word, what do you discover? Summarize your analysis in a paragraph that provides an overview of the values at play in Naylor's essay. (This two-column technique for analyzing ideology is described in Chapter 5, p. 77.)

2. How does the essay's title, "Mommy, What Does 'Nigger' Mean?" work to draw you into the reading? The title is punctuated as an excerpt from a conversation. What did that fact initially suggest to you about Naylor's approach to the subject matter? Is it an effective title? To explain why or why not, consider what kinds of expectations the title might set up in different readers. Then, imagine how Naylor might respond to an editor's suggestion that this title is too inflammatory. What arguments do you think she would make to keep the title as it is?

3. What do you remember about your own discovery of racism? Did it dawn on you as an abstract idea or through a specific, perhaps ugly, experience? What questions does Naylor's essay suggest to you as a way of exploring your own experience with the constellation of ideas about difference, hostility, threat, (in)equality, and (in)justice that have come to be associated with the term racism. Freewrite for at least ten minutes.

Joshua D. McColough (Student)

Seeking Answers to the Question of Divorce

Josh McColough (b. 1974) wrote this exploratory paper in the spring of 1996 for an undergraduate writing workshop at Marquette University, his alma mater. After several years working for an advertising agency in Chicago, he decided to pursue an MFA in creative nonfiction at the University of Iowa.

• *For Your Reading Log*

1. Has divorce ever affected you in any way? How close has it come to disrupting your life? Freewrite for a few minutes about your personal experience and feelings regarding divorce before you begin reading.

2. This is a student essay that has not undergone the formal editorial processes of publication. As you read it, imagine that it was written by one of your peers who is now seeking your honest response. When you finish reading, jot down your initial responses to the piece. What do you want to "say back" to McColough?

——————— • ———————

"The family in its old sense is disappearing from our land, and not only our free institutions are threatened, but the very existence of our society is endangered."
—Appeared in the Boston *Quarterly Review* in 1859

You never can tell what may go wrong. Marriage is a risk.   1
I'll tell you what it is—it's that people just aren't committed anymore.   2
Nobody wants to live with one person for *that* long. Humans live longer to- 3
day than in the days of marrying young and dying after 15 years of marriage.
Starter marriages—a first marriage designed to tide you over until you find 4
your real mate.
Sometimes it just doesn't work out. It takes two people, you know.   5
His parents are splitting up—after 32 years.   6
What is it now, 50 per cent? No, 62%.   7

Explanations, diversions, excuses, theories, statistics, but no answers. How do we 8
make sense of all this? The destructive forces of divorce impact society at its roots.
When institutions founded at the deepest personal level fail, the aftershock is
painfully experienced as more than just an explosion in the number of single-
parent families. Rejection, imbalance, suspicion, disillusionment, and despair dark
and dismal hang heavy over the joyous celebration of each new marriage. These

emotions can quickly replace the stability and promise that the exchange of wedding vows symbolizes.

9   I sink into the couch in our family room. Aunt Peggy and Uncle Max are separated. What about our traditional fondue dinner on New Year's Eve? The weekends up at the lake? All of our fun? We can still do all of this, right?

10   They are probably going to get a divorce.

11   NO! What about Katie and Stephen? When will they come over and play? A few kids in my class have divorced parents. They are the problem kids. The bullies, the recluses, the weird, the angry, the weak, the sad. I consider them the pitiful living truth that everyone needs parents—both of them. Don't you see? Aunt Peggy and Uncle Max have to get back together!

12   But for some reason, I know that Aunt Peggy and Uncle Max will never be "Aunt Peggy and Uncle Max" anymore. Never again. They become Aunt Peggy . . . and Uncle Max. And Katie and Stephen are shifted around depending upon the day of the week. But some day I should understand why this happens. I'm just a kid, and this is an adult problem. Mom will tell me really why this is happening . . . when I get older.

13   Becoming an adult offers little more understanding to the widespread dilemma of divorce. It just seems to become more common. Aunt Peggy . . . and Uncle Max were my first experience with divorce. Since then, I have become increasingly aware of every divorce. I am an active observer of numerous fractured families, a spectator of custody battles, a silent reflective bystander of strain and stress, pushing and pulling, tension . . . and release. I frantically grasp for anything that may suggest a general trend or pattern so that if I get married this painful ordeal can be avoided. But the only thing that I learn is that more marriages fail than are successful, and that "you just never know." Not exactly consoling words, but truthful.

14   The truth is that marriages can fail. The truth is that most marriages do fail. This is something that must be recognized if one is to have a full, mature appreciation of marriage. Having parents who have been married for over 30-some years clouds my efforts to understand the reasoning behind divorce. But it does provide me with a positive model for the institution of marriage.

15   Nevertheless, I remain uneasy with the idea of marriage simply because of divorce. It's a rather convoluted way of looking at things, much like being uneasy with life because of death. But contradictions don't stop some people from being constantly afraid that they could be killed in a car accident, have a stroke or heart attack, or simply expire at any moment.

16   I am at an interesting point in life. In less than two years, I proceed forth from the virtual bubble that school has provided for the last twenty or so years. I will enter the adult world, whether I like it or not. I will be forced to confront the future, make decisions about a career, a job, a place to live . . . on my own. The idea of marrying remains a distant goal, one that I talk about and approach as one approaches a sick friend, careful not to catch the disease.

17   The fact is, I have not been granted the epiphany that I was hoping for so many years ago when I first learned of the divorce of Aunt Peggy . . . and Uncle Max.

Indeed, I have been given the opposite of what I hoped for—the answer that there are no answers. Nothing here but statistics. Enter Disraeli: "There are three kinds of lies: lies, damn lies, and statistics." Right? Wrong. The statistics aren't lying. They are neither particularly optimistic nor shocking by today's standards. In fact, poking fun at the optimist's naïveté, one of my psychology textbooks uses this illustration regarding "Contemporary American Families: Dreams and Reality":

CULTURAL DREAM:	CULTURAL REALITY:
First marriage continues until the death of one spouse.	More than 60 per cent of all first marriages end in divorce.

In other words, "If you think 'till death do us part' is for real, you are dreaming." It's time to wake up.

I face this future armed with nothing more than an awe of the unknown 18 mixed with a greater respect for the risk involved in getting married. I see what happens when marriages fail. I go to class with a lot of them, hang out with them, am friends with them—the children, now adults, of divorced parents.

We are lucky enough to have grown up at a relatively new beginning in 19 American moral history. The tie between morality and divorce is gone. To many, this is a green light, a marital escape clause. "I want a divorce." It's an apathetic escapist cry heard more and more often in the last 25 years when the stresses and strains of marriage become too much to bear. Meanwhile, the casualties of divorce are left stranded, many too young to understand why their mommies and daddies no longer live together. This is enough to shatter the world of any child, at any age, living at any time period. No amount of psychological, guilt-free, it-isn't-your-fault-that-your-parents-are-divorced therapy can repair a child's loss of a primary role model, caretaker, educator. So these children are left to deal with it themselves, perhaps being told by overpriced psychologists and therapists that they shouldn't feel guilty, that it really is the *best* thing for everyone, that they really should be able to talk freely to their parents about their feelings. Being told how to feel everything, but never really understanding why . . . until they get older? Then they stand on the same shaky ground that I stand upon, looking toward the future, repulsed by statistics, wondering how to make sense of everything when the big realization of adulthood is that there are no certain answers.

I meet this on an individual level. The adults of divorce whom I know have 20 differing feelings about the effects it has had on their own lives. Some of them don't view it as any kind of barrier that will inhibit them from pursuing the joys of marriage. Others are terrified by the prospect of putting themselves, and possibly their children, through the same hell that they encountered when they were young. And there are those who claim divorce is inevitable, so they plan on multiple marriages.

Caught somewhere between the fear of marriage and the loathing of di- 21 vorce, I remain in a barren no man's land, stuck because of indirect brushes with divorce throughout my life. I know that nothing good comes easy. As much as my optimistic self wants to reject the idea, I also know this: we have to embrace divorce as a fact of modern life. Marriages can end in divorce. Most marriages end in divorce.

- ## *Thinking Critically About "Seeking Answers to the Question of Divorce"*

RESPONDING AS A READER

1. As the essay begins, what reasons does the author give you for reading it? Were you persuaded that the subject and McColough's engagement with it were significant? Why or why not?
2. What role does the text ask you to play in relation to McColough's very personal voice? Where were you most engaged with what he had to say? Where did you find yourself doubting or resisting him?
3. Are you satisfied with the way the essay ends? What ambiguities remain? Are they necessary ambiguities, or ambiguities that McColough needed to try to resolve?

RESPONDING AS A WRITER

1. Suppose that McColough wrote this essay in response to the Exploring a Question That Puzzles You assignment at the end of this chapter. What are its strengths and weaknesses? What suggestions would you give him for the next draft?
2. When McColough's classmates were workshopping this essay, he asked for feedback about two specific matters. First, was the collage organization effective? Second, did it fulfill a specific requirement to explore an issue of public, not just private, importance? What feedback would you give him on both these points?
3. What questions does this essay raise for you? How might you go about exploring possible answers?

Writing to Inquire and Explore

The texts in this chapter explore complex questions about how human beings live and work in community, questions that do not have clear-cut answers, problems that do not have ready solutions. The writing assignments below suggest ways in which you can use writing to explore comparable issues that are important to you.

EXPLORING A QUESTION THAT PUZZLES YOU

Choose a question that is difficult for you and others to resolve and explore it with a mix of personal narrative and researched information similar to that in most of the essays in this chapter. To make this a real exploration, not simply a report, work with a question, problem, or issue for which several apparent answers have been posed. Avoid "fake questions" on matters about which you already have a position, such as "Why doesn't this university impose a cap on tuition?" Use chronological organization and the first person as appropriate. Whether you find and express closure on the matter is up to you.

EXAMINING RHETORICAL STRATEGIES

One of the most important aspects of reading rhetorically is considering how a given author has constructed your role and responses within a text and whether this effort has been successful in getting you to change your mind about the subject matter in some way. For this assignment, evaluate the effectiveness of the exploratory rhetorical strategies in one of the texts in this chapter. Use the "Questions to Help You Read Explorations Rhetorically" on page 210 to guide your analysis. The purpose of your critique is to explain (1) the extent to which the author succeeded in deepening your thinking about the topic, and (2) how the exploratory approach contributed to that success or lack of success. Relate the effect of the author's rhetorical strategies to the evident overall purpose of the essay.

Feel free to use the first person in your analysis, but be sure to take into account possible responses and interpretations besides your own. Your points should be supported by evidence from the text and what you can glean about the context of original publication. As part of your preparation for writing, it may be particularly helpful to take separate looks at content and strategy in the text you have selected by using the descriptive *(does-says)* outline analysis described in Chapter 4 (p. 58).

EXTENDING THE CONVERSATION

There is more to be said about each of the topics explored by the texts in this chapter. Some of that "more" may come from your own questions, even your resistance to the texts; some may come from other published contributions to the ongoing conversation on the topic. For this assignment, we invite you to extend the conversation by (1) formulating your own question in response to one of the texts and (2) writing an exploratory essay about how you have wrestled with the question and how others have answered it. Use points from the author published here as a starting place for your exploration, and then use library sources to update, elaborate, or counter points in the original text. The texts themselves offer clues for where to begin your research: names of experts who may have published on the topic or who may be quoted elsewhere (for example, in the selections by Crossette and McGuire), publications that can be consulted for comparisons or readers' responses (for example, in Dillard), and, of course, concepts that you can use as search terms. (For additional guidance about finding reliable sources and incorporating them into your own writing, see Chapters 7 and 8.)

CHAPTER

11

Informing and Explaining

nformation and explanation lie at the heart of college study. You read informative materials to gain knowledge; your professors give lectures and lead discussions to explain difficult concepts and provide context for new ideas. You write informative papers and exams to demonstrate the knowledge you have gained, and then go off into the world to inform and explain to others what you have learned. End of story? Not at all. It would be naïve to think that the combination of information and explanation is a simple matter of transmitting facts from one mind to another via a page or screen. Effective presentation and explanation of information requires more than clear sentence structure and well-defined terms. It requires considerable rhetorical know-how. Reading such material effectively also requires good rhetorical skills so that you can determine whether the information has significance for you, how reliable it is, and what you can do with it.

Texts that inform and explain, also known as *expository* texts, share a rhetorical purpose of expanding their intended audience's understanding, or image, of the subject matter under discussion. The degree of change to be brought about in a given reader's views of the material depends upon the reader's already existing understanding and level of engagement with the subject. In its purest or prototypical form, informative writing asserts itself on the assumption that the writer knows something that the reader needs or wants to know and would be pleased to learn. However, this oversimplified prototype ignores the rhetorical elements present in nearly all expository texts. Readers' interest in a subject will vary. Readers don't always recognize that they need to know more about something. Furthermore, they won't pause to read just anybody's explanation of a given phenomenon. If taking in the new information will reconstruct previous thinking rather than simply expand it a bit, or if the new material brings unwelcome or threatening news, readers are likely to resist or reject what is said. The greater the likelihood of resistance from readers, the greater the writer's need to persuade as well as inform.

In this chapter, for example, consider how the assumptions about reader expectations implicit in Kathy Wollard's short newspaper pieces contrast with those in Peter Marin's article on homelessness. After opening with a reader's question, Wollard uses catchy comparisons (cool water versus intense heat; giggles versus pain) to move readers into her explanation. Marin, on the other hand, devotes five substantial paragraphs to anecdote and reflection before he states his purpose: "to explain at least some of that anger and fear [about homelessness], to clear up some of the confusion, to chip away at the indifference." Surely most readers will anticipate that the ideas in Marin's article will challenge their current views far more than Wollard's will, even if they know nothing at all about her subjects—mirages and hiccups.

What makes an informative or explanatory text good? You can probably list a few qualities by recalling what "worked" in materials that have taught you something, that have successfully expanded your image of their subject matter. Understanding a few of the essential qualities of good expository prose will enable you to assess the methods as well as the content of the texts in this chapter and, in turn, apply some of these strategies in your own writing.

An effective expository text gives readers a purpose for reading in the first place. Its author understands readers' need for information and establishes credentials for being taken seriously. Its vocabulary is understandable, and its organization meets readers' expectations. In certain contexts, especially scholarly journals, meeting readers' expectations involves following genre conventions, such as a distinct section devoted to a literature review (sometimes labeled as such, sometimes not). In other contexts, readers will be engaged best through a personal anecdote, or with graphic devices, or a page layout that enhances the ease of reading. Newspaper articles, for example, use boldface headings and short paragraphs to break up the grayness of big blocks of type in narrow columns. Similarly, headings and bulleted lists make it easy to locate key bits of information in this chapter's article from the *UC Berkeley Wellness Letter,* "Why Do Those #&*?@! 'Experts' Keep Changing Their Minds?" For some audiences, the best way to pique interest and convey information may be a question-and-answer format or a quiz.

A good expository text should offer something new, something interesting, either in the ideas presented or in what the writer has to say about them. Texts that intrigue us and hold our attention often suggest some tension between what we already know before we read and what we'll know after we finish. Texts that engage us make clear the significance of the information and explanations being presented. By indicating the subject's significance, the reading will suggest what readers will gain by continuing to read, why they should remember what they read, and how they might apply this newly gained understanding to their own professional or personal contexts. Of course, many writing assignments in school and on the job may call for what seems to be a fairly dry and straightforward presentation of information—as on an essay exam, for example, or a memo about new office procedures. But even in those cases, whether you are writing about the effectiveness of specific childhood vaccinations or a new method of reporting sales figures, your effectiveness in making your points clearly will be enhanced by your ability to communicate to your readers an understanding of what is significant in the text before them. As you read the various selections in this chapter, note how even the most apparently straightforward texts convey a sense of their subject's significance.

Effective writers have a fairly accurate sense of the degree of change they want and need to bring about in their readers' understanding of the subject at hand. They also can anticipate the degree of resistance their ideas will meet in those intended readers. The greater the resistance, the more carefully must they pave the way for the changed image. When the intended change in image is negative and the news probably unwelcome—for instance if something thought benign actually has harmful effects—the author's challenge is greater still.

Effective rhetorical readers are able to discern not only a writer's intended message but the strategies invoked for conveying it. (In the article from the *Wellness Letter*, the purpose is to help readers become more adept at this discernment when they read reports of medical research. Contrast its approach with the call for action in the *New England Journal of Medicine* editorial on the same subject by Marcia Angell and Jerome Kassirer in Chapter 15.) Rhetorical readers can detect assumptions a writer has made about their prior understanding of the subject; they can recognize how the writer has worked to counter their resistance to the message. The sharper the readers' recognition of how the writer is working to change their minds, the greater their freedom in deciding the extent to which they will resist or accept the new information and ideas.

A slight, and welcome, expansion of a reader's understanding of a phenomenon is rhetorically the simplest expository task, as in Wollard's two articles. In other situations, the reader's image may need more extensive adjustments. Marcy Gordon's article about credit cards starts out as an amusing history lesson but builds to a list of serious problems blamed on credit cards. In more personal statements, Paul Irgang and Nancy Mairs seek to clarify readers' understanding of people like themselves. Mairs's sharp images and challenging descriptions insist that readers reexamine their assumptions about being able to move around in the world. These writers, along with Marin, seem intent upon changing their readers' thinking in major ways. Nevertheless, we have grouped these pieces in this chapter with other more simply informative texts because, according to our rhetorical reading, an explanatory focus on subject matter dominates in them. (One of the writing assignments at the end of this chapter invites you to agree or disagree with this assessment.)

Finally, the short story at the end of the chapter, "Consent" by C. J. Hribal, offers a quite different way of thinking about explanation. The protagonist is confident that he understands a situation better than anyone else, but his view would alter certain people's worldviews so radically that he dare not explain.

Questions to Help You Read Informative and Explanatory Texts Rhetorically

As you read and work with the expository selections in this chapter, you will encounter differing assumptions about audience expectations and information needs. Use your rhetorical reading skills to assess what you can about each writer's purpose in relation to his or her original intended audience. The questions that follow will help you analyze the writers' aims and techniques for making their subjects intelligible and significant.

1. What techniques does the writer use to pique readers' interest and indicate the significance of the matter at hand? Were the techniques successful in engaging your interest? What role did they give you to play as a reader?

2. How does the writer apparently intend to change the reader's view of the subject or phenomenon at hand? Where would you place the selection on a continuum that runs from "adding new information to a reader's image" to "reconstructing a reader's image" of the subject matter?

3. What can you tell from the text about how the writer expects readers to react to it? Does he or she seem to expect us to be receptive to the points being made? How can you tell? What evidence is there of the writer attempting to smooth away resistance to the ideas presented?

4. What knowledge level does the writer assume readers have? Does the way information is presented match your own information needs? What background information is necessary to understand fully the points being made (for example, concepts, vocabulary, current events)?

5. Can you pinpoint a thesis statement in the selection? If not, what clues do you find that suggest the writer's purpose and central point?

6. Upon what claim to authority is the writer basing his or her points?

7. How is the selection marked by genre conventions? What do these tell you about the intended audience for the selection?

8. How has your thinking changed as a result of reading the selection? Why or why not? Try to pinpoint the places in the text where you resisted or assented to the writer's designs upon you.

Kathy Wollard

How Come?

These two short articles are from Kathy Wollard's (b. 1953) weekly science column in the Long Island newspaper *Newsday*. The column, distributed internationally through the Los Angeles Times Syndicate, is based on readers' questions about natural phenomena. It typically runs in science or health sections of newspapers and is available on the Internet. Wollard and her illustrator, Debra Solomon, have published *How Come?* (1993) and *How Come Planet Earth* (1999), two books collecting short texts similar to the ones included here.

• *For Your Reading Log*

1. As you read, note places in the texts that you find particularly engaging.
2. Immediately after you read each article, test your memory of the information in it by jotting down a quick explanation of why we see mirages and why we hiccup.

———————   •   ———————

Mirage Isn't a Figment of Your Imagination

"Why do you often see a patch of water on the road ahead, which disappears 1
when you near it?" asks K. R. Sushruth, a student in India.

A patch of water on the road on a sweltering day looks cool and refreshing 2
although you wonder why it hasn't evaporated in the heat.

Then, as you get near, it does "evaporate," disappearing into thin air. But 3
wait, another pool of water has appeared further down the road.

Soon you realize you can chase that patch of water down the highway all day 4
and never catch it. That's because the patch of water doesn't really exist—it's a
mirage.

The water-on-the-road mirage—fun for the family, especially on car trips— 5
is a version of the oasis-in-the-desert mirage.

In both cases, water appears to shimmer in the distance, only to vanish as 6
you approach. In cartoons, when a character sees a pool of water in the desert,
he's supposed to be out of his mind from heat and thirst.

But we can see mirages even from the air-conditioned comfort of our cars. 7
Mirages aren't tricks of the mind—they're as real as rainbows. Mirages are an intriguing fact of life on a planet with an atmosphere.

On the Moon, which has virtually no gases surrounding it, there are no mi- 8
rages. All day long the sky is black and starry. The rocky ground gets bright when
the sun shines, but there is no air to light up the sky.

9   But Earth is surrounded by a blanket of gases—nitrogen, oxygen and dozens more. When sunlight strikes gas molecules in Earth's sky, the blues of its hidden rainbow are scattered out into the sky, tinting the atmosphere blue.

10   What does our bright sky have to do with the water mirage? The patch on the road is not actually water, but a patch of sky.

11   Normally, blue light from the sky travels straight into your eyes, so you see the sky where it should be—above the Earth.

12   But a hot layer of air can change that. Heat rising from sun-baked asphalt warms the air above the road. So light streaming down from the sky passes from a layer of cooler, thicker air into the thinner, hot air a few feet above the hot blacktop.

13   As the edge of the light wave enters the thinner air, its way is clearer; it speeds up. But the rest of the wave, still traveling through the thicker air, lags. This makes the wave bend, so that instead of hitting the ground, it travels along it.

14   Then, the dragging of its slower top-half makes the light wave bend a second time—upward, toward you.

15   When the blue light strikes your eyes from near the ground, you see sky where asphalt should be. Since hot air is full of movement, the "sky" appears to shimmer.

16   When you drive nearer, however, the light is at the wrong angle for you to see, so the "water" disappears. It's the passengers in the car behind you who are glimpsing the mirage.

That Funny and Embarrassing Hiccup
May Actually Be Helpful for Your Body

1   "What makes us get the hiccups?" asks Angela Yang, a middle-school student, via e-mail.

2   Hiccups can provoke giggles, but they can also be embarrassing (hiccuping in church or in a quiet meeting) and painful (hiccuping for hours on end).

3   The record for hiccups: 28,000 in one day. Ouch! The hiccup culprit is the diaphragm, a dome-shaped sheet of muscle that lies across the top of the stomach just under the lungs. The diaphragm helps push air out of the lungs by expanding when we breathe out; it pulls down when we breathe in.

4   Hiccups happen when the diaphragm pushes up in a spasm, and the glottis, a part of the larynx (voice box), snaps shut. It's that sudden snap that causes the hic-ing sound. The control center for hiccups may actually be in the part of the spinal cord that runs through the neck. No one knows for sure.

5   At least since the time of the ancient Greeks and the physician Hippocrates, scientists have puzzled over hiccups. Most came to the conclusion that hiccups probably served no useful function—they were just an annoying body-glitch.

6   But some scientists think hiccups may perform a real job in the body. A clue to hiccups' possible usefulness comes from the fact that babies—and adults—often get hiccups when they've eaten too much too fast or consumed a lot of soda pop. In both cases, that means swallowing a lot of gas-air or carbon dioxide.

Gas swells the stomach, thrusting it up against the diaphragm. If the di- 7
aphragm then spasms, starting hiccups, something else happens: The sphincter
muscle at the bottom of the esophagus—the opening to the stomach—actually
widens. This allows gas to escape from the stomach up the esophagus, which is
why a hiccup is often followed by a belch. Presto: The pressure in the stomach
and on the diaphragm drops.

But when we belch, stomach acid and bits of food often come up along with 8
the gas. So some scientists say that when hiccups snap the glottis shut, it may prevent us from sucking the rising acid and food particles into the lungs. (Many people have asthma because of chronic "acid reflux.") If this theory is true, hiccups
may actually have a purpose!

Still, if they go on too long, hiccups are no fun. Which is why there are so 9
many hiccup "cures" floating around. Here's a short list: Eat a spoonful of
sugar, drink a cup of cold water (fast), breathe into a paper bag, bite on a
lemon, swallow chewed-up dry bread, cough, have someone scare you. The ancient Greeks advised tickling the nose with a feather, since a good sneeze will
often stop hiccups.

One trick that may actually work is forcefully exhaling all the air from your 10
lungs and briefly holding your breath. Another is to gently press in (and up) under your rib cage with the fingers of both hands. This applies pressure to your
diaphragm and often turns hiccups right off.

● *Thinking Critically About the "How Come" Articles*

RESPONDING AS A READER

1. Revisit the places you noted in your reading log where Wollard was particularly successful at engaging your interest. What do those spots have
   in common? Based on these examples, what generalizations can you
   make about her approach to writing about natural phenomena?
2. Try to identify specific details in both pieces that indicate Wollard's expectations of her potential readers' knowledge and attitudes. What does
   this textual information tell you about her intended audience and purpose?
3. What is the source of Wollard's authority in these articles? Why should
   we believe that she's right?

RESPONDING AS A WRITER

1. As you read over the quick explanations of mirages and hiccups that you
   wrote in your reading log, what do they tell you about Wollard's effectiveness as a writer who helps readers learn something? Working backward from your reading log, mark the places in the articles that you
   apparently remembered and understood the best. Then examine the
   wording and sentence structure Wollard used to present that specific information. What patterns do you see in the word choices or sentence
   structure of these particularly effective sentences or paragraphs? What

conclusions can you draw about the kind of writing that makes explanations effective?

2. Wollard's short paragraphs are typical of newspaper articles, which use
frequent paragraph indentations to break up the visual mass of gray
within narrow columns of type. For students of writing, these frequent
breaks have the additional advantage of creating distinct segments that
can be analyzed to reveal the article's organizational structure. The following steps will help you analyze Wollard's structure.

   a. Working with either the mirage or hiccups article, list what each paragraph segment *does* to accomplish the author's purpose of making the
   explanation clear to her readers.

   b. Note segments that in the wider format of this book's pages or the 8.5
   × 11 format of a college paper could be grouped together as a single
   paragraph.

   c. How does each new paragraph fit with the one it follows? For example, does the new paragraph extend the thought of the previous one,
   provide an example, offer a contrast, change directions? What other
   relationships between paragraphs do you see?

   d. When you compare your "does" list with that of a classmate who did
   the other article, what similarities do you find between the two articles' structures? (For more information about this kind of analysis, see
   Chapter 4, p. 58.)

3. In what ways would you expect encyclopedia articles about hiccups or
mirages to be different from Wollard's articles? Jot down some of your
expectations about the differences. Then make an actual comparison on
one of the topics, using the reference source of your choice, print or
electronic. Note differences between the reference writer's approach
and Wollard's in the following categories: (a) opening, (b) word choice,
(c) sentence style, (d) organization, and (e) apparent assumptions about
readers' knowledge and values. What does this comparison add to your
understanding of Wollard's strategies regarding audience and purpose?

Marcy Gordon

Once a Novelty, Now-Essential Credit Card Turns 50

Marcy Gordon is a Washington-based business writer for the Associated Press who writes frequently about credit and finance matters. The AP sent this article to member news organizations on March 7, 2000, as an "advance for use anytime." Many U.S. papers ran it as a feature story the following weekend.

● *For Your Reading Log*

1. Quickly scan the article to get a sense of its content, then jot down your expectation of what its main points will be.
2. When you finish reading, compare your original expectations with what you discovered as you read. What details contributed to the accuracy or inaccuracy of your initial perceptions of the article's purpose? Do you consider the outcome of your predictions to be a function of your scanning ability or of the way the article is written?

———————   ●   ———————

In the 1950s, dapper men with mustaches and fedoras used them to settle their bills 1 at Delmonico's, "21" or the Copacabana. They were a novelty for the affluent and the urbane, much like jet travel, at a time of postwar economic boom and optimism.

Today, we rely on them to pay for the mundane supplies of everyday life, from 2 groceries to gasoline.

The credit card, an idea begat 50 years ago when an absent-minded business- 3 man dining out left his wallet elsewhere, now provides financial convenience for an estimated 157 million Americans—close to the adult population of some 200 million.

But it's also been blamed for seducing millions of profligate spenders into 4 crushing debt and even bankruptcy. And fraudulent charges, by crooks and cyberpirates, cost companies big time.

Still, the credit card endures as an emblem of convenience and an instrument 5 of the democratization of credit.

It means "even the little guy can borrow," said Frederic Mishkin, a profes- 6 sor at Columbia University Business School in New York. In addition, he noted, "There's a tremendous convenience that allows us not to carry cash around."

For Chantal de Jonge Oudraat, of Washington, D.C., the cards' convenience 7 means that when she flies on her frequent trips to Europe, she often takes less than $20 cash.

"There are two things I check before I go on a trip: my passport and plastic," 8 she said.

De Jonge Oudraat, 43, carries five or six cards—close to the U.S. average. And 9 she uses her ATM card in machines overseas to get local currency.

10   Credit cards were paper, originally, like library cards. They didn't become plastic until 1959, a move by American Express to make them less vulnerable to fraud and easier to process.

11   The first charge card is said to have appeared in February 1950. Businessman Frank McNamara had dined at Major's Cabin Grill in Manhattan and, reaching for his wallet, realized he'd left it in another suit. Fortunately, his wife paid the tab, but McNamara wondered if a different solution could be found.

12   At a later meal at Major's, McNamara tried paying with a small cardboard card bearing his signature, which he dubbed a diner's club card, and signing for it. It worked: his being known at the restaurant probably helped. McNamara and his attorney founded Diners Club, now owned by banking giant Citigroup.

13   The first card was offered to 200 people, mostly McNamara's friends and acquaintances. Fourteen Manhattan restaurants initially agreed to accept it. By March 1951, the company claimed 42,000 Americans were carrying the card and more than 330 U.S. businesses were accepting it. Membership cost $3 a year.

14   At first, they were all charge cards, meaning that balances had to be paid in full each month. Bank credit cards, as we know them, buy now-pay later, were introduced in 1951 by Franklin National Bank in New York, which eventually became European American Bank.

15   Fast-forward to 2000. There are "affinity" credit cards that earn frequent flier miles or donations to your favorite charity, ATM cards, check cards, debit cards, smart cards, department store cards, gas cards and gift cards. There are credit cards with tiny ID photos or "smart chips" for security.

16   There are no-frills credit cards and, at the other end of the spectrum, a new premium card from American Express with a $1,000 annual fee that gives holders free airline and hotel upgrades, a personal travel counselor and their own concierge.

17   In a fiercely competitive business, banks try to sell their cards by offering seductively low "teaser" interest rates for several months. Still, the annual interest on credit cards in this country averages around 18 percent. Credit cards have become an extremely profitable business line for banks, which own the card networks.

18   We use credit cards to pay for everything—groceries, video rentals, stuff on the Internet, postage stamps, even taxes. Police use credit card receipts to help solve crimes. And credit cards are used all over the world: They were introduced in China in 1980.

19   An estimated 157 million Americans have at least one credit card or charge card, up from 122 million in 1990; 46 million have a valid passport; some 185 million have a driver's license.

20   "Don't leave home without it." . . . "It's everywhere you want to be." In TV ads, credit cards pay for priceless moments cooking stew with Grandma, visiting the Irish farm where Mom grew up, sharing tears with a close friend on her wedding day.

21   About 1.5 billion cards bulge in Americans' wallets and another 3 billion a year are hawked through the mail.

22   "Children, dogs, cats and moose are getting credit cards," Federal Reserve Chairman Alan Greenspan recently told the Senate Banking Committee.

23   While the heated competition has driven down interest rates, consumer groups and other critics say it has also driven credit card companies to abusively target marketing campaigns towards young people, especially college students.

About 70 percent of students at four-year colleges have at least one credit card, 24 and revolving debt on those cards averages more than $2,000, according to George-town University sociologist Robert Manning, who has studied credit card debt among college students. In the worst cases, he says, students are forced to drop out and work full time to pay off their debts. Some recent suicides by college students have been attributed to their despondency over mounting credit card debts.

There are other concerns: 25

- Federal regulators worry about increases in risky loans by banks— including credit cards—to people with poor credit histories. The higher-interest loans, called subprime loans, played a role in some of the eight U.S. bank failures last year.
- BestBank of Boulder, Colo., for example, sold high-interest credit cards as part of a travel-club membership to consumers nationwide with inferior credit records. Its failure drained some $232 million from the federal deposit insurance fund.
- In mid-January, someone pilfered thousands of credit card numbers from CD Universe, an Internet music seller. Described as the largest mass-cancellation of credit cards ever, it was soon followed by another blow to security when the credit card database of health products supplier Global Health Trax was opened to hackers for a few hours.

  And online travel agency Expedia recently said it would set aside $4 million to $6 million to compensate for fraudulent credit card purchases on its Web site.
- Set to go to trial in June is a Justice Department lawsuit against Visa and MasterCard, filed in October 1998, challenging the joint control of the two networks by the same group of big banks. The government also challenged rules imposed by Visa and MasterCard barring banks that issue their cards from doing business with other, smaller competing card networks, like American Express and Discover.
- The nation's biggest retailers, led by Wal-Mart Stores Inc., are seeking $8.1 billion in damages from Visa and MasterCard in federal court for alleged unfair domination of the debit card business, which the retailers say has pushed up stores' transaction fees and costs for consumers.

  In both cases, Visa and MasterCard, which together account for 75 percent of all credit card purchases in this country, are contesting the allegations. They maintain that consumers have unlimited choices in credit cards, with thousands of Visa and MasterCard member banks competing not only against rival brands but also among themselves by offering different rates, credit limits and other features. The companies say they shouldn't be forced to offer their competitors' products.

The stakes are high. Unpaid balances for the 80 million households with 26 credit card accounts now average $6,000 to $7,000, according to the Consumer Federation of America.

Fifty years ago, people saved money until they had enough to buy some- 27 thing, the idea behind the fast-fading Christmas Clubs, for example. Now, in our instant-gratification culture, people buy first and pay later—sometimes much later—with the help of plastic.

28   And sometimes, later turns into never. Personal bankruptcies in this country reached a record 1.4 million in 1998, despite the strong economy, up more than 300 percent since 1980. In some bankruptcies, credit card debts are erased; in others, they are repaid partially or over long periods of time.

29   Job loss, catastrophic illness and divorce are cited as frequent causes. But credit card companies say too many people simply have become irresponsible about their debts and have abused the bankruptcy court process as the social stigma of bankruptcy has weakened.

30   In the last few years, the banking industry has spent millions pushing legislation in Congress to make it tougher to sweep away debts through bankruptcy.

31   The bills, versions of which cleared the House last year and the Senate last month, apply new standards for determining whether people filing for bankruptcy should be forced to repay their debts under a court-approved reorganization plan rather than having them forgiven.

32   The Clinton administration, which supports rewriting the bankruptcy laws in principle, has criticized both the Senate and House versions as being too hard on debtors, but both bills passed with veto-proof margins.

33   Consumer groups and other opponents maintain the legislation favors corporate profits over the needs of families struggling with debt. They insist that the credit card companies share the blame by flooding consumers with solicitations to entice them into easy credit.

34   Still, about 43 percent of consumers pay off their credit card balances every month, the banking industry says.

35   From Frank McNamara's first office on the 24th floor of the Empire State Building, credit cards fanned out across the country, traversed oceans and eventually arrived in the farthest reaches of the Third World and the Internet. Next destination: outer space?

36   Alfred Bloomingdale, who succeeded McNamara as Diners Club president, mused in a 1959 magazine interview, "Where will it end? I don't see any limits. I think someday you're going to be able to charge anything."

• *Thinking Critically About "Once a Novelty, Now-Essential Credit Card Turns 50"*

RESPONDING AS A READER

1. This article establishes considerable tension between the amusing historical details in the opening paragraphs and the list of serious problems connected with credit cards toward the end. Does one aspect of the matter end up dominating? What evidence do you find of Gordon having one particular view of credit cards? In the end, what do you take her main purpose to be? Was she successful in accomplishing that purpose with you?

2. Like many newspaper articles, this piece uses the genre conventions of short paragraphs and a bulleted list to guide the reader's eye quickly

along narrow columns. How did those textual features facilitate or detract from your own reading in the quite different full page format of this book?

3. What assumptions does Gordon seem to have made about her reading audience's knowledge and opinions regarding credit cards? What evidence can you find in the text about how she expected readers to react to the mix of positive and negative information in the article? How does knowledge about the original publication context add to your analysis?

RESPONDING AS A WRITER

1. To suit local style and to fit with space constraints, local copy editors usually write the headlines for the wire service articles they print. The title we use here was suggested by the AP. We list below the headlines used by several newspapers and invite you to consider which best suits your understanding of the article's content and purpose.

   - "Credit Cards: 50 Years and Going Strong" *(St. Louis Post-Dispatch)*
     Subhead: "Forgotten Wallet in 1950 Leads to Credit for an Estimated 157 Million Americans"
   - "Diners Club Card Idea Spawned a Plastic Explosion" *(Milwaukee Journal Sentinel)*
     Subhead: "It All Started When a New York Businessman Forgot His Wallet at a Restaurant"
   - "A Humble Start for Today's Necessity" *(Los Angeles Times)*
     Subhead: "Finance: An Absent-minded Businessman Got Idea for Credit Cards When He Forgot to Take His Wallet to a Restaurant"
   - "Novelty of Affluent Revolves into Daily Phrase: Charge It!" *(Detroit News)*
     Subhead: "Credit Cards Give Us Convenience, Seduce Wallets"

     a. What do you perceive as the important differences among these titles? If the purpose of headlines and titles is to catch readers' attention and forecast content, which titles are better and worse choices?

     b. Given your rhetorical reading of the article, which title do you think is the most accurate *and* effective?

     c. Try your hand at writing a title/headline that engages interest and accurately indicates content. Including a subhead is optional.

2. What is your evaluation of the way Gordon handles the contradictory themes in her article, convenience and mounting debt? If this were not a news article but an essay for your class based on the "Explaining What You Know" assignment at the end of this chapter, what advice or feedback would you want to give her?

3. If you were researching a paper about the pros and cons of undergraduates having their own credit cards, what questions does this article suggest you should highlight in the paper? Which paragraphs in the article would be most useful to you? What clues does it offer about where to find additional information?

UC Berkeley Wellness Letter

Why Do Those #&?@! "Experts" Keep Changing Their Minds?*

This article on the difficulty of understanding news reports about medical research appeared originally in the *UC Berkley Wellness Letter,* a consumer publication that bills itself as "The Newsletter of Nutrition, Fitness, and Self-Care." Published since 1984 by the School of Public Health at the University of California, Berkeley, it carries no advertising and takes a skeptical attitude toward trendy remedies and diets. According to the newsletter's Website at www.berkeleywellness.com, its approach to wellness "emphasizes personal responsibility for making the lifestyle choices and self-care decisions that will improve the quality of your life." The *Wellness Letter*'s monthly eight-page issues, which subscribers receive by mail, typically include "how to" articles, question-and-answer columns, buying guides, quizzes, and detailed tables that rate the nutritional value of various prepared foods. This selection appeared in February 1996 as a two-page special report.

- *For Your Reading Log*

  1. Has someone in your family, or someone else you know, ever taken reports of medical breakthroughs too seriously? What happened? Take a few minutes to freewrite about any instances you know of involving overreaction to press reports about scientific research.
  2. News stories about science and health matters are quite common. What news of medical breakthroughs or health warnings have you become aware of in the last few months? What do you recall about your reaction at the time? What did you think about how the new findings might affect you or your loved ones?

———————   •   ———————

1 Let's say that for the last five years you've been paying close attention to health news as reported on TV and in newspapers. Perhaps you learned about antioxidants (notably vitamins E and C and beta carotene), which you can get both from foods and supplements. These antioxidants may help lower the risk of heart disease, cancer, cataracts, and other ills. The scientist who had told you this on the *Today* show was a handsome fellow in a good-looking suit (no rumpled Einstein he). He had led the groundbreaking study that had just appeared in *The Impeccable Journal of Medicine.* Not only was the evidence "very exciting," but he was taking hefty amounts of antioxidant supplements himself. So you started taking the pills. Next thing, you read that a study conducted in Finland showed that not only was beta carotene *not* protective against lung cancer, it ac-

tually seemed to increase the risk of getting it. Feeling deceived, you stopped taking your supplements and even gave up your daily carrot. You were tired of carrots anyway.

You may have seen something similar happen with oat bran (good one 2 week, outmoded the next), margarine (you switched to this supposed health food a few years ago, and now it's been tagged as an artery-clogger), DDT and breast cancer (first linked, then not), hot dogs and childhood leukemia (a headline-maker that soon pooped out, since even the researchers had a hard time explaining their findings), and household electricity (cancer again—but by then you had gotten bored). Do these folks just not know what they are talking about?

In fact, the experts don't change their minds as often as it may seem. This 3 newsletter, for example, never told you that margarine was a health food or that oat bran would solve your cholesterol problems. Both these foods were hyped by the media and by manufacturers—but most nutritionists never thought or said there was anything magic about them. A few researchers and journalists eagerly spread the idea that your power line and your electric toaster and clock could give you cancer. Most experts thought all along that the evidence was pretty thin. Headline writers change their minds more often than scientists.

Science is a process, not a product, a work in progress rather than a book of rules. 4 Scientific evidence accumulates bit by bit. This doesn't mean scientists are bumblers (though perhaps a few are), but that they are trying to accumulate enough data to get at the truth, which is always a difficult job. Within the circle of qualified, well-informed scientists, there is bound to be disagreement, too. The same data look different to different people. A good scientist is often his/her own severest critic.

The search for truth in a democracy is also complicated by 5

- Intense public interest in health
- Hunger for quick solutions
- Journalists trying to make a routine story sound exciting
- Publishers and TV producers looking for audiences
- Scientists looking for fame and grants
- Medical journals thirsting for prestige
- Entrepreneurs thirsting for profits

It pays to keep your wits about you as you listen, watch, and read. 6

The Search for Evidence

In general, there are three ways to look for evidence about health: 7

- **Basic research** is conducted in a laboratory, involving "test tube" or "in vitro" (within glass) experiments, or experiments with animals such as mice. Such work is vital for many reasons. For one, it can confirm observations or hunches and provide what scientists call plausible mechanisms for a theory. If a link between heart disease and smoking is suspected, laboratory experiments might show how nicotine affects blood vessels.

The beauty of lab research is that it can be tightly controlled. Its limitation is that what happens in a test tube or a laboratory rat may not happen in a free-living human being.

• **Clinical or interventional trials** are founded on observation and treatment of human beings. As with basic research, the "gold standard" clinical trial can and must be rigorously controlled. There'll be an experimental group or groups (receiving a bona-fide drug or treatment) and a control group (receiving a placebo, or dummy, treatment). A valid experiment must also be "blinded," meaning that no subject knows whether he/she is in the experimental or the control group. In a double-blind trial, the researchers don't know either.

But clinical trials have their limitations, too. The researchers must not knowingly endanger human life and health—there are ethics committees these days to make sure of this. Also, selection criteria must be set up. If the research is about heart disease, maybe the researchers will include only men, since middle-aged men are more prone to heart disease than women the same age. Or maybe they'll include only nurses, because nurses can be reliably tracked and are also good reporters. But these groups are not representative of the whole population. It may or may not be possible to generalize the findings. The study that determined aspirin's efficacy against heart attacks, for instance, was a well-designed interventional trial. But, for various reasons, nearly all the participants were middle-aged white men. No one is sure that aspirin works the same way for other people.

• **Epidemiologic studies.** These generate the most news because so many of them have potential public appeal. An indispensable arm of research, epidemiology looks at the distribution of disease ("epidemics") and risk factors for disease in a human population in an attempt to find disease determinants. Compared with clinical trials or basic research, epidemiology is beset with pitfalls. That's because it deals with people in the real world and with situations that are hard to control.

The two most common types of epidemiologic research are:

Case control studies. Let's say you're studying lung cancer. You select a group of lung cancer patients and match them (by age, gender, and other criteria) with a group of healthy people. You try to identify which factors distinguish the healthy subjects (the "controls") from those who got sick.

Cohort studies. You select a group and question them about their habits, exposures, nutritional intake, and so forth. Then you see how many of your subjects actually develop lung cancer (or whatever you are studying) over the years, and you try to identify the factors associated with lung cancer.

Pitfalls and Dead Ends

Epidemiologic studies cannot usually prove cause and effect, but can identify as-   8
sociations and risk factors. Furthermore, epidemiology is best at identifying
very powerful risk factors—smoking for lung cancer, for example. It is less good
at risk assessment when associations are weak—between radon gas in homes
and lung cancer, for example.

No matter how well done, any epidemiologic study may be open to criticism.   9
Here are just a few of the problems:

- People may not reliably report their eating and exercise habits. (How
  many carrots did you eat each month as an adolescent? How many last
  month? Few of us could say.) People aware of the benefits of eating vegetables may unconsciously exaggerate their vegetable consumption on a
  questionnaire. That's known as "recall bias."
- Hidden variables or "confounders" may cloud results. A study might indicate that eating broccoli reduces the risk of heart disease. But broccoli
  eaters may be health-conscious and get a lot of exercise. Was it the broccoli or the exercise?
- Those included in a study may seem to be a randomly selected, unbiased
  sample and then turn out not to be. For example, searching for a control
  group in one study, a researcher picked numbers out of the telephone
  book at random and called his subjects in the daytime. But people who
  stay home during the day may not be a representative sample. Those at

Words for the Wise

- ❏ **"May":** does *not* mean "will."
- ❏ **"Contributes to," "is linked to,"** or **"is associated with":** does *not* mean "causes."
- ❏ **"Proves":** scientific studies gather evidence in a systematic way, but one study, taken alone, seldom proves anything.
- ❏ **"Breakthrough":** this happens only now and then—for example, the discovery of penicillin or the polio vaccine. But today the word is so overworked as to be meaningless.
- ❏ **"Doubles the risk" or "triples the risk":** may or may not be mean-ingful. Do you know what the risk was in the first place? If the risk was 1 in a million, and you double it, that's still only 1 in 500,000. If the risk was 1 in 100 and doubles, that's a big increase.
- ❏ **"Significant":** a result is "statistically significant" when the associ-ation between two factors has been found to be greater than might occur at random (this is worked out by a mathematical formula). But people often take "significant" to mean "major" or "important."

home in the daytime might tend to be very young or very old, ill, or recovering from illness.
- Health effects, especially where cancer is concerned, may take 20 years or
more to show up. It's not always financially or humanly possible to keep
a study running that long.

Reading Health News in an Imperfect World

10 And this is only the half of it. Sometimes the flaws lie in the study, sometimes in
the way it has been promoted and reported. Science reporters may be deluged
with data. Many are expected to cover all science, from physics and astronomy
to the health effects of hair dyes. Sometimes health reporters may not even have
read the studies in question or may not understand the statistics.

11   Many medical organizations issue press releases. Some of these are excellent, and some aren't. Some deliberately try to manipulate the press, overstat-
ing the case, failing to provide context, and so forth. Researchers, institutions,
and corporations often hire public relations people to promote their work. These
people may actually know less than the enterprising reporter who calls to interview them.

12   Finally, people tend to draw their own conclusions, no matter what the article says.

However, the Bottom Line Is Pretty Good . . .

13 None of this means epidemiology doesn't work. *One study may not prove anything,
but a body of research, in which evidence accumulates bit by bit, can uncover the truth.*
Research into human health has made enormous strides and is still making
them. There may be no such thing as a perfect study, but here is only the briefest
list of discoveries that came out of epidemiologic research:

- Smoking is the leading cause of premature death in developed countries.
- High blood cholesterol is a major cause of coronary artery disease and
heart attack.
- Exercise is important for good health.
- Good nutrition offers protection against cancer; or, conversely, poor nu-
trition is a factor in the development of cancer.
- Obesity is a risk factor for heart disease, cancer, and diabetes.

14   The list could go on and on. We suggest that you retain a spirit of inquiry
and a healthy skepticism, but not lapse into cynicism. *The "flip-flops" you perceive
are often not flip-flops at all, except in the mind of some headline writer.*

15   There is a great deal of good reporting, and it's an interesting challenge to
follow health news. You don't believe everything you read or see on TV about
politics, business, or foreign relations, so it's no surprise that you shouldn't believe some health news. Luckily, there are many sources for health news—none
infallible, but some a lot better than others.

Some Commonsense Pointers

❏ **Don't jump to conclusions.** A single study is no reason for changing your health habits. Distinguish between an interesting finding and a broad-based public health recommendation.

❏ **Always look for context.** A good reporter—and a responsible scientist—will always place findings in the context of other research. Yet the typical news report seldom alludes to other scientific work.

❏ **If it was an animal study or some other kind of lab study, be cautious about generalizing.** Years ago lab studies suggested that saccharin caused cancer in rats, but epidemiologic studies later showed it didn't cause cancer in humans.

❏ **Beware of press conferences** and other hype. Scientists, not to mention the editors of medical journals, love to make the front page of major newspapers and hear their studies mentioned on the evening news. The fact that the study in question may have been flawed or inconclusive or old news may not seem worth mentioning. This doesn't mean you shouldn't believe anything. Truth, too, may be accompanied by hype.

❏ **Notice the number of study participants and the study's length.** The smaller the number of subjects and the shorter the time, the greater the possibility that the findings are erroneous.

❏ **Perhaps the most blatantly hyped research of late has been genetic.** But the treatment of human illness by altering human genes is still at a very early stage.

● **Thinking Critically About "Why Do Those #&*?@! 'Experts' Keep Changing Their Minds?"**

RESPONDING AS A READER

1. What problem does this special report set out to solve, and what reasons does it assert for seeking a solution? What does it *do* (as opposed to *say*) to try to accomplish this?

2. As the reading unfolds, what role does it give readers to play in the solution process? How might readers interact with the text differently if it were entitled, "Read Epidemiological Studies Carefully," and began with paragraph 3?

3. The playful title and introduction give little hint of the information-packed paragraphs and checklists that follow. How would you describe the writer's overall strategy for explaining this fairly complex topic to the newsletter's readers? What assumptions about readers' existing knowledge and information needs are signaled by the use of boxes, bulleted lists, and headings?

RESPONDING AS A WRITER

1. The complications of "the search for truth in a democracy" listed in paragraph 5 suggest the importance of being an alert media consumer no matter what the topic. What examples beyond the health area can you and your classmates think of that illustrate how these factors have interfered with the public's understanding of some process or phenomenon? Consider possible examples from a variety of areas, such as local and national politics, sports, and entertainment.

2. This tightly written article offers information that a college writer might find useful for many different kinds of papers. To practice your summary and paraphrase skills, write a *brief* summary of one of the article's main sections. Build a summary that you might incorporate into a paper after one of the following sentences. Limit your total length to no more than 75 words.

   a. The *UC Berkeley Wellness Letter* explains three different types of studies used for research on health matters.

   b. The *UC Berkeley Wellness Letter* warns that certain types of problems will create flaws in even very well done epidemiologic studies.

   c. Despite the problems inherent to epidemiologic studies, the *UC Berkeley Wellness Letter* says that "the bottom line is pretty good" in certain areas.

3. To test the usefulness of the *Wellness Letter*'s advice about reading scientific studies, apply its suggestions for careful reading to a current news report about a health-related scientific study. Use the Internet or a periodicals database to find an article written for a general audience in a well-known newspaper or magazine on a medical subject that interests you. Note the type of study reported and the language used about findings. Use the *Wellness Letter*'s "Words for the Wise" and "Common-sense Pointers" to analyze the importance of the news being reported. Then, write an informal letter or e-mail to a concerned friend or relative explaining how significant you think the study's findings are and why, given the *Wellness Letter*'s guidelines.

Amy R. Wolfson and Mary A. Carskadon

Sleep Schedules and Daytime Functioning in Adolescents

This is the research article that was the focus of the various introductions we presented in the rhetorical context exercise in Chapter 3. It presents impressive documentation that sleep loss interferes with adolescents' daytime functioning and links that finding to early school-opening times. *Child Development*, the journal in which it was published in August 1998, is an interdisciplinary refereed journal that includes empirical research articles, discussions of theory and policy, and literature reviews relevant to all aspects of human development from birth through adolescence. Originally reported at a 1996 conference, Wolfson and Carskadon's study received widespread press attention and has been influential in policy discussions about moving high school start times to 8 A.M. or later. The authors, both psychologists, are prominent sleep researchers with numerous scholarly publications credited to them. In the spring of 2000, they both served on a National Sleep Foundation task force cochaired by Carskadon that published *Adolescent Sleep Needs and Patterns*, a major research report and resource guide designed for general readers. Wolfson (b. 1960) teaches at the College of the Holy Cross in Worcester, Massachusetts, where the biography on her Web page notes that she "mentors undergraduates in the field of sleep research and has brought many trainees over the years to the Associated Professional Sleep Society meetings." Carskadon (b. 1947), who edited the *Encyclopedia of Sleep and Dreaming* (1993), is a professor in the Department of Psychiatry and Human Behavior at the Brown University School of Medicine in Providence, Rhode Island, where she directs the E.P. Bradley Hospital Sleep and Chronobiology Research Lab. (Note: the citation conventions used here follow the American Psychological Association system of author-date parenthetical citations, and a "references" list.)

• *For Your Reading Log*

1. Reading this study will offer you a good opportunity to explore the structure and content of a typical social science research article. The many internal citations and references to statistics may make reading this scholarly text seem like a daunting task; indeed, taking in every detail on a first reading would be extremely difficult. Despite the unfamiliarity of the genre, however, be assured that the main points are not difficult to follow. The article has clearly labeled sections, and the findings are interesting and important. Furthermore, the subject matter is something that many college students worry about and that all of us do—sleep.

   The discussion in Chapter 3 about matching reading strategy to genre and purpose suggests that probably very few people, even experts in the field, would read this text front to back, word for word. In fact, the abstract, literature review, and section labels actually help readers *not* read every word of every sentence, at least not initially. Instead, an expert reader would probably look for the material most relevant to his or her professional and personal interests. What will you do? As you determine your strategy for tackling this text, recall the advice in Chapter 4 about preparing to read. Take into account your existing knowledge of the article's significance as well as the context that leads you to read it (including both the way it is presented here and the comments your teacher made when assigning it). Then spend a few minutes writing in your log about your own purpose for reading and the reading strategy you think will work best for you.

2. What can you learn by reading this article? That question is always an important one to ask before diving into a text, especially one written for an audience of experts that does not include oneself. To answer the question, take time to read the article abstract carefully, then note in your log (a) the major question addressed by the study, (b) how the researchers set about trying to answer it, and (c) the gist of what they found out. Next, spot read through the article to get a sense of its organization and the major topics covered. Then you'll be ready to begin a full reading.

———————   •   ———————

Sleep and waking behaviors change significantly during the adolescent years. The objective of this study was to describe the relation between adolescents' sleep/wake habits, characteristics of students (age, sex, school), and daytime functioning (mood, school performance, and behavior). A Sleep Habits Survey was administered in homeroom classes to 3,120 high school students at 4 public high schools from 3 Rhode Island school districts. Self-reported total sleep times (school and weekend nights) decreased by 40–50 min across ages 13–19, $ps < .001$. The sleep loss was due to increasingly later bedtimes, whereas rise times were more consistent across ages. Students who described themselves as struggling or failing school (C's, D's/F's) reported that on school nights they obtain about 25 min less sleep and go to bed an average of 40 min later than A and B students, $ps < .001$. In addition, students with worse grades reported greater weekend delays of sleep schedule than did those with better grades. Furthermore, this study examined a priori defined *adequate* sleep habit groups versus *less than adequate* sleep habit groups on their daytime functioning. Students in the short school-night total sleep group (< 6 hr 45 min) and/or large weekend bedtime delay group (> 120 min) reported increased daytime sleepiness, depressive mood, and sleep/wake behavior problems, $ps < .05$, versus those sleeping longer than 8 hr 15 min with less than 60 min weekend delay. Altogether, most of the adolescents surveyed do not get enough sleep, and their sleep loss interferes with daytime functioning.

Introduction

1 Adolescence is a time of important physical, cognitive, emotional, and social change when the behaviors in one developmental stage are constantly challenged by new abilities, insights, and expectations of the next stage. Sleep is a primary aspect of adolescent development. The way adolescents sleep critically influences their ability to think, behave, and feel during daytime hours. Likewise, daytime activities, changes in the environment, and individual factors can have significant effects on adolescents' sleeping patterns. Over the last 2 decades, researchers, teachers, parents, and adolescents themselves, have consistently re-

ported that they are not getting enough sleep (Carskadon, 1990a; Carskadon, Harvey, Duke, Anders, & Dement, 1980; Price, Coates, Thoresen, & Grinstead, 1978; Strauch & Meier, 1988).

Although laboratory data demonstrate that adolescents probably do not 2 have a decreased need for sleep during puberty (Carskadon, 1990a; Carskadon et al., 1980; Carskadon, Orav, & Dement, 1983), survey and field studies show that teenagers usually obtain much less sleep than school-age children, from 10 hr during middle childhood to less than 7.5–8 hours by age 16 (Allen, 1992; Carskadon, 1982, 1990a, Williams, Karacan, & Hursch, 1974). Although sleeping less than when younger, over 54% of high school students in a Swiss study (Strauch & Meier, 1988) endorsed a *wish for more sleep*.

A consistent finding in studies of adolescent sleep patterns is that they tend 3 to stay up late. Price et al. (1978), for example, found that 60% of the eleventh and twelfth graders whom they surveyed stated that they "enjoyed staying up late." Another large survey study found that 45% of tenth to twelfth graders go to bed after midnight on school nights, and 90% retire later than midnight on weekends (Carskadon & Mancuso, 1988). Another consistent report (Bearpark & Michie, 1987; Petta, Carskadon, & Dement, 1984; Strauch & Meier, 1988) is that weekend total sleep times average 30–60 min more than school-night sleep times in 10- to 13/14-year-olds, and this difference increases to over 2 hr by age 18. Such data are usually interpreted as indicating that teenagers do not get enough sleep on school nights and then extend sleep on weekend nights to pay back a sleep debt. The most obvious explanation for the adolescent sleep debt appears to be a pattern of insufficient school-night sleep resulting from a combination of early school start times, late afternoon/evening jobs and activities, academic and social pressures, and a physiological sleep requirement that does not decrease with puberty (Carskadon, 1990b; Manber et al., 1995; Wolfson et al., 1995).

Many factors contribute to or are affected by increased daytime sleepiness 4 and inconsistent sleep schedules during the junior high and senior high school years. In the sections below, we review several key issues.

PUBERTY: SLEEP NEED, DAYTIME SLEEPINESS, AND CIRCADIAN PHASE DELAY

Several important changes directly affecting sleep patterns occur during the pu- 5 bertal years. One feature that seems not to change or to change in an unexpected direction is sleep need. A 6-year longitudinal summer sleep laboratory study of Carskadon and colleagues (1980) held the opportunity for sleep constant at 10 hr in children, who were 10, 11, or 12 years old at their first 3 night assessment. The research hypothesis was that with age, the youngsters would sleep less, reaching a normal adult sleep length of 7.5 or 8 hr by the late teens. In fact, the sleep quantity remained consistent at approximately 9.2 hours across all pubertal stages. Thus, these data clarified that sleep need is not reduced during adolescence. The longitudinal study of Carskadon and colleagues (1980) simultaneously demonstrated that daytime sleep tendency was increased at midpuberty. In other words, even though the amount of nocturnal sleep consumed by the adolescents did not decline during puberty, their midday sleepiness increased significantly at midpuberty and remained at that level (Carskadon et al., 1980, 1983). This finding was based on physician assessment of puberty using Tanner staging (Tanner, 1962) and a sensitive laboratory measure of sleepiness, the Multiple Sleep Latency Test (MSLT; Carskadon et al., 1986).

6   A significant change in the timing of behavior across adolescent development is a tendency to stay up later at night and to sleep in later in the morning than preadolescents, that is, to delay the phase of sleep (Carskadon, Vieira, & Acebo, 1993; Dahl & Carskadon, 1995). One manifestation of this process is that adolescents' sleep patterns on weekends show a considerable delay (as well as lengthening) versus weekdays, with sleep onset and offset both occurring significantly later. This sleep phase shift is attributed to psychosocial factors and to biological changes that take place during puberty. For example, in the longitudinal study described above, as children reached puberty, they were less likely to wake up on their own, and laboratory staff needed to wake them up (Carskadon et al., 1980). In fact, they likely would have slept more than 9 hr if undisturbed.

7   Carskadon and her colleagues have shown that this adolescent tendency to phase delay may be augmented by a biological process accompanying puberty. An association between self-reported puberty scores (Carskadon & Acebo, 1993) and phase preference (morningness/eveningness) scores of over 400 pre- and early pubertal sixth graders showed a delay of phase preference correlated with maturation stage (Carskadon et al., 1993). Morningness/eveningness is a construct developed to estimate phase tendencies from self-descriptions. Morning persons tend to arise early in the morning and have difficulty staying up late whereas night persons have difficulty getting up early in the morning and prefer staying up late. Whereas most people are somewhere between these extremes, the cohort value shifts during adolescence (Andrade, Benedito-Silva, & Domenice, 1993; Ishihara, Honma, & Miyake, 1990). A recent study examined the circadian timing system more directly in early adolescents by measuring the timing of melatonin secretion, for the first time demonstrating a biological phase delay in association with puberty and in the absence of psychosocial factors (Carskadon, Acebo, Richardson, Tate, & Seifer, 1997).

ENVIRONMENTAL CONSTRAINT: SCHOOL START TIME

8 Many U.S. school districts start school earlier at academic transitions, for example, elementary to junior high school and junior high school to senior high school. Earlier high school start time is a major externally imposed constraint on teenagers' sleep-wake schedules; for most teens waking up to go to school is neither spontaneous nor negotiable. Early morning school demands often significantly constrict the hours available for sleep. For example, Szymczak, Jasinska, Pawlak, and Swierzykowska (1993) followed Polish students aged 10 and 14 years for over a year and found that all slept longer on weekends and during vacations as a result of waking up later. These investigators concluded that the school duty schedule was the predominant determinant of awakening times for these students. Similarly, several surveys of high school students found that students who start school at 7:30 A.M. or earlier obtain less total sleep on school nights due to earlier rise times (Allen, 1991; Allen & Mirabile, 1989; Carskadon & Mancuso, 1988).

9   In a preliminary laboratory/field study, we evaluated the impact of a 65 min advance in school start time of 15 ninth graders across the transition to tenth

grade (Carskadon, Wolfson, Tzischinsky, & Acebo, 1995; Wolfson et al., 1995). The initial findings demonstrated that students slept an average of 40 min less in tenth grade compared with ninth grade due to earlier rise times, and they displayed an increase in MSLT measured daytime sleepiness. In addition, evening type students had more difficulty adjusting to the earlier start time than did morning types, and higher scores on the externalizing behavior problems scale (Youth Self-Report; Achenbach, 1991) were associated with less total sleep and later bedtimes (Brown et al., 1995; Wolfson et al., 1995).

DAYTIME BEHAVIORS

Very little research has assessed the relation between adolescents' sleep patterns 10 and their daytime behaviors. Although studies have concluded that associations between sleep/wake patterns and daytime functioning exist, the direction of this relation is not clear. Clinical experience shows that adolescents who have trouble adapting to new school schedules and other changes (e.g., new bedtimes and rise times, increased activities during the day, increased academic demands) may develop problematic sleeping behaviors leading to chronic sleepiness. Several studies indicate an association between sleep and stress. For example, a number of studies have found that sleep-disturbed elementary school-age children experience a greater number of stresses (e.g., maternal absence due to work/school; family illness/accident; maternal depressed mood) than non-sleep-disturbed children (Kataria, Swanson, & Trevathan, 1987). Likewise, sleepy elementary school-age children may have poorer coping behaviors (e.g., more difficulty recognizing, appraising, and adapting to stressful situations) and display more behavior problems at home and in school (Fisher & Rinehart, 1990; Wolfson et al., 1995).

ACADEMIC PERFORMANCE

Sleepy adolescents—that is, those with inadequate sleep—may also encounter 11 more academic difficulties. Several surveys of sample sizes ranging from 50 to 200 high school students reported that more total sleep, earlier bedtimes, and later weekday rise times are associated with better grades in school (Allen, 1992; Link & Ancoli-Israel, 1995; Manber et al., 1995). Epstein, Chillag, and Lavie (1995) surveyed Israeli elementary, junior high, and senior high school students and reported that less total sleep time was associated with daytime fatigue, inability to concentrate in school, and a tendency to doze off in class. Persistent sleep problems have also been associated with learning difficulties throughout the school years (Quine, 1992). Studies of excessive sleepiness in adolescents due to narcolepsy or sleep apnea have also reported negative effects on learning, school performance, and behavior (Dahl, Holttum, & Trubnick, 1994; Guilleminault, Winkle, & Korobkin, 1982).

SUMMARY OF FACTORS IMPOSING ON ADOLESCENTS' SLEEP/WAKE PATTERNS

The interplay among sleep/wake schedules, circadian rhythms, and behavior 12 during adolescence results in an increasing pressure on the nocturnal sleep period, producing insufficient sleep in many teenagers and, ultimately, changes in daytime functioning (Carskadon, 1995). For preadolescents, parents are more likely to set bedtimes, school begins later in the morning, and societal expectations favor long sleep. Prepubescent children are thus more likely to have earlier bedtimes and to wake up before the school day begins (Petta et al., 1984). In contrast, due to behavioral factors (social, academic, work-related), environmental constraints (school schedule), and circadian variables (pubertal phase delay), teenagers have later bedtimes, earlier rise times, and therefore, decreased time available to sleep (Carskadon, 1995). As a result, adolescents get to bed late, have difficulty waking up in the morning, and struggle to stay alert and to function successfully during the daytime.

13   Unfortunately, previous studies of adolescents' lifestyles (e.g., Hendry, Glendinning, Shucksmith, Love, & Scott, 1994) have failed to factor in these important developmental changes in sleep/wake patterns, and unanswered questions remain regarding the developmental changes in adolescent sleep/wake habits, the impact of adolescents' sleep habits on their daytime functioning (e.g., school performance), and the influence of the environment (e.g., school schedules) on teenagers' sleep. The present study examines more closely adolescents' sleep/wake habits and their association with several daytime behaviors using data from a large-scale survey. Such data are useful to assess generalizability of findings; furthermore, a large sample provides an opportunity to accentuate meaningful findings by setting the effect size (Cohen, 1988) and by examining extreme groups from the larger sample (Kagan, Resnick, & Gibbons, 1989).

14   The chief goal of this study is to document the association between adolescents' sleep/wake habits and daytime sleepiness, high school grades, depressed mood, and other daytime behaviors. Our study has three objectives: (1) to describe age, sex, and school differences in sleep/wake patterns; (2) to characterize the relation between self-reported high school grades and sleep/wake schedules; and (3) to compare daytime functioning in students on schedules we define a priori as *adequate* versus those adopting *less than adequate* schedules.

Method

MEASURES

15 In the fall of 1994, an eight page School Sleep Habits Survey was administered in homeroom classes to high school students at four public high schools from three Rhode Island school districts. School start times ranged from 7:10 A.M. to 7:30 A.M. All students who wanted to complete the survey did so unless their parent/guardian refused consent. The survey items queried students about usual sleeping and waking behaviors over the past 2 weeks. Chief variables include school-night and weekend night total sleep time (TST), bedtime, and rise time. To assess *sleep schedule regularity,* two additional sleep variables were derived: *weekend delay* is the difference between weekend bedtime and school-night bedtime, and *weekend oversleep* is the difference between weekend total sleep time and school-night total sleep time.

16   The survey also covered school performance (self-reported grades in school) and scales assessing daytime sleepiness, sleep/wake behavior problems (Carska-

don, Seifer, & Acebo, 1991), and depressive mood (Kandel & Davies, 1982). School performance was assessed by asking students, "Are your grades mostly A's, A's and B's, B's, B's and C's, C's, C's and D's, D's, or D's and F's?" These data were collapsed into four categories (mostly A's or A's/B's; mostly B's or B's/C's; mostly C's or C's/D's; mostly D's/F's).

The sleepiness scale consisted of total responses to items asking whether the [17] respondent had struggled to stay awake (fought sleep) or fallen asleep in 10 different situations in the last 2 weeks, such as in conversation, while studying, in class at school, and so on (Carskadon et al., 1991). The respondent was asked to rate his or her answer on a scale of 1 to 4 (1 = no to 4 = both struggled to stay awake and fallen asleep). Scores on the sleepiness scale range from 10 to 40 and coefficient alpha was .70.

The sleep/wake behavior problems scale included 10 items asking frequency [18] of indicators of erratic sleep/wake behaviors over the course of the last 2 weeks (e.g., arrived late to class because you overslept, stayed up past 3:00 A.M., needed more than one reminder to get up in the A.M., had an extremely hard time falling asleep, and so on; Carskadon et al., 1991). High school students were asked to rate the frequency of the particular behavior on a 5 point scale from everyday/night to never (5 = everyday, 1 = never). Scores range from 10 to 50, and coefficient alpha for the sleep/wake behaviors scale was .75.

The depressive mood scale (Kandel & Davies, 1982) queried the high school [19] students as to how often they were bothered or troubled by certain situations in the last 2 weeks. It consists of six items (e.g., feeling unhappy, sad, or depressed; feeling hopeless about the future), and three response categories were provided, ranging from not at all to somewhat too much (e.g., scored 1 to 3, respectively). The index of depressive mood was based on a total score and has high internal reliability (coefficient alpha was .79 for this sample and .79 in the original study; Kandel & Davies, 1982). The Pearson correlation between the Kandel and Davies six item, depressive mood scale and the SCL-90 scale is .72, and prior studies demonstrated that the scale has high test-retest reliability with adolescent samples ($r = .76$) over 5–6 month intervals (Kandel & Davies, 1982).

PARTICIPANTS

The survey was completed anonymously by 3,120 students, 395 students at School [20] A (rural), 1,077 at School B (urban), 745 at School C (suburban), and 903 at School D (suburban) (48% boys, 52% girls). The sample in Schools B and C comprised grades 10–12, whereas Schools A and D had ninth to twelfth graders. Approximately 8% of the students from schools A, C, and D and 17% from School B were eligible for free or reduced price lunches (State of Rhode Island Department of Education, 1994). Overall, the response rate was 88%. The students' ages ranged from 13 to 19 years (age 13–14, $n = 336$, age 15, $n = 858$, age 16, $n = 919$, age 17–19, $n = 988$). Over 91% of the students from Schools A, C, D reported that they were European American, whereas School B was more diverse (75% European American, 25% multiracial). On average, 81% of the students from all four schools reported that they live with both parents; 46% have older siblings, and 63% have younger siblings living in their homes. Eighty-six percent of their mothers *and* fathers were employed.

STATISTICAL METHODS

21 The findings are presented in three sections: (1) changes in sleep/wake habits according to age, sex, and school; (2) relation between high school grades and sleep/wake habits; and (3) an analysis of the differences in daytime functioning for students in extreme groups on several sleep parameters: short versus long school-night total sleep time, short versus long weekend oversleep, and small versus large weekend delay.

22 In the first two sections, multivariate analyses of variance (MANOVA) were used to examine age, sex, school, and grades in relation to the sleep/wake variables: total sleep time, bedtime, rise time, weekend delay, and weekend oversleep. Three multivariate analyses were computed: (1) school-night sleep variables, (2) weekend sleep variables, and (3) weekend delay and weekend oversleep. When significant multivariate effects were found, univariate effects were then examined using Bonferroni tests to determine significant group mean differences.

23 The large sample size in this study raises the possibility of finding many *statistically* significant results that have very small effect sizes, thus running the risk of overinterpreting inconsequential relations. To address this potential problem, we use an effect size criterion in addition to a statistical significance criterion for discussion and interpretation of those results most likely to prove meaningful in the long run. In the results section that follows, we restrict our discussion to those significant findings that also have effect sizes between what Cohen (1988) characterizes as small and medium. Specifically, a correlation of .20 is the effect size criterion, which is slightly smaller than the midpoint of Cohen's small ($r = .10$) and medium ($r = .30$) effects in terms of variance explained. For analysis of group differences, effects where two groups differ by more than one-third of the sample standard deviation are considered. Again, this is slightly lower than the midpoint between small ($d = .20$) and medium ($d = .50$) effect sizes (Cohen, 1988). (Note that we do not calculate exact effect sizes for our more complex analyses but simply wish to have a reasonable criterion for further consideration of effects most likely to have generalizable implications.) All *statistically* significant results, regardless of effect size, are noted in the tables that accompany the text.

Results

SLEEP/WAKE PATTERNS CHANGE ACROSS HIGH SCHOOL AGE GROUPS

24 Our analysis of age-related affects grouped data by four age ranges; Table 1 presents means, standard deviations, and F values for the sleep variables according to age. All school-night sleep variables were affected by age, multivariate $F(9, 6571) = 22.49$, $p < .001$. Specifically, average total sleep time decreased by approximately 40 min across the four age groups, $p < .001$, average school-night bedtimes were about 45 min later, $p < .001$, and average rise times about 10 min later, $p < .001$. Reported weekend sleep habits also showed age-related changes, multivariate $F(9, 6327) = 21.28$, $p < .001$. Average weekend total sleep time declined by about 50 min across the age groups, $p < .001$, as weekend night bedtimes shifted increasingly later, $p < .001$, differing by about 1 hr between the

Table 1   Means and Standard Deviations for School-Night and Weekend Sleep Variables by Age

Sleep/Wake Variable	13–14 Years (n = 336)	15 Years (n = 858)	16 Years (n = 919)	17–19 Years (n = 988)	F Value	Bonferroni
School-night TST	462	449	435	424	24.13***	14, 15 > 16 > 17
	(67)	(66)	(68)	(66)		
School-night bedtime	10:05 P.M.	10:20 P.M.	10:37 P.M.	10:51 P.M.	53.54***	14 < 15 < 16 < 17
	(49)	(55)	(58)	(58)		
School-night rise time	5:59 A.M.	6:00 A.M.	6:05 A.M.	6:10 A.M.	19.47***	14, 15 < 16 < 17
	(24)	(25)	(29)	(31)		
Weekend TST	567	564	549	518	32.53***	14, 15 > 16 > 17
	(100)	(104)	(108)	(114)		
Weekend bedtime	11:54 P.M.	12:06 A.M.	12:30 A.M.	12:49 A.M.	42.33***	14, 15 < 16 < 17
	(94)	(83)	(82)	(80)		
Weekend rise time	9:22 A.M.	9:40 A.M.	9:46 A.M.	9:32 A.M.	ns	⋯
	(85)	(104)	(107)	(107)		
Weekend oversleep	104	115	112	95	5.80**+	⋯
	(102)	(112)	(116)	(114)		
Weekend delay	89	88	92	95	ns	⋯
	(71)	(66)	(65)	(68)		

Note: TST refers to total sleep time (minutes). Weekend oversleep is the difference between weekend and school-night total sleep times and weekend delay is the difference between weekend and school-night bedtimes. Standard deviations, in parentheses, are in minutes; TST, weekend oversleep, and weekend delay are in minutes as well.
** $p < .01$; *** $p < .001$; + does not meet effect size criterion (e.g., effects where two groups differ by more than one-third of the sample standard deviation).

youngest and oldest teenagers. Weekend rise times did not change with age. Overall, weekend delay and weekend oversleep changed between ages 13 and 19, multivariate $F(6, 5060) = 3.93$, $p < .01$. Although this multivariate F is statistically significant, age group differences for weekend delay and weekend oversleep were too small (on the order of .1 SD) to meet our effect size criterion.

25   Although all four high schools had similarly early school start times (between 7:10 A.M. and 7:30 A.M.), students' school-night sleep habits varied among the schools, multivariate $F(9, 6571) = 12.76$, $p < .001$, due to differences in rise times, $p < .001$. In particular, students who attended the school with the earliest school start time (7:10) reported earlier rise times than students at the other schools (School A: $M = 5:53$ versus Schools B, C, D: $Ms = 6:04–6:09$, $ps < .01$). Although school differences occurred in reported average total sleep times and bedtimes, these group differences did not meet effect size criterion. Weekend sleep also varied among schools, multivariate $F(9, 6327) = 4.74$, $p < .001$; however, univariate differences for total sleep time, bedtime, and rise time did not meet our effect size criterion. Additionally, small differences among the schools on weekend delay and weekend oversleep were not meaningful based on the effect size criterion.

26   Few sex differences were identified. Female students reported different school-night sleep habits than their male peers, multivariate $F(3, 2700) = 41.36$, $p < .001$, due to female students reporting waking up earlier than males: females, $M = 5:58$ versus males, $M = 6:10$, $F(1, 2702) = 100.81$, $p < .001$. Boys and girls did not differ on reported school-night bedtimes, nor total sleep times. Overall, female students had greater weekend delays and weekend oversleeps than the male students, multivariate $F(2, 2530) = 6.67$, $p < .001$; however, univariate differences did not meet the effect size criterion. Female and male high school students did not report significant differences in weekend total sleep times, bedtimes, or rise times. The overall sample distributions of sleep patterns are displayed in Figure 1.

ACADEMIC PERFORMANCE AND SLEEP HABITS

27   Table 2 presents the analyses of sleep habits based on self-reported academic performance. In general, students with higher grades reported longer and more regular sleep, multivariate $F(9, 6571) = 8.91$, $p < .001$. Specifically, they reported more total sleep, $p < .001$, and earlier bedtimes, $p < .001$, on school nights than did students with lower grades. Post hoc analysis showed that these differences distinguished students reporting C's and worse from those reporting mostly B's or better. Students' weekend sleep habits also differed according to self-reported grades, multivariate $F(9, 6327) = 18.79$, $p < .001$. Specifically, A and B students reported earlier bedtimes and earlier rise times than did C and D/F students, $ps < .001$; however, self-reported grades did not distinguish the students on reported weekend total sleep. Finally, students with worse grades reported greater weekend delays of sleep schedule than did those with better grades, multivariate $F(6, 5060) = 18.22$, $p < .001$. Thus, C and D/F students reported going to bed on average about 2.3 hr later on weekends than on school nights versus a difference of about 1.8 hr for the A and B students, $ps < .001$. Students with D/F's reported longer weekend oversleeps than A, B, or C students; however, these differences did not meet the effect size criterion.

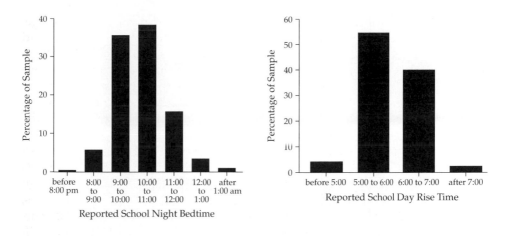

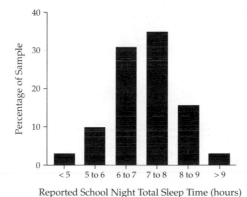

FIGURE 11.1   Sample Distributions of Sleep Patterns

DAYTIME FUNCTIONING OF STUDENTS WHO ADOPT *ADEQUATE* VERSUS *LESS THAN ADEQUATE* SLEEP HABITS

Data presented in the previous sections demonstrate that older high school stu- 28
dents sleep less and have later bedtimes than younger students, and those who
report a poor academic performance are more likely to sleep less, go to bed later,
and have more irregular sleep/wake habits. These descriptive findings, however,
do not explain whether especially short amounts of sleep and/or irregular schedules are associated with changes in daytime functioning. To describe more thoroughly the high school students who are obtaining minimal sleep and/or who
have irregular sleep schedules, we examined a priori defined groups based on
sleep variables that have been cited previously as having an impact on behavior, deriving our values from empirical data (Carskadon et al., 1980, 1983;
Carskadon, Keenan, & Dement, 1987). Other potentially important factors (e.g.,
history of sleep disorders) may covary with these, but data from our survey focused on total sleep and school-night versus weekend schedule changes.

The *extreme* groups of students were defined as follows: long (≥ 8 hr 15 min) 29
versus short (≤ 6 hr 45 min) school-night total sleep time; large (≥ 120 min)

Table 2 Means and Standard Deviations for School-Night and Weekend Sleep Variables by Grades

Sleep/Wake Variables	Self-Reported Grades				F Value	Bonferroni
	Mostly A's or A's/B's (n = 1,238)	Mostly B's or B's/C's (n = 1,371)	Mostly C's or C's/D's (n = 390)	Mostly D's/F's (n = 61)		
School-night TST	442 (62)	441 (66)	424 (74)	408 (94)	16.66***	A, B > C, D/F
School-night bedtime	10:27 P.M. (53)	10:32 P.M. (56)	10:52 P.M. (65)	11:22 P.M. (81)	24.58***	A, B < C, D/F
School-night rise time	6:02 A.M. (25)	6:05 A.M. (29)	6:10 A.M. (34)	6:09 A.M. (31)	ns	...
Weekend TST	547 (100)	547 (109)	534 (124)	549 (137)	ns	...
Weekend bedtime	12:06 A.M. (78)	12:29 A.M. (82)	1:09 A.M. (97)	1:33 A.M. (93)	51.32***	A < B < C, D/F
Weekend rise time	9:21 A.M. (97)	9:43 A.M. (103)	9:59 A.M. (113)	10:33 A.M. (160)	24.10***	A < B < C, D/F
Weekend oversleep	105 (101)	108 (114)	109 (130)	137 (159)	3.32*+	A, B, C < D/F
Weekend delay	99 (68)	117 (72)	137 (77)	133 (80)	26.53***	A < B < C, D/F

Note: TST refers to total sleep time (minutes). Weekend oversleep is the difference between weekend and school-night total sleep times, and weekend delay is the difference between weekend and school-night bedtimes. Standard deviations, in parentheses, are in minutes; TST, weekend oversleep, and weekend delay are in minutes as well.
* $p < .05$; ** $p < .01$; *** $p < .001$; + does not meet effect size criterion (e.g., effects where two groups differ by more than one-third of the sample standard deviation).

versus small (≤ 60 min) weekend delay; or high (> 120 min) versus low (< 60 min) weekend oversleep. High school students who had longer total sleep times, small weekend delays, or low weekend oversleeps were defined as having adopted *adequate* sleep habits, whereas students with shorter sleep times, large weekend delays or high weekend oversleeps were defined as having adopted *less than adequate* sleep habits. We compared these *extreme* groups on daytime and nighttime functioning. Table 3 displays means, standard deviations, and *F* values for depressive mood, sleepiness, and sleep/wake behavior problems for each of the sleep variable groups. (The demographic breakdown of these groups reflected the larger sample on age, sex, and school attendance.) Separate analyses of variance were calculated for each dependent variable (depressive mood, level of sleepiness, and sleep/wake behavior problems), with school-night total sleep time, weekend delay, weekend oversleep, and sex as independent variables. Age was analyzed as a covariate in these analyses.

Overall, adolescents who were in the groups defined as *less than adequate* sleep   30
habits reported increased behavioral difficulties in comparison to those we defined as *adequate sleepers*. Thus, students in the short total sleep group reported more sleep/wake behavior problems, such as arrived late to class because of oversleeping, tired or dragged out nearly every day, needed more than one reminder to get up, *ps* < .01, higher levels of depressive mood, *ps* < .001, and greater sleepiness, *ps* < .001, than those in the long sleep group. Similarly, adolescents in the large weekend delay group described more sleep/wake behavior problems, *ps* < .01, and greater daytime sleepiness, *ps* < .05, but no difference in depressed mood from those with small weekend delays. One exception was that the female students with large weekend delays reported increased depressive mood levels, *p* < .05. Adolescents in the high weekend oversleep group reported more sleep/wake behavior problems, *p* < .001, but no differences in depressed mood or sleepiness from those in the low oversleep group. No sex differences were found in self-reported sleep/wake behavior problems; however, females reported higher levels of depressed mood: females, *M* = 11.04, *SD* = 2.91 versus males, *M* = 9.20, *SD* = 2.68, *p* < .001, and daytime sleepiness: females, *M* = 15.26, *SD* = 3.59 versus males, *M* = 14.67, *SD* = 4.16, *p* ≤ .01, than did males.

Discussion

The principal aim of this research was to assess the relation between adolescents'   31
sleep/wake habits and their daytime functioning. The relatively high response rate (88%) obtained in this school-based study allows us to consider our findings representative of adolescents enrolled in moderate to large public high schools in this geographical region. The use of a self report questionnaire enabled us to gather timely information from a large student population.

HIGH SCHOOL STUDENTS' SLEEP LOSS AND IRREGULAR SLEEP/WAKE SCHEDULES

In particular, this sample of over 3,000 high school students reported lower to-   32
tal sleep (school and weekend nights) across ages 13–19. On school nights, the

Table 3 Means, Standard Deviations, and Analysis of Variance for Daytime Behavior Scales for *Adequate* Versus *Less Than Adequate* Sleepers

| Daytime Functioning Variables | Weekend Delay | | Weekend Oversleep | | School-Night TST | | F Values Sleep Variables | | | | | |
| | | | | | | | Delay | | Oversleep | | TST | |
	≤60 (n = 887)	≥120 (n = 928)	<60 (n = 972)	>120 (n = 1,411)	≥495 (n = 959)	≤405 (n = 1,207)	M	F	M	F	M	F
Depressive mood	10.13 (2.94)	10.35 (2.97)	9.92 (2.85)	10.42 (2.99)	9.48 (2.76)	10.79 (3.00)	ns	3.89*	ns	ns	10.80***	12.94***
Sleepiness	14.63 (3.71)	15.29 (3.98)	14.76 (3.82)	15.23 (3.81)	14.03 (3.51)	15.86 (4.01)	4.37*	6.45**	ns	ns	19.79***	29.77***
Sleep/wake behavior problems	19.10 (6.61)	21.80 (7.16)	19.33 (6.83)	21.22 (7.18)	18.48 (6.63)	22.17 (7.01)	13.17***	47.20***	17.83***	7.93**	16.15***	28.70***

Note: Weekend delay small = ≤60 min, large = ≥120 min; weekend oversleep short = <60 min, long = >120 min, and school-night TST long = ≥8 hr 45 min, short = ≤6 hr 15 min. M = effect for males, F = effect for females.
* $p < .05$; ** $p < .01$; *** $p < .001$.

mean total sleep decreased from 7 hr 42 min to 7 hr 4 min. Similarly, average weekend total sleep decreased from 9 hr 20 min to 8 hr 38 min. The sleep loss is due to increasingly later bedtimes in older teens, whereas rise times remain more consistent. The sleep habits of the students attending the four different high schools showed minimal differences, with the exception of school day rise time, which was significantly earlier for students attending the school with the earliest start time. Although the difference between 7:10 and 7:30 may appear slight, the impact on sleep patterns was meaningful.

Remarkably few differences were found between male and female high 33 school students' sleep/wake patterns. Female adolescents reported that they woke up 12 min earlier than their male peers on school mornings, a finding consistent with an earlier survey of high school students (Carskadon, 1990b) and a study of junior high school students in Taiwan (Gau & Soong, 1995). In the Gau et al. sample, however, the junior high school girls also reported less total sleep than the boys. We speculate that adolescent girls may be getting up earlier because they require more time to prepare for school and/or for family responsibilities.

Taken together, we conclude that most of these adolescents do not get 34 enough sleep. Our laboratory data indicate that optimal sleep length is about 9.2 hr in adolescents (Carskadon et al., 1980). Although individual differences in sleep need are likely, we note that 87% of our sample responded that they need more sleep than they get (median self-reported sleep need = 9 hr). Forty percent of the students reported that they went to bed after 11:00 P.M. on school nights, and 91% went to bed after 11:00 P.M. (67% after midnight) on weekends. Furthermore, 26% reported that they usually sleep 6.5 hr or less, and only 15% reported sleeping 8.5 hr or more on school nights (median = 7.5 hr). Nearly 70% of the students reported weekend delays of 60 min or more; on average, they reported oversleeping on weekends by nearly 1 hr and 50 min. Ninety-one percent of these high school students rise at 6:30 A.M. or earlier on school mornings, and 72% awaken at 9:00 A.M. or later on weekends.

These high school students' reported sleep/wake schedules are consistent 35 with the major trends in the field: (1) self-reported nocturnal sleep time declines across the adolescent years; (2) bedtimes during high school become later; and (3) teenagers show large variations between weekend and school-night sleep schedules (e.g., Carskadon, 1990a; Strauch & Meier, 1988; Szymczak et al., 1993). In comparison to data from Rhode Island high school students surveyed 8 years earlier, these students reported on average approximately 15–20 min less sleep per night on school nights, principally reflecting earlier rising times (Carskadon, 1990a). The developmental and secular trends raise concerns about patterns that may have negative effects on teenagers' waking behavior.

Not assessed in this survey is the impact of family factors on sleep patterns. 36 In the past, we have shown that parents tend to relinquish control of bedtime while increasing involvement with rising time as youngsters pass into adolescence (Carskadon, 1990a). In this particular sample, only 5.1% of students reported that parents set bedtimes on school nights; thus, the great majority of these youngsters set their own bedtime agenda. Over 80% of youngsters in this survey come from two-parent households in which both parents are employed, and we saw no differences between this cohort and those from single-parent homes on the major sleep variables. We propose that the biological and psychosocial processes favoring sleep delay in teens collide with early rising times mandated by schools and that even in the more well-regulated families the capacity for adequate adjustments may be limited.

SLEEP/WAKE HABITS AND SCHOOL PERFORMANCE

37 Our data support and extend findings from Kowalski and Allen (1995) and Link and Ancoli-Israel (1995) that students who described themselves as struggling or failing school (i.e., obtaining C's, D's/F's) report that they obtain less sleep, have later bedtimes, and have more irregular sleep/wake schedules than students who report better grades (i.e., A's, B's). In the Link and Ancoli-Israel survey of 150 high school students, students with self-reported higher grade point averages (GPA) slept more at night and reported less daytime sleepiness than students with lower GPAs. One explanation for these results is that students who get more sleep and maintain more consistent school/weekend sleep schedules obtain better grades because of their ability to be more alert and to pay greater attention in class and on homework. In contrast, Gau et al. (1995) found that younger students (junior high school age) on a highly competitive academic track reported shorter school and weekend night total sleep times, later bedtimes, and decreased daytime alertness than students in an alternative, less competitive program. Our data do not show a one-to-one relation between sleep patterns and grades. Certainly some students are able to function in school quite well with short amounts of sleep but may pay a price in other ways. Many students, however, may be too impaired by insufficient sleep to cope optimally with school demands. A major limitation of all of these studies is that they involve self-report; additional laboratory and field research are needed to clarify the direction of the relations among sleep loss, irregular sleep schedules, and academic performance and to assess other moderating and mediating variables, such as coping strategies, family rules, class schedules, and type of academic work.

ADDITIONAL CONSEQUENCES OF POOR SLEEP/WAKE HABITS

38 We have attempted to describe more thoroughly certain consequences of insufficient sleep and irregular sleep/wake schedules on adolescents' functioning by comparing extreme groups of students who reported patterns we defined as *adequate* versus *less than adequate* sleep/wake patterns. Students with short school-night sleep reported increased levels of depressed mood, daytime sleepiness, and problematic sleep behaviors in comparison to longer sleepers. Likewise, students with more irregular sleep schedules had more behavior problems. These data suggest that high school students with inadequate total sleep and/or irregular school-night to weekend sleep/wake schedules may struggle with daytime behavior problems. We interpret these findings to indicate that poor

sleep habits influence behavior and mood, acknowledging that in certain young-sters the cause-effect arrow may go in the opposite direction.

Researchers are just beginning to compile evidence relating emotional well- 39 being to sleep patterns. Our findings showing that teenagers with very short and irregular sleep/wake patterns have more daytime difficulties support the work of Morrison, McGee, and Stanton (1992), who compared four groups of 13- and 15-year-olds in New Zealand: those with no sleep problems, those indicating they needed more sleep only, those reporting difficulties falling asleep or main-taining sleep, and those with multiple sleep problems. These investigators found that adolescents in the sleep-problem groups were more anxious, had higher lev-els of depression, and had lower social competence than those in the no-sleep-problem group. Similarly, Carskadon et al. (1991) found that a pattern of short sleep in college-bound high school seniors was associated with reports of sleepi-ness and sleep problems in males and females, and with anxiety and depression in females. Moreover, in a study calling for ninth to twelfth graders to reduce their habitual sleep by 2 hr over 5 consecutive nights, dysphoric mood changes oc-curred during the reduced sleep period on both daily and weekly depressive mood scales (Carskadon et al., 1989).

We hypothesize that if adolescents had the opportunity to obtain more sleep 40 each night, they would experience fewer fluctuations in daily mood and fewer behavioral difficulties. In essence, we propose that adolescent moodiness may be in part a repercussion of insufficient sleep. The tendency for some adolescents to have reduced nocturnal sleep times and irregular schedules may have conse-quences that extend beyond daytime sleepiness to feelings of depression. On the other hand, depressed adolescents may be more inclined toward insufficient sleep and irregular schedules (Dahl et al., 1996). Additional in-depth laboratory and field assessment studies to probe the interplay between context, sleep/wake patterns, and daytime functioning of adolescents may enable us to tease apart some of these factors.

CAVEATS AND IMPLICATIONS

We are very concerned about the important information that we have obtained 41 from this large sample of high school students; however, certain caveats pertain. First, it is difficult to evaluate how representative the sample was, although the congruence between our findings and those from prior research (e.g., Carskadon, 1990a; Strauch & Meier, 1988) strongly suggests that the sample was quite typical. Whether our results hold for adolescents drawn from a wider so-cioeconomic and cultural background is an important issue for future studies. Second, the results of this study are based entirely on the adolescents' self-re-ports and suffer limitations because data are retrospective, based only on the last 2 weeks, and subjective. Multiple sources of measurement such as parent and teacher ratings, school record data, standardized test batteries, and sleep labo-ratory recordings would provide a more comprehensive and possibly more re-liable assessment than the current study. Our previous experience in laboratory studies indicates that such self-report data are well correlated with data ob-tained from daily sleep diaries or continuous activity monitoring, although we have not made a formal comparison. On the other hand, in a study of tenth grade students that included 2 weeks of diaries and activity monitoring followed by a laboratory assessment, we found an average sleep length on school nights of 6 hr, 53 min ($SD = 39$), very similar to self-report (Carskadon, Acebo, Wolfson, Tzischinsky, & Darley, 1997).

42   Third, because the survey was conducted in one geographic area, some caution should be taken in generalizing the findings. Fourth, because the study design was cross-sectional, no conclusions about long-term development and ramifications of inadequate sleep can be drawn. Future investigations should gather several weeks of sleep and behavioral data and consider following high school students over several years. Finally, because the data are cross-sectional it is difficult to demonstrate causal direction. Models that include parameters different than those included in the present study (e.g., home structure, parenting styles, school schedules, and so forth) could also account for variation in grades and/or sleep/wake schedules. Nevertheless, the present study extends the research on adolescent sleep in several ways: (1) to a large population of public high school students; (2) to a broader understanding of the association between sleep/wake habits, emotional well-being, and school performance in high school students from ages 13 to 19; and (3) to a clearer conceptualization of the risks for adolescents who obtain short amounts of sleep and/or experience erratic weekday-weekend sleep schedules on their daytime performance and mood.

43   Although self-report surveys have clear limitations, the implications of these data seem undeniable. First, schools need to take an active role and to examine sleep in the context of academic grades, test scores, truancy, behavioral difficulties, and other aspects of daytime functioning and adolescent development. Second, investigators in other fields who are concerned with adolescent development and well-being need to add the insights regarding adolescents' sleep into their studies and clinical work. Third, researchers, practitioners, and educators need to take interdisciplinary approaches to understanding and promoting the academic, health, and behavioral well-being of adolescents.

44   Adolescents confront a multitude of vulnerabilities, uncertainties, and changes. This developmental period is extremely eventful in terms of physiological, cognitive, and psychosocial development. Undoubtedly, most adolescents require more than 7 hr, 20 min (sample mean) of sleep to cope optimally with academic demands, social pressures, driving, and job responsibilities. Although adolescents may be differentially affected by pubertal changes in sleep/wake patterns, school start times, and academic responsibilities, the excessive sleepiness consequent to insufficient, erratic sleep is a potentially serious factor for adolescent development and behavioral well-being. The magnitude of the problem has been unrecognized because adolescent sleepiness is so widespread that it almost seems normal (Carskadon, 1990a). Steinberg and Darling (1994), Petersen, Silbereisen, and Soerensen (1993) and others have emphasized the importance of studying the context of adolescent development. The development of adolescent sleeping patterns cannot be understood without taking

into account school schedules and other contexts; likewise, adolescent development (psychosocial, cognitive, emotional) cannot be fully examined without considering sleep/wake factors.

Acknowledgments

This study was supported by funds from the National Institutes of Health, MH 45945. We thank Camille Brown, Catherine Darley, Francois Garand, Liza Kelly, Eric Kravitz, Christopher Monti, Orna Tzischinsky, and Beth Yoder for this assistance in gathering and coding data, and Christine Acebo and Ronald Seifer for their assistance regarding data analysis and interpretation of results. We would also like to thank the participating school districts in Rhode Island.

Addresses and Affiliations

Corresponding author: Amy R. Wolfson, College of the Holy Cross, Department of Psychology, Worcester, MA 01610; e-mail: AWolfson@Holycross.edu. Mary A. Carskadon is at Brown University School of Medicine.

References

Achenbach, T. (1991). *Manual for the Youth Self-Report and 1991 profile.* Burlington: University of Vermont Department of Psychiatry.

Allen, R. (1991). School-week sleep lag: Sleep problems with earlier starting of senior high schools. *Sleep Research, 20,* 198.

Allen, R. (1992). Social factors associated with the amount of school week sleep lag for seniors in an early starting suburban high school. *Sleep Research, 21,* 114.

Allen, R., & Mirabile, J. (1989). Self-reported sleep-wake patterns for students during the school year from two different senior high schools. *Sleep Research, 18,* 132.

Andrade, M. M., Benedito-Silva, E. E., & Domenice, S. (1993). Sleep characteristics of adolescents: A longitudinal study. *Journal of Adolescent Health, 14,* 401–406.

Bearpark, H. M., & Michie, P. T. (1987). Prevalence of sleep/wake disturbances in Sydney adolescents. *Sleep Research, 16,* 304.

Brown, C., Tzischinsky, O., Wolfson, A., Acebo, C., Wicks, J., Darley, C., & Carskadon, M. A. (1995). Circadian phase preference and adjustment to the high school transition. *Sleep Research, 24,* 90.

Carskadon, M. A. (1982). The second decade. In C. Guilleminault (Ed.), *Sleeping and waking disorders: Indications and techniques.* Menlo Park, CA: Addison-Wesley.

Carskadon, M. A. (1990a). Patterns of sleep and sleepiness in adolescents. *Pediatrician, 17,* 5–12.

Carskadon, M. A. (1990b). Adolescent sleepiness: Increased risk in a high-risk population. *Alcohol, Drugs, and Driving, 5/6,* 317–328.

Carskadon, M. A. (1995). Sleep's place in teenagers' lives. *Proceedings of the Biennial Meeting of the Society for Research in Child Development,* p. 32 (abstract).

Carskadon, M. A., & Acebo, C. (1993). A self-administered rating scale for pubertal development. *Journal of Adolescent Health Care, 14*, 190–195.

Carskadon, M. A., Acebo, C., Richardson, G. S., Tate, B. A., & Seifer, R. (1997). Long nights protocol: Access to circadian parameters in adolescents. *Journal of Biological Rhythms, 12*, 278–289.

Carskadon, M. A., Acebo, C., Wolfson, A., Tzischinsky, O., & Darley, C. (1997). REM sleep on MSLTS in high school students is related to circadian phase. *Sleep Research, 26,* 705.

Carskadon, M. A., Dement, W. C., Mitler, M. M., Roth, T., Westbrook, P. R., & Keenan, S. (1986). Guidelines for the Multiple Sleep Latency Test (MSLT): A standard measure of sleepiness. *Sleep, 9,* 519–524.

Carskadon, M. A., Harvey, K., Duke, P., Anders, T. F., & Dement, W. C. (1980). Pubertal changes in daytime sleepiness. *Sleep, 2,* 453–460.

Carskadon, M. A., Keenan, S., & Dement, W. C. (1987). Nighttime sleep and daytime sleep tendency in preadolescents. In C. Guilleminault (Ed.), *Sleep and its disorders in children.* New York: Raven Press.

Carskadon, M. A., & Mancuso, J. (1988). Sleep habits in high school adolescents: Boarding versus day students. *Sleep Research, 17,* 74.

Carskadon, M. A., Orav, E. J., & Dement, W. C. (1983). Evolution of sleep and daytime sleepiness in adolescents. In C. Guilleminault & E. Lugaresi (Eds.), *Sleep/wake disorders: Natural history, epidemiology, and long-term evolution* (pp. 201–216). New York: Raven Press.

Carskadon, M. A., Rosekind, M. R., Galli, J., Sohn, J., Herman, K. B., & Davis, S. S. (1989). Adolescent sleepiness during sleep restriction in the natural environment. *Sleep Research, 18,* 115.

Carskadon, M. A., Seifer, R., & Acebo, C. (1991). Reliability of six scales in a sleep questionnaire for adolescents. *Sleep Research, 20,* 421.

Carskadon, M. A., Vieira, C., & Acebo, C. (1993). Association between puberty and delayed phase preference. *Sleep, 16,* 258–262.

Carskadon, M. A., Wolfson, A., Tzischinsky, O., & Acebo, C. (1995). Early school schedules modify adolescent sleepiness. *Sleep Research, 24,* 92.

Cohen, J. (1988). *Statistical Power Analysis for the Behavioral Sciences.* Hillsdale, NJ: Erlbaum.

Dahl, R. E., & Carskadon, M. A. (1995). Sleep in its disorders in adolescence. In R. Ferber & M. Kryger (Eds.), *Principles and practice of sleep medicine in the child.* Philadelphia: WB Saunders.

Dahl, R. E., Holttum, J., & Trubnick, L. (1994). A clinical picture of childhood and adolescent narcolepsy. *Journal of the American Academy of Child and Adolescent Psychiatry, 33,* 834–841.

Dahl, R. E., Ryan, N. D., Matty, M. K., Birmaher, B., Alshabbout, M., Williamson, D. E., & Kupfer, D. J. (1996). Sleep onset abnormalities in depressed adolescents. *Biological Psychiatry, 39,* 400–410.

Epstein, R., Chillag, N., & Lavie, P. (1995). Sleep habits of children and adolescents in Israel: The influence of starting time of school. *Sleep Research, 24a,* 432.

Fisher, B. E., & Rinehart, S. (1990). Stress, arousal, psychopathology and temperament: A multidimensional approach to sleep disturbance in children. *Personality and Individual Differences, 11,* 431–438.

Gau, S-F., & Soong, W-T. (1995). Sleep problems of junior high school students in Taipei. *Sleep, 18,* 667–673.

Guilleminault, C., Winkle, R., & Korobkin, R. (1982). Children and nocturnal snoring: Evaluation of the effects of sleep related respiratory resistive load and daytime functioning. *European Journal of Pediatrics, 139,* 165–171.

Hendry, L. B., Glendinning, A., Shucksmith, J., Love, J., & Scott, J. (1994). The developmental context of adolescent life-styles. In R. K. Silbereisen & T. Eberhard (Eds.), *Adolescence in context: The interplay of family, school, peers, and work in adjustment* (pp. 66–81). New York: Springer-Verlag.

Ishihara, K., Honma, Y., & Miyake, S. (1990). Investigation of the children's version of the morningness-eveningness questionnaire with primary and junior high school pupils in Japan. *Perceptual and Motor Skills, 71,* 1353–1354.

Kagan, J., Resnick, J. S., & Gibbons, J. (1989). Inhibited and uninhibited types of children. *Child Development, 60,* 838–845.

Kandel, D. B., & Davies, M. (1982). Epidemiology of depressive mood in adolescents. *Archives of General Psychiatry, 39,* 1205–1212.

Kataria, S., Swanson, M. S., & Trevathan, G. E. (1987). Persistence of sleep disturbances in preschool children. *Pediatrics, 110,* 642–646.

Kowalski, N., & Allen, R. (1995). School sleep lag is less but persists with a very late starting high school. *Sleep Research, 24,* 124.

Link, S. C., & Ancoli-Israel, S. (1995). Sleep and the teenager. *Sleep Research, 24a,* 184.

Manber, R., Pardee, R. E., Bootzin, R. R., Kuo, T., Rider, A. M., Rider, S. P., & Bergstrom, L. (1995). Changing sleep patterns in adolescence. *Sleep Research, 24,* 106.

Morrison, D. N., McGee, R., & Stanton, W. R. (1992). Sleep problems in adolescence. *Journal of the American Academy of Child and Adolescent Psychiatry, 31,* 94–99.

Peterson, A. C., Silbereisen, R. K., & Soerensen, S. (1993). Adolescent development: A global perspective. In W. Meeus, M. de Goede, W. Kox, & K. Hurrelmann (Eds.), *Adolescence, careers and cultures* (pp. 1–34). New York: De Gruyter.

Petta, D., Carskadon, M. A., & Dement, W. C. (1984). Sleep habits in children aged 7–13 years. *Sleep Research, 13,* 86.

Price, V. A., Coates, T. J., Thoresen, C. E., & Grinstead, O. A. (1978). Prevalence and correlates of poor sleep among adolescents. *American Journal of Diseases of Children, 132,* 583–586.

Quine, L. (1992). Severity of sleep problems in children with severe learning difficulties: Description and correlates. *Journal of Community and Applied Social Psychology, 2,* 247–268.

State of Rhode Island Department of Education. (1994). *Rhode Island Public Schools 1994 District Profiles.* Providence: Rhode Island Department of Elementary and Secondary Education.

Steinberg, L., & Darling, N. (1994). The broader context of social influence in adolescence. In R. K. Silbereisen & T. Eberhard (Eds.), *Adolescence in context: The interplay of family, school, peers, and work in adjustment* (pp. 25–45). New York: Springer-Verlag.

Strauch, I., & Meier, B. (1988). Sleep need in adolescents: A longitudinal approach. *Sleep, 11,* 378–386.

Szymczak, J. T., Jasinska, M., Pawlak, E., & Swierzykowska, M. (1993). Annual and weekly changes in the sleep-wake rhythm of school children. *Sleep, 16*, 433–435.

Tanner, J. M. (1962). *Growth in adolescence.* Oxford: Blackwell.

Williams, R., Karacan, I., & Hursch, C. (1974). *EEG of human sleep.* New York: Wiley & Sons.

Wolfson, A. R., Tzischinsky, O., Brown, C., Darley, C., Acebo, C., & Carskadon, M. (1995). Sleep, behavior, and stress at the transition to senior high school. *Sleep Research, 24*, 115.

• *Thinking Critically About "Sleep Schedules and Daytime Functioning in Adolescents"*

RESPONDING AS A READER

1. It is likely that this text is one of the first scholarly articles you will have worked with closely. What have you discovered about the process of reading difficult material? What have you learned about the way scholars must present evidence to support their research conclusions? Use your reading log to reflect on the experience. Consider which parts of the text—other than the statistical discussions!—were more and less difficult to follow. Why? What made those stretches of text difficult to follow? What aspect of the text was easier to follow than you expected? What will you carry from this reading experience to other challenging assignments?

2. Make as long a list as you can of the ways in which this article follows conventions that are markedly different from articles in a general interest magazine or newspaper. How did these conventions of scholarly writing assist your reading and understanding? Where did they make it difficult to understand the material?

3. Initially, it may seem that the content of this article is so governed by genre conventions specifying how certain sections and headings should look that there is no room for the authors to put a personal mark on it. Yet many people who read the article are struck by the researchers' concern for adolescents who do not get enough sleep. Did this concern come across to you? Where and how amid all the technical details do they bring this issue alive? To put the question another way, what does the text tell us about why anyone should care about this research? Working alone or with your classmates, identify specific passages in the article that (a) connect with readers' everyday lives and (b) assert the significance of the subject matter.

RESPONDING AS A WRITER

1. The fourteen paragraphs in the introduction section of this article constitute what is known as a "review of the literature" (i.e., a review of relevant research). Their purpose is to explain how the study connects with previous research and why it was necessary. Try to explain in your own words, as if you were talking to a friend, why Wolfson and Carskadon undertook the study. What did they want to find out? Jot

down your best recollection of their purpose, then go back and examine the main points in the introduction to find material you can use to flesh out your notes to create a 50- to 100- word summary of the literature review. Your purpose in this summary is to explain the researchers' purpose. Your summary, like the literature review itself, should answer two important questions: (a) What had previous research established? (b) What questions did those findings raise for these researchers to explore? As you work, try to pinpoint a place *before* paragraph 14 where the discussion of previous research begins to establish the need for the current study, the place where someone who has read the abstract is likely to think, "Aha, I see where this is going now." Write for nonexpert readers interested in the subject; avoid quotations, and omit the citations of other research. You might open with a phrase such as, "By undertaking the study, Wolfson and Carskadon sought to. . . ."

2. What do your examination of the introduction and your composition of the summary reveal to you about the basic structure of literature reviews? Using paragraphs 1 through 14 as a model, what guidance would you be able to give someone who needs some help getting started on writing a literature review after assembling all the necessary articles?

3. Perhaps the most daunting aspect of this article is the detailed presentation of statistical findings in Tables 1–3 and the bar graphs in Figure 1. The exercise that follows is designed to help you discover what sense you can make of all this—a difficult task for nonexperts.

    Detailed presentation of statistical findings is essential to the credibility of the study. But is detailed understanding of them essential to your purposes as a reader? As we point out in the opening chapters of this book, dealing with difficult texts is part of effective rhetorical reading. How should you proceed? Avoid the statistics paragraphs? Try to understand every detail? Seek outside guidance (from experts or reference works)? Or accept the technical details at face value and try to understand the key points based on them? The appropriate decision will vary according to a reader's experience and purpose, of course. For this article, which you are reading in a book for writing students, we recommend the last option: accept the statistical findings as stated and focus on the points derived from them. We feel justified in recommending this because the article has been published in a reputable refereed journal; that means experts have already scrutinized the numbers. Like management executives who let technicians take care of technical matters, we who are not psychologists or statisticians should focus on the points most relevant to us. After all, even scientific researchers often rely on statisticians to help them with data analysis. (Notice that Wolfson and Carskadon acknowledge this kind of assistance at the end of the article.)

    Let's turn to the key points that Wolfson and Carskadon derive from their analysis of the statistical data. We list below five generic questions that rhetorical readers can use when reading about data analysis in a field where they are not experts. Working with one or two partners, examine the text to find answers to these questions and write out your answers in everyday language.

a. What questions do the researchers use the data to answer?
b. What answers do they emphasize as important in their discussion of findings?
c. What aspects of the data are highlighted by the graphical presentations (charts and tables)?
d. What problems, if any, do the authors acknowledge regarding their findings?
e. What are their recommendations for dealing with those problems in future studies?

As you look for answers to these questions, make maximum use of the text's genre conventions. For example, the purpose of a study is frequently articulated most clearly in the final paragraph of its literature review. More specific questions are implied in the headings that mark distinct sections under "Results." Try converting these headings into questions, then look for specific answers. You can check your conclusions by rereading the discussion section. Finally, examine the caveats and implications paragraphs to note the problems Wolfson and Carskadon acknowledge and their recommendations for future research.

Paul Irgang

When a Wet Vac Counts More Than a Ph.D.

Paul Irgang is a building maintenance technician at the University of Miami. This opinion piece appeared in the January 21, 2000 Chronicle of Higher Education, which calls itself "the academic world's No. 1 source of news and information." The article was subsequently reprinted by several building maintenance periodicals as well as posted on a number of Websites.

● *For Your Reading Log*

1. This article was originally published across four columns, with the opening epigraph in its own column on the left. As an experiment to see how epigraphs can influence a reader's response to a text, try the following procedure. *Put your hand or a piece of paper over the italic section*, read the essay's first two paragraphs, jot some notes about your response, and then go back to the epigraph and read the article straight through. How did the joke influence your perception of what Irgang has to say?

2. Whom do you know in the physical plant or facilities services department at your college or university? What's your sense of how this person feels about his or her job status in relation to faculty and students?

---- ● ----

Bringing up the rear of the circus parade were the elephants—eight majestic pachyderms with gleaming ivory tusks, enormous ears, and trunks swaying with each step. Fifty feet behind them was an old man carrying a shovel and pulling a yellow cart.

"Don't you ever get tired of scooping up elephant dung?" he was asked. "Why don't you pursue another line of work?"

He replied: "What, and leave show business?"

—Catskills "Borscht Belt" joke

At colleges and universities throughout the United States, physical-plant employees are often unappreciated and undervalued, the campus equivalent of Ralph Ellison's "invisible man."

Those of us who work in academe inhabit an unofficial, yet undeniable, caste system. Tenured Ph.D.'s constitute the Brahmin sect, followed by

untenured faculty and staff members and research associates, librarians, secretaries, food-service personnel, and, finally, the untouchables: physical-plant
employees.

3   If you can use a hammer and have a clean record—that is, no criminal convictions (arrests are OK, but no convictions)—you can get a job here at the University of Miami's department of facilities management (physical plant), where
I have been employed as a "building-maintenance worker II" for the past nine
years. (Note: If you are unable to use a hammer, you may still be eligible to become an administrator.)

4   Here at U.M., my colleagues and I are most appreciated whenever a hurricane with sustained winds of more than 150 m.p.h. approaches campus. It is usually during this "emergency-preparation phase" that our dean provides us with
a free catered lunch and unlimited kudos. When the impending storm is within
100 miles of Biscayne Bay, and the institution is officially closed, we are suddenly
given a new moniker—"essential personnel."

5   During these crisis situations the physical-plant team hunkers down, trying
to save not only the buildings, but years' and millions of dollars' worth of experiments in progress. Tissue samples must remain chilled by emergency gen-
erators. Irreplaceable 10,000-year-old ice-core samples must not be allowed to
thaw. Rare specimens of coral must be protected. Computers must be wrapped
in plastic, and kept dry and out of harm's way.

6   When the wind speed picks up, proficiency with a power saw becomes a
real asset. We board up windows. We man the pumps. We secure all objects
that have the potential to become destructive or deadly missiles during the
maelstrom.

7   Suddenly, the storm, influenced by a high-pressure system just offshore,
takes a sharp turn to the north. The university has dodged the bullet once again;
the danger has passed.

8   Within minutes the phone rings at the physical-plant department. It's one
of our associate deans: "Listen, I've been trying to get a light bulb replaced for
almost a week. How many of you guys does it take to screw in one of those
things?"

9   It is my sincere hope that all those involved in higher education begin to understand that the successful operation of a university campus demands a team
effort and that there are times when a man with a wet vac is as valuable as any
Ph.D. in theoretical physics.

10   Without the assistance of physical-plant employees, for how long would the
University of Notre Dame's golden dome remain golden? How long before Stanford's or Cornell's manicured lawns begin to resemble the brush and bramble of
some suburban bank in foreclosure? How long before all campuses decline and
decay into windblown shells, 20th-century Parthenons that only hint at the glory
that once was?

11   So, whether you're a professor or a student, an administrator or a secretary,
please treat all physical-plant employees with the dignity and respect they deserve. And remember, we have keys to everything.

• *Thinking Critically About "When a Wet Vac Counts More Than a Ph.D."*

RESPONDING AS A READER

1. Where in Irgang's essay did you find yourself most engaged, and where did you find yourself resisting? Try to account for these responses by pinpointing specific words and phrasings that you found effective or ineffective.

2. Irgang's first sentence asserts a point likely to cause discomfort for his audience of *Chronicle* readers—academic administrators and faculty. Yet he needs them to keep reading. How does he balance his intention of bringing negative ideas to readers' attention against his need to stave off any potential resistance to his ideas?

3. On what basis does Irgang assert authority regarding his subject matter? Taking the fact that he works as a "building-maintenance worker II" as just a beginning point, identify the other sources of credibility he establishes. How much of his effectiveness in the essay depends on *what* he says, and how much is a function of *how* he says it? In other words, to what extent can we say that his credibility stems from his rhetorical skill as well as his experience? Refer to specific places in the text to support your answers.

RESPONDING AS A WRITER

1. A common maxim for good writing is "show, don't tell," a phrase that asserts the value of using vivid detail to bring an idea to life. Where, specifically, do you see Irgang following this maxim? How does his use of detail help him make his points? Pick out one detail that had more impact on you than any other and compare your response to your classmates'.

2. Details alone cannot make an essay work. The language that a writer chooses to express them is also crucial. On your own or with a partner, go through the essay to highlight word choices that strike you as particularly original or even unexpected. How do they add to Irgang's overall effectiveness? To what extent do you see him choosing language that is likely to appeal to his academic audience?

3. Irgang's essay challenges what he calls the "unofficial, yet undeniable caste system" inhabited by university employees (a group that includes dishwashers as well as deans, remember). What values underlie his effort to change readers' understanding of how these employees do and should interact? According to his implicit assertions here, what makes work valuable? After freewriting for a few minutes in response to these questions, reread the essay to note both implicit and explicit references to values. Afterward, as you reflect further on the text, through writing or discussion, try to articulate any changes in your thinking that Irgang's essay has brought about.

Nancy Mairs

Body in Trouble

Nancy Mairs (b. 1943) is widely acclaimed for her autobiographical essays about her struggles with disabilities, including depression, agoraphobia, and multiple sclerosis, to which she has lost the use of her arms and legs. Her essay entitled, "On Being a Cripple," published in her book *Plaintext* (1986), first brought her to national attention. The essays collected in her five additional books characteristically confront readers with blunt language that asserts feminist values, explores difficult relationships, and depicts the difficulties presented by her disease. She once told a biographer, "In my writing I aim to speak the 'unspeakable.'" This essay comes from *Waisthigh in the World: A Life Among the Nondisabled*, published in 1996.

• *For Your Reading Log*

1. This essay is both intensely personal and conceptually abstract. As you read, "listen" to it carefully, marking key passages, bracketing points you don't understand, and jotting down questions as they occur to you. When you have the opportunity to compare the places you and your classmates found difficult, see how you can help each other deepen your understanding and then determine what patterns of difficulty remain.

2. As soon as you finish reading, freewrite in your log about your positive and negative responses to this text. Where does Mairs capture your belief most powerfully? Where do you find yourself resisting or doubting her assertions, perhaps wishing she would state things in a less forceful manner? Freewrite for 3 to 5 minutes from each perspective.

————————   •   ————————

1 In biblical times, physical and mental disorders were thought to signify possession by demons. In fact, Jesus's proficiency at casting these out accounted for much of his popularity among the common folk (though probably not among swine). People who were stooped or blind or subject to seizures were clearly not okay as they were but required fixing, and divine intervention was the only remedy powerful enough to cleanse them of their baleful residents.

2   Theologically as well as medically, this interpretation of the body in trouble now seems primitive, and yet we perpetuate the association underlying it. A brief examination of "dead" metaphors (those which have been so thoroughly integrated into language that we generally overlook their analogical origins) demonstrates the extent to which physical vigor equates with positive moral qualities. "Keep your chin up," we say (signifying courage), "and your eyes open" (alertness); "stand on your own two feet" (independence) "and tall" (pride); "look straight in the eye" (honesty) or "see eye to eye" (accord); "run rings around" (su-

periority). By contrast, physical debility connotes vice, as in "sit on your ass" (laziness), "take it lying down" (weakness), "listen with half an ear" (inattention), and get left "without a leg to stand on" (unsound argument). The way in which the body occupies space and the quality of the space it occupies correlate with the condition of the soul: it is better to be admired as "high-minded" than "looked down on" for one's "low morals," to be "in the know" than "out of it," to be "up front" than "back-handed," to be "free as a bird" than "confined to a wheelchair."

Now, the truth is that, unless you are squatting or six years old, I can never 3 look you straight in the eye, and I spend all my time sitting on my ass except when I'm taking it lying down. These are the realities of life in a wheelchair (though in view of the alternatives—bed, chair, or floor—"confinement" is the very opposite of my condition). And the fact that the soundness of the body so often serves as a metaphor for its moral health, its deterioration thus implying moral degeneracy, puts me and my kind in a quandary. How can I possibly be "good"? Let's face it, wicked witches are not just ugly (as sin); they're also bent and misshapen (crooked). I am bent and misshapen, therefore ugly, therefore wicked. And I have no way to atone.

It is a bind many women, not just the ones with disabilities, have historically 4 found themselves in by virtue of their incarnation in a sociolinguistic system over which they have had relatively little power. (Notice how virile the virtues encoded in the examples above.) Female bodies, even handsome and wholesome ones, have tended to give moralists fits of one sort or another (lust, disgust, but seldom trust). As everyone who has read the *Malleus Maleficarum* knows, "All witchcraft comes from carnal Lust which is in Women insatiable." If a good man is hard to find, a good woman is harder, unless she's (1) prepubescent, (2), senile, or (3) dead; and even then, some will have their doubts about her. It is tricky enough, then, trying to be a good woman at all, but a crippled woman experiences a kind of double jeopardy. How can she construct a world that will accommodate her realities, including her experience of her own goodness, while it remains comprehensible to those whose world-views are founded on premises alien or even inimical to her sense of self?

Disability is at once a metaphorical and a material state, evocative of other 5 conditions in time and space—childhood and imprisonment come to mind—yet "like" nothing but itself. I can't live it or write about it except by conflating the figurative and the substantial, the "as if" with the relentlessly "what is." Let me illustrate with an experience from a couple of years ago, when George and I went to a luncheon honoring the Dalai Lama, held at a large resort northwest of Tucson. Although we were not enrolled in the five-day workshop he had come here to lead, we found ourselves in the hallway when the meeting room disgorged the workshop participants—all fourteen hundred of them—into a narrow area further constricted by tables laden with bells, beads, and brochures. And let me tell you, no matter how persuaded they were of the beauty and sacredness of all life, not one of them seemed to think that any life was going on below the level of her or his own gaze. "Down here!" I kept whimpering at the hips and buttocks and bellies pressing my wheelchair on all sides. "Down here! There's a person down here!" My only recourse was to roll to one side and hug a wall.

6   Postmodern criticism, feminist and otherwise, makes a good deal of the concept of wall-hugging, or marginality, which is meant to suggest that some segment of the population—black, brown, yellow, or red, poor, female, lesbian, what have you—is shouldered to the side, heedlessly or not, by some perhaps more numerous and certainly more powerful segment, most frequently wealthy, well-educated Euro-American males. Regardless of the way marginality is conceived, it is never taken to mean that those on the margin occupy a physical space literally outside the field of vision of those in the center, so that the latter trip unawares and fall into the laps of those they have banished from consciousness unless these scoot safely out of the way. "Marginality" thus means something altogether different to me from what it means to social theorists. It is no metaphor for the power relations between one group of human beings and another but a literal description of where I stand (figuratively speaking): over here, on the edge, out of bounds, beneath your notice. I embody the metaphors. Only whether or not I like doing so is immaterial.

7   It may be this radical materiality of my circumstances, together with the sense I mentioned earlier that defect and deformity bar me from the ranks of "good" women, which have spurred me in the past, as they no doubt will go on doing, to put the body at the center of all my meditations, my "corpus," if you will. Not that I always write *about* the body, though I often do, but that I always write, consciously, *as* a body. (This quality more than any other, I think, exiles my work from conventional academic discourse. The guys may be writing with the pen/penis, but they pretend at all times to keep it in their pants.) And it is this—my—crippled female body that my work struggles to redeem through that most figurative of human tools: language. Because language substitutes a no-thing for a thing, whereas a body is pure thing through and through, this task must fail. But inevitable disappointment does not deprive labor of its authenticity.

8   And so I use inscription to insert my embodied self into a world with which, over time, I have less and less in common. Part of my effort entails reshaping both that self and that world in order to reconcile the two. We bear certain responsibilities toward each other, the world and I, and I must neither remove myself from it nor permit it to exclude me if we are to carry these out. I can't become a "hopeless cripple" without risking moral paralysis; nor can the world, except to its own diminishment, refuse my moral participation.

9   But is a woman for whom any action at all is nearly impossible capable of right action, or am I just being morally cocky here? After all, if I claim to be a good woman, I leave myself open to the question: Good for what? The most straightforward answer is the most tempting: Good for nothing. I mean really. I can stand with assistance but I can't take a step; I can't even spread my own legs for sex anymore. My left arm doesn't work at all, and my right one grows weaker almost by the day. I am having more and more trouble raising a fork or a cup to my lips. (It is possible, I've discovered, though decidedly odd, to drink even coffee and beer through a straw.) I can no longer drive. I lack the stamina to go out to work. If I live to see them, I will never hold my own grandchildren. These incapacities constitute a stigma that, according to social scientist Erving Goffman, removes me from normal life into a "discredited" position to relation to society.

From the point of view of the Catholic Church, to which I belong, however, 10
mine must be just about the ideal state: too helpless even for the sins other flesh
is heir to. After all, parties aren't much fun now that I meet the other revelers eye
to navel, and getting drunk is risky since I can hardly see straight cold sober. No
matter how insatiable my carnal Lust, nobody's likely to succumb to my charms
and sully my reputation. But I am, by sympathy at least, a Catholic *Worker,* part
of a community that wastes precious little time fretting about the seven dead-
lies, assuming instead that the moral core of being in the world lies in the care
of others, in *doing* rather than *being* good. How can a woman identify herself as
a Catholic Worker if she can't even cut up carrots for the soup or ladle it out for
the hungry people queued up outside the kitchen door? Physical incapacity certainly appears to rob such a woman of moral efficacy.

Well, maybe moral demands should no longer be placed on her. Perhaps 11
she ought simply to be "excused" from the moral life on the most generous of
grounds: that she suffers enough already, that she has plenty to do just to take
care of herself. This dismissive attitude tends to be reinforced when the woman
lives at the height of your waist. Because she "stands" no higher than a six-
year-old, you may unconsciously ascribe to her the moral development of a
child (which, in view of Robert Coles's findings, you will probably underesti-
mate) and demand little of her beyond obedience and enough self-restraint so
that she doesn't filch candy bars at the checkout counter while you're busy
writing a check. (God, I can't tell you how tempting those brightly wrapped
chunks are when they're smack up against your nose.) "Stature" is an intrinsic attribute of moral life, and the woman who lacks the one may be judged incapable of the other.

I am exaggerating here, of course, but only a little. Beyond cheerfulness and 12
patience, people don't generally expect much of a cripple's character. And certainly they presume that care, which I have placed at the heart of moral experience, flows in one direction, "downward": as from adult to child, so from well
to ill, from whole to maimed. This condescension contributes to what Goffman
calls "spoiled identity," though he does not deal satisfactorily with the damage
it inflicts: without reciprocity, the foundation of any mature moral relationship,
the person with a defect cannot grow "up" and move "out" into the world but
remains constricted in ways that make being "confined to a wheelchair" look
trivial. And so I would say that while it is all right to excuse me from making the
soup (for the sake of the soup, probably more than "all right"), you must never—
even with the best intentions, even with my own complicity—either enable or
require me to withdraw from moral life altogether.

So much for carrot-cutting, then, or any other act involving sharp instru- 13
ments. But wait! One sharp instrument is left me: my tongue. (Here's where
metaphor comes in hand.) And my computer keyboard is . . . just waist high.
With these I ought to be able to concoct another order of soup altogether (in
which I'll no doubt find myself up to my ears). In other words, what I can still
do—so far—is write books. Catholic Workers being extraordinarily tolerant of
multiplicity, on the theory that it takes all kinds of parts to form a body, this activity will probably be counted good enough.

The world to which I am a material witness is a difficult one to love. But I am not alone in it now; and as the population ages, more and more people—a significant majority of them women—may join me in it, learning to negotiate a chill and rubble-strewn landscape with impaired eyesight and hearing and mobility, searching out some kind of home there. Maps render foreign territory, however dark and wide, fathomable. I mean to make a map. My infinitely harder task, then, is to conceptualize not merely a habitable body but a habitable world: a world that wants me in it.

• *Thinking Critically About "Body in Trouble"*

RESPONDING AS A READER

1. How do you respond to the way Mairs presents herself in this essay? Do you find her self-portrayal credible? More specifically, do you imagine her as friendly or hostile? Does she come across as warm or cold? Strong or pathetic? To what aspects of her personality—as she conveys it here—do you respond most positively? Most negatively? If you were to spend a few hours with her, perhaps over dinner, what do you think would be the easiest and most difficult subjects to talk about?

2. Mairs discusses figurative language and uses it extensively as well. Working with a partner or group, make a list of the five or six nonliteral images here that you consider to be most important to the essay (go beyond those in her list of "dead" metaphors in the second paragraph). What emotional power do these images convey? What values are inherent in her choice of metaphor—for example, "childhood" and "imprisonment" for disability in paragraph 5?

3. What do you understand as Mairs's primary purpose in writing and publishing this essay? What is it that she most wants her readers to understand? To accept? To change?

RESPONDING AS A WRITER

1. The questions above ask you to tap into your responses as a reader. Now, to analyze from a writerly perspective how this essay works to accomplish its purposes, try taking it down to its bones. Use lists, mapping techniques, or whatever works best for you to answer the questions listed below. In the process, try to get outside the linear perspective of your moment-to-moment reading. Instead, zero in on what you take to be Mairs's core points and examine the web of connections she establishes among them and between you and them. Specifically:
   a. What is it that Mairs is seeking to explain?
   b. How is she doing it? (for example, through the use of anecdote, division into parts, analogy, reasoning, narrative, examples, etc.)
   c. How do her techniques for conveying her ethos and engaging readers' emotions assist with her explanatory project?

2. As a way of summing up your reading and analysis of this essay, try your hand at a four-sentence rhetorical précis that follows the model presented in Chapter 4 (p. 62). Follow precisely the form described there. The first sentence should state Mairs's primary point, the second should explain how she develops it, the third should indicate her purpose, and the fourth should describe her rhetorical strategies in relation to her readers. Adopt an academic, explanatory tone for an audience of readers who need a quick sense of what the essay is about and how it works.

3. In the end, how has "Body in Trouble" affected your thinking? In your reading log or as your teacher directs, compose a brief response that lays out any insights you've gained, new ways of thinking prompted by the essay, or questions that it has raised.

Peter Marin

Helping and Hating the Homeless

Peter Marin (b. 1936) is a poet, novelist, and essayist who lives in southern California, where he is a longtime advocate for homeless people. His most recent book of
essays, *Freedom and Its Discontents: Reflections on Four Decades of American Moral Experience* (1995), describes some of his friendships with homeless and marginalized
Americans. He is a contributing editor at *Harper's* magazine, where this essay was
published in January 1987. It is frequently read in college classes where students are
involved in community service programs.

• *For Your Reading Log*

1. Before you read, take a few moments to jot down your current understanding of why people become homeless. Note too the source of your
understanding—classes, experience on the streets, media reports, service
work, etc.

2. The first six paragraphs of Marin's essay constitute an introduction
based on personal experience, at the end of which he explains his purpose for writing. Pause in your reading after paragraph 6 and freewrite
for a few minutes about what you expect he will say and do in the rest
of the essay to fulfill that purpose. As you read the rest of the essay, put
a checkmark in the margin next to places where you find your expectations fulfilled or countered.

--------- • ---------

1   When I was a child, I had a recurring vision of how I would end as an old man:
alone, in a sparsely furnished second-story room I could picture quite precisely,
in a walk-up on Fourth Avenue in New York, where the secondhand bookstores
then were. It was not a picture which frightened me. I liked it. The idea of
anonymity and solitude and marginality must have seemed to me, back then, for
reasons I do not care to remember, both inviting and inevitable. Later, out of college, I took to the road, hitchhiking and traveling on freights, doing odd jobs here
and there, crisscrossing the country. I liked that too: the anonymity and the absence of constraint and the rough community I sometimes found. I felt at home
on the road, perhaps because I felt at home nowhere else, and periodically, for
years, I would return to that world, always with a sense of relief and release.

2   I have been thinking a lot about that these days, now that transience and
homelessness have made their way into the national consciousness, and especially since the town I live in, Santa Barbara, has become well known because of
the recent successful campaign to do away with the meanest aspects of its "sleeping ordinances"—a set of foolish laws making it illegal for the homeless to sleep

at night in public places. During that campaign I got to know many of the home-less men and women in Santa Barbara, who tend to gather, night and day, in a small park at the lower end of town, not far from the tracks and the harbor, un-der the roof-like, overarching branches of a gigantic fig tree, said to be the old-est on the continent. There one enters much the same world I thought, as a child, I would die in, and the one in which I traveled as a young man: a "marginal" world inhabited by all those unable to find a place in "our" world. Sometimes, standing on the tracks close to the park, you can sense in the wind, or in the smell of tar and ties, the presence and age of that marginal world: the way it stretches backward and inevitably forward in time, parallel to our own world, always present, always close, and yet separated from us—at least in the mind—by a gulf few of us are interested in crossing.

Late last summer, at a city council meeting here in Santa Barbara, I saw, close 3 up, the consequences of that strange combination of proximity and distance. The council was meeting to vote on the repeal of the sleeping ordinances, though not out of any sudden sense of compassion or justice. Council members had been pressured into it by the threat of massive demonstrations—"The Selma of the Eighties" was the slogan one heard among the homeless. But this threat that frightened the council enraged the town's citizens. Hundreds of them turned out for the meeting. One by one they filed to the microphone to curse the council and castigate the homeless. Drinking, doping, loitering, panhandling, defecating, urinating, molesting, stealing—the litany went on and on, was repeated over and over, accompanied by fantasies of disaster: the barbarian hordes at the gates, civ-ilization ended.

What astonished me about the meeting was not what was said; one could 4 have predicted that. It was the power and depth of the emotion revealed: the mindlessness of the fear, the vengefulness of the fury. Also, almost none of what was said had anything to do with the homeless people I know—not the ones I once traveled with, not the ones in town. They, the actual homeless men and women, might not have existed at all.

If I write about Santa Barbara, it is not because I think the attitudes at work 5 here are unique. They are not. You find them everywhere in America. In the last few months I have visited several cities around the country, and in each of them I have found the same thing: more and more people in the streets, more and more suffering. (There are at least 350,000 homeless people in the country, perhaps as many as 3 million.) And, in talking to the good citizens of these cities, I found, almost always, the same thing: confusion and ignorance, or simple indifference, but anger too, and fear.

What follows here is an attempt to explain at least some of that anger and 6 fear, to clear up some of the confusion, to chip away at the indifference. It is not meant to be definitive; how could it be? The point is to try to illuminate some of the darker corners of homelessness, those we ordinarily ignore, and those in which the keys to much that is now going on may be hidden.

The trouble begins with the word "homeless." It has become such an abstraction, 7 and is applied to so many different kinds of people, with so many different his-tories and problems, that it is almost meaningless.

8   Homelessness, in itself, is nothing more than a condition visited upon men and women (and, increasingly, children) as the final stage of a variety of problems about which the word "homelessness" tells us almost nothing. Or, to put it another way, it is a catch basin into which pour all of the people disenfranchised or marginalized or scared off by processes beyond their control, those which lie close to the heart of American life. Here are the groups packed into the single category of "the homeless":

- Veterans, mainly from the war in Vietnam. In many American cities, vets make up close to 50 percent of all homeless males.
- The mentally ill. In some parts of the country, roughly a quarter of the homeless would, a couple of decades ago, have been institutionalized.
- The physically disabled or chronically ill, who do not receive any benefits or whose benefits do not enable them to afford permanent shelter.
- The elderly on fixed incomes whose funds are no longer sufficient for their needs.
- Men, women, and whole families pauperized by the loss of a job.
- Single parents, usually women, without the resources or skills to establish new lives.
- Runaway children, many of whom have been abused.
- Alcoholics and those in trouble with drugs (whose troubles often begin with one of the other conditions listed here).
- Immigrants, both legal and illegal, who often are not counted among the homeless because they constitute a "problem" in their own right.
- Traditional tramps, hobos, and transients, who have taken to the road or the streets for a variety of reasons and who prefer to be there.

9   You can quickly learn two things about the homeless from this list. First, you can learn that many of the homeless, before they were homeless, were people more or less like ourselves: members of the working or middle class. And you can learn that the world of the homeless has its roots in various policies, events, and ways of life for which some of us are responsible and from which some of us actually prosper.

10   We decide, as a people, to go to war, we ask our children to kill and to die, and the result, years later, is grown men homeless on the street.

11   We change, with the best intentions, the laws pertaining to the mentally ill, and then, without intention, neglect to provide them with services; and the result, in our streets, drives some of us crazy with rage.

12   We cut taxes and prune budgets, we modernize industry and shift the balance of trade, and the result of all these actions and errors can be read, sleeping form by sleeping form, on our city streets.

13   The liberals cannot blame the conservatives. The conservatives cannot blame the liberals. Homelessness is the *sum total* of our dreams, policies, intentions, errors, omissions, cruelties, kindnesses, all of it recorded, in flesh, in the life of the streets.

14   You can also learn from this list one of the most important things there is to know about the homeless—that they can be roughly divided into two groups:

those who have had homelessness forced upon them and want nothing more than to escape it; and those who have at least in part *chosen* it for themselves, and now accept, or in some cases, embrace it.

I understand how dangerous it is to introduce the idea of choice into a dis- 15 cussion of homelessness. It can all too easily be used to justify indifference or brutality toward the homeless, or to argue that they are only getting what they "deserve." And yet it seems to me that it is only by taking choice into account, in all of the intricacies of its various forms and expressions, that one can really understand certain kinds of homelessness.

The fact is, many of the homeless are not only hapless victims but volun- 16 tary exiles, "domestic refugees," people who have turned not against life itself but against us, our life, American life. Look for a moment at the vets. The price of returning to America was to forget what they had seen or learned in Vietnam, to "put it behind them." But some could not do that, and the stress of trying showed up as alcoholism, broken marriages, drug addiction, crime. And it showed up too as life on the street, which was for some vets a desperate choice made in the name of life—the best they could manage. It was a way of avoiding what might have occurred had they stayed where they were: suicide, or violence done to others.

We must learn to accept that there may indeed be people, and not only vets, 17 who have seen so much of our world, or seen it so clearly, that to live in it becomes impossible. Here, for example, is the story of Alice, a homeless middle-aged woman in Los Angeles, where there are, perhaps, 50,000 homeless people. It was set down a few months ago by one of my students at the University of California, Santa Barbara, where I taught for a semester. I had encouraged them to go find the homeless and listen to their stories. And so, one day, when this student saw Alice foraging in a dumpster outside a McDonald's, he stopped and talked to her:

> She told me she had led a pretty normal life as she grew up and eventually went to college. From there she went on to Chicago to teach school. She was single and lived in a small apartment.
>
> One night, after she got off the train after school, a man began to follow her to her apartment building. When she got to her door she saw a knife and the man hovering behind her. She had no choice but to let him in. The man raped her.
>
> After that, things got steadily worse. She had a nervous breakdown. She went to a mental institution for three months, and when she went back to her apartment she found her belongings gone. The landlord had sold them to cover the rent she hadn't paid.
>
> She had no place to go and no job because the school had terminated her employment. She slipped into depression. She lived with friends until she could muster enough money for a ticket to Los Angeles. She said she no longer wanted to burden her friends, and that if she had to live outside, at least Los Angeles was warmer than Chicago.
>
> It is as if she began back then to take on the mentality of a street person. She resolved herself to homelessness. She's been out West since 1980, without a home or job. She seems happy, with her best friend being her cat. But the scars of memories still haunt her, and she is running from them, or should I say him.

18   This is, in essence, the same story one hears over and over again on the street. You begin with an ordinary life; then an event occurs—traumatic, catastrophic; smaller events follow, each one deepening the original wound; finally, homelessness becomes inevitable, or begins to seem inevitable to the person involved— the only way out of an intolerable situation. You are struck continually, hearing these stories, by something seemingly unique in American life, the absolute isolation involved. In what other culture would there be such an absence or failure of support from familial, social, or institutional sources? Even more disturbing is the fact that it is often our supposed sources of support—family, friends, government organizations—that have caused the problem in the first place.

19   Everything that happened to Alice—the rape, the loss of job and apartment, the breakdown—was part and parcel of a world gone radically wrong, a world, for Alice, no longer to be counted on, no longer worth living in. Her homelessness can be seen as flight, as failure of will or nerve, even, perhaps, as *disease*. But it can also be seen as a mute, furious refusal, a self-imposed exile far less appealing to the rest of us than ordinary life, but *better*, in Alice's terms.

20   We like to think, in America, that everything is redeemable, that everything broken can be magically made whole again, and that what has been "dirtied" can be cleansed. Recently I saw on television that one of the soaps had introduced the character of a homeless old woman. A woman in her thirties discovers that her long-lost mother has appeared in town, on the streets. After much searching the mother is located and identified and embraced; and then she is scrubbed and dressed in style, restored in a matter of days to her former upper-class habits and role.

21   A triumph—but one more likely to occur on television than in real life. Yes, many of those on the streets could be transformed, rehabilitated. But there are others whose lives have been irrevocably changed, damaged beyond repair, and who no longer want help, who no longer recognize the *need* for help, and whose experience in our world has made them want only to be left alone. How, for instance, would one restore Alice's life, or reshape it in a way that would satisfy *our* notion of what a life should be? What would it take to return her to the fold? How to erase the four years of homelessness, which have become as familiar to her, and as much a home, as her "normal" life once was? Whatever we think of the way in which she has resolved her difficulties, it constitutes a sad peace made with the world. Intruding ourselves upon it in the name of redemption is by no means as simple a task—or as justifiable a task—as one might think.

22   It is important to understand too that however disorderly and dirty and unmanageable the world of homeless men and women like Alice appears to us, it is not without its significance, and its rules and rituals. The homeless in our cities mark out for themselves particular neighborhoods, blocks, buildings, doorways. They impose on themselves often obsessively strict routines. They reduce their world to a small area, and thereby protect themselves from a world that might otherwise be too much to bear.

23   Pavlov, the Russian psychologist, once theorized that the two most fundamental reflexes in all animals, including humans, are those involving freedom and orientation. Grab any animal, he said, and it will immediately struggle to ac-

complish two things: to break free and to orient itself. And this is what one sees in so many of the homeless. Having been stripped of all other forms of connection, and of most kinds of social identity, they are left only with this: the raw stuff of nature, something encoded in the cells—the desire to be free, the need for familiar space. Perhaps this is why so many of them struggle so vehemently against us when we offer them aid. They are clinging to their freedom and their space, and they do not believe that this is what we, with our programs and our shelters, mean to allow them.

Years ago, when I first came to California, bumming my way west, the marginal 24 world, and the lives of those in it, were very different from what they are now. In those days I spent much of my time in hobo jungles or on the skid rows of various cities, and just as it was easier back then to "get by" in the easygoing beach towns on the California coast, or in the bohemian and artistic worlds in San Francisco or Los Angeles or New York, it was also far easier than it is now to survive in the marginal world.

It is important to remember this—important to recognize the immensity of 25 the changes that have occurred in the marginal world in the past twenty years. Whole sections of many cities—the Bowery in New York, the Tenderloin in San Francisco—were once ceded to the transient. In every skid-row area in America you could find what you needed to survive: hash houses, saloons offering free lunches, pawnshops, surplus-clothing stores, and, most important of all, cheap hotels and flop-houses and two-bit employment agencies specializing in the kinds of labor (seasonal, shape-up) transients have always done.

It was by no means a wonderful world. But it *was* a world. Its rituals were 26 spelled out in ways most of the participants understood. In hobo jungles up and down the tracks, whatever there was to eat went into a common pot and was divided equally. Late at night, in empties crisscrossing the country, men would speak with a certain anonymous openness, as if the shared condition of transience created among them a kind of civility.

What most people in that world wanted was simply to be left alone. Some 27 of them had been on the road for years, itinerant workers. Others were recuperating from wounds they could never quite explain. There were young men and a few women with nothing better to do, and older men who had no families or had lost their jobs or wives, or for whom the rigor and pressure of life had proved too demanding. The marginal world offered them a respite from the other world, a world grown too much for them.

But things have changed. There began to pour into the marginal world— 28 slowly in the sixties, a bit faster in the seventies, and then faster still in the eighties—more and more people who neither belonged nor knew how to survive there. The sixties brought the counterculture and drugs; the streets filled with young dropouts. Changes in the law loosed upon the streets mentally ill men and women. Inflation took its toll, then recession. Working-class and even middle-class men and women—entire families—began to fall into a world they did not understand.

At the same time the transient world was being inundated by new inhabi- 29 tants, its landscape, its economy, was shrinking radically. Jobs became harder to find. Modernization had something to do with it; machines took the place of men and women. And the influx of workers from Mexico and points farther south created a class of semipermanent workers who took the place of casual transient labor. More important, perhaps, was the fact that the forgotten parts of many cities began to attract attention. Downtown areas were redeveloped, reclaimed. The skid-row sections of smaller cities were turned into "old townes." The old hotels that once catered to transients were upgraded or torn down or became warehouses for welfare families—an arrangement far more profitable to the owners. The price of housing increased; evictions increased. The mentally ill, who once could afford to house themselves in cheap rooms, the alcoholics, who once would drink themselves to sleep at night in their cheap hotels, were out on the street—exposed to the weather and to danger, and also in plain and public view: "problems" to be dealt with.

30   Nor was it only cheap shelter that disappeared. It was also those "open" spaces that had once been available to those without other shelter. As property rose in value, the nooks and crannies in which the homeless had been able to hide became more visible. Doorways, alleys, abandoned buildings, vacant lots—these "holes" in the cityscape, these gaps in public consciousness, became *real estate*. The homeless, who had been there all the time, were overtaken by economic progress, and they became intruders.

31   You cannot help thinking, as you watch this process, of what happened in parts of Europe in the eighteenth and nineteenth centuries: the effects of the enclosure laws, which eliminated the "commons" in the countryside and drove the rural poor, now homeless, into the cities. The centuries-old tradition of common access and usage was swept away by the beginnings of industrialism; land became *privatized*, a commodity. At the same time something occurred in the cultural psyche. The world itself, space itself, was subtly altered. It was no longer merely to be lived in; it was now to be owned. What was enclosed was not only the land. It was also *the flesh itself*; it was cut off from, denied access to, the physical world.

32   And one thinks too, when thinking of the homeless, of the American past, the settlement of the "new" world which occurred at precisely the same time that the commons disappeared. The dream of freedom and equality that brought men and women here had something to do with *space*, as if the wilderness itself conferred upon those arriving here a new beginning: the Eden that had been lost. Once God had sent Christ to redeem men; now he provided a new world. Men discovered, or believed, that this world, and perhaps time itself, had no edge, no limit. Space was a sign of God's magnanimity. It was a kind of grace.

33   Somehow, it is all this that is folded into the sad shapes of the homeless. In their mute presence one can sense, however faintly, the dreams of a world gone a-glimmering, and the presence of our failed hopes. A kind of claim is made, silently, an ethic is proffered, or, if you will, a whole cosmology, one older than our own ideas of privilege and property. It is as if flesh itself were seeking, this one last time, the home in the world it has been denied.

34 Daily the city eddies around the homeless. The crowds flowing past leave a few feet, a gap. We do not touch the homeless world. Perhaps we cannot touch it. It remains separate even as the city surrounds it.

The homeless, simply because they are homeless, are strangers, alien—and 35
therefore a threat. Their presence, in itself, comes to constitute a kind of violence;
it deprives us of our sense of safety. Let me use myself as an example. I know,
and respect, many of those now homeless on the streets of Santa Barbara. Twenty
years ago, some of them would have been my companions and friends. And yet,
these days, if I walk through the park near my home and see strangers bedding
down for the night, my first reaction, if not fear, is a sense of annoyance and intrusion, of worry and alarm. I think of my teenage daughter, who often walks
through the park, and then of my house, a hundred yards away, and I am
tempted—only tempted, but tempted, still—to call the "proper" authorities to
have the strangers moved on. Out of sight, out of mind.

Notice: I do not bring them food. I do not offer them shelter or a shower in 36
the morning. I do not even stop to talk. Instead, I think: my daughter, my house,
my privacy. What moves me is not the threat of *danger*—nothing as animal as
that. Instead there pops up inside of me, neatly in a row, a set of anxieties, ones
you might arrange in a dollhouse living room and label: Family of bourgeois
fears. The point is this: our response to the homeless is fed by a complex set of
cultural attitudes, habits of thought, and fantasies and fears so familiar to us, so
common, that they have become a *second* nature and might as well be instinctive,
for all the control we have over them. And it is by no means easy to untangle this
snarl of responses. What does seem clear is that the homeless embody all that
bourgeois culture has for centuries tried to eradicate and destroy.

If you look to the history of Europe you find that homelessness first appears 37
(or is first acknowledged) at the very same moment that bourgeois culture begins to appear. The same processes produced them both: the breakup of feudal-
ism, the rise of commerce and cities, the combined triumphs of capitalism,
industrialism, and individualism. The historian Fernand Braudel, in *The Wheels
of Commerce*, describes, for instance, the armies of impoverished men and women
who began to haunt Europe as far back as the eleventh century. And the makeup
of these masses? Essentially the same then as it is now: the unfortunates, the
throwaways, the misfits, the deviants.

> In the eighteenth century, all sorts and conditions were to be found in this human
> dross . . . widows, orphans, cripples . . . journeymen who had broken their contracts,
> out-of-work labourers, homeless priests with no living, old men, fire victims . . . war
> victims, deserters, discharged soldiers, would-be vendors of useless articles, va-
> grant preachers with or without licenses, "pregnant servant-girls and unmarried
> mothers driven from home," children sent out "to find bread or to maraud."

Then, as now, distinctions were made between the "homeless" and the sup- 38
posedly "deserving" poor, those who knew their place and willingly sustained,
with their labors, the emergent bourgeois world.

> The good paupers were accepted, lined up and registered on the official list;
> they had a right to public charity and were sometimes allowed to solicit it out-
> side churches in prosperous districts, when the congregation came out, or in
> market places. . . .

When it comes to beggars and vagrants, it is a very different story, and different pictures meet the eye: crowds, mobs, processions, sometimes mass emigrations, "along the country highways or the streets of the Towns and Villages," by beggars "whom hunger and nakedness has driven from home." . . . The towns dreaded these alarming visitors and drove them out as soon as they appeared on the horizon.

39   And just as the distinctions made about these masses were the same then as they are now, so too was the way society saw them. They seemed to bourgeois eyes (as they still do) the one segment of society that remained resistant to progress, unassimilable and incorrigible, inimical to all order.

40   It is in the nineteenth century, in the Victorian era, that you can find the beginnings of our modern strategies for dealing with the homeless: the notion that they should be controlled and perhaps eliminated through "help." With the Victorians we begin to see the entangling of self-protection with social obligation, the strategy of masking self-interest and the urge to control as *moral duty*. Michel Foucault has spelled this out in his books on madness and punishment: the zeal with which the overseers of early bourgeois culture tried to purge, improve, and purify all of urban civilization—whether through schools and prisons, or, quite literally, with public baths and massive new water and sewage systems. Order, ordure—this is, in essence, the tension at the heart of bourgeois culture, and it was the singular genius of the Victorians to make it the main component of their medical, aesthetic, *and* moral systems. It was not a sense of justice or even empathy which called for charity or new attitudes toward the poor; it was *hygiene*. The very same attitudes appear in nineteenth-century America. Charles Loring Brace, in an essay on homeless and vagrant children written in 1876, described the treatment of delinquents in this way: "Many of their vices drop from them like the old and verminous clothing they left behind. . . . The entire change of circumstances seems to cleanse them of bad habits." Here you have it all: *vices, verminous clothing, cleansing them of bad habits*—the triple association of poverty with vice with dirt, an equation in which each term comes to stand for all of them.

41   These attitudes are with us still; that is the point. In our own century the person who has written most revealingly about such things is George Orwell, who tried to analyze his own middle-class attitudes toward the poor. In 1933, in *Down and Out in Paris and London*, he wrote about tramps:

In childhood we are taught that tramps are blackguards . . . a repulsive, rather dangerous creature, who would rather die than work or wash, and wants nothing but to beg, drink or rob hen-houses. The tramp monster is no truer to life than the sinister Chinaman of the magazines, but he is very hard to get rid of. The very word "tramp" evokes his image.

42   All of this is still true in America, though now it is not the word "tramp" but the word "homeless" that evokes the images we fear. It is the homeless who smell. Here, for instance, is part of a paper a student of mine wrote about her first visit to a Rescue Mission on skid row.

The sermon began. The room was stuffy and smelly. The mixture of body odors and cooking was nauseating. I remember thinking: how can these people share this facility? They must be repulsed by each other. They had strange habits and dispositions. They were a group of dirty, dishonored, weird people to me.

When it was over I ran to my car, went home, and took a shower. I felt extremely dirty. Through the day I would get flashes of that disgusting smell.

To put it as bluntly as I can, for many of us the homeless are *shit*. And our 43 policies toward them, our spontaneous sense of disgust and horror, our wish to be rid of them—all of this has hidden in it, close to its heart, our feelings about excrement. Even Marx, that most bourgeois of revolutionaries, described the deviant *lumpen* in *The Eighteenth Brumaire of Louis Bonaparte* as "scum, offal, refuse of all classes." These days, in puritanical Marxist nations, they are called "parasites"—a word, perhaps not incidentally, one also associates with human waste.

What I am getting at here is the *nature* of the desire to help the homeless— what 44 is hidden behind it and why it so often does harm. Every government program, almost every private project, is geared as much to the needs of those giving help as it is to the needs of the homeless. Go to any government agency, or, for that matter, to most private charities, and you will find yourself enmeshed, at once, in a bureaucracy so tangled and oppressive, or confronted with so much moral arrogance and contempt, that you will be driven back out into the streets for relief.

Santa Barbara, where I live, is as good an example as any. There are three 45 main shelters in the city—all of them private. Between them they provide fewer than a hundred beds a night for the homeless. Two of the three shelters are religious in nature: the Rescue Mission and the Salvation Army. In the mission, as in most places in the country, there are elaborate and stringent rules. Beds go first to those who have not been there for two months, and you can stay for only two nights in any two-month period. No shelter is given to those who are not sober. Even if you go to the mission only for a meal, you are required to listen to sermons and participate in prayer, and you are regularly proselytized—sometimes overtly, sometimes subtly. There are obligatory, regimented showers. You go to bed precisely at ten: lights out, no reading, no talking. After the lights go out you will find fifteen men in a room with double-decker bunks. As the night progresses the room grows stuffier and hotter. Men toss, turn, cough, and moan. In the morning you are awakened precisely at five forty-five. Then breakfast. At seven-thirty you are back on the street.

The town's newest shelter was opened almost a year ago by a consortium 46 of local churches. Families and those who are employed have first call on the beds—a policy which excludes the congenitally homeless. Alcohol is not simply forbidden *in* the shelter; those with a history of alcoholism must sign a "contract" pledging to remain sober and chemical-free. Finally, in a paroxysm of therapeutic bullying, the shelter has added a new wrinkle: if you stay more than two days you are required to fill out and then discuss with a social worker a complex form listing what you perceive as your personal failings, goals, and strategies—all of this for men and women who simply want a place to lie down out of the rain!

47   It is these attitudes, in various forms and permutations, that you find repeated endlessly in America. We are moved either to "redeem" the homeless or
to punish them. Perhaps there is nothing consciously hostile about it. Perhaps it
is simply that as the machinery of bureaucracy cranks itself up to deal with
these problems, attitudes assert themselves automatically. But whatever the case,
the fact remains that almost every one of our strategies for helping the homeless
is simply an attempt to rearrange the world *cosmetically*, in terms of how it looks
and smells to *us*. Compassion is little more than the passion for control.

48   The central question emerging from all this is, What does a society owe to its
members in trouble, and *how* is that debt to be paid? It is a question which must
be answered in two parts: first, in relation to the men and women who have been
marginalized against their will, and then, in a slightly different way, in relation
to those who have chosen (or accept or even prize) their marginality.

49   As for those who have been marginalized against their wills, I think the general answer is obvious: A society owes its members whatever it takes for them
to regain their places in the social order. And when it comes to specific remedies,
one need only read backward the various processes which have created homelessness and then figure out where help is likely to do the most good. But the real
point here is not the specific remedies required—affordable housing, say—but
the basis upon which they must be offered, the necessary underlying ethical notion we seem in this nation unable to grasp: that those who are the inevitable casualties of modern industrial capitalism and the free-market system are entitled,
by right, and by the simple virtue of their participation in that system, to whatever help they need. They are entitled to help to find and hold their places in the
society whose social contract they have, in effect, signed and observed.

50   Look at that for just a moment: the notion of a contract. The majority of
homeless Americans have kept, insofar as they could, to the terms of that contract. In any shelter these days you can find men and women who have worked
ten, twenty, forty years, and whose lives have nonetheless come to nothing.
These are people who cannot afford a place in the world they helped create. And
in return? Is it life on the street they have earned? Or the cruel charity we so
grudgingly grant them?

51   But those marginalized against their will are only half the problem. There remains, still, the question of whether we owe anything to those who are voluntarily
marginal. What about them: the street people, the rebels, and the recalcitrants,
those who have torn up their social contracts or returned them unsigned?

52   I was in Las Vegas last fall, and I went out to the Rescue Mission at the lower
end of town, on the edge of the black ghetto, where I first stayed years ago on
my way west. It was twilight, still hot; in the vacant lot next-door to the mission
200 men were lining up for supper. A warm wind blew along the street lined with
small houses and salvage yards, and in the distance I could see the desert's edge
and the smudge of low hills in the fading light. There were elderly alcoholics in
line, and derelicts, but mainly the men were the same sort I had seen here years
ago: youngish, out of work, restless and talkative, the drifters and wanderers for
whom the word "wanderlust" was invented.

At supper—long communal tables, thin gruel, stale sweet rolls, ice water— 53
a huge black man in his twenties, fierce and muscular, sat across from me. "I'm
from the Coast, man," he said. "Never been away from home before. Ain't sure
I like it. Sure don't like *this* place. But I lost my job back home a couple of weeks
ago and figured, why wait around for another. I thought I'd come out here, see
me something of the world."

After supper, a squat Portuguese man in his mid-thirties, hunkered down 54
against the mission wall, offered me a smoke and told me: "Been sleeping in my
car, up the street, for a week. Had my own business back in Omaha. But I got
bored, man. Sold everything, got a little dough, came out here. Thought I'd
work construction. Let me tell you, this is one tough town."

In a world better than ours, I suppose, men (or women) like this might not 55
exist. Conservatives seem to have no trouble imagining a society so well disci-
plined and moral that deviance of this kind would disappear. And leftists envision a world so just, so generous, that deviance would vanish along with
inequity. But I suspect that there will always be something at work in some men
and women to make them restless with the systems others devise for them, and
to move them outward toward the edges of the world, where life is always
riskier, less organized, and easier going.

Do we owe anything to these men and women, who reject our company and 56
what we offer and yet nonetheless seem to demand *something* from us?

We owe them, I think, at least a place to exist, a way to exist. That may not 57
be a *moral* obligation, in the sense that our obligation to the involuntarily marginal is clearly a moral one, but it is an obligation nevertheless, one you might
call an existential obligation.

Of course, it may be that I think we owe these men something because I have 58
liked men like them, and because I want their world to be there always, as a place
to hide or rest. But there is more to it than that. I think we as a society need men
like these. A society needs its margins as much as it needs art and literature. It
needs holes and gaps, *breathing spaces*, let us say, into which men and women can
escape and live, when necessary, in ways otherwise denied them. Margins guarantee to society a flexibility, an elasticity, and allow it to accommodate itself to
the natures and needs of its members. When margins vanish, society becomes
too rigid, too oppressive by far, and therefore inimical to life.

It is for such reasons that, in cultures like our own, marginal men and women 59
take on a special significance. They are all we have left to remind us of the nar-
rowness of the received truths we take for granted. "Beyond the pale," they somehow redefine the pale, or remind us, at least, that *something* is still out there, beyond
the pale. They preserve, perhaps unconsciously, a dream that would otherwise
cease to exist, the dream of having a place in the world, and of being *left alone.*

Quixotic? Infantile? Perhaps. But remember Pavlov and his reflexes coded 60
in the flesh: animal, and therefore as if given by God. What we are talking about
here is *freedom*, and with it, perhaps, an echo of the dream men brought, long ago,
to wilderness America. I use the word "freedom" gingerly, in relation to lives like
these: skewed, crippled, emptied of everything we associate with a full, or realized, freedom. But perhaps this is the condition into which freedom has fallen

among us. Art has been "appreciated" out of existence; literature has become an extension of the university, replete with tenure and pensions; and as for politics, the ideologies which ring us round seem too silly or shrill by far to speak for life. What is left, then, is this mute and intransigent independence, this "waste" of life which refuses even interpretation, and which cannot be assimilated to any ideology, and which therefore can be put to no one's use. In its crippled innocence and the perfection of its superfluity it amounts, almost, to a rebellion against history, and that is no small thing.

61   Let me put it as simply as I can: what we see on the streets of our cities are two dramas, both of which cut to the troubled heart of the culture and demand from us a response we may not be able to make. There is the drama of those struggling to survive by regaining their place in the social order. And there is the drama of those struggling to survive outside of it.

62   The resolution of both struggles depends on a third drama occurring at the heart of the culture: the tension and contention between the magnanimity we owe to life and the darker tending of the human psyche: our fear of strangeness, our hatred of deviance, our love of order and control. How we mediate by default or design between those contrary forces will determine not only the destinies of the homeless but also something crucial about the nation, and perhaps—let me say it—about our own souls.

• *Thinking Critically About "Helping and Hating the Homeless"*

RESPONDING AS A READER

1. How would you describe Marin's effort to engage readers and mold their response to what he has to say? To frame your answer, consider these aspects of his organization and style: (a) the sequence in which he leads us through different aspects of his subject matter, and (b) the way that he uses the pronouns "we" and "you."

2. In addition to his statement of intention in paragraph 6, where else do you see Marin stepping away from the flow of the essay to comment about how he intends to influence readers' thinking?

   a. What textual evidence can you find about how he expects readers to respond to those specific passages as well as to his overall presentation? Look for both explicit and implicit signals.

   b. What do you see Marin doing to foster a positive response? What does he do to smooth away a resisting or negative response? Work to pinpoint the exact language and try to remember your own response to it during your first reading of the essay.

3. Given your previous thoughts about homelessness and your expectations about the essay (as written in your reading log), to what extent would you say that you have engaged with the essay as Marin hoped readers would? When you analyze specific passages where you assented to or resisted his presentation, how do you account for the similarities

and differences between your response and what you think Marin would consider to be an ideal reader's response?

RESPONDING AS A WRITER

1. Marin takes up the subject of homelessness from a number of vantage points, drawing upon a wide variety of materials in the process. To examine how these different perspectives function in relation to his purposes, separate the essay into its major chunks and identify the formal strategy he uses to develop his points in each (e.g., cause and effect, definition, example, etc.). How does each chunk relate back to his statement of purpose in paragraph 6? Write out your understanding of these connections by completing one or more sentences similar to this one: "To accomplish his purpose of _____, Marin ___*[does X]*___." Be sure to describe what Marin does, not what he says. Choose verbs that indicate specifically what he is doing with the material, such as "defines _____" or "lists ____." You may want to write a series of sentences or one sentence that you complete with a bulleted list of Marin's techniques.

2. What overarching values and assumptions inform Marin's discussion of homelessness? To examine these in detail, follow the two-column process for analyzing ideology described in Chapter 5, page 77. In the left-hand column, list key terms Marin uses to signal what he values. In the right-hand column, enter the term(s) he explicitly uses to articulate values he opposes. If the opposite term is only implied, mark it with square brackets. If certain terms contain contrasting values, make two entries, labeling each to indicate the difference. Consider, for example, Marin's contrast in paragraph 36 of "danger" and "family of bourgeois fears." As you look at the lists you have developed, what do you discover about the pattern of values asserted in the essay? Summarize your analysis by writing a paragraph that explains the roles that several specific terms play within the whole.

3. It's been well over a decade since this article was published. How does Marin's description of homeless people's situations compare to current conditions in the municipality where your college or university is located? To extend the conversation and bring it up to date, use Marin's essay as a basis for generating questions that you and your classmates can explore to discover what services are available in your community to people who fall on hard economic times and what laws are in effect regarding panhandling, loitering, and sleeping out of doors.

Thomas Roepsch (Student)

America's Love Affair with Pizza: A Guilty Pleasure No More

When Thomas Roepsch (b. 1971) wrote this essay for an expository writing class at Marquette University, he was attending school part-time while working as owner/manager of an Italian restaurant. After selling his interest in the restaurant, he completed a B.S. in accounting and enrolled in law school. The assignment called for a paper that used outside research to counter a commonly held view of something that interested him. It specified that he make this a "good news" paper—that is, that he attempt to change readers' views about his topic from negative or skeptical to positive or at least accepting.

• **For Your Reading Log**

1. Given Roepsch's writing assignment, what does his title lead you to predict about what his paper will say?
2. This text is similar to papers you might respond to in a peer writing group. Try to engage with it the way you would when you work with your peers, whether your customary practice is to listen to papers read aloud or to examine drafts. Read it once fairly quickly and jot down some first impressions. Then read it a second time very carefully, noting specifically the places that you think work well, places that could be improved, and places where you have questions. Jot a few notes about these in your reading log, too, so that you can remember your original impressions for class discussion.

————————   •   ————————

1   The average American eats 46 slices, or 23 pounds, of pizza each year (Marston 28). Despite this popularity, pizza is commonly considered one of the poorest choices you can make when it comes to your health. Every pizza lover knows the guilt associated with devouring a greasy pizza straight out of the box, and health experts have been warning us for years that we would be much better off if we made every effort to avoid foods high in fat and cholesterol like pizza. New information, however, is changing the way nutritionists view pizza. According to a number of popular health magazines, experts have reexamined the pizza and are now finding it to be potentially an excellent way to get a fast, well-balanced meal from a single food item. And even more surprising, pizza is now being credited with the ability to save your life.

The most popular pizzas in America are topped with pork sausage, pep- 2
peroni, and layers of extra cheese, making them very high in cholesterol and fat.
According to an article in *Current Health*, the National Association of Pizza Op-
erators reported that we ate 371 million pounds of pepperoni and 2.2 billion
pounds of mozzarella on our pizzas last year (Denny 16). Meat and cheese are
the clear favorites when it comes to pizza. The beauty of pizza, however, is that
it can be topped with almost anything. Choosing the right toppings is the secret
to making pizza "health" food. Limiting the amount of cheese and meat is the
key. Top pizzas with more vegetables and go easy on the pepperoni and cheese,
and you will have provided yourself with a well-balanced meal.

Pizza makes a square meal because, unlike any other single food item, pizza 3
can satisfy all five of the United States Department of Agriculture's food groups
(Post 76). The crust is a very good source of complex carbohydrates, and a single slice of cheese pizza can provide a body with one fourth of its daily requirement of calcium (Denny 17). The wide variety of meat, poultry, and seafood
toppings available today all provide a good source of protein. Also, if you add
on the vegetables, you gain vitamins and minerals. Finally, and perhaps most importantly, don't forget to add extra sauce when ordering a healthy pizza.

The tomato sauce used in pizza is now being credited with helping to save 4
lives. Tomatoes contain lycopene (Seppa). This protein, in addition to giving the
tomato its color, is an antioxidant that is unlocked when tomatoes are cooked into
red sauces. The mutating elements of the cells in our body's tissues depend on
oxygen, and antioxidants like beta-carotene and lycopene limit the ability of
cells to mutate. Tomato sauces like those in pizza and pasta contain high levels
of lycopene and are credited with helping to prevent cells from mutating. In turn,
certain types of cancers are prevented. In a clinical study, researchers at Harvard
Medical School found significantly lower rates of prostate cancer among men
who ate pizza or other foods with tomato sauce at least twice a week (Seppa).
The study said that men who never ate tomato sauce were 21 to 34 percent more
at risk to develop prostate cancers.

Women are also able to benefit from the lycopene found in pizza sauce. 5
Wendy Marston, writing for *Health* magazine, reports that another study was
able to show a reduced risk of breast cancer in women who were eating foods
with tomato sauce on a regular basis (28). Researchers measured the levels of lycopene in the breast tissue of women and found that those who had high concentrations of the compound were less likely to have breast cancer. Another
recent *Health* article reports that a research team in Italy found that men and
women who ate at least seven servings of tomatoes a week were less likely to
have cancers of the stomach, colon, and rectum than individuals who only consumed two servings a week ("How to Slice")

It appears that the benefits of lycopene do not stop at combating cancer. The 6
compound has also been found to help prevent heart disease. A European study
of 1,300 men found that men with high concentrations of lycopene in the fat tissue of their bodies were half as likely to have a heart attack as men with low levels of lycopene (Marston 29).

7   Nutritionists warn, however, that this ability of lycopene is meaningless if you still want to top your pizza with a lot of high fat toppings. One study by Harvard University suggested, however, that the presence of fat is necessary for the absorption of lycopene by the body. Foods that contain the types of fats found in olive oil and mozzarella actually improve the body's ability to absorb lycopene. They found that the levels of lycopene are two and a half times higher in people who eat pizza rather than salad (Marston 29).

8   Pizza today is made with a limitless variety of toppings and ingredients. Spinach, artichokes, turkey, seafood, as well as other healthful and exotic choices are growing in popularity as pizza places try to satisfy changing tastes. You can order your pizzas any way you like, but it is important to remember that there are good pizzas and bad pizzas when it comes to your health. More vegetables and sauce but less meat and cheese are the key to a healthy pizza. In our fast-paced society, pizza is an ideal food—a quick, readily available food that you can eat with your fingers. But unlike other foods of this type, pizza can also be a square meal and a healthy choice.

Works Cited

Denny, Sharon. "Heap Health on Pizza." *Current Health* 2 Feb. 1999: 16–18. *Proquest Research Library*. Bell and Howell. Memorial Lib., Marquette Univ. 23 Feb. 2000 <http://proquest.umi.com>.

"How to Slice Your Cancer Risk." *Health* May 1999: 20.

Marston, Wendy. "Why Pizza's Better Than Ever." *Health* Jan.–Feb. 1998: 28–29.

Post, Robyn. "Pizza Can Save Your Life." *Men's Health* May 1997: 76+. *Proquest Research Library*. Bell and Howell. Memorial Lib., Marquette Univ. 23 Feb. 2000 <http://proquest.umi.com>.

Seppa, Nathan. "Tomato Compound Fights Cancer." *Science News* 24 Apr. 1999: 271.

• *Thinking Critically About "America's Love Affair with Pizza"*

RESPONDING AS A READER

1. In the opening paragraph, as Roepsch lays out his subject and the points he will make about it, what role does he assume in relation to his readers and in relation to his subject matter? What role does his approach give you, the reader, to play in relation to the text?
2. What does the text reveal about Roepsch's assumptions concerning his readers' knowledge and values? Is his presentation of the information appropriate for your knowledge level? How, specifically, does he work to accommodate possible differences in readers' information background?
3. What is the source of Roepsch's authority here? Is his use of his sources sufficiently convincing? What else might he have done? If his news were less welcome, or harder to believe—if he were writing, for example, to inform us that chocolate is a health hazard—what would he

have to do to make himself believable? (Don't worry, chocolate isn't dangerous as far as we know. Some studies even suggest that it is valuable as an antioxidant.)

RESPONDING AS A WRITER

1. What aspects of this paper do you find particularly effective? How might you apply his approach to your own writing?
2. What questions does the paper raise for you? Are they sufficiently answered? If not, what do you think Roepsch could have done to answer or forestall such questions?
3. The second reading log question asked you to jot down notes about this paper as if you were reading it for a peer review group. As you look over your notes, what points might you raise about his style in the paper? How effective are his word choices? Where might he consider some changes? How about the structure of the sentences themselves? Does the reader move smoothly from one to another? Are there spots where the structure gets tedious or difficult to follow? Again, what advice would you give Roepsch for possible revision? (This is a pretty good paper, but you can undoubtedly find ways that it could be better still. As you consider your response, realize that few writers asking for feedback find it helpful to hear, "Everything's fine.")

C. J. Hribal

Consent (Fiction)

A Wisconsin native, C. J. Hribal (b. 1956) won the Associated Writing Programs 1999 short fiction award for *The Clouds in Memphis* (2000), in which this story appears. He is a professor at Marquette University in Milwaukee, Wisconsin, and frequently teaches in the graduate writing program at Warren Wilson College in Asheville, North Carolina. Hribal's other books include the collection *Matty's Heart* (1984) and the novel *American Beauty* (1987). "Consent" was first published in 1995 by the literary quarterly *Witness* in a special issue on rural America.

• *For Your Reading Log*

1. This story presents differing explanations of a painful event. As a way of keeping track of your engagement with the story the narrator presents, stop at several points during your reading to predict what will happen next. We suggest stopping after paragraphs 3, 12, 21, and 40. At each of these points, freewrite for three or four minutes about how the story is unfolding. Be sure to note details in the text that lead you to your predictions.

2. Immediately after you finish reading the story, write down your responses to it. Freewrite about your emotional responses and any questions you have about the events and people portrayed. To give yourself a good basis for discussion and further writing, spend at least five minutes writing and reflecting while the story is fresh in your mind.

———————   •   ———————

1 Porter Atwood's Chevy Blazer screeches to a halt behind Clayton Jones's police cruiser and a county ambulance. He hears somebody say the county sheriff is on his way. The cars are lined up one two three on Atwood Lane, one of six serpentine roads in Atwood Acres that bear his or his family's name. Porter wipes his face with his handkerchief and makes a mental note to have Leo Puhl at the dealership check his brakes. They might be due. Porter doesn't want to hear any screeches or squeaks when he brakes, just the shower of stones and the slurred crush of gravel. A cloud of gravel dust drifts off behind him, mingling with the white haze of a clean and hot blue day.

2   He mops his face again, then puts the handkerchief in his pocket. He's here in Atwood Acres because on this very day it has become a real and true subdivision, a place distinct from the fields it used to be. There are enough of these new people to make it so. They've achieved a kind of critical mass, outnumbering the farmers and the townies, and what they call things is what things will come to be called. And nobody's going to call it Matty Keillor's anymore, or you-know-

that-subdivision-Porter-cobbled-together-from-Matty's-eighty-and-the-Brudecki's-and-the-old-Schniederbaum-place. From now on it's going to be called by its proper, true and real name.

Atwood Acres has had its first drowning.   3

Porter mops his face again quickly. He's florid. All his weight seems to be go-   4
ing to the balls of his feet and his cheeks. He used to be tight-bodied. The woman he used to sleep with before he was married to his wife, Deniece, used to lick ice cream off his washboard stomach with her tongue. But now Porter is awash in excess flesh, and grease oozes out of him every time the mercury climbs above sixty. The machine of his body labors, tries to keep up with the demands made by the loose folds of flesh on his belly, the dewlaps on his throat, the soft ripplings of fat that dip down his rib cage as though he were melting. He has become the ice-cream cone itself. He thinks of that woman again, the woman who liked him before Deniece. He recalls the bright pink blob of her tongue making its way up and down his belly hair, but for the life of him he can't remember her name.

Straightening his string tie as he heads toward the knot of people gathered   5
behind the Surhoff place (dentist from Neenah, upset that the two-and-a-half acre lots on Atwood Cove were already taken), Porter hopes it happened in a pool. Personally he finds pools an abomination. Deniece forced him to install one for their kids, but both the girls go skinny-dipping with their boyfriends in the quarry, same as everybody else. It's the one thing about Augsbury he wouldn't change: the quarry.

That pool went in what? three years ago? It's amazing how much he's let   6
himself go since then. He would almost be embarrassed about the weight gain except that it seems like an outward sign of his success. Girth equals greatness. Though not so great that he can throw his weight around in his own home. Deniece makes him swim in the pool, has at first curtailed and then forbidden Porter's quarry visits. She knows, she says, what goes on down there. Porter mops his face again and thinks, Pools. Medallions of stupidity.

He goes over to the knot of people around the Surhoff's above ground pool,   7
but it turns out these are the squeamish onlookers, moms with kids who've corralled their youngsters and won't let them get any closer. The more serious gathering of the morbidly curious is by the ravine. Clayton Jones is there, as are the paramedics with their gurney and lockboxes.

When this was fields that ravine was a bit of a problem. Cows grazed right to   8
the edge and the spring run-off carved deep crumbling erosion channels in its scoured, plum-colored banks. When he first bought this field he let it sit a few years before he had it lotted. He needed that ravine as a selling point. A creek, good drainage—that field needed time to restore itself. The erosion cuts needed time to heal themselves, the crumbling banks time to acquire some cattails, the scrub trees along the banks time to look less like Halloween scarecrows—that haunted, lonely look people like in landscape paintings but not in their own backyard. Never mind that their lawnmowers would eat things right down to the nubbins again and the erosion would start all over. What he needed was picturesque weeds.

He got them, and the lots sold nicely. Better than he hoped, really. Feeling   9
pleased, Porter has to remind himself to wipe the smile off his face when he

clamps a solicitous hand on Clayton Jones's shoulder and asks, "What's happened here, Clay?"

10   Jones indicates the gurney. "You got eyes. See for yourself."

11   Porter steals a quick glance. It's not a Surhoff kid. This boy is older. Eight, eleven? As he's gotten older he's lost his ability to distinguish kids by their ages. They all look so big. This kid, though, doesn't. He's thin and his ribs show. He's one of those kids whose limbs look like match sticks; their scapulas stick out like wings when they reach behind themselves to scratch their backs. It would have been years before the flesh on this kid's body caught up with those willowy limbs.

12   Nobody knows the boy who's drowned. He's a playmate of somebody else's kid, drawn here by the newness of the big houses and his friend telling him that after yesterday's thunderstorm the ravine is running thick and brown, a good day for sending radio controlled boats, plastic boats, construction paper boats, pieces of bark, anything that floats down the newly revived current. Bikes are clumped or dumped all along the bank. The grass at the top is matted and muddy, trampled under bare and sneakered feet. It was a regular field day. Whole regattas were launched and disappeared.

13   Porter peers down the bank. The water's running fast, but it's only a foot deep, maybe two or three at the channel's deepest. It's amazing how little water you need to drown in. He's heard of six-month-olds drowning in three inches of water in the bathtub when the parent looks away for just a moment. Ten-month-olds drowning in a toilet. He's even heard of infants drowning without getting wet. Placed on unbaffled water beds, the child sleeps in the warmth of the receiving plastic which eventually conforms to the shape of the baby's mouth. Surrounded by water, dreaming of the womb, the child returns there. It's too tiny to lift its head to save itself.

14   Usually these ravine and river drownings, though, happen in springtime. The creek's swollen with run off, sometimes four or five or eight feet deep, and the kids, not knowing this, dare each other, or sometimes a single kid, alone, will dare itself to cross the turgid water, will lose its footing, and be swept away. Sometimes the kids will string a rope across a ravine or creek and ford the creek that way. The current is surprisingly strong, however, and young hands weak. They find the body miles away sometimes, usually amid a collection of branches where some municipality has screened its culverts. The child looks like something you find in drain traps. Wet, matted, limp, greasy.

15   This kid, though, nobody knows what happened to this kid. But edging over the ravine, conscious of where his feet meet the ravine's crumbling muddy edge and conscious, too, of the child's drowned body a few feet behind him, Porter can guess. These kids were playing with their boats. It was a lazy summer day, kids were scattered up and down the ravine, and there was the constant huzzing of crickets and the voices of children. This kid, or maybe a kid he knew, or maybe a kid he wanted to know, owned one of these radio controlled boats. It got away from him. Maybe the transmitter was weak, maybe the surging of the current was able to overpower the boat's tiny motor, maybe it got tangled in a floating branch and wouldn't heed the call of its owner. Most of these kids

wouldn't care that much about losing a boat. They can afford to lose just about anything. Some screeching, a heaved sigh from their parents, a quick trip to Toys R Us, and everything is back to the way it was before, maybe even better if they were able to cajole their parents into something bigger. But this kid couldn't do that. This was it; it was his only boat and if he lost it there wouldn't be another. Or maybe, not having the money for a radio controlled anything, the kid thought that about the boat's owner as well—that if he lost it there would be the inconsolable grief over the loss plus the yelling of the parents. So whether to reclaim what was his, or to impress the boat's owner, maybe get a turn at operating it himself, the kid slogs out the ten or fifteen feet to where the boat is hung up in the branches. The branches themselves are hung up. Maybe they're caught against a rock, or maybe against some other branches growing close to the water's edge and the boat's mired someplace inside them. The boat has a white hull and blue gunwales. Its tiny motor is whirring and can be heard over the intermittent gurgle and rush of the creek. The kid has volunteered to get his friend's boat. At first, the water's only ankle deep. It gets knee deep when he gets to the branches. There's more branch than he thought. He can't simply reach into the tangle and retrieve his friend's boat. A spider walks a tightroped filament of web from one leaf to another, quavering as the leaf does in the light breeze. A mosquito buzzes in the boy's ear. He slaps at it, the buzzing resumes at the base of his neck, by his other ear. His jeans are rolled to his knees but the cuffs are soaking wet. Something drifts past his calf. Instinctively he reaches down to scratch, panicking a little. Recently he's seen for the first time *The African Queen.* His parents rented it. Leech! he thinks, his heart racing, but it's only a leaf. He brushes it aside, knocks the spider off its tightrope just out of spite. The spider spins away on the current, he loses sight of it. Maybe it found a new leaf or twig, maybe not. He forgets about it. The sun's hot on the back of his neck but his legs feel cool The creek bottom is muddy and rocky both and his shoes are filling with silt. His feet feel squishy. He stands there wriggling his toes inside his canvas sneakers until he's called back to his task by his impatient, lordly friend. The friend with the boat who will be the kid's friend only if he retrieves the boat.

But it's not that easy. The boat is trapped in a nest of branches, tucked between them in such a way he can't just reach in and grab it. He has to penetrate the nest. At the same time he has to be careful. If he just pushes himself inside there he could set the whole mess moving and the boat might swamp or get away. So he eases himself between the branches. It's an oak tree these branches came from. They still have last year's leaves on them. They're russet and the twigs break easily. Must have been a lightning kill. He can almost feel the residual electricity. His feet, his fingers are tingling. Perhaps it's because he knows now what he must do. The oak branches, always gnarly, have formed a kind of dome, and to retrieve his friend's boat he must submerge himself and then resurface inside the dome. There are too many branches to simply throw it aside. How did that thing get in there, anyway? 16

Perhaps at this point the boy turned to shout something at his better-heeled companion. Perhaps he told him what he was planning on doing—the quick duck, the resurfacing inside the dome of brown leaves. He would be a hero to all of them. 17

18   There were other boys in the creek or on the banks, surely, Porter thinks. There was a scattering of bikes there when he came down, and he saw one or two boys with wet jeans and muddy feet and plastered hair. Towels over their heads like monk cowls. Porter recalls seeing these things. He remembers them shivering in the heat.

19   What next? he wonders. Did he go under, get a belt loop caught on a branch, did he struggle, lose his footing, panic? If he thrashed, would the boy who owned the boat, or any of the other boys notice? And noticing, would they do anything or simply stand there, horrified and fascinated? Maybe where those branches form a dome there's a sinkhole, and stepping into it he lost contact with the surface and face up, sliding, he wound up underneath the dome of branches and was held in place by them. It would be as though he were being pulled by his feet. Pinned, held in place by branches and current, his thrashings lost under the many branches that held him. Even if he screamed it would only hasten his drowning.

20   Another thought occurs to Porter, and it has to do with Porter's knowledge of the male species in adolescence. Those boys gathered at the top of the ravine or standing on rocks where the current meets the bank—what's to prevent them from doing what they usually do when boys gather?

21   Pick on the most vulnerable. The new kid from one of those cracker-box ranch houses in the cheesier section of the subdivision. The white trash ghetto, you've heard your parents say.

22   There are plenty of rocks. Nice hefty granite ones, rocks as big as your fist. You're up high, you've got the numbers, he's down below, disoriented from ducking under those branches and trying to find his way through the fertilizer-laced water. You wait till he surfaces, spluttering, unsure of his footing, and then you start raining rocks down upon him. KaCHUSH! KaCHUSH! The geysers and spray are magnificent. Sometimes the rocks come down next to each other and you can hear the clack of their meeting just a second before the geyser. Hey! he yells. Quit it! Stop it! Stop it, hey, quit it! Ouch!

23   Somebody catches him on the shoulder. Everybody laughs. Then somebody has the bright idea of going with whole handfuls of rocks—clumps of mud and gravel and pebbles, whatever your fist closes around—and flinging them shotgun style at the now cowering, weeping kid. Then it's a mixture—gravel and clumps of mud from some kids, the bigger rocks from those higher up. The kid is spluttering, confused, crying, bent over, humiliated, ducking beneath the water and resurfacing to fresh fusillades. Sometimes he's bent over with his face in the water, his back taking the blows; other times he's upright, imploring them, begging them to stop, his arms raised to ward off blows and to surrender. Finally—this is the part that now seems inevitable—one catches him on the crown or by his temple just as he's surfacing. Got 'im! somebody yells. Got 'im a good one! Did you see that?

24   They throw stones for maybe ten or fifteen more seconds. They're waiting, poised, for him to resurface. He's staying under longer this time. Maybe he's hoping to wait them out, the silly dink. Another scattering of plips, plooshes, thlupps and clacks. One kid rolls down the biggest boulder he can move. It tumbles lazily down the embankment, then gathers speed just as it reaches the bottom, and

seemingly catapults itself several feet out into the creek a yard away from where that new boy is hiding in his nest of oaks. The KaCHUSH! this time is tremendous. That oughta make him pee his pants!

Then nothing for a long time. No movement. Two or three minutes elapse. 25 Some pebbles trickle down the embankment and plop into the water. In the general silence they sound ominous.

"Maybe he's hiding," somebody says. 26

"Yeah, maybe he cut one of them reed things. I saw a movie on Nickelodeon 27 where a guy did that. These guys were shooting arrows at him so he ducked into these reeds and breathed through them till the king's horsemen and these arrow guys went away. Arrow Flynn, my mom said it was. The reed guy, I mean."

"Maybe he got away," somebody else says. "Maybe he got out from under- 28 neath those branches and he swam away."

"Dummy! We'd see him if he swam away. He's still there. He's just hiding." 29 And the speaker of this remark throws another handful of gravel at the kid's bower. Some stones hit branches, others plop directly into the water.

Everyone becomes immediately aware of how hot the day seems. And how 30 irritating it is to be kept waiting. And how uncomfortable it is to fight off what is suddenly an inchoate but nagging sense of blame, responsibility, and guilt.

What happens next Porter's not sure about. Maybe one of the boys screams 31 out, "I see him! I see him!" and they gather around and they do see him, a ghost in the water. Or maybe they look at each other for a few moments of panicked silence and then they scatter, gathering here again only when they hear the sirens.

One of them had to have called. He checks this with Clayton. Yes, it was a 32 child's voice, very excited, saying that they could see somebody on the bottom of the creek in Atwood Acres. They didn't stay on the line long enough to identify themselves. They were shouting, nearly hysterical. Then they hung up. No way to trace who it might have been, and upon arriving, Clayton makes one half-hearted attempt to determine who it was—"It would be really helpful if one of you boys, whoever it was called, would step forward"—and gives up on that for now. Porter eyes the kids who stand in clutches near enough the body to be a part of what's going on. A few mothers are with them, their hands protectively on their kid's shoulders.

They find the boy up under the branches almost as if he'd been sleeping 33 there. The blue and white boat is still bobbing in the tangle. Now we have something. The boy whose boat it is—he's still clutching the remote as though he could get everything going again if he just keeps turning the dial, pulling the trigger—steps forward under Clayton's prodding. "Just tell me what you saw, son." And the boy says that he saw the kid go under the branches trying to retrieve his boat and they waited and then he didn't come out again. He speaks haltingly, but what he says, to Porter's ear, which is used to hearing lies, sounds rehearsed, insincerely apologetic. "We waited," the boy says. "We waited and waited and waited and we waited but Kenny—" Somebody nudges this kid.

"Danny," the nudger says, "the kid said his name was Danny." 34

"—Danny," the boat boy continues, "Danny didn't show up again." 35

"Who called me?" Clayton asks. "Who called the ambulance?" 36

37　　"I did," the boat boy says.

38　　"And why didn't you try getting your friend out right away?"

39　　"I was freaking, sir. I was really afraid. I was afraid the same thing was going to happen to me." He shivers involuntarily.

40　　"Please, officer," the boy's mother says. "I'm sure you can see they're scared out of their minds. Can't you leave well enough alone?"

41　　Up until now Porter hasn't been able to—hasn't really wanted to—take a close look at the drowned boy. Just that first cursory glance trying to determine if it was anybody he knew. He looks now. The boy has a spider webbing of hair over his forehead and his lips are blue. His cheeks and eyelids have that bloated quality, and there is the tiniest suggestion of baby fat around his hips, that puffing of very pale flesh over his pant loops. His arms are skinny but his belly's full. That could be from the water, though. Or maybe he was recently a chubby kid and was just now hitting puberty, the baby fat stretching itself over willowy bone.

42　　He looks like a child on ice, sleeping.

43　　Then he sees what confirms everything he's previously imagined: a bruise the size and color of a pomegranate on his shoulder. An abrasion on his cheek—that could be from the branches—and a bruised spot, quarter-sized, above his right temple. There's the slightest inkling of an indentation where the forehead and the hairline meet.

44　　The kid was wearing jeans and underwear, socks and sneakers.

45　　Such a pitifully easy target.

46　　For the briefest of moments Porter Atwood wants to see justice done. Check out that bruise, he wants to say to the paramedics, who are already packing up. The one on the shoulder, there, and the one by the temple. Clayton, check these kids for dirt under their fingernails, for gravel dust on their palms. Put the screws to them. Drill them for the truth. A boy died here. The least we can give him is honesty.

47　　The boy's mother doesn't even know he's dead yet.

48　　But Porter knows these boys. Knows them in the sense that they look familiar. He sold their parents these houses or the lots they were built on. These kids were the bored ones kicking at the wall boards in the models, leaving scuff marks. These were the boys he had to keep his eyes on. Not that there was anything to steal, but if there was, he knew they'd steal it. He has a sense about these things. He knows what happened, he knows what's been done. It would have happened like this, the way he imagined. He has learned to trust his gut feelings on these things, the same as he does when he's calculating to himself how much a farmer's willing to give up to get off the land that feeds him, and how much a buyer's willing to spend for that same piece of earth. His success depends on appearing absolutely disinterested to both.

49　　So Porter satisfies himself by nodding and saying in his mind only, Yes, it would have happened like this. And out loud he says, to the boys and their mothers, to Clayton and the paramedics and all the interested bystanders, to all these people who've bought from him and who want their tranquility restored, who want this unreasonable chaos put into a box, out loud he says, "What a tragedy.

What a horrible, horrible tragedy. What a horrible accident. Really, we must take up a collection for the boy's family. I'll personally see that this is taken care of."

There, he's done it. He's done what he could. He walks back to his car con- 50
scious of his weight, his blubber, really, all that acquired flesh, and puts a new cigar between his teeth. On the way he runs into the mother, a wan woman of thirty, maybe thirty-five, it's hard to tell once these women start having children, especially a woman like this, short and slightly-boned. She comes toward him, but her focus is clearly on what's behind him. She's wringing her hands, clutch-ing her elbows, not willing to believe what she already knows. No, Porter Atwood thinks as she flutters past him, No. She will not get the truth from me. Kenny's or Danny's or whoever that kid's mother is will have to find out her own truth. He's not helping. Porter Atwood has already done what he could.

● *Thinking Critically About "Consent"*

RESPONDING AS A READER

1. As you and your classmates compare the freewrites in your reading logs, what patterns emerge among your predictions, responses, and questions? How accurately did people predict the way the plot would unfold? What details provided either reliable or misleading clues? What did you and the others find most compelling about the story? What was perplexing?

2. Once we become immersed in the world of a story, it's often difficult to recall exactly how we got there. To revisit your introduction to Porter At-wood and Atwood Acres, go back over the story's very first paragraph and try to reconstruct your moment-by-moment reading experience. Consider carefully the effect of the way the paragraph unfolds word by word, sentence by sentence. What is the sequence in which details pile up? What images and expectations does the sequence create? If this were all you knew about Porter Atwood, what would you think of him?

3. The story is told mostly through Porter Atwood's eyes, yet he is not the narrator. How does this separation between the story's main character and its third-person narrator affect your understanding of the unfold-ing events? How does the separation affect your understanding of At-wood himself?

RESPONDING AS A WRITER

1. A good way to develop ideas for a paper on a work of fiction is to locate places in the text where events, motivations, or ideas are unclear or am-biguous. Look for places where the text doesn't provide clear explana-tions about why people are the way they are or why events unfold as they do. Review the questions you jotted down immediately after you finished reading "Consent." Separate the *factual questions* for which the text offers clear, definite answers from *problematic questions* for which the text offers more than one explanation. This second set will be more

fruitful for starting discussion and developing a paper. (For some questions, the text will offer no clues at all. These unanswerable or *speculative questions* might be interesting to talk about, but since they go beyond the scope of the text that you actually read, they should be put aside.)

Within your list of problematic questions, consider which are the most important to a reader's understanding of the story. Some will no doubt involve side details, but others are likely to get at important issues, or *themes*, that shape the story and reveal its significance. On your own or with your classmates, choose two or three questions that you think would be interesting to pose for class discussion. Be prepared to explain why you think these are significant enough to explore in discussion and possibly in a paper.

2. Another productive way to find a focus for a paper about a work of fiction is to identify places where something changes in a major way. Exploration of the change, or *turning point*, and its possible significance can lead you to valuable insights about the themes woven through the story. Apply this idea to "Consent" by noting places where events, characters, or perceptions (even the narrative point of view) change. Again on your own or with a group of classmates, develop a short list of questions that you think are worth group discussion. Be prepared to explain and advocate for the importance of your questions.

3. We have placed "Consent" at the end of a group of texts that inform and explain. What is the role of explanation in this story? What does and does not get explained? What does the text indicate about why that is the case? Who does and does not understand those explanations? What is left unexplained? From whose perspective? Again, what does the text suggest about why that happens?

Writing to Inform and Explain

The texts in this section present samples of explanatory writing intended for readers with significantly different interests and backgrounds—from scientists to hiccuping children. The variety demonstrates different kinds of challenges that readers and writers face when they decide to explain a phenomenon. The discussion questions that accompany each text are designed to help you appreciate content and recognize a variety of reader-oriented writing strategies that you can try out in your own written work. The assignment prompts below invite you to apply what you've learned about information and explanation by analyzing writers' methods in depth and trying out similar approaches when you write about subjects that are important to you.

EXPLAINING WHAT YOU KNOW

We invite you to try your hand at the informative and explanatory strategies you have seen at work in this chapter. Write an essay that will enlarge your readers' understanding of a subject by providing new information or a clear explanation. Choose a subject that you already know well or something that you are interested in learning more about. Your specific goal is to write an informative or explanatory piece that alters readers' commonly held but incomplete or incorrect view of something. Consider carefully how you will bring something new to your readers that will enhance their understanding of the subject under discussion. Also consider the kinds of changes your new material will bring to your readers' view of your subject. To what extent can you expect them to welcome "good news" in your explanation? To what extent can you expect them to resist "bad news" in what you have to say?

Structure your organization and content carefully to maximize your paper's influence on your readers' understanding of your subject matter. Before you write, jot down notes to yourself about how you want to change your readers' thinking about your subject matter. Then, after you have written a draft, test it against your notes to see if it accomplishes the expository task you set for yourself.

EXAMINING RHETORICAL STRATEGIES

When is information really argument, explanation really advocacy? The texts by Irgang, Mairs, and Marin in this chapter all are presented as informative, explanatory articles. However, each has a serious stake in changing our views of something. This assignment invites you to look closely at two of these texts to compare their strategies for engaging readers in a way that will smooth away resistance to the sometimes uncomfortable ideas they present. Do you consider one to be more effective than the other? If so, how and why? Should either or both be in a different section of this book? Why? (You may wish to consult the section of Chapter 2 called "A Further Look at Writers' Purposes," on p. 21.)

   Organize your paper to support a thesis that states how you define the purposes of the two articles you choose, and then devote the bulk of your paper to
explaining similarities and differences in the two writers' strategies for gaining
readers' confidence and overcoming any readers' resistance. Provide textual evidence to support your points.

EXTENDING THE CONVERSATION

The UC Berkeley *Wellness Letter* article uses conflicting reports about antioxidants as a starting point for its explanation of how to be a discerning reader of
headline-grabbing stories of medical research. It was published in the mid-
1990s, when these conflicting findings from antioxidant studies were a big
news story. What is the current thinking about antioxidants? Find the most recent reports you can on the subject and write an academic, thesis-driven report
on the advice that experts currently offer about the role antioxidants should
play in our diet.

C H A P T E R

12

Analyzing and Interpreting

Much of what we read every day in newspapers and magazines or watch on television involves analysis and interpretation. Political analysts, for example, write about public policy issues in order to educate the public. Sports columnists explain a particular game's outcome by analyzing the performance of the teams and players. Film critics discuss movies in terms of the cinematography, acting, plot, special effects, and so on. In many of these cases, analysis and interpretation are the means to another end. The political analyst may dissect a policy issue in order to persuade readers to share her opinion regarding it, or the film critic may analyze a movie's features to make an evaluative argument. However, unlike texts whose primary aim is to persuade, evaluate, or explain, analytical texts aim first and foremost at understanding a perplexing subject, often by examining how it works, why it is as it is, or what it means.

Analytical texts (and writing assignments for that matter) constitute a common kind of academic prose. In general, analytical texts try to find meaningful patterns in complex data. They try to clarify a puzzling phenomenon by studying its constituent parts and by looking for underlying patterns, cause/effect relationships, and so on. Your psychology textbook, for example, introduces you to Freud's analysis of the psyche in terms of the id, ego, and superego. Your history textbook offers multiple explanations of the causes of the Civil War: economic, geographic, and sociological. Your English instructor asks you to read three different essays about Hawthorne's short story, "Rappacini's Daughter," each of which uses a different literary critical method to analyze and interpret the story. What all of these texts have in common is that they "take apart" a particular phenomenon (event,

337

concept, issue, or text) in order to see it differently and understand it more fully, and they "put it back together" in order to offer a "fresh" interpretation or conclusion, a new theory or explanation.

We can better understand how analysis and interpretation work together by taking a closer look at the definitions of these two key words. The word *analysis* comes from a Greek word that means "to dissolve, loosen, or undo." The act of "unraveling" a particular phenomenon or dividing it into its constituent parts allows us to see it from new perspectives. The result disrupts our quick holistic determination of its meaning, enabling us to see connections we have not heretofore seen and encouraging us to think of explanations or interpretations we had not thought of before. *Interpretation* derives from an Old French word that means "to negotiate, translate, or explain," and the branch of study dedicated to the "science" of interpretation is called *hermeneutics* after Hermes, the Greek messenger god. The writer offers an interpretation or translation of a text's or phenomenon's meaning and delivers this "message" to others. Important to note, the first dictionary definition of *to interpret* is "to explain to oneself" the meaning of something. Taken together, these definitions suggest that the act of interpretation is always a matter of negotiation among possible meanings, of deciding upon one translation rather than another, of making sense of things for oneself before passing on that understanding to another.

Although these definitions of *analysis* and *interpretation* imply that analysis precedes and forms the basis for interpretation, analysis itself is inevitably guided by prior assumptions or interpretive frameworks. For example, economists analyze various economic indicators in order to make predictions based on particular economic theories; school officials analyze various student test scores to determine the success of a school's curriculum according to certain definitions of academic achievement. In both cases, the data identified as significant—that is, the economic indicators and student test scores—as well as the theories used to interpret the data reveal the economist's or educator's beliefs or assumptions about how the economy works or what is significant in terms of school achievement. Kenneth Burke, the rhetorical theorist we referred to several times in the early chapters of this book, coined the phrase "terministic screens" to refer to this chicken-and-egg relationship between analysis and interpretation. According to Burke's theory, the "terms" we use to articulate and understand our perceptions "screen" or direct those perceptions: "any nomenclature necessarily directs the attention into some channels rather than others." For example, if we call a person sleeping on a city heating grate a "homeless person," the word "homeless" implicitly directs attention to economic issues and larger social causes. But if we call the person a "wino," alcoholism immediately comes to mind, thus focusing attention on an individual problem rather than on a socioeconomic problem. In Burke's view, the terms we use to take something apart and put it back together to create new meaning are inevitably shaped by our terministic screens, which entail various assumptions, beliefs, and values.

As the examples of the economist and educator suggest, the whole process of analysis and interpretation is central to our efforts to understand complex phenomena, generate new knowledge, and make important decisions. Thus, readings that analyze and interpret participate in ongoing conversations within disciplines, professions, and the public sphere. They offer tentative explanations or answers to questions that puzzle us. What does this new migration pattern of birds mean?

What accounts for the success of this urban renewal plan over another or this treatment for schizophrenia over another? How are we to understand the concluding scene in Spike Lee's *Do the Right Thing*? What does it mean that some advertisers in the 1990s used models whose look has been described as "heroin chic"?

To summarize: effective analytical and interpretive texts begin by identifying a key question or area of uncertainty. Their method is to examine the parts of the subject systematically in order to see how these parts are related to each other and to the whole. Texts that analyze and interpret pay close attention to detail and often make the implicit features of the subject explicit and therefore available to interpretation. The goal of analytical texts is new understanding. The opening selection in this chapter, Kirk Savage's "The Past in the Present," for example, analyzes and interprets the significance of public memorials; the short essays by Sarah Boxer and Roland Barthes interpret cultural practices and objects. At the center of Toni Cade Bambara's short story "The Lesson" is the issue of interpretation, and this dramatic portrayal of the subjectivity involved in interpretation invites the reader, in turn, to analyze and interpret the meaning of the story.

• *Questions to Help You Read Analysis and Interpretation Rhetorically*

1. What phenomenon is the writer analyzing and interpreting? What is puzzling about this phenomenon to the writer and presumably to readers?
2. What question or purpose seems to guide the writer's analysis and interpretation? Is the writer trying to understand how something works? Why it is as it is? What it means? Why does the writer believe it is important to understand this phenomenon in new ways?
3. How does the writer go about taking this phenomenon apart? What parts of the whole does the writer select for scrutiny? What assumptions does this selection reveal?
4. What, if any, organizational principles direct this writer's analysis? (Examples might be comparison or contrast, identification of causes or effects, classification of parts, or division into preconceived structural categories such as the exposition, rising action, climax, and denouement of a dramatic plot.)
5. What terministic screens seem to guide this writer's analysis and interpretation? What key terms are repeated in the essay? Which terms have a positive meaning, which a negative meaning?
6. If the author cites other writers or texts, what is her or his purpose in doing so? Which are cited to back up this writer's interpretation? Which to show how this writer is modifying or challenging another's interpretations or ideas?
7. What other ways are there of taking apart or analyzing this phenomenon?
8. What other interpretations are possible?
9. What aspects of this writer's analysis and interpretation are convincing? Which unconvincing? Why?

Kirk Savage

The Past in the Present: The Life of Memorials

Long interested in public monuments, Kirk Savage (b. 1958) is author of *Standing Soldiers, Kneeling Slaves: Race, War, and Monument in Nineteenth-Century America* (1998), which won the John Hope Franklin Prize for the best book in American studies in 1998. Savage teaches the history of art and architecture at the University of Pittsburgh and continues to investigate contemporary representations of slavery and emancipation in American public sculpture. As Savage explains in the introduction to *Standing Soldiers,* public space continues to be a "representational battleground, where many different social groups fight for access and fight for control of the images that define them."

"The Past in the Present: The Life of Memorials" appeared in *Harvard Design Magazine* (HDM) in the fall of 1999. HDM, which is published by Harvard University's Graduate School of Design in cooperation with MIT Press, features "critical explorations of key contemporary issues and practices connected to the built environment." Each issue is organized around a particular theme, such as "What Is Nature Now?" or "Constructions of Memory," which was the theme of the issue in which "The Past in the Present" appeared. Not surprisingly, articles in HDM tend to be scholarly in their treatment of various topics; Savage follows the *Chicago Manual of Style* citation conventions here, using sequential superscript note numbers that refer to *endnotes* at the end of the article.

• *For Your Reading Log*

1. The term *memorial* includes monuments, museums, sculptures, and holiday celebrations, any structure or occasion intended as a reminder of a person or event. Examples of memorial structures include the Vietnam War Memorial and Holocaust Museum in Washington as well as the equestrian statue of a local hero in a town square. Think of a memorial that you have visited, either recently or as a child or adolescent. What was your response to this memorial? What, if any, meaning did the experience have for you? Take a few minutes to describe this experience and your memories of the memorial itself in your reading log.

2. In "The Past in the Present," Savage offers various theories about the cultural meaning of memorials, particularly monuments. As you read his essay, mark what you believe to be key passages. After you have completed the essay, go back to the passages you have marked, and try to translate these ideas into your own words in your reading log. If you cannot explain them, then formulate questions about the meaning to raise in class.

——————— • ———————

In an office park in suburban Los Angeles, set within a pristine landscape garden 1
designed by Isamu Noguchi, there is a funny monument made of piled stones; the
artist dubbed it *The Spirit of the Lima Bean* (1982). Back in the heyday of allegorical
sculpture, at the turn of the past century, citizens were likely to encounter the *Spirit
of Truth,* or the *Spirit of Fire,* or maybe even the *Spirit of Electricity*—but never the
spirit of an ordinary legume. Yet Noguchi's lima-bean monument is more than a
joke on an old sculptural genre; it gestures to a lost way of life from the Southern
California of his youth. If the lima bean lives in spirit in this garden, the nearby
farms that once produced actual lima beans are long gone, victims of a relentless
process of displacement in which Noguchi's own work participates.

The *Spirit of the Lima Bean* could easily stand as an emblem for a whole school 2
of thought that sees modern collective memory as a phenomenon of rupture and
loss. According to this school, only when the past has slipped away—becoming
a "foreign country" in David Lowenthal's famous phrase—do we begin to mark
and commemorate it. Or to paraphrase Pierre Nora, it is when we stop experiencing memory spontaneously from within that we begin to "design" memory,
to create its external signs and traces, such as monuments and museums and historic buildings.[1] According to this way of thinking, the intensifying proliferation
of the external signs of memory in the contemporary built environment signals the
death of a more organic cultural memory that supposedly existed in the hazy pre-
modern past. Thus we can add "the death of memory" to the other assorted
deaths—of art, of the author, etc.—that cultural critics have been eager to identify.

But if this sort of lament is increasingly common, we often fail to acknowledge 3
its long genealogy. Long before Robert Musil declared that "there is nothing in this
world as invisible as a monument,"[2] many observers were complaining that public monuments were inert, even "dead," worth little by comparison to a memory
that "lived" within people's hearts. Ironically, even at ceremonies marking the construction of public monuments, this sort of rhetoric became commonplace. As the
orator at the 1867 cornerstone-laying for the first soldiers' monument at the Antietam battlefield affirmed, "Let statues or monuments to the living or the dead
tower ever so high, the true honor, after all, is not in the polished tablet or tower-
ing column, but in that pure, spontaneous, and unaffected gratitude and devotion
of the people that enshrines the memory of the honored one in the heart, and trans-
mits it from age to age long after such costly things have disappeared."[3] This idea
dates back to Pericles's famous funeral oration for the Athenian war dead, in
which he argued that the most distinguished monument is the one "planted in the
heart rather than graven on stone."[4] The contrast between heart and stone—between spontaneity and fabrication, feeling and obligation—obviously calls into
question the authenticity and efficacy of built forms of remembering.

Embedded in the very process of memorial building, then, is a longstand- 4
ing anxiety about monuments. Today, as we are experiencing an explosion of interest in erecting public monuments, it is useful to explore whether this anxiety
is still—or was ever—justified. Of particular interest to me are the new monuments to the Civil Rights movement, because they revisit many of the issues—
stated and unstated—that we as a nation struggled with at the end of the last
century in trying to come to grips with the legacy of the Civil War.

5   Why lavish time and money on monuments, especially if "true" memory indeed resides elsewhere? During the great age of the public monument in the
United States, from the mid-19th through the early 20th century, monument proponents were armed with a well-rehearsed response. Monuments did not replace the "true" memory within people's hearts, they claimed; rather, monuments
were tangible proof of that inner memory. Thus were monuments construed as
the most conspicuous sign that a national people understood and valued its own
history.[5] In the United States, the dominant notion of history has been that of a
people dedicated to progress. Public monuments helped to celebrate and cement
this progressive narrative of national history. To do so, monuments had to instill
a sense of historical closure. Memorials to heroes and events were not meant to
revive old struggles and debates but to put them to rest—to show how great men
and their deeds had made the nation better and stronger. Commemoration was
a process of condensing the moral lessons of history and fixing them in place for
all time; this required that the object of commemoration be understood as a completed stage of history, safely nestled in a sealed-off past. Until the 18th century,
statues were made of living kings, a practice that continued in the early years of
the United States when the state of Virginia erected Houdon's statue of George
Washington in 1796, three years before his death. By the 19th century, however,
it was generally believed that monumental heroes—like Noguchi's lima bean—
should be dead and gone, their life histories closed.[6] (At Washington's death,
some writers rejoiced that now he could do nothing to tarnish his reputation; it
was safe for eternity. They could not foresee that DNA testing might alter a president's reputation two centuries after his death.) Similarly, historical events had
to be decisively over: wars won (or lost), acts of statesmanship consummated.

6   This logic of commemoration drastically shriveled history. Women, non-
whites, laborers, and others who did not advance the master narrative of progress
defined by a white male elite had little place in the commemorative scheme, except perhaps as the occasional foil by which heroism could be better displayed.
This kind of commemoration sought to purify the past of any continuing conflict
that might disturb the carefully crafted national narrative. Perhaps the most dramatic example of this in the United States is the commemoration of emancipation
in the aftermath of the Civil War.

7   The abolition of black slavery in 1865 constituted more of a beginning than
an end—the beginning of a long period of intense contestation over the meaning of "freedom" that would, at the end of the 19th century, culminate tragically
in a renewed era of the repression of African Americans. Yet as early as 1866, de-
signers of monuments were proposing to "commemorate" emancipation in the
form of monuments to Abraham Lincoln. To become an object of commemoration, emancipation needed to be understood as a finished act rather than an unresolved process. Thus the struggle for freedom was condensed into a single
human decision—Lincoln's Emancipation Proclamation—even though this action freed only the slaves in Confederate territory, leaving slavery intact in the
Union. Similarly, the decisive role played by slaves themselves in their own liberation had to be repressed for two crucial reasons: their actions distracted from
the main point of the historical episode, which was the moral glory of the white

leader; and their historical struggle against slavery prefigured their continuing struggle for equal rights. A complex and disputed historical process was thus reduced to the stroke of a pen and the waving of a piece of a paper, a work of individual, isolated genius. Most notorious of the memorials that embody this flawed understanding is the so-called Emancipation Monument in Washington (1876), funded but not designed by African Americans; in this monument, a standing Lincoln with one hand on the proclamation appears to be blessing a kneeling slave whose chains have been magically sundered.[7]

By trying to lock up the past in a prefabricated narrative of progress, monuments such as these can, as Lowenthal and Nora suggest, work to destroy the sense of a past that still lives within us—a past that helps us define the problems and opportunities we face in the present. Yet the processes of making and experiencing a public memorial always have the potential to undermine the monument's appearance of fixity. The world around a monument is never fixed. The movement of life causes monuments to be created, but then it changes how they are seen and understood. The history of monuments themselves is no more closed than the history they commemorate. 8

To see this at work, we need only glance at Monument Avenue in Richmond, Virginia, which, since the Civil Rights movement, has become a locus of great controversy. This stately boulevard takes its name from the five colossal monuments to Confederate generals and leaders erected along its length between 1890 and 1929, the first and most prominent an equestrian statue of Robert E. Lee. The Lee Monument and its successors worked to strengthen a canonical narrative of the Confederate past—a saga of white valor and statesmanship. The closure of history embodied so effectively in these monuments was part of a larger strategy engineered by the white elite to legitimate its authority in the so-called New South. Sensing that a threat to the avenue's Confederate integrity would be a threat to this version of history, the avenue's defenders long claimed that it was a sacred precinct and therefore exempt from historical processes of change. But like all monumental precincts, Monument Avenue has no choice but to participate in history. The avenue originated in a real estate scheme supported by a nephew of Robert E. Lee, and from the first it was embroiled in local and state politics.[8] When the black majority finally took control of local government and an African American was elected governor in the late 1980s, the Confederate bastion began to crack. A protracted battle ensued when various proposals were made to place monuments to civil rights heroes on the avenue. Ultimately the battle ended in compromise: the African American chosen for commemoration was black tennis star and native son Arthur Ashe, whose monument was erected in 1996 and located just beyond the five Confederate statues. Although not a political figure, Ashe was an educated and articulate African American who spent his last years campaigning for better AIDS education. The white Richmonders who fought the Ashe Monument worried, rightly, that its presence would profoundly alter Monument Avenue. Now the procession of Confederate heroes, icons of white supremacist rule in Richmond and the New South, culminates ironically in an emblem of exactly the sort of black citizenry the Confederacy feared, outlawed, and fought. 9

10   But the battles are far from over. Recently, a large portrait of Robert E. Lee was hung on a new riverfront walk in Richmond, only to be removed because of protests from African-American leaders. While the protesters asserted that Lee had fought to keep their ancestors enslaved, the Sons of Confederate Veterans argued that Lee was "a hero of all Virginians" and that removing his picture was a "desecration."[9] This dispute is similar to one that occurred in 1871, when white legislators moved to purchase a portrait of Lee for the Virginia State Capitol, and it recalls scattered protests that took place as the Lee Monument was being constructed.[10] These disputes remind us that there is no single or unified experience of a commemorative image, and conflict often centers on *whose* experience the image tacitly recognizes and legitimates.

11   The essential problem is not that "true" inner memory has disappeared, as Nora would assert. On the contrary, inner memory is alive and kicking: it is the force of living memory that makes the external forms of commemoration meaningful and controversial. The historical memory of the Confederacy is profoundly fractured, and its competing versions continue to be nourished by organizations dedicated to remembering as well as by the oral traditions of families descended from slaves and soldiers alike. Commemorative imagery always has the potential to bring these less visible currents of memory into public contention. For a century, Confederate sympathizers had a near monopoly on public memory in the South; having now lost that monopoly, they are trying to position themselves as "Confederate Americans" with their own right to representation in a multicultural society.[11] Their new ethnic posture is disingenuous, however, given their continuing efforts to claim Lee as a hero for everyone. Lee can be their hero but he is not an African-American hero, nor will he be as long as the memory of slavery remains a vital part of the African-American community.

12   The Civil Rights movement is a more recent, indeed personal memory for its surviving participants; but the commemorative issues it raises resemble those of the Civil War. As an object of commemoration, the Civil Rights movement would appear to offer an ideal opportunity to improve on the dismal precedent of emancipation. The public realm is far more accessible to African Americans today than during Reconstruction, when they had virtually no opportunity to influence the design of any public monument, even those they funded themselves. Today African-American communities not only are acknowledged as monument consumers, but they also have the political leverage to sponsor and design public monuments. Still, the commemorative enterprise of our own time presents a striking parallel to the dilemma posed by emancipation. The 20th-century movement for civil rights picked up where emancipation left off, and this long continuous history remains unfinished. While the civil rights era has its martyrs, milestones, and tangible accomplishments that provide grist for the commemorative mill, the movement has evolved, fractured, and continued to struggle toward the elusive goal of racial equality. The legacy of the movement's heroic past continues to be disputed in conflicts over affirmative action, school and housing desegregation, and economic opportunity. The key question then becomes: will commemorating this heroic past make it recede further from the present, or can commemoration challenge us to grapple with that past's complicated legacy?

Much of the civil rights memorial activity has been in Alabama, where mon- 13
uments erected over the past decade run the gamut of commemorative solutions.
At one extreme is Maya Lin's memorial at the Southern Poverty Law Center in
Montgomery: abstract, contemplative, anchored by its elegant presentation of objective historical fact. Against a backdrop inscribed with Martin Luther King, Jr.'s
famous words, "until justice rolls down like waters and righteousness like a
mighty stream," a black marble "table" bathed in water displays a circular time
line of events from 1954 to 1968, with the names of several dozen martyrs interspersed with a record of judicial decisions and political actions. Like her Vietnam
Veterans Memorial in Washington, the Civil Rights Memorial condenses historical process into a sequence of verifiable events and sacrifices with a definite beginning and end; interpretation of this "closed" historical period, however, is left
to the individual viewer who is encouraged by the flowing water and the serene
surfaces to reflect on history's meaning.[12] At the other extreme is a group of figurative monuments in Kelly Ingram Park in Birmingham, which try to draw the
viewer back into the tumult of the past. Several works designed by James Drake
along a path named Freedom Walk commemorate the brutal police repression
of the famous marches in the spring of 1963. In one work, the walkway passes
between two vertical slabs, from which bronze attack dogs emerge on either side
and lunge into the pedestrian's space. In another, the walkway leads through an
opening in a metal wall faced by two water cannons; just off the walk, by the
wall, are two bronze figures of African Americans, a man crumpled to the ground
and a woman standing with her back turned against the imagined force of the
water. Integrated into the pedestrian experience of the park, these monuments
invite everyone—black or white, young or old—to step for a moment into someone else's shoes, those of an innocent victim of state-sponsored terror.

At first glance, Drake's works appear to direct the viewer's experience more 14
imperiously than Lin's does. But Lin's memorial to the Civil Rights movement is
far more of a guided experience than her earlier memorial to Vietnam veterans.
While the Vietnam Memorial is notable for the absence of any statement glorify-
ing the cause or linking the war deaths to any lasting achievement, the Civil
Rights Memorial obviously valorizes its cause with the quotation from King, and
its time line links human sacrifices to tangible accomplishments. At the Vietnam
Memorial, the absence of customary explanations of warfare and death forces the
visitor to supply her own. In the Montgomery monument, the moral of the story
is already part of the package. Yet aspects of the monument work against this neat
closure of history. The very circularity of the time line is ambivalent: on the one
hand, it suggests completeness; on the other, return and repetition. Unlike a textbook time line, that of the memorial is neither linear nor progressive. And it ends
not with an accomplishment but with King's assassination, a tragedy whose im
plications remain to this day unresolved. Unanswered questions are formulated.
Where might we have gone with him? Where have we gone without him?

For all their obvious drama, Drake's monuments are unpredictable in their im- 15
pact. In a sense, they are victim monuments: they do not represent the human vic-
timizer but instead position the viewer as the target of his unseen evil.[13] No single
critic can hope to explain or even describe how such a monument affects viewers.

As visitors assume the imagined position of the victim, they do not leave their own selves, their inner memories and life experiences, behind. While the monuments are supposed to make history seem less remote, they might have the opposite effect on some visitors, who might see them as emblematic of a barbaric past, long gone. Others might wonder whether the abuses of the past have been rectified; they might connect the repressive tactics of the early '60s with the police brutality that has lately been so much in the headlines. Some might leave Kelly Ingram Park with the message that the fight is behind them; others might feel inspired to continue the struggle in new ways. These simple predictions don't even begin to exhaust the possible divisions—based on race, class, gender, political persuasion, life history, and so on—that can inspire radically different responses to the same work.

16   The design of public monuments is obviously important; but design cannot claim to engineer memory. The inner memories of a culture profoundly shape how its monuments are experienced and lived. The fate of the civil rights memorials will ultimately depend upon how the movement itself is remembered and reinterpreted in the complex reality of the present. In this light, one of the most promising projects is one not yet designed. Last year in Wilmington, North Carolina, a coalition of politicians, business leaders, citizens, and academics sponsored a year-long series of community events and small-group dialogues to commemorate and reexamine one of the most shameful episodes of Southern history: the white supremacist riot of 1898 that destroyed the local black press, attacked black businesses, and forced a legally elected interracial administration to resign from power. The centennial observances in 1998 were partly about history—about setting the historical record right, giving the African-American community the opportunity to voice its own "inner" memory of the past handed down over generations. But even more important, the observances were intended to create a framework for the future based on ongoing dialogue, mutual understanding, and community action. Dozens of interracial discussion groups, each with a trained facilitator, met for a year; local institutions such as the police, banks, and chamber of commerce reevaluated and revised their practices. A monument has been envisaged as one part of this broader effort.[14] Whatever its design, its success or failure will inevitably be linked to the success of the city's campaign to recast itself. The experience of the monument—the "lesson" of the monument—will be affected by the community's efforts to bridge the racial divide. If this North Carolina city can work toward genuine racial justice, then the monument commemorating this struggle will not become an obsolete marker of a disconnected past but an agent of consciousness in a changing world.

Notes

1. David Lowenthal, *The Past Is a Foreign Country* (Cambridge: Cambridge University Press, 1985); Pierra Nora, "Between Memory and History: Les Lieux de Memoire," *Representations* 26 (Spring 1989), 7–25.

2. Robert Musil, "Monuments," in *Posthumous Papers of a Living Author,* trans. Peter Wortsman (Hygiene, Colorado: Eridanos Press, 1987), 61.

3. *History of Antietam Cemetery* (Baltimore: J. W. Woods, 1869), 4.

4. Thucydides, *History of the Peloponnesian War,* trans. Charles Forster Smith (Cambridge: Harvard University Press, 1928), II: 43.

5. Great men like Washington needed no monuments, many argued, but a nation's people needed to erect monuments to great men to show the nation's gratitude; this was the thrust of Thomas Carlyle's famous argument in "Hudson's Statue," in *Latter-Day Pamphlets* (New York, 1903; orig. 1850).

6. Monuments to living heroes are extremely rare in the 19th century. A Reconstruction-era federally sponsored project for a monument to Abraham Lincoln on the Capitol grounds (never executed) received intense criticism for its inclusion of figures of several contemporaries of Lincoln then living.

7. Kirk Savage, *Standing Soldiers, Kneeling Slaves: Race, War, and Monument in Nineteenth-Century America* (Princeton: Princeton University Press, 1997), 52–128.

8. Ibid., 148–152.

9. Craig Timberg, "Confederate Image Casts Shadow," *Washington Post,* June 4, 1999, B-1.

10. *Richmond Dispatch,* January 18, 1871 and January 20, 1871; Savage, 137–138, 151–154.

11. Craig Timberg, "Richmond Is Seeking a Civil Solution," *Washington Post,* June 17, 1999, B-1. The United Daughters of the Confederacy used the term Confederate Americans in their recent website posting, but the term surfaced during the conflict over the Ashe monument as well.

12. See Daniel Abramson, "Maya Lin and the 1960s: Monuments, Time Lines, and Minimalism," *Critical Inquiry* 22 (Summer 1996), 679–709.

13. Victim monuments of this sort are a recent phenomenon. War memorials in the United States, for example, almost never represented wounded soldiers or men under attack; soldier statues nearly always restored the soldier's body to an intact, vigilant figure—elevated on a pedestal, of course, which deliberately distanced him from the viewer's space. Also in Kelly Ingram Park is a controversial monument that does depict a white policeman and dog attacking an African-American male.

14. A thorough account of these activities is in the self-published *Centennial Record* (Wilmington, N.C.: 1898 Centennial Foundation, 1998).

• *Thinking Critically About "The Past in the Present: The Life of Memorials"*

RESPONDING AS A READER

1. In paragraph 5, Savage raises a key question: "Why lavish time and money on monuments, especially if 'true' memory indeed resides elsewhere?" Although he never answers this question directly, he does so indirectly. What, in your own words, is his answer? Does he convince you that this is an important question? What other questions does he implicitly raise regarding monuments?

2. Throughout the essay, Savage discusses specific monuments such as the Emancipation Monument and Drake's monuments in Birmingham to illustrate his ideas. Which of the examples did you find most engaging or most helpful in clarifying a particular idea or debate?

3. Part of Savage's analysis involves presenting and weighing the ideas of others. In particular, he refers several times to the ideas of Pierre Nora. How does Savage position his ideas in relation to Nora's? What does this contribute to his overall analysis?

RESPONDING AS A WRITER

1. Savage organizes his analysis primarily through contrasts. For example, he contrasts memories graven on the heart with those graven on stone, the meaning of the Lee Monument with that of the Ashe Monument on Monument Avenue in Richmond, Virginia, and so on. Make a list of what you consider to be key contrasts in terms, examples, and ideas, and then use these to write a paragraph summarizing Savage's main points about monuments.

2. Return to the memorial you wrote about in your reading log, and reconsider its meaning in light of Savage's ideas. Does this memorial represent the older logic of commemoration that sees history as finished or a new logic that sees history as still unfolding? Write a paragraph recording your insights.

3. In the last paragraph of the essay, Savage refers to a project in Wilmington, North Carolina, where a memorial is being planned to commemorate "one of the most shameful episodes of Southern history: the white supremacist riot of 1898 that destroyed the local black press, attacked black businesses, and forced a legally elected interracial administration to resign from power." This memorial has not yet been designed. Working on your own or with a small group of classmates, propose a design for this memorial, and write a letter to the city council of Wilmington arguing for the appropriateness of your design.

Sarah Boxer

I Shop, Ergo I Am:
The Mall as Society's Mirror

Sarah Boxer (b. 1959) is a cultural critic who writes regularly for the *New York Times*. Her particular interests are in popular culture, contemporary art, and critical theory. In "I Shop, Ergo I Am: The Mall as Society's Mirror," published March 28, 1998 in the *New York Times,* Boxer offers a brief cultural history of shopping as well as an analysis of the meaning of contemporary trends in shopping. Boxer's title alludes to the famous statement made by French philosopher Rene Descartes about the relationship between cognition and one's sense of self: "I think; therefore, I am."

• *For Your Reading Log*

1. As Boxer reports in this article, the academic field known as cultural studies analyzes ordinary activities such as "eating fast food, buying a house in the suburbs, watching television and taking vacations at Disneyland." A subspeciality in this field is what Boxer calls "shopping studies." Does shopping strike you as a serious subject for academic inquiry? Why might a scholar be interested in studying the history of shopping or current shopping behaviors?
2. Write a short entry in your reading log about your attitudes toward shopping and your shopping habits.

In certain academic circles, "shop till you drop" is considered a civic act. If you 1 follow cultural studies—the academic scrutiny of ordinary activities like eating fast food, buying a house in the suburbs, watching television and taking vacations at Disneyland—you will know that shopping is not just a matter of going to a store and paying for your purchase.

How you shop is who you are. Shopping is a statement about your place in 2 society and your part in world cultural history. There is a close relationship, even an equation, between citizenship and consumption. The store is the modern city-state, the place where people act as free citizens, making choices, rendering opinions and socializing with others.

If this sounds like a stretch, you're way behind the times. The field of cul- 3 tural studies, which took off in England in the 1970's, has been popular in this country for more than a decade.

The intellectual fascination with stores goes back even further. When the 4 philosopher Walter Benjamin died in 1940, he was working on a long study of the Paris arcades, the covered retail passageways, then almost extinct, which he called the "original temples of commodity capitalism." Six decades later, the study of shopping is well trampled. Some academics have moved on from early classical work on the birth of the department store and the shopping arcade to the shopping malls of the 1950's and even the new wide aisles of today's factory outlets and superstores—places like Best Buy, Toys "R" Us and Ikea.

5   Historically, the age of shopping and browsing begins at the very end of the 18th century. In a paper titled "Counter Publics: Shopping and Women's Sociability," delivered at the Modern Language Association's annual meeting, Deidre Lynch, an associate professor of English at the State University of New York in Buffalo, said the word "shopping" started to appear frequently in print around 1780. That was when stores in London started turning into public attractions.

6   By 1800, Ms. Lynch said, "a policy of obligation-free browsing seems to have been introduced into London emporia." At that point, "the usual morning employment of English ladies," the 18th-century writer Robert Southey said, was to "go a-shopping." Stores became places to socialize, to see and be seen. Browsing was born.

7   The pastime of browsing has been fully documented. Benjamin wrote that the Paris arcades, which went up in the early 1800's, created a new kind of person, a professional loiterer, or flaneur, who could easily turn into a dangerous political gadfly. The philosopher Jurgen Habermas, some of his interpreters say, has equated consumer capitalism with the feminization of culture. And now some feminists, putting a new spin on this idea, are claiming the store as the place where women first became "public women."

8   By imagining that they owned the wares, women were "transported into new identities," Ms. Lynch said. By meeting with their friends, they created what feminist critics like Nancy Fraser and Miriam Hansen call "counter publics," groups of disenfranchised people.

9   Some feminists point out that as shoppers, women had the power to alter other people's lives. Women who spent "a summer's day cheapening a pair of gloves" without buying anything, as Southey put it, were "fortifying the boundaries of social class," Ms. Lynch said. They were "teaching haberdashers and milliners their place," taunting them with the prospect of a purchase and never delivering. It may not have been nice, but it was a sort of political power.

10   Women could also use their power for good. In 1815, Ms. Lynch points out, Mary Lamb wrote an essay called "On Needlework," urging upper-class ladies who liked to do needlework as a hobby to give compensatory pay to women who did it to make a living. Lamb's biographer recently noted that this was how "bourgeois women busily distributed the fruits of their husbands' capitalist gains in the name of female solidarity."

11   The idea that shopping is a form of civil action naturally has its critics. In one of the essays in a book titled "Buy This Book," Don Slater, a sociologist at the University of London, criticized the tendency of many academics to celebrate "the productivity, creativity, autonomy, rebelliousness and even . . . the 'authority' of the consumer." The trouble with this kind of post-modern populism is that it mirrors "the logic of the consumer society it seeks to analyze," he said. Such theo-

ries, without distinguishing between real needs and false ones, he suggested, assume that shoppers are rational and autonomous creatures who acquire what they want and want what they acquire.

Another critic, Meaghan Morris, author of an essay called "Banality in Cultural Studies," has faulted academics for idealizing the pleasure and power of shopping and underestimating the "anger, frustration, sorrow, irritation, hatred, boredom and fatigue" that go with it. 12

The field of shopping studies, whatever you think of it, is now at a pivotal point. In the 19th century, emporiums in London and arcades in Paris turned shopping into social occasions; in the 20th century, academics turned shopping into civic action; and in the 21st century, it seems that megastores will bring us into a new, darker era. 13

Shoppers' freedoms are changing. According to Robert Bocock, writing in "Consumption," the mall walkers of today do not have the rights that the flaneurs of the 19th century had. "In the United States, 'policing' of who is allowed entry to the malls has become stricter in the last two or three decades of the 20th century." 14

In superstores, the role of shoppers has changed even more radically. Superstores are warehouses that stock an astounding number of goods picked out at a national corporate level, said Marianne Conroy, a scholar of comparative literature at the University of Maryland. Shoppers educate themselves about the goods and serve themselves. Thus, the superstore effectively "strips shopping of its aura of sociality," Ms. Conroy said. There is no meaningful interaction between the salespeople and the shoppers or among the shoppers. The shoppers' relationship is not with other people but with boxes and shelves. 15

Does the concept of the shopper as citizen still hold? The real test is to see how the citizen-shopper fares at the superstore. In a paper she delivered to the Modern Language Association, titled "You've Gotta Fight for Your Right to Shop: Superstores, Citizenship and the Restructuring of Consumption," Ms. Conroy analyzed one event in the history of a superstore that tested the equation between shopping and citizenship. 16

In 1996 Ronald Kahlow, a software engineer, decided to do some comparison shopping at a Best Buy outlet store in Reston, Va., by punching the prices and model numbers of some televisions into his laptop computer. When store employees asked him to stop, he refused and was arrested for trespassing. The next day, Mr. Kahlow returned with a pen and paper. Again, he was charged with trespassing and handcuffed. 17

When he stood trial in Fairfax County Court, he was found not guilty. And, as Ms. Conroy observed, the presiding judge in the case, Donald McDonough, grandly equated Mr. Kahlow's comparison shopping to civil disobedience in the 1960's. Mr. Kahlow then recited Robert F. Kennedy's poem "A Ripple of Hope," and the judge said, "Never has the cause of comparison shopping been so eloquently advanced." 18

At first, Ms. Conroy suggested they both might have gone overboard in reading "public meaning into private acts," but then she reconsidered. Maybe, she said, it's just time to refine the model. 19

20   Ms. Conroy suggested that consumerism should be seen no longer as the way citizens exercise their rights and freedoms but rather as "an activity that makes the impact of economic institutions on everyday life critically intelligible." In other words, shoppers in superstores are like canaries in the mines. Their experience inside tells us something about the dangers lurking in society at large.

21   What does one man's shopping experience at Best Buy tell us about the dangers of modern life in America? The fact that Mr. Kahlow was arrested when he tried to comparison shop shows that even the minimal rights of citizen-shoppers are endangered, said Ms. Conroy. Not only have they lost a venue for socializing, but they are also beginning to lose their right to move about freely and make reasoned choices.

22   Without the trappings of sociability, it's easier to see what's what. Stores used to be places that made people want to come out and buy things they didn't know they wanted. And they were so seductive that by the end of the 20th century they became one of the few sites left for public life. But in the superstores, the flaneurs and the consumer-citizens are fish out of water. They have nowhere pleasant to wander, no glittering distractions, no socializing to look forward to and no escape from the watchful eyes of the security guards. If this is citizenship, maybe it's time to move to another country.

● *Thinking Critically About "I Shop, Ergo I Am"*

RESPONDING AS A READER

1. What kind of a relationship does Boxer try to establish with readers? What roles does she invite readers to play? Point out particular passages that support your answer.

2. What's the effect of the background information Boxer offers about studies of shopping in earlier eras (paragraphs 5–13)? What kind of connection do you see between these studies and more recent studies of superstores (paragraphs 15–22)? How does Boxer help you to understand this relationship?

3. What seems to be Boxer's purpose in writing this essay? What new perspective does this article offer readers?

RESPONDING AS A WRITER

1. Boxer quotes a number of experts in this short article. List three scholars that she quotes, and explain briefly what you believe to be her purpose in citing each. How does she use the ideas supplied by them to develop her points?

2. To what extent does your experience in superstores confirm or counter Boxer's interpretation of them? Write a brief response to her claims based on your own experiences with superstores.

3. Throughout the essay Boxer cites scholars who claim that shopping has always offered people certain kinds of identities—"the public woman," the free citizen who can make choices, and so on. Think of a contemporary shopping practice like shopping by catalogue or online, and offer a brief interpretation of the identity or identities offered by this kind of shopping.

Roland Barthes

Toys

Roland Barthes (1915–1980) was one of the most influential critical theorists of the twentieth century. A French intellectual, trained in the classics and philology, Barthes was a leading figure in developing semiotic theory, a critical method that views cultural artifacts of all sorts—literature, fine art, fashion, sports—as a system of signs that can be analyzed and interpreted. Among his best known books are *Writing Degree Zero* (1967), *The Pleasure of the Text* (1975), and *The Rustle of Language* (1984). "Toys" is taken from *Mythologies* (1972), a collection of short essays analyzing a wide range of cultural artifacts such as wrestling and margarine.

● **For Your Reading Log**

    1. As a child, what was your favorite toy? Write a short entry in your reading log describing this toy and explaining why it was your favorite.

    2. As you read through this essay, mark Barthes's key statements about the meaning of French toys.

——————— ● ———————

1 French toys: One could not find a better illustration of the fact that the adult Frenchman sees the child as another self. All the toys one commonly sees are essentially a microcosm of the adult world; they are all reduced copies of human objects, as if in the eyes of the public the child was, all told, nothing but a smaller man, a homunculus to whom must be supplied objects of his own size.

2   Invented forms are very rare: a few sets of blocks, which appeal to the spirit of do-it-yourself, are the only ones which offer dynamic forms. As for the others, French toys *always mean something*, and this something is always entirely socialized, constituted by the myths or the techniques of modern adult life: the army, broadcasting, the post office, medicine (miniature instrument-cases, operating theaters for dolls), school, hair styling (driers for permanent-waving), the air force (parachutists), transport (trains, Citroëns, Vedettes, Vespas, petrol stations), science (Martian toys).

3   The fact that French toys *literally* prefigure the world of adult functions obviously cannot but prepare the child to accept them all, by constituting for him, even before he can think about it, the alibi of a Nature which has at all times created soldiers, postmen and Vespas. Toys here reveal the list of all the things the adult does not find unusual: war, bureaucracy, ugliness, Martians, etc. It is not so much, in fact, the imitation which is the sign of an abdication, as its literalness: French toys are like a Jivaro head, in which one recognizes, shrunken to the size of an apple, the wrinkles and hair of an adult. There exist, for instance, dolls which urinate; they have an esophagus, one gives them a bottle, they wet their

nappies; soon, no doubt, milk will turn to water in their stomachs. This is meant to prepare the little girl for the causality of housekeeping, to "condition" her to her future role as mother. However, faced with this world of faithful and complicated objects, the child can only identify himself as owner, as user, never as creator; he does not invent the world, he uses it: There are, prepared for him, actions without adventure, without wonder, without joy. He is turned into a little stay-at-home householder who does not even have to invent the mainsprings of adult causality; they are supplied to him ready-made: He has only to help himself, he is never allowed to discover anything from start to finish. The merest set of blocks, provided it is not too refined, implies a very different learning of the world: Then, the child does not in any way create meaningful objects, it matters little to him whether they have an adult name; the actions he performs are not those of a user but those of a demiurge. He creates forms which walk, which roll, he creates life, not property: Objects now act by themselves, they are no longer an inert and complicated material in the palm of his hand. But such toys are rather rare: French toys are usually based on imitation, they are meant to produce children who are users, not creators.

The bourgeois status of toys can be recognized not only in their forms, which   4 are all functional, but also in their substances. Current toys are made of a graceless material, the product of chemistry, not of nature. Many are now molded from complicated mixtures; the plastic material of which they are made has an appearance at once gross and hygienic, it destroys all the pleasure, the sweetness, the humanity of touch. A sign which fills one with consternation is the gradual disappearance of wood, in spite of its being an ideal material because of its firmness and its softness, and the natural warmth of its touch. Wood removes, from all the forms which it supports, the wounding quality of angles which are too sharp, the chemical coldness of metal. When the child handles it and knocks it, it neither vibrates nor grates, it has a sound at once muffled and sharp. It is a familiar and poetic substance, which does not sever the child from close contact with the tree, the table, the floor. Wood does not wound or break down; it does not shatter, it wears out, it can last a long time, live with the child, alter little by little the relations between the object and the hand. If it dies, it is in dwindling, not in swelling out like those mechanical toys which disappear behind the hernia of a broken spring. Wood makes essential objects, objects for all time. Yet there hardly remain any of these wooden toys from the Vosges, these fretwork farms with their animals, which were only possible, it is true, in the days of the craftsman. Henceforth, toys are chemical in substance and color; their very material introduces one to a coenaesthesis of use, not pleasure. These toys die in fact very quickly, and once dead, they have no posthumous life for the child.

• *Thinking Critically About "Toys"*

RESPONDING AS A READER

1. Barthes analyzes toys according to their form and function as well as their substance. What are his chief criticisms of the form and function of

French toys? His chief criticisms of their substance? Does he adequately explain and illustrate his analysis?

2. In paragraph 4, Barthes speaks almost poetically about the value of wood as a material for making toys. In his view, why is the material toys are made of important? Do you agree? Why or why not?

3. To what larger social issues does Barthes connect his critique of French toys?

RESPONDING AS A WRITER

1. Do the criticisms Barthes offers of French toys of the 1950s apply to contemporary American toys? Write a paragraph in which you answer this question by citing specific examples of contemporary American toys to support your opinion. Feel free to raise issues other than those raised by Barthes in your critique of contemporary American toys.

2. What ideology or terministic screen informs Barthes's analysis? Make a list with the terms Barthes values in one column and the terms he doesn't value in another. What do these sets of oppositions suggest about his ideology and worldview?

3. Think of a toy besides wooden blocks that you believe would meet with Barthes's approval. If you can't think of a real toy, make up one. Write a short ad-type description of this toy, urging parents to buy it.

Toni Cade Bambara

The Lesson (Fiction)

Toni Cade Bambara (1939–1995) was a prominent civil rights activist, author, and educator until her untimely death from cancer in 1995. Through her writing, Bambara portrays the lives of urban African Americans, particularly women, with depth and richness. Bambara also wrote several screenplays, including *Zora,* a film about the life of Zora Neale Hurston, and *The Bombing of Osage,* a film about an incident in Philadelphia in which the African American mayor used lethal force against a group of black militants. Her best known books of fiction include *Gorilla, My Love* (1972), a collection of short stories that includes "The Lesson," and two novels—*The Salt Eaters* (1980) and *If Blessings Come* (1987).

• *For Your Reading Log*

1. Can you remember an experience in which an adult—a parent, teacher, or adult friend—was trying to teach you something you didn't want to learn? Take a few minutes to write in your reading log about your memories of resisting this adult lesson.

2. As you read through this story, mark passages that seem key in the unfolding of the plot.

———————   •   ———————

Back in the days when everyone was old and stupid or young and foolish and   1
me and Sugar were the only ones just right, this lady moved on our block with
nappy hair and proper speech and no makeup. And quite naturally we laughed
at her, laughed the way we did at the junk man who went about his business like
he was some big-time president and his sorry-ass horse his secretary. And we
kinda hated her too, hated the way we did the winos who cluttered up our
parks and pissed on our handball walls and stank up our hallways and stairs so
you couldn't halfway play hide-and-seek without a goddamn gas mask. Miss
Moore was her name. The only woman on the block with no first name. And she
was black as hell, cept for her feet, which were fish-white and spooky. And she
was always planning these boring-ass things for us to do, us being my cousin,
mostly, who lived on the block cause we all moved North the same time and to
the same apartment then spread out gradual to breathe. And our parents would
yank our heads into some kinda shape and crisp up our clothes so we'd be presentable for travel with Miss Moore, who always looked like she was going to
church, though she never did. Which is just one of the things the grown-ups
talked about when they talked behind her back like a dog. But when she came
calling with some sachet she'd sewed up or some gingerbread she'd made or
some book, why then they'd all be too embarrassed to turn her down and we'd

get handed over all spruced up. She'd been to college and said it was only right that she should take responsibility for the young ones' education, and she not even related by marriage or blood. So they'd go for it. Specially Aunt Gretchen. She was the main gofer in the family. You got some ole dumb shit foolishness you want somebody to go for, you send for Aunt Gretchen. She been screwed into the goalong for so long, it's a blood-deep natural thing with her. Which is how she got saddled with me and Sugar and Junior in the first place while our mothers were in a la-de-da apartment up the block having a good ole time.

2   So this one day Miss Moore rounds us all up at the mailbox and it's puredee hot and she's knocking herself out about arithmetic. And school suppose to let up in summer I heard, but she don't never let up. And the starch in my pinafore scratching the shit outta me and I'm really hating this nappy-head bitch and her goddamn college degree. I'd much rather go to the pool or to the show where it's cool. So me and Sugar leaning on the mailbox being surly, which is a Miss Moore word. And Flyboy checking out what everybody brought for lunch. And Fat Butt already wasting his peanut-butter-and-jelly sandwich like the pig he is. And Junebug punchin on Q.T.'s arm for potato chips. And Rosie Giraffe shifting from one hip to the other waiting for somebody to step on her foot or ask her if she from Georgia so she can kick ass, preferably Mercedes's. And Miss Moore asking us do we know what money is, like we a bunch of retards. I mean real money, she say, like it's only poker chips or monopoly papers we lay on the grocer. So right away I'm tired of this and say so. And would much rather snatch Sugar and go to the Sunset and terrorize the West Indian kids and take their hair ribbons and their money too. And Miss Moore files that remark away for next week's lesson on brotherhood, I can tell. And finally I say we oughta get to the subway cause it's cooler and besides we might meet some cute boys. Sugar done swiped her mama's lipstick, so we ready.

3   So we heading down the street and she's boring us silly about what things cost and what our parents make and how much goes for rent and how money ain't divided up right in this country. And then she gets to the part about we all poor and live in the slums, which I don't feature. And I'm ready to speak on that, but she steps out in the street and hails two cabs just like that. Then she hustles half the crew in with her and hands me a five-dollar bill and tells me to calculate 10 percent tip for the driver. And we're off. Me and Sugar and Junebug and Flyboy hanging out the window and hollering to everybody, putting lipstick on each other cause Flyboy a faggot anyway, and making farts with our sweaty armpits. But I'm mostly trying to figure how to spend this money. But they all fascinated with the meter ticking and Junebug starts laying bets as to how much it'll read when Flyboy can't hold his breath no more. Then Sugar lay bets as to how much it'll be when we get there. So I'm stuck. Don't nobody want to go for my plan, which is to jump out at the next light and run off to the first bar-b-que we can find. Then the driver tells us to get the hell out cause we there already. And the meter reads eight-five cents. And I'm stalling to figure out the tip and Sugar say give him a dime. And I decide he don't need it bad as I do, so later for him. But then he tries to take off with Junebug's foot still in the door so we talk about his mama something ferocious. Then we check out that we on Fifth Av-

enue and everybody dressed up in stockings. One lady in a fur coat, hot as it is. White folks crazy.

"This is the place," Miss Moore say, presenting it to us in the voice she uses 4 at the museum. "Let's look in the windows before we go in."

"Can we steal?" Sugar asks very serious like she's getting the ground rules 5 squared away before she plays. "I beg your pardon," say Miss Moore, and we fall out. So she leads us around the windows of the toy store and me and Sugar screamin, "This is mine, that's mine, I gotta have that, that was made for me, I was born for that," till Big Butt drowns us out.

"Hey, I'm going to buy that there."   6

"That there? You don't even known what it is, stupid."   7

"I do so," he say punchin on Rosie Giraffe. "It's a microscope."   8

"Whatcha gonna do with a microscope, fool?"   9

"Look at things."   10

"Like what, Ronald?" ask Miss Moore. And Big Butt ain't got the first notion. 11 So here go Miss Moore gabbing about the thousands of bacteria in a drop of water and the somethinorother in a speck of blood and the million and one living things in the air around us is invisible to the naked eye. And what she say that for? Junebug go to town on that "naked" and we rolling. Then Miss Moore ask what it cost. So we all jam into the window smudgin it up and the price tag say three hundred dollars. So then she ask how long'd take for Big Butt and Junebug to save up their allowances. "Too long," I say. "Yeh," adds Sugar, "outgrown it by that time." And Miss Moore say no, you never outgrow learning instruments. "Why, even medical students and interns and," blah, blah, blah. And we ready to choke Big Butt for bringing it up in the first damn place.

"This here costs four hundred eighty dollars," say Rosie Giraffe. So we pile 12 up all over her to see what she pointin out. My eyes tell me it's a chunk of glass cracked with something heavy, and different-color inks dripped into the splits, then the whole thing put into a oven or something. But for $480 it don't make sense.

"That's a paperweight made of semi-precious stones fused together under 13 tremendous pressure," she explains slowly, with her hands doing the mining and all the factory work.

"So what's a paperweight?" asks Rosie Giraffe.   14

"To weigh paper with, dumbbell," say Flyboy, the wise man from the East.   15

"Not exactly," say Miss Moore, which is what she say when you warm or 16 way off too. "It's to weigh paper down so it won't scatter and make your desk untidy." So right away me and Sugar curtsy to each other and then to Mercedes who is more the tidy type.

"We don't keep paper on top of the desk in my class," say Junebug, figuring 17 Miss Moore crazy or lyin one.

"At home, then," she say. "Don't you have a calendar and a pencil case and 18 a blotter and a letter-opener on your desk at home where you do your homework?" And she know damn well what our homes look like cause she nosys around in them every chance she gets.

"I don't even have a desk," say Junebug, "Do we?"   19

20   "No. And I don't get no homework neither," says Big Butt.

21   "And I don't even have a home," say Flyboy like he do at school to keep the white folks off his back and sorry for him. Send this poor kid to camp posters, is his specialty.

22   "I do," says Mercedes. "I have a box of stationery on my desk and a picture of my cat. My godmother bought the stationery and the desk. There's a big rose on each sheet and the envelopes smell like roses."

23   "Who wants to know about your smelly-ass stationery," say Rosie Giraffe fore I can get my two cents in.

24   "It's important to have a work area all your own so that . . ."

25   "Will you look at this sailboat, please," say Flyboy, cuttin her off and pointin to the thing like it was his. So once again we tumble all over each other to gaze at this magnificent thing in the toy store which is just big enough to maybe sail two kittens across the pond if you strap them to the posts tight. We all start reciting the price tag like we in assembly. "Handcrafted sailboat of fiberglass at one thousand one hundred ninety-five dollars."

26   "Unbelievable," I hear myself say and am really stunned. I read it again for myself just in case the group recitation put me in a trance. Same thing. For some reason this pisses me off. We look at Miss Moore and she lookin at us, waiting for I dunno what.

27   "Who'd pay all that when you can buy a sailboat set for a quarter at Pop's, a tube of glue for a dime, and a ball of string for eight cents? It must have a motor and a whole lot else besides," I say. "My sailboat cost me about fifty cents."

28   "But will it take water?" say Mercedes with her smart ass.

29   "Took mine to Alley Pond Park once," say Flyboy. "String broke. Lost it. Pity."

30   "Sailed mine in Central Park and it keeled over and sank. Had to ask my father for another dollar."

31   "And you got the strap," laugh Big Butt. "The jerk didn't even have a string on it. My old man whaled on his behind."

32   Little Q.T. was staring hard at the sailboat and you could see he wanted it bad. But he too little and somebody'd just take it from him. So what the hell. "This boat for kids, Miss Moore?"

33   "Parents silly to buy something like that just to get all broke up," say Rosie Giraffe.

34   "That much money it should last forever," I figure.

35   "My father'd buy it for me if I wanted it."

36   "Your father, my ass," say Rosie Giraffe getting a chance to finally push Mercedes.

37   "Must be rich people shop here," say Q.T.

38   "You are a very bright boy," say Flyboy. "What was your first clue?" And he rap him on the head with the back of his knuckles, since Q.T. the only one he could get away with. Though Q.T. liable to come up behind you years later and get his licks in when you half expect it.

39   "What I want to know is," I says to Miss Moore though I never talk to her, I wouldn't give the bitch that satisfaction, "is how much a real boat costs? I figure a thousand'd get you a yacht any day."

"Why don't you check that out," she says, "and report back to the group?" 40
Which really pains my ass. If you gonna mess up a perfectly good swim day least
you could do is have some answers. "Let's go in," she say like she got something
up her sleeve. Only she don't lead the way. So me and Sugar turn the corner to
where the entrance is, but when we get there I kinda hang back. Not that I'm
scared, what's there to be afraid of, just a toy store. But I feel funny, shame. But
what I got to be shamed about? Got as much right to go in as anybody. But somehow I can't seem to get hold of the door, so I step away for Sugar to lead. But she
hangs back too. And I look at her and she looks at me and this is ridiculous. I
mean, damn, I have never ever been shy about doing nothing or going nowhere.
But then Mercedes steps up and then Rosie Giraffe and Big Butt crowd in behind
and shove, and next thing we all stuffed into the doorway with only Mercedes
squeezing past us, smoothing out her jumper and walking right down the aisle.
Then the rest of us tumble in like a glued-together jigsaw done all wrong. And
people lookin at us. And it's like the time me and Sugar crashed into the Catholic
church on a dare. But once we got in there and everything so hushed and holy
and the candles and the bowin and the handkerchiefs on all the drooping heads,
I just couldn't go through with the plan. Which was for me to run up to the altar and do a tap dance while Sugar played the nose flute and messed around in
the holy water. And Sugar kept givin me the elbow. Then later teased me so bad
I tied her up in the shower and turned it on and locked her in. And she'd be there
till this day if Aunt Gretchen hadn't finally figured I was lying about the boarder
takin a shower.

Same thing in the store. We all walkin on tiptoe and hardly touchin the games 41
and puzzles and things. And I watched Miss Moore who is steady watchin us like
she waiting for a sign. Like Mama Drewery watches the sky and sniffs the air and
takes note of just how much slant is in the bird formation. Then me and Sugar
bump smack into each other, so busy gazing at the toys, 'specially the sailboat. But
we don't laugh and go into our fat-lady bump-stomach routine. We just stare at
that price tag. Then Sugar run a finger over the whole boat. And I'm jealous and
want to hit her. Maybe not her, but I sure want to punch somebody in the mouth.

"Whatcha bring us here for, Miss Moore?" 42

"You sound angry, Sylvia. Are you mad about something?" Givin me one of 43
them grins like she tellin a grown-up joke that never turns out to be funny. And
she's lookin very closely at me like maybe she planning to do my portrait from
memory. I'm mad, but I won't give her that satisfaction. So I slouch around the
store bein very bored and say, "Let's go."

Me an Sugar at the back of the train watchin the tracks whizzin by large then 44
small then gettin gobbled up in the dark. I'm thinkin about this tricky toy I saw
in the store. A clown that somersaults on a bar then does chin-ups just cause you
yank lightly at his leg. Cost $35. I could see me askin my mother for a $35 birthday clown. "You wanna who that costs what?" she'd say, cocking her head to the
side to get a better view of the hole in my head. Thirty-five dollars could buy new
bunk beds for Junior and Gretchen's boy. Thirty-five dollars and the whole
household could go visit Granddaddy Nelson in the country. Thirty-five dollars
would pay for the rent and the piano bill too. Who are these people that spend

that much for performing clowns and $1,000 for toy sailboats? What kinda work they do and how they live and how come we ain't in on it? Where we are is who we are, Miss Moore always pointin out. But it don't necessarily have to be that way, she always adds then waits for somebody to say that poor people have to wake up and demand their share of the pie and don't none of us know what kind of pie she talkin about in the first damn place. But she ain't so smart cause I still got her four dollars from the taxi and she sure ain't getting it. Messin up my day with this shit. Sugar nudges me in my pocket and winks.

45   Miss Moore lines us up in front of the mailbox where we started from, seem like years ago, and I got a headache for thinkin so hard. And we lean all over each other so we can hold up under the draggy-ass lecture she always finishes us off with at the end before we thank her for borin us to tears. But she just looks at us like she readin tea leaves. Finally she say, "Well, what do you think of F.A.O. Schwarz?"

46   Rosie Giraffe mumbles, "White folks crazy."

47   "I'd like to go there again when I get my birthday money," says Mercedes, and we shove her out the pack so she has to lean on the mailbox by herself.

48   "I'd like a shower. Tiring day," says Flyboy.

49   Then Sugar surprises me by sayin, "You know, Miss Moore, I don't think all of us here put together eat in a year what that sailboat costs." And Miss Moore lights up like somebody goosed her. "And?" she say, urging Sugar on. Only I'm standin on her foot so she don't continue.

50   "Imagine for a minute what kind of society it is in which some people can spend on a toy what it would cost to feed a family of six or seven. What do you think?"

51   "I think," say Sugar pushing me off her feet like she never done before, cause I whip her ass in a minute, "that this is not much of a democracy if you ask me. Equal chance to pursue happiness means an equal crack at the dough, don't it?" Miss Moore is besides herself and I am disgusted with Sugar's treachery. So I stand on her foot one more time to see if she'll shove me. She shuts up, and Miss Moore looks at me, sorrowfully I'm thinkin. And somethin weird is goin on. I can feel it in my chest.

52   "Anybody else learn anything today?" lookin dead at me. I walk away and Sugar has to run to catch up and don't even seem to notice when I shrug her arm off my shoulder.

53   "Well, we got four dollars anyway," she says.

54   "Uh-hunh."

55   "We could go to Hascombs and get half a chocolate layer and then go to the Sunset and still have plenty money for potato chips and ice cream sodas."

56   "Uh-hunh."

57   "Race you to Hascombs," she say.

58   We start down the block and she gets ahead which is OK by me cause I'm going to the West End and then over to the Drive to think this day through. She can run if she want to and even run faster. But ain't nobody gonna beat me at nuthin.

● *Thinking Critically About "The Lesson"*

RESPONDING AS A READER

1. The story is narrated from the point of view of Sylvia, though she is re-counting this story some time after the event, after the "days when everyone was old and stupid or young and foolish and me and Sugar were the only ones just right." What does this line suggest about how the narrator's perspective has changed over time? What details of the story seem to be from this older, wiser perspective? What details from the narrator's perspective as a young child?

2. What other perspectives, besides the narrator's, are introduced? What do these other perspectives add to the story?

3. Consult your reading log notes, and construct a map or outline of the plot. Since plots usually involve some kind of conflict, how would you define the conflicts that set this story in motion? What is Sylvia's initial attitude toward the outing to F.A.O. Schwartz? What is her attitude toward Miss Moore and her attempts to educate the children and refine their behavior? What is the climactic moment or turning point in the story? How do you interpret the denouement or the outcome of the plot?

RESPONDING AS A WRITER

1. Look carefully at the language of the story, particularly the use of dialect and humor. Find three or four particular passages that you find espe-cially effective, and write about what these uses of language contribute to the story.

2. How do you interpret the meaning of the title? Reread the passages in which the characters discuss the microscope, paperweight, and sailboat. What lesson or lessons are being taught in these passages? What lesson or lessons are learned by the end of story? By whom? Use evidence from the text to back up your answer.

3. When Sylvia enters F.A.O. Schwartz, she feels uncharacteristically shy and ashamed. Why does she have these feelings? How are these feelings connected to the lesson or lessons she learns?

Geoffrey Miller

Waste Is Good

Evolutionary psychologist Geoffrey Miller is a senior research fellow at the Economic and Social Research Council in Britain. Miller has written numerous scholarly articles on subjects such as evolutionary psychology, sexual selection theory, evolutionary simulations, and the psychology of marketing, advertising, and consumer behavior. A recent book is entitled *Courting Minds.* In February 1999, "Waste Is Good" was published in *Prospect*, a British journal, which advertises itself as *"the* magazine for the intellectually curious general reader who appreciates finely written essays across the spectrum of political, intellectual, and cultural debate."

● ***For Your Reading Log***

  1. Geoffrey Miller's field of expertise is evolutionary psychology, a highly specialized field that may be unfamiliar to you. What predictions can you make about the essay's content given the blurb that follows the title?

     Evolutionists used to be puzzled by the wastefulness of the peacock's tail. Now they believe that almost everything in nature that we find beautiful or impressive has been shaped by wasteful sexual display. Sexual display also lies at the root of culture, consciousness and modern consumerism.

  2. This essay will require close reading, and you may have difficulty understanding Miller's arguments the first time you read the essay. Mark passages that you find difficult to understand and formulate questions about them. After you have finished reading, look up the terms and references you did not understand.

—————   ●   —————

¹ At the top of Sennheiser's range is the "Orpheus Set," stereo headphones which retail for £9,652. They are finely crafted headphones, no doubt. But to most ears, they deliver a sound quality not greatly superior to a pair of £25 Vivanco SR250s, which have received several "best value" awards. As an evolutionary psychologist considering contemporary human culture, I wonder this: why would evolution produce a species of anthropoid ape that feels it simply must have the Sennheisers, when the Vivancos would stimulate its ears just as well?

² The standard Darwinian account of consumerism is that natural selection shaped us to have certain preferences and desires which free markets fulfil by providing various goods and services. For example, sugars were rare and nutritionally valuable in Pleistocene Africa, so we evolved a taste for sweets, which

chocolate and cola manufacturers now fulfil—or perhaps exploit. This theory can explain many features of many products, and seems to give the Darwinian seal of approval to free-market consumerism.

However, this theory of evolved preferences can't explain the Sennheiser effect. 3 The nominal function of stereo headphones is to deliver a private soundscape, an acoustic virtual reality. We might expect headphones to be judged and priced in proportion to their sound quality. But they are not. The marketing people at Sennheiser know that Orpheus Sets are bought mainly by rich men, young or middle-aged, who are on the mating market, openly or tacitly. Their 400-times greater cost than the Vivancos is a courtship premium. While the Vivancos are merely good headphones, the Sennheisers are peacock's tails and nightingale's songs. Buyers of many top-of-the-range products understand that their price is a benefit, not a cost. It keeps poorer buyers from owning the product, thereby making it a reliable indicator of a possessor's wealth and taste. We want Sennheisers not for the sounds they make in our heads, but for the impressions they make in the heads of others.

Thorstein Veblen understood all this a century ago, with his theory of con- 4 spicuous consumption, outlined in *The Theory of the Leisure Class*. Yet Veblen's sociological insight did not connect in any obvious way with natural science. This missing link can now be made via a branch of evolutionary biology called sexual selection theory.

From this biological viewpoint, consumerism is what happens when a smart 5 ape, evolved for sexual self-promotion, attains the ability to transform the raw material of nature into a network of sexual signals and status displays. It transmutes a world made of quarks into a world of tiny, unconscious courtship acts— every signal becomes sexual. Yet most sexual signals go unrecognised and unreciprocated. The result is the phenomenon we call modern civilisation, with its glory and progress, to be sure, but also with its colossal waste and incalculable alienation. The alienation of the modern consumer, the disappointment that sets in when the Sennheisers fail to deliver what they promise (not good sounds, but good mates) is not new. It may simply represent a deeper alienation of our selves from our sexual displays.

Understanding consumerism requires understanding a little bit about the evo- 6 lutionary process of sexual selection. Sexual selection is basically what happens when sexually-reproducing animals pick their sexual partners according to criteria which are consistent across generations. Darwin first realised that if peahens consistently prefer to mate with peacocks which have tails brighter and longer than average, then peacock tails must evolve to be ever brighter and longer over evolutionary time. Peacock genes, no matter how useful for survival, can only make it into the next generation if they are carried in peacock bodies with long, bright tails. Thus, sexual selection can be even more powerful than selection for survival itself. Evolution is driven not just by survival of the fittest, but reproduction of the sexiest.

Many sexually-selected traits, such as peacock tails, whale songs and male hu- 7 man aggressiveness, are so costly in time, energy and risk, that they severely reduce survival chances, but evolved, none the less, for their reproductive benefits.

Until recently, biologists assumed that these costs of sexually-selected traits were incidental to their courtship function. But Israeli biologist Amotz Zahavi has been winning many converts to his view that these costs are an adaptive feature rather than a maladaptive fault of sexual signals. His book, *The Handicap Principle* (1997), argues that sexually-selected traits, such as peacock tails, *must* be costly handicaps in order to be reliable indicators of an animal's fitness as a potential mate and parent.

8   Zahavi's "handicap principle" identifies a tension between natural selection (for survival) and sexual selection (for attracting mates), and waste is at the heart of that tension. Waste in sexual displays guarantees that there will be some correlation between survival ability and reproductive success. On the one hand, waste is the bridge between natural and sexual selection: only the healthiest peacocks can develop big tails. But it is also the chasm between them: the tail's wastefulness, its uselessness for survival, is precisely what makes it a sexual trait.

9   Zahavi's logic is the same as Veblen's conspicuous consumption. If big, bright, peacock tails were cheap to grow, easy to maintain and light to carry around, any old peacock could sport one, no matter how unhealthy, hungry or parasite-ridden he was. The tails would carry no information about peacock quality if they carried no increased costs. In Zahavi's view, the real reason why peacock tails are so big, bright, heavy and cumbersome, is that only very healthy, fit, strong, well-fed peacocks can afford such tails. Because very fit peacocks tend to have fit sons and daughters which are more likely to survive and reproduce, peahens benefit by choosing big-tailed peacocks. Peahens which preferred shorter-than-average tails did not leave many descendants, because their offspring were less fit than average. Large peacock tails, like luxury Sennheiser headphones, are specifically designed not to be affordable by every individual. So, sexual selection favours both the preference for costly sexual displays, and the displays themselves.

10   The handicap principle suggests that prodigious waste is a necessary feature of sexual courtship. A clever peahen who read Veblen would understand that peacocks as a species would be better off if they didn't have to waste so much energy growing big tails (which are useless for survival). But as individual males and females, they have irresistible incentives to grow the biggest tails they can afford, or to choose sexual partners with the biggest tails they can attract (in order to ensure mating success). In nature, showy waste is the only guarantee of truth in advertising.

11   Conspicuous consumption is the modern human analogue of the peacock's tail: a handicap that reveals quality by wasting resources. Consumerism is a sort of ritualisation of conspicuous consumption, where people display their wealth and taste by owning widely recognised products of well-known cost.

12   Advertising based on image, as opposed to product features, attempts to create a sexual-signalling niche for each such product. This requires demonstrating a three-way relationship between product, potential consumer, and pool of potential mates appreciating the act of consumption. The cola advert must show the cola, the cola-buyer and the cola-buyer-watcher. It must pretend that it is al-

ready common knowledge that drinking the cola is cool, in order for the cola to qualify as an effective sexual signal. The advertising must lift the product from unrecognised thing to consensual object of desire.

The difficulties in comprehending this leap of faith are similar to the diffi- 13 culties that evolutionary biologists had, for over a century, in understanding how peacock's tails could evolve. Logically, there seems nowhere for the process to get off the ground. If peahens didn't already prefer long bright tails, why should males evolve them? But if males didn't already have long bright tails, why should females prefer them? Likewise, if women don't already prefer men who drive Porsches, why should any men buy Porsches? But if no men drive Porsches, why should women develop any preference for Porsche-drivers? The history of sexual selection theory is the story of how biologists solved this chicken-and-egg problem. Details aside, the answer is that evolution does it gradually, through continuous escalation of both mate preferences (analogous to consumer tastes) and courtship traits (analogous to product quality).

Yet the cultural evolution of products as sexual signals need not follow the 14 same gradual dynamics as the genetic evolution of peacock tails. Mass advertising can jump-start the process by showing fake men (actors) driving not-yet-available Porsches, and fake women winking at them. The whole signaling system based on the product can be posited, all at once, in the virtual reality of advertising before a single product is sold or a single sexual prospect is impressed.

When we buy a product because of image-based advertising, we buy into a 15 sexual signaling system. But it is a hypothetical system, not a real one. It was invented by a few advertising executives for a client's profits. It was not evolved over millions of years by our ancestors to improve their children's fitness. This can create problems. Gullible people may act as if the hypothetical signal system had already been accepted as real. They may spend more time displaying virtual signals (advertised products) than real, biologically validated signals (wit, creativity, kindness). They may become frustrated when their virtual signals are ignored, and may increase their shopping rather than improve their character. The result can be pathological, a runaway consumerism in which an individual gets lost in a semiotic wilderness, searching for sexual signalling systems in all the wrong places.

This analysis raises another fundamental question: what is the link between 16 biological fitness and monetary wealth in modern societies? Clearly, one's ability to buy things is a reliable indicator of one's wealth, but is wealth a reliable indicator of fitness? Politically, the right has posited a tight relationship between monetary wealth and biological fitness, and the left has denied such a link. The right views money as liquid fitness, accumulated by virtue of innate, heritable biological abilities such as intelligence and ambition, and translated into manifest symbols of success. The left puts money in a domain of culture, class and history supposedly divorced from biology. Scientifically, the relationship between wealth and fitness remains unresolved. The right cites the high correlation between intelligence and wealth, and the strong contribution of genetics to intelligence. The left points out that according to the standard biological measure of fitness— number of offspring—the rich and bright do not show higher fitness than the poor or the uneducated; indeed, it is often the opposite. So perhaps consumerism

derives from sexual-display instincts which evolved under earlier, more polygamous, conditions.

17   As we have seen, one problem with consumerism is that advertising can raise
unrealistic expectations about the sexual signaling power of products. Another
problem is that even the most effective signals cannot improve everyone's mating success. Sexual competition is a zero-sum game. Some individuals attract
good mates; others don't. Heartbreak is inevitable, given that human mating requires mutual consent, and given that people differ markedly in physical, mental and social attractiveness. Not every man can command a harem of 5,000 like
the first emperor of China. Not every woman can cycle through eight husbands
like Elizabeth Taylor.

18   Yet, if the costs of sending sexual signals become very high, a society's mating system can become a negative-sum game, costing everyone more time,
money, effort and risk. Two generations ago, Japanese couples did not bother
with buying engagement rings. Then the De Beers diamond cartel, through an
advertising campaign in the 1970s, convinced Japanese women that they de-
served a ring just like western women. A new standard was imposed: Japanese
men must spend at least two months' salary on a colourless lump of carbon to
demonstrate their romantic commitment. Japanese marriages are probably no
happier than a generation ago, but De Beers is richer.

19   In thousands of such cases, consumerism leads to costlier signals of wealth,
more taxing signals of taste and riskier signals of physical courage. They are endless treadmills of personal mating effort, often without social benefit. Sexual
competition is one domain where improved technology does not usually improve average human welfare.

20   The sexual-signaling imperatives of consumerism introduce another form of
waste: they give consumers little incentive to get good value for their money.
Britain seems strangely comfortable with its oligopolies, cartels and retail-price-
maintenance agreements. These artificially inflate the price of cars, clothes, books
and consumer electronics by up to 50 per cent above their prices in the US. If the
point of buying a Porsche is to get a good A-to-B machine for the money, these
cartels seem pathological. But if the point is to advertise one's wealth and status, it does not much matter how the prices are set. As long as the prices are common knowledge in the mating market, each car model reliably signals the
owner's wealth level. In sexual signaling, price differences are much more important than absolute prices. But in human welfare terms, the reverse is true. Sexual signaling undermines economic efficiency. Marketing products as courtship
gifts gives businesses and governments great power over the buyers of those
products, because it makes consumer activism look like the economic equivalent
of erectile dysfunction. Only those who can't afford them complain about the un-
fairness of the prices and the taxes.

21   As one moves from courtship gifts to more pragmatic consumption, prices
drop, profits fall and free-market competitiveness takes hold. Cultures differ in
the boundaries they draw between courtship goods and ordinary goods. Yet
every culture retains a core of courtship products or luxury goods with which people fall in love, conspicuously casting aside their roles as rational economic agents.

Humans are unusual because both men and women buy these courtship 22
products. In most species, especially most mammals, conspicuous sexual display
is a male activity. The traditional biological view can explain why men buy be-
spoke suits, sports cars and country houses, but not why any women would ever
love to shop. However, biologists are adding some nuances to Darwin's view of
the active male courting the passive female. New research reveals that male animals of many species are choosier about their sexual partners than Darwin suspected, and females of many species have evolved their own versions of wasteful
sexual display. The female baboon's bright red genital swelling serves the same
function as the peacock's tail. In our species, sexual choice is mutual and sexual
display is mutual, so both sexes can be seen at the January sales.

Veblen's biographers often argue that his contempt for conspicuous consump- 23
tion reflects the frugality of his Norwegian ancestors encountering America's
Gilded Age. Sub-Arctic, subsistence protestantism meets Boston, bourgeois luxury—and shakes its head in disapproval. Veblen claimed that he used "waste"
as a neutral term, but his indignation at consumerist signalling shows through
every example he analyses. Must we follow his moral crusade against waste?

Evolutionary theorists did so for many decades and, until recently, it kept 24
them from understanding sexual selection. Veblen's peak was Darwin's trough.
By 1900, sexual selection theory was viewed as Darwin's worst blunder. Then,
in the 1930s, the biologists of the Modern Synthesis combined Darwinian selection theory and Mendelian genetics. The great synthesisers such as Julian Hux-
ley, Ernst Mayr and JBS Haldane recognised that sexual selection could produce
extravagant, wasteful signals, but they did not approve of such profligacy. They
thought that it was bad for the species, bad for evolutionary progress and generally pathological. Their disdain for the biological waste of courtship was identical to Veblen's disdain for the cultural waste of consumerism. They revived
natural selection, but left sexual selection to rot for another 50 years. Even when
Zahavi first proposed his "handicap principle" more than two decades ago, biologists couldn't believe that nature could favour such wasteful signaling.

Like Veblen, most evolutionary biologists embraced a machine aesthetic that 25
celebrated efficiency, good engineering and form following function. Veblen
shared HG Wells's vision of a technocratic utopia run by enlightened engineers,
from which all traces of conspicuous signaling and invidious comparison were
eradicated. But the revival of sexual selection has changed all that. Many evolu-
tionists now recognise that almost everything in nature which we find beautiful
or impressive has been shaped for wasteful display, not for pragmatic efficiency.
Flowers, fruits, butterfly wings, bowerbird nests, nightingale songs, mandrill
faces, elephant tusks, elk antlers, humpback whale songs, firefly lights, fiddler
crab claws, lion manes, swordfish tails and human language have all been shaped
by sexual selection. Waste can be fun. Sexual signaling can be sublime. Evolution
for invidious comparison can be creative rather than pathological. Modern evo-
lutionists have become more comfortable in celebrating wasteful signalling.

In fact, because each sexually-reproducing species can be viewed as a dif- 26
ferent sexual signalling system, the proliferation of these systems is what creates
biodiversity itself. Without so many varieties of waste, our planet would not host

so many species. There may be a hidden irony in an environmentalism which worships biodiversity but despises consumerism: what if both result from the same imperatives of sexual signalling?

27   Contra Veblen, consumerist waste has some overlooked benefits. Courtship products bought in a money-based economy have unusual features which make them less wasteful than most sexual signals. First, being material objects, they last longer than the courtship dances, songs and ritual combats of most species. Once our species started using material culture for sexual display, we could accumulate and even inherit large numbers of objects that improve not just our status, but our quality of life. Consumer durables such as houses, cars and appliances, acquired partially for sexual display, stick around long after courtship ends.

28   More importantly, consumerism entails a social circulation of value rather than a solo act of waste. Compare the peacock's tail to a Porsche. Both are expensive to their displayer. But when the peacock pays the growth and maintenance costs of his tail, he doesn't transfer any value to any other member of his species. He simply burns the energy, and the energy is gone. By contrast, when the Porsche-buyer pays for the car, he transfers money to the seller, who transfers some to the manufacturer, and hence to the manufacturer's employees and shareholders. The only real waste in the production of the Porsche is whatever extra steel, leather, fuel, labour and human ingenuity goes into its production compared to an ordinary car. Its price premium is not waste in any broader social sense, because the price is transferred to others within society.

29   This is an important effect. Ever since the automation of agriculture and manufacturing, an increasing number of us have been employed, directly or indirectly, to produce wasteful consumerist displays for other people. If an asexual species invented automation, most of them would lose their jobs permanently. They would have no domain of waste to soak up the material surplus their technology gives them. In our sexual species, the demand for wasteful sexual displays is unbounded, so we need never fear mass permanent unemployment, as long as consumerism persists.

30   Consumerism redistributes not just money, but status. Advertising posits products as sexual signals, but the product-buyers are not the only people to benefit from a product's sexual status. The status trickles out in all directions, along the entire chain of production and consumption. Porsche advertises. Buyers of new Porsches reap the status benefits of that advertising. But so do Porsche salesmen, Porsche executives, Porsche factory workers, Porsche shareholders, Porsche mechanics, receivers of gift Porsches, and buyers and inheritors of used Porsches. Although a physical product can only be owned by one individual, its sexual status value can be enjoyed by anyone associated with its production, financing, marketing or consumption. In this sense, consumerism automatically redistributes sexual status from the wealthy to the suppliers of their status. This lends consumerism an egalitarian aspect utterly alien to sexual competition in most species.

31   This more positive attitude towards wasteful signalling may be good for the scientific analysis of waste, but is it the best attitude for fostering sustainable human societies? Surprisingly, biology suggests that the answer may be yes. All

sexually-reproducing animals face a trade-off between courtship effort and parenting effort. The more time and energy you waste on showing how sexy you are, the less time and energy you have for raising offspring.

The same trade-off seems to hold for humans. With the industrial revolution, urbanisation and the rapid increase in consumerism came the demographic transition: a dramatic reduction in numbers of children. Sexual competition intensified so much that the products of sexual reproduction were delayed. Consumerism is soaking up the time and energy that our ancestors used to devote to having large families. Instead of spending our 20s taking care of our first six toddlers, as our ancestors would have done, we spend our 20s acquiring a university education, launching our careers, buying stuff, going to movies, taking vacations and worrying about status. Conspicuous consumption or conspicuous children, it is difficult to attend to both.   32

A well-intentioned, Veblenesque reduction in the waste of sexual signalling might reverse the demographic transition and create a population explosion. People like to keep busy. If a state decided to eliminate conspicuous consumption by outlawing luxury goods, costly entertainment, status differences between occupations and so on, people might just marry younger and pump out more offspring. In fact, eliminating conspicuous consumption and other forms of wasteful sexual signalling would mean eliminating most of what we consider to be human culture. It would roll back the evolutionary clock a couple of million years, trying to recreate an Australopithecine lifestyle of small-brained primates bored to death, and surrounded by babies.   33

It is not difficult for evolution to achieve mere sustainability. Trilobites flourished for hundreds of millions of years, enjoying their low-consumption, low-waste, sexually unsophisticated lifestyle. They were a model of Veblenesque rationality and efficiency. But waste is what makes things interesting.   34

For at least a million years, our species has been engaged in a great evolutionary experiment: to explore the wonderland of wasteful sexual signalling. An increasing number of evolutionary psychologists believe that many aspects of the human mind were shaped by sexual selection. In my view, language, art, music, humour and clothing were the first of our new wasteful signals to evolve. Other varieties of sexual waste—religion, philosophy, literature—followed.   35

The last century has seen a dramatic increase in a new form of sexual waste: conspicuous consumption, which translates a primordial logic of how to show off from biology to technology. This brings some problems, as we have seen. We may too easily forget our innate biological capacities for display—language, creativity, intelligence. We may rely too much on Sennheisers. But perhaps our critiques of consumerism go too far when they condemn waste in general, as Veblen did. Sexual waste is what made our species what it is. We are creatures of waste, evolved to burn off our time, our energy, our very lives to show that we can do so better than our sexual competitors. The human brain, that most expensively wasteful organ, that ultimate biological luxury, is our original bonfire of the vanities.   36

Human consciousness itself may have evolved partly through sexual selection as a sort of wasteful display. Suppose, during the evolution of language, that our ancestors chose mates who were better able to articulate a wider range   37 of perceptions and concepts. That new criterion of mate choice would dramatically speed up the development of language and consciousness. Such a process would not make the mindless principles of sexual signalling any more rational, or conscious. But rather than consciousness evolving as a neutral executive that co-ordinates our behaviour and experiences, it may have evolved as a showpiece, an amusement park designed to entertain others. Full of sound and fury, it may signify nothing more than our biological fitness, to those who consider merging their genes with ours.

38   If used vigorously and frequently, the mind often delivers the courtship effects it evolved to produce. It impresses potential mates with facts, memories, hopes, ambitions, sensitivities, tastes, empathies and—perhaps its greatest trick—the illusion of boundless, authentic, conscious subjectivity. To work this courtship magic, the mind convinces us that we have an authentic, conscious subjectivity, and that the contents of our consciousness are uniquely worth communicating to others.

39   The human body is a patchwork of traits evolved for survival (legs, lungs, teeth) and traits evolved for sexual attraction (breasts, buttocks, beards, penises, lips). But human consciousness may have evolved as pure display, like a peacock's tail which needs no peacock body as its anchor. Perhaps human consciousness evolved to have exactly the forms and functions required for effective courtship. Perhaps the most intimate parts of our minds evolved through our most intimate relationships. In short, consciousness may be a product rather than a factory, a wasteful status symbol perfectly adapted to its consumers by sexual selection, evolution's ingenious marketing department.

40   Where does this leave those of us who value the life of the mind? Perhaps equating ourselves with our vain, babbling, concept-spewing consciousness is no more authentic a lifestyle than identifying with an expensive, well-advertised possession. Intellectualism and consumerism may be equally alienated modes of existence, if over-identification with one's sexual signals counts as alienation.

41   This seems especially true of intellectualism in the style of the *New York Review of Books,* wherein acquaintance with a few big names (Freud, Nietzsche, Foucault, Bellow, Kristeva, Sontag, Borges) suffices to display membership in a cultural elite. These names have become the debased coinage in the libidinal economy of the bespectacled. Their ideas become mere gambits for coffee-house courtship. Europe's cultural icons are conveniently packaged as American products. Their only distinction is that they are marketed by New York book reviewers and essayists rather than New York advertising firms, and their acquisition cost is a university education rather than a price in dollars. Intellectual alienation no longer has any roots in the existentialism of Dostoevsky, Kafka or Sartre. It has become the same alienation felt by any other consumer buying products as sexual signals. And intellectual debate, too often, is carried out with the same bombast as lunching bond-dealers on the merits of Mercedes versus Porsche, or the Seychelles versus Mauritius: signallers signalling their signals are best.

Perhaps it was always thus. Philosophy originated in sophistry, competitive 42
public displays of prowess in reasoning and arguing. Universities were founded
to teach dead languages, useless rituals, and a nodding acquaintance with Aristotle to a leisured class of priests. As Veblen noted, an English degree from Oxford was the premier badge of conspicuous leisure for centuries. Only with the
rise of science have the intellectual varieties of wasteful display achieved any
cognitive link to reality or any pragmatic link to social progress. Most intellectual display throughout history may have been waste in Veblen's sense. Yet
those human achievements and insights we most value would never have been
produced without our sexual instincts for waste.

• *Thinking Critically About "Waste Is Good"*

RESPONDING AS A READER

1. Miller opens his essay with the question: "Why would evolution produce a species of anthropoid ape that feels it simply must have the
   Sennheisers [top-of-the-line headphones], when the Vivancos [a much
   cheaper brand of headphones] would stimulate its ears just as well?"
   Clearly, Miller's main interest is not in headphones per se. What role
   does this specific question play in the way he organizes the essay? What
   is the effect of calling humans "a species of anthropoid ape"? How does
   the way he poses the question presume certain kinds of answers and exclude other kinds?

2. Miller uses scientific-sounding language in paragraph 5 to explain sexual selection theory. How does this language reflect his effort to reach
   the audience defined by the magazine? What is your response as a
   reader? Try to restate his answer in everyday language.

3. Miller frequently refers to the work of Thorstein Veblen and Amotz Zahavi. Briefly summarize their key ideas—conspicuous consumption (Veblen) and the handicap principle (Zahavi)—as represented by Miller.
   How does Miller use their ideas to forward his own argument? At what
   points does he agree with them? At what points does he disagree with
   either or both of them?

RESPONDING AS A WRITER

1. After arriving at what he considers to be the answer to his question, Miller
   uses this theory to interpret phenomena such as consumerism, advertising, and human progress generally. Because he writes so authoritatively,
   it is easy to forget that the basis for his interpretations is a theory or interpretation itself, and not the only possible interpretation. Take one of his
   assertions—for example, "Conspicuous consumption is the modern human analogue of the peacock's tail: a handicap that reveals quality by
   wasting resources" (paragraph 11)—and analyze its logic. Are there other
   explanations for this phenomenon? Other factors that he doesn't mention?
   What assumptions are implicit in his assertion? Are they valid?

2. In paragraph 12, Miller offers his theory about how ads work, using the theory of sexual signaling. Find an ad that either bears out or challenges his theory, and write a brief explanation of how the ad illustrates (or refutes) Miller's theory.

3. In the last section of the article, Miller explains the benefits of "consumerist waste," which is thought by many to be negative. What are the benefits he names? Though he acknowledges that there are some negative consequences of consumerist waste, he does not specify or detail these negative consequences. What are some of those negative consequences? What groups of people or interest groups might object to Miller's emphasis on the benefits of consumerist waste?

Natalie Angier

Men, Women, Sex, and Darwin

A founding and former staff member of *Discovery* magazine, Natalie Angier (b. 1958) has been a science writer for *Time* and is currently a science writer for the *New York Times*. In 1991, she won a Pulitzer Prize for beat reporting based on ten features she had written on a variety of topics, including scorpions, sexual infidelity in the animal kingdom, and the molecular biology of the cell cycle. Her books include *Natural Obsessions* (1988) about the world of cancer research and *Woman: An Intimate Geography* (1999), a "guided tour" of the female body. "Men, Women, Sex, and Darwin," published in the *New York Times Magazine* on February 21, 1999, is taken from *Woman: An Intimate Geography*. In this essay, Angier challenges the interpretations of male-female behavior offered by evolutionary psychologists such as Geoffrey Miller, whose essay precedes this one.

• *For Your Reading Log*

1. What are your beliefs about the innate differences between males and females? What parts do culture and nature play in these differences? To what extent do you believe "biology is destiny"? Write a short entry in your reading log in which you respond to these questions.
2. Spot read Angier's essay, following the suggestions in Chapter 4 (p. 50), and make some predictions about the stance she will take in relation to the questions raised in the preceding reading log question.

———————   •   ———————

Life is short but jingles are forever. None more so, it seems, than the familiar ditty, variously attributed to William James, Ogden Nash and Dorothy Parker: "Hoggamus, higgamus, / Men are polygamous, / Higgamus, hoggamus, / Women monogamous."

Lately the pith of that jingle has found new fodder and new fans, through the explosive growth of a field known as evolutionary psychology. Evolutionary psychology professes to have discovered the fundamental modules of human nature, most notably the essential nature of man and of woman. It makes sense to be curious about the evolutionary roots of human behavior. It's reasonable to try to understand our impulses and actions by applying Darwinian logic to the problem. We're animals. We're not above the rude little prods and jests of natural and sexual selection. But evolutionary psychology as it has been disseminated across mainstream consciousness is a cranky and despotic Cyclops, its single eye glaring through an overwhelmingly masculinist lens. I say "masculinist" rather than "male" because the view of male behavior promulgated by hard-core evolutionary psychologists is as narrow and inflexible as their view of womanhood is.

3   I'm not interested in explaining to men what they really want or how they should behave. If a fellow chooses to tell himself that his yen for the fetching young assistant in his office and his concomitant disgruntlement with his aging wife make perfect Darwinian sense, who am I to argue with him? I'm only proposing here that the hard-core evolutionary psychologists have got a lot about women wrong—about some of us, anyway—and that women want more and deserve better than the cartoon Olive Oyl handed down for popular consumption.

4   The cardinal premises of evolutionary psychology of interest to this discussion are as follows: (1) Men are more promiscuous and less sexually reserved than women are. (2) Women are inherently more interested in a stable relationship than men are. (3) Women are naturally attracted to high-status men with resources. (4) Men are naturally attracted to youth and beauty. (5) Humankind's core preferences and desires were hammered out long, long ago, a hundred thousand years or more, in the legendary Environment of Evolutionary Adaptation, or E.E.A., also known as the ancestral environment, also known as the Stone Age, and they have not changed appreciably since then, nor are they likely to change in the future.

5   In sum: Higgamus, hoggamus, Pygmalionus, Playboy magazine, eternitas. Amen.

6   Hard-core evolutionary psychology types go to extremes to argue in favor of the yawning chasm that separates the innate desires of women and men. They declare ringing confirmation for their theories even in the face of feeble and amusingly contradictory data. For example: Among the cardinal principles of the evo-psycho set is that men are by nature more polygamous than women are, and much more accepting of casual, even anonymous, sex. Men can't help themselves, they say: they are always hungry for sex, bodies, novelty and nubility. Granted, men needn't act on such desires, but the drive to sow seed is there nonetheless, satyric and relentless, and woman cannot fully understand its force. David Buss, a professor of psychology at the University of Texas at Austin and one of the most outspoken of the evolutionary psychologists, says that asking a man not to lust after a pretty young woman is like telling a carnivore not to like meat.

7   At the same time, they recognize that the overwhelming majority of men and women get married, and so their theories must extend to different innate mate preferences among men and women. Men look for the hallmarks of youth, like smooth skin, full lips, and perky breasts; they want a mate who has a long childbearing career ahead of her. Men also want women who are virginal and who seem as though they'll be faithful and not make cuckolds of them. The sexy, vampy types are fine for a Saturday romp, but when it comes to choosing a marital partner, men want modesty and fidelity.

8   Women want a provider, the theory goes. They want a man who seems rich, stable and ambitious. They want to know that they and their children will be cared for. They want a man who can take charge, maybe dominate them just a little, enough to reassure them that the man is genotypically, phenotypically, eternally, a king. Women's innate preference for a well-to-do man continues to this day, the evolutionary psychologists insist, even among financially independent and professionally successful women who don't need a man as a provider. It was adap-

tive in the past to look for the most resourceful man, they say, and adaptations can't be willed away in a generation or two of putative cultural change.

And what is the evidence for these male-female verities? For the difference 9 in promiscuity quotas, the hard-cores love to raise the example of the differences between gay men and lesbians. Homosexuals are seen as a revealing population because they supposedly can behave according to the innermost impulses of their sex, untempered by the need to adjust to the demands and wishes of the opposite sex, as heterosexuals theoretically are. What do we see in this ideal study group? Just look at how gay men carry on! They are perfectly happy to have hundreds, thousands, of sexual partners, to have sex in bathhouses, in bathrooms, in Central Park. By contrast, lesbians are sexually sedate. They don't cruise sex clubs. They couple up and stay coupled, and they like cuddling and hugging more than they do serious, genitally based sex.

In the hard-core rendering of inherent male-female discrepancies in promis- 10 cuity, gay men are offered up as true men, real men, men set free to be men, while lesbians are real women, ultrawomen, acting out every woman's fantasy of love and commitment. Interestingly, though, in many neurobiology studies gay men are said to have somewhat feminized brains, with hypothalamic nuclei that are closer in size to a woman's than to a straight man's, and spatial-reasoning skills that are modest and ladylike rather than manfully robust. For their part, lesbians are posited to have somewhat masculinized brains and skills—to be sportier, more mechanically inclined, less likely to have played with dolls or tea sets when young—all as an ostensible result of exposure to prenatal androgens. And so gay men are sissy boys in some contexts and Stone Age manly men in others, while lesbians are battering rams one day and flower into the softest and most sexually divested girlish girls the next.

On the question of mate preferences, evo-psychos rely on surveys, most of 11 them compiled by David Buss. His surveys are celebrated by some, derided by others, but in any event they are ambitious—performed in 37 countries, he says, on six continents. His surveys, and others emulating them, consistently find that men rate youth and beauty as important traits in a mate, while women give comparatively greater weight to ambition and financial success. Surveys show that surveys never lie. Lest you think that women's mate preferences change with their own mounting economic clout, surveys assure us that they do not. Surveys of female medical students, according to John Marshall Townsend, of Syracuse University, indicate that they hope to marry men with an earning power and social status at least equal to and preferably greater than their own.

Perhaps all this means is that men can earn a living wage better, even now, 12 than women can. Men make up about half the world's population, but they still own the vast majority of the world's wealth—the currency, the minerals, the timber, the gold, the stocks, the amber fields of grain. In her superb book "Why So Slow?" Virginia Valian, a professor of psychology at Hunter College, lays out the extent of lingering economic discrepancies between men and women in the United States. In 1978 there were two women heading Fortune 1000 companies; in 1994, there were still two; in 1996, that number had jumped all the way to four. In 1985, 2 percent of the Fortune 1000's senior-level executives were women; by

1992, that number had hardly budged, to 3 percent. A 1990 salary and compensation survey of 799 major companies showed that of the highest-paid officers and directors, less than one-half of 1 percent were women. Ask, and he shall receive. In the United States the possession of a bachelor's degree adds $28,000 to a man's salary but only $9,000 to a woman's. A degree from a high-prestige school contributes $11,500 to a man's income but subtracts $2,400 from a woman's. If women continue to worry that they need a man's money, because the playing field remains about as level as the surface of Mars, then we can't conclude anything about innate preferences. If women continue to suffer from bag-lady syndrome even as they become prosperous, if they still see their wealth as provisional and capsizable, and if they still hope to find a man with a dependable income to supplement their own, then we can credit women with intelligence and acumen, for inequities abound.

13   There's another reason that smart, professional women might respond on surveys that they'd like a mate of their socioeconomic status or better. Smart, professional women are smart enough to know that men can be tender of ego—is it genetic?—and that it hurts a man to earn less money than his wife, and that resentment is a noxious chemical in a marriage and best avoided at any price. "A woman who is more successful than her mate threatens his position in the male hierarchy," Elizabeth Cashdan, of the University of Utah, has written. If women could be persuaded that men didn't mind their being high achievers, were in fact pleased and proud to be affiliated with them, we might predict that the women would stop caring about the particulars of their mates' income. The anthropologist Sarah Blaffer Hrdy writes that "when female status and access to resources do not depend on her mate's status, women will likely use a range of criteria, not primarily or even necessarily prestige and wealth, for mate selection." She cites a 1996 New York Times story about women from a wide range of professions—bankers, judges, teachers, journalists—who marry male convicts. The allure of such men is not their income, for you can't earn much when you make license plates for a living. Instead, it is the men's gratitude that proves irresistible. The women also like the fact that their husbands' fidelity is guaranteed. "Peculiar as it is," Hrdy writes, "this vignette of sex-reversed claustration makes a serious point about just how little we know about female choice in breeding systems where male interests are not paramount and patrilines are not making the rules."

14   Do women love older men? Do women find gray hair and wrinkles attractive on men—as attractive, that is, as a fine, full head of pigmented hair and a vigorous, firm complexion? The evolutionary psychologists suggest yes. They believe that women look for the signs of maturity in men because a mature man is likely to be a comparatively wealthy and resourceful man. That should logically include baldness, which generally comes with age and the higher status that it often confers. Yet, as Desmond Morris points out, a thinning hairline is not considered a particularly attractive state.

15   Assuming that women find older men attractive, is it the men's alpha status? Or could it be something less complimentary to the male, something like the following—that an older man is appealing not because he is powerful but because in his maturity he has lost some of his power, has become less marketable and desirable and potentially more grateful and gracious, more likely to make

a younger woman feel that there is a balance of power in the relationship? The rude little calculation is simple: He is male, I am female—advantage, man. He is older, I am younger—advantage, woman. By the same token, a woman may place little value on a man's appearance because she values something else far more: room to breathe. Who can breathe in the presence of a handsome young man, whose ego, if expressed as a vapor, would fill Biosphere II? Not even, I'm afraid, a beautiful young woman.

In the end, what is important to question, and to hold to the fire of alterna- 16 tive interpretation, is the immutability and adaptive logic of the discrepancy, its basis in our genome rather than in the ecological circumstances in which a genome manages to express itself. Evolutionary psychologists insist on the essential discordance between the strength of the sex drive in males and females. They admit that many nonhuman female primates gallivant about rather more than we might have predicted before primatologists began observing their behavior in the field—more, far more, than is necessary for the sake of reproduction. Nonetheless, the credo of the coy female persists. It is garlanded with qualifications and is admitted to be an imperfect portrayal of female mating strategies, but then, that little matter of etiquette attended to, the credo is stated once again.

"Amid the great variety of social structure in these species, the basic theme . . . 17 stands out, at least in minimal form: males seem very eager for sex and work hard to find it; females work less hard," Robert Wright says in "The Moral Animal." "This isn't to say the females don't like sex. They love it, and may initiate it. And, intriguingly, the females of the species most closely related to humans—chimpanzees and bonobos—seem particularly amenable to a wild sex life, including a variety of partners. Still, female apes don't do what male apes do: search high and low, risking life and limb, to find sex, and to find as much of it, with as many different partners, as possible; it has a way of finding them." In fact female chimpanzees do search high and low and take great risks to find sex with partners other than the partners who have a way of finding them. DNA studies of chimpanzees in West Africa show that half the offspring in a group of closely scrutinized chimpanzees turned out not to be the offspring of the resident males. The females of the group didn't rely on sex "finding" its way to them; they proactively left the local environs, under such conditions of secrecy that not even their vigilant human observers knew they had gone, and became impregnated by outside males. They did so even at the risk of life and limb—their own and those of their offspring. Male chimpanzees try to control the movements of fertile females. They'll scream at them and hit them if they think the females aren't listening. They may even kill an infant they think is not their own. We don't know why the females take such risks to philander, but they do, and to say that female chimpanzees "work less hard" than males do at finding sex does not appear to be supported by the data.

Evo-psychos pull us back and forth until we might want to sue for whiplash. 18 On the one hand we are told that women have a lower sex drive then men do. On the other hand we are told that the madonna-whore dichotomy is a universal stereotype. In every culture, there is a tendency among both men and women to adjudge women as either chaste or trampy. The chaste ones are accorded esteem. The trampy ones are consigned to the basement, a notch or two below goats in social status. A woman can't sleep around without risking terrible retribution, to her reputation, to her prospects, to her life. "Can anyone find a single culture in which women with unrestrained sexual appetites aren't viewed as more aberrant than comparably libidinous men?" Wright asks rhetorically.

19   Women are said to have lower sex drives than men, yet they are universally punished if they display evidence to the contrary—if they disobey their "natural" inclination toward a stifled libido. Women supposedly have a lower sex drive than men do, yet it is not low enough. There is still just enough of a lingering female infidelity impulse that cultures everywhere have had to gird against it by articulating a rigid dichotomy with menacing implications for those who fall on the wrong side of it. There is still enough lingering female infidelity to justify infibulation, purdah, claustration. Men have the naturally higher sex drive, yet all the laws, customs, punishments, shame, strictures, mystiques and antimystiques are aimed with full hominid fury at that tepid, sleepy, hypoactive creature, the female libido.

20   "It seems premature . . . to attribute the relative lack of female interest in sexual variety to women's biological nature alone in the face of overwhelming evidence that women are consistently beaten for promiscuity and adultery," the primatologist Barbara Smuts has written. "If female sexuality is muted compared to that of men, then why must men the world over go to extreme lengths to control and contain it?"

21   Why indeed? Consider a brief evolutionary apologia for President Clinton's adulteries written by Steven Pinker, of the Massachusetts Institute of Technology. "Most human drives have ancient Darwinian rationales," he wrote. "A prehistoric man who slept with 50 women could have sired 50 children, and would have been more likely to have descendants who inherited his tastes. A woman who slept with fifty men would have no more descendants than a woman who slept with one. Thus, men should seek quantity in sexual partners; women, quality." And isn't it so, he says, everywhere and always so? "In our society," he continues, "most young men tell researchers that they would like eight sexual partners in the next two years; most women say that they would like one." Yet would a man find the prospect of a string of partners so appealing if the following rules were applied: that no matter how much he may like a particular woman and be pleased by her performance and want to sleep with her again, he will have no say in the matter and will be dependent on her mood and good graces for all future contact; that each act of casual sex will cheapen his status and make him increasingly less attractive to other women; and that society will not wink at his randiness but rather sneer at him and think him pathetic, sullied, smaller than life? Until men are subjected to the same severe standards and threat of censure as women are, and until they are given the lower hand in a so-called casual encounter from the start, it is hard to insist with such self-satisfaction that, hey, it's natural, men like a lot of sex with a lot of people and women don't.

22   Reflect for a moment on Pinker's philandering caveman who slept with 50 women. Just how good a reproductive strategy is this chronic, random shooting of the gun? A woman is fertile only five or six days a month. Her ovulation is concealed. The man doesn't know when she's fertile. She might be in the early stages of pregnancy when he gets to her; she might still be lactating and thus not

ovulating. Moreover, even if our hypothetical Don Juan hits a day on which a woman is ovulating, the chances are around 65 percent that his sperm will fail to fertilize her egg; human reproduction is complicated, and most eggs and sperm are not up to the demands of proper fusion. Even if conception occurs, the resulting embryo has about a 30 percent chance of miscarrying at some point in gestation. In sum, each episode of fleeting sex has a remarkably small probability of yielding a baby—no more than 1 or 2 percent at best.

And because the man is trysting and running, he isn't able to prevent any of 23 his casual contacts from turning around and mating with other men. The poor fellow. He has to mate with many scores of women for his wham-bam strategy to pay off. And where are all these women to be found, anyway? Population densities during that purportedly all-powerful psyche shaper the "ancestral environment" were quite low, and long-distance travel was dangerous and difficult.

There are alternatives to wantonness, as a number of theorists have empha- 24 sized. If, for example, a man were to spend more time with one woman rather than dashing breathlessly from sheet to sheet, if he were to feel compelled to engage in what animal behaviorists call mate guarding, he might be better off, reproductively speaking, than the wild Lothario, both because the odds of impregnating the woman would increase and because he'd be monopolizing her energy and keeping her from the advances of other sperm bearers. It takes the average couple three to four months of regular sexual intercourse to become pregnant. That number of days is approximately equal to the number of partners our hypothetical libertine needs to sleep with to have one encounter result in a "fertility unit," that is, a baby. The two strategies, then, shake out about the same. A man can sleep with a lot of women—the quantitative approach—or he can sleep with one woman for months at a time, and be madly in love with her—the qualitative tactic.

It's possible that these two reproductive strategies are distributed in discrete 25 packets among the male population, with a result that some men are born philanderers and can never attach, while others are born romantics and perpetually in love with love; but it's also possible that men teeter back and forth from one impulse to the other, suffering an internal struggle between the desire to bond and the desire to retreat, with the circuits of attachment ever there to be toyed with, and their needs and desires difficult to understand, paradoxical, fickle, treacherous and glorious. It is possible, then, and for perfectly good Darwinian reason, that casual sex for men is rarely as casual as it is billed.

It needn't be argued that men and women are exactly the same, or that hu- 26 mans are meta-evolutionary beings, removed from nature and slaves to culture, to reject the perpetually regurgitated model of the coy female and the ardent male. Conflicts of interest are always among us, and the outcomes of those conflicts are interesting, more interesting by far than what the ultra-evolutionary psychology line has handed us. Patricia Gowaty, of the University of Georgia, sees conflict between males and females as inevitable and pervasive. She calls it sexual dialectics. Her thesis is that females and male vie for control over the means of reproduction. Those means are the female body, for there is as yet no such beast as the parthenogenetic man.

Women are under selective pressure to maintain control over their repro- 27 duction, to choose with whom they will mate and with whom they will not—to exercise female choice. Men are under selective pressure to make sure they're chosen or, barring that, to subvert female choice and coerce the female to mate against her will. "But once you have this basic dialectic set in motion, it's going to be a constant push-me, pull-you," Gowaty says. That dynamism cannot possibly result in a unitary response, the caricatured coy woman and ardent man. Instead there are going to be some coy, reluctantly mating males and some ardent females, and any number of variations in between.

28   "A female will choose to mate with a male whom she believes, consciously or otherwise, will confer some advantage on her and her offspring. If that's the case, then her decision is contingent on what she brings to the equation." For example, she says, "the 'good genes' model leads to oversimplified notions that there is a 'best male' out there, a top-of-the-line hunk whom all females would prefer to mate with if they had the wherewithal. But in the viability model, a female brings her own genetic complement to the equation, with the result that what looks good genetically to one woman might be a clash of colors for another."

29   Maybe the man's immune system doesn't complement her own, for example, Gowaty proposes. There's evidence that the search for immune variation is one of the subtle factors driving mate selection, which may be why we care about how our lovers smell; immune molecules may be volatilized and released in sweat, hair, the oil on our skin. We are each of us a chemistry set, and each of us has a distinctive mix of reagents. "What pleases me might not please somebody else," Gowaty says. "There is no one-brand great male out there. We're not all programmed to look for the alpha male and only willing to mate with the little guy or the less aggressive guy because we can't do any better. But the propaganda gives us a picture of the right man and the ideal women, and the effect of the propaganda is insidious. It becomes self-reinforcing. People who don't fit the model think, I'm weird, I'll have to change my behavior." It is this danger, that the ostensible "discoveries" of evolutionary psychology will be used as propaganda, that makes the enterprise so disturbing.

30   Variation and flexibility are the key themes that get set aside in the breathless dissemination of evolutionary psychology. "The variation is tremendous, and is rooted in biology," Barbara Smuts said to me. "Flexibility itself is the adaptation." Smuts has studied olive baboons, and she has seen males pursuing all sorts of mating strategies. "There are some whose primary strategy is dominating other males, and being able to gain access to more females because of their fighting ability," she says. "Then there is the type of male who avoids competition and cultivates long-term relationships with females and their infants. These are the nice, affiliative guys. There's a third type, who focuses on sexual relationships. He's the consorted. . . . And as far as we can tell, no one reproductive strategy has advantages over the others."

31   Women are said to need an investing male. We think we know the reason. Human babies are difficult and time consuming to raise. Stone Age mothers needed husbands to bring home the bison. Yet the age-old assumption that male parental investment lies at the heart of human evolution is now open to serious question. Men in traditional foraging cultures do not necessarily invest resources in their offspring. Among the Hadza of Africa, for example, the men hunt, but

they share the bounty of that hunting widely, politically, strategically. They don't deliver it straight to the mouths of their progeny. Women rely on their senior female kin to help feed the children. The women and their children in a gathering-hunting society clearly benefit from the meat that hunters bring back to the group. But they benefit as a group, not as a collection of nuclear family units, each beholden to the father's personal pound of wildeburger.

This is a startling revelation, which upends many of our presumptions about 32 the origins of marriage and what women want from men and men from women. If the environment of evolutionary adaptation is not defined primarily by male parental investment, the bedrock of so much of evolutionary psychology's theories, then we can throw the door wide open and ask new questions, rather than endlessly repeating ditties and calling the female coy long after she has run her petticoats through the Presidential paper shredder.

For example: Nicholas Blurton Jones, of the University of California at Los 33 Angeles, and others have proposed that marriage developed as an extension of men's efforts at mate guarding. If the cost of philandering becomes ludicrously high, the man might be better off trying to claim rights to one woman at a time. Regular sex with a fertile woman is at least likely to yield offspring at comparatively little risk to his life, particularly if sexual access to the woman is formalized through a public ceremony—a wedding. Looked at from this perspective, one must wonder why an ancestral woman bothered to get married, particularly if she and her female relatives did most of the work of keeping the family fed from year to year. Perhaps, Blurton Jones suggests, to limit the degree to which she was harassed. The cost of chronic male harassment may be too high to bear. Better to agree to a ritualized bond with a male and to benefit from whatever hands-off policy that marriage may bring, than to spend all of her time locked in one sexual dialectic or another.

Thus marriage may have arisen as a multifaceted social pact: between man 34 and woman, between male and male and between the couple and the tribe. It is a reasonable solution to a series of cultural challenges that arose in concert with the expansion of the human neocortex. But its roots may not be what we think they are, nor may our contemporary mating behaviors stem from the pressures of an ancestral environment as it is commonly portrayed, in which a woman needed a mate to help feed and clothe her young. Instead, our "deep" feelings about marriage may be more pragmatic, more contextual and, dare I say it, more egalitarian than we give them credit for being.

If marriage is a social compact, a mutual bid between man and woman to con- 35 trive a reasonably stable and agreeable microhabitat in a community of shrewd and well-armed members, then we can understand why, despite rhetoric to the contrary, men are as eager to marry as women are. A raft of epidemiological studies have shown that marriage adds more years to the life of a man that it does to that of a woman. Why should that be, if men are so "naturally" ill suited to matrimony?

What do women want? None of us can speak for all women, or for more than 36 one woman, really, but we can hazard a mad guess that a desire for emotional parity is widespread and profound. It doesn't go away, although it often hibernates under duress, and it may be perverted by the restrictions of habitat or culture into something that looks like its opposite. The impulse for liberty is congenital. It is the ultimate manifestation of selfishness, which is why we can count on its endurance.

•   *Thinking Critically About "Men, Women, Sex, and Darwin"*

RESPONDING AS A READER

1. What is Angier's attitude toward evolutionary psychologists and their theories? How do both what she says and how she says it communicate this attitude? Find particular passages that reveal her attitude directly through what she says and passages that reveal her attitude indirectly through her tone, choice of words, and so on.

2. In paragraph 3, she explains her purpose in writing this essay: "I'm not interested in explaining to men what they really want or how they should behave. . . . I'm only proposing here that the hard-core evolutionary psychologists have got a lot about women wrong." According to Angier, what are the negative effects of the popularly disseminated opinions of evolutionary psychologists? Who is her intended audience? What kind of a change in perspective is she trying to accomplish in this article?

3. What kind of image (or images) does Angier create of herself in the text? Do you find her trustworthy, likeable, and knowledgeable? If so, what in the text contributes to your positive assessment of her image? If not, what contributes to your negative assessment of her image?

RESPONDING AS A WRITER

1. In paragraph 4, Angier outlines the five cardinal premises held by evolutionary psychologists that she wishes to challenge. Make a chart in which you list the position of evolutionary psychologists on one side and the alternate interpretation or position of Angier (and other researchers that she cites) on the other side. After you have completed the chart, write a paragraph or two about which side is more persuasive to you and why.

2. Despite her disagreement with evolutionary psychologists on many points, she does agree with them on some points. For Angier, it is a combination of cultural and biological changes that accounts for human behavior. An example of her balanced approach begins in paragraph 34, where she calls marriage "a reasonable solution to a series of cultural challenges that arose in concert with the expansion of the human neocortex." Revisit the reading log entry in which you recorded your opinion about the nature versus culture debate. Has Angier succeeded in changing your opinion in any way? If so, how has it changed? Why? If not, why not?

3. To understand more clearly Angier's purpose in writing this essay, write a rhetorical précis of it.

Heather Wendtland (Student)

Rebellion Through Music

Heather Wendtland (b. 1978) is a student at the University of Wisconsin–Milwaukee, where she is majoring in sociology and minoring in psychology. After completing her undergraduate degree, she may apply to law school. She wrote "Rebellion Through Music" for a second-semester composition class in which she was assigned to analyze and interpret a cultural phenomenon.

● *For Your Reading Log*

1. What kind of music did you listen to in high school? Why was this music appealing to you? Did your friends share your taste in music? What were your parents' or guardians' attitudes toward this music?
2. What do you think of efforts to put restrictions on rock and rap lyrics that promote violence or make derogatory comments about various groups of people? Should such music carry a warning label? Should it be sold only to people over a certain age? Should it be banned from the radio? Write a short paragraph in which you state your position on this issue.

———————   ●   ———————

Oh, the memories of the Vanilla Nation, my group of girlfriends from high 1 school! I can still remember riding around and still hear us singing Snoop Doggy Dog's lyrics about "b*tches gettin it on" and "sippin' on the gin and juice." Unfortunately, though, we weren't rollin' in a six-four on Crenshaw in South Central Los Angeles. We were cruisin' on College Avenue in Appleton in what we lovingly referred to as the "Eggplant." It was my 92 purple Ford Taurus, and it was forever bumpin' to the music we loved. We were what Norman Mailer would describe as the "White Negroes" of Appleton, and I was the Vanilla Queen. However, let it be known that none of us were what Master P would call "Thug Girls," nor were we a gang. We were, though, a group of girls loving rap music. But the truth of the matter was the things that we sang about in the "Eggplant" were never reality for us. We were all virgins, none of us drank really, we didn't even know where to buy chronic, African Americans were scarce in our town, and our idea of fun was going to a small truck stop for pancakes every Friday and getting back late for school. The funny thing was, we still had this fascination with rap and hip-hop music. We loved the stuff and ate it up like crazy, even though we never really had a damn clue what the lyrics of rappers like Snoop Doggy Dog, Notorious BIG, and Tupac were actually talking about. To us it was music to dance to and interpret in our own ways.

2   Why did we love entertainers and songs we knew we should hate? I can think of many reasons, but mainly it just felt good to know that something we liked was bad. It felt empowering. It allowed us to express aggressive feelings that are unacceptable for girls, and it annoyed the hell out of adults, which was very satisfying at the time.

3   Both Mary Gaitskill in "An Ordinariness of Monstrous Proportions" and Joan Morgan in "The Nigga Ya Hate to Love" articulate similar feelings. Specifically, Gaitskill writes about her love of Axl Rose, and Morgan her love of Ice Cube. Each explains how she found strength in the rebel's voice, despite her recognition of all the negatives in this "inspirational" voice.

4   In her essay, Gaitskill discusses her attraction to two "bad boys," Brad, a kid she knew in junior high school, and rock musician Axl Rose. Both, she says, let her feel things she knew she should not. She remembers Brad as being "particularly clever and maddeningly cute" and describes Axl Rose as "obviously sexy" (272-4). But it was not only their physical attractiveness that appealed to her, it was their actions as well. She describes how Brad picked on special-ed students. Even though his actions "made her sick," they gave her an intense rush and put a certain angry energy into the air (272). Axl Rose did the same thing for her though he "picked on" minorities and women rather than special-ed kids. Gaitskill knew Axl's lyrics were politically incorrect, and she did not blame the groups that he insulted for not liking him, but she could not deny how he made her feel an intense "ferocity." She saw her obsession with both Brad and Axl as "a result of a disavowal of [her own] aggressiveness and meanness" (273). Gaitskill realizes that both Axl and Brad let her express herself in an unconventional way for a woman: "I imagine that girls, even more than boys, could look at Axl Rose and feel intense delight at seeing him embody their unexpressed ferocity and thus experience it temporarily through him" (273).

5   For Joan Morgan, it was Ice Cube's lyrics that offered this sense of empowerment and vicarious expression of aggressive feelings. In "The Nigga Ya Hate to Love," Morgan explains the appeal of Ice Cube by recounting two incidents that occurred during a trip she and her friends took to ultra-white Martha's Vineyard. On the way there, Morgan and two friends were listening to Ice Cube's latest album, *AmeriKKKa's Most Wanted.* After listening to Side A, one of her friends says, "Joan, you know this m*therf*cka must be bad if he can scream b*tch at me ninety-nine times and make me want to sing it" (249). It gave us, we realized, a "sense of pleasure that is almost perverse" (250).

6   On the ferry back from Martha's Vineyard, she witnessed another kind of empowerment offered by Ice Cube's music. The situation involved "a carload of black folks behind [us] playing Ice Cube stupid loud" and "carloads of white folks looking over at the car, extremely uncomfortable" (251). In observing this scene, Morton imagines the empowerment the carload of African Americans must have felt in forcing their music upon the whites who had no choice but to listen. However, Morgan also realizes that this music is not entirely positive for the black community. She knows that calling women b*tches and celebrating the use of drugs has negative effects on the future of African Americans. Morgan sums up both points by stating, "That's the problem with unmitigated black rage.

It grabs white people by the jugular with one hand, and strangles black folks with the other" (251).

As for my Vanilla Nation, we used the rap group Bone Thugs-N-Harmony 7 as an outlet for our feelings. The Bone lyric used by Vanilla Nation to describe how we felt told listeners to look them in the eye and say what they could see. This idea was important to us because we wanted adults to look deeper than just our surface. At first glance they could only see our youth, color, and gender. It made us angry that those things were all they saw. All that we wanted them to do was to look into our eyes and see the truth: that under the surface we were strong and independent.

The Vanilla Nation felt as Morgan and her friends did when listening to Ice 8 Cube. Even though the Bone Thugs-N-Harmony called us "b*tches," we still wanted to sing along. Ironically, perhaps, degrading women was a part of the music we listened to. To us, it was simply the music that made us want to get out there and to shake our booty and want "to get some" (even though we weren't). We knew the songs didn't send positive messages, but we still sang them anyway.

Similarly, the Vanilla Nation could identify with the empowerment felt by the 9 "black folks in the carload behind" described by Joan Morgan. We have been in their situation, and it was so invigorating. It was exhilarating to know that you were making ultra conservative white Americans listen to what they thought was complete rubbish. The best thing was they couldn't turn it off. No words can describe our complete sense of elation when we would go into an Appleton gas station and blast my Lil' Kim. It was especially gratifying when Lil' Kim would shout lyrics about "d*cks and pu**ies." To adults listening, these were especially outrageous coming from a woman. This made it even more offensive, because people have been conditioned to believe such things should never be said by women, even though they have been spoken thousands of times by a man. You could tell by their looks, which were priceless, that they felt it was unacceptable. However, to us, there was nothing that could beat the pleasure we got from putting our music out there and knowing full well that it was offending those in our presence.

It seems the Vanilla Nation, like Gaitskill and Morgan, got something out of 10 music that wasn't exactly politically correct. We loved music that degraded, knowing full well that it did so. These songs and lyrics were outlets for hidden feelings. It allowed us the five minutes of freedom that we so urgently needed. Like the chorus of rapper Mase's song "Bad Boys" says, bad, bad boys made us feel good.

Works Cited

Bone Thugs-N-Harmony. *The Art of War*. Ruthless Records, 1997.

Gaitskill, Mary. "An Ordinariness of Monstrous Proportions." *Rock She Wrote: Women Write About Rock, Pop, and Rap*. Ed. Evelyn McDonnell and Ann Powers. New York: Dell, 1995. 271–75.

Mase. *Harlem World*. MBG/Arista/Bad Boy Entertainment, 1997.

Morgan, Joan. "The Nigga Ya Hate to Love." *Rock She Wrote: Women Write About Rock, Pop, and Rap*. Ed. Evelyn McDonnell and Ann Powers. New York: Dell, 1995. 247–52.

• *Thinking Critically About "Rebellion Through Music"*

RESPONDING AS A READER

1. What kind of an image(s) does Wendtland create of herself and her high school group of friends, the Vanilla Nation? What details in the text serve to create this image? How do you think the adults at the gas station in Appleton interpreted the behavior of Wendtland and the Vanilla Nation? What is your response to the image(s) Wendtland creates of herself and the Vanilla Nation?

2. What does Wendtland's citation of the articles by Gaitskill and Morgan contribute to her essay? How does her use of these sources affect her authority as a writer?

3. What appear to be Wendtland's intentions in writing this essay (besides the obvious one of fulfilling her teacher's assignment)? What kind of an effect do you think Wendtland hopes her essay will have on readers?

RESPONDING AS A WRITER

1. What does Wendtland's use of profanity, hip-hop slang, and offensive language contribute to this essay? How necessary was this language or these references to her purpose in the essay? What effect would it have on the essay if she eliminated these aspects of her essay? Briefly explain.

2. Wendtland suggests that it is ironic that she and her friends found it empowering to listen to and sing lyrics that degraded women. In addition to the reasons she suggests for this irony, what other reasons can you think of for these young women's attraction to songs whose lyrics degrade women?

3. If you were a member of a peer response group, what kind of feedback would you give Wendtland to help her revise and strengthen her paper?

Writing to Analyze and Interpret

The selections in this chapter analyze and interpret a range of phenomena from monuments to white suburban girls' love of gangsta rap. These readings illustrate a variety of analytical strategies that can be used to shed new light on puzzling subjects: Kirk Savage uses contrasts to illustrate differing interpretations of the meaning of memorials; Natalie Angier breaks evolutionary psychologists' theories into five "cardinal premises" which she then critiques one by one; Roland Barthes divides his analysis of toys into their form and function; and Heather Wendtland examines the causes for her past behavior. The assignments below offer opportunities to understand analytical writing more deeply by trying your own hand at analyzing and interpreting.

OFFERING AN INTERPRETATION

Choose a cultural object or phenomenon, and write an analysis and interpretation that enables others to understand and see it differently. The key here is to use analysis and interpretation to challenge and extend your readers' understanding, to make them think critically or imaginatively about an ordinary object or phenomenon that in your opinion they take for granted or misunderstand. Your goal is new understanding, not evaluation of the object or phenomenon. Roland Barthes, for example, in his collection of essays *Mythologies*, from which the "Toys" essay was taken, interprets the cultural meaning of a variety of ordinary objects particular to 1950s France—margarine, wrestling, striptease, steak and chips, the French flag. Following a similar approach, you might take a familiar object like the television remote control or the now ubiquitous cell phone or Palm Pilot and interpret its meaning in ways that go beyond the obvious and the predictable. Or you might take a less familiar object or phenomenon, say, a new trend in fashion or music, to analyze and interpret for readers who may not understand the meaning of this phenomenon.

EXAMINING RHETORICAL STRATEGIES

Choose one of the essays in this chapter, and note the strategies the author uses to analyze and interpret. How does she or he "take apart" the subject and how does this taking apart lead to various conclusions regarding it? What assumptions or perspectives inform the author's interpretation? For example, Angier analyzes the arguments of evolutionary biologists from a feminist perspective. How is this perspective evident, and how does it shape her interpretation? More important, perhaps, how does the author's perspective affect your response to the interpretation? What appears to be the author's purpose in writing this interpretation and to whom is this interpretation directed? How effective is she or he in accomplishing this purpose?

EXTENDING THE CONVERSATION

In "The Past in the Present," Kirk Savage argues that memorials do not function the way many observers (for example, Pierre Nora) think they do. Choose a local or national memorial about which there has been some controversy. (You might choose to follow up on one of the memorials that Kirk Savage mentions in his article.) Research the history of this memorial and the controversies surrounding it. Look for articles or commentaries on the memorial, analyze the memorial itself, and use all of this data to interpret its meaning and the issues at stake in the controversy. Is the controversy about the original design or location? Is the controversy about the meaning or message of the design? Is the controversy due to changes in the monument's meaning over time? Does the memorial mean something different to various members of the community? Connect your interpretation and ideas to those of Savage and/or other cultural critics (his citations might provide a starting point), and write a paper that analyzes and interprets this memorial and the cultural work it performs.

13

Taking a Stand

The authors you will read in this chapter want to change your mind—unless you already agree with them. They seek to demonstrate the superiority of their views and the flaws in competing views. Their technique is argument, the presentation of claims supported by reasons and evidence. Their arguments move forward on the basis of assumptions that the authors believe they share with their readers. To enhance their readers' identification with these assumptions, the authors choose rhetorical strategies intended to emphasize their own authority and to engage readers' values and emotions. Some of the authors attempt to soothe readers' responses by qualifying their claims. Others try to persuade readers by focusing on what's wrong with the opposition's claims.

These writers want their readers to adopt their viewpoint and reject opposing ideas. Readers must decide whether to agree. From the perspective of rhetorical reading, however, mere agreement is not the only matter at stake. How the argument is constructed—its reasoning, its authority, its appeal to readers—must be examined as part of determining an argument's effectiveness. Rhetorical reading goes beyond the simplified "yes-no" binaries that grab headlines. For college students, and for college graduates in the workplace and public sphere, the intellectual work of reading arguments entails analysis of the rhetorical strategies at work in a given text. In academic work, a careful analysis of an argument will distinguish a good argument from a flawed one on the basis not just of its content, but its method. In this chapter we present concepts of argumentation that will allow you to perform this kind of analysis, analysis that will make your reading skills more productive as well as give you a persuasive edge in your own writing.

Texts that take a stand attempt to reconstruct a skeptical reader's image of the subject matter. As readers, if we are to make an intelligent decision about whether we will let that new image replace our previous ideas, we must read carefully and critically. We must analyze the structure of the arguments and recognize the authors' persuasive methods. We must evaluate their claims to authority, examine the reliability and relevance of their supporting evidence, and scrutinize the reasoning that binds the argument together. We must consider both explicit claims and implicit assumptions. We must read with a critical awareness that allows us to pinpoint exactly what is at issue not just from the arguer's perspective, but from the perspective of others who have a stake in the matter, who may disagree.

You might reasonably ask how the selections we label in this chapter as "texts that take a stand" are different from those in the earlier sections of this anthology. After all, you might say, every author, no matter the specific occasion and purpose, seeks to convince readers of the validity of his or her own perspective. You would be making a good point. In the eyes of many experts, all written texts constitute at least an implicit argument. Indeed, in the thesis-driven context of academic writing, the verb "argue" is commonly used to refer to a wide variety of writing, even when the specific aim is primarily explanatory or analytical and nothing particularly controversial is involved.

What we feature in this chapter, however, are texts in which a persuasive aim dominates. The authors here and in the chapters that follow on special types of arguments (evaluations and proposals) address subjects that are recognizably in dispute; they have the direct intention of persuading readers to see the given subject their way. These writers' claims and the reasoning that supports them extend beyond explaining subject matter. They take up questions on which the public or a given segment of it has not been able to agree. The views of their intended audience govern their rhetorical decisions. These authors expect their readers to resist, and so they engage them as people who need to be convinced. They want to change our minds.

For the careful rhetorical reader, the question is, does a given author succeed? Will your mind be changed? What makes a particular argument successful, or not?

Argument and Public Life

Although we have pointed out that writers of arguments anticipate resistance and so work to counter opposing views, we must hasten to point out that the exchange of arguments through reading and writing is ultimately not a matter of winning or losing but a process of seeking truth in situations where reasonable people disagree about what constitutes "truth." In fact, competing arguments provide a means of inquiring into the best way to understand these situations and to choose the best course of action to resolve them. The goal of argument may be best understood not as competition but as cooperation.

We are using the term *argument* to signal concepts more complex than simple "yes-no" disputes. Not every disagreement represents a genuinely arguable issue. People frequently disagree over matters that depend simply upon personal preferences. Coke or Pepsi? Alternative or country? Classical or jazz? You and your friends or family may disagree, perhaps intensely, but your preferences have little impact on others. Agreeing to disagree, you move on. Arguable issues, in contrast, extend beyond the personal. They arise when members of a community must decide how to address a question of common concern but are faced with more than one reasonable response. Rhetoric, the art of persuasion, developed in ancient times precisely because human beings constantly confront situations in which certainty about the best belief or action is not possible but decisions must nevertheless be made about how to proceed. These discussions about finding the best course of action to take, known as *deliberative arguments*, typically depend not on determining empirical truth but on using reasons and persuasion to negotiate differences and contingencies. Finding the best options, in other words, is a rhetorical matter, and often a task for argumentation.

The argument texts in this chapter take a stand by asserting positions on issues that are part of ongoing deliberations about how public life is best understood and managed. If everybody agreed on everything—which accomplishments are most praiseworthy, which policies will foster the greatest good, and how occasional disputes should be adjudicated—civic arguments would be rare. But human beings do not live in circumstances of certainty. As even a quick glance at a newspaper will tell you, perceptions vary, resources are limited, interests compete, values clash. From neighborhoods to international treaty organizations, humans must deliberate over options and make decisions together. Whether the decision concerns funding for a new community library or ethical use of new biological technologies, there's bound to be disagreement.

Indeed, many political theorists have argued that dissent is essential to democracy. The outcome of the resulting deliberative process will depend upon who is persuaded by what set of claims and counterclaims. Politicians give speeches, editors write editorials, pundits debate, columnists write op-ed pieces, citizens write letters to the editor. We read, think, discuss, listen, argue back. Advocates take stands and try to convince others to join them. Eventually, elections are held, court cases heard, decisions made. Then another round begins as the effectiveness of those decisions comes under scrutiny.

Why Should You Agree? Claim, Reason, Evidence, and Assumption

The basic frame of any argument is a claim and a reason (sometimes called a subclaim or a premise). This frame and the way that a given writer elaborates it into a network of reasoning constitute an argument's *logos*, its logical power. What makes the logos of an argument convincing is the way that its elements are connected with each other. To evaluate the effectiveness of an argument and determine whether it earns your assent, you need to analyze how all its components work together. What follows is a description of the four major components of an argument's logos along with a key analytical question to use to pinpoint each of them within a text.

- **Claim:** The point being argued, the author's answer to the question at issue. *Ask, "What's the main point, the one toward which everything else builds?"*
- **Reason** (sometimes called a premise): A subclaim that links the evidence to the main claim, usually with a logical conjunction such as "because." *Ask, "Why is the central point here said to be true/a good idea?"*

  Persuasive arguments are likely to offer several different reasons in support of their claim. Some reasons can be immediately supported with evidence. For example, if we said, "Reject this proposal for expanding the town library because it will be extremely costly," we could immediately provide data about the costs without confusing our audience. Other reasons depend for their support on still other reasons. For example, if we said, "We should legalize drugs because doing so will get the government out of our private lives," we would have to make further arguments about both how such legalization would get the government out of private lives and why that would be a good thing.
- **Evidence** (sometimes referred to as *grounds* or *data*): Factual support that provides the particulars, details, and specifics to validate the reason. *Ask, "What empirical information is presented to support this claim and reason?"*

  To evaluate evidence, consider whether it is sufficient, typical, accurate, current, and relevant. Regarding the point above about the high cost of the library, we would need to evaluate the data about costs. For the point about legalizing drugs, we would need to evaluate the idea that legalizing drugs would get the government out of our private lives, and, perhaps, examine evidence that the government is, in fact, in our private lives, or that its involvement in our lives is a function of drug laws. Clarification is called for.

Whether the evidence and reason adequately support a claim depends upon the reader's acceptance of the next element:

- **Assumption** (sometimes referred to as *warrant*): The stated or unstated values and beliefs that authorize the given reason and demonstrate the connection between the evidence and the claim. Assumptions may be explicitly stated and argued for or left unstated under the presumption that the audience already holds these values or beliefs. *Ask, "What values or beliefs are being asserted here as a bridge between evidence and claim?"*

  The first example above clearly assumes that cost should be the determining factor in a decision about the project. Supporters of the library project may forward counterclaims that other factors are more important than cost, but the assumption that drives the given argument is clear. If the writer suspected that some readers would not put first priority on cost, then he might devote part of his argument to the importance of cost. The second example assumes that getting the government out of our private lives is desirable and is of paramount consideration regarding the legalization of drugs. For most readers, the logic of this assumption would need to be argued. (Statements that elaborate on or otherwise support an argument's basic assumptions are sometimes called *backing*.)

In your analysis of arguments, you will need to consider several additional factors beyond logos that influence the persuasiveness of a claim and its support. You should examine the dynamics of *ethos*, the ways in which the writer seems credible and gains the reader's trust, and *pathos*, the ways in which the writer engages the presumed audience's interests, emotions, and imagination. You should also examine how the writer handles opposing cases, a place where ethos and pathos may be particularly revealing. Are known and potential objections to the argument summarized and countered fairly? Does the author appropriately qualify or limit the scope of the claims? ("*Unless* other funding sources become available, this library project is too expensive.") Does the author concede that the opposition has raised valuable points? ("*While it is true that* the existing library facility is inadequate, the current plan goes well beyond what is necessary to solve the problem.")

The extent to which a given claim needs evidence to support its reasons, backing to support its basic assumptions, or both, will depend upon the subject matter, the context in which the argument is articulated, and the presumed audience's attitude toward the subject. To illustrate, let's move to a practical situation, family members shopping for a new car. The decision-making process they face provides us with a homespun example of the deliberative arguments so common in public discourse. With one child in college and another graduating from high school next year, everyone agrees that low cost should be the deciding factor, so attention turns to the evidence about cost, which seems to give the nod to Car A. However, the family financial whiz contends that this car, although lower in purchase price, will be more expensive to insure and maintain than Car B. Then circumstances suddenly change. One of the grandparents receives a windfall commission for a special project and offers it for the car purchase. Now the specifics of cost are no longer a major concern. Cars A and B are no longer at the top of anyone's list, and the basis for the decision is in dispute because the family members no longer share the same assumptions about which criteria should apply. One parent contends that safety is primary; the other argues that comfort on long trips to two different college campuses must be considered. Meanwhile, the college student suggests that commitment to minimizing environmental impact means they should buy one of the new hybrid cars, and the high school student advocates for a sporty-looking car that will be easy to park. These criteria point in very different directions and are not as easily compared or reconciled as cost estimates are. Before they can decide what car to buy, this family must negotiate among the competing beliefs and values so that they can agree upon criteria for selecting the new car.

What's Really at Issue?

For rhetorical readers, a key element of argument analysis is identifying the way advocates phrase not only their claims, but the questions—explicit and implicit—that they intend those claims to answer. It's evident that arguments arise because different parties answer questions differently. What is often less evident is that the parties presenting opposing arguments may have quite different understandings of what is at issue. They are mounting arguments that answer different questions. Yet, as the changing situation of our car-shopping family suggests, the shape of an argument depends in major ways on how an issue is defined. Conflicts that arise because of opposing interests and limited resources are familiar to us all, from childhood squabbles over toys to major labor strikes caused by the difficulty of reconciling workers' desires for higher pay with management's desires to hold costs down. However, even when a goal is agreed upon, everything from fundamental values to the details of procedures may eventually be contested. People who share the same values may nevertheless disagree about policies or procedures because they cannot agree on how to translate those values into practical actions or on how to gauge the consequences of a particular course of action. (See, for example, the conflicting views about the effects of a law requiring trigger locks in Kathleen Parker's two op-ed columns in this chapter.) In a still more difficult matter, consider the complexities of trying to establish guidelines for the ethical use of new genetic technologies. What constitutes "ethical" use? Who should establish guidelines? Who should be included in the agreement process? Would the guidelines be legally binding? Who has the authority to make them so? Which technologies would be covered? Would there be an appeals procedure? Each question opens the floor to new claims and counterclaims as conflicts over resources, interests, and values come into focus.

Classical rhetoric offers us a set of conceptual categories for analyzing the ways in which questions are posed and issues defined. These categories, known as the *stases*, are defined by the type of issue that separates disputants in an argument. The word *stasis*, derived from the Greek word *stand*, indicates the point at which agreement comes to a halt. Although originally used as a way to "invent" or find and develop arguments, these categories offer modern readers an equally powerful tool for analyzing the claims in arguments they hear or read and discerning what issues lie at the heart of a given controversy. For example, the family shopping for a car initially faced a question in the *stasis of fact:* Which car would be the most economical? When the family's financial situation changed, the type of claims competing in their deliberations changed as well, from factual claims about economy to claims about comfort, safety, and style that can be categorized in the *stasis of values*. To reach a decision, the family had to decide which of those values claims offered them the greatest good.

In Table 13.1 we present the six stasis categories that we consider to be the most useful for the critical analysis called for in college reading assignments. These categories will serve to guide your analysis of the argument texts in this chapter and in other classes as well. To illustrate the differences among the stasis

Table 13.1 What Kind of Question Is at Issue? Using Stasis Categories for Argument Analysis

Sample Argument Issues

Is Y guilty of Z's murder?	How safe is our municipal water supply?	Should children under twelve be required by law to wear bicycle helmets?	To protect children from Internet pornography, should we place content filters on Internet terminals in public libraries?

Stasis of Fact: Does X exist? Did X occur?

Did Y kill Z?	What pollutants are present in the drinking water?	What is the evidence that bicycle helmets save lives and prevent injuries?	Do children access pornography via library computer terminals?

Stasis of Definition: What kind of thing is this? What category of things does it fit? What does the category label mean?

Y did kill Z, but was it murder? Self-defense? An accident?	What kind of pollutants are "safe" or "unsafe"? What do "safe" and "unsafe" mean in this case?	Is the wearing of bicycle helmets a "government matter" or a "private matter"?	Does limiting public access to the Internet through library computer terminals equal "censorship"? Is access to information equal to free speech? Does limiting access to information violate librarians' definition of their responsibilities? What is "pornography"?

Stasis of Cause or Consequence: What caused this thing? What will happen because of it?

What, specifically, caused Z's death?	What is the source of unsafe pollutants? What effect will they have on human health? In what concentration? How much will it cost to get rid of them?	Would a bicycle helmet law significantly reduce injuries? What would enforcement cost? Will poor children have to stop riding bikes because they can't afford helmets?	How effective are the available filtering technologies? Will they actually block pornography without blocking valuable information? Will limits on one kind of information lead to limits on other types? Do limits on access threaten democracy?

continued

Table 13.1 *continued*

Stasis of Interpretation, Including Similarity and Analogy: What does this mean? What is it like that we already understand?			
How do we understand the interactions between Y and Z before the death? Was Z threatening Y?	How reliable is the data interpretation in the tests for these pollutants and their effects?	Is the bicycle helmet safety issue more like automobile seat belts (a public matter already covered by law) or more like non-skid strips in bathtubs (a private matter)?	What makes a given piece of material "pornographic"?

Stasis of Value: Is this thing good or bad?			
Was Y's killing of Z justified?	How bad (dangerous) are the pollutants? Can we tolerate a certain level of contaminants in the municipal water supply?	Does the value of reducing children's injuries outweigh the value of keeping government out of people's private lives?	Does free access to information have value equal to free speech? Does that outweigh the value of protecting children from pornographic Internet sites?

Stasis of Policy and Procedures: What should be done? How should it be done? Who has the authority to do it?			
Y is a diplomat. Can he be tried in a U.S. court?	The major sources of the pollution in our drinking water are in another state. Who has the authority and the ability to address the problem?	How will a bicycle helmet law be enforced?	How would a filtering law be implemented and enforced? To whom should concerned parents speak about their library's Internet policy?

categories, the table provides generic questions that define each stasis. To illustrate how the stases can generate lines of inquiry useful for both analyzing and developing argument claims, the table lists specific sample questions that apply each stasis category to the four controversies listed at the top. These specific questions demonstrate how the stases can be applied, but by no means cover all possibilities for developing an argument relevant to the issues listed. You will undoubtedly be able to think of additional questions and claims. As you examine the table, consider how certain questions are more likely to be raised by advocates on one side of an issue than on another.

As the sample questions illustrating the stasis categories in Table 13.1 suggest, significant controversies will involve claims and counterclaims in more than one category. In fact, some experts consider the categories to be progressively inclusive because claims in one stasis typically depend upon claims in a stasis preceding it. Questions of evaluation and policy, in particular, depend upon prior claims related to definition, consequence, or interpretation, and claims in these categories depend on the ones preceding them. Definitions usually depend upon facts, for example; causes and consequences typically determine how the meaning of a phenomenon is interpreted. In turn, agreement and disagreement about definitions, consequences, and interpretations all play a role in questions about the extent to which something should be valued as good or bad. Finally, answers to questions in all of the first five categories play important—and perhaps competing—roles in decisions about how to proceed.

One cause of disagreement among disputants in a controversy is that various voices in the conversation focus on different stases so that all the disputants can't be clearly lined up as "pro" or "con" on an issue. For example, in the sample controversy of whether the state should require that children under twelve wear bicycle helmets, one person, believing strongly in the safety value of helmets, might spend an entire argument providing evidence that wearing helmets would prevent many serious injuries and save lives. The next person might oppose the law but not be interested in the question of safety. This person might believe that the government has too many rules and regulations and hence argue that wearing bicycle helmets is purely a private matter between children and their parents. These two arguments don't speak to each other at all. The first disputant is arguing a stasis of fact (wearing helmets can prevent injuries). The second disputant is arguing a stasis of definition. (What constitutes "public matters" in contrast to "private matters"? According to this person's definition of "public concern," the government doesn't have jurisdiction to force kids to wear bicycle helmets any more than it has jurisdiction to make kids under twelve eat their vegetables.) Still a third person might oppose the proposed law by focusing on a stasis of consequence, that the law is unenforceable. (Passing this law would put police in the impossible situation of having to card kids—"Are you twelve, sonny?"—and then fine their parents.)

When opponents define the issue so differently that they do not even address, perhaps even perceive, each other's concerns, controversies persist and become intractable. You and your classmates can undoubtedly think of a number of policy debates that boil down to stand-offs such as rights versus values, safety versus freedom, or environmental preservation versus economic expansion. Readers trying to understand the complexities of such debates must recognize not just the major claims on each side but what those claims, and the defining questions to which they respond, reveal about what the opposing parties perceive to be at the heart of the issue.

Questions to Help You Read
Arguments Rhetorically

The list of questions below summarizes the advice provided in this chapter about analyzing and evaluating argument texts. Choose relevant questions to guide your analysis for both discussion and writing.

1. What question is this argument addressing? What kind of question (stasis) is it?
2. What is the central claim?
3. How is the claim supported with reasons and evidence? What are the basic assumptions about values and beliefs upon which this argument depends?
4. Evaluate the evidence. Is it sufficient? Relevant? Reliable? Timely (in relation to the date of original publication)?
5. What point(s) does the author seem to think provide the strongest support for the argument's central claim? Do you agree?
6. How are opposing cases handled? Consider (a) what the author seems to think are the strongest and weakest point(s) for the opposing cases, (b) whether the opposition is treated fairly, and (c) whether appropriate qualifiers and concessions are used (not necessary in every argument).
7. How does the author establish his or her authority on this subject? What specific qualities of arrangement and style create *ethos* here? Which are the most engaging or off-putting? (See Chapter 5 for discussion of *ethos* and *pathos*.)
8. What specific qualities of the piece did you find engaging or off-putting? What assumptions does the author seem to be making about the concerns and views of the intended audience for this argument? How would you describe this author's use of *pathos*—the strategies used for appealing to these readers' emotions and imaginations?
9. Overall, how has your mind been changed by this argument? How convincing was it? What are your reservations? Try to pinpoint places in the text where you resist or grant assent to the writer's claims.

Web Pages for the Million Mom March and Second Amendment Sisters Rally, May 2000

Marching For and Against Guns and Gun Controls

Calling citizens to demonstrate their support for or against a cause by marching on Washington has a long tradition in U.S. history. On Mother's Day of 2000, May 14, thousands of citizens converged on the national mall to take opposing stands on federal gun control legislation in two competing demonstrations: the Million Mom March (MMM) and the Second Amendment Sisters Armed Informed Mothers March (SAS-AIMM). The two Web pages reproduced here (Figures 13.1 and 13.2) convey the gist of the two organizations' positions as they called for marchers to join each demonstration. In their mission statement, MMM organizers announced themselves as "dedicated to the mission of educating our children and our country about the life-threatening danger of guns" and called for Congress to pass "common sense gun legislation" by the date of the march, something that did not happen. SAS-AIMM organized a rally for the day of the march to counter the MMM message and oppose such legislation. (National Public Radio reported the next morning that several hundred thousand people gathered around the MMM stage near Capitol Hill, while a "small group of gun owners' rights advocates" joined the SAS-AIMM rally near the Washington Monument. Parallel MMM rallies/marches were held in seventy other cities.)

Unlike the rest of the "take a stand" arguments presented in this chapter, these two Web pages rely on visual appeals for their effect. We invite you to use your rhetorical reading skills to analyze the arguments proclaimed in them through both verbal and visual expression. Posted before the marches and gradually revised afterward, the groups' Web materials offered much more information than we can present in these two screen captures, of course. For example, as viewers scrolled through the SAS-AIMM page, they could watch a video, sign a petition, and take a quiz about their attitude toward gun control legislation. The MMM site offered opportunities to join a mailing list, view a photo gallery, send e-mail, learn about the group's history and goals, and even print a MMM logo to use on signs for the march. The likelihood of reader/surfers staying at any Website long enough to take up such invitations depends largely on the effectiveness of the initial screen presentation, which is what the questions below are designed to help you analyze. We start by asking you to try to capture in your reading log your own gut-level, nonanalytical responses.

● *For Your Reading Log*

1. The visual design of both pages has definite emotional implications. Working with just one page at a time, try to imagine what your initial emotional reactions to each one would have been if you had encountered it in full color on your computer screen. To help you do this, we'll describe the color used on each page.

- The MMM page featured pastels: lavender for what you see as gray background at the top, bright pink for the first six lines of the poster set against it, soft pink inside the letters of the main headline, and pale orange, green, and turquoise on the flower just to its left. The intense pink of the poster's words was repeated in the marching figures and on the MMM gun logo's squiggle, flower outlines, and the word "Mom." A turquoise ribbon trailing from the multicolored flower on the left defined the left margin of the black-on-white text, which continued from what you can see to stipulate a ten-step plan for reaching the organization's goals. Those multicolored pastel petals were repeated in the large flower at the upper right as each of the links was activated.
- In contrast, the SAS-AIMM page featured primary colors: blue lettering on a gray-speckled white background with repeating darker gray watermarks of a handgun. The first letter of each word in the headline and the entire first word of each paragraph were red, as was the "self defense" link under the black-and-white photo.

With these images in mind, jot down the ideas the pages inspire and the emotional responses you have to them.

2. Again working one page at a time, close the book and jot down what you remember about the ideas expressed by each screen and how they were expressed. Note only the most memorable aspects of each screen. What made the strongest impression on you in each?

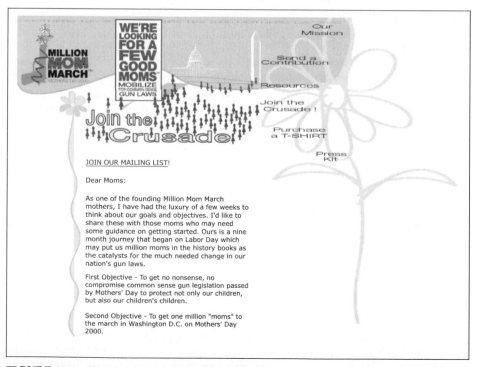

FIGURE 13.1   Web page for Million Mom March

Second Amendment Sisters, Inc.

If you are a woman (or a man) who has ever felt threatened or been attacked, or needed a restraining order against a violent ex, then you know what fear and powerlessness mean.

If you have ever wondered what it would be like to never have to be so powerless again, we can help you.

But, we need your help too! There is a group of women who want to take away, or severely infringe on your right to protect yourself and your family. They call their effort the Million Mom March.

We need you to help us send a Million Moms of our own, to let Congress know that these women do not speak for all mothers!

ALIVE
ALIVE
ALIVE
ALIVE
ALIVE

Protect yourself.
Stop the predator.
Re-load. Call 911.

Self Defense, A Basic Human Right

FIGURE 13.2 Web page for Second Amendment Sisters Armed Informed Mothers March

● *Thinking Critically About the Calls to March For and Against Guns and Gun Controls*

RESPONDING AS A READER

1. What is the central argument of each of these pages? What predominates, the message of "join us" or the purpose of each demonstration?

2. Taking a more analytical approach, consider how you read the visual content of these two pages. Divide two sheets of paper—one for each Web page—into two columns. Use the left column for "what I see" and the right for "meaning I infer." Put yourself in a scenario of someone who's looking at the page and considering whether to join each demonstration. In the first column, note all the visual details that capture your attention. Then, on your own or with a partner, use the second column for notes about how you read these details; that is, what meaning does each suggest? How does that meaning connect with each page's central argument?

3. Putting aside your own attitude toward guns and gun control, evaluate the total effect of each page from a neutral standpoint. In terms of immediate goals, which page seems more likely to convince a sympathetic viewer to come to Washington? In terms of the causes that each supports, which page seems more likely to convince an undecided viewer of the validity of its position? If you answer these two questions differently, how do you account for the difference?

RESPONDING AS A WRITER

1. How would you translate into words the *ethos* created by each page? That is, on what basis does each organization claim authority on the gun control issues at hand? Again trying to take up a neutral analytic stance, what do you see as the strengths and flaws of each presentation?

2. What assumptions does each page seem to make about the concerns and opinions of its audience? From a neutral position, how would you

translate each page's use of *pathos*? What do you find more and less effective in each?

3. What does the title of each organization—"Million Mom March" and
"Second Amendment Sisters"—tell you about the *logos* and underlying
assumptions that govern each group's goals? Both rallies featured emotional testimonials from women whose lives had been marked by gun
use. At the MMM rally, these women told the crowd stories about their
children who had been killed by guns. At the SAS-AIMM rally, the
speakers told stories about how using a gun had saved their own or their
children's lives. The broader arguments for and against each of these organizations' positions were reported and debated extensively in the media at the time and continue to influence American political debate. But
on Web pages such as these, the reasoning behind each position must be
presented in a nutshell. For each position, write out a brief summarizing claim with reasons, then add a sentence that articulates the underlying assumptions driving the claim. How would the testimonials at
each rally function implicitly within the structure of those arguments?

Kathleen Parker

About Face

Syndicated columnist Kathleen Parker (b. 1951) writes for the *Orlando Sentinel* and appears regularly in *USA Today* and the *Jewish World Review*. Her writing focuses on issues related to family, children, and gender, typically from a political perspective that is to the right of center. The two op-ed columns presented here in which Parker first supports then opposes government-mandated trigger locks, were published three days apart. The first commentary appeared in the *Milwaukee Journal Sentinel* on Sunday, March 5, 2000, less than a week after a six-year-old boy in Michigan killed a first-grade classmate with a handgun he had found in the house where he was living temporarily without his parents. The paper published the second on March 8.

• *For Your Reading Log*

1. Before you read either of these columns, spend some time freewriting about your ideas concerning trigger locks. Should their use be required by law? Why or why not? If you don't have a position on the matter, consider and write out the questions you would want answered before you could decide on a position.

2. As indicated in the titles and headnote, the first of Parker's columns advocates government-mandated trigger locks and the second reverses that position. Before you read, try to predict her primary reasoning in each case. Given the context of the shooting death to which she is responding, what reasons and assumptions do you predict Parker uses in the first column to support her advocacy of trigger locks? Given what you know of arguments for and against gun control, how do you expect her reasoning to change in the second column?

——————— • ———————

For Starters, We Can Require Trigger Locks

Another shooting, another child dead, another round of debate. This time, the 1
age and innocence of both victim and shooter push the limits of rational thought.

Unlike previous school shootings, all too familiar now, there's no easy tar- 2
get for our contempt. No cult to despise, no black trench coat to repel, no pattern of weird behavior to suggest we should have known. Just two little kids, caught in the crosshairs of an accidental moment.

One of them, Kayla Rolland, 6, is dead. The other, a 6-year-old boy whose 3
name had not been released at this writing, is in the custody of a relative.

4   Last week's tragedy at Buell Elementary School near Flint, Mich., poses more questions than answers. Foremost, where does one place blame? Can we blame a first-grader who comes to school with a loaded gun he found on the floor of his home? Can we blame a school for not checking the book bags of children just four years out of diapers? Can we blame parents for not being good enough parents?

5   You bet we can blame parents, and we should. We also should blame anyone who opposes the simplest of precautions against such tragedies, such as trigger locks on handguns. Locks aren't a cure, but they're the least we can do to protect children from the adults who pretend to be their parents.

6   I realize the world is full of slobs, and most of them are engaged in procreation. There's not much we can do about that fact, absent a dictatorship and parental licensing, an increasingly attractive option—as long as I get to be dictator.

7   But there is something we can do about parents who refuse to behave responsibly and to take charge of their progeny.

8   Early reports suggested that the shooter was himself a victim, the offspring of a chaotic home and drug culture. He lived in a "flophouse" with his mother, a man known as an uncle and a younger sibling.

9   The gun he brought to school had been reported stolen in December. Investigators also found a stolen 12-gauge shotgun in the boy's home.

10   So these are not the Cleavers or the Huxtables or even the Simpsons. A product of such a home predictably will wind up on a rap sheet one of these days. Better that he steal a car at 16 than kill a classmate at 6.

11   But there you have it. No amount of understanding, compassion or empathy will bring peace to Kayla's parents or to the millions of others who rightfully fear sending their children to school. The time for punitive action against parents is overdue. Someone has to step up to the plate and be held accountable for this child sacrifice.

12   Prosecutors say they'll seek involuntary manslaughter charges against the man they say once had the gun.

13   Any adult who leaves a weapon around for a young child to take to school is negligent, no yes-buts. Adults may be unable to prevent older children from procuring firearms, either through theft or purchase (Columbine killers Dylan Klebold and Eric Harris come to mind), but a half-witted monkey can keep a pistol from a 6-year-old. If you have guns, lock them up.

14   When someone dies because you didn't properly tend to home and child, you bear a responsibility.

15   Regardless of how the judicial system resolves the issue of culpability in this case, we can immediately insist on trigger locks for all firearms, especially handguns. To accept anything less is irresponsible and a crime against common sense, for which we all share blame.

Revisiting the Issue of Trigger Locks

1 Quick, somebody sell me a bridge over the Sahara before I grow a brain.

2   I don't know how to explain my recent lapse in common sense. Was my body snatched by an idiot pod?

I'm talking about my last column ("For Starters, We Can Require Trigger 3 Locks," March 5) in which I reacted to the shooting of one first-grader by another first-grader. I urged tough consequences for adults whose carelessness results in a shooting by a child. So far, so good.

Then, I apparently lost consciousness and urged trigger locks for all weapons. 4 Who said that? Surely not I, the daughter of a responsible gun collector who taught me to handle and shoot guns safely as soon as I could hold a rifle. My father must be banging his head against heaven's gate. He taught me better.

Among his more valuable lessons was the lawyerly advice that an unen- 5 forceable law is a bad law. A law that makes trigger locks mandatory is about as useful as a law that requires daily showering. You can force gun dealers to sell locks, but you can't force gun owners to use them.

Thanks to readers who managed to remain rational in the wake of the terri- 6 ble Michigan incident that claimed the life of 6-year-old Kayla Rolland, I've been born again. To the one Colorado reader who agreed with my first knee-jerk response, sorry. The Sahara Bridge Builders Association wants you, too.

The better solution to this and other gun tragedies is to make the conse- 7 quences for irresponsible gun ownership so severe that such accidents become rarer than sensible government. Responsible gun ownership might include the use of trigger locks—I'd like to think so—but a law mandating them is little more than a political pacifier.

Irresponsible gun owners aren't going to use trigger locks. And responsible 8 gun owners aren't going to leave handguns lying on the floor, as was the case in the Michigan shooting.

The child who killed Kayla, police say, took a stolen .32 semiautomatic to 9 school. The boy was living in a crack house, where trigger locks were about as likely as a well-balanced meal. Or even a real bed.

The boy slept on a couch in the living room of a run-down house inhabited 10 by his 21-year-old uncle and another man, who was 19. The boy's mother left the child and his 8-year-old brother with the uncle about two weeks ago when she was evicted from her nearby home. The boy's father is in prison.

It is ridiculous to suppose that someone who deals in drugs and guns will 11 take the extra step of attaching trigger locks. You can picture the thought process: "Boy, this crack sure smacks good. But, whoa, I forgot to lock the trigger on that piece I stole yesterday. What am I thinking?"

"Thinking" is the operative word here, and I've got a turtle's lead on the 12 lowlife who left a child to play with a lethal weapon. There is only one reasonable conclusion: Make adults pay for crimes committed by children.

Prosecutors are heading in that direction. In Michigan, police arrested one 13 of the men and charged him with involuntary manslaughter for allegedly allowing the boy access to the gun. The boy's mother has been accused of neglect.

Trigger locks are a good idea. They're also readily available and cost as little 14 as $10. I can't imagine why anyone with young children in the house wouldn't use them.

But a law insisting on the use of trigger locks would be as effective as laws 15 insisting that people not steal or use drugs, or a law requiring them to be good parents.

- ## *Thinking Critically About "For Starters, We Can Require Trigger Locks" and "Revisiting the Issue of Trigger Locks"*

RESPONDING AS A READER

1. Did your experience of reading Parker's two columns confirm or contradict your predictions? To track her reasoning, work up a basic outline of her primary claims regarding trigger locks in each of the two columns with the reasons, evidence, and assumptions that support them.
2. In the second column, what is Parker's basis for attacking her previous position? What differences are there in the way she counters the opposing position in each of the columns?
3. How have Parker's two pieces deepened or changed your thinking about the trigger locks issue? About handgun regulation in general? About gun safety in general? What specific aspects of these texts did you find particularly compelling or particularly repellent?

RESPONDING AS A WRITER

1. Parker is known for the informal conversational style of her columns. To examine the details of her style, work with the column of your choice to note which sentences (or parts of sentences) contribute directly to the line of reasoning that supports her primary claim about trigger locks, which ones provide background information, and which ones provide neither. What is the function of this material? How does it contribute to Parker's credibility? To her audience appeal? To her overall effectiveness?
2. Parker is known for her unexpectedly playful word choices and phrasing. Working again from the column of your choice, list the words that you consider to be unexpected or unusual in a political commentary. Next to each word, write what would have been a more conventional way to express the idea(s). What does Parker accomplish by making the unexpected choice? Choose three or four of these that you find most interesting and compare them to your classmates' choices.
3. Writing op-ed columns is more difficult than it may appear because content must be condensed to fit strict length limits. (These two have fewer than 600 words.) To understand Parker's approach to this tight structure more fully, try summarizing one of these columns in 100 words. Then condense your summary even further and add commentary about her method by using the model in Chapter 4 to develop a four-sentence rhetorical précis of the column. (See p. 62.)

Arnold Wolfendale and Seth Shostak

Is There Other Intelligent Life in the Universe? An Exchange of Letters

This exchange of letters debating the possibility of extraterrestrial intelligence was published in the June 2000 issue of the British monthly *Prospect*, which focuses on political and cultural issues and makes its contents available to an international readership via the World Wide Web. Sir Arnold Wolfendale (b. 1927), who answers the title question with a firm "No," takes the first turn in the debate. An Emeritus Professor of Physics at the University of Durham in England, he is an expert on cosmic rays and magnetic fields and served as Astronomer Royal from 1991 through 1995. He is well known in the United Kingdom for his work fostering public understanding of science. Seth Shostak (b. 1943), who answers "Yes," holds a Ph.D. in astronomy and has served since 1989 as public programs scientist at the nonprofit Search for Extraterrestrial Intelligence (SETI) Institute in Mountain View, California, where he oversees the SETI Website and writes articles and books, including *Sharing the Universe* (1998).

● *For Your Reading Log*

1. What do you know about the search for extraterrestrial intelligence?
2. What do you believe about extraterrestrial intelligence? Do you think we are alone in the universe?

———————   ●   ———————

27th April 2000

Dear Seth Shostak,

It is 400 years since Giordano Bruno was burnt at the stake for heresy. He believed that the earth was not at the centre of the universe and that life on Earth was not unique. He was right about the former, but what about the latter? 1

Asked the question "are we alone in the Universe?" most people believe that the answer is "no," even when the question specifies that life elsewhere must be able to communicate with us in an intelligible form. Supporters of the "life is unique" brigade have a big hill to climb. Let me start the ascent. 2

The argument of those who believe that we are not alone runs as follows. There are many stars in the galaxy (many more in the Universe) and many have planets. A large fraction of these will have the conditions necessary for our kind of life: oxygen, water, and so on. It is then only one step to the evolution of intelligent life, et voila: "Life is common." End of problem. 3

True, planets are quite common around other stars, and their presence has been demonstrated by a number of scientists using the techniques of optical 4 astronomy; it should not be long before planets with the ingredients of life are detected. Moreover, the recent work on the Mars meteorite, with the possible detection of bacteria-style fossils, is intriguing. Although there is considerable argument about the accuracy of these findings, free water was found on the early Martian surface and there may well be elementary life beneath the surface now. It would not be surprising if elementary life—Martian-style—were common.

5   It is the next step—a step which took 3 billion years on Earth—which worries me: the transition from elementary biological systems (perhaps extending as far as lower animals) to the polished intelligent beings who now inhabit Earth. My worries are twofold.

6   The first concerns the factors which can snuff out life before it reaches the intelligent category. Setting aside naturally occurring problems of climate, fertility and so on, there are astronomical hazards associated with the impact of extraterrestrial bodies, enhanced emissions from the Sun, and effects from other stars. This problem is arousing considerable interest, not least because the U.S. military has found a new enemy to replace the Russians. Although it looks as though Earth could last a billion years before the doomsday comet arrives, this period could be much shorter if smaller comets, or even near-misses, were seriously to disturb the climate. The situation may be much worse on other "earths" if the comet rain were denser, which is quite likely because the Earth is protected by Jupiter. Also our Sun is, fortunately, very quiescent—which is why we are here—although it is likely that dramatic solar flares occur every 1 million years. Many other stars are much less stable, with prospects for life on their planets correspondingly reduced.

7   When allowance is made for these factors, the odds on "life is common" are considerably reduced. But what clinches the argument is my second difficulty. This concerns the answer to the question: where are they? We, on Earth, have probably only about 1 billion years to go before the solar radiation level renders life unbearable and we have to leave. Certainly, in about 4 billion years, the Sun will run out of fuel and swell alarmingly. When we ask "where are they?" we are not asking "why have we not detected any signals from them?" but rather, "why are they not here in person?" The point is that, if intelligent life were common, there should have been colonisation by the inhabitants of planets around the many other stars which have come to the end of their lives. If the "people" leaving the other planets were similar to us, Earth would have seemed an appealing place to settle. But there is no evidence of their presence.

8   The simplest conclusion is that these other civilisations do not exist. What, then, is the point of spending large sums searching for their signals using radio receivers (Jodrell Bank, Arecibo, and so on)? My own view is that there is a good case to be made for such spending and for the work of your own institute, dedicated to the Search for Extraterrestrial Intelligence (SETI). For a start, the "we are alone" argument could be wrong. And something unexpected in another area—perhaps of purely astronomical interest—might be discovered. Furthermore, there is the stimulus to technology from the development of your listening equipment. But I remain sceptical about hearing "them" out there.

Yours,
Arnold Wolfendale

28th April 2000

Dear Arnold Wolfendale,

You do me a disservice. You don't believe the intelligent extraterrestrials are 9 out there, and yet you think that I and my colleagues should continue to bang away searching for them—not so much because we might succeed, but because we could stumble upon some intriguing spin-off. This is like encouraging James Cook to sail to the South Pacific by appealing to his possible contribution to ship design.

You begin with the currently accepted view that planets capable of incubat- 10 ing life are probably common. I agree, of course. Indeed, estimates of the numbers of planets which populate our galaxy are usually tallied in tens of billions. You then concede that biology will likely spring up on many of these other worlds; once more, I concur. But you then argue (along with Peter Ward and Donald Brownlee in their recent book *Rare Earth*) that while life may be commonplace, intelligent life—the kind which could make its presence known via radio signals hurled across the vast spaces between the stars—is rare, and possibly absent altogether. In this view, we inhabit an enormous galactic zoo populated by lesser creatures. Humans, you suggest, are the smartest things in the Milky Way. This is a nice point of view, at least for humans. But given the enormity of the Universe, and the lesson against cosmic hubris first taught by Copernicus, we should be suspicious of this proposition. You offer two reasons why we should not expect extraterrestrial companions. The first is that the slow progression from simple to sentient life will often be stopped in its evolutionary tracks. Intelligence on Earth was slow in coming. It has been 3.6 billion years since life arose on our planet, and 600 million years since the Cambrian explosion of complex, multicellular creatures. This long R&D phase before nature produced humans does suggest that the whole process is vulnerable to even a rare catastrophe. But one didn't happen here—and Earth is not likely to be an astronomical rarity.

Certainly there have been mass extinctions, the most famous being the de- 11 struction of three-fourths of all species—most notably the dinosaurs—65 million years ago. This disaster was probably caused by a rock from space—an asteroid or comet—about 10km in size. But neither this nor any of the other calamities to befall our planet (including at least one period of global glaciation) have succeeded in terminating biology. The chain of life has snaked unbroken through every disaster for over 3.5 billion years.

Life is durable. And, as you say, we should probably thank Jupiter for keep- 12 ing the inner solar system relatively free of large comets (although Jupiter also pulls some of these missiles our way). But there is no reason to think that large planets able to deflect lethal rubble from the cradles of life are scarce. Indeed, planet-hunters have found that at least 3 per cent of Sun-like stars have Jupiter-like planets.

Your second argument is that aliens should be in the neighbourhood—driven 13 to colonisation by imploding stars—but they are not. This argument, as you know, dates from a remark by the physicist Enrico Fermi in 1950. Indeed, it provoked a cottage industry of research intended to explain how aliens might be plentiful, but poor travellers. Many of these explanations are reasonable. For example, Frank Drake has noted the daunting cost of interstellar travel and concluded that few civilisations would do it, thus limiting the number of colonies. Others have pointed out that colonisation efforts always run out of steam. Even insects which specialise in "colonising" vegetation by chewing it full of holes don't devour the entire forest.

14　　In other words, it could be that the lack of apparent alien presence in our neighbourhood tells us nothing. After all, *Homo sapiens* has been wandering the globe for 100,000 years and yet there are still places where I can go and be out of sight of all humans and their artifacts. Within 200kms of my home is barren desert, devoid of any sign of the hundreds of millions of people who populate the continent. A native of Nevada might logically—but incorrectly—infer that his family was the lone clot of humans in America. You are like this putative Nevada native.

15　　It was not long ago—a matter of decades—that the existence of life elsewhere was considered a radical idea among astronomers. Nearby planets seemed brutally inhospitable, and the complexity of life suggested that even a simple bacterium was an improbable project that nature would seldom complete. But you now admit that biology may not be such a rare phenomenon after all. I would suggest that evolution to intelligence is a far less daunting proposition than creating the initial living cells. And if the first has taken place on a huge scale, then the second will often occur.

Yours,
Seth Shostak

2nd May 2000

Dear Seth,

16　　You say that I do you a "disservice" by pointing out that there may be spinoffs from your search. Clearly you're a member of the "all or nothing" brigade—a risky stance if you fail to find those signals. In this context, you mention my hero, Captain Cook. Well, one of his key contributions to knowledge was the testing of a John Harrison chronometer. (Harrison was after the Longitude Prize of 1714—£20,000—for devising a method of determining longitude at sea to a high degree of accuracy. He took on the astronomical establishment, who wanted to use stellar, planetary and lunar positions to do the job, and beat them with his superb horological technique.)

17　　Back to the aliens. You refer to the tens of billions of planets in our galaxy. You are right, but the number in the right range of size, which have gentle stars, not subject to alarming disturbances, with appropriate climate and so on, is probably no more than 1 million—and could be many fewer. So, if the likelihood of intelligent life evolving is less than one in a million, we are alone—in our galaxy, at least. "One in a million" sounds like a small probability, but it would be a remarkably high probability for life to evolve into intelligent beings capable of communicating with us in a manner we can understand. And if you abandon the idea of "life like us," how will you identify its signals?

18　　Now to Fermi's question: where are they? I'm waiting to hear some better "cottage industry explanations" for avoiding the horns of this dilemma. Even the best example you quote—Frank Drake's point about the cost of interstellar travel—is a nonstarter. If there are many civilisations in the galaxy, as you suggest, then quite a large fraction will be ahead of us technically, and quite able to send out large numbers of their "people." After all, the drawing to an end of the possibility of life on a planet should be a great spur to innovation; I hope you can recognise SOS calls in extraterrestrial languages.

Yours,
Arnold

3rd May 2000

Dear Arnold,

You are overly impressed with Fermi's throwaway comment. The galaxy is 19 an enormous place, with hundreds of billions of stars splayed across formidable tracts of unexplored real estate. You have strolled down to the local beach, found no whales or walruses, and concluded that it is improbable that the ocean could be home to large mammals.

I have already suggested several reasons why sophisticated alien societies 20 might be common, but still undiscovered by us (more can be found in my book, *Sharing the Universe*). In particular, the galaxy might be "urbanised," but we could be located in an uninteresting rural area. In addition, I would urge caution in assuming that tomorrow's technology (which the aliens presumably have) will solve the difficulties inherent in interstellar travel, à la Star Trek. Physics, not engineering, is the real problem. Gallivanting from star to star at any reasonable speed is stupendously costly in terms of the required energy. To draw any conclusions from our isolation is premature. We have not done much hunting for signs of nearby alien intelligence, and it is unclear whether we would recognise them anyway.

Cut to the nub of your argument: you grant the probable existence of tens of 21 billions of planets in the Milky Way. You then make the odd statement that only 1 million or fewer of these worlds will enjoy the conditions necessary for spawning biology. Where, in heaven's name, do you get this number? Sun-like stars, which account for one in ten of the galaxy's stellar complement, are incredibly stable producers of light. True, we don't know what fraction of the Milky Way's billions of planets will have the conditions required for life, but in our own solar system three worlds are believed to be capable of cooking up a bit of biology: Earth, Mars, and one of Jupiter's moons, Europa. That's three among nine planets which could have produced life. So how do you justify the claim that only 1 million of the galaxy's tens of billions of worlds might be carpeted with biology?

I suspect that life is common, and that proof will come in the form of dis- 22 coveries to be made on Mars and Europa within the next 20 years. But you have a valid point when you question whether a sizeable fraction of living worlds will produce intelligent life, capable of building the powerful transmitters which would make them detectable by our radio telescopes. Maybe that fraction is small. Only once (twice, if you count the Neanderthals) has nature evolved an intelligent species on this planet, and this high IQ experiment may have been an unlikely accident. But note that there has been a substantial increase in relative brain size for several classes of earthly mammals in the last 50 million years. Most of today's furry creatures are a lot brainier than the dinosaurs who stomped over our planet not so long ago. This at least suggests that sentience has real survival value, and nature will often produce it.

23   Intelligence may or may not frequently raise its cerebral head, but I suspect that it is a durable phenomenon when it does so. The whole point of SETI is to find out if this is the case. We hunt for simple, narrow-band signals—a sure sign of beings with a good grasp of physics and engineering—which keeps the search as culturally nonspecific as possible. We don't worry too much about how the aliens are constructed.

Yours,
Seth

4th May 2000

Dear Seth,

24   You talk about the galaxy being "an enormous place, with hundreds of billions of stars splayed across formidable tracts of unexplored real estate." But we're trying to work out statistical probabilities—and even one billion stars with a probability of intelligent life per star (or solar system) of much less than one in a billion makes us almost certainly unique.

25   You also admit that "it's unclear whether we would recognise them [alien signals] anyway." You are a glutton for punishment! Your life is dedicated to looking for an unrecognisable needle in a giant haystack. To recap: the odds against extraterrestrial intelligence—capable of communicating with us in an intelligible way—are very high. But because of the likelihood of something astronomically interesting turning up—and "just in case"—please keep at it.

Yours,
Arnold

6th May 2000

Dear Arnold,

26   Of course we're trying to work out probabilities. My point is that if, as you say, we are alone in the Milky Way, then the odds against the evolution of intelligent life must be more than an imposing thousand to one, or a daunting million to one—they must be billions to one. This seems unrealistically high odds against intelligent life when we know that there are around half a trillion stars in our galaxy alone. If our Sun were extraordinary, or if planets were rare, then there would be a rationale for such irrational odds. Neither is the case. Indeed, I have yet to hear of one peculiarity of our situation which could so sharply distinguish us. If astronomy has taught us anything in the past 400 years, it is that every time we thought we enjoyed a unique cosmic situation, we were wrong.

Yours,
Seth

- *Thinking Critically About "Is There Other Intelligent Life in the Universe?"*

RESPONDING AS A READER

1. To understand the debate between these two thinkers fully, create an idea map that tracks the reasons each gives in support of his "yes" or "no" answer to the title question. Then add, perhaps with different pens or pencils, points about which they agree (for example, that many planets are capable of incubating life), and finally, their rebuttals of each other's points. (See, for example, Shostak's rebuttals in paragraphs 10 through 12 of Wolfendale's claim that astronomical hazards lower the chances of life having survived on other planets beyond basic stages.)
2. Now try to articulate the unstated assumptions that each man uses to carry the reasoning from his evidence to his claim.
3. What question seems to you to pose the most significant sticking point between these two scientists' conflicting views? Which of the categories of the stasis question types in Table 13.1 (p. 395) does it fit? In your view, which of the two men makes the more convincing case in response to that question? Why?

RESPONDING AS A WRITER

1. How would you describe the personalities that Wolfendale and Shostak establish in these letters? What is each man's method for doing this? Point to specific passages for analysis. Which man did you find more likable? How did this likableness interact with your evaluation of the arguments each set forward?
2. This direct exchange provides a good opportunity for examining how the writers restate each other's positions and forward counterarguments. Find an instance that you consider particularly well handled and one you consider flawed. How could it have been improved? What does this back-and-forth reveal about what each of these writers seems to consider his opponent's strongest and weakest cases?
3. Do you find this exchange of letters to be an effective means of conveying the complexity of this scientific debate to nonscientists? Why or why not? What other topics might be suitable for this type of article? What topics would not be suitable? Why?

Martin Luther King Jr.

Statement by Alabama Clergymen and Letter from Birmingham Jail

The Reverend Martin Luther King Jr. (1929–1968) is known worldwide for his leadership of the civil rights movement in the United States and for his advocacy of nonviolent protests in pursuit of equality before the law for African Americans. This famous letter was written after he was arrested and put into solitary confinement on Good Friday in 1963 for defying a court order forbidding him and 132 others from participating in demonstrations in Birmingham, Alabama. King, a Baptist minister, is responding to a statement from eight white Alabama clergymen urging that demonstrations cease, which ran as a full page ad in the *Birmingham News* on the day he was arrested. This well-known explanation of his intent to keep protesting against racial prejudice is said to have begun as scribbled notes in the margins of the newspaper and on scraps of toilet paper. The resulting letter, dated four days after his arrest, was originally published as a pamphlet by the American Friends Service Committee. The version we present here, obtained from the Website of the Martin Luther King Jr. Papers Project at Stanford University, appeared in King's 1964 book, *Why We Can't Wait*. We include as well the text of the statement from the clergymen.

• *For Your Reading Log*

1. To draw together your expectations about the argument King makes in support of nonviolent protests advocating civil rights, freewrite about what you know about his thinking on this issue. If you have read the letter before, freewrite about what you remember of King's argument.
2. Before you read King's letter, read the statement from the Alabama clergy, then turn to your reading log to record your understanding of its primary point and to predict (perhaps recall) the reasoning King uses to reject it.

——————— • ———————

Statement by Alabama Clergymen

12 April 1963

1 We the undersigned clergymen are among those who, in January, issued "An Appeal for Law and Order and Common Sense," in dealing with racial problems in Alabama. We expressed understanding that honest convictions in racial matters could properly be pursued in the courts, but urged that decisions of those courts should in the meantime be peacefully obeyed.

Since that time there had been some evidence of increased forbearance and 2
a willingness to face facts. Responsible citizens have undertaken to work on various problems which cause racial friction and unrest. In Birmingham, recent
public events have given indication that we will have opportunity for a new constructive and realistic approach to racial problems.

However, we are now confronted by a series of demonstrations by some of 3
our Negro citizens, directed and led in part by outsiders. We recognize the natural impatience of people who feel that their hopes are slow in being realized.
But we are convinced that these demonstrations are unwise and untimely.

We agree rather with certain local Negro leadership which has called for hon- 4
est and open negotiation of racial issues in our area. And we believe this kind of
facing of issues can best be accomplished by citizens of our own metropolitan
area, white and Negro, meeting with their knowledge and experience of the local situation. All of us need to face that responsibility and find proper channels
for its accomplishment.

Just as we formerly pointed out that "hatred and violence have no sanction in 5
our religious and political traditions," we also point out that such actions as incite
to hatred and violence, however technically peaceful those actions may be, have
not contributed to the resolution of our local problems. We do not believe that these
days of new hope are days when extreme measures are justified in Birmingham.

We commend the community as a whole, and the local news media and law 6
enforcement officials in particular, on the calm manner in which these demonstrations have been handled. We urge the public to continue to show restraint
should the demonstrations continue, and the law enforcement officials to remain
calm and continue to protect our city from violence.

We further strongly urge our own Negro community to withdraw support 7
from these demonstrations, and to unite locally in working peacefully for a better Birmingham. When rights are consistently denied, a cause should be pressed
in the courts and in negotiations among local leaders, and not in the streets. We
appeal to both our white and Negro citizenry to observe the principles of law and
order and common sense.

Signed by:

C.C.J. Carpenter, D.D., LL.D., Bishop of Alabama

Joseph A. Durick, D.D., Auxiliary Bishop, Diocese of Mobile-Birmingham

Rabbi Milton L. Grafman, Temple Emanu-El, Birmingham, Alabama

Bishop Paul Hardin, Bishop of the Alabama–West Florida Conference of the
Methodist Church

Bishop Nolan B. Harmon, Bishop of the North Alabama Conference of the
Methodist Church

George M. Murray, D.D., LL.D., Bishop Coadjutor, Episcopal Diocese of
Alabama

Edward V. Ramage, Moderator, Synod of the Alabama Presbyterian Church
in the United States

Earl Stallings, Pastor, First Baptist Church, Birmingham, Alabama

Letter from Birmingham Jail

My Dear Fellow Clergymen:

1   While confined here in the Birmingham city jail, I came across your recent statement calling my present activities "unwise and untimely." Seldom do I pause to answer criticism of my work and ideas. If I sought to answer all the criticisms that cross my desk, my secretaries would have little time for anything other than such correspondence in the course of the day, and I would have no time for constructive work. But since I feel that you are men of genuine good will and that your criticisms are sincerely set forth, I want to try to answer your statements in what I hope will be patient and reasonable terms.

2   I think I should indicate why I am here in Birmingham, since you have been influenced by the view which argues against "outsiders coming in." I have the honor of serving as president of the Southern Christian Leadership Conference, an organization operating in every southern state, with headquarters in Atlanta, Georgia. We have some eighty-five affiliated organizations across the South, and one of them is the Alabama Christian Movement for Human Rights. Frequently we share staff, educational and financial resources with our affiliates. Several months ago the affiliate here in Birmingham asked us to be on call to engage in a nonviolent direct-action program if such were deemed necessary. We readily consented, and when the hour came we lived up to our promise. So I, along with several members of my staff, am here because I was invited here. I am here because I have organizational ties here.

3   But more basically, I am in Birmingham because injustice is here. Just as the prophets of the eighth century B.C. left their villages and carried their "thus saith the Lord" far beyond the boundaries of their home towns, and just as the Apostle Paul left his village of Tarsus and carried the gospel of Jesus Christ to the far corners of the Greco-Roman world, so am I compelled to carry the gospel of freedom beyond my own home town. Like Paul, I must constantly respond to the Macedonian call for aid.

4   Moreover, I am cognizant of the interrelatedness of all communities and states. I cannot sit idly by in Atlanta and not be concerned about what happens in Birmingham. Injustice anywhere is a threat to justice everywhere. We are caught in an inescapable network of mutuality, tied in a single garment of destiny. Whatever affects one directly, affects all indirectly. Never again can we afford to live with the narrow, provincial "outside agitator" idea. Anyone who lives inside the United States can never be considered an outsider anywhere within its bounds.

5   You deplore the demonstrations taking place in Birmingham. But your statement, I am sorry to say, fails to express a similar concern for the conditions that brought about the demonstrations. I am sure that none of you would want to rest content with the superficial kind of social analysis that deals merely with effects and does not grapple with underlying causes. It is unfortunate that demonstrations are taking place in Birmingham, but it is even more unfortunate that the city's white power structure left the Negro community with no alternative.

In any nonviolent campaign there are four basic steps: collection of the facts 6
to determine whether injustices exist; negotiation; self-purification; and direct action. We have gone through all these steps in Birmingham. There can be no gain-
saying the fact that racial injustice engulfs this community. Birmingham is
probably the most thoroughly segregated city in the United States. Its ugly
record of brutality is widely known. Negroes have experienced grossly unjust
treatment in the courts. There have been more unsolved bombings of Negro
homes and churches in Birmingham than in any other city in the nation. These
are the hard, brutal facts of the case. On the basis of these conditions, Negro leaders sought to negotiate with the city fathers. But the latter consistently refused
to engage in good-faith negotiation.

Then, last September, came the opportunity to talk with leaders of Birming- 7
ham's economic community. In the course of the negotiations, certain promises
were made by the merchants—for example, to remove the stores' humiliating
racial signs. On the basis of these promises, the Reverend Fred Shuttlesworth and
the leaders of the Alabama Christian Movement for Human Rights agreed to a
moratorium on all demonstrations. As the weeks and months went by, we realized that we were the victims of a broken promise. A few signs, briefly removed,
returned; the others remained.

As in so many past experiences, our hopes had been blasted, and the shadow 8
of deep disappointment settled upon us. We had no alternative except to prepare
for direct action, whereby we would present our very bodies as a means of laying our case before the conscience of the local and the national community.
Mindful of the difficulties involved, we decided to undertake a process of self-
purification. We began a series of workshops on nonviolence, and we repeatedly
asked ourselves: "Are you able to accept blows without retaliating?" "Are you
able to endure the ordeal of jail?" We decided to schedule our direct-action program for the Easter season, realizing that except for Christmas, this is the main
shopping period of the year. Knowing that a strong economic withdrawal program would be the by-product of direct action, we felt that this would be the best
time to bring pressure to bear on the merchants for the needed change.

Then it occurred to us that Birmingham's mayoralty election was coming up 9
in March, and we speedily decided to postpone action until after election day.
When we discovered that the Commissioner of Public Safety, Eugene "Bull"
Connor, had piled up enough votes to be in the run-off, we decided again to postpone action until the day after the run-off so that the demonstrations could not
be used to cloud the issues. Like many others, we waited to see Mr. Connor defeated, and to this end we endured postponement after postponement. Having
aided in this community need, we felt that our direct-action program could be
delayed no longer.

You may well ask: "Why direct action? Why sit-ins, marches and so forth? Is- 10
n't negotiation a better path?" You are quite right in calling for negotiation. Indeed,
this is the very purpose of direct action. Nonviolent direct action seeks to create
such a crisis and foster such a tension that a community which has constantly refused to negotiate is forced to confront the issue. It seeks so to dramatize the issue

that it can no longer be ignored. My citing the creation of tension as part of the work of the nonviolent-resister may sound rather shocking. But I must confess that I am not afraid of the word "tension." I have earnestly opposed violent tension, but there is a type of constructive, nonviolent tension which is necessary for growth. Just as Socrates felt that it was necessary to create a tension in the mind so that individuals could rise from the bondage of myths and half-truths to the un-fettered realm of creative analysis and objective appraisal, so must we see the need for nonviolent gadflies to create the kind of tension in society that will help men rise from the dark depths of prejudice and racism to the majestic heights of un-derstanding and brotherhood.

11   The purpose of our direct-action program is to create a situation so crisis-packed that it will inevitably open the door to negotiation. I therefore concur with you in your call for negotiation. Too long has our beloved Southland been bogged down in a tragic effort to live in monologue rather than dialogue.

12   One of the basic points in your statement is that the action that I and my as-sociates have taken in Birmingham is untimely. Some have asked: "Why didn't you give the new city administration time to act?" The only answer that I can give to this query is that the new Birmingham administration must be prodded about as much as the outgoing one, before it will act. We are sadly mistaken if we feel that the election of Albert Boutwell as mayor will bring the millennium to Bir-mingham. While Mr. Boutwell is a much more gentle person than Mr. Connor, they are both segregationists, dedicated to maintenance of the status quo. I have hope that Mr. Boutwell will be reasonable enough to see the futility of massive resistance to desegregation. But he will not see this without pressure from devo-tees of civil rights. My friends, I must say to you that we have not made a single gain in civil rights without determined legal and nonviolent pressure. Lamen-tably, it is an historical fact that privileged groups seldom give up their privileges voluntarily. Individuals may see the moral light and voluntarily give up their un-just posture; but, as Reinhold Niebuhr has reminded us, groups tend to be more immoral than individuals.

13   We know through painful experience that freedom is never voluntarily given by the oppressor; it must be demanded by the oppressed. Frankly, I have yet to engage in a direct-action campaign that was "well timed" in the view of those who have not suffered unduly from the disease of segregation. For years now I have heard the word "Wait!" It rings in the ear of every Negro with piercing familiar-ity. This "Wait" has almost always meant "Never." We must come to see, with one of our distinguished jurists, that "justice too long delayed is justice denied."

14   We have waited for more than 340 years for our constitutional and God-given rights. The nations of Asia and Africa are moving with jetlike speed toward gain-ing political independence, but we still creep at horse-and-buggy pace toward gaining a cup of coffee at a lunch counter. Perhaps it is easy for those who have never felt the stinging darts of segregation to say, "Wait." But when you have seen vicious mobs lynch your mothers and fathers at will and drown your sisters and brothers at whim; when you have seen hate-filled policemen curse, kick and even kill your black brothers and sisters; when you see the vast majority of your twenty million Negro brothers smothering in an airtight cage of poverty in the midst of

an affluent society; when you suddenly find your tongue twisted and your speech stammering as you seek to explain to your six-year-old daughter why she can't go to the public amusement park that has just been advertised on television, and see tears welling up in her eyes when she is told that Funtown is closed to colored children, and see ominous clouds of inferiority beginning to form in her little mental sky, and see her beginning to distort her personality by developing an unconscious bitterness toward white people; when you have to concoct an answer for a five-year-old son who is asking: "Daddy, why do white people treat colored people so mean?", when you take a cross-country drive and find it necessary to sleep night after night in the uncomfortable corners of your automobile because no motel will accept you; when you are humiliated day in and day out by nagging signs reading "white" and "colored"; when your first name becomes "nigger," your middle name becomes "boy" (however old you are) and your last name becomes "John," and your wife and mother are never given the respected title "Mrs."; when you are harried by day and haunted by night by the fact that you are a Negro, living constantly at tiptoe stance, never quite knowing what to expect next, and are plagued with inner fears and outer resentments; when you are forever fighting a degenerating sense of "nobodiness"—then you will understand why we find it difficult to wait. There comes a time when the cup of endurance runs over, and men are no longer willing to be plunged into the abyss of despair. I hope, sirs, you can understand our legitimate and unavoidable impatience.

You express a great deal of anxiety over our willingness to break laws. This 15 is certainly a legitimate concern. Since we so diligently urge people to obey the Supreme Court's decision of 1954 outlawing segregation in the public schools, at first glance it may seem rather paradoxical for us consciously to break laws. One may well ask: "How can you advocate breaking some laws and obeying others?" The answer lies in the fact that there are two types of laws: just and unjust. I would be the first to advocate obeying just laws. One has not only a legal but a moral responsibility to obey just laws. Conversely, one has a moral responsibility to disobey unjust laws. I would agree with St. Augustine that "an unjust law is no law at all."

Now, what is the difference between the two? How does one determine 16 whether a law is just or unjust? A just law is a man-made code that squares with the moral law or the law of God. An unjust law is a code that is out of harmony with the moral law. To put it in the terms of St. Thomas Aquinas: An unjust law is a human law that is not rooted in eternal law and natural law. Any law that uplifts human personality is just. Any law that degrades human personality is unjust. All segregation statutes are unjust because segregation distorts the soul and damages the personality. It gives the segregator a false sense of superiority and the segregated a false sense of inferiority. Segregation, to use the terminology of the Jewish philosopher Martin Buber, substitutes an "I-it" relationship for an "I-thou" relationship and ends up relegating persons to the status of things. Hence segregation is not only politically, economically and sociologically unsound, it is morally wrong and sinful. Paul Tillich has said that sin is separation. Is not segregation an existential expression of man's tragic separation, his awful estrangement, his terrible sinfulness? Thus it is that I can urge men to obey the

1954 decision of the Supreme Court, for it is morally right; and I can urge them to disobey segregation ordinances, for they are morally wrong.

17   Let us consider a more concrete example of just and unjust laws. An unjust law is a code that a numerical or power majority group compels a minority group to obey but does not make binding on itself. This is *difference* made legal. By the same token, a just law is a code that a majority compels a minority to follow and that it is willing to follow itself. This is *sameness* made legal.

18   Let me give another explanation. A law is unjust if it is inflicted on a minority that, as a result of being denied the right to vote, had no part in enacting or devising the law. Who can say that the legislature of Alabama which set up that state's segregation laws was democratically elected? Throughout Alabama all sorts of devious methods are used to prevent Negroes from becoming registered voters, and there are some counties in which, even though Negroes constitute a majority of the population, not a single Negro is registered. Can any law enacted under such circumstances be considered democratically structured?

19   Sometimes a law is just on its face and unjust in its application. For instance, I have been arrested on a charge of parading without a permit. Now, there is nothing wrong in having an ordinance which requires a permit for a parade. But such an ordinance becomes unjust when it is used to maintain segregation and to deny citizens the First-Amendment privilege of peaceful assembly and protest.

20   I hope you are able to see the distinction I am trying to point out. In no sense do I advocate evading or defying the law, as would the rabid segregationist. That would lead to anarchy. One who breaks an unjust law must do so openly, lovingly, and with a willingness to accept the penalty. I submit that an individual who breaks a law that conscience tells him is unjust, and who willingly accepts the penalty of imprisonment in order to arouse the conscience of the community over its injustice, is in reality expressing the highest respect for law.

21   Of course, there is nothing new about this kind of civil disobedience. It was evidenced sublimely in the refusal of Shadrach, Meshach and Abednego to obey the laws of Nebuchadnezzar, on the ground that a higher moral law was at stake. It was practiced superbly by the early Christians, who were willing to face hungry lions and the excruciating pain of chopping blocks rather than submit to certain unjust laws of the Roman Empire. To a degree, academic freedom is a reality today because Socrates practiced civil disobedience. In our own nation, the Boston Tea Party represented a massive act of civil disobedience.

22   We should never forget that everything Adolf Hitler did in Germany was "legal" and everything the Hungarian freedom fighters did in Hungary was "illegal." It was "illegal" to aid and comfort a Jew in Hitler's Germany. Even so, I am sure that, had I lived in Germany at the time, I would have aided and comforted my Jewish brothers. If today I lived in a Communist country where certain principles dear to the Christian faith are suppressed, I would openly advocate disobeying that country's antireligious laws.

23   I must make two honest confessions to you, my Christian and Jewish brothers. First, I must confess that over the past few years I have been gravely disappointed with the white moderate. I have almost reached the regrettable conclusion that the Negro's great stumbling block in his stride toward freedom

is not the White Citizen's Counciler or the Ku Klux Klanner, but the white moderate, who is more devoted to "order" than to justice; who prefers a negative peace which is the absence of tension to a positive peace which is the presence of justice; who constantly says: "I agree with you in the goal you seek, but I cannot agree with your methods of direct action"; who paternalistically believes he can set the timetable for another man's freedom; who lives by a mythical concept of time and who constantly advises the Negro to wait for a "more convenient season." Shallow understanding from people of good will is more frustrating than absolute misunderstanding from people of ill will. Lukewarm acceptance is much more bewildering than outright rejection.

I had hoped that the white moderate would understand that law and order 24 exist for the purpose of establishing justice and that when they fail in this purpose they become the dangerously structured dams that block the flow of social progress. I had hoped that the white moderate would understand that the present tension in the South is a necessary phase of the transition from an obnoxious negative peace, in which the Negro passively accepted his unjust plight, to a substantive and positive peace, in which all men will respect the dignity and worth of human personality. Actually, we who engage in nonviolent direct action are not the creators of tension. We merely bring to the surface the hidden tension that is already alive. We bring it out in the open, where it can be seen and dealt with. Like a boil that can never be cured so long as it is covered up but must be opened with all its ugliness to the natural medicines of air and light, injustice must be exposed, with all the tension its exposure creates, to the light of human conscience and the air of national opinion before it can be cured.

In your statement you assert that our actions, even though peaceful, must be 25 condemned because they precipitate violence. But is this a logical assertion? Isn't this like condemning a robbed man because his possession of money precipitated the evil act of robbery? Isn't this like condemning Socrates because his unswerving commitment to truth and his philosophical inquiries precipitated the act by the misguided populace in which they made him drink hemlock? Isn't this like condemning Jesus because his unique God-consciousness and never-ceasing devotion to God's will precipitated the evil act of crucifixion? We must come to see that, as the federal courts have consistently affirmed, it is wrong to urge an individual to cease his efforts to gain his basic constitutional rights because the quest may precipitate violence. Society must protect the robbed and punish the robber.

I had also hoped that the white moderate would reject the myth concerning 26 time in relation to the struggle for freedom. I have just received a letter from a white brother in Texas. He writes: "All Christians know that the colored people will receive equal rights eventually, but it is possible that you are in too great a religious hurry. It has taken Christianity almost two thousand years to accomplish what it has. The teachings of Christ take time to come to earth." Such an attitude stems from a tragic misconception of time, from the strangely irrational notion that there is something in the very flow of time that will inevitably cure all ills. Actually, time itself is neutral; it can be used either destructively or constructively. More and more I feel that the people of ill will have used time much more effectively than have the people of good will. We will have to repent in this generation not merely for the hateful words and actions of the bad people but for the appalling silence of the good people. Human progress never rolls in on wheels of inevitability; it comes through the tireless efforts of men willing to be co-workers with God, and without this hard work, time itself becomes an ally of the forces of social stagnation. We must use time creatively, in the knowledge that the time is always ripe to do right. Now is the time to make real the promise of democracy and transform our pending national elegy into a creative psalm of brotherhood. Now is the time to lift our national policy from the quicksand of racial injustice to the solid rock of human dignity.

27   You speak of our activity in Birmingham as extreme. At first I was rather disappointed that fellow clergymen would see my nonviolent efforts as those of an extremist. I began thinking about the fact that I stand in the middle of two opposing forces in the Negro community. One is a force of complacency, made up in part of Negroes who, as a result of long years of oppression, are so drained of self-respect and a sense of "somebodiness" that they have adjusted to segregation; and in part of a few middle-class Negroes who, because of a degree of academic and economic security and because in some ways they profit by segregation, have become insensitive to the problems of the masses. The other force is one of bitterness and hatred, and it comes perilously close to advocating violence. It is expressed in the various black nationalist groups that are springing up across the nation, the largest and best-known being Elijah Muhammad's Muslim movement. Nourished by the Negro's frustration over the continued existence of racial discrimination, this movement is made up of people who have lost faith in America, who have absolutely repudiated Christianity, and who have concluded that the white man is an incorrigible "devil."

28   I have tried to stand between these two forces, saying that we need emulate neither the "do-nothingism" of the complacent nor the hatred and despair of the black nationalist. For there is the more excellent way of love and nonviolent protest. I am grateful to God that, through the influence of the Negro church, the way of nonviolence became an integral part of our struggle.

29   If this philosophy had not emerged, by now many streets of the South would, I am convinced, be flowing with blood. And I am further convinced that if our white brothers dismiss as "rabble-rousers" and "outside agitators" those of us who employ nonviolent direct action, and if they refuse to support our nonviolent efforts, millions of Negroes will, out of frustration and despair, seek solace and security in black-nationalist ideologies—a development that would inevitably lead to a frightening racial nightmare.

30   Oppressed people cannot remain oppressed forever. The yearning for freedom eventually manifests itself, and that is what has happened to the American Negro. Something within has reminded him of his birthright of freedom, and something without has reminded him that it can be gained. Consciously or unconsciously, he has been caught up by the *Zeitgeist*, and with his black brothers of Africa and his brown and yellow brothers of Asia, South America and the Caribbean, the United States Negro is moving with a sense of great urgency toward the promised land of racial justice. If one recognizes this vital urge that has engulfed the Negro community, one should readily understand why public

demonstrations are taking place. The Negro has many pent-up resentments and latent frustrations, and he must release them. So let him march; let him make prayer pilgrimages to the city hall; let him go on freedom rides—and try to understand why he must do so. If his repressed emotions are not released in nonviolent ways, they will seek expression through violence; this is not a threat but a fact of history. So I have not said to my people: "Get rid of your discontent." Rather, I have tried to say that this normal and healthy discontent can be channeled into the creative outlet of nonviolent direct action. And now this approach is being termed extremist.

But though I was initially disappointed at being categorized as an extremist, 31 as I continued to think about the matter I gradually gained a measure of satisfaction from the label. Was not Jesus an extremist for love: "Love your enemies, bless them that curse you, do good to them that hate you, and pray for them which despitefully use you, and persecute you." Was not Amos an extremist for justice: "Let justice roll down like waters and righteousness like an ever-flowing stream." Was not Paul an extremist for the Christian gospel: "I bear in my body the marks of the Lord Jesus." Was not Martin Luther an extremist: "Here I stand; I cannot do otherwise, so help me God." And John Bunyan: "I will stay in jail to the end of my days before I make a butchery of my conscience." And Abraham Lincoln: "This nation cannot survive half slave and half free." And Thomas Jefferson: "We hold these truths to be self-evident, that all men are created equal..." So the question is not whether we will be extremists, but what kind of extremists we will be. Will we be extremists for hate or for love? Will we be extremists for the preservation of injustice or for the extension of justice? In that dramatic scene on Calvary's hill three men were crucified. We must never forget that all three were crucified for the same crime—the crime of extremism. Two were extremists for immorality, and thus fell below their environment. The other, Jesus Christ, was an extremist for love, truth and goodness, and thereby rose above his environment. Perhaps the South, the nation and the world are in dire need of creative extremists.

I had hoped that the white moderate would see this need. Perhaps I was too 32 optimistic; perhaps I expected too much. I suppose I should have realized that few members of the oppressor race can understand the deep groans and passionate yearnings of the oppressed race, and still fewer have the vision to see that injustice must be rooted out by strong, persistent and determined action. I am thankful, however, that some of our white brothers in the South have grasped the meaning of this social revolution and committed themselves to it. They are still too few in quantity, but they are big in quality. Some—such as Ralph McGill, Lillian Smith, Harry Golden, James McBride Dabbs, Ann Braden and Sarah Patton Boyle—have written about our struggle in eloquent and prophetic terms. Others have marched with us down nameless streets of the South. They have languished in filthy, roach-infested jails, suffering the abuse and brutality of policemen who view them as "dirty nigger-lovers." Unlike so many of their moderate brothers and sisters, they have recognized the urgency of the moment and sensed the need for powerful "action" antidotes to combat the disease of segregation.

Let me take note of my other major disappointment. I have been so greatly 33 disappointed with the white church and its leadership. Of course, there are some notable exceptions. I am not unmindful of the fact that each of you has taken some significant stands on this issue. I commend you, Reverend Stallings, for your Christian stand on this past Sunday, in welcoming Negroes to your worship service on a nonsegregated basis. I commend the Catholic leaders of this state for integrating Spring Hill College several years ago.

34   But despite these notable exceptions, I must honestly reiterate that I have been disappointed with the church. I do not say this as one of those negative critics who can always find something wrong with the church. I say this as a minister of the gospel, who loves the church; who was nurtured in its bosom; who has been sustained by its spiritual blessings and who will remain true to it as long as the cord of life shall lengthen.

35   When I was suddenly catapulted into the leadership of the bus protest in Montgomery, Alabama, a few years ago, I felt we would be supported by the white church. I felt that the white ministers, priests and rabbis of the South would be among our strongest allies. Instead, some have been outright opponents, refusing to understand the freedom movement and misrepresenting its leaders; all too many others have been more cautious than courageous and have remained silent behind the anesthetizing security of stained-glass windows.

36   In spite of my shattered dreams, I came to Birmingham with the hope that the white religious leadership of this community would see the justice of our cause and, with deep moral concern, would serve as the channel through which our just grievances could reach the power structure. I had hoped that each of you would understand. But again I have been disappointed.

37   I have heard numerous southern religious leaders admonish their worshipers to comply with a desegregation decision because it is the law, but I have longed to hear white ministers declare: "Follow this decree because integration is morally right and because the Negro is your brother." In the midst of blatant injustices inflicted upon the Negro, I have watched white churchmen stand on the sideline and mouth pious irrelevancies and sanctimonious trivialities. In the midst of a mighty struggle to rid our nation of racial and economic injustice, I have heard many ministers say: "Those are social issues, with which the gospel has no real concern." And I have watched many churches commit themselves to a completely other-worldly religion which makes a strange, un-Biblical distinction between body and soul, between the sacred and the secular.

38   I have traveled the length and breadth of Alabama, Mississippi and all the other southern states. On sweltering summer days and crisp autumn mornings I have looked at the South's beautiful churches with their lofty spires pointing heavenward. I have beheld the impressive outlines of her massive religious-education buildings. Over and over I have found myself asking: "What kind of people worship here? Who is their God? Where were their voices when the lips of Governor Barnett dripped with words of interposition and nullification? Where were they when Governor Wallace gave a clarion call for defiance and hatred? Where were their voices of support when bruised and weary Negro men and women decided to rise from the dark dungeons of complacency to the bright hills of creative protest?"

39   Yes, these questions are still in my mind. In deep disappointment I have wept over the laxity of the church. But be assured that my tears have been tears of love.

There can be no deep disappointment where there is not deep love. Yes, I love the church. How could I do otherwise? I am in the rather unique position of being the son, the grandson and the great-grandson of preachers. Yes, I see the church as the body of Christ. But, oh! How we have blemished and scarred that body through social neglect and through fear of being nonconformists.

There was a time when the church was very powerful—in the time when the [40] early Christians rejoiced at being deemed worthy to suffer for what they believed. In those days the church was not merely a thermometer that recorded the ideas and principles of popular opinion; it was a thermostat that transformed the mores of society. Whenever the early Christians entered a town, the people in power became disturbed and immediately sought to convict the Christians for being "disturbers of the peace" and "outside agitators." But the Christians pressed on, in the conviction that they were "a colony of heaven," called to obey God rather than man. Small in number, they were big in commitment. They were too God-intoxicated to be "astronomically intimidated." By their effort and example they brought an end to such ancient evils as infanticide and gladiatorial contests.

Things are different now. So often the contemporary church is a weak, inef- [41] fectual voice with an uncertain sound. So often it is an archdefender of the status quo. Far from being disturbed by the presence of the church, the power structure of the average community is consoled by the church's silent—and often even vocal—sanction of things as they are.

But the judgment of God is upon the church as never before. If today's [42] church does not recapture the sacrificial spirit of the early church, it will lose its authenticity, forfeit the loyalty of millions, and be dismissed as an irrelevant social club with no meaning for the twentieth century. Every day I meet young people whose disappointment with the church has turned into outright disgust.

Perhaps I have once again been too optimistic. Is organized religion too [43] inextricably bound to the status quo to save our nation and the world? Perhaps I must turn my faith to the inner spiritual church, the church within the church, as the true *ekklesia* and the hope of the world. But again I am thankful to God that some noble souls from the ranks of organized religion have broken loose from the paralyzing chains of conformity and joined us as active partners in the struggle for freedom. They have left their secure congregations and walked the streets of Albany, Georgia, with us. They have gone down the highways of the South on tortuous rides for freedom. Yes, they have gone to jail with us. Some have been dismissed from their churches, have lost the support of their bishops and fellow ministers. But they have acted in the faith that right defeated is stronger than evil triumphant. Their witness has been the spiritual salt that has preserved the true meaning of the gospel in these troubled times. They have carved a tunnel of hope through the dark mountain of disappointment.

I hope the church as a whole will meet the challenge of this decisive hour. [44] But even if the church does not come to the aid of justice, I have no despair about the future. I have no fear about the outcome of our struggle in Birmingham, even if our motives are at present misunderstood. We will reach the goal of freedom in Birmingham and all over the nation, because the goal of America is freedom. Abused and scorned though we may be, our destiny is tied up with America's destiny. Before the pilgrims landed at Plymouth, we were here. Before the pen of Jefferson etched the majestic words of the Declaration of Independence across the pages of history, we were here. For more than two centuries our forebears labored in this country without wages; they made cotton king; they built the homes of their masters while suffering gross injustice and shameful humiliation—and yet out of a bottomless vitality they continued to thrive and develop. If the inexpressible cruelties of slavery could not stop us, the opposition we now face will surely fail. We will win our freedom because the sacred heritage of our nation and the eternal will of God are embodied in our echoing demands.

45   Before closing I feel impelled to mention one other point in your statement that has troubled me profoundly. You warmly commended the Birmingham police force for keeping "order" and "preventing violence." I doubt that you would have so warmly commended the police force if you had seen its dogs sinking their teeth into unarmed, nonviolent Negroes. I doubt that you would so quickly commend the policemen if you were to observe their ugly and inhumane treatment of Negroes here in the city jail; if you were to watch them push and curse old Negro women and young Negro girls; if you were to see them slap and kick old Negro men and young boys; if you were to observe them, as they did on two occasions, refuse to give us food because we wanted to sing our grace together. I cannot join you in your praise of the Birmingham police department.

46   It is true that the police have exercised a degree of discipline in handling the demonstrators. In this sense they have conducted themselves rather "nonviolently" in public. But for what purpose? To preserve the evil system of segregation. Over the past few years I have consistently preached that nonviolence demands that the means we use must be as pure as the ends we seek. I have tried to make clear that it is wrong to use immoral means to attain moral ends. But now I must affirm that it is just as wrong, or perhaps even more so, to use moral means to preserve immoral ends. Perhaps Mr. Connor and his policemen have been rather nonviolent in public, as was Chief Pritchett in Albany, Georgia, but they have used the moral means of nonviolence to maintain the immoral end of racial injustice. As T. S. Eliot has said: "The last temptation is the greatest treason: To do the right deed for the wrong reason."

47   I wish you had commended the Negro sit-inners and demonstrators of Birmingham for their sublime courage, their willingness to suffer and their amazing discipline in the midst of great provocation. One day the South will recognize its real heroes. They will be the James Merediths, with the noble sense of purpose that enables them to face jeering, and hostile mobs, and with the agonizing loneliness that characterizes the life of the pioneer. They will be old, oppressed, battered Negro women, symbolized in a seventy-two-year-old woman in Montgomery, Alabama, who rose up with a sense of dignity and with her people decided not to ride segregated buses, and who responded with ungrammatical profundity to one who inquired about her weariness: "My feets is tired, but my soul is at rest." They will be the young high school and college students, the young ministers of the gospel and a host of their elders, courageously and nonviolently sitting in at lunch counters and willingly going to jail for conscience's

sake. One day the South will know that when these disinherited children of God sat down at lunch counters, they were in reality standing up for what is best in the American dream and for the most sacred values in our Judaeo-Christian heritage, thereby bringing our nation back to those great wells of democracy which were dug deep by the founding fathers in their formulation of the Constitution and the Declaration of Independence.

Never before have I written so long a letter. I'm afraid it is much too long to 48 take your precious time. I can assure you that it would have been much shorter if I had been writing from a comfortable desk, but what else can one do when he is alone in a narrow jail cell, other than write long letters, think long thoughts and pray long prayers?

If I have said anything in this letter that overstates the truth and indicates 49 an unreasonable impatience, I beg you to forgive me. If I have said anything that understates the truth and indicates my having a patience that allows me to settle for anything less than brotherhood, I beg God to forgive me.

I hope this letter finds you strong in the faith. I also hope that circumstances 50 will soon make it possible for me to meet each of you, not as an integrationist or a civil rights leader but as a fellow clergyman and a Christian brother. Let us all hope that the dark clouds of racial prejudice will soon pass away and the deep fog of misunderstanding will be lifted from our fear-drenched communities, and in some not too distant tomorrow the radiant stars of love and brotherhood will shine over our great nation with all their scintillating beauty.

Yours for the cause of Peace and Brotherhood,
Martin Luther King Jr.

● *Thinking Critically About "Letter from Birmingham Jail"*

RESPONDING AS A READER

1. King and the people to whom he was responding voice arguments that not only are directly opposed to each other but grow out of very different conceptions of what questions the citizens of Birmingham, and of the United States, should be addressing at that moment. Working with both texts, identify the underlying question/issue that each addresses, then identify how King transforms the central issue in the Alabama clergy's newspaper ad into the issue he feels must be addressed.

2. Although King is at odds with his fellow clergymen, he devotes much of his argument to invoking values he believes his audience shares with him. What are these values, and how does he use them in his argument?

3. At the end of the first paragraph, King says he will try to answer the clergymen's statements in what he hopes will be "patient and reasonable terms." Do you think he was successful in achieving that tone? Your context of reading is, of course, quite different from the context of those Alabama pastors in 1963, but consider carefully King's appeals to *ethos* and *pathos* and try to assess how readers from different political perspectives might have responded at the time.

RESPONDING AS A WRITER

1. What aspects of this document spoke most strongly to you? Focusing on the *how* more than the *what* of King's writing, examine the paragraph or paragraphs that you found most effective and use textual details to explain how King's technique worked to engage you.

2. To deepen your understanding of how King's letter is constructed, prepare a descriptive outline of it as described in Chapter 4 by dividing it into chunks and then jotting down what each of these major chunks *does* and *says*. (See p. 58.)

3. Few of us will be called to write a document such as King's, but many of us will be faced with the necessity of refuting ideas we oppose or explaining why we advocate a difficult action opposed by others. The historical importance of King's letter goes well beyond its pragmatic beginnings as a counterargument; nevertheless, it offers considerable food for thought about strategies for composing one. How would you generalize in a few sentences what King has *done* (as opposed to *said*) in this letter? What can you learn from it about strategies of argument?

Andrew Sullivan

Let Gays Marry

A high-profile advocate of gay marriage, Andrew Sullivan (b. 1963) is an openly gay conservative journalist who is a practicing Roman Catholic. He is a senior editor at the *New Republic* and publishes often in periodicals such as the *New York Times Book Review* and the *Advocate*, the national gay and lesbian newsmagazine. Sullivan's frequently controversial writing often highlights commonalities between gay and straight people. Born and raised in England, he holds a Ph.D. in political science from Harvard and has authored several books, including *Virtually Normal: An Argument About Homosexuality* (1995) and *Love Undetectable* (1999). This opinion piece appeared in the June 3, 1996, issue of *Newsweek* as part of the magazine's coverage of the U.S. Supreme Court's overturning of a Colorado constitutional amendment that would have prohibited any antidiscrimination legislation protecting homosexuals. Sullivan's mention of Bill Bennett in the final paragraph refers to the conservative leader's opinion piece in the same issue opposing gay marriage.

● *For Your Reading Log*

1. Before you read this "take a stand" argument, pause to articulate your current thinking about gay marriage. Should it be legal? Why or why not?
2. What are the main opposition arguments that Sullivan needs to address? What do you predict his reasoning will be based upon?

●

"A state cannot deem a class of persons a stranger to its laws," declared the 1 Supreme Court last week. It was a monumental statement. Gay men and lesbians, the conservative court said, are no longer strangers in America. They are citizens, entitled, like everyone else, to equal protection—no special rights, but simple equality.

For the first time in Supreme Court history, gay men and women were seen 2 not as some powerful lobby trying to subvert America, but as the people we truly are—the sons and daughters of countless mothers and fathers, with all the weaknesses and strengths and hopes of everybody else. And what we seek is not some special place in America but merely to be a full and equal part of America, to give back to our society without being forced to lie or hide or live as second-class citizens.

That is why marriage is so central to our hopes. People ask us why we want 3 the right to marry, but the answer is obvious. It's the same reason anyone wants the right to marry. At some point in our lives, some of us are lucky enough to meet the person we truly love. And we want to commit to that person in front of our family and country for the rest of our lives. It's the most simple, the most natural, the most human instinct in the world. How could anyone seek to oppose that?

4   Yes, at first blush, it seems like a radical proposal, but, when you think about it some more, it's actually the opposite. Throughout American history, to be sure, marriage has been between a man and a woman, and in many ways our society is built upon that institution. But none of that need change in the slightest. After all, no one is seeking to take away anybody's right to marry, and no one is seeking to force any church to change any doctrine in any way. Particular religious arguments against same-sex marriage are rightly debated within the churches and faiths themselves. That is not the issue here: there is a separation between church and state in this country. We are only asking that when the government gives out civil marriage licenses, those of us who are gay should be treated like anybody else.

5   Of course, some argue that marriage is by definition between a man and a woman. But for centuries, marriage was by definition a contract in which the wife was her husband's legal property. And we changed that. For centuries, marriage was by definition between two people of the same race. And we changed that. We changed these things because we recognized that human dignity is the same whether you are a man or a woman, black or white. And no one has any more of a choice to be gay than to be black or white or male or female.

6   Some say that marriage is only about raising children, but we let childless heterosexual couples be married (Bob and Elizabeth Dole, Pat and Shelley Buchanan, for instance). Why should gay couples be treated differently? Others fear that there is no logical difference between allowing same-sex marriage and sanctioning polygamy and other horrors. But the issue of whether to sanction multiple spouses (gay or straight) is completely separate from whether, in the existing institution between two unrelated adults, the government should discriminate between its citizens.

7   This is, in fact, if only Bill Bennett could see it, a deeply conservative cause. It seeks to change no one else's rights or marriages in any way. It seeks merely to promote monogamy, fidelity and the disciplines of family life among people who have long been cast to the margins of society. And what could be a more conservative project than that? Why indeed would any conservative seek to oppose those very family values for gay people that he or she supports for everybody else? Except, of course, to make gay men and lesbians strangers in their own country, to forbid them ever to come home.

• Thinking Critically About "Let Gays Marry"

RESPONDING AS A READER

1. What point does Sullivan seem to consider to be the strongest support for his argument that gay marriage should be legal? Whether you agree with his ultimate point or not, do you agree that this is his strongest argument? If not, what is? Why?

2. In a relatively short space, Sullivan summarizes and counters several powerful arguments against gay marriage. Tracing his reasons and evidence in each counterargument, what do you discover about the values

and assumptions he asserts as shared with his opponents? With his *Newsweek* audience?

3. How has reading Sullivan's argument changed your thinking about gay marriage—even if he hasn't convinced you or you already agreed with him, what aspect of this text showed you a new way of understanding some aspect of this issue?

RESPONDING AS A WRITER

1. What aspects of this opinion column did you find most engaging and/or most off-putting? Why? Analyze specific points in the text that invoked a strong reaction in you. How would you describe his strategy for dealing with potential resistance from readers?

2. Sullivan's core assertion that gay marriage is "a deeply conservative cause" is an unexpected one. What does Sullivan mean by "conservative"? To understand fully the values he asserts here, apply the ideology analysis technique in Chapter 5 (p. 77) to key terms in Sullivan's argument. Using two columns, list on the left the words that signal the values Sullivan is asserting to support his argument and rebut his opponents. In the right column, write the opposing term, using brackets if it is only implied. Summarize your analysis by writing a paragraph no longer than seven sentences that *explains but does not argue for or against* Sullivan's assertion that support of gay marriage is an issue that should appeal to conservatives.

3. How would you describe the persona that Sullivan presents here? What specific wording, sentence strategies, or organizational decisions contribute to this impression? What does his technique suggest to you as an effective way for writers to assert themselves when writing about highly controversial topics such as this?

Sallie Tisdale

Should a Boy Be Expelled for Thought Crimes?

Sallie Tisdale (b. 1957) is a freelance writer who contributes frequently to a wide variety of print periodicals such as *Audubon*, *Self*, the *New Yorker*, and *Harper's*, where she serves as a contributing editor. A native of Oregon, she began her career as a nurse and first began writing about medical issues. The subjects of her books include hospitals, nursing homes, sexuality, and salt, including most recently *The Best Thing I Ever Tasted: The Secret of Food* (2001). She describes herself as an advocate of the essay and often leads writing workshops on college campuses. This article was published in the popular "Mothers Who Think" department of the online magazine *Salon* in November 1998.

● *For Your Reading Log*

1. What's your prediction of how Tisdale will answer the question she poses in her title? What makes you think that even without reading the text? What does the term "thought crimes" mean to you? Write out a tentative definition and imagine several examples.
2. Keep track of your moment-by-moment response to reading Tisdale's argument by pausing to note in a sentence or so your reaction to specific chunks of the text: after paragraphs 3, 8, 10, 17, and 20.

─────────   ●   ─────────

1   I wrote my first short story in Mrs. Hurley's fourth-grade class, when I was 8 years old. I had been reading science fiction for a few years, and my story was a suitably allegorical tale of a young woman bent on collecting bronzed souvenirs of the most important "firsts" in her life. At the end, her minions roll in her newest souvenir—her first lover.

2   I was really pleased with this story, especially with the shocker of an ending. I handed it to Mrs. Hurley without a doubt.

3   My mother taught fifth grade a few doors down the hall, and Maxine Hurley was one of my mother's best friends. They spent that afternoon's recess huddled on the playground, supervising us with one eye each while they mulled over the possibly dire implications of my murderous fantasy. I watched and was gratified to know how exciting my story proved to be. I wasn't punished, though I did spend several afternoons that year and the next doing a battery of entertaining tests with the school counselor.

4   This memory comes back to me because a 16-year-old boy named James LaVine was expelled from high school in Blaine, Wash., last month because he

wrote a poem. The poem was not a class assignment; LaVine has written poetry for several years. The poem in question is called "Last Words." It's written in the first person and is a narrative about killing 28 people and then committing suicide.

I think it's important to note that James LaVine had not been in any partic- 5 ular trouble with the school before, except for a one-day suspension last year for getting in a fight. He's not shown himself to have a particularly short fuse or an urge to solve every problem with force. He doesn't appear to have an inordinate interest in weapons or bombs. He is able to make friends. He has not shown a desire to inflict harm on animals or start fires. He does not, in other words, en-gage in any of the behaviors commonly associated with impending violence in teenagers. LaVine was expelled solely because his poem described murder.

After LaVine was sent home from school, sheriff's deputies came to his 6 house and read the poem, too. They considered whether he could be committed against his will to a psychiatric ward and subjected to involuntary testing. Since the poem doesn't name the school, the deputies were forced to conclude that he hadn't actually made a threat, and they let him be.

At first, the school district was calling this an "emergency" expulsion, based 7 on the fear of "an immediate and continuing danger." But in the words of a let-ter sent to the student's parents, the district claimed that LaVine had committed "violations of Blaine High School discipline policy" by showing his teacher a poem that was "of a nature significant enough to be classified as dangerous."

James LaVine was not just suspended for a few days, while everybody put 8 their heads together and thought things through. He was expelled, meaning he could not return to school without district permission or court intervention. He stayed out of school, in fact, nearly all of October, and was allowed to return only after agreeing to go through psychological testing voluntarily—something his family accepted because the alternative might have meant months of legal wrangling.

I live in the Northwest, not far from Springfield, Ore., where 15-year-old Kip 9 Kinkel made headlines last May when he opened fire on classmates in his school, after killing his parents at home. Here in Kip Kinkel Land, people are a bit sen-sitive about violent teenage boys. But Kinkel, like the other high school killers we've seen in the news this year, showed a clear pattern of violence over several years. It was in stories he wrote, class reports and conversations; in his hobbies and obsession with weapons and bombs; and in repeated problems with be-havior. Kinkel brought a gun to school; his parents had asked for professional help with their son. Authorities in Springfield had every reason to be wary of Kinkel, but they treated him with benign indifference.

James LaVine is guilty of nothing more—or less—important than express- 10 ing a frightening thought. Blaine High School didn't choose to call his parents or even schedule a conference. They went for the throat, in a socially violent act of rejection and petty-mindedness.

I spoke with James yesterday. He's a bit laconic, rather tired of the whole fuss 11 and clearly glad to be back in school. He's switched English classes, partly to catch up with his work, though being with a teacher other than the one who called out the dogs is probably for the best. I asked him if he liked the poem.

12   "I'm proud of it," he said. "I'm proud of most of my work. Otherwise, I wouldn't have taken it to school."

13   Breean Beggs, James LaVine's lawyer, isn't through with the school district. He wants the disciplinary letter expunged from LaVine's record and the school district to apologize.

14   "They expelled him because they thought he might be depressed and that he fit some profile of school killers—a profile in their own minds," Beggs told me. "They shifted the burden of proof to him and said, 'You have to prove to us you're not dangerous because you're a creative writer.'"

15   James wants the letter out, too. "It's really hurting me in my file. Future employers might see that and not hire me. I was planning on going into the Marine Corps. They won't take me with that there."

16   Gordon Dolman, the school superintendent in Blaine, refused to speak to me. Beggs told me that when he'd mentioned the possibility of a lawsuit, a representative of the district told him to go right ahead. They were far less worried about the damages for violating a student's rights than the damages that might follow a violent episode, a precedent Beggs finds "disturbing."

17   So should we all. Why would anyone, especially an educator, be surprised to find out that an American high school boy thinks about murder? It's a subject worth many millions of dollars to novelists and screenwriters, and not exactly a new subject for artists. Why, for that matter, would an educator want to smother that boy's expression on something ubiquitous in common discourse? If there had been actual violence at Blaine High School, grievance and trauma counselors would have poured in to help the student body cope—perhaps by writing poems.

18   I asked James if he'd been inspired by recent events. He said no and explained in words very like those of other writers.

19   Teachers always told him, he said, that "you get the most powerful effect with the first person. I just get a feeling and I write, and I don't know what's going to come out until I get to the end of the poem."

20   James LaVine is back in school now, and perhaps he'll get into the Marine Corps yet. I can just imagine the school district proudly displaying his picture if he succeeds—weapon at the ready, trained to kill. But the image I keep returning to is that of a cadre of sheriff's deputies standing around analyzing the hidden messages in his poem. It's a curiously pleasing picture. I wonder what they would have thought of Edgar Allan Poe's "Annabel Lee." After all, Poe named names.

- ● *Thinking Critically About "Should a Boy Be Expelled for Thought Crimes?"*

  RESPONDING AS A READER

  1. What assumptions does Tisdale apparently make about how her readers will react to her assertions? Do those assumptions hold true in your case? As you review the notes you made about your unfolding reaction to the text, what do you discover about where you were drawn in to Tisdale's reasoning and where you resisted it? What specific aspects of the

text can you identify that account for these responses? How do your responses to specific sections compare to those of your classmates?

2. Tisdale's argument focuses on a specific incident. What more general claims are implied about how "thought crimes" should be handled by schools and law enforcement agencies? How persuasive do you find Tisdale's points about the specific incident to be? Do you respond the same way to the implicit more general argument? Why or why not?

3. What counterarguments might someone make to Tisdale's specific claims as well as her implied more general claims? How would you describe Tisdale's handling of alternative points of view in this text?

RESPONDING AS A WRITER

1. To explore Tisdale's approach to argument, develop a four-sentence rhetorical précis of it as described in Chapter 4 (p. 62). Follow the model carefully so that your first sentence provides bibliographic information and a restatement of the thesis, the second sentence summarizes support, the third sentence captures your understanding of her purpose, and the fourth sentence describes her technique for appealing to her intended audience.

2. It has been said that Tisdale's twice monthly "Second Thoughts" pieces for *Salon*'s "Mothers Who Think" (MWT) department helped define the style and popularity of that feature. To discover whether this column is typical to her approach, what questions would you want to investigate about the style of Tisdale's other MWT columns? To formulate some study questions, refer to specific features of this text to identify characteristics of her style. If you can access *Salon*'s online archives, select a few of Tisdale's pieces at random and use your questions to compare her aims and techniques there to this text. (Note: Tisdale was published in MWT from January 1998 to June 1999. A 1997 "manifesto" about MWT's purpose was posted at <http://www.salon.com/june97/mothers/mamafesto970616.html>.

3. The years since Tisdale's column was published have seen additional school violence and given authorities more experience with both responding to apparently troubled students and attempting to prevent violent incidents. If you had an opportunity to interview Tisdale now about what she wrote in 1998, what would you want to ask her about her position on the matter and the way she presents it here? Working with your classmates, jot down all the questions that occur to you, then sort them into three categories: (1) neutral, (2) implicit or explicit agreement with her "Thought Crimes" column, and (3) implicit or explicit opposition to it. What differences in wording determine the category a question belongs in? Revise the material you have so that you have at least three questions for each category.

George Orwell

A Hanging (Fiction)

This short story, frequently mistaken as an essay, was one of the earliest works of George Orwell, one of the twentieth century's best known political essayists and novelists (*Animal Farm* [1945] and *1984* [1948]). Orwell is the pseudonym of Eric Blair (1903–1950), who was born in Bengal, India, where his father worked for the colonial government, and educated in England. After graduating from Eton College, a prestigious secondary school, instead of attending university he volunteered as an officer with the Indian Imperial Police in Burma, where this short story is set. After five years, he returned to England on medical leave and announced he would pursue a career as a writer. Describing himself as a "democratic socialist," Orwell/Blair had grave misgivings about the abstract political philosophies that drove the major conflicts of the times (e.g., colonialism, fascism, communism). "A Hanging" was published in the English literary magazine *Adelphi* in 1931, and later in Orwell's collection, *Shooting an Elephant and Other Essays* (1950). Blair died at the age forty-six from complications of tuberculosis, which he is thought to have contracted in Burma.

● **For Your Reading Log**

1. A short story author's creation of a narrator is crucial for establishing the point of view through which readers engage with the story's events. As you read, pay particular attention to details that reveal something about the character who is telling the story, such as his role in the events, how others regard him, or what he cares about. Mark the text or jot notes in your reading log about these points to use as a resource when you work with the "Thinking Critically" questions that follow the story.

2. As soon as you finish reading, freewrite for several minutes about what interests you about the story and the most important question it has prompted in you about its events or ideas.

———————   ●   ———————

1   It was in Burma, a sodden morning of the rains. A sickly light, like yellow tinfoil, was slanting over the high walls into the jail yard. We were waiting outside the condemned cells, a row of sheds fronted with double bars, like small animal cages. Each cell measured about ten feet by ten and was quite bare within except for a plank bed and a pot for drinking water. In some of them brown, silent men were squatting at the inner bars, with their blankets draped round them. These were the condemned men, due to be hanged within the next week or two.

2   One prisoner had been brought out of his cell. He was a Hindu, a puny wisp of a man, with a shaven head and vague liquid eyes. He had a thick, sprouting mustache, absurdly too big for his body, rather like the mustache of a comic man

on the films. Six tall Indian warders were guarding him and getting him ready for the gallows. Two of them stood by with rifles and fixed bayonets, while the others handcuffed him, passed a chain through his handcuffs and fixed it to their belts, and lashed his arms tight to his sides. They crowded very close about him, with their hands always on him in a careful, caressing grip, as though all the while feeling him to make sure he was there. It was like men handling a fish which is still alive and may jump back into the water. But he stood quite unresisting, yielding his arms limply to the ropes, as though he hardly noticed what was happening.

Eight o'clock struck and a bugle call, desolately thin in the wet air, floated   3
from the distant barracks. The superintendent of the jail, who was standing apart from the rest of us, moodily prodding the gravel with his stick, raised his head at the sound. He was an army doctor, with a gray toothbrush mustache and a gruff voice. "For God's sake, hurry up, Francis," he said irritably. "The man ought to have been dead by this time. Aren't you ready yet?"

Francis, the head jailer, a fat Dravidian in a white drill suit and gold specta-   4
cles, waved his black hand. "Yes sir, yes sir," he bubbled. "All iss satisfactorily prepared. The hangman iss waiting. We shall proceed."

"Well, quick march, then. The prisoners can't get their breakfast till this job's   5
over."

We set out for the gallows. Two warders marched on either side of the pris-   6
oner, with their rifles at the slope; two others marched close against him, gripping him by arm and shoulder, as though at once pushing and supporting him. The rest of us, magistrates and the like, followed behind. Suddenly, when we had gone ten yards, the procession stopped short without any order or warning. A dreadful thing had happened—a dog, come goodness knows whence, had appeared in the yard. It came bounding among us with a loud volley of barks and leapt round us wagging its whole body, wild with glee at finding so many human beings together. It was a large woolly dog, half Airedale, half pariah. For a moment it pranced around us, and then, before anyone could stop it, it had made a dash for the prisoner, and jumping up tried to lick his face. Everybody stood aghast, too taken aback even to grab the dog.

"Who let that bloody brute in here?" said the superintendent angrily. "Catch   7
it, someone!"

A warder detached from the escort charged clumsily after the dog, but it   8
danced and gamboled just out of his reach, taking everything as part of the game. A young Eurasian jailer picked up a handful of gravel and tried to stone the dog away, but it dodged the stones and came after us again. Its yaps echoed from the jail walls. The prisoner, in the grasp of the two warders, looked on incuriously, as though this was another formality of the hanging. It was several minutes before someone managed to catch the dog. Then we put my handkerchief through its collar and moved off once more, with the dog still straining and whimpering.

It was about forty yards to the gallows. I watched the bare brown back of the   9
prisoner marching in front of me. He walked clumsily with his bound arms, but quite steadily, with the bobbing gait of the Indian who never straightens his knees. At each step his muscles slid neatly into place, the lock of hair on his scalp danced up and down, his feet printed themselves on the wet gravel. And once,

in spite of the men who gripped him by each shoulder, he stepped lightly aside to avoid a puddle on the path.

10   It is curious; but till that moment I had never realized what it means to destroy a healthy, conscious man. When I saw the prisoner step aside to avoid the puddle, I saw the mystery, the unspeakable wrongness, of cutting life short when it is in full tide. This man was not dying, he was alive just as we are alive. All the organs of his body were working—bowels digesting food, skin renewing itself, nails growing, tissues forming—all toiling away in solemn foolery. His nails would still be growing when he stood on the drop, when he was falling through the air with a tenth-of-a-second to live. His eyes saw the yellow gravel and the gray walls, and his brain still remembered, foresaw, reasoned—even about puddles. He and we were a party of men walking together, seeing, hearing, feeling, understanding the same world; and in two minutes, with a sudden snap, one of us would be gone—one mind less, one world less.

11   The gallows stood in a small yard, separate from the main grounds of the prison, and overgrown with tall prickly weeds. It was a brick erection like three sides of a shed, with planking on top, and above that two beams and a crossbar with the rope dangling. The hangman, a gray-haired convict in the white uniform of the prison, was waiting beside his machine. He greeted us with a servile crouch as we entered. At a word from Francis the two warders, gripping the prisoner more closely than ever, half led, half pushed him to the gallows and helped him clumsily up the ladder. Then the hangman climbed up and fixed the rope round the prisoner's neck.

12   We stood waiting, five yards away. The warders had formed in a rough circle round the gallows. And then, when the noose was fixed, the prisoner began crying out to his god. It was a high, reiterated cry of "Ram! Ram! Ram! Ram!" not urgent and fearful like a prayer or cry for help, but steady, rhythmical, almost like the tolling of a bell. The dog answered the sound with a whine. The hangman, still standing on the gallows, produced a small cotton bag like a flour bag and drew it down over the prisoner's face. But the sound, muffled by the cloth, still persisted, over and over again: "Ram! Ram! Ram! Ram! Ram!"

13   The hangman climbed down and stood ready, holding the lever. Minutes seemed to pass. The steady, muffled crying from the prisoner went on and on, "Ram! Ram! Ram!" never faltering for an instant. The superintendent, his head on his chest, was slowly poking the ground with his stick; perhaps he was counting the cries, allowing the prisoner a fixed number—fifty, perhaps, or a hundred. Everyone had changed color. The Indians had gone gray like bad coffee, and one or two of the bayonets were wavering. We looked at the lashed, hooded man on the drop, and listened to his cries—each cry another second of life; the same thought was in all our minds: oh, kill him quickly, get it over, stop that abominable noise!

14   Suddenly the superintendent made up his mind. Throwing up his head he made a swift motion with his stick. "Chalo!" he shouted almost fiercely.

15   There was a clanking noise, and then dead silence. The prisoner had vanished, and the rope was twisting on itself. I let go of the dog, and it galloped im-

mediately to the back of the gallows; but when it got there it stopped short, barked, and then retreated into a corner of the yard, where it stood among the weeds, looking timorously out at us. We went round the gallows to inspect the prisoner's body. He was dangling with his toes pointed straight downwards, very slowly revolving, as dead as a stone.

The superintendent reached out with his stick and poked the bare brown 16 body; it oscillated slightly. "*He's* all right," said the superintendent. He backed out from under the gallows, and blew out a deep breath. The moody look had gone out of his face quite suddenly. He glanced at his wristwatch. "Eight minutes past eight. Well, that's all for this morning, thank God."

The warders unfixed bayonets and marched away. The dog, sobered and 17 conscious of having misbehaved itself, slipped after them. We walked out of the gallows yard, past the condemned cells with their waiting prisoners, into the big central yard of the prison. The convicts, under the command of warders armed with lathis, were already receiving their breakfast. They squatted in long rows, each man holding a tin pannikin, while two warders with buckets marched around ladling out rice; it seemed quite a homely, jolly scene, after the hanging. An enormous relief had come upon us now that the job was done. One felt an impulse to sing, to break into a run, to snigger. All at once everyone began chattering gaily.

The Eurasian boy walking beside me nodded towards the way we had 18 come, with a knowing smile: "Do you know sir, our friend (he meant the dead man) when he heard his appeal had been dismissed, he pissed on the floor of his cell. From fright. Kindly take one of my cigarettes, sir. Do you not admire my new silver case, sir? From the boxwallah, two rupees eight annas. Classy European style."

Several people laughed—at what, nobody seemed certain.   19

Francis was walking by the superintendent, talking garrulously: "Well, sir, 20 all has passed off with the utmost satisfactoriness. It was all finished—flick! Like that. It iss not always so—oah, no! I have known cases where the doctor was obliged to go beneath the gallows and pull prisoner's legs to ensure decease. Most disagreeable!"

"Wriggling about, eh? That's bad," said the superintendent.   21

"Ach, sir, it iss worse when they become refractory! One man, I recall, clung 22 to the bars of his's cage when we went to take him out. You will scarcely credit, sir, that it took six warders to dislodge him, three pulling at each leg. We reasoned with him, 'My dear fellow,' we said, 'think of all the pain and trouble you are causing to us!' But no, he would not listen! Ach, he was very troublesome!"

I found that I was laughing quite loudly. Everyone was laughing. Even the 23 superintendent grinned in a tolerant way. "You'd better all come out and have a drink," he said quite genially. "I've got a bottle of whiskey in the car. We could do with it."

We went through the big double gates of the prison into the road. "Pulling 24 at his legs!" exclaimed a Burmese magistrate suddenly, and burst into a loud chuckling. We all began laughing again. At the moment Francis' anecdote seemed extraordinarily funny. We all had a drink together, native and European alike, quite amicably. The dead man was a hundred yards away.

• *Thinking Critically About "A Hanging"*

RESPONDING AS A READER

1. Our editorial decision to include this story in a selection of texts that "take a stand" is based not on Orwell's articulation of a formal argument but on the way his narrator draws readers' attention to certain details. Have we made a good decision? When you finished reading, did you feel you had read a statement of someone's stand on an issue? To answer, analyze your response to the details you noted in your reading log. Which engages you most powerfully? How do they work together to focus the story and take a stand?

2. Finding political abstractions distasteful, Orwell focused on concrete details. The argument of this story, for example, remains largely indirect. The story is narrated in the first person, yet the narrator tells us directly about what he was thinking only at one point. Did the narrator's reflections in paragraph 10 about the rain puddle surprise you? If so, what previous details led you to expect something else at that point? If not, what details prepared you for this expression of his attitude?

3. How important to your experience of the story is the opening line, "It was in Burma...."? *What* was in Burma?

RESPONDING AS A WRITER

1. How would you describe the relationship Orwell establishes between the narrator and his readers? What draws readers into the life of the story?

2. When you and your classmates compare responses to the reading log prompts and the questions above, what patterns of agreement and disagreement emerge? What generalizations do these patterns suggest about *how* Orwell tells the story as well as about *what* he tells in it?

3. Questions that a text prompts in you as you read are frequently an excellent starting place for good group discussions and can lead to good paper topics, especially when the text suggests more than one possible answer or more than one way of understanding a particular passage or series of events. What important questions about "A Hanging" remain unanswered for you? What is it about the question(s) or possible answers that makes them important to your understanding of the story?

Sofia Collins (Student)

Good Intentions in the Anti-Sweatshop Movement

Sofia Collins (a pseudonym) wrote this opinion piece for her campus newspaper in the fall of 2000 after several students were arrested at a department store protest against the low wages paid to workers overseas by some apparel manufacturers.

● *For Your Reading Log*

1. What do you know about the anti-sweatshop movement in which many college students became active in the late 1990s? As far as you know, what are their concerns and goals? How effective have they been? Take a few minutes to write out your thoughts on this issue.
2. How do you think you would react if your shopping trip with friends to a mall department store were interrupted by a group of demonstrators carrying banners that called upon you to boycott that very store because it sold clothing or shoes that could not be certified "sweat free." Use your reading log to imagine several different courses of action you might take in the situation described; then explain which of these you would take, and why.

———————   ●   ———————

The arrest of two students at the Southridge demonstration against sweatshop 1 wages counters the popular image of college students wallowing in social and political indifference. Such protests have revived issues such as unionization, fair labor, and free trade at a time when economic prosperity allows many of us to shop for yet another new pair of sneakers or jeans without much thought about what they cost—or where they were made, by whom, under what conditions.

Like the authors of recent columns in the *Record*, I find it heartening that stu- 2 dent activists are leading the campaign against sweatshops. Ray Schultz's clearheaded and detailed letter gave me food for thought: much of the denim and khaki I wear was probably sewn by outsourced workers in developing countries under conditions that violate most U.S. health and safety standards. The protesters and their supporters say that these workers are paid between two and eleven percent of what their U.S. counterparts would earn. The prospect of working eighteen hours a day in dangerous conditions for about thirty cents an hour is appalling. Yet I must raise a voice of protest against the protests. Despite noble intentions, such protests are unintentionally paternalistic and predictably ineffective.

Too many activists have focused almost exclusively on the matter of higher pay. 3 Their arguments for "a living wage" in foreign clothing factories are vulnerable to the criticism of economic experts who contend that raising the wages of apparel workers around the globe is an unrealistic goal. Echoing arguments against a higher minimum wage in this country, these economists say that increased wages for sweatshop workers would have negative effects such as inflation and job reduction. However, both sides are actually sidestepping more crucial issues.

4   Rather than concentrating on raises for sweatshop workers, activists should direct their efforts toward more feasible ways of correcting the numerous injustices in the global apparel industry. While the low wages are certainly objectionable, even more disturbing are the hazardous conditions under which they work for unreasonably long hours. But probably the biggest impediment to establishing fair work environments abroad are many companies' stringent prohibitions against labor unions, the most effective institutions for protecting workers' rights.

5   The current fixation on asking multinational corporations to pay workers fair wages demonstrates a fundamentally protectorate mentality. Many well-intentioned students epitomize the paternalistic characteristics often associated with the United States because they assume the role of self-appointed advocates for poor, third world laborers. Instead of making arguments to American shoppers on behalf of the sweatshop workers, a more effective approach would be to address the corporations and insist on the workers' right to unionize. Organized unions would empower workers to demand of their employers what the workers deem important rather than what Americans assume they need.

6   Perhaps the most important contribution anti-sweatshop activists can make is redefining the debate, making it more comprehensive and more sensitive to the potential pitfalls of good intentions. By promoting and supporting the unionization of sweatshop laborers, activists can draw international attention to these workers' plight and pressure manufacturers to extend workers' rights. Most importantly, this less paternalistic advocacy would focus on empowering workers to assert their own human rights.

● *Thinking Critically About "Good Intentions in the Anti-Sweatshop Movement"*

RESPONDING AS A READER

1. At what point did you realize that Collins did not approve of the protesters' goals? Did you find her tactic of delaying this major point to be effective? Why or why not?

2. As you were reading, how did your previous knowledge and opinions about the anti-sweatshop movement affect your responses to Collins's points? How do you imagine someone with a prior perspective very different from yours, whether negative or positive, informed or uninformed, would react as the piece unfolded? What evidence do you find in the text that Collins was considering readers with varying opinions and/or levels of knowledge as part of her intended audience?

3. Which sentence(s) in the argument did you find most engaging or sympathetic? Which sentence(s) did you find most off-putting? What could Collins have done—other than assert a different opinion—to increase your positive responses and decrease your negative ones?

RESPONDING AS A WRITER

1. This piece was actually too long for publication. It needs to be shorter by twenty-five words. What should Collins cut? Working with a partner, role-play Collins and a copy editor trying to agree on how to shorten it to fit the available space. Consider several different ways to cut out twenty-five words *as well as* Collins's likely counterarguments about what would be lost if those particular words were dropped. Compare results with your classmates to see if the group can agree on a slightly shorter version of the column that all the "Sofia's" will accept.

2. Imagine a continuum for describing arguments with the labels "confrontational" at one end and "cooperative" at the other. Where would you place Collins's piece? Why? Do you think this aspect of the article enhances or detracts from its effectiveness? (For more information about cooperative arguments that seek common ground, see Chapter 16.)

3. To what extent have reading this opinion column and considering the questions posed here about it affected your thinking about the anti-sweatshop movement? Has Collins educated you? Has she earned your agreement with her opinion? Be prepared to explain exactly what aspects of her argument were more and less convincing to you.

Writing to Take a Stand

The authors represented in this section use a variety of argument strategies to accomplish their purposes. In the discussion questions that accompany the texts, we have invited you to explore different facets of their claims and strategies, putting special emphasis on how they engage their readers. The writing assignments below are designed to give you a chance to apply your new knowledge about argument strategies by analyzing published work and/or writing an argument that takes a stand.

TAKING A STAND OF YOUR OWN

Write an essay in which you attempt to persuade your readers to accept your stand rather than a competing one on an issue of public concern. Choose an arguable issue and supply your readers with adequate background and a clear explanation of the question(s) at issue. Decide whether you are primarily addressing someone opposed to your position or someone undecided about the issue, then adjust your strategies accordingly. As you work to articulate your claims and reasons, you will need to consider what kinds of evidence will be most persuasive to the audience you are addressing. How informed are your readers about the subject? You will need to decide how much to spell out the assumptions and reasoning that will link your evidence to your claims, so think carefully about the assumptions you share with your target audience. Try to predict where that audience will resist your points. Your paper should anticipate such objections and summarize opposing views fairly.

EXAMINING RHETORICAL STRATEGIES

We invite you to extend your study of argument strategies by writing a rhetorical analysis of two or three short opinion pieces by one writer. A local or nationally syndicated columnist who is published regularly is the perfect subject for this analysis because these writers' success depends not just on their argument skills but also on their ability to convey a personality that brings readers back to them. To begin, find in the newspaper or on the Internet two or three sample arguments by the same political, entertainment, or sports columnist (a person of your choice or as your teacher directs). Whether you choose arguments on similar or unrelated subjects, be sure that they address an arguable issue and take a stand. Expressions of personal taste will not work for this assignment. (It is unlikely that you'll find an "about face" similar to Parker's.) Use the "Questions to Help You Read Arguments Rhetorically" on page 400 as a basis for careful rhetorical reading of the argument structure, appeals, and stylistic techniques in each piece. Pay careful attention to similarities among them. Then articulate and support a thesis statement that focuses on what the pieces have in common in (1) the way issues are framed, (2) the type of reasoning used, and (3) the style through which the writer engages readers. Since you will be analyzing only two or three writings by this writer, take care not to overgeneralize; instead, use qualifiers to signal that you realize you are working from a limited sample (for example, "If Raspberry's approach here is typical . . ."). Be sure to provide sufficient textual evidence to support your points.

EXTENDING THE CONVERSATION

Letters to the editor and readers' op-ed articles provide an important forum for public opinion in both local and national communities. People write to newspaper and magazine editors (and to radio and TV stations) in hopes that their opinions and arguments will be published or broadcast to the community at large. Sometimes these letters and columns make specific comments about recently published material, including other readers' comments; sometimes they bring up a new or not recently discussed issue in hopes of getting it in the public eye. Whatever their purpose, writers of such letters and columns face intense competition for a small amount of available space. The pieces must be carefully crafted to gain an editor's approval for publication. Take a look at the letters section of a newspaper in your community. What trends do you see over several issues? Which letters make you want to talk back to them? Why?

Now, go public. Write a brief op-ed column or letter to the editor for your local paper in which you comment upon both content and strategy in a recently published piece. Follow the length restrictions of the publication where the argument to which you are responding was published. Remember that you need to reach a multilayered audience: editor, original writer, the reading public. Make your point clearly and succinctly, and include at least one sentence either praising or critiquing one of the rhetorical techniques the other letter writer used. The choice of actually mailing the letter is up to you, but we imagine you will want to see if your letter is chosen for publication.

Note: This assignment focuses on print publications specifically because of the competition for space there. It will be a valuable exercise to work within those constraints rather than with the wide open rhetorical choices on the Internet, where postings in many venues are typically not limited by space.

CHAPTER

14

Evaluating and Judging

E valuating and making judgments is an everyday occurrence in our personal, work, and school lives. Sometimes our daily judgments involve little conscious deliberation—what to wear, what to eat for breakfast, where to park on campus (actually, that may be a highly strategic judgment on some campuses!). At other times, we carefully analyze a situation and weigh our options before making a judgment. Think about what your decision-making process might be if you were choosing an apartment. You would probably read the rental section of your newspaper carefully, noting the apartment's location and square footage, calculating the monthly rent plus utilities, visiting various apartments, comparing their advantages and disadvantages, and talking it over with friends and family. Because a decision such as this is of great consequence to your daily life, not to mention your pocketbook, you would undoubtedly take the time to make a careful judgment. Although we may be more aware of it in consequential decision making, all judgments and evaluations involve *criteria*—that is, standards we use to measure the quality or value of something.

You also encounter other people's evaluations on a daily basis. You read movie reviews and sports writers' ranking of teams; you listen to friends' evaluations of the latest music CDs, or your econ professor's discussion of the pros and cons of raising the interest rate in the current economic climate. Each of these cases involves stated or unstated criteria—the movie's cinematography, the strength of a football team by position, and so on. At the end of the semester, many students are also asked to evaluate their courses and teachers based on a specific set of criteria: organization of course material, use of class time, value of the assignments, and so on.

Not surprisingly, much of the reading and writing that you will do in college involves evaluation and judgment. Writing researchers Barbara Walvoord and Lucille McCarthy, for example, found that many college writing assignments take the form of good/better/best questions:

Good: Is X good or bad?

Better: Which is better—X or Y?

Best: Which is the best among available options? What is the best solution to a given problem?

Even writing assignments that do not involve evaluation as their central aim often require you to make evaluative decisions as part of your writing process. All papers that require research, for example, require you to evaluate and select sources based on certain criteria, a topic we discuss in Chapter 7, where we offer guidelines for this kind of evaluation. College reading assignments also frequently involve good/better/best questions. In your history class, for example, you may read contrary opinions about whether it was right or wrong (good or bad), necessary or unnecessary (the best option under the circumstances) to have dropped the bomb on Hiroshima and Nagasaki to end World War II. In your English class, you might read literary criticism arguing that Toni Morrison's *Song of Solomon* is a better novel than *Beloved,* despite the latter's greater popularity.

As may be apparent, readings that evaluate and judge are often a form of argument. At issue in evaluative arguments are questions of value. In making claims about value, writers offer criteria-based reasons and evidence for their judgments just as they do in other kinds of arguments. For example, the critic who argues that *Song of Solomon* is a better novel than *Beloved* may cite richness of character development, novelty of plot, and evocativeness of style as her reasons for making the judgment she does. In doing so, she would be using criteria that are commonly accepted standards for judging the merits of literary texts. Others may quarrel with her assessment, but to do so they would have to use the same commonly accepted criteria to demonstrate differing judgments or they would have to argue that other criteria are more relevant.

Since evaluations are by definition judgmental, ethos presents a particular challenge for writers of evaluation. To be credible, writers must establish their credentials for making the judgments that they do. At the same time, they must avoid the impression of superiority or condescension toward their subject or audience. Sometimes, to be sure, satire and sarcasm may work as a form of negative evaluation as long as the reader is willing to be positioned as an ally in denigrating the subject at hand. However, a sarcastic tone and style can just as easily backfire if readers do not agree that the subject deserves such treatment. Generally, evaluative writers are most effective when they create a knowledgeable and fair-minded ethos.

Although evaluative arguments may appear straightforward—either you like something or you don't, either you think something is harmful or not—this appearance is deceptive. Successful evaluative arguments are challenging both to write and to read. To make convincing evaluative claims, writers must establish clear and appropriate criteria and then offer evidence that the particular subject meets or fails to meet the stated criteria. If the criteria are inappropriate or if the evidence doesn't match the established criteria, the evaluation will not be persuasive. For example, one would not use criteria appropriate for evaluating indie art films to evaluate a blockbuster Hollywood action film, nor would one cite the charitable giving of a best-selling author as evidence about the quality of his new novel. Before accepting the claims made by an evaluative text, rhetorical readers should consider whether the criteria reflect shared values and common standards for assessing this kind of phenomena and whether the evidence fits the established criteria and sufficiently supports the evaluative claims.

Yet another matter to consider in reading and writing evaluative texts is the role of context and purpose in establishing criteria. If, for example, a supervisor is evaluating the performance of her staff, the criteria she chooses to use in her evaluation (or the criteria that are set for her to use) will be determined by the work involved and individual employee's roles and responsibilities. Similarly, the purpose and use to which performance reviews are put in her company will shape the content and tone of her evaluations. If it is a company that sees performance reviews as formative—that is, as a way of strengthening their employees' abilities—then she might feel quite free to name specific weaknesses and recommend steps the employee might take to address those weaknesses. If, however, performance reviews are seen as summative judgments that are regularly used to fire employees or deny them merit pay, a supervisor might downplay employee weaknesses or refer to them obliquely in order to protect the employees under her charge (unless, of course, she wants to get them fired!). Both the writer and reader of performance reviews need to understand the context and purpose since the judgments made in these reviews have material consequences for those reviewed. As this example suggests, both context and purpose influence the criteria selected as well as the potential consequences of the judgment, and rhetorical readers are well advised to be mindful of both.

A further issue to consider is whether relative or absolute standards are appropriate. Making a judgment based on relative standards assumes that ideal standards cannot be met and that a judgment must therefore be made using relative standards—judging what is good or better, not what is best. The danger in using relative standards is in overpraising the mediocre. However, making a judgment based on absolute or ideal standards can lead to overly negative judgments, for few performances meet ideal standards. If, for example, you were reviewing a high school drama performance, you would probably not apply the ideal standards used to judge professional actors, directors, and so on. Such application would undoubtedly result in a withering and demoralizing review. At the same time, one could argue that applying these ideal standards might motivate the high school thespians to work harder and achieve a higher level of performance. Although most situations call for the application of relative, not ideal, standards, it is important to be alert for situations that may call for the application of ideal, or at least, less compromised standards. The issue of relative versus absolute standards is a thorny one, requiring writers to consider the potential effects of their evaluation and readers to consult their own values as they assess the value judgments of others.

Although judgments based on relative criteria are much more common than those based on ideal criteria, occasionally a case is made for something or someone being the "best" in a particular category. For example, some basketball commentators argue that Michael Jordan is the "best" to ever play the game of basketball while others dispute that judgment. In a 1999 special millennium issue, the *New York Times Magazine* featured articles about "the best" of the millennium—best invention, best herb, best pope, best joke, you name it. The articles, two of which are included in this chapter, have two kinds of purposes: to entertain or to offer a serious commentary on our cultural values and beliefs. Some combine these two purposes. As Frank Rich explains in the lead article, "Why the Best?," the authors of these articles recognize the impossibility of making any absolute judgments about their subjects and elect instead to offer their evaluations as a form of cultural commentary: "the Best is most likely to provide a snapshot of our own time, not a definitive guide to that vast expanse of past time we seek to pillage." The larger point is that all judgments and evaluations are shaped by the evaluator's worldview and values and, consequently, reveal as much about the person making the judgment as they do about the thing being judged. To read evaluative texts rhetorically, one must take into account the ideology that informs the judgments being made.

To establish their criteria for judgment, evaluative writers often call on methods that involve other aims, such as to inform and analyze. Articles in *Consumer Reports*, for example, aim to inform as well as to "argue" that a particular product is better than other products in its class. Movie reviews use analysis and interpretation to make their judgments. Though all of the readings in this chapter offer evaluations, some include other purposes as well. Jared Diamond, for example, explains the complicated factors that lead to inventions as part of his re-evaluation of Gutenberg's contribution to the millennium's "best" invention, the printing press. Joyce Millman's "The Addictive Spectacle of Maternal Reality" and Rhonda Downey's "Through the Looking Glass" interpret as well as evaluate the cultural significance of two different types of television shows.

At times, authors of evaluative texts stop short of making a value judgment, allowing readers to draw their own conclusions based on the author's analysis of the positive and negative qualities of the phenomenon being evaluated. For example, Laurence Zuckerman, whose essay "Words Go Right to the Brain, But Can They Stir the Heart?" is included in this chapter, declines to answer directly the question posed in his title. Rather he invites readers to draw their own conclusions about the effects of PowerPoint presentations.

Finally, the readings in this chapter illustrate that what is at stake in a given evaluation varies considerably. In the case of Alison Lurie's "A Perfect Set of Teeth," there is very little of consequence at stake. Her evaluation of the taken-for-granted zipper is meant mainly to amuse. By contrast, a great deal is at stake for Rhonda Downey in her evaluation of the negative stereotypes of African Americans perpetuated by television sitcoms.

Questions to Help You Read
Evaluative Texts Rhetorically

Asking the following questions of the texts you read in this chapter offers you practice in the very activity this chapter discusses: evaluating and judging. The questions below imply criteria by which you can evaluate and judge the effectiveness of these texts. Additionally, they offer guidance for writing your own evaluations.

1. What question of value is at issue? Is it a question of whether something is beneficial or harmful? A question of whether something is good, better, or best? Is this question of value stated explicitly or only implied?
2. What criteria are stated or implied? Are the terms clearly defined? Does the writer use relative or ideal criteria? Are the criteria appropriate to the subject being evaluated and to the situation?
3. Does the author offer evidence that the subject being evaluated meets or fails to meet the stated or implied criteria? What kind of evidence is offered—quantitative or qualitative? Does the author offer sufficient evidence to convince you of his or her judgment? Does the author use analogy or comparison as evidence for his or her evaluation? If so, are such analogies or comparisons appropriate and convincing?
4. What's the author's purpose? Is the author merely trying to inform you of his or her judgment, or is she or he trying to persuade you to take some action based on that evaluation? What, if anything, is at stake in this evaluation?
5. What kind of knowledge or authority does the author assert as a qualification for making this judgment?
6. What kind of a persona or personality does the author create in the text? That is, do the author's tone and attitude toward the subject being judged convince you that he or she is fair-minded, someone whose judgment is worthy of respect?

Jared Diamond

Invention Is the Mother of Necessity

Jared Diamond (b. 1937), a professor of physiology at the UCLA School of Medicine, is the author of several widely acclaimed "trade" books—that is, books written for nonscientists—as well as the author of numerous scholarly articles. His books include *Guns, Germs, and Steel: The Fates of Human Societies* (1997) and *Why Is Sex Fun? The Evolution of Human Sexuality* (1997). In 1985, Diamond received a MacArthur Foundation "Genius" Award, and in 1998 a Pulitzer Prize for *Guns, Germs, and Steel*. An expert in bird ecology and evolutionary physiology, Diamond is both praised and criticized for his interdisciplinarity as well as for his unconventional theories. For example, in *Guns, Germs, and Steel*, Diamond argues that the peoples of Europe and Asia were successful in conquering others because of an accident of geography that made it possible for them to develop advanced weaponry, immunity to disease, and certain social structures. In this essay on the "best invention" of the past 1,000 years, written for the *New York Times Magazine* April 18, 1999 issue on millennial "bests," Diamond demonstrates both his broad knowledge and his inclination to play the iconoclast.

•   *For Your Reading Log*

1. This article ran with the following subtitle: "Gutenberg didn't invent the printing press—and other surprises from 1,000 years of ingenuity." What expectations does this subtitle create for you?

2. As mentioned in the headnote, this article was published with a group of other articles in anticipation of the new millennium. Given the information you have about the rhetorical context—occasion, place of publication, and author—what do you predict about the article's level of difficulty and interest to you?

————   •   ————

1   My 11-year-old twin sons just told me what they learned today in school. "Daddy, Johannes Gutenberg invented the printing press, and that was one of the greatest inventions in history." I learned that, too, when I was a child. I suspect that the same view is taught in most other American and European schools. What we are told about printing is partly true, or at least defensible. Personally, I would rate it as the best single "invention" of this millennium. Just think of its enormous consequences for modern societies. Without printing, millions of people wouldn't have read quickly, with no transmission errors, Martin Luther's 95 Theses, the Declaration of Independence, the Communist Manifesto or other world-changing texts. Without printing, we wouldn't have modern science. Without printing, Europeans might not have spread over the globe since 1492,

because consolidation of initial European conquests required the emigration of thousands of would-be conquistadors motivated by written accounts of Pizarro's capture of the Incan emperor Atahualpa.

So I agree with half of what my kids were taught—the part about the importance of printing. But things get more complicated when you credit this invention specifically to Gutenberg, or even when you credit him with just the printing press itself. Gutenberg did much more than invent the printing press— and much less than invent printing. A more accurate rendering of his achievements would be something like the following legalistic sentence: "Gutenberg played a major practical and symbolic role in independently reinventing, in a greatly improved form and within a more receptive society, a printing technique previously developed in Minoan Crete around 1700 B.C., if not long before that." 2

Why did Gutenbergian printing take off while Minoan printing didn't? 3 Therein lies a fascinating story that punctures our usual image of the lonely and heroic inventor: Gutenberg, James Watt, Thomas Edison. Through his contribution to the millennium's best invention, Gutenberg gave us the millennium's best window into how inventions actually unfold. Even American and European schoolchildren reared on Gutenberg hagiography soon learn that China had printing long before Gutenberg. Chinese printing is known to go back to around the second century A.D., when Buddhist texts on marble pillars began to be transferred to the new Chinese invention of paper via smeared ink. By the year 868, China was printing books. But most Chinese printers carved or otherwise wrote out a text on a wooden block instead of assembling it letter by letter as Gutenberg did (and as almost all subsequent printers using alphabetic scripts have also done). Hence the credit for what Gutenberg invented is also corrected from "printing" to "printing with movable type": that is, printing with individual letters that can be composed into texts, printed, disassembled and reused.

Have we now got the story right? No, Gutenberg still doesn't deserve credit 4 even for that. By about 1041, the Chinese alchemist Pi Sheng had devised movable type made of a baked-clay-and-glue amalgam. Among the subsequent inventors who improved on Pi Sheng's idea were Korea's King Htai Tjong (cast-bronze type, around 1403) and the Dutch printer Laurens Janszoon (wooden type with hand-carved letters, around 1430). From all those inventors, it's convenient (and, I think, appropriate) to single out Gutenberg for special credit because of his advances—the use of a press, a technique for mass-producing durable metal letters, a new metal alloy for the type and an oil-based printing ink. We also find it convenient to focus on Gutenberg as a symbol because he can be considered to have launched book production in the West with his beautiful Bible of 1455.

But a form of printing with movable type was invented far earlier by an un- 5 named printer of ancient Crete in the Minoan age. The proof of Minoan printing can be found in a single baked-clay disk, six inches in diameter. Found buried deep in the ruins of a 1700 B.C. palace at Phaistos on Crete, the disk is covered on both sides with remarkable spiraling arrays of 241 symbols constituting 45 different "letters" (actually, syllabic signs), which were not deciphered until a couple of years

ago. A recent decipherment identifies the signs' language as an ancient form of
Greek that predates even Homer.

6   Astonishingly, the symbols of the Phaistos disk weren't scratched into the
clay by hand, as was true of most ancient writing on clay, but were instead
printed by a set of punches, one for each of the 45 signs. Evidently, some ancient
Cretan predecessor of Pi Sheng beat him to the idea by 2,741 years. Why did Minoan printing die out? Why was Renaissance Europe ready to make use of the
millennium's best invention while Minoan Crete was not?

7   Technologically, the Minoans' hand-held punches were clumsy. The early
Minoan writing system itself, a syllabary rather than an alphabet, was so am-
biguous that it could be read by few people and used for only very particular
kinds of texts, perhaps only tax lists and royal propaganda. Chinese printing's
usefulness was similarly limited by China's own nonalphabetic writing system.
To make Minoan printing efficient would have required technological advances
that did not occur until much later, like the creation of paper, an alphabet, improved inks, metals and presses.

8   I mentioned that Gutenberg is part not only of the millennium's best invention but also of its best insight into how our usual view of inventions often
misses the point. Coming up with an invention itself may be the easy part; the
real obstacle to progress may instead be a particular society's capacity to utilize
the invention. Other famously premature inventions include wheels in pre-
Columbian Mexico (relegated to play toys because Mexican Indians had no draft
animals) and Cro-Magnon pottery from 25,000 B.C. (What nomadic hunter-
gatherer really wants to carry pots?)

9   The technological breakthroughs leading to great inventions usually come
from totally unrelated areas. For instance, if a queen of ancient Crete had
launched a Minoan Manhattan Project to achieve mass literacy through improved printing, she would never have thought to emphasize research into
cheese, wine and olive presses—but those presses furnished prototypes for
Gutenberg's most original contribution to printing technology. Similarly, American military planners trying to build powerful bombs in the 1930's would have
laughed at suggestions that they finance research into anything so arcane as
transuranic elements.

10   We picture inventors as heroes with the genius to recognize and solve a society's problems. In reality, the greatest inventors have been tinkerers who loved
tinkering for its own sake and who then had to figure out what, if anything, their
devices might be good for. The prime example is Thomas Edison, whose phono-
graph is widely considered to be his most brilliant invention. When he built his
first one, in 1877, it was not in response to a national clamor for hearing
Beethoven at home. Having built it, he wasn't sure what to do with it, so he drew
up a list of 10 uses, like recording the last words of dying people, announcing
the time and teaching spelling. When entrepreneurs used his invention to play
music, Edison thought it was a debasement of his idea.

11   Our widespread misunderstanding of inventors as setting out to solve society's problems causes us to say that necessity is the mother of invention. Actually, invention is the mother of necessity, by creating needs that we never felt

before. (Be honest: did you really feel a need for your Walkman or CD player long before it existed?) Far from welcoming solutions to our supposed needs, society's entrenched interests commonly resist inventions. In Gutenberg's time, no one was pleading for a new way to churn out book copies: there were hordes of copyists whose desire not to be put out of business led to local bans on printing.

The first internal-combustion engine was built in 1867, but no motor vehi- 12 cles came along for decades, because the public was content with horses and railroads. Transistors were invented in the United States, but the country's electronics industry ignored them to protect its investment in vacuum-tube products; it was left to Sony in bombed-out postwar Japan to adapt transistors to consumer-electronics products. Manufacturers of typing keyboards continue to prefer our inefficient qwerty layout to a rationally designed one.

All these misunderstandings about invention pervade our science and tech- 13 nology policies. Every year, officials decry some areas of basic research as a waste of tax dollars and urge that we instead concentrate on "solving problems": that is, applied research. Of course, much applied research is necessary to translate basic discoveries into workable products—a prime example being the Manhattan Project, which spent three years and $2 billion to turn Otto Hahn and Fritz Strassman's discovery of nuclear fission into an atomic bomb. All too often, however, the world fails to realize that neither the solutions to most difficult problems of technology nor the potential uses of most basic research discoveries have been predictable in advance. Instead, penicillin, X-rays and many other modern wonders were discovered accidentally—by tinkerers driven by curiosity.

So forget those stories about genius inventors who perceived a need of so- 14 ciety, solved it single-handedly and transformed the world. There has never been such a genius; there have only been processions of replaceable creative minds who made serendipitous or incremental contributions. If Gutenberg himself hadn't devised the better alloys and inks used in early printing, some other tinkerer with metals and oils would have done so. For the best invention of the millennium, do give Gutenberg some of the credit—but not too much.

● Thinking Critically About "Invention Is the Mother of Necessity"

RESPONDING AS A READER

1. What did you initially expect Diamond to evaluate? At what point did you begin to realize that he was actually going to evaluate something other than what you initially thought? What effect did this surprising reversal have on you as a reader?

2. According to what criteria does Diamond argue that the printing press is the "millennium's best invention"? What evidence does he use to support this claim? What evidence does he offer to support his re-evaluation of Gutenberg's achievement (paragraph 2)? What implicit criteria does he suggest for re-evaluating the achievements of those credited with an invention?

3. Why does Diamond think it is important to change people's minds about the process of invention? What are possible consequences of this change in perspective?

RESPONDING AS A WRITER

1. Diamond's essay is densely packed with facts, yet he tries to lighten his essay with anecdotes, humor, and other strategies meant to engage reader interest. Find examples of these strategies and evaluate their effectiveness in enlivening the essay and engaging your interest.

2. The title inverts the word order of the proverb "Necessity is the mother of invention." First, consider the meaning of this proverb. Does it seem to be true in terms of your knowledge of scientific discoveries and/or your personal experience? Second, consider the meaning of his reversal of the proverb. Does he persuade you of the validity of his claim? Freewrite your responses to these questions.

3. Do you agree with Diamond's claim that inventions "create needs that we never felt before"? He cites the CD player and Walkman. Can you think of other inventions that have occurred during your lifetime that created needs you and others never felt before? Take a few minutes to jot down your ideas.

Alison Lurie

A Perfect Set of Teeth

Alison Lurie's (b. 1926) work includes novels, short fiction, literary nonfiction, and children's fiction. A professor of American literature at Cornell University, Lurie is editor of *The Oxford Book of Modern Fairy Tales* and coeditor of the Classics of Children's Literature, 1631–1932 book series. In 1985, she won a Pulitzer Prize in fiction for *Foreign Affairs*, a novel about the relationship that develops between two professors who are in London to do research. Her most recent novel is *The Last Resort: A Novel* (2000). "A Perfect Set of Teeth" is taken from the *New York Times Magazine* issue on the millennial best. Lurie's topic is the "best fashion."

● *For Your Reading Log*

1. Accompanying the original article were a subtitle—"There's nothing sexier than a zipper"—and a 1960s photograph of a man unzipping a woman's black leather motorcycle jacket. What do the title, subtitle, and photograph suggest to you about the tone and focus of the article?

2. If you were asked to write a short essay on the "best fashion," what would you write about? Take a few minutes and freewrite about what you would select and why.

———————   ●   ———————

> Zip! I was reading Schopenhauer last night.
> Zip! And I think that Schopenhauer was right. . . .
> Zip! I'm an intellectual.
>
> —Lorenz Hart, "Zip," from "Pal Joey"

The zipper is probably the only clothes fastener to have been the star of a Broadway song. When the highbrow strip-tease artist in "Pal Joey" shed bits of her shiny costume, she demonstrated the zipper's amazing properties, of which the most remarkable is speed. 1

The zipper revolutionized not only dressing, but also undressing, and in the process changed relations between the sexes. For centuries, getting your clothes on and off was a slow, awkward process. It was also precarious: hooks came undone, drawstrings knotted or broke, pins made holes in you and in the fabric, buttons popped, buttonholes tore. 2

For years, getting dressed took a long time, while getting undressed could take so long that it might be dangerous. Medieval knights bled to death on the battlefield before they could be extricated from their tin-can armor. In the 18th 3 and 19th centuries, formal gowns might have had 30 buttons, and underneath them fashionable women were laced into corsets that made it impossible for them to take a deep breath. They often fainted, and sometimes suffered permanent damage before they were freed.

4   The creation of the zipper took several decades. The original "clasp locker" exhibited by Whitcomb L. Judson at the World's Columbian Exposition in 1893 was clumsy and bulky. Many inventors, some of them women, worked to perfect it. Finally, in 1917, Gideon Sundback patented the device we know today. In World War I, his "hookless fasteners" appeared on life vests and flying suits for the Army and Navy; and the B. F. Goodrich Company, which gave the zipper its name, put it on galoshes in the 1920's. But it wasn't until the 1930's that zippers were light and flexible enough to be used on fashionable clothing.

5   At first, zippers, always made of metal, were usually concealed by flaps of fabric. In the 1960's, however, they came out into the open as part of the 60's look. Bright-colored, supersize zippers ran up the front of stiff plastic or cotton pique mini-dresses, making women look as if they were wearing the covers of small kitchen appliances.

6   The other postwar apotheosis of the zipper was the biker look. Marlon Brando set the style in "The Wild One," and today black leather jackets still bristle with shiny metal zippers that suggest not only secrecy (all those little pockets) but speed and violence—and also sex.

7   As a film expert I know says, "When you're talking about zippers, you're already talking about sex." A dress that fastens with a row of buttons is a romantic challenge. A man needs patience, skill and charm to get you out of it. A zipper, especially if it is partly unfastened, is a sort of silent come-on; but the kind of sex it suggests is passionate and immediate rather than romantic and long-term. Peeling your girlfriend (or your boyfriend) is the work of a moment.

• *Thinking Critically About "A Perfect Set of Teeth"*

RESPONDING AS A READER

1. What seems to be Lurie's definition of *fashion*? How is it similar to or different from the definition implicit in your reading log entry on the "best fashion"?
2. What criteria does Lurie offer for her selection of the zipper as the "best fashion"? How effectively does her use of examples match these criteria?
3. Is Lurie serious about her selection of the zipper as the best fashion? What in the text makes you believe she is? What in the text makes you believe she isn't?

RESPONDING AS A WRITER

1. Reread the last paragraph. Why do you think she concluded the essay this way?

2. Is it possible to establish criteria that people generally would agree upon when it comes to fashion? Why or why not?
3. Return to your freewriting in your reading log and consider your choice of a best fashion. What criteria did you use to make your selection? How would you characterize your selection? Serious? Playful? Satirical? If you were to develop this into a short essay, what tone would you take? To what kind of audience might you direct this essay?

Laurence Zuckerman

Words Go Right to the Brain,
but Can They Stir the Heart?

Laurence Zuckerman, a staff writer for *Time* magazine and regular contributor to the *New York Times*, writes frequently on technology and culture. This article, published in the *New York Times* in 1999, offers a commentary on the communicative effectiveness of PowerPoint, a presentation program created by Microsoft to assist public speakers in organizing and creating visual aids for their talks. The article is accompanied by a photograph of Dr. Martin Luther King Jr. delivering his famous "I Have a Dream" speech. Above the photograph, as if projected onto a screen behind King, an image of a PowerPoint slide presents his speech as follows:

I HAVE A DREAM

Dreams include:
- sons of former slaves and slave owners will have a sit-down
- skin color out; content of character in
- black and white children hold hands
- black men = white men

Freedom is scheduled to ring in:

New York, Mississippi, Georgia, Alabama, Tennessee, California

• *For Your Reading Log*

1. How familiar are you with PowerPoint? Have you seen any PowerPoint presentations in class or at work? Have you ever used PowerPoint yourself? If so, what's your assessment of its value to speakers as well as to audiences? If not, do you think such a program might be useful to speakers and audiences? Why?
2. Whether or not you are familiar with the content of King's speech, what does the above presentation suggest to you about the effects of PowerPoint on King's speech?

———————   •   ———————

1 Good Morning.
2   The title of today's presentation is: "The Effect of Presentation Software on Rhetorical Thinking," or "Is Microsoft Powerpoint Taking Over Our Minds?"

- I will begin by making a joke.
- Then I will take you through each of my points in a linear fashion.
- Then I will sum up again at the end.

Unfortunately, because of the unique format of this particular presentation, we will not be able to entertain questions. 3

Were Willy Loman to shuffle through his doorway today instead of in the late 1940's, when Arthur Miller wrote "Death of a Salesman," he might still be carrying his sample case, but he would also be lugging a laptop computer featuring dozens of slides illustrating his strongest pitches complete with bulleted points and richly colored bars and graphs. 4

Progress? Many people believe that the ubiquity of prepackaged computer software that helps users prepare such presentations has not only taken much of the life out of public speaking by homogenizing it at a low level, but has also led to a kind of ersatz thought that is devoid of original ideas. 5

Scott McNealy, the shoot-from-the-lip chairman and chief executive of Sun Microsystems, who regularly works himself into a lather criticizing the Microsoft Corporation, announced two years ago that he was forbidding Sun's 25,000 employees to use Powerpoint, the Microsoft presentation program that leads the market. (The ban was not enforced.) Some computer conferences have expressly barred presenters from using slides as visual aids during their talks, because they think it puts too much emphasis on the sales pitch at the expense of content. 6

Psychologists, computer scientists and software developers are more divided about the effect of Powerpoint and its competitors. Some are sympathetic to the argument that the programs have debased public speaking to the level of an elementary school filmstrip. 7

"The tools we use to shape our thinking with the help of digital computers are not value free," said Steven Johnson, the author of "Interface Culture," a 1997 study of the designs used to enable people to interact with computers. 8

Mr. Johnson uses Powerpoint himself (for example, during a recent talk he gave at Microsoft) but nonetheless said, "There is a certain kind of Powerpoint logic that is brain numbing." 9

Presentation programs are primarily used for corporate and sales pitches. Still, the approach has leaked into the public discourse. Think of Ross Perot's graphs or President Clinton's maps. Critics argue such programs contribute to the debasement of rhetoric. "Try to imagine the 'I have a dream' speech with Powerpoint," said Cliff Nass, an associate professor of communication at Stanford University who specializes in human-computer interaction. Other people, however, have made the opposite argument, saying that Powerpoint has elevated the general level of discourse by forcing otherwise befuddled speakers to organize their thoughts and by giving audiences a visual source of information that is a much more efficient way for humans to learn than by simply listening. 10

"We are visual creatures," said Steven Pinker, a psychology professor at the Massachusetts Institute of Technology and the author of several books about cognition including "The Language Instinct." "Visual things stay put, whereas sounds fade. If you zone out for 30 seconds—and who doesn't?—it is nice to be able to glance up on the screen and see what you missed." 11

Mr. Pinker argues that human minds have a structure that is not easily reprogrammed by media. "If anything, Powerpoint, if used well, would ideally reflect the way we think," he said. 12

13   But Powerpoint too often is not used well, as even Mr. Pinker admitted. He is on a committee at M.I.T. that is updating the traditional writing requirement to include both speech and graphic communication. "M.I.T. has a reputation for turning out Dilberts," he said. "They may be brilliant in what they do, but no one can understand what they say."

14   Visual presentations have played an important part in business and academia for decades, if not centuries. One of the most primitive presentation technologies, the chalkboard, is still widely used. But in recent years the spread of portable computers has greatly increased the popularity of presentation programs.

15   Just as the word processing programs eliminated many of the headaches of writing on a typewriter, presentation software makes it easy for speakers to create slides featuring text or graphics to accompany their talks. The programs replace the use of overhead projectors and acetate transparencies, which take time to create and are more difficult to revise. Most lecture halls and conference rooms now feature screens that connect directly to portable computers, so speakers can easily project their visual aids.

16   The secret to Powerpoint's success is that it comes free with Microsoft's best-selling Office software package, which also features a word processing program and an electronic spreadsheet. Other presentation programs, like Freelance from I.B.M.'s Lotus division and Corel Corporation's Presentations, also come bundled with other software, but Office is by far the most successful, racking up $5.6 billion in sales last year.

17   Because most people do not buy Powerpoint on its own, it is difficult to tell how many actual users there are. Microsoft says that its surveys show that, compared with two years ago, twice as many people who have Office are regular users of Powerpoint today, and that three times as many Office users have at least tried the program. Anecdotal evidence indicates an explosion in the use of Powerpoint.

18   For instance, the program is used for countless sales pitches every day both inside and outside a wide variety of companies. It is de rigueur for today's M.B.A. candidates. The Dale Carnegie Institute, which imbues its students with the philosophy of the man who wrote the seminal work "How to Win Friends and Influence People," has a partnership with Microsoft and offers a course in "high-impact presentations" at its 170 training centers in 70 countries. Microsoft has incorporated into Powerpoint many templates based on the Carnegie programs and has even incorporated the Carnegie course into the program's help feature.

19   Powerpoint is so popular that in many offices it has entered the lexicon as a synonym for a presentation, as in "Did you send me the Powerpoint?"

20   The backlash against the program is understandable. Even before the advent of the personal computer, there were those who argued that speeches with visual aids stressed form over content. Executives at International Business Machines Corporation, the model of a successful corporation in the 1950's, 60's and 70's, were famous for their use of "foils," or transparencies.

21   "People learned that the way to get ahead wasn't necessarily to have good ideas," wrote Paul Carroll in "Big Blues," his 1993 study of I.B.M.'s dramatic decline in the era of the personal computer. "That took too long to become apparent. The best way to get ahead was to make good presentations."

Critics make many of the same claims about Powerpoint today. "It gives you 22
a persuasive sheen of authenticity that can cover a complete lack of honesty," said
John Gage, the chief scientist at Sun Microsystems, who is widely respected in
the computer industry as a visionary.

Academic critics echo the arguments made by Max Weber and Marshall 23
McLuhan ("The medium is the message") that form has a critical impact on
content.

"Think of it as trying to be creative on a standardized form," Mr. Nass said. 24
"Any technology that organizes and standardizes tends to homogenize."

Powerpoint may homogenize more than most. In the early 1990's Microsoft 25
realized that many of its customers were not using Powerpoint for a very powerful reason: They were afraid. Steven Sinofsky, the Microsoft vice president in
charge of the Office suite, said that writer's block was an issue for people using
word processors and other programs but the problem was worse with Powerpoint because of the great fear people had of public speaking.

"What would happen was that people would start up Powerpoint and just 26
stare at it," he said.

Microsoft's answer was the "autocontent wizard," an automated feature 27
that guides users through a prepared presentation format based on what they are
trying to communicate. There are templates for "Recommending a Strategy,"
"Selling a Product," "Reporting Progress" and "Communicating Bad News."

Since 1994, when it was first introduced, the autocontent wizard in Power- 28
point has become increasingly sophisticated. About 15 percent of users, Mr.
Sinofsky said, now start their presentations with one of those templates. The latest version of Powerpoint, which will be released this month, will feature an even
more powerful wizard. The new version also includes thousands of pieces of clip
art that the program can suggest to illustrate slides. There is even a built-in
presentation checker that will tell you whether your slides are too wordy, or that
your titles should be capitalized while bullet points should be lower case.

Many see the best antidote to the spread of Powerpoint in a graphic medium 29
that is expanding even faster than the use of presentation software: the Web.
Whereas Powerpoint presentations are static and linear, the Web jumps around,
linking information in millions of ways. Mr. Gage of Sun tries to use the Web to
illustrate his many public speeches, though a live Internet connection is not as
readily available at lecterns these days as a cable that can connect a notebook
computer to a screen for a Powerpoint presentation.

"Powerpoint is just a step along the way because you can't click on a Pow- 30
erpoint presentation and get the details," said Daniel S. Bricklin, who developed
the first electronic spreadsheet for P.C.'s and more recently a program called Trel-
lix that puts Web-like links into documents.

Mr. Bricklin said the Web, like any new medium, required new forms of com- 31
position just as the headlines and opening paragraphs of newspaper articles
helped readers skim for the most information.

But he does not bemoan the popularity of presentation software. "It was a 32
lot worse," he said, "when people got up with their hands in their pockets,
twirling their keys, going 'Um um um.'"

• *Thinking Critically About "Words Go Right to the Brain, but Can They Stir the Heart?"*

RESPONDING AS A READER

1. What is the effect of Zuckerman's decision to present the introductory paragraph as a PowerPoint presentation? What connections do you see between this opening and the graphic of King's speech? What do these two examples of PowerPoint make you expect in the rest of the essay? Is this expectation fulfilled?

2. Do you find the criteria Zuckerman uses to evaluate the effect of PowerPoint on speakers and audiences to be appropriate and convincing?

3. Who are Zuckerman's intended readers in terms of age, educational background, social class, and profession? Are you part of this intended audience? Explain your answer by citing various allusions, terms, and statements in the text.

RESPONDING AS A WRITER

1. Zuckerman presents both negative and positive evaluations of Power-Point's effects. Do you find his presentation balanced? Make a list of the advantages and disadvantages he mentions. What do you think his opinion is of PowerPoint—favorable, unfavorable, or mixed? Offer evidence to support your answer. Does Zuckerman ever really answer the question he poses in the title? If so, what is his answer? If not, why not?

2. Zuckerman quotes Steven Johnson as saying, "The tools we use to shape our thinking with the help of digital computers are not value free." What do you think Johnson means? Offer a paraphrase of this statement, and try to think of an example that illustrates Johnson's point.

3. Make a list of situations in which you think a PowerPoint presentation might be appropriate and effective and a list of situations in which it would not be appropriate nor effective. What criteria did you use to decide? Choose one of the situations in which you think a PowerPoint presentation would not be appropriate, say, a marriage proposal, and create a mock PowerPoint presentation.

Michael Kinsley

The Morality and Metaphysics of Email

In 1996, Michael Kinsley (b. 1951) became editor-in-chief of the online journal *Slate* when it was founded by Microsoft Corporation. Formerly an editor of the *New Republic* and *Harper's*, two intellectually highbrow journals, Kinsley has written extensively about politics and culture. In addition to his experiences as an editor and writer, Kinsley has served as the moderator of two television shows that feature political debate, CNN's *Crossfire* and *Firing Line*. "The Morality and Metaphysics of Email" was published in 1996 by *Forbes ASAP*, which focuses on the latest developments in technology and its impact on business. Like its parent publication, *Forbes ASAP* is written for business professionals, economists, stockbrokers, financial advisors, and others particularly interested in keeping up with financial issues.

• *For Your Reading Log*

1. To what extent is e-mail a part of your work, school, and/or personal life? Would you rank yourself a frequent, moderate, or infrequent user, or a nonuser? If e-mail plays at least some small part in your life, list the ways in which you use e-mail and write a brief entry in your reading log about your attitude toward it. If you are an infrequent or nonuser, explain why. Is it circumstance or personal choice?
2. Even if you are a nonuser, to what extent do you believe we've become an "e-mail culture"?

———————   •   ———————

The way the new technology has affected my working life most directly has nothing in particular to do with what I am producing. My product happens to be an Internet-based magazine, but this particular innovation would be just as transforming if my business were manufacturing paper clips. The innovation is email. 1

Until I came to Microsoft in January, I had never worked for a big corporation. So I was having a hard time sorting out all my new impressions. What was 2 Microsoft (which prides itself, of course, on being a different kind of corporation) and what was (despite Microsoft's pretensions) corporate America in general? Shortly after I arrived, I met someone who'd just joined Microsoft from Nintendo North America—a similar high-tech, postindustrial, shorts-and-sandals sort of company, one would suppose. So I asked him, How is Microsoft different? He said, "At Microsoft, the phone never rings." And it's almost true. The ringing telephones that TV producers use as an all-purpose background noise to signify a business setting are virtually silent at Microsoft. At least in terms of intracompany communications, probably 99 percent take place through email. If you should happen to get an old-fashioned phone call, you may well be informed of that fact by email, even if the person who took the message is within eye-contact range.

3   Microsoft may still be a bit ahead of most of the rest of the country in developing an email culture, but I suspect it's only a tiny bit. Email is inevitable. Nineteen eighty-nine was the year you stopped asking people, "Do you have a fax machine?" and started asking, "What is your fax number?" Nineteen ninety was the year you started being annoyed (and, by around Christmastime), incredulous that anyone in the business or professional world would not have a fax number. Similarly, 1996 is the year you stopped asking people, "Do you have email?" and started asking, "What is your email address?" By the end of 1997 you will be indignant if anyone you're doing business with expects you to go to the trouble of communicating by less convenient methods.

4   This is an almost entirely positive development. Convenience aside, email is a marvelous medium of communication. It combines the immediacy of telephone or face-to-face talk with the thoughtfulness (or at least the opportunity for thoughtfulness) of the written word. At *Slate* we find it a wonderfully productive way to bounce around editorial ideas. And we use it in the online magazine as a medium of policy debate that we find intellectually superior to television chat.

5   Email has eased the burden of putting out a national magazine of politics and culture from Redmond, Washington (which is not the center of the universe, whatever some of its denizens may think). With a small budget and staff, we could not ordinarily afford to have a headquarters in Redmond plus bureaus in Washington and New York. But email enables us to spread the "headquarters" staff over all three places. Our East Coast representatives can pick up the local vibes in the traditional metropolitan manner (i.e., lunch) then plug back into Redmond in the modern manner (i.e., email). If you use email dozens of times a day—and save it—you end up with a pretty complete record of your activities and thoughts. As someone who (like many others) aspires to keep a diary but lacks the self-discipline, I find this comforting. Lawyers, of course, find it alarming, but you can't please everybody.

6   A social advantage of email is its egalitarianism. It's another blow to the old corporate culture in which Mr. Bigshot dictates letters and memos and the secretary types them, folds them, mails them, opens them at the receiving end, files them, and so on. Is there anyone in the business world who still thinks that he or she is too important to type? If so, that person had better wake up. Refusing to use a keyboard will soon be as anachronistic as, say, refusing to speak on the telephone.

7   To be sure, egalitarianism has its limits. The ease and economy of sending email, especially to multiple recipients, makes us all vulnerable to any bore, loony, or commercial or political salesman who can get our email address. It's still a lot less intrusive than the telephone, since you can read and answer or ignore email at your own convenience. But as normal people's email starts mounting into the hundreds daily, which is bound to happen, filtering mechanisms and conventions of etiquette that are still in their primitive stage will be desperately needed.

8   Another supposed disadvantage of email is that it discourages face-to-face communication. At Microsoft, where people routinely send email back and forth all day to the person in the next office, this is certainly true. Some people believe

this tendency has more to do with the underdeveloped social skills of computer geeks than with Microsoft's role in developing the technology email relies on. I wouldn't presume to comment on that. Whether you think email replacing live conversation is a good or bad thing depends, I guess, on how much of a misanthrope you are. I like it.

Historians looking back on our time, I suspect, will have no doubt that the arrival of email was a good thing. For decades now historians have been com- 9 plaining about the invention of the telephone. By destroying the art of letter writing, telephones virtually wiped out the historians' principal raw material. Email, however, has reversed that development. Historians of the twenty-first century will be able to mine rich veins of written-and-stored material. People's daily lives will be documented better than ever before. Scholars specializing in the twentieth century will be at a unique disadvantage compared both with their colleagues writing about the nineteenth or earlier centuries and with those writing about the twenty-first or later.

So 1996 is not just the year business embraced email. In a way, it is the year history started again.   10

● *Thinking Critically About "The Morality and Metaphysics of Email"*

RESPONDING AS A READER

1. Kinsley offers a sequence of criteria to support his claim that "email is a marvelous medium of communication." What does this particular sequence of criteria contribute to his overall argument? Do you find his reasons persuasive and his evidence adequate?
2. How does his status as a newcomer to corporate America generally and to a high-tech corporation specifically affect his credibility?
3. Kinsley compares e-mail to the fax machine (paragraph 3) and to the telephone (paragraphs 4 and 9). What do these comparisons contribute to his evaluation of e-mail?

RESPONDING AS A WRITER

1. In paragraphs 7 and 8, Kinsley lists some disadvantages of e-mail. Does he emphasize these disadvantages sufficiently? Can you think of other disadvantages that he fails to mention?
2. Kinsley claims the "social advantage of email is its egalitarianism." Do you agree? Explain why or why not, and offer evidence from your own experience for your answer.
3. Although Kinsley does not develop this point, in the final paragraphs he suggests that e-mail has again made written communication important. If you are a regular user of e-mail, take a few minutes to freewrite about the impact of e-mail on your writing process and on the new forms of writing you have observed.

Joe Queenan

Web Sites Dedicated to Being Simple Without Giving Up Affluence

Joe Queenan (b. 1950) is a cultural critic and freelance writer who writes about everything from politics and movies to fast food restaurants. His satirical stance toward
his many subjects is suggested in such book titles as *Imperial Caddy: The Rise of Dan
Quayle and the Fall of Practically Everything Else* (1992) and *Red Lobster, White Trash, and
the Blue Lagoon: Joe Queenan's America* (1998). Queenan, a former editor at *Forbes* magazine, has written articles for popular magazines such as *Spy, Gentleman's Quarterly,
TV Guide, Rolling Stone,* and *Time.* This commentary appeared in the *New York Times*
on March 23, 2000, beneath an article entitled "The Frantic Race to Exploit the Complications of Simplification," which was based on an interview with Susan Wyland,
the editor of *Real Simple.*

• *For Your Reading Log*

1. What does Queenan's title suggest about his attitude toward his subject?
2. As you read through the article, mark passages that support or contradict your prediction.

——————— • ———————

1   On 02Simplify, a Web site devoted to streamlining daily life, there is a guide to
planning a New Year's Eve party that contains 62 tips, not one of them "Buy
more tequila." There is also a guide to starting a rock band that includes 18 hints
like "Obtain your instrument, learn the basics" and "Don't forget tuning!"
Clearly, the online simplification industry has a ways to go before it is ready to
offer the public a truly indispensable product.

2   Simplicity has evolved into a secular religion for affluent Americans in recent years, making a likable but neurotic class of people feel even more uncomfortable with themselves. At heart, simplicity buffs yearn for an earlier, simpler
time when people did not have BMWs, villas in Tuscany and 401Ks, because they
had simplified their lives by being poor. Since no one these days actually wants
to give up the villas in Tuscany or be poor, the alternative is to read books and
magazine articles about how simple life would be if only it were not so complicated. Clinically, this is best described as vicarious Shakerism.

3   Philosophically, the simplicity movement derives from the belief that if one
could only reduce paperwork, one's children would be less annoying. Because
the simplicity movement proceeds from the flawed assumption that material
supplied by journalists can help simplify anything, it is probably doomed. But
before it fizzles, it will almost certainly manage to support a number of content-
driven, advertisement-laden Web sites.

Two addresses worthy of attention are RealSimple.com and O2Simplify. 4
com, a feature provided by Oxygen, the Web site devoted to women and those
who think like them. RealSimple.com is the official Web site of the magazine
Real Simple. As such it will offer not only sample articles from the magazine,
but also chat rooms where les nouveaux simples can talk about simple things
in a simple way. For example, RealSimple.com, the Web page, explains that
Real Simple, the magazine, will show how to "create family rituals that make
lasting memories." In the past, this might have meant eating together or going
to Chip's lacrosse game. But now it seems the whole family might want to log
on to the RealSimple.com chat room and talk with other people about creating
"islands of calm." When the kids grow up they can reminisce about e-mailing
complete strangers with the toll-free numbers of credit card companies that do
not charge annual fees.

O2Simplify is a more complicated simplification tool, consisting of innu- 5
merable lists. Also, there is a certain class bias. For example, in a section devoted
to hiring a nanny, O2Simplify suggests buying surveillance equipment, but it
never once mentions learning a foreign language so one might actually be able
to chat with the person who is raising the kids. And O2Simplify ignores the
nanny's needs, perhaps assuming that nannies who wish to simplify can visit
Oxygen4Nannies.com, which, alas, does not yet exist.

None of the foregoing is meant to suggest that simplicity sites are useless, 6
trendy or foolish. O2Simplify's iconoclastic guide to simplifying St. Patrick's Day
(no booze) is a welcome addition to the science of streamlining, and Real
Simple.com, the Web site, enables visitors to send friends gift subscriptions to
Real Simple, the magazine, always a nice surprise for anyone expecting another
three years of Industry Week.

Still, it is clear that online simplicity remains so complicated that a few nav- 7
igational guides are needed. Here then are seven ways to simplify the use of simplicity Web sites:

1. Get rid of all but one of your credit cards so you won't have to read any
   more articles online about getting rid of all but one of your credit cards.
2. Get better-looking. A considerable amount of online simplification material is devoted to improving your looks, which you wouldn't have to
   read about if you weren't so plain.
3. Hire a nanny to raise your kids, eliminating the need to read online articles about child-rearing. Tell your nanny to e-mail you reports of the
   kids' progress, preferably in a language you speak.
4. If a guide to simplifying something contains more than 60 helpful hints,
   accept the fact that some things cannot be simplified.
5. Get rid of half your friends, creating more time to visit simplicity Web
   sites. Tell your ex-friends to do the same. If everyone in America had
   fewer friends, life would be much simpler.
6. Move to Nebraska. You can read the article in Real Simple, the magazine,
   about why you should move to Nebraska later. Meanwhile, just pack up
   and go.

7. Hire a college student or impoverished senior to visit simplicity Web sites and prepare a precis of all the ways you can make your life simpler. Better yet, let the nanny do it.

• *Thinking Critically About "Web Sites Dedicated to Being Simple Without Giving Up Affluence"*

RESPONDING AS A READER

1. What made you laugh as you read this article? What roles does this humor invite the reader to play in relation to the simplicity movement and those caught up in it?
2. To whom is this article directed? At those who are likely to already share Queenan's opinion about this movement? At those who have created simplicity Websites? At people who visit these Websites and take this movement seriously? Find evidence in the text to support your answer.
3. Queenan compares several simplicity Websites in the course of this article. What criteria does he use to make his comparison? Besides the Websites, what else is Queenan evaluating in this article? What leads you to this conclusion?

RESPONDING AS A WRITER

1. The word *simple* has a double meaning throughout the article. Find two or three examples of this play on words and jot down some notes about the effect he achieves in these passages.
2. Although the article is clearly meant to be humorous, do you think Queenan has any serious points to make? If so, what are they? If not, why don't you think so?
3. What do you believe to be Queenan's underlying values and ideology? Use the ideology analysis technique presented in Chapter 5 (p. 77) to answer this question. How are these values and worldview revealed in this article?

Joyce Millman

The Addictive Spectacle
of Maternal Reality

Joyce Millman is a media critic who frequently publishes her work in the online magazine *Salon* as well as in publications such as the *New York Times*. Her special interest is television, and she has written critical reviews of such popular shows as *The Sopranos* and *NYPD Blue*. In this article published on August 13, 2000 in the regularly featured television/radio section of the the *New York Times*, Millman evaluates the reality TV show *A Baby Story*, which premiered on cable's Learning Channel in 1998.

• *For Your Reading Log*

1. Is there a reality TV show that you watch? If so, which show is it? What draws you to this show? If not, what have you heard about reality TV shows? What do you think accounts for the emergence and popularity of such shows?
2. Have you ever seen a film of an actual childbirth or witnessed a birth firsthand? What were your reactions, particularly your emotional reactions? How similar was this experience to portrayals of childbirth on television shows or in the movies?

——————— • ———————

Nine years ago, before "Survivor," before "Big Brother," before "The Real World," even, I was introduced to reality programming of the most intimate sort. It was thrilling and disturbing. It made me want to look away. It made me want to look back again. I think it even made me nauseous. But then everything made me nauseous, because I was pregnant. This was the final week of Lamaze class and my spouse and I and our classmates were finally watching the Movie. 1

Most Lamaze classes screen a variation of the Movie, a natural childbirth documentary depicting actual couples experiencing labor and delivery. The only part I remember clearly is the one in which the woman serenely labored at home in her rocking chair, then strolled over to the hospital to give unmedicated birth with nary a groan. The two other vignettes involved long, hard labors that were clearly not helped any by the magical pain-dulling techniques we'd spent a month learning about. 2

As Lamaze propaganda, the movie was a bust; it was a much better endorsement for the value of an epidural (or for being knocked out cold with a large mallet). And it was seat-squirmingly embarrassing—you felt sorry for the hard-laboring women and their terrified mates, so vulnerable and exposed in what should be a private moment. I snickered at the dorky intrusiveness of it all. Yet 3 each time a woman gave her final triumphant push and out came a slippery baby, I was surprised by the tears welling up in my eyes. I became, truth be told, a tad verklempt. And I wasn't the only one, judging from the sniffles around me. I chalked it up to hormones, confident it would pass once I was back to my old un-expectant self.

4   One afternoon last year, I turned on my TV and stumbled upon a sight that instantly took me back to Lamaze class. There, in my living room, was a woman in labor, with a doctor and nurses urging her to push, a husband at her head telling her to breathe and a half-dozen family members crowded around the foot of the bed watching her (discreetly draped) nether region as if it were a wide-screen TV. O.K., that part was weird. But the rest of the scene was just like the Movie—right down to the sobby lump in my throat. I had found "A Baby Story," a reality series on cable's Learning Channel that follows expectant couples through the last weeks of pregnancy and into the delivery room. It's like watching a Lamaze movie every day, except that you don't have to do the breathing exercises.

5   Since its premier in late 1998, "A Baby Story" has become the Learning Channel's most popular daytime series among adult women, drawing 3.8 million viewers a week. Two consecutive half-hour episodes are broadcast each weekday (beginning at 2 p.m.), sandwiched between "A Dating Story" and "A Wedding Story" (now there's a chronology that probably gives conservatives fits). A five-hour "Baby Story" marathon is scheduled for—of course—Labor Day.

6   Who the heck watches "A Baby Story"? I imagine the audience is made up of women like me, years removed from new motherhood, but whose scary, overpowering new-mom instinct never quite got turned all the way back to "off." And it doesn't take much for the floodgates to open. We'd sell our own grandmothers to hold an infant and get a fix of that intoxicating scent known as "new baby's head." Childbirth is a test of a woman's stamina, proof of her body's power. It's an unbelievably heady feeling giving birth, probably akin to winning a marathon (but how many of us ever win a marathon?). "A Baby Story" expertly taps that rush of maternal giddiness.

7   Hopelessly addictive, "A Baby Story" provides an undeniable voyeuristic tingle; not only do you get a peek at one of life's most awesome, intimate spectacles, you get to see how your birthing performance rated in the overall scheme of things. It's like childbirth porn—complete with unflattering lighting, sometimes muddy sound and decidedly nonprofessional stars. And it's shamelessly formulaic. Each episode of "A Baby Story" opens with the expectant couple in their living room talking about how they met, how long they've been together and why they've decided to have this baby. If it's a first baby, the episode features the obligatory "couple goes shopping" scene, where the wide-eyed mom-and dad-to-be are played like violins by the baby-goods-store clerk (yes, you must have this electric diaper wipe warmer!). If the couple already have a child, the shopping scene is replaced by one in which the parents tout the joys of big brother or sisterhood to their firstborn.

8   Then, halfway through the episode, the drama of labor begins and it's time for the couple to go to the hospital (pausing, of course, to notify the 60 or so relatives and friends they want to take with them). The passing of the hours is

quaintly signaled by (I swear) shots of the hospital room clock. The episode's climax—the mommy shot, if you will—comes when the determined woman gives one last mighty push (her private parts are blurred in postproduction) and the doctor holds aloft the slick, wiggly bundle. As the new parents cuddle their baby, happy tears glistening on their cheeks, a winsome acoustic guitar tune fills the soundtrack. The music could have been lifted straight from an episode of "thirtysomething," and why not? Both shows are about couples totally absorbed in new parenthood—as if no one had ever had a baby before them.

Part of the allure of the new reality programming is its mean-spiritedness; 9 we watch "Survivor" and "Big Brother" so we can laugh at the obnoxious exhibitionists whose lives are on display. But "A Baby Story" is virtually alone among reality series in the dignity it accords its subjects. Oh, I'm not saying you won't chortle at the naivete of some of these couples, fluttering around stocking up on frilly little baby clothes and fancy, useless gadgets. But "A Baby Story" is, for the most part, generous and respectful (if that can be said of a show that presents birth as entertainment).

The producers solicit couples for the show through an announcement at 10 the end of each episode, and through the program's Web page, http://tlc. discovery.com/tlcdaytime/babystory/newkids.html. Oddly, though, these cattle calls have not resulted (on air, anyway) in a circus of shameless Springer-esque attention seekers. No, these appear to be ordinary people who approach the show as an opportunity to create the deluxe version of a keepsake home video.

What strikes you most about the couples on "A Baby Story" is how thought- 11 ful and committed they seem. "A Baby Story" presents a variety of parents-to-be—white, African-American, Latino, Orthodox Jewish, Mormon, blue-collar, yuppie, rural, urban, deaf—and a panorama of parenting philosophies. My favorite parents-to-be were the Philadelphia couple, both boho artists, who decided to name their soon-to-be-born daughter Liberty, decorated her nursery with Springsteen posters and kitschy Americana and devised a touchingly kooky "commitment to parenthood" ceremony in which they invited family and friends to join them for a day at a steam train amusement park to conjure memories of what it felt like to be a kid.

In one aspect, though, every story on "A Baby Story" is the same: all of these 12 babies are wanted. (For those seeking hardcore, depressing childbirth stories, the Learning Channel offers the occasional prime-time reality series "Maternity Ward," a production of New York Times Television, which documents unwed teenagers giving birth in public hospitals—the fathers of the babies are never there—and shows us the harrowing medical complications that "A Baby Story" leaves out.) Which is not to say that "A Baby Story" has an agenda, that it's an advertisement for (take your pick) family planning or the pro-life movement. It's just that it presents childbirth under the best, most hopeful of circumstances.

I used to wonder if my Lamaze instructor was nuts. A perky mother of 13 three, she attended several births a week, observing the deliveries of friends, family members, students and probably total strangers, too. If you've seen one birth, haven't you seen them all? At the time, I didn't get it, but now I do. "A Baby

Story" freezes that four-handkerchief moment of perfect joy, when, gazing upon their newborn, parents are filled with gratitude and humility. As any parent knows, the trick is to hold onto those delivery room feelings through the anxiety-filled, exhausting, increasingly complicated years that follow. And that's why "A Baby Story" keeps you coming back for more; it makes you remember why you signed on for this in the first place.

• *Thinking Critically About "The Addictive Spectacle of Maternal Reality"*

RESPONDING AS A READER

1. How does Millman go about establishing her credibility as an evaluator of *A Baby Story*?
2. How would you describe Millman's attitude toward *A Baby Story*? Toward reality shows in general? What role does she offer her readers to play in relation to these shows?
3. Do you think the intended audience is primarily women or, even more specifically, women who have given birth? What, if anything, does Millman do to engage a broader range of readers? Did you consider yourself part of her audience? Why or why not?

RESPONDING AS A WRITER

1. At what points in the text do you find yourself most engaged? What effect does her use of personal anecdotes have on your response to this article?
2. Millman describes *A Baby Story* as "addictive." How does Millman explain this addiction? Do you find certain television shows to be addictive? Take a few minutes to speculate about why you find a particular show addictive.
3. Millman's article suggests that there's sometimes a disconnection between our thoughts and our feelings. That is, we can be consciously aware that our emotions are being manipulated by a TV advertisement or show, yet still find ourselves reacting emotionally, perhaps in the way the makers of the ad or show intended. Try to recall a time when watching television triggered this kind of reaction in you, then freewrite for a few minutes to reflect on this response. Compare your experience with those of your classmates to generate possible explanations.

M. G. Lord

En Garde, Princess!

M(ary) G(race) Lord (b. 1955) is a nationally syndicated editorial cartoonist who works for *Newsday*. Lord's cartoons are known for their bold and biting social commentary; however, her cultural criticism extends beyond cartooning. She is a commentator for National Public Radio and an investigative journalist. Author of *Forever Barbie: The Unauthorized Biography of a Real Doll* (1995), she is currently working on a cultural history of NASA's Jet Propulsion Lab. "En Garde, Princess!" appeared in the online magazine *Salon* on October 27, 2000, in the regularly featured "Mothers Who Think" department.

● *For Your Reading Log*

1. This article was originally accompanied by the subhead "For the first time ever, Barbie may have a challenger who can kick her anorexic butt." What do the title and this subhead suggest about the tone and style of this article? Log on to http://www.salon.com. What commonalities do you discover among the article titles you find? How would you describe the *Salon* style and attitude? Who is the intended audience?

2. Lord's title and first paragraph use military or battle metaphors to discuss the competition between Barbie and the Get Real Girls dolls. As you read this article, mark the examples of military metaphors that occur throughout the article.

——————— ● ———————

If I were Barbie, the 11-and-a-half-inch princess who has dominated the doll 1 world since 1959, I would keep an eye on the newly formed SWAT team of action figures known as Get Real Girls. I wouldn't raise the pink drawbridge or dump the radio-controlled alligators into the moat. Not just yet, anyway. But I would watch my bony little back.

I do not say this lightly. As the author of "Forever Barbie: The Unauthorized 2 Biography of a Real Doll," I know that the princess has systematically annihilated each and every one of her competitors, beginning in 1963, when Marx Toys introduced a shabby wannabe, Miss Seventeen, with whom Barbie swiftly wiped the nursery floor. There were legal issues involved, but they did not ultimately matter. Miss Seventeen was a wreck—jaundiced skin, shoddily implanted hair, a veritable Miss Teen Runaway—and kids simply didn't want her. Consequently, when I was asked to evaluate these new pretenders to Barbie's throne, I knew I had to move fast. Barbie's challengers do not tend to last long.

When I saw the Get Real Girls, however, I was thrown off guard. These 3 dolls are far from slipshod wannabes. And the time seems right for a toy-world upset. Last year, something happened at Mattel that had once seemed impossible: Jill Barad, the company's Barbie-identified, pink-suit-wearing (a bubblegum shade) juggernaut of a CEO, resigned—after making such a mess of the company that its stock lost 70 percent of its value. If Barad, who built the Barbie line from about $250 million (when she arrived as a low-level manager in the 1980s) to $1.7 billion last year, could suffer a reversal of fortune, why not Barbie herself? This warranted a closer look: at Barbie and Barad, and the new, punchy young upstarts, the Get Real Girls and their creator, Julz Chavez.

4   The Get Real team has six members: Gabi, a soccer player, Corey, a surfer, Skylar, a snowboarder, Nakia, a basketball player, Claire, a scuba diver, and Nini, a mountaineer. You won't find these girls in toeshoes or figure skates. They are a tough, muscular lot, whose swelling biceps and chiseled abdominals are as much inspired by Brandi Chastain, the U.S. soccer player best known for ripping off her shirt after last year's World Cup victory, as by the original pumped-up action figure, GI Joe. (In fact, if you do rip the shirt off a Get Real Girl, you will find a trim little sports bra covering up a modest package in place of Barbie's bare, bullet-shaped bosoms.)

5   Chavez is not your archetypal doll designer. A cousin to César Chavez, the legendary 1960s labor leader, she worked in toy development for 15 years, several of which were spent behind the fuchsia ramparts of Barbie's own manufacturer, Mattel. Chavez's dolls, however, do not bear a trace of fuschia. Their boxes are blue and orange.

6   "Our stealth name for the project, while we were working on it, was, 'No Pink,'" Chavez told me over coffee recently. But the defiant moniker didn't make it to market. "If you call a concept 'No Pink,' Mattel will come after you big time," she explained.

7   Mattel will usually come after you anyway. In the fall of 1985, for example, the Barbie team learned from undercover sources that Hasbro was planning to release Jem, a new rock star fashion doll, the following February. "Within minutes," a former Mattel executive told me, "we had a war council." Within an hour, they had a plan: Pull together a rock group for Barbie. Although Barbie and the Rockers hurt Jem's sales, the Hasbro doll destructed on her own. At 12 inches tall, she looked like a surly drag queen in Barbie's clothes. "If you're going to go up against General Motors," a dealer in collector merchandise explained, "you'd better be the same size."

8   Similarly, in 1991, Barbie's most recent challenger, Happy to Be Me, fizzled after a promising start. From Allure to People magazine, journalists applauded her alleged "realistic" proportions—closer to the Get Real Girls' 33-24-33 than to Barbie's (roughly) 40-18-22. But the doll did not live up to its press. Created by a Midwestern mom who lacked toy industry experience, Happy was produced cheaply and badly. The doll was repulsive—from its lackluster wardrobe, which seemed to consist solely of frumpy housecoats, to its sparse clumps of hair, scattered so meagerly that the total effect recalled Sen. William Proxmire's hair transplant.

9   It satisfied neither girls' craving for an over-the-top prom queen nor their mothers' desire for a tasteful, realistic role model. Like Barbie, Happy looked like she belonged in a trailer park, but if Barbie was cast in the role of neighborhood

slut, Happy was the careworn housewife who had let herself go. She may have been happy to be herself, but it was obvious, even to kids, that she had extremely low standards.

The Get Real Girls, by contrast, are beautifully designed miniatures. If nothing else, Chavez's experience at Mattel taught her that details matter. The Get Real Girls are equipped with meticulous replicas of the sporty styles that modern girls covet—exquisite zippered backpacks, painted hiking boots, two-tone beach slippers. Chavez says her girls would "look great in a tight black dress," even if they had to steal it from Barbie. And despite their slightly obtrusive ball-like joints, I am inclined to agree (even if their sneaker-ready feet mean that they must pair their cocktail dresses with sensible flats). They also have great, shiny, abundant hair. This is a crucial asset, since "hairplay," as Mattel market research types call it, is a big draw for girls. "Each doll," Chavez reminded me, "comes with a hairbrush." 10

These dolls express the ethos of their time, which has changed considerably in the 40 years since Barbie first wobbled out in her steep stiletto mules. Today, the adjective "ladylike" has bitten the dust. Parents encourage daughters to sweat and grunt in physical competition, and even supermodels sport muscles obtained by logging hours at the gym. Chastain, immortalized in her sports bra, is a role model for girls, one that meets with the approval of most middle-class parents. 11

Although Mattel equipped its princess for such country-club sports as tennis, at the time of her creation, the idea of a woman participating in a so-called extreme sport was inconceivable. In the 1960s, even swaggering gym teacher types rarely engaged in anything more vigorous than golf or bowling. Barbie, to be sure, has been issued paraphernalia for rougher sports, but with her '60s-era pinup girl figure, she looks ridiculous in a basketball uniform—as if she borrowed it for a photo shoot and cannot wait to give it back. 12

And the Internet may do for the Get Real Girls what television advertising did for Barbie. In 1955, Mattel became the first toy company to broadcast commercials during children's programs that were aimed directly at underage viewers. Before this time, children were not thought of as significant consumers, and no company had made a large-scale attempt to shape or exploit their buying habits. 13

Chavez's site speaks directly to girls. It is reminiscent of the early Barbie commercials, in which the doll was deliberately portrayed in a subversive way that, during market research sessions, had unnerved parents and delighted kids. Back then, of course, subversive meant unabashedly sexy. The Get Real Girls are subversive in a different way: jocky, and up-to-date on music that may be grating to parental ears. At the Get Real Girl site, users can choose among "dance," "groove," "lounge" and "tune out" sounds. Every single music selection had a thumping beat that irritated me immensely—a sure sign that kids will groove on the music. 14

It isn't as if Barbie doesn't have her own Web site. She does. It's just shockingly uncool and hopelessly out of date. Hit an icon labeled "Storytelling," for example, and you are assaulted by insipid harp music reminiscent of Walt Disney's TV show during the 1950s. 15

16   Although GetRealGirl.com is intended to sell dolls, it does not promote specific products by other manufacturers. "I don't want to tell kids that you have to buy brands to be cool," Chavez explained. "We will not post banner ads on our site." (On the other hand, Chavez does encourage kids to obtain certain accessories, even if their makers aren't specified. "I wish I had an MP3 player like Sky does," Corey, for example, laments in the course of her adventure.) The deemphasis on brands, however, places Chavez in sharp contrast to Barad, who coaxed high-end manufacturers like Ferrari to license Barbie-size versions of their products as a way to teach brand recognition to kids.

17   Born Julia Chavez in 1962, Chavez shortened her name to Julz when, after graduating from the California College of Arts and Crafts, she applied for jobs designing toys not specifically intended for girls. As Julia, she got polite rejections; as Julz, she was invited to show her portfolio. In person her gender was abundantly clear: When I met her, she was chic, thin and stylishly turned out in a turtleneck and leather jacket.

18   Yet her demeanor was a far cry from that of Barad, who made grossly exaggerated femininity her trademark. Barad dressed to intimidate: The suit she wore when I met her while researching my book cost more than my car. During company presentations, she would often dance, cheerleader fashion, to music from product promotions—a practice that appalled Wall Street. "This may be very infectious in a sales presentation at a toy company," an industry analyst told the New York Times, "but you are not accustomed to seeing it at banker presentations."

19   Chavez was never much of a fan of froufrou femininity. Neither Chavez nor her sisters ever owned a Barbie. This did not present a problem until she arrived at Mattel, and was told that all new employees must accept an upscale porcelain version of the doll. "I made it so far without a Barbie," she told them, "I'm not going to start now." When they gave her a hard time, she reluctantly accepted a porcelain Ken.

20   One of 10 children raised by her father, a farmworker, Chavez was born in Yuma, Ariz., and came of age in Southern California. The Arizona years were hard, in no small part because of the discrimination visited on Mexican-Americans. "We were thrown out of restaurants because my father was too dark," she recalled.

21   Chavez based the Get Real Girls on her real-life friends—athletes like Olympic cyclist Stephanie McKnight and former professional surfer Candace Woodward. She claims that out of all her dolls, she feels the strongest affinity for Gabi, the Brazilian-American soccer player, who, like her, is biracial.

22   I asked Chavez for the details on the Get Real Girls' lives: How old are they? Are they still in school? Have they turned pro? Chavez picked up a blue and orange package and read the girls' biographies off the back of the box. Nini plans to steady archaeology. Claire intends to be a vet. "But Nakia," Chavez said slyly, "might turn pro. I'm not sure yet."

23   And where are the tennis players? Aren't Venus and Serena Williams inspiring girls left and right? This question seemed to hit a nerve. The sisters, Chavez said, "made a deal with another company."

Inspired by her cousin, Chavez has been vigilant about labor practices in- 24
volved in the making of her dolls. The Get Real Girls, like Barbie, are made in
China. But before Chavez would permit production to begin, she visited the factory to make sure workers had adequate on-site living facilities and received sufficient breaks. (If Barad ever did anything along these lines, she did not tell me
or any other journalist.)

In the past, Barbie has, of course, navigated shoals that shipwrecked Mattel 25
executives. In 1978, for example, Ruth Handler, the Mattel co-founder who is considered by many to be the closest thing Barbie has to a mother, pleaded no contest to charges of conspiracy, mail fraud and falsifying Securities and Exchange
Commission information. She was sentenced to a 41-year prison sentence and a
$57,000 fine, which the judge later suspended. He did, however, require that she
devote 500 hours each year for five years to community service and pay $57,000
to fund an occupational "rehab" center for convicted felons. Barbie, however, suffered only a temporary setback. No competitors managed to exploit her weakness. Roughly 15 years later, when Barad arrived, Barbie sales reached their
highest point ever.

Mattel's Teflon resiliency over the past 40 years does not signal doom for the 26
Get Real Girls, who, despite their hipster spunk and pumped-up swagger, are
still far from perfect. But it does suggest a different way to interpret victory. For
the girls to crush Barbie, they don't have to eradicate her. They just have to beat
her up a bit, punch a few holes in her sales. Even a tiny dent would be historic,
the first such inroad of its kind.

Sparring with the girls might just build Barbie's character—after they break 27
her plastic jaw.

● *Thinking Critically About "En Garde, Princess!"*

RESPONDING AS A READER

1. In this article, Lord assesses the Get Real Girls' chances of dethroning
   Barbie by comparing the dolls according to various criteria. What are
   those criteria and what judgments do they lead Lord to make?
2. How does Lord use her historical knowledge of Barbie to establish her
   credibility as a judge?
3. Why does Lord compare Barad, the power behind Barbie's success for
   many years, and Chavez, the creator of the Get Real Girls, as well as the
   dolls? What criteria does she use to compare these two women? What
   does her evaluation of the two doll sponsors/creators contribute to her
   evaluation of the dolls?

RESPONDING AS A WRITER

1. Review the military metaphors and references you noted in your log.
   Why are such metaphors appropriate? List all of the ways in which this
   is a battle. What stakes are involved in winning or losing this battle?

2. Lord claims that "these dolls express the ethos of their time, which has changed considerably in the forty years since Barbie first wobbled out in her steep stiletto mules" (paragraph 11). What images of women are communicated by these two lines of dolls? What messages do these two lines of dolls communicate to young girls about the role and status of women in our society? In your opinion, do the changes suggested in the differences between these two doll lines reflect actual changes in the status of women?

3. Lord briefly compares the two Websites set up for the dolls: Barbie.com and GetRealGirl.com. Log on to these two sites and make your own comparison about their effectiveness and appeal.

Sandra Cisneros

Barbie-Q (Fiction)

Sandra Cisneros (b. 1954) is a poet and fiction writer known for her appeal to children and young adult readers as well as adults. Much of her work draws on her own ethnic and family background as the only daughter among the eight children of her Mexican father and Chicana mother. She was born in Chicago, but the family moved frequently between Mexico and the United States. She is known for her short, lyrical narratives, which are collected in two books so far, *House on Mango Street* (1984) and *Woman Hollering Creek* (1991), where "Barbie-Q" was first published, a collection of interior monologues from Mexican Americans. Cisneros has been awarded fellowships from the National Endowment for the Arts and the MacArthur Foundation and has taught as a guest writer at numerous secondary schools, colleges, and universities.

• *For Your Reading Log*

1. What expectations does the title of this story raise for you? What associations does "Barbie-Q" bring to mind? Freewrite for several minutes, trying to think of as many possibilities as possible.

2. What do you remember about make-believe games from your childhood in which you and your friends were imitating adults you knew or were familiar with from television?

————————   •   ————————

for Licha

Yours is the one with mean eyes and a ponytail. Striped swimsuit, stilettos, sunglasses, and gold hoop earrings. Mine is the one with bubble hair. Red swimsuit, stilettos, pearl earrings, and a wire stand. But that's all we can afford, besides one extra outfit apiece. Yours, "Red Flair," sophisticated A-line coatdress with a Jackie Kennedy pillbox hat, white gloves, handbag, and heels included. Mine, "Solo in the Spotlight," evening elegance in black glitter strapless gown with a puffy skirt at the bottom like a mermaid tail, formal-length gloves, pink chiffon scarf, and mike included. From so much dressing and undressing, the black glitter wears off where her titties stick out. This and a dress invented from an old sock when we cut holes here and here and here, the cuff rolled over for the glamorous, fancy-free, off-the-shoulder look.

Every time the same story. Your Barbie is roommates with my Barbie, and my Barbie's boyfriend comes over and your Barbie steals him, okay? Kiss kiss kiss. Then the two Barbies fight. You dumbbell! He's mine. Oh no he's not, you stinky! Only Ken's invisible, right? Because we don't have money for a stupid-looking boy doll when we'd both rather ask for a new Barbie outfit next Christmas. We have to make do with your mean-eyed Barbie and my bubblehead Barbie and our one outfit apiece not including the sock dress.

3   Until next Sunday when we are walking through the flea market on Maxwell Street and *there!* Lying on the street next to some tool bits, and platform shoes with the heels all squashed, and a fluorescent green wicker wastebasket, and aluminum foil, and hubcaps, and a pink shag rug, and windshield wiper blades, and dusty mason jars, and a coffee can full of rusty nails. *There!* Where? Two Mattel boxes. One with the "Career Gal" ensemble, snappy black-and-white business suit, three-quarter-length sleeve jacket with kick-pleat skirt, red sleeveless shell, gloves, pumps, and matching hat included. The other, "Sweet Dreams," dreamy pink-and-white plaid nightgown and matching robe, lace-trimmed slippers, hairbrush and hand mirror included. How much? Please, please, please, please, please, please, please, until they say okay.

4   On the outside you and me skipping and humming but inside we are doing loopity-loops and pirouetting. Until at the next vendor's stand, next to boxed pies, and bright orange toilet brushes, and rubber gloves, and wrench sets, and bouquets of feather flowers, and glass towel racks, and steel wool, and Alvin and the Chipmunks records, *there!* And *there!* And *there!* And *there!* and *there!* and *there!* and *there!* Bendable legs Barbie with her new page-boy hairdo. Midge, Barbie's best friend. Ken, Barbie's boyfriend. Skipper, Barbie's little sister. Tutti and Todd, Barbie and Skipper's tiny twin sister and brother. Skipper's friends, Scooter and Ricky. Alan, Ken's buddy. And Francie, Barbie's MOD'ern cousin.

5   Everybody today selling toys, all of them damaged with water and smelling of smoke. Because a big toy warehouse on Halsted Street burned down yesterday—see there?—the smoke still rising and drifting across the Dan Ryan expressway. And now there is a big fire sale at Maxwell Street, today only.

6   So what if we didn't get our new Bendable Legs Barbie and Midge and Ken and Skipper and Tutti and Todd and Scooter and Ricky and Alan and Francie in nice clean boxes and had to buy them on Maxwell Street, all water-soaked and sooty. So what if our Barbies smell like smoke when you hold them up to your nose even after you wash and wash and wash them. And if the prettiest doll, Barbie's MOD'ern cousin Francie with real eyelashes, eyelash brush included, has a left foot that's melted a little—so? If you dress her in her new "Prom Pinks" outfit, satin splendor with matching coat, gold belt, clutch, and hair bow included, so long as you don't lift her dress, right?—who's to know.

• *Thinking Critically About "Barbie-Q"*

RESPONDING AS A READER

1. How does the title work with the story? Go back to your reading log notes about the expectations it raised and consider how these were expanded. Compare your ideas with those of your classmates.
2. This is a very short story, yet filled with evocative detail. Reread it to consider exactly how these details worked to engage you. Where did you

smile? Where did you laugh? Where did you resist what the speaker was telling you? Where were you surprised?

3. Consider the effect of this monologue on you as a reader. Did you find yourself accepting the role of the "you" that Cisneros has her narrator address? When you compare your reading experience and responses to those of your classmates, what similarities and differences are apparent?

RESPONDING AS A WRITER

1. What do the details tell readers about the character of the story's narrator? What can you infer about her age, personality, and values? How does that sense of her change as the story unfolds? Try to pinpoint the places where Cisneros signals the changes through the details as well as through plot development.

2. What is this story about? Is it about toys, or something more? What is it doing in this chapter on texts that evaluate? Who's evaluating what? How? Why?

3. Use the ideology exercise in Chapter 5 (p. 77) to examine the values set forth by the narrator. What does she value? What are the stated or implied opposites of those values? To what extent does your analysis reveal an author behind the narrator?

Rhonda Downey (Student)

Through the Looking Glass

Rhonda Downey (b. 1973) is a community education major at the University of Wisconsin–Milwaukee. In addition to being a student, she is a research assistant at the Social Development Commission, an agency that awards grants to community groups that offer programs to inner-city residents—job training, day care, after-school tutoring, and so on. After graduation, she intends to go on to graduate school. This essay was written for a first-year writing class in which she was asked to analyze and evaluate a particular cultural image or phenomenon.

- *For Your Reading Log*

    1. Downey analyzes the representations of African Americans in two TV sit-coms of the 1990s. Think of a current sitcom that features an underrepresented group. How is this character (or group of characters) represented? Do they challenge or reinforce stereotypes related to this group?
    2. As you read Downey's essay, mark passages where you agree or disagree with her assessment.

——————— • ———————

1   The American media have always played an important part in many Americans' formulations of certain beliefs and ideals. The media have promoted everything from the ideal beauty image (white, tall, blonde, blue-eyed) to patriotism. With worldwide access to American media, many people outside of our culture get their impressions of what Americans look like, behave like, and value from media images. This global sharing of information sounds like a great idea. It should be. However, throughout America's history the media have often misconstrued the cultural images of its minorities, particularly African Americans.

2   The new wave of African American television shows in the 1990s showed promise. They provided recognition that African Americans do watch television and would like to view themselves portrayed in a positive manner. Shows like *Family Matters* and *Martin* both included committed, loving relationships be-tween the lead male and female characters. They had a caring circle of friends and extended families. Both shows dealt with at least one character doing some kind of community service. These shows were also enormously popular with the black audience (and white) and long running. These shows sound great, don't they? They challenge racial stereotypes and create a positive image of African Americans, don't they? Most people would agree. Unfortunately, after evaluat-ing these cultural images, I have come to disagree.

3   The first show, *Family Matters*, is about an extended, working- to middle-class African American family. The cast consists of a father, mother, son, daughter,

grandmother, aunt, and cousin all residing in the same house. The father is a policeman. The mother works, as I recall, but is seen mostly in the home. The children are obedient, polite, and loving. The matriarch grandmother doles out
precious lessons about life, family ties, and cultural pride.

The show seems to want to imitate life for southern Blacks where extended, 4
large families were prevalent. Keeping close family ties and staying strong to survive both as a family and as a people were extremely important. In the past, dark-
skinned African Americans were never the main characters in any television
show or film. The exclusively dark-skinned family featured in this program
seems to try to rectify that. Nevertheless, the antics of the characters do damage
to the cultural image of African Americans. The father is an obese, dark man with
protruding eyes and big lips. He reminds me of some sort of old-time caricature.
The wife has similar features, however more toned down. The grandmother
gives me the impression of some sort of "mammy-figure" used to sell molasses
or laundry soap. The actions of the husband are always harebrained, although
well intentioned. The wife has to then undo the damage caused by his deeds and
schemes gone awry. The entire family can be very loud at times, especially the
husband, adding to the myth that African Americans are prone to be loud, bois-
terous, and unruly. The producer and writers of this show had to have had the
best intentions, but the remnants of old-time minstrel shows and black caricatures are still prevalent.

The second show, *Martin*, features the leading man in the title role. Martin 5
Lawrence is an African American, male comedian turned actor whose stand-up
comedy appeals mostly to the black, urban audience. This show's cast consists
of Martin, his long-time love, Gina, his two best friends, and his girlfriend's best
friend. All are young, vibrant, and on promising career tracks. The skin tones
vary, as they do among African Americans. The show's leading character is
known by many in real life to be a highly successful businessman and marketer.
In the show, he gives people what they want in terms of humor. I used to find
the show funny, too. I used to love watching this program. It was one of my favorites. However, while living in the dorms and watching this program with a
mainly white audience, I started to feel different. We were no longer laughing
with the show's characters. We were laughing at them. They were not fully developed characters with real substance and meaning, but were flat caricatures
that danced, wiggled, and did any dignity-sacrificing thing for a laugh. I looked
at how my housemates were viewing the characters. I listened to the kinds of remarks that they made. Somehow, I felt exposed, embarrassed, and betrayed. I
wanted to either turn off the TV set or run and hide. It made me think about the
way *Martin* was just some sort of updated version of *Good Times*; Martin was just
a revamped J.J. A perfect example of a buffoon, scuffling and shuffling for the
laughs and the dollars.

If I were from another planet and needed to get information on the varieties 6
of earthlings, what would I conclude? What if I were going to be a foreign exchange student and I used American popular television to gather information on
my hosts? What would I conclude? While I was living in the dorms, one of these
questions was answered. A student from Japan explained to me the reason she

did not like to visit my roommate with me present or wait in the room alone with me while my roommate returned. She said the only knowledge she has ever had has come from old black exploitation films like *Shaft*, *Coffy*, and *Superfly* as well as television programs where the villains were usually black thugs and prostitutes. She felt the African Americans were an undesirable people, the lowest on the totem pole, and she would do best not to interact with them at all. She thought the African Americans would rub off on her.

7   The images that the media project about our various cultures are subtle, but strong. American media, leaders in the promotion of ethnic peace and harmony, should examine more closely the images they project.

• *Thinking Critically About "Through the Looking Glass"*

RESPONDING AS A READER

1. What criteria does Downey use to evaluate the representation of African Americans on *Family Matters* and *Martin*? Are these criteria a convincing basis for judging the beneficial or detrimental effects of these images of African Americans? Are there additional criteria she might have used to make her judgment?
2. How do you interpret the meaning of Downey's title, "Through the Looking Glass"?
3. Who seems to be the intended audience (or audiences), and what is Downey's purpose in writing this evaluation?

RESPONDING AS A WRITER

1. How does Downey go about establishing her credibility to judge or evaluate representations of African Americans on sitcoms?
2. If you were a member of Downey's peer response group, what advice might you give her for strengthening her paper?
3. Downey writes about 1990s sitcoms featuring African American characters. Have the representations of African Americans changed since then? Explain your answer with examples.

Writing to Evaluate and Judge

MAKING AN EVALUATION

Option A: Assume that you have been asked to write an essay about "the best" something—you fill in the blank. Using the *New York Times Magazine* essays about millennium "bests" as models, choose either a serious or light class of things about which to make a judgment about the best. Some of the other topics included in the *Times* issue might suggest possibilities: best toy, best joke, best magic trick, best come-from-behind victory. Even if your evaluation is humorous or meant mainly to entertain, you should make sure you articulate clear criteria and offer evidence that matches these criteria.

Option B: Write a review of a book, movie, musical performance, or restaurant in which you evaluate your chosen subject according to appropriate criteria. For example, you might evaluate a restaurant in the category of best ethnic restaurant, best Sunday brunch, or best Friday night fish fry. Or evaluate a movie in the category of "action thriller" or "film noir." Use your familiarity with this category of events, places, or performances to establish criteria for judging the success or quality of whatever you are evaluating, and provide ample evidence to support your claims. Your essay should offer a clear purpose for your evaluative claim. What changed perspective or new insight do you want your readers to have of your subject?

EXAMINING RHETORICAL STRATEGIES

Choose one of the evaluative readings and analyze the text in terms of its purpose and rhetorical strategies. What question of value is at issue for this writer? Are the criteria or basis for the writer's judgment directly stated or implied? Appropriate? Well supported with evidence? What is the writer's purpose in making this evaluation and how successful is she or he in achieving this purpose? Be sure to offer textual evidence to support your analysis and, perhaps, evaluation of this text.

EXTENDING THE CONVERSATION

Choose one of the evaluative arguments in this chapter, and write your own evaluation of the same (or similar) object, performance, or phenomenon but with the goal of offering a different judgment or evaluation. For example, you might choose one of the essays that evaluates a new technology like e-mail or Power-Point and offer your own judgment about its value or effects. Or you might wish to take Rhonda Downey's or Joyce Millman's essay as a starting point and offer your own evaluation of the social impact of reality TV or sitcoms that feature minority characters. Yet another possibility is to visit one of the Websites mentioned in Joe Queenan's essay and offer your own assessment of its worth or the values it promotes. Or visit the Barbie and Get Real Girls Websites, and make a comparative evaluation of their effectiveness.

CHAPTER

15

Proposing Solutions

exts that propose solutions ask readers to take an action, which may sometimes be a new way of thinking. For example, a member of the local community writes an editorial in the college newspaper, proposing that university officials take concrete steps to curb late-night, drunken student parties in the neighborhood surrounding campus. The employee of a start-up dot.com company submits a written proposal for delivering products quickly and reliably. A politician outlines her plan for saving social security in a policy statement distributed to the press. An op-ed writer argues that Americans must change their attitude toward energy consumption before resources are depleted.

The ability to evaluate the proposals of others and write effective proposals ourselves is essential to responsible citizenship and professional success. As citizens we are constantly inundated with policy proposals to solve everything from deterioration of the local library facilities to global warming. To make informed decisions, we need to be able to analyze the reasoning and evidence offered in such proposals and evaluate their soundness and feasibility. Similarly, the ability to write persuasive proposals is called for in nearly all professions—engineering, architecture, medicine, arts, nonprofit management, to cite just a few examples.

As a form of argument, proposals include all the features of arguments—claims, reasons, evidence, counterarguments, and assumptions. Generally, proposals involve one or more of the following goals: (1) specific, concrete action; (2) acceptance, rejection, or modification of a policy; and/or (3) a change in outlook or values. The readings in this chapter illustrate all of these goals, usually in combination. For example, in "Consider the Study of Peace," Kathryn Sipiorski calls on members of the Marquette University community to consider the idea that

491

nonviolent values can be taught and to take practical action to create courses that promote peace and nonviolence. Similarly, Peter Singer in "The Singer Solution to World Poverty" calls for a change in outlook followed by concrete action on the part of the American public at large. Specifically, Singer asks readers to see themselves as responsible for world hunger and, therefore, as responsible for doing something about it by donating substantial proportions of their income to poverty relief efforts. In "The Case for Allowing Kidney Sales," J. Radcliffe-Richards and other experts in medical ethics propose reconsideration and possible rejection of the current policy prohibiting the sale of kidneys by live donors.

The audience for proposals is those who are in a position to act on the proposal either directly or indirectly. To persuade the audience that the proposed action is feasible, beneficial, and better than other proposals, writers need to appeal to their audience's assumptions, values, and interests. Sipiorski addresses her proposal to the Marquette University community, an audience able to take various types of actions in relation to her proposal. Students who read her proposal might request such courses; faculty might propose and teach them. To persuade them of the need for action, she appeals to their concerns about recent violence at a local school. "The Case for Allowing Kidney Sales," published in a British medical journal, is directed primarily at medical and health care professionals, the group charged with implementing the current policy and best positioned to lobby successfully for the policy's reversal. The writers assume this audience understands the problems that result from the shortage of kidneys for transplants as well as the ethical arguments that support the prohibition of kidney sales by live donors. Since the ethical arguments are the greatest obstacle to changing current law, they focus mainly on challenging those arguments.

Effective proposals have three components: *description of the problem, proposal of a solution,* and *justification.* How fully each of these components is developed will depend entirely upon the nature and goal of the proposal as well as upon the rhetorical situation. If the audience is quite familiar with the problem—for example, as would be the case of medical professionals reading "The Case for Allowing Kidney Sales"—then the writers need not spend much time dramatizing the problem's urgency to their readers. If, by contrast, the audience is not familiar with nor concerned about the problem, then the writer's main task is to make the problem present or compelling to the audience. In deciding upon how to introduce the problem, the proposal writer needs to ask questions such as the following: How familiar are people with this problem? Whom does it affect? Whom am I trying to persuade of my solution—only those directly affected or others who might be indirectly affected? If people aren't concerned about this problem, why aren't they? What would make them concerned?

Likewise, the degree to which the writer needs to spell out in detail the proposed solution depends upon the writer's purpose, the nature of the solution, and the audience's background knowledge. Some proposals require detailed explanation if their aim is to convince the audience to take concrete action. Other proposals may require little explanation of the proposed solution because the writer's chief aim is to persuade the audience that there is a problem about which they ought to be concerned. For example, an advertising firm that wishes to persuade a client to accept its proposal for a new ad campaign will need to provide detailed information: test-market data, a detailed cost analysis, a plan for dissemination, a timetable for launching the campaign, and so on. By contrast, writers who propose new approaches to complex social issues may choose, as do Weston and Oates in this chapter, to present their recommendations in general terms because they feel they need to change people's thinking about the issue before recommending more specific actions.

Often the most important aspect of the proposal is the justification section where the writer must persuade the audience that the solution is beneficial, feasible, and better than other possible solutions. To justify their solutions, proposal writers typically argue from principle, consequence, and precedent or analogy. That is, they may appeal to principles, values, or assumptions shared with the audience; to consequences that the audience will agree are good or bad; or to precedents or analogies of similar cases in which their proposed solution was justified and successful. Let's look at each type of argument based on passages drawn from "The Case for Allowing Kidney Sales":

> [I]f we are to deny treatment to the suffering and dying we need better reasons than our own feelings of disgust. (**Argument from principle**)

> Dialysis is a wretched experience for most patients, and is anyway rationed in most places and simply unavailable to the majority of patients in most developing countries. (**Arguments from consequence**)

> Trying to end exploitation [of the poor who sell their kidneys] by prohibition is rather like ending slum dwelling by bulldozing slums: it ends the evil in that form, but only by making things worse for the victims. (**Argument from analogy**)

To summarize: Proposals involve one or more of the following goals: (1) specific, concrete action; (2) acceptance, rejection, or modification of a policy; and (3) a change in outlook or values. In order to achieve these goals, proposal writers must tailor their description of the problem, presentation of the solution, and justification in terms of their audience's values and assumptions and the situation at hand. Some of the proposals in this chapter address issues that are of broad concern to many—environmental policy, world hunger, health care—while others address issues that are of particular concern to university communities.

Questions to Help You Read Proposals Rhetorically

The following questions are designed to guide your analysis of the proposals you read. In addition, these questions offer useful guides for composing and revising your own proposals.

1. How does the writer go about introducing the problem? Does the writer describe the problem in enough detail to give the problem presence? What strategies does the writer use to make the problem seem compelling? If the writer chooses not to describe the problem in detail, can you speculate about why? What is he or she assuming about the audience's background knowledge and concerns? Do these assumptions seem justified?

2. Does the author seem to have the expertise or authority to propose a sound solution? On what do you base your judgment about the author's credibility—the person's public reputation? Or do you base your judgment on the way in which the writer establishes credibility in the text itself by creating a persona that is knowledgeable, concerned, respectful of other opinions, reasonable, and/or practical?

3. What is the solution proposed? How does the author go about presenting it? Does the author provide adequate detail for the intended audience?

4. How does the author go about justifying the solution? To what extent does the writer use arguments from principle, consequence, precedent, and/or analogy? What do these strategies reveal about the author's view of the audience's values, interests, and concerns?

5. Is the author's reasoning sound? Does he or she back up claims with reasons and evidence? Does the author anticipate readers' objections, offer counterarguments, and/or acknowledge alternative solutions? If not, do you think such anticipation, acknowledgment, and counterargument would have made the author's proposal stronger?

Anthony Weston

The Need for Environmental Ethics

Anthony Weston (b. 1954) teaches philosophy at Elon College in North Carolina. His publications include *Toward Better Problems* (1992) and *A Practical Companion to Ethics* (1996). *Toward Better Problems*, the book from which this excerpt is taken, was first introduced in Chapter 3 (p. 36) of this textbook. As we explained there, *Toward Better Problems* applies pragmatic philosophy to pressing ethical issues of our time: abortion, animal rights, the environment, and justice. However, Weston's aim in this book is not so much to solve these complex ethical problems as it is to transform these problematic situations into more manageable or "better" problems. "The Need for Environmental Ethics" is the opening section of the chapter on the environment. Other sections of this chapter include "Beyond Anthropocentrism," where Weston proposes that we move beyond our purely "human-centered" perspective to consider and respect nature "in its own right," and "Integrative Strategies in Environmental Politics," where Weston proposes seeking common ground in the fight for more enlightened environmental policies.

● **For Your Reading Log**

1. Choose a particular environmental issue, and write a short entry in your log about your knowledge and concerns about this issue. If you have little or no knowledge about environmental issues, write about why you think that is so.
2. As you read Weston's text, annotate passages with which you strongly agree or disagree.

──────────   ●   ──────────

We are beginning to struggle with the intimation that something is seriously 1
wrong with our relation to the natural world. It is a little like suspecting cancer but not wanting to know. But the danger signs are all around us. Garbage dumped a hundred miles off the Atlantic coast is now washing up annually on beaches. The federal government is continuing its increasingly desperate search for a way to dispose of the highly toxic radioactive wastes that American nuclear reactors have been generating since they began operating, so far without any permanent disposal plan at all. A state-sized chunk of South American rain forest is slashed, cut, or burned every year, in large part to clear land to graze beef cattle, though the resultant pasture is of marginal quality and will be reduced to desert within ten years. And our society, affluent beyond the wildest dreams of our ancestors and most of the rest of the human race, increasingly fortifies itself inside artificial environments—we see the countryside through the windshield or the airplane window, we "learn about nature" by watching TV specials about

endangered African predators—while outside of our little cocoons the winds laugh for no one and increasingly, under pressure of condominiums and shopping malls, the solace of open space is no more.

2   Short-term solutions of course suggest themselves. If the seas can no longer be treated as infinite garbage pits, we say, let us incinerate the garbage instead. Rain forest cutting could be curtailed by consumer action if North Americans paid a little more for home-grown meat. Sooner or later, we suppose, "science" will figure out something to do with nuclear wastes. And so on. This kind of thinking too is familiar. The problems may seem purely practical, and practical solutions may be in sight. Environmental ethics, however, begins with the suspicion that something far deeper is wrong, and that more fundamental change is called for.

Beyond Ecological Myopia

3 For one thing, these "solutions" are short term indeed, and ignore or obscure the structural crises that underlie the immediate problems. Incinerating trash just treats the air as a waste dump instead of the sea, with consequences that even proponents of incineration admit are unpredictable. The only workable short-term solution is recycling, and the only workable long-term solution is to stop producing so much garbage in the first place, especially materials that are not biodegradable. But this calls for an entirely different way of thinking: for greater respect for the earth, more awareness of the dynamics and the limits of the wider world, and more insistent reminders that our children's children will inherit the world we are "trashing." And these new ways of thinking in turn call for a different way of living. Sometimes the practical demands are not so very difficult—using paper cups instead of styrofoam is hardly a major lifestyle change—but even this calls for a kind of mindfulness that today we lack. In the background is the suggestion that we need to recognize systematic ecological constraints on economic activity, a kind of constraint that is still unfamiliar and controversial, at least in America.

4   Nuclear wastes are an even clearer case. Even proponents admit that long after the normal operation of nuclear power plants is past, we will be left with enormously toxic waste products from their operation, including the reactors themselves, which after their forty or so years generating electricity may take hundreds of thousands of years to drop back to safe levels of radioactivity. Operating wastes are presently stored at reactor sites and in temporary federal storage areas and tanks, most of them nearly full and some notoriously already leaking. It is not obvious that there is any adequate permanent disposal method. Burying the wastes, even in the most apparently stable site, puts all future life at the mercy of geological changes, which are virtually certain over hundreds of thousands of years. Meanwhile, no state or community will voluntarily accept the proposed storage facilities, let alone have the wastes shipped, as they must be, by truck or rail, across half the nation.

5   Public opposition to nuclear power focuses, for the most part, on the danger of accidents: on the dangers of injury to *us*. But the waste problem mortgages

the entire future of the earth. Any significant leakage would be devastating. Even very low-level leakage will cause genetic damage, not just to humans, but to all plants and animals, which over generations can have immense consequences. Again, then, our habitual short-term perspective comes into question; again an ecological point of view suggests radical change.

Finally, the devastation of the rain forests too is motivated almost exclusively 6 by short-term and commercial considerations. Since the land can be bought very cheaply (or can simply be expropriated), nothing stands in the way of the most shortsighted and complete exploitation. The soil, however, is very poor—rain forests are self-sustaining and self-nurturing systems, biotic efflorescences that virtually run of themselves—and so exploitation is complete indeed. In ten years the land will not even support cattle. Like the bare hills of the Mediterranean stripped of their forests by the ancients and since irreparably eroded, the land will become unable to support any life at all. And so for the sake of a few more years of slightly cheaper hamburgers we are turning the most exquisite jungle in the world into desert, and along with it threatening up to 60 percent of the world's plant and animal species, many of them unknown, with unknown medicinal and other benefits, not to mention the completely unpredictable climatic effects of turning enormous areas of the world's wettest ecosystems into the world's driest, the loss of atmospheric recharge, and so on.

Like our willingness to saddle our descendants with radioactive wastes into 7 the unimaginably distant future, our willingness to sacrifice the unknown potentials of rain forest ecosystems to the most trivial and short-term advantage shows an astonishing arrogance toward the human future. And to recognize this disproportion is already to take a major ethical step. Merely to take our own descendants seriously might well require a different way of life. That alone may be enough to require of us a far more respectful and conserving attitude toward the earth, and certainly requires us to avoid making massive, little-understood, and irreversible ecological changes, like destroying the rain forests or leaving genetically lethal wastes to the perpetual guardianship of our children's children's children. *Maybe* the most pressing and vital interests of the race could justify such a thing. Maybe we could justify turning some of the rain forests into deserts if in some unimaginable crisis only ravaging the rain forests could save life on earth. But ten years of slightly cheaper meat does not justify it. Maybe our children could understand reactor waste left littering the landscape of the future if the electricity it made possible saved civilization from some unheard-of threat, or accomplished some great task. But the "need" to run air conditioners is the saddest of excuses. Especially when the alternative is not even so serious as having to sweat in the summer, God forbid, but merely requires designing slightly more energy-efficient appliances and building houses that aren't heat sinks in the sun. Traditional cultures know how to build naturally cool houses. Only we seem to have lost the ability.

"Environmental ethics," then, urges upon us at minimum a much more mind- 8 ful and longer-term attention to the way we interact with and depend on nature. It urges attention to everything from the medicinal and nutritional uses of rain forest plants to the psychic need for open spaces and various kinds of ecological dependence of which we are not yet even aware. The implications are radical. We need to think of the earth itself in a different way: not as an infinite waste sink, and not as a collection of resources fortuitously provided for our use, but as a complex system with its own integrity and dynamics, far more intricate than we understand or perhaps *can* understand, but still the system within which we live and on which we necessarily and utterly depend. We must learn a new kind of respect.

● *Thinking Critically About "The Need for Environmental Ethics"*

RESPONDING AS A READER

1. In this excerpt, Weston takes on the challenge of trying to make the long-term threats to the environment vividly present for the reader. Which of these threats seems most urgent or compelling to you? Is it Weston's presentation or your prior knowledge that makes this issue "present" for you?
2. Why does he believe short-term practical solutions are inadequate? What reasons and evidence does he offer to support this claim? Are his reasoning and evidence persuasive to you as a reader?
3. Find examples of arguments from principle, consequence, and precedent/analogy. Which of these arguments does he rely on most heavily?

RESPONDING AS A WRITER

1. How feasible or likely are the "fundamental" changes Weston calls for in people's thinking and behavior? What are the barriers to these changes?
2. Weston's task in trying to get readers to share his concerns and outlook is challenging. In his opinion these problems are, in large part, a result of Americans' arrogance, short-sightedness, and greed. How can he challenge Americans to question their behavior and values without alienating them and turning them off? What strategies does he use to criticize without alienating? How does he try to win over readers, establish a bond with them, and appeal to their interests? How successful is he in managing this balance between critique and solidarity?
3. Perhaps one of the most subtle and powerful persuasive techniques that Weston uses is the appeal to readers' emotions. Find some examples and assess their effectiveness.

John Oates

Why a Prime Model for Saving Rain Forests Is a Failure

John Oates (b. 1944) is a professor of anthropology at Hunter College and the Graduate School of the City University of New York. His research focuses on primate social behavior, ecology, conservation, and zoo-geography. Currently he is studying the factors that influence the distribution and abundance of African rain-forest monkeys, which has led to an even deeper political commitment to conservation issues. His most recent book is *Myth and Reality in the Rain Forest: How Conservation Strategies Are Failing in West Africa* (1999). "Why a Prime Model for Saving Rain Forests Is a Failure" appeared on January 14, 2000, in the *Chronicle of Higher Education*, a periodical read mainly by university faculty and administrators.

● *For Your Reading Log*

1. When you hear the phrase "save the rain forests," what comes to mind? What political stance and people do you associate with this slogan? In terms of social/political issues about which you have concern, where might this issue rank? Near the top or bottom? Somewhere in the middle? Write a brief entry in your log about why this issue ranks where it does in your hierarchy of concerns.

2. Read the first three paragraphs of Oates's essay, and write out the definitions of the following terms based on what you can infer from their use in context: *sustainable development, economic development, renewable resources,* and *nonrenewable resources.* What expectations do these three paragraphs set up regarding Oates's proposal?

--- ● ---

In the last 20 years, the size of tropical rain forests—and the number of animals 1 in them—has declined drastically, although money for conserving those forests has become more plentiful. We have made protecting the forests an international priority, but we are not doing a good job of it.

The problem is that many conservationists have embraced the goal of sus- 2 tainable development, which is badly defined and may well be unworkable. Economic growth—a component of most definitions of development—usually requires the consumption of at least some nonrenewable resources; and even where stable systems of agriculture can be constructed around renewable resources, those systems inevitably displace natural ecosystems.

In any case, we cannot achieve both sustainable development and conserva- 3 tion's original goal of protecting largely unspoiled habitats. The pressures of human population growth and general economic development have led people to clear forests to make farms, plantations, roads, and towns. Nonetheless, conservationists continue to support development, out of financial and political expediency.

4   During the 1960s and early 1970s, two major international conservation groups—IUCN-The World Conservation Union and the World Wide Fund for Nature, known in the United States as the World Wildlife Fund—began or adopted many conservation projects in tropical regions, and the number of parks and other protected areas in rain forests began to increase markedly. As the quantity of projects grew, IUCN racked up a substantial budget deficit; it was bailed out in 1976 by the newly founded United Nations Environment Programme.

5   From that point on, ICUN, the W.W.F., and UNEP became regular collaborators. UNEP, founded to improve the condition of the human environment, supplied much of the financial support for a strategy of world conservation that was formulated by IUCN and published, in 1980, as a joint report by the three organizations. Rather than focusing on the creation of nature reserves around the world—the original goal of IUCN—the strategy stressed the concept of sustainable development.

6   Another new source of money for conservation in the 1970s was development organizations such as the U.S. Agency for International Development and the World Bank. Those organizations faced increasing criticism because so many of the projects they sponsored in the tropics—such as new dams and highways—were disrupting the environment. In response, they began to make money available for projects that linked development with conservation—in at least one case, in Nigeria, involving agricultural development inside a forest reserve.

7   Politicians in developing countries supported the new integration of conservation with development, because they had felt that international agencies were giving wildlife protection precedence over economic development for humans. Naturally, conservation groups, which had previously relied chiefly on donations from individuals, were happy to have the additional funds. Linking conservation and development seemed to be a solution that would benefit everyone involved, as well as protect natural ecosystems.

8 The marriage of conservation and development has been a disaster for much of tropical nature. Most of the integrated conservation-and-development projects that I know of have failed to protect the environment, and they have rarely achieved sustainable development either. Like the majority of pure development projects, they are designed to fit the short-term financial strategies of their sponsoring agencies. The projects typically have three-to-five-year budgets, even though conservation efforts should focus on the very long term. Large amounts of money are released over short periods of time, promoting lavish and unsustainable spending, and sometimes corruption. Most of the projects are managed by highly paid consultants, often resented by local professionals, whose salaries can be less then one-thousandth of that of a consultant.

9   The projects usually emphasize local economic and agricultural development. But if the work is at all successful, it both increases the impact on the ecosystem of the people already in the area and attracts migrants. As Andrew Noss, a scientist at the Wildlife Conservation Society, said in a review of one proj-

ect in the Central African Republic, many Africans will readily move, even to a remote area, to exploit new economic opportunities.

Because most international agencies' policies stress helping people, rather 10 than preserving the environment, few integrated conservation-and-development projects make the rigorous policing of protected areas a high priority. Those in charge of the projects typically believe that if people have viable economic alternatives, they will voluntarily refrain from exploiting forest resources. By contrast, land-management policies in developed countries do not rely on that comforting idea, based on the myth that humans will attempt to live in harmony with nature if given the chance. Instead, industrialized countries recognize the human tendency to exploit any available resource until it is exhausted; as a result, they have zoning regulations.

As John Terborgh, a tropical ecologist at Duke University, and others have 11 made clear, we are on the verge of a crisis: Many animal species in the tropics face extinction, as their ecosystems are reduced to smaller and smaller fragments, each of which is under increasing pressure from human-population growth and economic development. Strong action is necessary to prevent the crisis, and academics can play a role in the solution.

Scientists such as Terborgh and the primatologist Thomas Struhsaker, also at 12 Duke, have become convinced, as I have, that a much greater effort must be made to protect tropical parks and reserves from human interference—while some large, relatively untouched natural ecosystems remain. Without better protection, through policing of the sites and enforcement of laws against exploiting the resources, many of those ecosystems and the species they support will soon be gone forever. Many tropical countries have already set aside about 5 percent of their land area as reserves. Turning over that amount of land to development would have only a marginal economic effect for humans, yet it would have a devastating impact on millions of other species.

The money to create new parks, and to protect them and the existing ones, 13 would probably have to come, for the time being, from the citizens of rich countries, given that the economies of many developing countries—particularly in Africa—are not in good shape.

Through their governments' financial support of organizations such as the 14 World Bank, the citizens of developed countries are now subsidizing the conservation-and-development projects that are harming rain forests. If that money were allocated instead to independent trust funds, income from the funds could pay indefinitely for the basic protection of many tropical parks. Some organizations, such as Conservation International, have already helped establish trust funds for tropical conservation.

Such investments should be accompanied by increased efforts to instill a 15 greater appreciation for nature—beyond its material value—among people, especially children, in developing countries. That is not a hopeless cause. Children everywhere tend to be fascinated by animals and plants, and that interest can lead up to public support for protecting nature. India is an excellent example of a densely populated country whose citizens, though mostly very poor, show widespread respect for other living things and generally support government-run conservation areas.

16   Teaching science and natural history in primary schools can be an effective way to reach children. Natural-history books are now in short supply in many tropical countries, as are movies and videos about wildlife. Spending money on educational resources would be an excellent investment; so would improving the often awful zoos in cities of developing countries, and including exhibits on conservation.

17   Finally, biologists should be more vocal in their criticism of current conservation policies. Only a few, such as Terborgh and Struhsaker, have so far made public statements about the lack of logic, and the danger, in promoting sustainable development.

18   Over the years, many academics have refrained from directly criticizing international conservation organizations on the ground that those groups are only trying to do their best under difficult circumstances—if we undermine them, who will be left to fight for conservation? Many biologists working in the tropics have also depended for their research funds on conservation organizations, a practice that surely has inhibited criticism.

19   Before it is too late, more academics should apply the critical thinking in which they are specially trained to the problems of tropical conservation, and speak out about the logical flaws in current policies. Biologists in particular have an obligation to do what they can to preserve nature. They are the experts, the logical defenders of the natural world.

- ### *Thinking Critically About "Why a Prime Model for Saving Rain Forests Is a Failure"*

RESPONDING AS A READER

1. In the first section of the article, Oates explains why and how the current model (sustainable development) for saving the rain forest came about. Why do you think he spends so much time explaining the history of this model for readers?

2. What's wrong with this model according to Oates? List as many reasons as you can find. Does he provide convincing evidence for his claim that this model is a failure? What criteria does he use to determine that this model is a failure?

3. What seem to be Oates's goals in making the proposals he does to readers of the *Chronicle of Higher Education*? What changes in policy, perspective, and/or practical action does he propose to his intended audience?

RESPONDING AS A WRITER

1. There are three parts to Oates's article signaled by spacing. (Part I includes paragraphs 1–7; Part II, paragraphs 8–11; and Part III, paragraphs 12–19.) Write a descriptive outline as explained in Chapter 4 (p. 58) in

which you write a *does* and *says* statement for each section. What does your outline reveal about Oates's rhetorical strategies?

2. Throughout the article, Oates refers to various sets of competing values: for example, nonrenewable resources versus renewal resources, wildlife protection versus economic development for humans. List all of the competing values you can find in this article. For Oates, these competing values cannot be reconciled, and he makes clear which side of these values debates he is on. Do you agree that these competing values are irreconcilable? What arguments might a supporter of the current sustainable development model offer to rebut Oates's arguments?

3. What kind of justification—arguments on principle, consequence, or precedent/analogy—does Oates offer for the actions he proposes? Assume you are a member of Oates's intended audience. How persuasive do you find his justification for action, change in policy, or outlook?

Peter Singer

The Singer Solution to World Poverty

Australian philosopher Peter Singer (b. 1946) has been called the "world's most controversial ethicist." Known for his radical stands on such issues as animal rights and euthanasia, Singer now teaches at Princeton University, where his appointment in 1999 was met by vigorous protests from right-to-life groups. His best-known books include *Animal Liberation: A New Ethics for Our Treatment of Animals* (1975), *Practical Ethics* (1993), and *Rethinking Life and Death: The Collapse of Our Traditional Ethics* (1995). "The Singer Solution to World Poverty," published in the *New York Times Magazine* on September 5, 1999, deals with an issue that Singer takes very seriously. In an interview with the *New York Times*, Singer revealed that he gives one-fifth of his income to famine-relief agencies.

• *For Your Reading Log*

1. Where does world hunger rank in your list of social and moral concerns? How easy or difficult do you find it to identify with this problem on an international scale? How easy or difficult do you find it to identify with this problem on a local level?

2. What's your response to the title, "The Singer Solution to World Poverty"? What image does this conjure up of the author, who has named a solution to world poverty after himself?

————— • —————

1 In the Brazilian film "Central Station," Dora is a retired schoolteacher who makes ends meet by sitting at the station writing letters for illiterate people. Suddenly she has an opportunity to pocket $1,000. All she has to do is persuade a homeless 9-year-old boy to follow her to an address she has been given. (She is told he will be adopted by wealthy foreigners.) She delivers the boy, gets the money, spends some of it on a television set and settles down to enjoy her new acquisition. Her neighbor spoils the fun, however, by telling her that the boy was too old to be adopted—he will be killed and his organs sold for transplantation. Perhaps Dora knew this all along, but after her neighbor's plain speaking, she spends a troubled night. In the morning Dora resolves to take the boy back.

2   Suppose Dora had told her neighbor that it is a tough world, other people have nice TV's too, and if selling the kid is the only way she can get one, well, he was only a street kid. She would then have become, in the eyes of the audience, a monster. She redeems herself only by being prepared to bear considerable risks to save the boy.

3   At the end of the movie, in cinemas in the affluent nations of the world, people who would have been quick to condemn Dora if she had not rescued the boy

go home to places far more comfortable than her apartment. In fact, the average family in the United States spends almost one-third of its income on things that are no more necessary to them than Dora's new TV was to her. Going out to nice restaurants, buying new clothes because the old ones are no longer stylish, vacationing at beach resorts—so much of our income is spent on things not essential to the preservation of our lives and health. Donated to one of a number of charitable agencies, that money could mean the difference between life and death for children in need.

All of which raises a question: In the end, what is the ethical distinction be-   4 tween a Brazilian who sells a homeless child to organ peddlers and an American who already has a TV and upgrades to a better one—knowing that the money could be donated to an organization that would use it to save the lives of kids in need?

Of course, there are several differences between the two situations that   5 could support different moral judgments about them. For one thing, to be able to consign a child to death when he is standing right in front of you takes a chilling kind of heartlessness; it is much easier to ignore an appeal for money to help children you will never meet. Yet for a utilitarian philosopher like myself—that is, one who judges whether acts are right or wrong by their consequences—if the upshot of the American's failure to donate the money is that one more kid dies on the streets of a Brazilian city, then it is, in some sense, just as bad as selling the kid to the organ peddlers. But one doesn't need to embrace my utilitarian ethic to see that, at the very least, there is a troubling incongruity in being so quick to condemn Dora for taking the child to the organ peddlers while, at the same time, not regarding the American consumer's behavior as raising a serious moral issue.

In his 1996 book, "Living High and Letting Die," the New York University   6 philosopher Peter Unger presented an ingenious series of imaginary examples designed to probe our intuitions about whether it is wrong to live well without giving substantial amounts of money to help people who are hungry, malnourished or dying from easily treatable illnesses like diarrhea. Here's my paraphrase of one of these examples:

Bob is close to retirement. He has invested most of his savings in a very rare   7 and valuable old car, a Bugatti, which he has not been able to insure. The Bugatti is his pride and joy. In addition to the pleasure he gets from driving and caring for his car, Bob knows that its rising market value means that he will always be able to sell it and live comfortably after retirement. One day when Bob is out for a drive, he parks the Bugatti near the end of a railway siding and goes for a walk up the track. As he does so, he sees that a runaway train, with no one aboard, is running down the railway track. Looking farther down the track, he sees the small figure of a child very likely to be killed by the runaway train. He can't stop the train and the child is too far away to warn of the danger, but he can throw a switch that will divert the train down the siding where his Bugatti is parked. Then nobody will be killed—but the train will destroy his Bugatti. Thinking of his joy in owning the car and the financial security it represents, Bob decides not to throw the switch. The child is killed. For many years to come, Bob enjoys owning his Bugatti and the financial security it represents.

8   Bob's conduct, most of us will immediately respond, was gravely wrong. Unger agrees. But then he reminds us that we, too, have opportunities to save the lives of children. We can give to organizations like Unicef or Oxfam America. How much would we have to give to one of these organizations to have a high probability of saving the life of a child threatened by easily preventable diseases? (I do not believe that children are more worth saving than adults, but since no one can argue that children have brought their poverty on themselves, focusing on them simplifies the issues.) Unger called up some experts and used the information they provided to offer some plausible estimates that include the cost of raising money, administrative expenses and the cost of delivering aid where it is most needed. By his calculation, $200 in donations would help a sickly 2-year-old transform into a healthy 6-year-old—offering safe passage through childhood's most dangerous years. To show how practical philosophical argument can be, Unger even tells his readers that they can easily donate funds by using their credit card and calling one of these toll-free numbers: (800) 367-5437 for Unicef; (800) 693-2687 for Oxfam America.

9   Now you, too, have the information you need to save a child's life. How should you judge yourself if you don't do it? Think again about Bob and his Bugatti. Unlike Dora, Bob did not have to look into the eyes of the child he was sacrificing for his own material comfort. The child was a complete stranger to him and too far away to relate to in an intimate, personal way. Unlike Dora, too, he did not mislead the child or initiate the chain of events imperiling him. In all these respects, Bob's situation resembles that of people able but unwilling to donate to overseas aid and differs from Dora's situation.

10   If you still think that it was very wrong of Bob not to throw the switch that would have diverted the train and saved the child's life, then it is hard to see how you could deny that it is also very wrong not to send money to one of the organizations listed above. Unless, that is, there is some morally important difference between the two situations that I have overlooked.

11   Is it the practical uncertainties about whether aid will really reach the people who need it? Nobody who knows the world of overseas aid can doubt that such uncertainties exist. But Unger's figure of $200 to save a child's life was reached after he had made conservative assumptions about the proportion of the money donated that will actually reach its target.

12   One genuine difference between Bob and those who can afford to donate to overseas aid organizations but don't is that only Bob can save the child on the tracks, whereas there are hundreds of millions of people who can give $200 to overseas aid organizations. The problem is that most of them aren't doing it. Does this mean that it is all right for you not to do it?

13   Suppose that there were more owners of priceless vintage cars—Carol, Dave, Emma, Fred and so on, down to Ziggy—all in exactly the same situation as Bob, with their own siding and their own switch, all sacrificing the child in order to preserve their own cherished car. Would that make it all right for Bob to do the same? To answer this question affirmatively is to endorse follow-the-crowd ethics—the kind of ethics that led many Germans to look away when the Nazi atrocities were being committed. We do not excuse them because others were behaving no better.

We seem to lack a sound basis for drawing a clear moral line between Bob's 14 situation and that of any reader of this article with $200 to spare who does not donate it to an overseas aid agency. These readers seem to be acting at least as badly as Bob was acting when he chose to let the runaway train hurtle toward the unsuspecting child. In the light of this conclusion, I trust that many readers will reach for the phone and donate that $200. Perhaps you should do it before reading further.

Now that you have distinguished yourself morally from people who put 15 their vintage cars ahead of a child's life, how about treating yourself and your partner to dinner at your favorite restaurant? But wait. The money you will spend at the restaurant could also help save the lives of children overseas! True, you weren't planning to blow $200 tonight, but if you were to give up dining out just for one month, you would easily save that amount. And what is one month's dining out, compared to a child's life? There's the rub. Since there are a lot of desperately needy children in the world, there will always be another child whose life you could save for another $200. Are you therefore obliged to keep giving until you have nothing left? At what point can you stop?

Hypothetical examples can easily become farcical. Consider Bob. How far 16 past losing the Bugatti should he go? Imagine that Bob had got his foot stuck in the track of the siding, and if he diverted the train, then before it rammed the car it would also amputate his big toe. Should he still throw the switch? What if it would amputate his foot? His entire leg?

As absurd as the Bugatti scenario gets when pushed to extremes, the point it 17 raises is a serious one: only when the sacrifices become very significant indeed would most people be prepared to say that Bob does nothing wrong when he decides not to throw the switch. Of course, most people could be wrong; we can't decide moral issues by taking opinion polls. But consider for yourself the level of sacrifice that you would demand of Bob, and then think about how much money you would have to give away in order to make a sacrifice that is roughly equal to that. It's almost certainly much, much more than $200. For most middle-class Amerians, it could easily be more like $200,000.

Isn't it counterproductive to ask people to do so much? Don't we run the risk 18 that many will shrug their shoulders and say that morality, so conceived, is fine for saints but not for them? I accept that we are unlikely to see, in the near or even medium-term future, a world in which it is normal for wealthy Americans to give the bulk of their wealth to strangers. When it comes to praising or blaming people for what they do, we tend to use a standard that is relative to some conception of normal behavior. Comfortably off Americans who give, say, 10 percent of their income to overseas aid organizations are so far ahead of most of their equally comfortable fellow citizens that I wouldn't go out of my way to chastise them for not doing more. Nevertheless, they should be doing much more, and they are in no position to criticize Bob for failing to make the much greater sacrifice of his Bugatti.

At this point various objections may crop up. Someone may say: "If every cit- 19 izen living in the affluent nations contributed his or her share I wouldn't have to make such a drastic sacrifice, because long before such levels were reached, the resources would have been there to save lives of all those children dying from lack of food or medical care. So why should I give more than my fair share?" Another, related, objection is that the Government ought to increase its overseas aid allocations, since that would spread the burden more equitably across all taxpayers.

20   Yet the question of how much we ought to give is a matter to be decided in the real world—and that, sadly, is a world in which we know that most people do not, and in the immediate future will not, give substantial amounts to overseas aid agencies. We know, too, that at least in the next year, the United States Government is not going to meet even the very modest United Nations-recommended target of 0.7 percent of gross national product; at the moment it lags far below that, at 0.09 percent, not even half of Japan's 0.22 percent or a tenth of Denmark's 0.97 percent. Thus, we know that the money we can give beyond that theoretical "fair share" is still going to save lives that would otherwise be lost. While the idea that no one need do more than his or her fair share is a powerful one, should it prevail if we know that others are not doing their fair share and that children will die preventable deaths unless we do more than our fair share? That would be taking fairness too far.

21   Thus, this ground for limiting how much we ought to give also fails. In the world as it is now, I can see no escape from the conclusion that each one of us with wealth surplus to his or her essential needs should be given most of it to help people suffering from poverty so dire as to be life-threatening. That's right: I'm saying that you shouldn't buy that new car, take that cruise, redecorate the house or get that pricey new suit. After all, a $1,000 suit could save five children's lives.

22   So how does my philosophy break down in dollars and cents? An American household with an income of $50,000 spends around $30,000 annually on necessities, according to the Conference Board, a nonprofit economic research organization. Therefore, for a household bringing in $50,000 a year, donations to help the world's poor should be as close as possible to $20,000. The $30,000 required for necessities holds for higher incomes as well. So a household making $100,000 could cut a yearly check for $70,000. Again, the formula is simple: whatever money you're spending on luxuries, not necessities, should be given away.

23   Now, evolutionary psychologists tell us that human nature isn't sufficiently altruistic to make it plausible that many people will sacrifice so much for strangers. On the facts of human nature, they might be right, but they would be wrong to draw a moral conclusion from those facts. If it is the case that we ought to do things that, predictably, most of us won't do, then let's face that fact head-on. Then, if we value the life of a child more than going to fancy restaurants, the next time we dine out we will know that we could have done something better with our money. If that makes living a morally decent life extremely arduous, well, then that is the way things are. If we don't do it, then we should at least know that we are failing to live morally decent life—not because it is good to wallow in guilt but because knowing where we should be going is the first step toward heading in that direction.

24   When Bob first grasped the dilemma that faced him as he stood by that railway switch, he must have thought how extraordinarily unlucky he was to be placed in a situation in which he must choose between the life of an innocent child and the sacrifice of most of his savings. But he was not unlucky at all. We are all in that situation.

● *Thinking Critically About "The Singer Solution to World Poverty"*

RESPONDING AS A READER

1. As you read through this controversial proposal, mark the places in the text where you had the strongest reaction—either positive or negative. Compare the places you marked with those marked by your classmates. Did you have similar reactions? If not, what accounts for your differing reactions as readers?

2. What kind of a relationship does Singer try to establish with readers? At times, he speaks directly to the reader: for example, "Now you, too, have the information you need to save a child's life" (paragraph 9); "Perhaps you should do it [reach for the phone and donate $200] before reading further" (paragraph 14). Do you think he believes most readers will do what he asks? If not, why does he address the reader in this way?

3. Throughout the article, Singer tries to anticipate and address readers' objections to his proposal in paragraph 22. How successful do you think he is in doing this? Can you think of objections to his proposal that he doesn't address?

RESPONDING AS A WRITER

1. Play the believing and doubting game with Singer's proposal. That is, first write down all of the reasons that you believe Singer's proposal to be a solution to the problem of world poverty. Then write down all of the reasons that you doubt his proposal to be a solution to the problem of world poverty. (For further discussion of this activity, see p. 81 in Chapter 5.)

2. For the most part, Singer chooses to appeal to readers' reason and logic rather than to their emotions. Why do you think Singer chose this approach? Do you think this was a wise decision? What role does emotion play in the way Singer attempts to engage readers? How might he have appealed to readers' emotions differently, and to what effect?

3. Singer uses two analogies to justify his argument about our moral responsibility to donate a significant amount of our income to save the lives of starving children—Dora's moral dilemma in *Central Station* and Bob's moral dilemma in deciding whether or not to save his Bugatti or the child. In your own words, explain how he uses each analogy to justify his argument. Are you persuaded that these situations are analogous to our situation in choosing whether or not to give money to alleviate world poverty? Singer says, basically, that "any reader of this article with $200 to spare who does not donate it to an overseas aid agency" is behaving as Bob did in not throwing the switch to save the child. Do you agree? Why or why not?

Marcia Angell and Jerome Kassirer

Clinical Research—What Should the Public Believe?

Marcia Angell (b. 1939) is editor-in-chief of the prestigious *New England Journal of Medicine* (NEJM). A pathologist by training, Angell is the author of *Science on Trial: The Clash of Medical Evidence and the Law in the Breast Implant Case.* Angell is known for her commitment to patients' rights, ethical values in medicine, high standards for clinical research, and cautious dissemination of research results. Her coauthor, Jerome Kassirer (b. 1932), is the former editor-in-chief of NEJM and an internist by training. A medical educator as well as a former editor and practicing physician, Kassirer shares Angell's concern for high ethical standards and rigor in medical research.

   In 1994 "Clinical Research—What Should the Public Believe?" appeared in the editorial section of NEJM, a journal for health care professionals. Its articles on medical research are frequently the subject of news reports. Although the essay is an opinion piece, the authors use the same documentation conventions that they would if they were writing a scientific article. NEJM's citation system follows *Index Medicus,* which is similar to that used in many other scientific journals. This system numbers citations consecutively through the text and then lists them in a reference section according to the order they appeared in the text. If a work is cited again later in the text, its initial citation number is repeated. This scholarly care in an editorial suggests that opinions need to be backed up by evidence if they are to be credible to the scientific community.

● *For Your Reading Log*

   1. Are there particular health issues that you follow in news reports or magazines? Perhaps you perk up your ears when you hear a report about the latest weight-loss drugs or treatments for cancer or mental illness. Why does this particular health topic interest you? How much stock do you put in the reports you hear in the popular media? Write a journal entry in response to these questions.

   2. The authors claim that most Americans believe that good health is a matter of living right. Do you believe this to be true? If so, what lifestyle choices have you made to try to ensure good health—exercise, a healthy diet, abstinence from smoking or drinking? If you do not believe this to be true, why not? What is your attitude toward the American preoccupation with healthy living? Make a few notes in response to these questions.

——————— ● ———————

1 Americans have become increasingly avid for news of clinical research that they feel will improve their health or extend their lives. This is particularly true of research about diet or lifestyle. To many Americans, as Fitzgerald points out

elsewhere in this issue of the *Journal,* good health is largely a matter of living right.[1] They believe that they can ward off many if not most diseases and disability simply by knowing what foods to eat, what supplements to consume, and what leisure activities to pursue. This belief is fed by the new emphasis on preventive medicine as a solution to rising costs in health care. Thus, research on how diet and lifestyle affect health is of personal and intense interest to many Americans. Millions now eat low-fat, high-fiber diets, take antioxidant supplements, drink alcohol only in moderation, stay slim, and exercise regularly.

But there are problems. Health-conscious Americans increasingly find themselves beset by contradictory advice. No sooner do they learn the results of one research study than they hear of one with the opposite message. They substitute margarine for butter, only to learn that margarine may be worse for their arteries.[2] They are told to eat oat bran to lower their cholesterol[3, 4] but later learn that the bran they dutifully ate may be useless.[5] They substitute low-calorie saccharin for high-calorie sugar, only to hear that some researchers find an association between saccharin and bladder cancer,[6] while other researchers do not.[7] They exercise because they are told that it is good for their hearts, only to learn that exercise may increase the immediate risk of sudden death.[8–10] Most recently, vitamin E and beta carotene, long touted for their ostensible role in preventing cancer, were found in a large study to be no better and possibly worse than placebo.[11] And now, a study reported elsewhere in this issue of the *Journal* concludes that antioxidants are probably not helpful in preventing cancer of the colon,[12] although earlier studies found that they are.[13, 14]

Not surprisingly, the existence of all these contradictory reports has not escaped the attention of the media. When the recent study of the effects of vitamin E and beta carotene was published, many of the major newspapers and newsmagazines carried stories complaining about the problem. Ellen Goodman, a popular syndicated columnist, seemed to feel betrayed. She spoke of "planned obsolescence" in research, as though the problem were a conspiracy by scientists to confuse the public.[15] The recent analysis of the risks of margarine[2] prompted the *New York Times* to editorialize, under the title "Diet Roulette," "No wonder health-conscious Americans often feel they just can't win."[16] Why can't researchers get it straight the first time?

In our view the problem is not in the research but in the way it is interpreted for the public. In addition, the public itself must bear some responsibility for its unrealistic expectations. (Why should every scientific study reported in the media be a "win" for them?) We here review some of the features of clinical research that are often misunderstood by both the media and the public.

What medical journals publish is not received wisdom but rather working papers. Each of these is meant to communicate to other researchers and to doctors the results of one study. Each study becomes a piece of a puzzle that, when assembled, will help either to confirm or to refute a hypothesis. Although a study may add to the evidence about a connection between diet or exercise and health, rarely can a single study stand alone as definitive proof. In part, this is because there may be unappreciated biases in the works. For example, those who consume high-fiber diets or take antioxidant supplements may be healthier than those who do not, for reasons that have nothing to do with the diet or the supplements. As was discussed in an earlier editorial, we may not always control adequately for these confounding factors.[17] In fact, we may not even know about them. Even when there are no such problems, the results of a study can still be due to chance. Nearly all studies of connections between lifestyle and health deal with probabilities. Chance cannot be ruled out even when it is highly unlikely. Finally, results that are valid in one population may not be in another. The vitamin-E-and-beta-carotene study was performed in male Finnish smokers. There is no reason to believe that their response to antioxidants would be different from the response of women, nonsmokers, or people in different age groups, but it might be. Thus, nearly every clinical research study should be seen as preliminary. No matter how important the conclusions, they should usually be considered tentative until a body of evidence accumulates pointing in the same direction. For example, the now overwhelming evidence that cigarette smoking is extremely dangerous was accumulated bit by bit over many years.

6   Doctors know that clinical research rarely advances in one giant leap; instead, it progresses incrementally. For this reason, the practice of medicine, as well as clinical research, is inherently conservative. Doctors are reluctant to change their practices overnight, for good reason. (Unfortunately, they do not always communicate this reason adequately to their patients.) And researchers often end their reports with the phrase, "More work is required," which is more than a bromide. But because of the public's keen interest in new medical findings, the media may be less conservative. They are serving a public that believes passionately that the more we can learn about what to eat or how to live, the longer we will live. And neither the public nor the media are inclined to wait for confirmatory studies. Often, the media reports are exaggerated or oversimplified. Even when a report itself is circumspect, headline writers may sensationalize the story. For example, the headline over a story reporting that the GUSTO trial[18] found tissue plasminogen activator (t-PA) given after an acute myocardial infarction to be only slightly better than streptokinase (mortality, 6.3 percent vs. 7.3 percent) read, "Anti-Clotting Therapy Found to Spare Lives."[19] While technically true, this is nevertheless misleading.

7   There are many ways the media could improve the way they interpret science to the public. In our view the most important would be to pay closer attention to the following caveats. First, an association between two events is not the same as a cause and effect. For example, prenatal care is associated with better perinatal outcomes, but we do not yet know that it is the reason for the better outcomes. Second, demonstrating one link in a postulated chain of events does not mean that the whole chain is proved. For example, if a screening test for prostate cancer is effective, that does not mean it will save lives.[20] Third, probabilities are not the same as certainties. For example, a study showing that alcohol causes a 30 percent increase in the risk of breast cancer does not mean that a woman who drinks no alcohol will not get breast cancer (nor that she will inevitably get breast cancer if she does drink).[21] And fourth, the way a scientific result is framed can greatly affect its impact. For example, the results of the GUSTO trial could be framed in three ways: t-PA was 14 percent more effective than streptokinase; t-PA lowered the mortality from 7.3 percent to 6.3 percent; or t-PA increased the survival rate from 92.7 percent to 93.7 percent. All three ways are accurate, but they produce

very different impressions on readers. The media would do a much better job of reporting medical research if they considered these four caveats explicitly.

Finally, the public at large needs to become much more sophisticated about [8] clinical research, particularly epidemiology. Unfortunately, that is unlikely to happen as long as science education in the United States is so poor. Even with improvements in science education, however, no one could expect people to go to medical journals and evaluate the evidence themselves. But it would be possible for people to learn enough about the scientific method to know that there are very few breakthroughs in clinical research and that claims of a breakthrough should be regarded warily. In particular, they should not rush to change their diets or habits on the basis of reports of one study. Any one study should be regarded as tentative, the more so if the results are spectacular or at odds with the evidence accumulated so far. And the public should remember that the media may sometimes make more of a study than the results warrant.

Although we would all like to believe that changes in diet or lifestyle can [9] greatly improve our health, the likelihood is that, with a few exceptions such as smoking cessation, many if not most such changes will produce only small effects. And the effects may not be consistent. A diet that is harmful to one person may be consumed with impunity by another. Furthermore, any change in diet or lifestyle will almost inevitably involve some sort of trade-off—for example, risking sports injuries in order to enjoy that physiologic advantages of exercise. The subject of trade-offs is considered in more detail by Keeney elsewhere in this issue.[22]

What is called for is more moderation in our response to news of clinical research. Every study reported in the media does not require an all-or-nothing response in our diet or lifestyle. In general, we should not embrace the conclusions of a study until other studies support them. Reserving judgment in this way, without succumbing to antiscientific nihilism, is the best protection against being whipsawed by media reports of clinical research. People who felt betrayed when they learned of a new study showing that vitamin E and carotene do not protect against cancer should ask themselves why they so readily believed that antioxidants had this effect in the first place and why they now believe that there is no such effect.

References

1. Fitzgerald FT. The tyranny of health. *N Engl J Med* 1994;331:196-8.

2. Willett WC, Ascherio A. Trans fatty acids: are the effects only marginal? *Am J Public Health* 1994; 84:722-4.

3. Kirby RW, Anderson JW, Sieling B, et al. Oat-bran intake selectively lowers serum low-density lipoprotein cholesterol concentrations of hypercholesterolemic men. *Am J Clin Nutr* 1981;34:824-9.

4. Anderson JW, Story L, Sieling B, Chen W-JL, Petro MS, Story J. Hypocholesterolemic effects of oat-bran or bean intake for hypercholesterolemic men. *Am J Clin Nutr* 1984;40:1146-55.

5. Swain JF, Rouse IL, Curley CB, Sacks FM. Comparison of the effects of oat bran and low-fiber wheat on serum lipoprotein levels and blood pressure. *N Engl J Med* 1990;322:147-52.

6. Howe GR, Burch JD, Miller AB, et al. Artificial sweeteners and human bladder cancer. *Lancet* 1977;2:578-81.

7. Hoover RN, Strasser PH. Artifical sweeteners and human bladder cancer: preliminary results. *Lancet* 1980;1:837-40.

8. Mittleman MA, Maclure M, Tofler GH, Sherwood JB, Goldberg RJ, Muller JE. Triggering of acute myocardial infarction by heavy physical exertion—protection against triggering by regular exertion. *N Engl J Med* 1993;329:1677–83.

9. Willich SN, Lews M, Lowel H, Arntz H-R, Schubert F, Schroder R. Physical exertion as a trigger of acute myocardial infarction. *N Engl J Med* 1993;329:1684-90.

10. Curfman GD. Is exercise beneficial or hazardous to your heart? *N Engl J Med* 1993;329:1730-1.

11. The Alpha-Tocopherol, Beta Carotene Cancer Prevention Study Group. The effect of vitamin E and beta carotene on the incidence of lung cancer and other cancers in male smokers. *N Engl J Med* 1994;330:1029-35.

12. Greenberg ER, Baron JA, Tosteson TD, et al. A clinical trial of antioxidant vitamins to prevent colorectal adenoma. *N Engl J Med* 1994;331:141-7.

13. Bostick RM, Potter JD, McKenzie DR, et al. Reduced risk of colon cancer with high intake of vitamin E: the Iowa Women's Health Study. *Cancer Res* 1993;53:4230-7

14. Roncucci L, Di Donato P, Carati L, et al. Antioxidant vitamins or lactulose for the prevention of the recurrence of colorectal adenomas. *Dis Colon Rectum* 1993;36:227-34.

15. Goodman E. To swallow or not to swallow: that is the new vitamin question. *Boston Globe*. April 17, 1994:A27.

16. Diet roulette. *New York Times*. May 20, 1994:A26.

17. Angell M. The interpretation of epidemiologic studies. *N Engl J Med* 1990;323:823-5.

18. The GUSTO Investigators. An international randomized trial comparing four thrombolytic strategies for acute myocardial infarction. *N Engl J Med* 1993;329:673-82.

19. Lehman BA. Cancer drug is found to have heart benefit. *Boston Globe*. September 2 1993:3.

20. Blood test's value in early prostate cases. *New York Times*. August 25, 1993:C10

21. Willett WC, Stampfer MJ, Colditz GA, Rosner BA, Hennekens CH, Speizer FE. Moderate alcohol consumption and the risk of breast cancer. *N Engl J Med* 1987;316:1174-80.

22. Keeney RL. Decisions about life-threatening risks. *N Engl J Med* 1994;331:193-6.

● *Thinking Critically About "Clinical Research—What Should the Public Believe?"*

RESPONDING AS A READER

1. What problem does this editorial address? How do Angell and Kassirer go about giving the problem "presence" for readers? Are they successful in making you feel that this is an important problem with serious negative consequences?

2. To accomplish their persuasive aim, Angell and Kassirer must explain the ways in which the public misunderstands the nature of clinical research. How informative was this article to you as a reader? What, if any, of this information was new to you? Do they provide adequate explanation and examples to correct the misunderstandings they name?

3. Angell and Kassirer propose practical actions on the part of both the media and the public (paragraphs 7–10). How likely do you think either group is to take the practical actions recommended? Why or why not?

RESPONDING AS A WRITER

1. In paragraph 7, Angell and Kassirer suggest three ways of reporting the results of a study comparing two different treatments (t-PA and streptokinase) for heart attack patients. They claim that while all three ways of stating the results are accurate, each produces "very different impressions on readers." Take each statement, and explain your interpretation of its meaning, paying close attention to the word choice in each statement. What are the differences in the meanings suggested by these three statements?

2. In paragraph 9, Angell and Kassirer say that "many if not most such changes [in diet or lifestyle] will produce only small effects . . . [and] any change in diet or lifestyle will almost inevitably involve some sort of trade-off." What's the function of this paragraph in the context of their overall argument? Imagine that you're talking about the importance of healthy lifestyle choices with a friend who eats a lot of junk food and never exercises. Your friend cites the ideas of these two medical experts to support his claim that changes in diet and lifestyle are pointless. How could you counter your friend's argument? What logical flaws or errors in reasoning do you find either in their original claims or in your friend's use of them?

3. Find a recent newspaper or magazine article reporting the results of clinical research, and analyze it in light of Angell and Kassirer's article. Does the headline sensationalize the findings? Does the article explain the circumstances and limitations of the study itself or offer qualifications about its results? Are there any particular claims that you suspect are exaggerated, misleading, or oversimplified? Write a paragraph in which you report these clinical findings in terms that Angell and Kassirer would find acceptable.

Janet Radcliffe-Richards et al.

The Case for Allowing Kidney Sales

British philosopher Janet Radcliffe-Richards, a faculty member at the Milton Keynes Open University in the United Kingdom, is lead author of a team of eight—which includes lawyers, doctors, medical sociologists, and philosophers—who wrote "The Case for Allowing Kidney Sales." The article was originally presented at the International Forum for Transplant Ethics and later published on June 27, 1998, in the Department of Ethics section of *The Lancet*, a weekly British medical journal that publishes a wide range of medical articles. For example, the issue in which this article appeared included a story on "UK 'Bristol Case' Doctors Found Guilty of Shaken-Baby Syndrome" in the News section, a scientific report on "Death from Heroin Overdose: Findings from Hair Analysis" in the Early Reports section, and an article entitled "If Children's Lives Are Precious, Which Children?" in the Health and Human Rights section.

   The Lancet uses a citation system similar to that used by the *New England Journal of Medicine* and other scientific journals in which citations are numbered consecutively through the text except for repeated citations. In the reference list, the numbered citations appear in the order in which they were first cited in the text.

●   *For Your Reading Log*

   1. What effect does this team of authors' diverse professional credentials have on your expectations about the authoritativeness of this article? Read the first paragraph of the article. What relationships do you see between the rhetorical situation they outline in this opening paragraph and their diverse professional backgrounds?
   2. Are you familiar with the ethical debates surrounding organ transplants? Make a few notes about your background knowledge, opinions, and questions about this issue.

———————   ●   ———————

1   When the practice of buying kidneys from live vendors first came to light some years ago, it aroused such horror that all professional associations denounced it[1,2] and nearly all countries have now made it illegal.[3] Such political and professional unanimity may seem to leave no room for further debate, but we nevertheless think it important to reopen the discussion.

2   The well-known shortage of kidneys for transplantation causes much suffering and death.[4] Dialysis is a wretched experience for most patients, and is anyway rationed in most places and simply unavailable to the majority of patients

in most developing countries.[5] Since most potential kidney vendors will never become unpaid donors, either during life or posthumously, the prohibition of sales must be presumed to exclude kidneys that would otherwise be available. It is therefore essential to make sure that there is adequate justification for the resulting harm.

Most people will recognise in themselves the feelings of outrage and disgust   3 that led to an outright ban on kidney sales, and such feelings typically have a force that seems to their possessors to need no further justification. Nevertheless, if we are to deny treatment to the suffering and dying we need better reasons than our own feelings of disgust.

In this paper we outline our reasons for thinking that the arguments com-   4 monly offered for prohibiting organ sales do not work, and therefore that the debate should be reopened.[6,7] Here we consider only the selling of kidneys by living vendors, but our arguments have wider implications.

The commonest objection to kidney selling is expressed on behalf of the ven-   5 dors: the exploited poor, who need to be protected against the greedy rich. However, the vendors are themselves anxious to sell,[8] and see this practice as the best option open to them. The worse we think the selling of a kidney, therefore, the worse should seem the position of the vendors when that option is removed. Unless this appearance is illusory, the prohibition of sales does even more harm than first seemed, in harming vendors as well as recipients. To this argument it is replied that the vendors' apparent choice is not genuine. It is said that they are likely to be too uneducated to understand the risks, and that this precludes informed consent. It is also claimed that, since they are coerced by their economic circumstances, their consent cannot count as genuine.[9]

Although both these arguments appeal to the importance of autonomous   6 choice, they are quite different. The first claim is that the vendors are not competent to make a genuine choice within a given range of options. The second, by contrast, is that poverty has so restricted the range of options that organ selling has become the best, and therefore, in effect, that the range is too small. Once this distinction is drawn, it can be seen that neither argument works as a justification of prohibition.[7]

If our ground for concern is that the range of choices is too small, we cannot   7 improve matters by removing the best option that poverty has left, and making the range smaller still. To do so is to make subsequent choices, by this criterion, even less autonomous. The only way to improve matters is to lessen the poverty until organ selling no longer seems the best option; and if that could be achieved, prohibition would be irrelevant because nobody would want to sell.

The other line of argument may seem more promising, since ignorance does   8 preclude informed consent. However, the likely ignorance of the subjects is not a reason for banning altogether a procedure for which consent is required. In other contexts, the value we place on autonomy leads us to insist on information and counselling, and that is what it should suggest in the case of organ selling as well. It may be said that this approach is impracticable, because the educational level of potential vendors is too limited to make explanation feasible, or because no system could reliably counteract the misinformation of nefarious middlemen and profiteering clinics. But even if we accepted that no possible vendor could be competent to consent, that would justify only putting the decision in the hands of competent guardians. To justify total prohibition it would also be necessary to show that organ selling must always be against the interests of potential vendors, and it is most unlikely that this would be done.

9   The risk involved in nephrectomy is not in itself high, and most people regard it as acceptable for living related donors.[10] Since the procedure is, in principle, the same for vendors as for unpaid donors, any systematic difference between the worthwhileness of the risk for vendors and donors presumably lies on the other side of the calculation, in the expected benefit. Nevertheless the exchange of money cannot in itself turn an acceptable risk into an unacceptable one from the vendor's point of view. It depends entirely on what the money is wanted for.

10   In general, furthermore, the poorer a potential vendor, the more likely it is that the sale of a kidney will be worth whatever risk there is. If the rich are free to engage in dangerous sports for pleasure, or dangerous jobs for high pay, it is difficult to see why the poor who take the lesser risk of kidney selling for greater rewards—perhaps saving relatives' lives,[11] or extricating themselves from poverty and debt—should be thought so misguided as to need saving from themselves.

11   It will be said that this does not take account of the reality of the vendors' circumstances: that risks are likely to be greater than for unpaid donors because poverty is detrimental to health, and vendors are often not given proper care. They may also be underpaid or cheated, or may waste their money through inexperience. However, once again, these arguments apply far more strongly to many other activities by which the poor try to earn money, and which we do not forbid. The best way to address such problems would be by regulation and perhaps a central purchasing system, to provide screening, counselling, reliable payment, insurance, and financial advice.[12]

12   To this it will be replied that no system of screening and control could be complete, and that both vendors and recipients would always be at risk of exploitation and poor treatment. But all the evidence we have shows that there is much more scope for exploitation and abuse when a supply of desperately wanted goods is made illegal. It is, furthermore, not clear why it should be thought harder to police a legal trade than the present complete ban.

13   Furthermore, even if vendors and recipients would always be at risk of exploitation, that does not alter the fact that if they choose this option, all alternatives must seem worse to them. Trying to end exploitation by prohibition is rather like ending slum dwelling by bulldozing slums: it ends the evil in that form, but only by making things worse for the victims. If we want to protect the exploited, we can do it only by removing the poverty that makes them vulnerable, or, failing that, by controlling the trade.

14   Another familiar objection is that it is unfair for the rich to have privileges not available to the poor. This argument, however, is irrelevant to the issue of organ selling as such. If organ selling is wrong for this reason, so are all benefits available to the rich, including all private medicine, and, for that matter, all pub-

lic provision of medicine in rich countries (including transplantation of donated organs) that is unavailable in poor ones. Furthermore, all purchasing could be done by a central organisation responsible for fair distribution.[12]

It is frequently asserted that organ donation must be altruistic to be accept- 15 able,[13] and that this rules out payment. However, there are two problems with this claim. First, altruism does not distinguish donors from vendors. If a father who saves his daughter's life by giving her a kidney is altruistic, it is difficult to see why his selling a kidney to pay for some other operation to save her life should be thought less so. Second, nobody believes in general that unless some useful action is altruistic it is better to forbid it altogether.

It is said that the practice would undermine confidence in the medical pro- 16 fession, because of the association of doctors with money-making practices. That, however, would be a reason for objecting to all private practice; and in this case the objection could easily be met by the separation of purchasing and treatment. There could, for instance, be independent trusts[12] to fix charges and handle accounts, as well as to ensure fair play and high standards. It is alleged that allowing the trade would lessen the supply of donated cadaveric kidneys.[14] But although some possible donors might decide to sell instead, their organs would be available, so there would be no loss in the total. And in the meantime, many people will agree to sell who would not otherwise donate.

It is said that in parts of the world where women and children are essentially 17 chattels there would be a danger of their being coerced into becoming vendors. This argument, however, would work as strongly against unpaid living kidney donation, and even more strongly against many far more harmful practices which do not attract calls for their prohibition. Again, regulation would provide the most reliable means of protection.

It is said that selling kidneys would set us on a slippery slope to selling vi- 18 tal organs such as hearts. But that argument would apply equally to the case of the unpaid kidney donation, and nobody is afraid that will result in the donation of hearts. It is entirely feasible to have laws and professional practices that allow the giving or selling only of non-vital organs. Another objection is that allowing organ sales is impossible because it would outrage public opinion. But this claim is about western public opinion: in many potential vendor communities, organ selling is more acceptable than cadaveric donation, and this argument amounts to a claim that other people should follow western cultural preferences rather than their own. There is, anyway, evidence that the western public is far less opposed to the idea, than are medical and political professionals.[15]

It must be stressed that we are not arguing for the positive conclusion that 19 organ sales must always be acceptable, let alone that there should be an unfettered market. Our claim is only that none of the familiar arguments against organ selling works, and this allows for the possibility that better arguments may yet be found.

Nevertheless, we claim that the burden of proof remains against the de- 20 fenders of prohibition, and that until good arguments appear, the presumption must be that the trade should be regulated rather than banned altogether. Furthermore, even when there are good objections at particular times or in particular places, that should be regarded as a reason for trying to remove the objections, rather than as an excuse for permanent prohibition.

21   The weakness of the familiar arguments suggests that they are attempts to justify the deep feelings of repugnance which are the real driving force of prohibition, and feelings of repugnance among the rich and healthy, no matter how strongly felt, cannot justify removing the only hope of the destitute and dying. This is why we conclude that the issue should be considered again, and with scrupulous impartiality.

References

1   British Transplantation Society Working Party. Guidelines on living organ donation. *BMJ* 1986; 293: 257-58.

2   The Council of the Transplantation Society. Organ sales. *Lancet* 1985; 2: 715-16.

3   World Health Organization. A report on developments under the auspices of WHO (1987-1991). WHO 1992 Geneva. 12-28.

4   Hauptman PJ, O'Connor KJ. Procurement and allocation of solid organs for transplantation. *N Engl J Med* 1997; 336: 422-31.

5   Barsoum RS. Ethical problems in dialysis and transplantation: Africa. In: Kjellstrand CM, Dossetor JB, eds. Ethical problems in dialysis and transplantation. Kluwer Academic Publishers, Netherlands. 1992: 169-82.

6   Radcliffe-Richards J. Nephrarious goings on: kidney sales and moral arguments. *J Med Philosph.* Netherlands: Kluwer Academic Publishers, 1996; 21: 375-416.

7   Radcliffe-Richards J. From him that hath not. In: Kjellstrand CM, Dossetor JB, eds. Ethical problems in dialysis and transplantation. Netherlands: Kluwer Academic Publishers, 1992: 53-60.

8   Mani MK. The argument against the unrelated live donor, ibid. 164.

9   Sells RA. The case against buying organs and a futures market in transplants. *Trans Proc* 1992; 24: 2198-202.

10 Daar AD, Land W, Yahya TM, Schneewind K, Gutmann T, Jakobsen A. Living-donor renal transplantation: evidence-based justification for an ethical option. *Trans Reviews* (in press) 1997.

11 Dossetor JB, Manickavel V. Commercialisation: the buying and selling of kidneys. In: Kjellstrand CM, Dossetor JB, eds. Ethical problems in dialysis and transplantation. Netherlands: Kluwer Academic Publishers, 1992: 61-71.

12 Sells RA. Some ethical issues in organ retrieval 1982-1992. *Trans Proc* 1992; 24: 2401-03.

13 Sheil R. Policy statement from the ethics committee of the Transplantation Society. *Trans Soc Bull* 1995; 3: 3.

14 Altshuler JS, Evanisko MJ. *JAMA* 1992; 267: 2037.

15 Guttmann RD, Guttmann A. Organ transplantation: duty reconsidered. *Trans Proc* 1992; 24: 2179-80.

• *Thinking Critically About "The Case for Allowing Kidney Sales"*

RESPONDING AS A READER

1. What is the current policy in regard to allowing the sale of kidneys by live donors? What circumstances led to the current policy? Do the authors present the rationale for the current policy fairly?

2. Why do you think the authors appeal mostly to readers' reason rather than to their emotions? Find examples of their rational treatment of potentially emotional issues (for instance, their use of the term "live vendors" to refer to those who sell their kidneys). What effect did this treatment have on your response?

3. What is their primary purpose in writing this article? Are they proposing a change in policy, a practical action, or a change of perspective on an issue? What is the effect of their decision to wait until the concluding paragraphs to spell out their counterproposal?

RESPONDING AS A WRITER

1. Since the authors are dealing with a controversial subject, they devote most of the article to addressing the objections readers may have to their proposal to reopen and reconsider the sale of kidneys. Indeed, they set up a point-counterpoint structure in this article, responding to opponents' positions point by point. Choose one point that they address (for example, most vendors are the "exploited poor," vendors don't have a free choice, or vendors are too uneducated to make an informed choice), and analyze the reasoning the authors use to counter this objection. What reasons do they offer for reaching a different conclusion? How satisfactorily do they address the concerns of their opponents? After you have analyzed their reasoning on this point, write a brief response in which you either agree or disagree with their position on this point.

2. The authors use argument from analogy at several points in the article—for example, "if the rich are free to engage in dangerous sports for pleasure . . . it is difficult to see why the poor . . . should be thought so misguided as to need saving from themselves" (paragraph 10) ; there are "many other activities by which the poor try to earn money, and which we do not forbid" (paragraph 11). How persuasive are these arguments by analogy? Briefly explain your answer.

3. Imagine that you are taking a course in medical ethics and have been required to write a rhetorical précis of this article. Use the instructions for writing a rhetorical précis, found in Chapter 4 (p. 62).

Kenneth Bruffee

Binge Drinking as a Substitute for a "Community of Learning"

Kenneth Bruffee (b. 1934) is a professor of English and the director of the Scholars Program and the Honors Academy at Brooklyn College, City University of New York. A nationally known leader in the collaborative learning movement, Bruffee is the author of *Collaborative Learning: Higher Education, Interdependence and the Authority of Knowledge* (1990) and other books and articles on the subject. Advocates of collaborative learning believe that students learn more effectively when they work together to solve problems and understand complex information. In writing classrooms, collaborative learning often takes the form of peer response groups where student writers give and receive feedback on their writing. Collaborative learning theorists believe that students' learning is enhanced when they are actively engaged and when they feel a sense of community within the classroom. This essay was published in 1999 in the *Chronicle of Higher Education,* a journal whose readers include faculty, administrators, and other higher education professionals.

• *For Your Reading Log*

1. Is excessive drinking a problem on your campus? If so, how much of a problem is it? What efforts have campus officials made to curb it? How successful have they been?
2. In this article, Kenneth Bruffee claims that "most college students make few friends through their classes until late in their college careers, if at all." Does your experience confirm or disconfirm this claim? Write a short entry in your reading log about this experience.

———————— • ————————

1 The Harvard School of Public Health found in 1993 that binge drinking is widespread on American college campuses, particularly among members of fraternities and sororities. The school's most recent report documents the disturbing fact that binge drinking has not declined in the five years since that first study. Even though the proportion of students who declare themselves teetotalers is slightly larger, the effects of binge drinking continue to be widespread and severe. They range from poor grades to destruction of property, assault, drunk driving, and death.

2   To stem the tide of binge drinking, colleges have tried closing fraternities and sororities, punishing heavy drinkers, enlisting the help of liquor-store owners, and banning alcohol on their campuses. So far, those efforts have largely failed. One reason may be that missing from most of them, and from most research on the subject, is an understanding of why first-year students join fraternities and sororities in the first place.

I know why I joined one, many more years ago than I care to mention. I ar- 3
rived on that gracious, learned, sophisticated campus to find myself among people—professors, administrators, upperclassmen (yes, all were men in those
days)—who were committed (it seemed to me) to making me feel just how green,
scared, lonely, and small-town I was. They all seemed vexed that I wasn't already
what they hoped I would become. Administrators told me how much I had to learn
and how hard I had to work to learn it. Professors told me how little they valued
what I already knew, and how trivial and misleading would be anything that I
learned from anyone but themselves. I was an intrusive rube. I didn't belong.

Most of my fellow freshmen seemed committed to making me feel like a 4
rube, too. Today I think I know why, though I certainly did not know it then.
They were trying as hard as I was to conceal from everyone, including themselves, that they, too, were green, scared, lonely, and small-town.

I joined a fraternity because I wanted, desperately, to belong. 5

Fraternity members were the only people on the campus who seemed to know 6
what it meant to feel like a rube, who knew the depth and overwhelming intensity
of an 18-year-old's need to belong. They knew how to marshal and exploit that
need, because they'd been there themselves not long before. Fraternities seemed
to be the only place on the campus with a ready supply of friends for freshmen.

There were certainly no friends to be had where I thought I would achieve 7
my most consequential goals as a college student—in my classes. I made no
friends there until my last year in college, and then only by chance. Even today,
most college students make few friends through their classes until late in their
college careers, if at all.

That's one reason college students become binge drinkers. 8

Such a claim may sound like some kind of bad joke, so I hasten to explain. 9

Most of the talk about binge drinking, the research into it, and the adminis- 10
trative attempts to curb it assume a sharp distinction between the "academic" and
the "social" connections of college students with their peers. Students also make
that distinction. If you ask a cross section of college students about their friends,
some may say they occasionally talk with a few of them about their course work
and (if they admit at all to such eccentricities) their intellectual and aesthetic interests. With the rest of their friends, they'll say, such topics seldom come up.

It's peculiar, when you think about it, that most American colleges do not help 11
entering students make friends through their course work. Presumably, one goal
of liberal education is to enrich life with the kind of conversation that comes with
substantive friendship. And when colleges actively provide students with the opportunity to make friends through their classes, they eagerly grasp the chance.

A study of 183 students who entered Brooklyn College in the fall of 1987 and 12
took courses that were organized into "learning communities"—in which the
same group of students was registered for three courses together—showed that
73 per cent agreed with the statement that the experience "helps students make
new friends more easily." The retention rate of the students studied was 73 per
cent, compared with the college's normal average of 59 per cent.

Many students who do make it to their junior or senior years are likely to con- 13
cede (if only in private) that most of their friendships then tend to merge social
interests with academic and aesthetic interests—from pursuing genetic research

to listening to Mozart concertos. By then, their sense of belonging is rooted in the academic major they have chosen and in the new interests they have developed in elective courses.

14   Of course, some freshmen arrive on the campus in the company of old high-school friends. But those students, too—most of them similarly green, scared, lonely 18-year-olds—feel the pressing need to belong to the new world they have entered. And they, too, are willing to belong on any terms, even terms that require them to continue to keep their curiosity and thought deeply buried.

15   Those are the terms of membership that fraternities and sororities offer. In return, these social clubs provide companionship that is predictable, reliable, aesthetically unimaginative, and intellectually unchallenging. So-called "wild parties" and the binge drinking that fuels them are misguided attempts to breathe life into stultifying conventionality.

16   In contrast, many traditional college classrooms—organized around lectures and class discussions—offer surprise, change, and intellectual stimulation. But their structure emphasizes individual mastery, self-sufficiency, and exclusion of outside distractions. While encouraging individual achievement, such courses often foster little substantive social interaction among students.

17   Colleges can do a great deal more than they generally do to make classrooms a source of social engagement around substantive issues. One approach is collaborative learning and related ways of organizing course work into learning communities, team projects, and peer tutoring.

18   Research can guide colleges in such efforts. We need to know whether collaborative learning actually does help students bring to the surface suppressed curiosity and thought, and, if so, how. Most of all, we need to know whether collaborative learning—especially, but not exclusively, during the first year of college—can give students opportunities to make friends in settings that are not merely social, vapid encounters, and, as a result, reduce the social desperation that drives students to binge drinking.

19   Granted, research is unlikely to show that collaborative learning is a universal solution to social problems at colleges. Research certainly will not demonstrate that collaborative learning alone can empty out fraternity and sorority houses.

20   But I am confident that research will show that collaborative learning can give entering college students a chance to experience a refreshingly new kind of social intimacy with their peers. It could help American colleges chip away at the problem of binge drinking, by helping to generate social cohesion, civil discourse, and yes, even friendship among young people who arrive on campuses green, scared, lonely, and small-town.

● *Thinking Critically About "Binge Drinking as a Substitute for a 'Community of Learning'"*

RESPONDING AS A READER

1. Bruffee spends only a sentence at the end of paragraph 1 describing the problem and the negative consequences of binge drinking. Why do you think he spends so little time trying to give the problem presence? If he

were writing this essay for an audience of students, how might his handling of the problem differ?

2. His main evidence for the claim that insecurity, loneliness, and a wish
   to belong cause students to join fraternities and sororities and engage in
   binge drinking comes from his experience in college many years ago.
   While this evidence might be persuasive to the faculty who read the
   Chronicle of Higher Education, is this evidence persuasive to you as a
   reader? Why or why not?

3. What practical actions is Bruffee proposing? What kind of justification
   does he offer for his proposal—arguments from consequence, principle,
   or precedent/analogy?

RESPONDING AS A WRITER

1. Bruffee's solution depends upon whether or not his assessment of a key
   reason for binge drinking is accurate. Do you agree with Bruffee's claim
   that loneliness and a wish to belong are key reasons for excessive drinking and wild parties? What other equally important factors does he ignore?

2. In recent years, colleges have taken a number of steps to curb binge
   drinking, from advertising campaigns intended to make students aware
   of the dire results of binge drinking to more recent campaigns that acknowledge the inevitability of drinking and encourage moderation.
   How would you evaluate the success of these various efforts? How successful do you think Bruffee's solution would be?

3. If you were to make a proposal to discourage binge drinking or to minimize the negative consequences of drinking on your campus, what
   would you propose? Make some notes toward such a proposal.

Kathryn Sipiorski (Student)

Consider the Study of Peace

Kathryn Sipiorski (b. 1977) graduated from Marquette University in 1999 and now attends medical school. She wrote this editorial for a composition assignment that asked for a "call to action" regarding a community concern. At the time, there had been several fatal shootings at local schools. She submitted this essay to the student paper, which published it in May 1996.

• *For Your Reading Log*

1. Have you ever written a letter to the editor of your school or local newspaper? If so, what issue prompted you to write? What was your purpose? Was your letter published, and if so, what response did your letter receive? If you have never written such a letter, can you think of issues or situations that might prompt you to write a letter to the editor?
2. Are you familiar with peace studies programs or courses? What do you predict that Sipiorski's arguments for the study of peace will be?

———————   •   ———————

1 "It was another senseless act in this interminable urban warfare. . . ." This is how a *Milwaukee Journal Sentinel* editorial began, entitled "Let's teach youngsters to settle disputes peaceably."

2   Although this article made several references to the tragic death of David Fajardo at South Division High School, the prevalence of senseless violence unfortunately extends beyond a few freak incidents.

3   Fajardo's death may have been the result of an argument over lunch money. It is a sad truth that incidents where trivial events turn violent and fatal can be found daily in newspapers, on television, and in our immediate communities. An elderly man shot and killed his wife because he did not want to care for her. A few months after Israeli leader Yitzak Rabin died for peace, Isreali guns have yet to remain silent. And the leading cause of death among black male teens is gunshots. Are we doomed to live in a world where cheerleading competitions lead to murder?

4   It is doubtful Fajardo studied the great figures of nonviolent resistance like Gandhi, Jesus, and Martin Luther King Jr. as extensively as he studied the Civil War or the atomic bomb. The chances are he witnessed many more fights and arguments than he compromised or peacefully resolved.

Example of Marquette

5 The emphasis of violence over nonviolence in society is evident at Marquette. For example, there are twelve courses on the subject of crime or violence spread among the history, philosophy, criminology, and sociology departments. Theol-

ogy of Non-Violence is, however, the only course that specifically explores the alternative to violence and is focused on historical examples of peaceful human interaction on social, political, and cultural levels.

Learning about wars and studying the tendencies of crime and violence are 6 indisputably necessary to gain an understanding of past and present atrocities. No matter how well the causes for World War I are understood, studying methods of avoiding war remain neglected. In *The Progressive,* Jan. 1991, Colman McCarthy, a professor of peace studies at American University, wrote, "Criticizing the way of violence is hollow unless we can offer solutions." In history books, entertainment, and on the streets there is an imbalance in our exposure to violence. There need to be efforts to increase peaceful behaviors.

Community Responsibility

As members of the Marquette community, we have the resources and ability to ex- 7 pand peace education. We can balance the war, crime, and violence courses by developing courses like McCarthy's Peace and World Order and the Politics of Nonviolence. We need to draw attention to individuals on campus and in the community who have been dedicated to nonviolence. We can emphasize peaceful conflict resolution and evaluate situations where peace has prevailed and failed.

Most important, we can all personally accept our roles in moving toward a 8 peaceful community by committing ourselves to nonviolence. Reading the works of Gandhi, King, Dorothy Day, Joan Baez, and Tolstoy can expand our awareness and help to form a new mentality. Peace is a passive force achieved only by active minds. Every fight that is avoided or conflict that is calmly resolved could symbolize a life like Fajardo's saved. As members of the Marquette community, we have the ability to nurture, harvest, and distribute the fruits of nonviolence.

● *Thinking Critically About "Consider the Study of Peace"*

RESPONDING AS A READER

1. What kind of impression of Sipiorski is created in this editorial? How credible do you find her to be as a spokesperson for the study of peace? What aspects of the text contribute to your sense of her credibility or lack of credibility?

2. How does Sipiorski go about introducing the problem? Although the problem clearly had "presence" for members of her university community at the time, does she make it sufficiently present for you as a reader? If not, what might she have done to make the problem more present for you?

3. Sipiorski argues from both consequence and principle. Find passages in her editorial where she argues from principle. How effective are these arguments to you as a reader?

RESPONDING AS A WRITER

1. In paragraph 4, Sipiorski argues from consequence, suggesting that the disproportionate exposure to violent actions as opposed to peaceful

ones contributes to violence in our society. What kinds of cause/effect assumptions is she making in this paragraph? Cite evidence that supports and/or evidence that refutes her reasoning from consequence.

2. In the last paragraph, she sums up her argument in a paradoxical statement: "Peace is a passive force achieved only by active minds." What does she mean? Do you believe this to be true? Write a paragraph or two in response to this statement.

3. Imagine that you are a member of the university that Sipiorski is addressing, and write a letter to the editor responding to Sipiorski's letter.

Writing to Propose a Solution

PROPOSING A SOLUTION

Think of a problem that genuinely concerns you and for which you have a solution to propose. Write an essay that proposes this solution to a particular audience. You may wish to write this essay as an editorial to your school or local paper, or you may wish to make your proposal to a school official, political figure, or work supervisor. In planning and writing your proposal, consider the following questions:

- Do you need to convince this audience that the problem is a problem?
- How will you go about introducing this problem?
- What kind of a solution are you proposing: a specific action, policy, or change of outlook that will lead to policy change and/or action?
- How much detail regarding the solution will you need to provide for your intended audience?
- What kind of evidence will you need to provide to persuade your audience of your proposal's feasibility and benefits?
- What kind of arguments or combination of arguments will you use in your justification section?
- What objections might your audience have and how will you address those objections?
- What alternate proposals exist and how will you support your claim that yours is the better solution?

EXAMINING RHETORICAL STRATEGIES

Choose one of the proposal essays in this chapter (or one that your teacher assigns) and analyze the author's rhetorical strategies. In a sense, your essay will evaluate the proposal using the features of effective proposals mentioned in this chapter as your criteria. Is the description of the problem sufficient and does it persuade you as a reader that the problem is compelling? Is the solution presented in adequate detail for the intended audience? What arguments does the writer use to justify his or her proposal, and are these convincing? Does the author ignore or acknowledge fairly competing solutions and possible consequences? Is the author credible? The effectiveness of your essay will depend upon your use of textual evidence to support your evaluative claims.

EXTENDING THE CONVERSATION

Several of the readings in this chapter propose a change in university policy, curriculum, or both. Sipiorski suggests that courses in nonviolence and peace studies might contribute to creating a less violent society. Bruffee proposes that the formation of learning communities might be one solution to binge drinking on the part of students, particularly first-year college students. Angell and Kassirer recommend, as one of several proposals, that students be taught enough about the scientific method to be critical consumers of the reported results of clinical research.

Using one of these articles as your starting point, write a proposal that either extends or counters the solutions offered in one of these articles. Perhaps, for example, you have an alternative recommendation for reducing the problem of excessive drinking by college students. In your proposal, briefly refer to other proposals (like Bruffee's or others on your campus) and point out their limitations before moving on to propose, explain, and justify your solution. To write such a proposal, you will need to conduct some research. That research may involve examining the undergraduate catalog for particular kinds of courses, interviewing faculty, administrators or students, and tracking down other articles about the issue.

CHAPTER

16

Seeking Common Ground

*I*t may be that uncertainty, disagreement, and outright conflict are inescapable aspects of human life. But must these difficulties lead to incivility and violence? The authors of the texts presented in this chapter would say "no."

Most of the essays and articles throughout this book have the explicit purpose of demonstrating that a particular way of looking at things is better than another. The authors contend—sometimes explicitly, sometimes implicitly—that their way of thinking about their subject is better informed, is more likely to have good results, or is even morally superior to other views of the matter. Readers expect such clarity and advocacy. The fabric of democratic discourse is woven with challenges to and defenses of commonly accepted views and status quo policies. Through the exchange, people figure out what they think, why, and what course of action to take. Assertive, even contentious, debate is not only common, but expected. The same is true of academic research and writing. From applied sciences to the humanities and arts, the work of scholars is to challenge accepted understandings of phenomena—to build new knowledge by questioning, enlarging, and reconstructing what's been understood so far.

But can these competing attempts to change listeners' and readers' minds go too far? Does the noise and rancor of public debate sometimes make it difficult for productive discussion and decision making to proceed? In recent years, a growing number of people have answered "yes" to such questions and have sought ways to "lower the decibel level" of public controversies. Deborah Tannen, author of the first selection in this chapter, urges readers to distinguish between "having an argument" (often an unpleasant experience) and "making an argument" (a potentially productive effort). In tune with her pleas, "civility" and "common ground" have become watchwords in the media; some members of Congress have even attended civility workshops. Schoolchildren learn conflict resolution skills, and people on opposing sides of the abortion rights issue have joined forces to work toward their shared goals of fewer teen pregnancies and more adoptions.

Can such efforts at establishing common ground flourish in a world seemingly filled with racial, ethnic, and religious rivalries, even hatreds? The authors in this chapter explore possibilities for debates that are more civil, relationships that are less rancorous. They consider whether and how even intractable moral issues and ethnic conflicts can be, if not resolved, at least tamed into reasonable conversations. Their levels of optimism vary.

Even though several centuries of rhetoricians and teachers have analyzed the structure and components of arguments, we do not have a specific outline of a "rhetoric of common ground" to draw upon as an analytical method. However, a template for rhetorical reading of opposing arguments is suggested by the basic guidelines for conflict resolution that educator Aida Michlowski lays out in her article in this chapter about peaceable classrooms. Analysis that looks for common ground might involve (1) determining the central question at issue, (2) understanding what type of conflict this is (e.g., values, interpretation, or other *stasis* categories) and what is at stake (e.g., money, prestige, freedom, quality of life, or life itself), and (3) detecting possible points of agreement between the competing positions.

In another selection, Sydney Callahan suggests how participants in a controversy might go about creating texts in which a writer extends a hand toward opposing views instead of pounding the table to assert his or her own particular view. Callahan describes four specific tactics for discussing—and arguing about —deeply felt and difficult issues within a family. Her points about civility and respect dovetail with the principles of what has come to be known as "Rogerian argument," which is based on principles of careful listening and empathy that were developed by the psychologist Carl Rogers. The key element of this approach is reducing threat. Instead of focusing on what's wrong with an opposing position (an inherently threatening move), the writer who follows Rogerian principles will emphasize points of agreement between the positions and work to convey understanding and respect for opposing views, even though, in the end, the writer holds a different position. Rogerian arguments feature careful restatement of an opponent's position, suggestion of broad areas of agreement between opposed positions, and delayed statements of the author's own claim or thesis. Advocates of this approach to communication emphasize that an effective restatement of the opposition's claims is meant to convey understanding, not compromise.

Analogies to this written process of exchange are evident in the speaking and listening work that takes place in conflict resolution or mediation groups. For example, in the model for participation in the Common Ground Network for Life and Choice (whose activities are described in Faye Ginsburg's article in this chapter), individual members take turns explaining their positions and the rationale behind them *without trying to convince anyone else.* Then they listen while someone with an opposing view "says back" what was heard. Only when the first person is satisfied that the restatement accurately reflects his or her views does the group move on to the next person. Crucial to this process is participants' recognition that listening to and restating unfamiliar (even distasteful) ideas does not obligate one to adopt those ideas.

The selections in this chapter offer new ways of approaching controversies and conflicts. These texts describe, recommend, and demonstrate what it is like to seek common ground. In the end, their primary goal is to reduce tension and create understanding—between opposed political and moral views and between cultural differences. As you read, consider the ways in which deepening someone's understanding of an idea is a form of changing that person's mind.

Questions to Help You Read Rhetorically About Common Ground

In the selections that follow, pay particular attention to the way writers describe and use techniques for moving readers beyond polarized positions. The questions below will help guide your analysis. Some are similar to those you would use to analyze any text. Others focus on the specifics of moving readers to common ground.

1. What has caused the conflict among the people or groups involved in the issue at hand? For example, do they have different, perhaps competing, goals and incompatible values? Are they competing for the same limited resources?
2. What type(s) of disagreement does the author of the given text identify as the chief impediment to agreement between the parties in the controversy? What kind of question is at issue? (See Table 13.1, pp. 397–398.) What differences are there in the ways the people involved in the dispute define the question that is at issue?
3. What is the writer's central claim or proposal, and how is it developed in terms of evidence, reasoning, and assumptions?
4. What possibility of common ground is evident in the text?
5. What does the writer apparently presume about the intended audience's attitude toward and engagement with the subject?
6. What specific efforts to "lower the decibel level" and "reduce threat" can you identify in the text? If you are working with an explicit argument, examine carefully the treatment of opposing views and try to identify specific places where the writer is using Callahan's "rules" or Rogerian principles of "listening" and reducing threat.
7. How do you imagine various parties involved in the controversy would respond to (a) the way their positions are depicted in the text and (b) the points the author is advocating?
8. If the text has changed your mind, try to identify the specific content point or rhetorical strategy that brought about that change. How extensive has that change been? If your thinking hasn't changed, what else could the writer have done to earn your agreement?

Deborah Tannen

The Triumph of the Yell

Deborah Tannen (b. 1945), a linguistics professor at Georgetown University, has published many academic articles and books as well as short stories and poems. She became known to the general public with the 1990 publication of *You Just Don't Understand: Women and Men in Conversation*, which examines gender differences in conversational style. She once told an interviewer that she sees as one of her missions "the presentation of linguistic research to a general audience—as a means of understanding human communication and improving it." This opinion essay was published in the *New York Times* in January 1994. The points she makes here became the germ of her 1998 book, *The Argument Culture*.

•   *For Your Reading Log*

1. Where have you observed a public, staged debate—that is, a situation in which two people known to have opposed views were invited to present them? What did you enjoy about it? What did you find uncomfortable?
2. Tannen makes a distinction between "making an argument" and "having an argument." Without having read the article, what's your sense of the difference between these two concepts?

———————   •   ———————

1   I put the question to a journalist who had written a vitriolic attack on a leading feminist researcher: "Why do you need to make others wrong for you to be right?" Her response: "It's an argument!"

2   That's a problem. More and more these days, journalists, politicians and academics treat public discourse as an argument—not in the sense of making an argument, but in the sense of having one, of having a fight.

3   When people have arguments in private life, they're not trying to understand what the other person is saying. They're listening for weaknesses in logic to leap on, points they can distort to make the other look bad. We all do this when we're angry, but is it the best model for public intellectual interchange? This breakdown of the boundary between public and private is contributing to what I have come to think of as a culture of critique.

4   Fights have winners and losers. If you're fighting to win, the temptation is great to deny facts that support your opponent's views and present only those facts that support your own.

5   At worst, there's a temptation to lie. We accept this style of arguing because we believe we can tell when someone is lying. But we can't. Paul Ekman, a psychologist at the University of California at San Francisco, has found that even

when people are very sure they can tell whether or not someone is dissembling, their judgements are as likely as not to be wrong.

If public disclosure is a fight, every issue must have two sides—no more, no 6 less. And it's crucial to show "the other side," even if one has to scour the margins of science or the fringes of lunacy to find it.

The culture of critique is based on the belief that opposition leads to truth: 7 when both sides argue, the truth will emerge. And because people are presumed to enjoy watching a fight, the most extreme views are presented, since they make the best show. But it is a myth that opposition leads to truth when truth does not reside on one side or the other but is rather a crystal of many sides. Truth is more likely to be found in the complex middle than in the simplified extremes, but the spectacles that result when extremes clash are thought to get higher ratings or larger readership.

Because the culture of critique encourages people to attack and often mis- 8 represent others, those others must waste their creativity and time correcting the misrepresentations and defending themselves. Serious scholars have had to spend years of their lives writing books proving that the Holocaust happened, because a few fanatics who claim it didn't have been given a public forum. Those who provide the platform know that what these people say is, simply put, not true, but rationalize the dissemination of lies as showing "the other side." The determination to find another side can spread disinformation rather than lead to truth.

The culture of critique has given rise to the journalistic practice of con- 9 fronting prominent people with criticism crouched as others' views. Meanwhile, the interviewer has planted an accusation in readers' or viewers' minds. The theory seems to be that when provoked, people are spurred to eloquence and self-revelation. Perhaps some are. But others are unable to say what they know because they are hurt, and begin to sputter when their sense of fairness is outraged. In those cases, opposition is not the path to truth.

When people in power know that what they say will be scrutinized for weak- 10 nesses and probably distorted, they become more guarded. As an acquaintance recently explained about himself, public figures who once gave long, free-wheeling press conferences now limit themselves to reading brief statements. When less information gets communicated, opposition does not lead to truth.

Opposition also limits information when only those who are adept at ver- 11 bal sparring take part in public discourse, and those who cannot handle it, or do not like it, decline to participate. This winnowing process is evident in graduate schools, where many talented students drop out because what they expected to be a community of intellectual inquiry turned out to be a ritual game of attack and counterattack.

One such casualty graduated from a small liberal arts college, where she 12 "luxuriated in the endless discussions." At the urging of her professors, she decided to make academia her profession. But she changed her mind after a year in an art history program at a major university. She felt she had fallen into a "den of wolves." "I wasn't cut out for academia," she concluded. But does academia have to be so combative that it cuts people like her out?

13   In many university classrooms, "critical thinking" means reading some-one's life work, then ripping it to shreds. Though critique is surely one form of critical thinking, so are integrating ideas from disparate fields and examining the context out of which they grew. Opposition does not lead to truth when we ask only "What's wrong with this argument?" and never "What can we use from this in building a new theory, and a new understanding?"

14   Several years ago I was on a television talk show with a representative of the men's movement. I didn't foresee any problem, since there is nothing in my work that is anti-male. But in the room where guests gather before the show I found a man wearing a shirt and tie and a floor-length skirt, with waist-length red hair. He politely introduced himself and told me he liked my book. Then he added: "When I get out there, I'm going to attack you. But don't take it personally. That's why they invite me on, so that's what I'm going to do."

15   When the show began, I spoke only a sentence or two before this man nearly jumped out of his chair, threw his arms before him in gestures of anger and be-gan shrieking—first attacking me, but soon moving on to rail against women. The most disturbing thing about his hysterical ranting was what it sparked in the stu-dio audience: they too became vicious, attacking not me (I hadn't had a chance to say anything) and not him (who wants to tangle with someone who will scream at you?) but the other guests: unsuspecting women who had agreed to come on the show to talk about their problems communicating with their spouses.

16   This is the most dangerous aspect of modeling intellectual interchange as a fight: it contributes to an atmosphere of animosity that spreads like a fever. In a society where people express their anger by shooting, the result of demonizing those with whom we disagree can be truly demonic.

17   I am not suggesting that journalists stop asking tough questions necessary to get at the facts, even if those questions may appear challenging. And of course it is the responsibility of the media to represent serious opposition when it ex-ists, and of intellectuals everywhere to explore potential weaknesses in others' arguments. But when opposition becomes the overwhelming avenue of inquiry, when the lust for opposition exalts extreme views and obscures complexity, when our eagerness to find weaknesses blinds us to strengths, when the atmos-phere of animosity precludes respect and poisons our relations with one another, then the culture of critique is stifling us. If we could move beyond it, we would move closer to the truth.

● *Thinking Critically About "The Triumph of the Yell"*

RESPONDING AS A READER

1. How extensive is Tannen's central claim here? When she takes issue with the belief that opposition leads to truth, is she at odds with those who say vigorous dissent is essential for democracy to thrive? What tex-tual evidence supports your view?
2. What type of argument particularly bothers Tannen? Is she more con-cerned with *how* an argument is conducted or with *what* it is about ?

3. How do you respond to Tannen's own argument? What is compelling about it for you? Where do you resist it? Why?

RESPONDING AS A WRITER

1. How would you explain where Tannen draws the line between productive and nonproductive exchanges in a controversy?
2. How does Tannen draw her readers to her point of view? Examine her text closely to trace its development in relationship to the way it engages readers.
3. Consider an instance of the "culture of critique" that you have witnessed recently—in person, through broadcast media, or in print, either on paper or on the Web. If the person you most sympathized with in the dispute requested your advice about achieving a more productive exchange by applying Tannen's ideas, what advice would you give?

Sidney Callahan

Fight Fierce but Fair: And Practice at Home

Sydney Callahan (b. 1933), a retired professor of psychology, is a widely published author and lecturer. She and her husband Daniel, both Roman Catholic ethicists, have frequently spoken and written about their opposing views on bioethical issues. They published *Abortion: Understanding Differences* in 1984. The essay we present here explains how they keep peace within the family despite their disagreements. It was published in February 1994 in *Commonweal*, a biweekly edited by Catholic laypeople, which, according to its Website, focuses on "topical issues of the day" and "the links between 'worldly' concerns and religious beliefs."

- ### *For Your Reading Log*

  1. "Good family fights prepare you for the larger world of democratic conflict," Callahan begins. Do you agree? Before you read the essay, reflect in writing about how your family handles disagreements about public issues. How do you manage to keep peace?
  2. Given only the background information above, the essay title, and its first sentence, what do you feel you already know about the personal *ethos* Callahan brings to this text? As you read, pay attention to details that reinforce or alter your initial impressions.

——————— • ———————

1 Good family fights prepare you for the larger world of democratic conflict. If you learn to fight well and fairly at home, you can contribute to the civic struggle necessary to keep a pluralistic society moving. I'm constantly advocating my causes in public debate, but during family holidays I'm kept in fighting trim by late-night arguments with my adult children.

2 Home debating seems natural to me because I constantly argued with my strong-minded father, who came from a good Southern prejudiced stock (lapsed Calvinist division). He refused to reform his racist, militaristic, atheistic, anti-intellectual views quickly enough for me. But as I married young (forty years this June so I was a bride of nine), my basic combat training and maneuvering skills in argument have come from frequent marital, martial engagements.

3 It's no secret that my husband Dan and I have had private and public disagreements on religious and ethical issues, as for instance over abortion. Dan takes a moderate prochoice position and I am more militantly prolife. At least we've produced a book and a few articles detailing those internal conflicts.

A magazine reporter once called to ask me how we could continue to stay 4
married since we disagreed so vigorously over abortion. I replied that after so
many decades we had so many deep and serious conflicts between us that we
hardly noticed the abortion disagreement at all! When the young interviewer
(unmarried) didn't laugh, I quickly explained that this was my attempt at a joke,
as in irony. You know, like the comment of the obese Herman Kahn, who once
said, "Inside this fat man there lives another fat man."

Thankfully, and not hopefully, Dan thinks these kinds of sallies are funny, 5
and makes plenty himself. Obviously this marriage can be saved. A shared sense
of humor is the best bonding agent or glue I know of to keep friends, spouses,
and adult children sticking around.

Disagreements abound but agreement abounds more. Dan and I, and my 6
children, friends, and relations agree about more things than we disagree. One
of the most critical agreements that Dan and I share is our joint commitment to
the Callahan guidelines for conducting civilized debate. If we could convince the
larger world of these rules (painfully acquired from experience in public debates
on abortion), we could make a great contribution to cleaning up our polluted
public discourse.

Rule Number 1: Be obsessively civil, courteous, and charitable in your use 7
of language. Words never are "mere words" (as Catharine A. MacKinnon, the
prominent feminist theorist, has written). But those who regularly use words (including prominent feminists) should take care to be absolutely accurate in their
facts and remain calm enough to argue sans hyperbolic thrusts issued with nasty
sneers of contempt. (A list of all the known offenders against this rule would take
up all the space of charity.)

Rule Number 2 follows from number one: Always show respect for your op- 8
ponents and assume their good will and sincerity (even if you might harbor a
wee doubt or two in your heart). Address what your opponents say not what you
infallibly detect to be their hidden agenda or underlying motives. After all, only
the Shadow knows what evil lurks in the heart of men and women, so take the
magnanimous high road, even if it doesn't heap coals of fire on your opponent's
head, à la Saint Paul.

Rule Number 3 may sometimes conflict with the personnel available for de- 9
bate: Try to argue against the best representative of your opposition, and not
against a strawperson, or the other side's most repellent fanatic extremist—
that's too easy, and "unsportspersonlike behavior unbefitting a gentleperson."

When attacked by an incoherent ranter, veritably foaming at the mouth, or 10
when confronted by a cowed novice too inept to give his or her side's best arguments, present them yourself. If you can't state the opposing side's arguments better than they can, and then show why the position is unsatisfactory, you
haven't done your homework. Why should serious differences be decided by
which side has the most crazies roaming around its fringes?

Rule Number 4 demands the most intellectual integrity and honesty: Admit 11
the price of following your own position. Every side in a serious disagreement
has some weaknesses, otherwise all reasonable and intelligent persons of good

will would agree already. Unfortunately, it's easy to see the looming drawbacks of your opponents' arguments but difficult to admit that your own solution includes risks and difficulties. A truly unflinching mind can confront a choice between lesser evils and say, "Yes, I am willing to say no to this or that demand, even at the price of legal coercion." Or in another kind of argument, "No, I don't think it wrong to let people abuse their freedom and make mistakes."

12   Americans are all too human. We hate to face dilemmas or scenarios which don't have happy endings. We want everything at the same time, even if the demands are logically contradictory. Perhaps more than anything else, we hate sustained argument and hard-focused thinking.

13   But the right sort of family training can produce people able to persevere in arguments and willing to confront, to persuade, to win through to a higher ground or a better consensus. As the British officer instructed his troops, "One, two, three, and repeat your fire—without rancor."

14   Friendly firefights or the learned ability to listen and "respectfully disagree," take practice. You must fully understand that those who disagree with you and have different positions in politics, sex, religion, or whatever, are not despicable people. (Or if they are despicable, it's not because of their dreadful opinions.)

15   We can resolve to play by the rules of civil and charitable debate. Who knows? By attentive, polite listening to all sides of conflicted encounters in and out of the family, you can learn new things. Your father sometimes did know best, your spouse has had a well-taken point or two, and even your adult children may be onto something you need to know. Let's keep the home fires burning for the greater good of the body politic. Or for the commonweal?

● *Thinking Critically About "Fight Fierce but Fair"*

RESPONDING AS A READER

1. How were your initial impressions of Callahan's *ethos* confirmed or altered as you read? Choose a few specific details that you found particularly effective in the way she conveyed this ethos, then compare your responses to those of your classmates.

2. What underlying question drives this essay? How would you describe the reasoning Callahan uses to respond to it? When you examine her claims, reasons, evidence, and assumptions, what aspects of her argument do you find most and least compelling?

3. In paragraph 12, Callahan suggests that her assertions about the value of debate are countercultural. Do you agree or disagree that "more than anything else, we [Americans] hate sustained argument and hard-focused thinking?" What role does this point play in your response to her larger argument?

RESPONDING AS A WRITER

1. Callahan says here that despite the well-known disagreements she and her husband have about abortion and other ethical issues, "agreement

abounds more" in their life together. Her primary elaboration of this is, of course, the four Callahan rules. What explicit values and implicit assumptions do you find in her presentation of these rules? Use the two-column analysis technique presented in Chapter 5 (p. 77) to scrutinize the paragraphs where she explains these rules, then write a short paragraph summarizing what you discover.

2. When you reflect upon intense discussions about public issues that you've had with people close to you (whether literally family members or not), which of Callahan's rules strikes you as the most difficult to apply? Why? Would the same difficulties apply when you write for an audience less familiar to you?

3. Composing a written argument to be read by a teacher, fellow students, and/or strangers in the general public is, of course, quite different from the live give-and-take of a family debate about hot topical issues. How, in your view, do the Callahan guidelines translate effectively as guidelines for writing effective arguments?

Aida A. Michlowski

From Conflict to Congruence

Aida A. Michlowski (b. 1944) is a professor of education at Marian College in Fond du Lac, Wisconsin, where she teaches courses in education and law. A licensed attorney, she has practiced law as a mediator and a guardian ad litem (child advocate) and has given numerous presentations locally and nationally on conflict resolution, negotiation, mediation, and team building. This overview of techniques for fostering a "peaceable classroom" was the lead article in a special issue on conflict resolution of the *Kappa Delta Pi Record* (Spring 1999). The refereed journal is published by Kappa Delta Pi, an international honor society dedicated to scholarship and excellence in education. The conventions used by the journal for citations follow the *Chicago Manual of Style* author-date system.

• *For Your Reading Log*

1. This scholarly article uses headings and other typographical conventions to mark sections and highlight terms being defined. Give yourself two minutes to scan the text, taking advantage of these textual clues and spot reading as appropriate, then jot down what you've learned about its purpose and content.
2. Now personalize this preview by reflecting in writing for a few minutes about any experiences you or a member of your family has had with peace education or peer mediation. If you don't have experience related to such programs, write instead about conflicts you or someone close to you have experienced or witnessed in a school setting. Then, given this background, articulate a personal purpose for reading this article. What questions specifically relevant to your experience might it answer?

———————   •   ———————

1 Conflict resolution has found its way from the courtroom to the classroom, from kindergarten to college. Since the founding of the National Association for Mediation in Education in 1984, school-based conflict-resolution programs have increased from fifty to more than 5,000 in the United States (National Institute for Dispute Resolution 1994). As it continues to grow in acceptance, conflict resolution may yet become "the fourth R" in basic education.

2   Conflict is a natural occurrence that can happen when two or more individuals interact. In schools, the interests of students versus students and students versus teachers are at times congruent and at other times in conflict. Congruence means balance, harmony, and conformity. To transform conflict into congruence, teachers and students must understand the nature of conflict, what causes it, and how to manage it creatively and constructively.

Conflict is variously defined as a difference of unwavering opinions, a col- 3
lision of mutually exclusive interests, a battle of potent wills, and a clashing of
incompatible personalities. Maurer (1991, 2) has noted that "conflict is not a
state of being, but, rather an active process, which over time takes on various dimensions and dynamics." Whether it becomes destructive or constructive depends on how conflict is managed (Deutsch 1973). Ignored or suppressed, or if
confronted with aggression and anger, conflict becomes destructive. Managed
positively, conflict becomes a constructive experience resulting in a win-win situation. When schools foster a positive climate, conflicts become opportunities for
growth (Johnson and Johnson 1995).

The three major types of conflicts are (1) conflict of goals—when students 4
have incompatible ideas or opinions, but only one can be realized; (2) conflict of
needs—when students want different things, but only one can be met; and (3)
conflict over resources—when students want the same thing, but only one can
have it. These clashes may escalate or de-escalate depending on the classroom
climate. A classroom with a highly competitive and intolerant atmosphere
and/or an authoritarian teacher tends to foster an "I win; you lose" disposition
instead of an "I win; you win" attitude. Implementing conflict-resolution programs, however, enables teachers to change the classroom climate into a culture
of caring and congruence.

Methods of Resolution

The peaceful resolution of conflict follows a logical scheme. It begins with dis- 5
puting individuals attempting to find a solution through negotiation. When negotiation fails, neutral third parties become involved in mediation and, if
necessary, arbitration.

Negotiation advocates conflict resolution through partnership that improves 6
and sustains the relationship between two individuals (Weeks 1992). It becomes
desirable when there is a balance of power and both parties' needs can be met
(Fisher and Ury 1991). Negotiation is a bilateral process with two disputants trying to work out an agreement or a settlement without the intervention of a third
party. It begins with negotiators stating their positions and describing their goals,
needs, and wants. Negotiators then generate options and search for common
ground. If negotiation is successful, it ends with a mutually beneficial solution. If
the negotiators fail to resolve their conflict, the next alternative is peer mediation.

Peer mediation adheres to the principles of caring confrontation, using a neu- 7
tral third party to assist the disputants in reaching a win-win agreement. It focuses on the solution of the immediate problem and the preservation of the
relationship (Schmidt 1994). It also directs participants to use prosocial behaviors and positive communication skills.

Peer mediation involves at least three people—the two parties in conflict and 8
a third, neutral person who acts as mediator. It is a voluntary process that follows certain protocols. First, the mediator opens the session with an introductory statement and sets the ground rules: no interruptions, no physical or verbal
abuse, and no lying. Second, the complainant presents his or her case, defines the

conflict, states what happened, and expresses his or her feelings in a nonblaming manner. Third, the respondent presents his or her side of the issue, states what happened, and expresses his or her feelings in a nondefensive manner. Fourth, the mediator restates and summarizes the information. He or she may ask questions for clarification. Fifth, the mediator asks the disputants to propose a win-win solution, taking care not to offer advice or criticism. Sixth, if and when an agreement is reached, the mediator writes the agreement in the form of a contract and both disputants sign it. If the disputants cannot agree, then the mediation reaches an impasse, at which point the mediator ends the session and advises the disputants either to try the mediation process again or pursue another form of conflict resolution such as arbitration.

9   *Arbitration* is considered the conflict resolution of last resort, because it is employed only after the disputants have tried negotiation and mediation without success. It involves the intervention of a disinterested third party, such as a teacher, a guidance counselor, or the principal. Voluntary arbitration occurs when students ask an adult to intervene. Compulsory arbitration occurs when students are unable to resolve their conflict through negotiation and mediation. The arbitrator, acting as "judge and jury," hears both sides and makes a final judgment. The disputants must abide by the arbitrator's decision.

Objectives and Outcomes

10 Data on conflict-resolution programs is limited (Lam 1989). The few studies that have been conducted, though, have turned up some interesting revelations. Among the findings:

- Objective: Make students and teachers aware of alternative ways to handle conflict, such as cooperation and affirmation, and improve communication and problem-solving skills. Outcome: Ten out of ten possible teachers developed an understanding of constructive conflict, and forty-five out of fifty students used conflict-resolution strategies (Korn 1994). In addition, third-grade students became aware of their options and learned how to communicate more effectively (Moreau 1994).
- Objective: Teach students to handle interpersonal conflicts in positive, nonviolent ways and replace antisocial behaviors (blaming, bossing, tattling, and pushing) with prosocial behaviors (listening and talking). Outcome: Conflict time declined and prosocial skills usage increased when conflict-resolution strategies were taught to twenty second- and third-grade students (Bastianello 1989).
- Objective: Offer alternative disciplinary measures, increase attendance, improve academic performance, and avoid suspensions and expulsions. Outcome: Discipline referrals for antisocial behaviors decreased and students got along with their peers and felt good about school (Satchel 1992).
- Objective: Encourage students to transfer their knowledge and skills of conflict prevention and resolution to their family and community. Outcome: Kindergartners applied newly acquired problem-solving skills at home (DeMasters and King 1994).

Curriculum Approaches

The two major approaches to establishing conflict-resolution programs in schools 11
are the "cadre approach" and the "total student body approach" (Johnson and
Johnson 1995). The cadre approach trains a small group of students and teachers.
The total student body approach teaches all students and staff. Conflict-resolution programs often exist as stand-alone modules. Examples include classroom
discipline, peace education, multicultural perspective, and just community.

Classroom discipline is the most common form of conflict resolution. As dis- 12
ciplinarians, though, teachers respond to classroom confrontations in different
ways. Among the personal styles: "No-nonsense" firmly enforces class rules.
"Smoothing" maintains the status quo. "Ignoring" lets the conflict fizzle out.
"Problem solving" assumes that conflicts always equal problems that must be
solved. "Compromising" encourages listening and settling for smaller victories
(Kriedler 1984).

Peace education proposes that conflict resolution is best taught in the context 13
of a caring community. Nonviolent alternatives to dispute resolution and a new
generation of peacemakers are at the core of peace education (Crawford and Bodine 1996; Hinitz and Stomfay-Stitz 1996). Two distinct yet similar delivery systems exist: The Peaceable Classroom focuses on social responsibility, a sense of
unity, and a spirit of cooperation. The Peaceable School is a comprehensive program extending from personal peace to global peace (Bodine, Crawford, and
Schrumpf 1994).

Multicultural perspective seeks to minimize conflict by teaching team build- 14
ing, consensus, self-expression, tolerance, and acceptance. The purpose is not to
eliminate cultural differences but to use them in positive and productive ways
(Educators for Social Responsibility 1991).

Just community is not usually viewed as part of a conflict resolution program; 15
however, it can help prevent conflict when implemented in schools. Based on the
concept of moral development, just community recommends teaching moral
content such as kindness, truthfulness, and fairness (Power, Higgins, and
Kohlberg 1989). In addition to teacher-led peer dialogues about hypothetical
moral dilemmas, the entire school practices a democratic way of life wherein students have significant input in establishing policies.

Teaching Strategies

Teaching conflict resolution must be developmental and sequential. The type of 16
strategy used will depend on a variety of factors, including grade level, issues
causing the conflict, student and teacher training, and available resources (Sprick
1995). Among the techniques that educators have found effective:

- Role playing exploits drama as a teaching tool (Pipkin and DiMenna
  1989). First, the teacher describes the conflict scenario and sets the background that simulates real-life situations. Second, the teacher assigns the
  roles to the participants. Third, the students act out their roles. They are
  free to improvise as long as they stay in character. The teacher remains in

the background, stepping in only to ask leading questions if the players become stuck or get lost in tangents. Finally, at a critical point of conflict, the teacher freezes the role-play and asks the audience for alternative solutions and possible outcomes. A variation of this exercise constitutes additional role players standing next to the main characters and acting as their alter egos. The alter egos then verbalize what they think the main characters really might mean.

- Storytelling enables children to learn creative ways to resolve their conflicts (Shatles 1992). The teacher tells a story about a contrived situation or retells one from a book. When the story reaches its point of conflict, the teacher stops and asks the class to brainstorm solutions. Suggestions are listed on a board, and a consensus must be reached by choosing the best solution. An extension to this exercise includes students writing and/or illustrating their own endings to popular fairy tales.

- Conflict games are effective attention-getters. "Walk in the Shoes of the Other," for example, helps students understand both sides of a conflict. The game begins with two pairs of cutout footprints on the classroom floor. The disputing students face each other, stand on the footprints, and take turns relating differences, similarities, and ways in which they can become friends.

- Humor uses laughter as pacifier. It is difficult to stay angry while laughing. Although conflict is no laughing matter, learning to deal with it in a positive manner need not be all doom and gloom. The Bluegrass Alley Clowns of Kentucky, for example, teach conflict resolution to children through their clown capers. Members of the troupe use funny skits, jokes, stories, and magic tricks to communicate the message of peace.

- Mnemonics and metaphors are creative ways of teaching conflict resolution. They conform to Gardner's (1993) theory of multiple intelligences and brain-based education (Caine and Caine 1991). These teaching tools use meaningful associations by making the strange familiar and the familiar strange. For example, "The Seven C's of Conflict Resolution" (communication, cooperation, caring, compromise, choice, change, and congruence) can be introduced by applying the jigsaw technique. The teacher divides the class into seven groups, with each group assigned a C word. Members of the first grouping serve as experts, so they must understand their C word well enough to teach it to others. After a period of time, the teacher regroups the class for a second grouping comprised of the seven C words. Experts from the first grouping take turns presenting their C word until everyone in the group understands the seven C's of conflict resolution. To apply the lesson, the teacher guides the class in preparing a recipe and baking a cake or other treat with seven ingredients starting with the letter C.

17   Changing conflict into congruence is not always an easy task, but it is a worthwhile endeavor. Conflict-resolution programs should aim to do more than resolve present conflicts among students and reduce violence and destructive behavior; they must also help students learn how to solve problems, make wise de-

cisions, take full responsibility for their actions, and face the consequences of their decisions.

Hopefully, students will first try to resolve their conflicts through peaceful 18 negotiation. When they cannot reach an agreement, they must know how to get the help of a peer mediator. When peer mediation fails, they should seek the assistance of an adult through arbitration. If students and teachers are successful in making peace within themselves and with each other, a peaceable classroom in a peaceable school will soon evolve.

References

Bastianello, S. 1989. Implementation of a program for teaching conflict resolution strategies in a primary classroom. ERIC ED 315 182.

Bodine, R., D. Crawford, and F. Schrumpf. 1994. *Creating the peaceable school: A comprehensive program for teaching conflict resolution.* Champaign, Ill.: Research Press.

Caine, R. N., and G. Caine. 1991. *Making connections: Teaching and the human brain.* Menlo Park, Calif.: Addison-Wesley.

Crawford, D., and R. Bodine. 1996. Conflict resolution education: A guide to implementing programs in schools, youth-serving organizations, and community and juvenile justice settings program report. Washington, D.C.: Office of Juvenile Justice and Delinquency Prevention. ERIC ED 404 426.

DeMasters, R. H., and E. S. King. 1994. Conflict resolution: Teaching social skills in a kindergarten classroom. ERIC ED 373 905.

Deutsch, M. 1973. *The resolution of conflict: Constructive and destructive processes.* New Haven, Conn.: Yale University Press.

Educators for Social Responsibility. 1991. Dealing with differences: Conflict resolution in our schools. ERIC ED 371 983.

Fisher, R., and W. Ury. 1991. *Getting to yes: Negotiating agreement without giving in.* New York: Houghton-Mifflin.

Gardner, H. 1993. *Multiple intelligences: The theory in practice.* New York: Basic Books.

Hinitz, B. F., and A. Stomfay-Stitz. 1996. Dream of peace, to dare to stay the violence, to do the work of the peacemaker. Paper presented at the Annual Conference of the Association for Childhood Education International, 11-13 April, Minneapolis, Minn. ERIC ED 394 733.

Johnson, D. W., and R. T. Johnson. 1995. *Reducing school violence through conflict resolution.* Alexandria, Va.: Association for Supervision and Curriculum Development.

Korn, J. 1994. Increasing teachers' and students' levels of conflict resolution and peer mediation strategies through teachers and student training programs. ERIC ED 375 944.

Kreidler, W. 1984. *Creative conflict resolution: More than 200 activities for keeping peace in the classroom.* Glenview, Ill.: Scott, Foresman & Co.

Lam, J. A. 1989. *The impact of conflict resolution programs on schools: A review and synthesis of the evidence,* 2d ed. Amherst, Mass.: National Association for Mediation in Education.

Maurer, R. E. 1991. *Managing conflict: Tactics for school administrators.* Boston: Allyn and Bacon.

Moreau, A. S. 1994. Improving social skills of third grade students through conflict resolution training. ERIC ED 375 334.

National Institute for Dispute Resolution. 1994. A survey of schools, dispute resolution
programs across the country. *NIDR News* 1(7): 6-9.

Pipkin, W., and S. DiMenna. 1989. Using creative dramatics to teach conflict resolution:
Exploiting the drama/conflict dialectic. *Journal of Humanistic Education and Development*
28(2):104-12.

Power, F. C., A. Higgins, and L. Kohlberg. 1989. *Lawrence Kohlberg's approach to moral education.* New York: Columbia University Press.

Satchel, B. 1992. Increasing prosocial behavior of elementary students in grades K-6
through a conflict resolution management program. ERIC ED 347 607.

Schmidt, F. 1994. *Mediation: Getting to win-win!* Miami, Fla.: Peace Education Foundation.

Shatles, D. 1992. Conflict resolution through children's literature. New York: The Teachers Network. ERIC ED 344 976.

Sprick, R. S. 1995. *Stop, think, plan: A school-wide conflict resolution strategy training video.*
Eugene, Ore.: Teaching Strategies, Inc.

Weeks, D. 1992. *The eight essential steps to conflict resolution: Preserving relationships at work,
at home, and in the community.* New York: Tarcher/Putnam.

• *Thinking Critically About "From Conflict to Congruence"*

RESPONDING AS A READER

1. The reading log assignment asked you to articulate a personal purpose
   for reading this article. Did the article enable you to satisfy your purposes for reading? How accurate was your initial understanding of the
   article's purpose? Were you able either to find answers to the ques-
   tion(s) you articulated or to find in the text a reference that might be a
   better source?

2. On what basis is Michlowski's credibility asserted in this text? How
   would you describe the *ethos* that she establishes for herself as author?
   What textual evidence supports your answers?

3. What does Michlowski seem to have assumed to be readers' previous at-
   titude(s) toward and knowledge of her subject matter? What is your assessment of how she intended to change attitudes and understanding?
   In what ways did she succeed or not in relation to your own attitude and
   understanding?

RESPONDING AS A WRITER

1. Unlike many scholarly articles in education, this one does not begin
   with an abstract that previews its contents. What essential points would
   need to be included in such an abstract? Try your hand at writing a brief
   summary of the article—fewer than 75 words—that could be used in an
   annotated bibliography or published above the article as a summarizing preview. (See the discussion on composing a summary in Chapter
   4, p. 59.)

2. Consider a conflict—major or minor—that you have recently had with someone. How do Michlowski's categories for types of conflicts help you understand the sources of conflict in a different way than before? What does her description of resolution methods suggest might have been a better way of resolving it than whatever happened? What might still be a good way of working out the conflict?
3. Now consider an unresolved conflict currently in the news, one about which you can readily find opposing statements from at least two perspectives published during the last week or two. (The brevity of letters to newspaper editors makes them particularly good sources of clearly stated opposing views.) Again try out Michlowski's concepts for analyzing and resolving matters. How applicable are those ideas when you look specifically at textual statements of opposing views?

Faye Ginsburg

The Anthropology of Abortion Activism

In this opinion article, Faye Ginsburg (b. 1952) discusses what she learned from her anthropological research on grassroots abortion activism and praises the accomplishments of activists who have worked cooperatively in Common Ground groups. The article appeared in the January 26, 1996, issue of the *Chronicle of Higher Education*, a weekly newspaper that is widely read by college and university administrators, staff, and faculty. Ginsburg is a professor of anthropology at New York University and director of the graduate Program in Culture and Media there. Her book-length report of this research, *Contested Lives: The Abortion Debate in an American Community* (1998), won numerous awards.

• *For Your Reading Log*

1. As you will learn from her article, Ginsburg's findings go against some common views of abortion activism. As part of recalling relevant background knowledge, write in your log about your image of people who are involved in abortion activism on either side. Alternatively, if you yourself have been active regarding this issue, consider the stereotypes you think others may have of people who side with you or stereotypes that you may have once had about either group.

2. As further preparation for reading, try to imagine what goals "pro-life" and "pro-choice" activists might agree upon. What beliefs and assumptions do you think they might share either about public policy issues or about productive ways to handle debate and conflict?

———————   •   ———————

1   Like many people who are drawn to anthropology, I wanted to conduct research that would debunk common stereotypes about "natives." Unlike my colleagues who departed for distant shores to earn their Ph.D.'s in the early 1980s, I was drawn to the abortion issue in the United States. Why does it excite such profound emotions and political virulence in our society? What motivates activists? What kind of political activity occurs beyond the rhetoric and polarizing demonstrations organized by the leaders of both sides? Perhaps most important, I wanted to see whether activists in both camps could find any new, more-creative ways to deal with each other and the controversy surrounding abortion.

2   I felt that the abortion debate needed the kind of research that anthropologists and other qualitative social scientists undertake: studies that try to understand people as part of a community, getting to know them over time and in

context, so that we can see the world from their point of view and comprehend why certain issues become more pressing than others in their lives.

Unfortunately, except for a few sociological works, such as James Davison 3 Hunter's *The Culture Wars* and Kristen Luker's *The Politics of Motherhood*, as well as the historian Rickie Solinger's *The Abortionist*, most scholarly and popular writing on abortion seems to rely on stereotypes.

Journalists generally have focused on the most-violent aspects of the con- 4 flict—the headline-grabbing protests at clinics by Operation Rescue and the murders of two doctors and three clinic workers by activists invoking what they considered to be the "Christian" principle of "justifiable homicide." And surveys and statistical research have relied on multiple-choice questions about variables assumed to influence attitudes on abortion, such as religion, income, or education.

Much of this research is enormously valuable. For example, the stability of 5 public opinion on the issue for more than two decades—with half to two thirds of the public favoring abortion in some circumstances—is a stunning bit of data that has frustrated many an activist trying to push legislative change.

Yet such work does not provide a rounded, complex sense of who the activists 6 are, the diversity of opinion and philosophical divisions within each side of the debate, or where new political possibilities for a solution to the conflict might emerge.

Scholarship can help place current "news" in the historical context of the ebb 7 and flow of social movements. For example, the extreme violence that has characterized anti-abortion activism in the 1990s is a relatively new phenomenon. Through the mid-1980s, most activists on both sides of the issue were moderates—people who felt strongly but were fundamentally committed to public civility, such as nonconfrontational protests and attempts to enact legislation.

Moderates still make up the majority of activists, but their presence is much 8 harder to detect as radicals engage in deliberately provocative acts. Yet, despite all the clamor among activists and the shifting positions of politicians, the legality of abortion, established by the Supreme Court's 1973 decision in *Roe v. Wade*, has remained largely unchanged. And the confrontational and violent tactics of anti-abortion extremists have turned off some potential supporters and aggravated philosophical differences among pro-lifers. Some more-moderate opponents of abortion have begun focusing on activities such as educational programs on fetal development and centers that try to help women with prenatal and obstetric care.

Academic work that looks beyond the front-page stories can help to illumi- 9 nate new political possibilities that offer a brave counterpoint to the atmosphere of increasing violence. In a number of small cities, activists have grown tired of the polarized battles and are trying to find alternative ways to accomplish their agendas at the grassroots level. At a time when our country and the rest of the world seem dominated by the politics of hate, it seems especially important to locate and study how people are finding more-constructive ways to accomplish their political and social ends.

I was fortunate to encounter some of this activity while doing field research 10 on grassroots abortion activists during the 1980s. My work focused on the small, prairie city of Fargo, N.D., where the opening of the Fargo Women's Health Organization in 1981—the first, and still the only, clinic in the state to offer abortion services—has provoked continuing local controversy. In Fargo, I witnessed some remarkable political creativity among activists on both sides, especially those involved in a group called Pro-Dialogue. For a brief time, those activists dared to step out of their stereotyped positions; they tried to imagine a way to work on their different agendas that was driven not by hate and violence, but by a desire to use the political process to improve the conditions faced by pregnant women.

11   Pro-Dialogue was formed during a meeting of the North Dakota Democratic Women's Caucus in March 1984, in preparation for that year's state Democratic convention. A pro-choice plank on abortion was proposed for the state party's platform, and, after much debate, was defeated. A woman who found she had friends arguing on both sides of the issue suggested a compromise position based on areas of agreement. The result read: "The North Dakota Democratic party believes public policy on abortion should provide some positive alternatives which would stress effective sex education, continued research on safer means of contraception, improved adoption services, support for parents of exceptional children, and economic programs which make it possible for parents to both raise children with love and pursue a productive work life."

12   Pro-Dialogue expired after only a few years, when Fargo—like many small American cities—was subject to prolonged anti-abortion protests by extremists from outside the community. Compared with the recent years of violence, Pro-Dialogue represented only a fragile moment in the abortion conflict.

13   But fragility is not the same as insignificance. In the past five years, the germ of the idea that emerged in Fargo a decade ago has begun to blossom independently; groups have formed around the country, made up of pro-choice and pro-life activists determined to find alternatives to divisive rhetoric and violence. Like strong families, these groups are finding ways to tolerate differences among their members and work toward common goals, such as helping women with difficult pregnancies. They have created an organization called the Common Ground Network for Life and Choice, whose members are trying to work together on issues such as teen-age pregnancy, ways to provide adequate resources for impoverished mothers and children, and guidelines for protests at abortion clinics.

14   When I first heard about Common Ground, I thought that it must have been founded by people who were interested in the abortion issue but had not put themselves on the front lines. In fact, exactly the opposite was true. Groups have emerged in places where the abortion battle has been the most prolonged and divisive—Buffalo, Milwaukee, Boston, St. Louis, and even Pensacola, Fla., the site of several abortion-clinic bombings in the 1980s and the murders of two doctors and one clinic worker in the 1990s. Indeed, one of the first local Common Ground groups to form was begun by the principal adversaries in the 1989 Supreme Court case, *Webster v. Reproductive Health Services,* a decision that allowed states to impose restrictions on abortion services, such as banning the use of public funds for counseling or for providing abortions.

15   Following that ruling, B. J. Isaacson Jones, the woman who directed the largest abortion clinic in St. Louis, and Andrew Puzder, the leading anti-abortion lawyer in Missouri, decided to find areas in which the two sides could work to-

gether. The efforts of the group they founded have resulted in legislation in Missouri providing assistance to drug-addicted pregnant women. Last year, the group issued a position paper on "Adoption as Common Ground."

Creative political imagination can flower in many different ways, inspiring 16 people to protest peacefully, to dehumanize their opponents, or to commit murder in God's name. Public and even scholarly understanding of why people are driven to particular forms of activism is as rare as deep knowledge of the "exotic" people whom anthropologists and other social scientists traditionally have studied. Ethnographic research on a divisive issue such as abortion can give much-needed visibility to people who are trying to create new, positive action on social and political issues.

Perhaps if more attention had been paid to groups such as Fargo's Pro- 17 Dialogue in the mid-1980s, we might have had a Common Ground network much earlier, which might have helped to prevent the murders of the past few years. Much as Margaret Mead studied other cultures, in part, to help Americans rethink their own cultural habits, contemporary anthropologists and other social scientists can, by the cases they choose to study and write about, help to redefine the way we think about cultural conflict and its resolution.

Social movements are built on trust and dialogue as well as on disagree- 18 ment, but cooperative actions rarely attract as much media coverage as violent forms of protest do. Yet in an era of profound cynicism, when distrust of any one unlike ourselves seems to dominate politics, it is crucial for academics to focus more research on people whose actions contradict our stereotypes. Such analyses can help expand and reframe the public discourse on controversial issues and, in the abortion debate, remind us of the key concern that seems to have been lost: how we can make our society more supportive of women in their childbearing years, and help people have and raise children under the best possible circumstances.

• *Thinking Critically About "The Anthropology of Abortion Activism"*

RESPONDING AS A READER

1. In a nutshell, what are Ginsburg's major points about abortion activism and about anthropology? Her article is marked by a theme of unexpected findings and surprising choices. Read through it again to trace instances of these surprises and consider how her treatment of them contributes to her overall points.

2. What does Ginsburg seem to assume about her intended audience's interest in her subject and existing attitude about the two major topics she addresses? What methods does she use to attempt to change her readers' minds?

3. What specific possibilities for establishing common ground between opposing groups are evident in this text?

RESPONDING AS A WRITER

1. Did you find Ginsburg's presentation of surprising information persuasive? What surprised you in this text? Write a brief paragraph describing your response to her text, pinpointing specific places where you found her presentation to be effective or flawed.

2. Examine Ginsburg's organizational strategy by preparing a descriptive outline as explained in Chapter 4 (p. 58), stating what each paragraph or section "does" as well as "says" to move the reader toward Ginsburg's concluding points.

3. We include this article in this chapter because it describes common ground activities undertaken by activists in perhaps the most intractable controversy in recent decades. But is the article itself an example of a text that seeks common ground? As you examine its content and technique to answer that question, decide whether Ginsburg devotes adequate attention to the activities and concerns of both sides of the abortion issue. Use textual evidence to support your answer when you and your classmates compare responses. To assist your analysis, you may want to use the technique described in Chapter 5 (p. 77) for examining binaries.

Michael X. Delli Carpini and Scott Keeter

What Should Be Learned Through Service Learning?

The opening paragraph of this examination of different approaches to teaching political science explicitly asserts the possibility of "common ground." The article was published in a special section on "Service Learning in Political Science" in the September 2000 issue of *PS: Political Science and Politics*, the journal of the American Political Science Association (APSA). As the list of references indicates, the authors, Michael Delli Carpini (b. 1953) and Scott Keeter (b. 1951), also wrote together the 1996 book, *What Americans Know About Politics and Why It Matters*. Delli Carpini, a professor of political science at Barnard College, Columbia University, was serving as director of the public policy program of the Pew Charitable Trusts when the article was published. Keeter is a professor of government and politics at George Mason University, where he teaches courses on political analysis and survey research. *PS* is a scholarly journal that uses a blind review process in which neither authors nor reviewers are identified. The system for parenthetical citations used in the journal follows the *Style Manual for Political Science*, which is issued by the APSA.

● **For Your Reading Log**

1. To prepare for reading this article, jot a few sentences about what you understand to be the goal of political science as a discipline. Given that, what would you say the goal of undergraduate political science classes is from the faculty point of view? From the students' point of view?
2. Now consider the second major topic of the article. How would you define service learning? How is doing service learning different from just volunteering? Write from what your own experience tells you or from what you understand from the terms themselves.

——————— ● ———————

Service learning is typically distinguished from both community service and tra- 1
ditional civic education by the integration of study with hands-on activity outside the classroom, typically through a collaborative effort to address a community problem (Ehrlich 1999, 246). As such, service learning provides opportunities and challenges for increasing the efficacy of both the teaching and practice of democratic politics. To better understand these opportunities and challenges, it is necessary to make explicit the goals of service learning and to consider how these goals intersect those of more traditional approaches to teaching about government and politics. We believe that one place these sometimes

competing models could find common ground is in the learning of factual knowledge about politics.

2   Underlying the pedagogy of service learning are the beliefs that a central mission of civic education is to produce active, engaged citizens and that this mission is more likely to be accomplished by allowing young Americans to directly experience "politics" as part of their education. As noted by Frantzich and Mann, this view is very compatible with the stated mission of the American Political Science Association:

> The founding of the [APSA] in 1903 marked the evolution of political science as a distinct academic discipline in colleges and universities. At the time, two educational objectives were claimed for the emerging discipline: citizenship and training for careers in public service. . . . For the student, direct experience was recommended to supplement formal instruction in government and politics. (1997, 193)

3   Frantzich and Mann went on to show that, while the definitions of public service and citizenship have evolved over time, training for both through a combination of classroom and "real world" experiences has remained a central responsibility for the discipline.

4   Despite this longstanding commitment to developing good citizens, there remains a tension between the educational and civic goals of the discipline. Not all members of our profession would agree that developing active citizens is or should be part of our mission. Perceiving political science as a discipline that observes, critiques, and seeks to understand public life can easily (and justifiably) lead individuals to embrace a teaching philosophy that dictates transmitting knowledge and cultivating a critical perspective rather than encouraging participation. Indeed, some political science theory and research suggests that, for some Americans at least, civic and political engagement is irrational, unnecessary, ineffective, and even harmful (see, e.g., Berelson 1952; Downs 1957; Edelman 1988; Ginsberg 1982; Neuman 1986; Olson 1971).

5   Being more dedicated to transmitting knowledge than creating engaged citizens would not automatically lead one to reject the value of experiential learning, but it would lead one to consider it valuable only to the extent that it enhances a student's understanding of government and politics. In short, a factual orientation would lead one to design service learning experiences that increased learning (of a certain kind) rather than service.

6   Of course, the choice between transmitting knowledge and creating engaged citizens is seldom so stark as this. It is fair to assume that most political science instructors believe there is a connection between understanding government and politics and being an effective citizen, even if they never ask students to experience public life as part of their coursework. Similarly, few advocates for service learning as a means for creating more engaged citizens would deny the importance of putting one's real-world experiences into the broader context provided by readings, lectures, discussions, and writing assignments. The challenge facing instructors, therefore, lies in clarifying the relationship between classroom

and experiential learning. Put another way, the questions all instructors, whatever their teaching philosophy, must answer are "What does the experience of participating in public life add to classroom learning?" and "What does classroom learning add to the participatory experience?" While there are numerous ways one might attempt to answer these questions, we suggest that one good answer to both is factual knowledge about politics.

At first blush, the learning of political facts would seem far removed from the goals and approaches most centrally identified with either the service learning movement or current thinking about effective classroom instruction. The central objective of service learning is the development of lifelong habits of engagement in democratic citizenship. Indeed, service learning is often held up as an alternative to the dry, objectified, often context-free memorization of facts associated with traditional classroom civics. At the same time, even those who believe classroom learning is valuable in and of itself often emphasize the teaching of skills such as critical thinking or effective argument over the learning of specific facts. 7

While we agree that rote memorization of facts does little to create either engaged citizens or educated students (Niemi and Junn 1999), we also believe that imparting factual knowledge about politics is necessary, if not sufficient, for creating both. Consider the current paradox: America's youth are highly engaged with volunteer activity and yet very disengaged from traditional political activity; they are more trusting of government than their elders and yet feel much less politically efficacious (National Election Studies 1998). Young people want to help solve society's problems, but most do not see how what the government does can worsen or ameliorate these problems. And those who do see this connection often lack the practical knowledge of the issues, players, and rules to be able to participate in politics effectively. Political knowledge is a key to seeing these connections and to understanding how to affect the system. 8

Being informed increases the likelihood that a citizen will have opinions about the issues of the day and that those opinions will be stable over time and consistent with each other. It produces opinions that are arguably more closely connected to one's values, beliefs, and objective conditions. It facilitates participation in public life that effectively connects one's opinions with one's actions. And it promotes greater support for democratic values such as tolerance (Delli Carpini and Keeter 1996). Put simply, while one can debate the amount or content of information a person "needs" to know, it is difficult to imagine either an educated student or an engaged citizen who is unfamiliar with the substance, key actors, institutions, and processes of politics. 9

Granting that factual knowledge is a prerequisite for becoming an educated and engaged citizen, we can begin to answer the two-part question posed above. One anticipated outcome of service would be the learning of political facts. There are reasons to expect this. Research suggests that knowledge is both a spur to political interest and involvement and a consequence of such interest and involvement, often offsetting more structural correlates of knowledge such as class, gender, or ethnicity (Delli Carpini and Keeter 1996; Junn 1991; Leighley 1991; Tan 1980). Further, political learning is more likely to occur when the information is directly relevant to one's immediate circumstances and behaviors. It is likely that 10 a service learning experience, properly constituted, could activate interest and demonstrate relevance in ways that would increase a student's receptivity to and retention of factual knowledge. In addition, how much an individual learns about politics is closely tied to the opportunity to learn. Well-designed service learning projects would expose students to a great deal of essential contextual information about substantive issues, key political actors, the law, policy making, political participation (and the barriers thereto), and other fundamentals of the operation of the political system, all of which would increase the likelihood of political learning.

11   All of the above suggests that including service as part of students' educational experience can increase their motivation and opportunity to learn about politics, which in turn could increase the likelihood of their continued engagement in public life. Indirect evidence for this can be found in the *National Assessment of Educational Progress 1998 Report Card for the Nation* (U.S. Department of Education 1999), which found that students who engaged in some form of volunteerism in their community (either through schools or on their own) scored higher on a test of civic knowledge than did those who had not engaged in this kind of activity.

12   The key to success is likely to be found in the nature of the service experience and how well the experience is integrated into the classroom. Effective programs provide opportunities that are likely to lead students to both "bump into" and actively seek out information about politics that is relevant to their activities. At the same time, this specific information will be more easily learned, more likely to be retained, and more likely to be connected to broader kinds of political knowledge if the classroom curriculum is integrated with the service experience. It is in the classroom that specific, often disparate service experiences can be tied to larger issues of government and politics, helping to instill not only factual knowledge but also the motivations and skills likely to increase learning over time.

13   Research is needed on several fronts. What is the impact of service learning on both short- and long-term gains in knowledge? What specific kinds of service experiences and teaching techniques enhance this learning? At what age (or ages) is service learning likely to be most effective? But we already know enough to expect that the combination of experiential and classroom education—when properly designed—can be an effective way to produce citizens who are both educated observers of the political scene and more active participants in public life.

References

Berelson, Bernard. 1952. "Democratic Theory and Public Opinion." *Public Opinion Quarterly* 16: 313–30.

Delli Carpini, Michael X., and Scott Keeter. 1996. *What Americans Know about Politics and Why It Matters*. New Haven: Yale University Press.

Downs, Anthony. 1957. *An Economic Theory of Democracy*. New York: Harper and Row.

Edelman, Murray. 1988. *Constructing the Political Spectacle*. Chicago: University of Chicago Press.

Ehrlich, Thomas. 1999. "Civic Education: Lessons Learned." *PS: Political Science and Politics* 32 (June): 245–50.

Frantzich, Stephen, and Sheilah Mann. 1997. "Experiencing Government: Political Science Internships." In *Experiencing Citizenship: Concepts and Models for Service Learning in Political Science*, ed. Richard Battistoni and William E. Hudson. Washington, DC: American Association for Higher Education.

Ginsberg, Benjamin. 1982. *The Consequences of Consent*. Reading, MA: Addison-Wesley.

Junn, Jane. 1991. "Participation and Political Knowledge." In *Political Participation and American Democracy*, ed. William Crotty. New York: Greenwood Press.

Leighley, Jan. 1991. "Participation as a Stimulus of Political Conceptualization." *Journal of Politics* 53: 198–211.

National Election Studies. 1998. *1998 PostElection Study* <www.umich.edu/~nes/archives/studies.phtml>. Ann Arbor: Center for Political Studies, University of Michigan.

Neuman, Russell. 1986. *The Paradox of Mass Politics: Knowledge and Opinion in the American Electorate*. Cambridge, MA: Harvard University Press.

Niemi, Richard, and Jane Junn. 1999. *Civic Education: What Makes Students Learn*. New Haven: Yale University Press.

Olson, Mancur. 1971. *The Logic of Collective Action: Public Goods and the Theory of Groups*. Cambridge, MA: Harvard University Press.

Tan, Alexis. 1980. "Mass Media Use, Issue Knowledge and Political Involvement." *Public Opinion Quarterly* 44: 241–48.

U.S. Department of Education, National Center for Education Statistics. 1999. "Focus on Civics" <http://nces.ed.gov/nationsreportcard/civics/civics.asp>. *National Assessment of Educational Progress 1998 Report Card for the Nation*. Washington, DC: U.S. Department of Education.

• *Thinking Critically About "What Should Be Learned Through Service Learning?"*

RESPONDING AS A READER

1. Written for an audience of university faculty, this article is part of an ongoing conversation about what should be taught in political science classrooms, and how. Students, although not part of the intended audience, are likely to consider themselves interested onlookers regarding the issues being discussed. How difficult was it for you to catch the drift of the conversation that the article joins about teaching goals and methods? What specific passages in the text helped you understand the main positions that Delli Carpini and Keeter identify? What specific passages were more difficult? Reexamine these passages and try to pinpoint what made them clear or difficult. Some possible sources of difficulty include word choices, complex syntax, and references to unknown people or ideas.

2. What type of conflict is represented by the issue these authors are examining? What is at stake for each side? What might proponents of each

view consider to be threatening; that is, what might they fear losing if the other perspective dominates political science pedagogy?

3. What role do Delli Carpini and Keeter create for themselves as they discuss the differing approaches to teaching political science? Does their interest in explaining how competing models can find common ground appear to stem from a preference for one model over the other, from a desire to resolve a damaging disagreement, or, perhaps, from a neutral, scholarly standpoint? Find places in the text that both support and potentially counter your interpretation.

RESPONDING AS A WRITER

1. To discover whether a journal is "refereed"—that is, whether submitted material must be approved by expert reviewers before it is published—it is usually necessary to examine the editor/publisher's statement of purpose and procedures, known as the masthead. But the fact that a given journal is intended for a scholarly audience is usually readily apparent. What features of this text—beyond the bibliographic references—mark it as a scholarly article?

2. What techniques do the authors use to establish a "common ground" tone in the article? Look for specific aspects of wording, sentence structure, and organization that would likely be different in an article that explicitly advocated for one approach to teaching over another. What additional features contribute to or detract from this tone?

3. Extend your readerly response to the Responding as a Reader question above about Delli Carpini and Keeter's role in the article by using a variation of the two-column technique explained in Chapter 5 for examining a text's ideology. The main binary in the article sets service learning against "more traditional approaches to teaching about government and politics" (paragraph 1). Put each of these two at the head of a column, then list the values and qualities that the authors associate with each. Use plus and minus signs to identify the positive or negative value spin that the authors give the term; if the term is used neutrally, leave it unmarked. Then see if you can identify an opposing term in the other column. As you analyze the lineup of terms, what do you discover about the authors' assertion of common ground between the two pedagogies? Is your initial readerly response confirmed or countered?

Mel White

Open Letter from Mel White to Jerry Falwell

The letter presented here is the first of a series that gay rights leader Mel White (b. 1940) wrote to fundamentalist Christian preacher Jerry Falwell asking him to accept White's homosexuality, and, on a larger scale, the full humanity of all sexual minorities. An evangelical minister for thirty years, White at one time was a major figure on the religious right. As a ghostwriter for leaders such as Oliver North and Pat Robertson, he was sometimes asked to write antigay materials; he even wrote Falwell's autobiography, as the letter here indicates. White's own autobiography, *Stranger at the Gate: To Be Gay and Christian in America* (1994), relates his story of coming to terms with his sexual orientation. His letters to Falwell are posted on the Website of Soulforce, an activist organization founded by White and his partner Gary Nixon. Its principles are evident at the top of the Soulforce page, where a banner flanked by profiles of Martin Luther King Jr. and Mahatma Ghandi reads, "Join our Network of Friends Learning Nonviolence from Gandhi and King Seeking Justice for God's Lesbian, Gay, Bisexual and Transgendered Children."

● *For Your Reading Log*

1. Based on any background knowledge you have about Mel White and Jerry Falwell and the information about rhetorical context supplied above, what do you surmise lies at the root of the conflict between White and Falwell? What do you predict White will say?

2. When you finish reading White's letter, before turning to the analysis questions that follow the letter, return to your log to record your experience of reading the letter. What surprised you? What moved you emotionally? When you finished, how did you feel about White and his ideas?

———————— ● ————————

June 5, 1999

Dear Jerry,

I've been reading your autobiography again. It still moves me. And I'm not just saying that because I wrote it. Strength for the Journey inspires and informs readers because you talk about your failures and not just your success.   1

I'm especially moved by those twenty short pages in Chapter Eleven that describe your transformation from 1964, when you were a staunch segregationist, to 1968, when you baptized the first black member of Thomas Road Baptist Church.   2

3   When I asked you what happened in four short years to change your mind about segregation, you told me stories about the African-Americans you had known and loved from childhood.

4   "It wasn't the Congress, the courts, or the demonstrators," you assured me. "It was Lewis, the shoeshine man, and Lump Jones, the mechanic, and David Brown, the sensitive, loving black man without a wife or family who lived for most of his adult life in the backroom of our large family home in Lynchburg."

5   It was obvious that you really cared about those black men, especially David Brown. "He was a good man," you told me. "He helped my mother with the cooking and cleaning. He cared for me and my brother Gene when we were children. He bathed and fed us both. He was like a member of our family."

6   Then, one day, you and Gene found David Brown lying unconscious and unattended in the lobby of Lynchburg's General Hospital. One portion of his head and face had been crushed from a severe blow with a dull pipe or the barrel of a pistol. He suffered cuts and bruises over his entire body; yet because he was black, he lay dying in that waiting room for forty-eight hours without medical help. You and your brother intervened but your friend was permanently damaged by the racist thugs who left him for dead and by the racist hospital policies that denied him treatment in time.

7   Do you remember how your eyes filled with tears when you told me, "I am sorry that I did not take a stand on behalf of the civil rights of David Brown and my other black friends and acquaintances during those early years."

8   I knew from the sound of your voice, Jerry, that you are still sorry that you did not take a stand for equality in those early years of ministry. Nevertheless, after condemning President Johnson's Civil Rights legislation as an act of "Civil wrong" and after preaching fervently against integration, you had the courage to acknowledge your sinfulness and to end your racist ways.

9   "In all those years," you told me, "it didn't cross my mind that segregation and its consequences for the human family were evil. I was blind to that reality. I didn't realize it then, but if the church had done its job from the beginning of this nation's history, there would have been no need for the civil rights movement."

10   Well said, friend. But now I have to ask you one more time. Has it ever crossed your mind that you might be just as wrong about homosexuality as you were about segregation? Could it be that you are blind to a tragic new reality, that the consequences of your anti-homosexual rhetoric are as evil for the human family as were your sermons against integration? Have you even thought about the possibility that you are ruining lives, destroying families, and causing endless suffering with your false claims that we are "sick and sinful," that we "abuse and recruit children," that we "undermine family values."

11   In the 1950s and 60s, you misused the Bible to support segregation. In the 1990s you are misusing it again, this time to caricature and condemn God's gay and lesbian children. Once you denied black Christians the rights (and the rites) of church membership. Now it's gay, lesbian, bisexual, and transgendered Christians you reject.

For ten years we've been collecting samples of your dangerous and mis- 12
leading rhetoric against homosexuals. We have file drawers filled with your
antigay mass-mailings to raise funds and mobilize volunteers. We have audio
and video collections of your antigay sermons and your antigay radio and television broadcasts. Coupled with your regular appearances on Nightline, Geraldo, and Larry King Live, and your ability to attract media attention (as you did
with Tinky Winky) you have become one of the nation's primary sources of misinformation about homosexuality and homosexuals. You are saying things about
us that are NOT true, terrible things with tragic consequences in our lives and
in the lives of those we love.

Please, Jerry, hear your own words about segregation and apply them to my 13
homosexual sisters and brothers. "I can see from the earliest days of my new faith
in Christ," you told me, "that God had tried to get me to understand and to acknowledge my own racial sinfulness. In Bible College, the Scriptures had been
perfectly clear about the equality of all men and women, about loving all people equally, about fighting injustice, and about obeying God and standing against
the immoral and dehumanizing traditions of man."

The Scriptures are still clear about the equality of all men and women. The 14
Scriptures are still clear about loving all people equally. The Scriptures are still
clear about fighting injustice and standing against the immoral and dehumanizing traditions of man. Why can't you apply THOSE Scriptures to us instead of
the six verses you misuse over and over again to clobber and condemn GLBT
[gay, lesbian, bisexual, and transgendered] people?

For years you supported the "immoral and dehumanizing traditions" used 15
to persecute people of color. Then, finally, the Spirit of Truth set you free. Now,
you are a supporter of "immoral and dehumanizing traditions" used to persecute
homosexuals. Please, Jerry, let the Spirit of Truth set you free again.

Thank you for meeting with me last year to hear the evidence that we are 16
God's children, too, but it was obvious during our meeting (and in your avalanche
of antigay rhetoric that followed) that you were not taking that evidence seriously.

Today, I begin a series of open letters to you reviewing the evidence one more 17
time. Where I am wrong, correct me and I will confess my error. I hope you will
do the same. Let this be a genuine public dialogue. I'm hoping that TOGETHER
we can negotiate an end to your tragic misinformation campaign against us. If
you refuse to hear the evidence again, if you insist on continuing your false and
inflammatory rhetoric, then we will have no other option but to mobilize people of faith across this nation to conduct a serious nonviolent direct action against
your Untruths in the spirit of Gandhi and King.

In this series of open letters, I'm going to do my best to summarize the psy- 18
chological, psychiatric, scientific, medical, historical, personal and biblical evidence that demonstrates clearly that homosexuality is neither a sickness nor a
sin. I'm putting all this material together one more time in the hopes that God
will change your mind and heart about us. In the meantime, you learned that it
wasn't data that changed your mind about segregation. It was knowing its victims and sharing their suffering.

19   How many lesbian or gay people do you know, Jerry? Have you invited closeted gay or lesbian members of your staff and congregation to tell you what it feels like to be ridiculed and condemned endlessly by their pastor? Have you invited closeted gay or lesbian students at Liberty or Liberty graduates to share the pain your endless attacks have caused them? We know at least one gay student who killed himself after being expelled from your university because of his sexual orientation. Your eyes filled with tears when you thought of a black man lying unattended in a Lynchburg hospital. How will you feel when you finally realize that you have been the source of even worse suffering in the lives of those you love and serve.

20   Please, Jerry, read Chapter Eleven of your autobiography once again. After years of blindly and enthusiastically supporting segregation, you heard God's voice, admitted your error, and changed your ways. Now, after years of blindly and enthusiastically supporting anti-homosexual ignorance and bigotry, will you stop long enough to hear God's voice again?

Sincerely,

Mel White

• *Thinking Critically About "Open Letter from Mel White to Jerry Falwell"*

RESPONDING AS A READER

1. Although a reader (especially Falwell) may surmise where the opening paragraphs of the letter are leading, White doesn't directly address his purpose until well into the text. What do you take to be his organizational strategy? What is the common ground that White suggests he and Falwell share?

2. How does White portray the core conflict between Falwell and himself? Would you call this a conflict of goals, needs, or resources? What other description might apply instead? Try to articulate the fundamental questions at issue in this conflict. Using the stasis categories in Table 13.1 (pp. 397–398), decide how you would categorize the question(s) you articulated. Given White's portrayal of Falwell's position, does it seem likely that the two sides would agree about what underlying issue it is that separates them?

3. White's argument works with two types of commonalities and similarities: between White and Falwell, and between Falwell's earlier change of heart and the one White is currently asking him to make. To take a second look at these intuitive and ultimately emotional connections, use the argument analysis terminology (claims, reasons, evidence, and assumptions) from Chapter 13 to work out the line of reasoning White is not only using but proposing to Falwell.

RESPONDING AS A WRITER

1. To analyze White's strategy in this letter, review our description of Rogerian argument (p. 532) as a means of reducing threat between antagonistic opponents. How does White's letter match with the features we describe?

2. How would you describe White's use of *pathos* in this letter? He once knew his intended audience very well. What specific word choices and details of evidence can you pinpoint as reflecting values Falwell can be assumed to hold?

3. As a means of solidifying your understanding of the Rogerian "listening" approach to argument that White's letter exemplifies, prepare a brief digest of its contents and methods according to the pattern for a rhetorical précis described in Chapter 4 (p. 62).

Salim Muwakkil

Aaron the "Wiggah"

Salim Muwakkil (b. 1947) is senior editor of *In These Times*, a nonprofit, left-leaning, political newsmagazine in Chicago, and a contributing columnist with the *Chicago Tribune*. His reflective narrative about the "boundary jumping" of one of his students appeared in a special 1999 campus diversity issue of *CommonQuest: The Magazine of Black-Jewish Relations*, which is published jointly by the American Jewish Committee and Howard University. The seminar Muwakkil writes about, part of the urban studies program of the Associated Colleges of the Midwest, was entitled "Distorted Images: African American Images in the Media."

• *For Your Reading Log*

1. This essay is based on a high school student's explorations of racial and cultural differences. Before you read it, reflect in your log about your own cultural explorations. What experiences have taken you away from your cultural home base either literally or figuratively? What's the furthest you've traveled into another culture? What happened? Freewrite for at least 10 minutes.

2. Now take a look at your experiences from outside yourself. How do you imagine your explorations appeared to people from your home culture? From the new culture?

———————   •   ———————

1   I pegged Aaron as soon as I spotted him on the first day of class: the type of student who pushes limits and tests boundaries. His baggy garb, hulking posture and sullen demeanor were cultural semaphores: Aaron was a white hip hop kid. (The subversive quality of rap music with its tough ghettocentricity has held a strong fascination for certain white youth from its inception.) Aaron wasn't my first white student to display hip hop leanings and, quite frankly, I was happy to see another one—such students seem to share a questing and stimulating intelligence. But Aaron was more committed than his predecessors, a true aficionado.

2   I teach a college seminar in Chicago that employs an experimental pedagogy. Our students, mostly juniors and seniors from liberal arts schools across the country, spend a semester in Chicago where they are immersed in the dynamics of urban life and dip into the city's swirling cultural events. We encourage them to abandon their traditional comfort zones and drift in those currents. Adventurous students like Aaron sometimes get in over their heads. There was the time, for instance, when he referred to the only black seminar member as "my

niggah." Aaron had spent the previous night in a hip hop club and insisted he was using the phrase as a term of endearment, as he had all night. The object of the term was not endeared; I spent most of class time that day quashing a beef between the two. It wasn't easy; after all, Aaron had a point. "My niggah" *is* a term of endearment in most precincts of the "Hip Hop Nation."

Wholesale incorporation of the "n-word" into hip hop culture has sparked 3 furious debate within the African-American community. Some say hip hop has performed an act of etymological alchemy; others question if such a loathsome symbol of racist subordination can ever be a word of a different color.

In one way, Aaron's enthusiastic embrace of the word suggests that a process 4 of transformation already is underway. Those who use the word with malicious intent still may be able to inflict pain, but they're brandishing a weakening weapon. The way the word is being so relentlessly denuded, it's possible that one day it could be totally defused. In fact, the way Aaron saw things, that already has happened. But not many people see things as Aaron.

Although rap music has begun to dominate the record charts, hip hop culture 5 remains outside the mainstream. Whites who embrace hip hop still are regarded as being on the fringe, and it was even more so a few years back during Aaron's Chicago semester. White youth who express affection for African-American cultural forms these days are dismissed as *wiggers,* that is white niggers. Perhaps *wiggah* is more accurate morphologically since *niggah* is the appropriate hip hop pronunciation. These boundary jumpers usually are mocked by both whites and blacks. They are condemned as juvenile poseurs who irreverently toy with alternative identities, "culture vultures" who exploit black creativity for their own cultural sustenance or sometimes as haplessly naive romantics seeking emotional proximity to an oppressed but exoticized caste. Derided as "wannabes" by some blacks and "nigger lovers" by some whites, they are blistered with vitriol from both sides of the racial divide.

Aaron hated the word *wiggah,* but he also knew he exemplified it. His will- 6 ingness to examine the phenomena via his own example offered an opportunity to explore issues of racial identity and the consequence of white supremacy.

Other seminar members immediately said they understood why some 7 whites would hate wiggahs, but why would blacks? Didn't Aaron's open affection for a musical genre so deeply connected to African-American culture actually make him an ally in the struggle to topple racial barriers? Why should he be derided for crossing cultural boundaries? Isn't he courageously bucking powerful incentives by embracing a culture other whites deem beneath them? If racism is a form of ethnocentrism writ large, why are wiggahs like Aaron condemned for decentering ethnicity?

But the immediate assumption that blacks would welcome whites' identity 8 switching derives from a presumption implicit in U.S. culture: "Whiteness" is normative. By condescending to appreciate black culture, wiggahs may be making a humanitarian gesture, but this role of cultural adventurer seeking novelty among the exotics is what so incenses many blacks. These conflicting views kept our seminar consistently lively.

9   These are issues with long and complicated pedigrees. Where does appreciation end and appropriation begin? The boundaries Aaron seeks to ignore were formed from a history of deliberate social practice. Traditional Western Afrophobia and antebellum/Jim Crow exigencies of enforced white supremacy affected all cultural exchanges between enslaved Africans and Euro-Americans for most of this country's formative years; the pattern is deeply etched.

10   The history of those exchanges generally has favored the white majority in that commercial exploitation of African-American cultural capital disproportionately benefited whites. Because of this history, many African Americans look askance at any majority interest in their cultural products lest they be commodified for others' profit or "museumed" for voyeuristic distractions.

11   The view from my class suggests that wiggahs may turn out to be lead scouts in our multicultural future. Although by semester's end the students came to understand African Americans' anxiety about cultural appropriation, they also learned to appreciate Aaron's transgressions of ethnic boundaries. The wiggah and "his niggah" became best of friends, and they remain close today.

• *Thinking Critically About "Aaron the 'Wiggah'"*

RESPONDING AS A READER

1. In what ways, besides the obvious cross-cultural experience, does Aaron's story exemplify various concepts of common ground discussed in this chapter?

2. In what ways does Muwakkil's essay critique concepts of common ground discussed in this chapter?

3. The previous two questions referred to the text "Aaron the 'Wiggah'" in two different ways. When you read the text the first time, which did you read, the story or the essay? How would you describe the primary difference between the two different focuses or emphases we are suggesting by our change in terms?

RESPONDING AS A WRITER

1. Why do you suppose it was easier for Aaron to consider the word "niggah" as having been transformed (paragraph 4) than for his African American classmate to see it that way? How would you explain to a newcomer from a third culture the complex overlapping of positive and negative values in the meanings and uses of both "niggah" and "wiggah"?

2. Seeking to explain the conflicting views of white cultural adventurers that "kept our seminar consistently lively" (paragraph 8), Muwakkil says that African Americans are wary of being "commodified for others' profit or 'museumed' for voyeuristic distractions" (paragraph 10). What does he mean? Using context and the familiar meanings of the nouns "commodity" and "museum," work to develop a nutshell definition of

the verbs-turned-adjectives Muwakkil uses. Then write a one- or two-sentence paraphrase of the point he makes as he tries to explain why wiggahs are derided within the musical culture they admire so.

3. Muwakkil asks where appreciation ends and appropriation begins (paragraph 9). Did your initial reflections in your reading log about adventuring away from your home culture involve movement toward or away from a more dominant culture? What new perspectives on that experience does your reading of both the story and the essay in this text offer you? Is there an overlapping of appreciation and appropriation there? From whose perspective?

Jenny Trinitapoli (Student)

Public Libraries and Internet Filters: Protection Versus Access

Jenny Trinitapoli (b. 1977) received her B.A. in Latin American Studies at Marquette University in 1999. She has studied and traveled extensively in South America, including a year in Chile on a Fulbright Fellowship. Her future plans include a Ph.D. in sociology and a career that combines academic work with international service. She wrote this analysis of the controversy about Internet filters in public libraries in response to the Extending the Conversation assignment at the end of this chapter, finishing it in early 2001 just before leaving the United States to work in Brazil for a year.

● *For Your Reading Log*

1. The case against the 1998 Child Online Protection Act has been described by *New York Times* reporter David Stout as "an agonizing conflict between the cherished right of free speech and the profound duty to watch over children." Which side of that conflict between rights and duties do your basic instincts lead you to favor? Why? As you consider the issue, what questions are sparked in you that Trinitapoli's paper might answer? Freewrite for several minutes.

2. What kind of common ground can you envision for a controversy that is defined this way? Freewrite again for several minutes.

———————— ● ————————

1 The Internet revolution has increased our access to more of the world's information than ever before, but in doing so it has also brought about a number of conflicts and problems regarding the types of material that both children and adults can see and read on their computer screens. Among the most passionate of these issues is the controversy about whether public libraries should install Internet filters that will restrict access to controversial material. The debate has focused primarily on protecting children from cyberporn (Internet pornography) but also addresses whether Websites that detail bomb making, advocate white supremacy, encourage drug use, or promote other controversial subjects should be accessible from public computer terminals. At the heart of this controversy are serious values issues about decency, safety, and freedom of information—and the role of government in guaranteeing all of the above to its citizens. Torn between conflicting allegiances to their communities and to their profession, librarians are finding themselves in the middle of this controversy.

2 Before it adjourned in December 2000, Congress passed a $450 billion spending bill to which it had attached a mandate that schools and libraries must use

Internet filters or lose federal funding for technology (Hopper). This law, the Children's Internet Protection Act (CIPA, Public Law 106-554), is sure to face court challenges from the American Civil Liberties Union (ACLU), the American Library Association (ALA), and other groups concerned about the First Amendment. But the law's supporters contend that it is framed in a way that will withstand challenges this time, particularly because of the tie to federal funding. Two previous efforts at protecting the public, especially children, from indecent or dangerous material on the Internet have floundered in the courts. The Supreme Court ruled the 1996 Communications Decency Act (CDA) unconstitutional, and two federal courts have supported injunctions against enforcement of the 1998 Children's Online Protection Act (COPA) (Stout).

The new law, if it passes constitutional muster, will definitely change the way   3 public libraries provide Internet access. In the spirit of the First Amendment, public libraries have long operated under an open-access policy that provides full access to all material for all patrons, regardless of age. Such policies did not become subject to fervent criticism until libraries began providing open access to the Internet. Groups such as Keep the Internet Decent and Safe (KIDS) and the American Family Association (AFA) have pressured local libraries since the mid-90s to use software filters to block pornography and other material that could be harmful to minors (Blankenhorn). Conscious of First Amendment free speech issues, these groups propose to protect children through "client-side" filters rather than try to regulate Internet expression, which the Supreme Court ruling against the CDA declared to be constitutionally protected. Those who advocated for the filtering rules in CIPA decried the ease with which anyone can reach pornographic sites via computers without filters. Although it is illegal for a store owner to sell even mainstream pornography to a minor, they argued, children can easily access much more explicit material at the public library.

For librarians, the forced choice between installing filters on their public com-   4 puters or giving up federal funds presents a powerful conflict of values. While the well-being of children is certainly a compelling interest, placing filters on public computers directly threatens librarians' professional commitment to intellectual freedom. The ALA has taken a strong stance against filtering and declared its intention to challenge CIPA in court (American Library Association). The librarians' organization holds firmly to its policy of open access to patrons of all ages, applying its philosophy regarding books and nonprint materials to the Internet, which it deems a public forum also deserving of constitutional protection. The ALA argues that while schools, businesses, and other members of the private sector are free to use Internet filters as they see fit, libraries are local government agencies and cannot begin to restrict the exchange of information, regardless of the medium.

Values arguments dominate the other side of the debate as well. Websites   5 sponsored by the AFA and KIDS invoke a community of decency and accuse public libraries of refusing to protect children from the perils of the Internet. The AFA offers a kit that concerned parents can use to mobilize others to insist upon filters at the library. "All across America local citizens are taking back control of their local libraries. YOU CAN TOO!" proclaims their Website (AFA Special Projects). The kit includes a video, a guide for approaching and evaluating local libraries, a model ordinance, sample arguments for rebutting the ALA position, and news articles "exposing the dangers of Internet porn." The values agenda of some pro-filter groups sometimes goes farther. For example, at the Family Friendly Libraries Website, the list of "Basic Documents" includes one entitled "Homosexual Ideology Within the Library System" (Gounaud).

6   Neither side questions the fact that not all material on the Internet is meant for children's viewing; advocates both for and against filters express concern about the ease with which children might be exposed unintentionally to inappropriate sites. The real values issue that divides these advocates has to do with the question of what the proper role of government is in relation to information access and which entities are responsible for keeping kids safe when they use the Internet.

7   The ALA defines the role of a librarian as one of advising and assisting users in selecting information resources, and insists that public librarians, unlike some school librarians, do not serve in loco parentis: "Only parents and legal guardians have the right and responsibility to restrict their children's—and only their own children's—access to any electronic resource" ("Questions and Answers"). Since libraries neither require parental consent for a child to hold a library card nor prohibit children from checking out adult material, restricting children's access to the Internet, the ALA says, would be inconsistent with the rights and responsibilities they already award children. As a Website from the School of Information Studies at Syracuse University points out, advocates for restricted access for minors respond that the analogy to physical materials owned by a given library is faulty because the Internet makes it impossible for librarians any longer to select (and thus control) the materials they make available to their patrons ("Internet Filtering"). Those advocates argue that filters are good because they will enable librarians to regain control of the information they provide.

8   The question of who or what is actually *capable* of keeping kids safe on the Internet may be the bottom line issue. This practical matter is often clouded over by the intensity of the values debate. CIPA mandates a technological solution: filters. But the inaccuracy of filters, along with their vulnerability to hacking, is one of the chief practical objections raised by librarians and other opponents of filtering. While it is definitely feasible that a child might inadvertently stumble upon a pornographic Website while using an unfiltered library computer, or might accidentally see pornographic images on another patron's unfiltered screen, groups such as the ACLU and ALA are deeply concerned that it's just as likely, perhaps more likely, that software filters will block constitutionally protected material. "No filtering software successfully differentiates constitutionally protected speech from illegal speech on the Internet," the ALA said in its press release announcing its plans to challenge CIPA (American Library Association). Software filters designed to block pornography often block important information on AIDS prevention, for example, and have prohibited users from viewing sites about Mars exploration or chicken breasts while failing to catch more subtly explicit vocabulary such as "Dolly Does Dave" (Minow).

9   Peacefire, a group whose motto is "Open Access for the Net Generation," regularly publicizes lists of nonpornographic sites that have been filtered out by one filtering software product or another (Haselton). Perhaps of even greater

practical significance is the fact that in response to the passage of CIPA, Peace-fire has posted on its Website software that, it says, "can disable all popular Win-dows censorware" ("Peacefire.exe").

In the October 2000 report of Congress's COPA Commission, these practical 10 matters trumped all the competing values issues. The commission specifically recommended against a federal mandate for library filtering, having concluded that "no single technology or method will effectively protect children from harm-ful material online" ("Executive Summary"). When the report was released to the press, panel members acknowledged that they had in effect come down on the side of free speech because existing technology cannot distinguish between con-stitutionally protected and unprotected text and images (Johnson). The *San Fran-cisco Chronicle* reported that at a hearing last summer the founder of Peacefire, Bennett Haselton, had shown the panel filtering software that blocked part of COPA's own Website (Kirby).

Even though Congress has ignored the COPA commission's clear opposition 11 to a filtering law, the group's most lasting contribution may come from the com-mon ground implicit in its validation of concerns on both sides of the contro-versy. The commission's primary recommendation is that government and business together undertake a major education campaign to promote consumer awareness of methods for keeping children safe online ("Recommendations"). Other recommendations call for

- promotion of acceptable use policies by government and industry that would be voluntarily implemented by public institutions
- establishment of an independent, nongovernmental facility devoted to test-ing child protection technologies and disseminating findings to the public
- industry commitment to improving child protection mechanisms and making them available online
- an improved system for labeling, rating, and identifying content of both old and new media
- government encouragement of technology for improving child safety on the Internet
- more aggressive law enforcement against violations of federal and state obscenity laws

By affirming First Amendment rights as well as parental fears, by warning 12 the public about the limitations of filtering software, and by calling for both im-proved technology and wider discussion about Internet safety, these recommen-dations make clear the broad area of shared concerns on both sides of the controversy. These recommendations are valuable regardless of eventual court findings about the constitutionality of CIPA because the difficulties of inefficient technology, polarized positions, and parent-child disagreements will remain. Li-braries and librarians should be at the center of local conversations and educa-tion campaigns about Internet safety. Such conversations would add depth and perspective to the cause of protecting children on the Internet and might also fa-cilitate greater understanding not just of the values that separate filter proponents and opponents, but the practical challenges and core values that they share. Perhaps before long the public library will once again be just one space out of many where children decide whether they will obey established parental limits.

Works Cited

AFA Special Projects. "Library Internet Filtering Packet." Home page. American Family Association. 19 Jan. 2001 <http://www.afa.net/lif/packet.asp>.

American Library Association. "American Library Association Votes to Challenge CIPA." Home page. 18 Jan. 2001. 19 Jan. 2001 <http://www.ala.org/news/v7n1/cipa.html>.

Blankenhorn, Dana. "Filtering." Almanac of Internet Politics. Policy.Com. 27 Nov. 2000 <http://www.policy.com/reports/blankenhorn/filter.html>.

COPA Commission. "Executive Summary." Final Report. Home page. 20 Oct. 2000. Internet Caucus Advisory Committee. 4 Dec. 2000 <http://www.copacommission.org/report/executivesummary.shtml>.

---. "Recommendations." Final Report. Home page. 20 Oct. 2000. Internet Caucus Advisory Committee. 4 Dec. 2000 <http://www.copacommission.org/report/recommendations.shtml>.

Gounaud, Karen Jo. "Homosexual Ideology within the Library System." Family Friendly Libraries. 26 July 2000. 27 Nov. 2000 <http://www.fflibraries.org/>.

Haselton, Bennett. "Amnesty Intercepted: Global Human Rights Groups Blocked by Web Censoring Software." Peacefire. 12 Dec. 2000. 21 Dec. 2000 <http://www.peacefire.org/amnesty-intercepted/>.

Hopper, D. Ian. "New Law Will Require Use of Internet Filters." Milwaukee Journal Sentinel 20 Dec. 2000, final ed.: 6A.

"Internet Filtering: What It's All About." Librarians in the 21st Century. 8 May 2000. School of Information Studies, Syracuse University. 21 Dec. 2000 <http://istweb.syr.edu/21stcenlib/>.

Johnson, Carrie. "Panel Doesn't Push School Porn Filters." Washington Post 21 Oct. 2000, final ed.: E1. Lexis-Nexis Academic Universe. Reed-Elsevier. Memorial Lib., Marquette Univ. 3 Dec. 2000 <http://web.lexis-nexis.com/universe>.

KIDS: Keep the Internet Decent and Safe. Home page. 4 Apr. 1999. 10 Dec. 2000 <http://www.garlic.com/~robthrr/KIDS/>.

Kirby, Carrie. "Net Filters Should Be a Choice, Not Requirement, Panel Says." San Francisco Chronicle 20 Oct. 2000, final ed.: B2. Lexis-Nexis Academic Universe. Reed-Elsevier. Memorial Lib., Marquette Univ. 3 Dec. 2000 <http://web.lexis-nexis.com/universe>.

Minow, Mary. "Filters and the Public Library: A Legal and Policy Analysis." First Monday 2.12: Dec. 1997. University of Illinois at Chicago Library. 10 Dec. 2000 <http://www.firstmonday.dk/issues/issue2_12/minow/>.

"Peacefire.exe." Peacefire.Org 21 Dec. 2000 <http://peacefire.org/bypass/>.

"Questions and Answers: Access to Electronic Information, Services, and Networks: An Interpretation of the Library Bill of Rights." American Library Association. 9 Jan. 2001. 19 Jan. 2001 <http://www.ala.org/alaorg/oif/oif_q&a.html>.

Stout, David. "U.S. Court Rules Against Online Pornography Law." <u>New York Times</u> 23 June 2000, late ed.: A16. <u>Lexis-Nexis Academic Universe</u>. Reed Elsevier. Memorial Lib., Marquette Univ. 11 Dec. 2000 <http://web.lexis-nexis.com/universe>.

● *Thinking Critically About "Public Libraries and Internet Filters"*

RESPONDING AS A READER

1. How similar were Trinitapoli's ideas about common ground between the conflicting positions on filtering to the ideas you wrote about in your reading log? Did you find her suggestions convincing?
2. What seemed to be Trinitapoli's assumptions about her audience's attitude toward and engagement with the controversy over Internet filters at public libraries? Did you feel that you were part of her intended audience?
3. How do you imagine a member of Congress who supported the Children's Internet Protection Act would respond to this text? A member of Family Friendly Libraries? A librarian at your local public library? A teenager whose parents have installed filtering software at home? Bennett Haselton of Peacefire?

RESPONDING AS A WRITER

1. Where do you see Trinitapoli making specific moves that seem designed to demonstrate her appreciation of different people's perspectives about this controversy? Do you find this effort credible? Why or why not? What could have been omitted or added to increase the paper's effectiveness?
2. Writing that seeks to explain and mediate among conflicting viewpoints can be extremely difficult to organize. Use the descriptive outline technique described in Chapter 4 (p. 58) to pinpoint the function of each paragraph in this text in terms of what it "does" and "says." Describe the writer's organizational strategy as briefly as you can.
3. How successful has Trinitapoli been in meeting the goals specified in the Extending the Conversation assignment at the end of this chapter? If you were in a peer review group together, what suggestions or advice would you want to give her for revising this draft?

Writing to Seek Common Ground

This chapter's texts have suggested a number of approaches through which differences can be explored and, although perhaps not resolved, understood more clearly. The assignments here offer you several different ways to try out these ideas in your own writing in relation to difficult issues that hold special significance for you.

MOVING TOWARD COMMON GROUND

Write an argument essay that seeks common ground between you and a resistant audience that opposes your view. Your essay should devote as much of its space to expressing an understanding of opposition views as it does to explaining and advocating your own position. The following steps will help you develop your essay.

- Choose a controversial issue that is important to you.
- As you explore ideas for your argument, begin by believing and then doubting your own position. Apply Sidney Callahan's Rule Number 4 and "admit the price of following your own position" (p. 536).
- Consider why those who oppose you find your position threatening. How can you alleviate that sense of threat?
- Do research as necessary to understand the central issues for people who hold opposing views on this matter—both their surface claims and their underlying values.
- Lay out as extensively as possible the area of shared goals and values (common ground) between your view and one that opposes it.
- Compose a delayed-thesis argument that clearly presents the commonality between you and the opposing position yet advocates persuasively for your views.

EXAMINING RHETORICAL STRATEGIES

Without taking sides, explain the claims and strategies of two representative opposing arguments in a public controversy of your choice. Your goal is to help readers understand both the underlying issues and the way that advocates for each side make their cases. From a neutral vantage point, use everything you know about rhetorical reading to analyze two representative arguments and explain to your readers answers to the following questions:

1. What is the central question at issue?
2. Is it the same question for both sides?
3. What kinds of evidence, reasoning, and assumptions do the writers use to make their cases?

4. What other qualities of tone, style, audience engagement, and appeals to authority characterize the arguments?
5. What common ground can you find between the two sides?
6. What basic disagreements make this matter so difficult to resolve?

EXTENDING THE CONVERSATION

We invite you to look for and assert common ground. Focus on a difficult issue familiar to you in which you see a greater possibility for agreement, if not complete resolution, than those engaged in argument about the issue apparently do. Examine several different published positions regarding the matter, then enter the conversation with your own point of view. Your goals for this assignment are as follows:

- Present background as necessary to contextualize the issue and various people's positions regarding it.
- Explain to your own readers what you understand to be the difficult issues at the heart of the controversy.
- Use argument analysis and the description of stasis categories in Chapter 13 (p. 397) to describe how the different parties approach the controversy.
- Point to common ground that exists within the conflicting positions.
- Recommend some steps that might bring about a resolution or at least a lessening of intensity or negative feelings.

You may wish to work with one of the difficult issues suggested in this chapter's readings, with a matter raised by other readings in this book, or with readings relevant to an issue currently under discussion in your local community or in the national media. As with any text seeking to draw others to common ground, your main points should assert ideas about how the various sides can recognize and perhaps act upon commonalities in their positions—not the supremacy of one side over the other.

A P P E N D I X

———————————— ● ————————————

Building a Citation

roviding accurate, conventionally formatted documentation of your sources will enhance your own authority as well as give your readers essential information for follow-up. In the examples below we use Modern Language Association (MLA) style to provide basic models for the citations on your works cited lists. For guidance about creating in-text citations that refer readers to these lists, see Chapter 8. If you don't find a category here that matches the type of source you need to cite, consult the current edition of the *MLA Handbook for Writers of Research Papers*, which is almost certainly available in your library's reference section, or go to the online source for MLA style that your library or writing center recommends.

Basic Guidelines for Works Cited Lists

These important guidelines will help you format your works cited lists according to MLA citation conventions. Remember: your works cited list is an integral part of your paper. It conveys to your readers both the reliability of your sources and the care with which you have approached your writing project. In other words, the quality of your list testifies to your own credibility as an author.

1. Your list of works cited should begin on a separate page at the end of your paper with the title "Works Cited" centered at the top. Include in this list only materials you refer to in the body of your paper. Use double spacing throughout.

2. Arrange all citations alphabetically according to the author's last name. If the source lists no author, begin with the title, fitting it into the overall alphabetical order. When alphabetizing, ignore *the, a,* and *an* in article and book titles and drop them from periodicals titles; for example, *The New Yorker* should be listed as *New Yorker.*

3. Use the "hanging indent" format illustrated in the model citations so that the first line of each citation starts at the left margin and subsequent lines are indented a half inch. This format helps readers find the word(s) from an in-text citation quickly.

To avoid omissions and confusion, we urge you to add citations to your works cited lists *while you are composing and integrating sources into your paper.* An easy way to do this is to keep open a separate computer file for a given paper's works cited list and add to it as you add outside material to your paper. Working this way will help you avoid last-minute scrambles to recover missing bibliographic information. As part of final proofreading, check to be sure that each of your in-text citations matches a full citation on your works cited list. This process will reveal not only any citations missing from the list but also any in-text citations that were accidentally deleted during revision. If you discover citations listed during your early drafting that are no longer relevant to your final paper, just delete them.

Citation Formats for Books

INFORMATION TO INCLUDE

The MLA citation format for books presents information in the following sequence. Items should be separated by periods.

1. **Author,** last name first
   • If no author's name appears, begin with the title.

2. **Title of work**
   • In MLA style, capitalize all words of a title (except *the, a,* and short prepositions) even if they are not capitalized in the original.
   • Titles of books are underlined; titles of separate works collected within books are placed in quotation marks. Note: in our sample citations we follow the MLA style for research papers and scholarly manuscripts by using underlining instead of italics for the titles of books, periodicals, and Web pages. We recommend that you do the same. Underlining is easier to see than italics, which vary greatly in different fonts and tend to be more difficult to read. In academic work submitted for a grade, underlining will provide the clearest format for your readers. If you wish to use italics, check with your instructor.

3. **Publication information as follows (note punctuation):** City, State: Publisher, date. For example: Carbondale, IL: Southern Illinois UP, 1991.
   - Shorten publishers' names—e.g., shorten "Random House, Inc." to "Random" and "University Press" to "UP."
   - Consult the book's title and copyright pages for the place of publication. If the city is well known (e.g., Philadelphia), you don't need to list the state. Otherwise, use the postal code abbreviation for the state (e.g., Portsmouth, NH).

4. **For a specific work within a book, the first and last page numbers.**
   For example, pages for a chapter or article that begins on page 350 and ends on page 356 would noted this way: 350-356.

MODEL CITATIONS

Book by One Author
Radway, Janice A. <u>Reading the Romance: Women, Patriarchy, and Popular Literature</u>. Chapel Hill: U North Carolina P, 1984.

Book with Two or Three Authors
Brooke, Robert, Ruth Mirtz, and Rick Evans. <u>Small Groups in Writing Workshops: Invitations to a Writer's Life</u>. Urbana, IL: NCTE, 1994.
Lutz, Catherine A., and Jane L. Collins. <u>Reading National Geographic</u>. Chicago: U of Chicago P, 1993.
   - Note the commas after the first and second authors' names.
   - Use regular name order for the second and subsequent authors.

Using "et al." for More Than Three Authors
In MLA style, when a book or article has more than three authors, you may list all names or you may use "et al." ("and others") after the first name.

Mabey, Nick, Stephen Hall, Clare Smith, and Sujata Gupta. <u>Argument in the Greenhouse: The International Economics of Controlling Global Warming</u>. London: Routledge, 1997.
OR
Mabey, Nick, et al. <u>Argument in the Greenhouse: The International Economics of Controlling Global Warming</u>. London: Routledge, 1997.

Two or More Works by the Same Author
Alphabetize first by the author's name, then by the works' titles. On the second and any subsequent entries, instead of the author's name, type three hyphens, a period, and then the title.

Quindlen, Anna. <u>How Reading Changed My Life</u>. New York: Ballantine, 1998.
---. "It's the Cult of Personality." <u>Newsweek</u>. 14 Aug. 2000: 68.
---. <u>One True Thing</u>. New York: Random, 1994.

Book with Corporate Author

In this sense "corporate" means authored by any group where individual members are not identified.

Consumer Reports Books Editors. <u>New Car Buying Guide 2000</u>. Tulsa, OK: Educational Development Corp., 2000.

Hayward Gallery. <u>Rhapsodies in Black: Art of the Harlem Renaissance</u>. Berkeley: U of California P, 1997.

Book with No Author Listed

<u>Strong Hearts: Native American Visions and Voices</u>. New York: Aperture, 1995.

Translated Book

Aristotle. <u>On Rhetoric: A Theory of Civic Discourse</u>. Trans. George A. Kennedy. New York: Oxford UP, 1991.

If your discussion primarily concerns the translation, begin the citation with the translator's name, followed by "trans." Include the author after the title, preceded by the word "by."

Kennedy, George A., trans. <u>On Rhetoric: A Theory of Civic Discourse</u>. By Aristotle. New York: Oxford UP, 1991.

Edited Collection

Citations for these follow the book models above, with the label "ed." or "eds." inserted after the last editor's name.

Ward, Harold, ed. <u>Acting Locally: Concepts and Models for Service-Learning in Environmental Studies</u>. Washington, DC: American Association for Higher Education, 1999.

Severino, Carol, Juan C. Guerra, and Johnnella E. Butler, eds. <u>Writing in Multicultural Settings</u>. New York: MLA, 1997.

Selection from an Edited Collection

Present inclusive (i.e., first and last) page numbers for the selection as a separate item after the date.

Christian-Smith, Linda K. "Voices of Resistance: Young Women Readers of Romantic Fiction." <u>Beyond Silenced Voices: Class, Race, and Gender in U.S. Schools</u>. Ed. Lois Weis and Michelle Fine. New York: State U of New York P, 1993. 169-89.

"The Dream of the Rood." <u>Longman Anthology of British Literature</u>. Ed. David Damrosch, et al. Vol. 1A. New York: Longman, 1999. 120-24.

Welch, James. "Christmas Comes to Moccasin Flat." <u>A Geography of Poets</u>. Ed. Edward Field. New York: Bantam, 1979. 43.

If the selection is from a book that collects work by one author, use the same format, including an editor only if relevant.

Hribal, C. J. "Consent." <u>The Clouds in Memphis</u>. Amherst, MA: U of Massachusetts P, 2000. 55-67.

Williams, William Carlos. "The Red Wheelbarrow." <u>Selected Poems</u>. New York: New Directions, 1968. 30.

Work Reprinted in an Anthology

When information about the original publication date and venue are important but your page references are from a reprinted version, use the following format to provide publication information for both versions.

Beck, Evelyn Torton. "From 'Kike' to 'JAP': How Misogyny, Anti-Semitism, and Racism Construct the 'Jewish American Princess.'" <u>Sojourner</u> Sept. 1988: 18-26. Rpt. in <u>Race, Class, and Gender</u>. Ed. Margaret L. Andersen and Patricia Hill Collins. 2nd ed. Belmont, CA: Wadsworth, 1995. 87-95.

Introduction, Preface, Foreword, or Afterword of a Book

Hirsch, Edward. Introduction. <u>Transforming Vision: Writers on Art</u>. By Art Institute of Chicago. Boston: Little, 1994. 9-11.

Second or Later Edition of a Book

A book without an edition notation is probably a first edition. If a later edition is noted, include it between the title and the publication information because content and page numbers have probably changed since the first edition.

White, Edward M. <u>Teaching and Assessing Writing</u>. 2nd ed. San Francisco: Jossey-Bass, 1994.

Multivolume Works

Volume information comes after any edition note and immediately before publication information. List only the volumes you discuss or use.

Citation for an Entire Work

Baym, Nina, et al., eds. <u>Norton Anthology of American Literature</u>. 5th ed. 2 vols. New York: Norton, 1999.

Citation for Material Within a Volume

Melville, Herman. "Bartleby the Scrivener." <u>Norton Anthology of American Literature</u>. Ed. Nina Baym et al. 5th ed. Vol. 1. New York: Norton, 1999. 2330-55.

Book from a Series

If the title page or page preceding it indicates that the book is part of a series, place the series name without underlining or quotation marks then the series number immediately before the publication information.

Folsom, Marcia McClintock, ed. <u>Approaches to Teaching Austen's</u> Pride and Prejudice. Approaches to Teaching World Lit. 45. New York: MLA, 1993.

Special Considerations When Titles Include Titles

To indicate that a book title includes the title of another book, omit the underlining on the included title.

Sten, Christopher. <u>Sounding the Whale:</u> Moby-Dick <u>as Epic Novel</u>. Kent, OH: Kent State UP, 1996.

To indicate a short story or essay title within a book title, include the quotation marks for the shorter title as well as the underlining for the book title.

Dock, Julie Bates, ed. <u>Charlotte Perkins Gilman's "The Yellow Wall-Paper" and the History of Its Publication and Reception: A Critical Edition and Documentary Casebook</u>. University Park, PA: Pennsylvania State UP, 1998.

Reference Books

Cite material from reference books as you would work in a collection, but omit the editor's name. If the article is signed, begin with the author's name. If contents are arranged alphabetically, you may omit volume and page. If the reference work is well known and appears in frequent editions, full publication information is not needed.

Material from Familiar Source Arranged Alphabetically

"Rembrandt." <u>The New Encyclopedia Britannica</u>. 1998.

Material from Less Familiar Source Arranged Alphabetically

Blasing, Mutlu Konuk. "Poetry: Since 1960." <u>Benet's Reader's Encyclopedia of American Literature</u>. New York: Harper, 1991.
"Hegira." <u>Merriam-Webster's Dictionary of Allusions</u>. Springfield, MA: Merriam-Webster, 1999.

Material from Less Familiar Source with Multiple Sections

"Kentucky Living." <u>Magazines for Libraries</u>. New Providence, NJ: Bowker, 2000. 382.

Specific Dictionary Definition Among Several

"Story." Def. 9. <u>Random House Dictionary of the English Language</u>. 2nd ed. 1987.

Cross References

When you cite several works from the same collection, avoid repetition and save space by using one main entry to which citations for specific works within it can refer. Note the absence of punctuation between the editor's name and the page numbers.

Atwan, Robert. Foreword. Hoagland ix-xii.
Hoagland, Edward, ed. <u>The Best American Essays 1999</u>. Boston: Houghton Mifflin, 1999.
---. "Introduction: Writers Afoot." Hoagland xiii-xix.
Metcalf, Ben. "American Heartworm." Hoagland 173-84.

Citation Formats for Articles in Periodicals

Periodicals are increasingly making full text of their contents available in both paper and electronic form through library databases or subscription services and through their own Websites. As a result, students frequently have difficulty determining how to cite periodicals in a manner that indicates how they retrieved them. This section of the appendix presents model citations for periodicals published on paper. Several of these model citations demonstrate how to include information about electronic retrieval of the print item. The next section of the appendix will present models for citing materials published *only* on the World Wide Web.

To help you follow the list of information items to include when citing periodical material, we first present three generic MLA citation models for materials from print periodicals. These models vary only in terms of how the material was accessed.

Basic Model for Print Article Retrieved in Print

Author. "Article Title." <u>Periodical Title</u> date: pages.

As you will see in the examples we provide below, the format for publication information that comes after the title varies according to the type of periodical cited; furthermore, additional information may be required for special types of articles.

When the material from the print periodical is accessed electronically, the information about electronic access is added *after* full information about print publication, including original page numbers.

Basic Model for Print Article Retrieved Through Database

Author. "Article Title." <u>Periodical Title</u> date: pages. <u>Database Name</u>. Database Company. Library, Place. Date accessed <http://url.fordatabasemainpage.com>.

When the material is accessed electronically not from a library database service but directly from a magazine, newspaper, or wire service Website, the citation moves directly from the print page numbers to the date accessed and Web address.

Basic Model for Print Article Retrieved Through Periodical's Website

Author. "Article Title." <u>Periodical Title</u> date: pages. Date accessed <http://url.periodicalsite.com/otherdetails/html>.

INFORMATION TO INCLUDE

The MLA citation structure for print periodicals (magazines, journals, newspapers, and newsletters) presents information in the following sequence:

1. **Author,** last name first
   - If no author's name appears, begin with the title.

2. Title of the work (e.g., essay, article, story, poem) in quotation marks

- MLA format calls for capitalizing all words of a title except *the*, *a*, and short prepositions even if they are not capitalized in the original headline.

3. Title of the periodical, underlined

4. Publication date, with volume, issue, or edition as relevant

- Omit punctuation between the periodical title and date; insert a colon between date and page numbers.
- Provide volume numbers only for scholarly journals.
- Include issue numbers only for scholarly journals that paginate each issue separately or that list only issue numbers.
- Include edition information in newspaper citations when available.

5. Page number(s)

- If the article appears on consecutive pages, provide both the first and last page number.
- If the pages are not consecutive, provide only the first page number followed by a plus sign. *Note:* When you consult only the electronic version of a print text, you may not have sufficient information to provide a page number to use in an in-text citation for a quote or paraphrase; *nevertheless, the citation in your works cited list must provide accurate pagination information for the print version* in one of these two formats.

6. Electronic retrieval information as relevant

If you retrieved the material electronically from a library database or subscription service, include the following sequence of information items immediately after the page number(s) for the print version. Note that each of the first three items is followed by a period.

Name of Database. Underline this.

Name of Database Company (if different from database).

Library, University (or municipality if public library). Can be abbreviated.

Date accessed

<Web address for database home page>. This is known as the Uniform Resource Locator or URL.

If you retrieved the material directly from the publication's Website, skip the three items about the database and include only the date accessed and specific URL for the article.

- Never use punctuation between the date you accessed the material and the URL. The effect is an implicit sentence: "on X date I found this material at the following address."
- Be sure to use angle brackets on URLs and include a period at the end of the citation. If a URL must continue to a second line, break it only after a slash mark.

MODEL CITATIONS

Work from Scholarly Journal with Continuous Pagination Through Each Volume

Original Paper Version

Krabill, William, et al. "Greenland Ice Sheet: High-Elevation Balance and Peripheral Thinning." Science 289 (2000): 428-30.

Electronic Version Retrieved Through Library Database

Krabill, William, et al. "Greenland Ice Sheet: High-Elevation Balance and Peripheral Thinning." Science 289 (2000): 428-30. Academic Search Elite. EBSCO Publishing. Memorial Lib., Marquette Univ. 15 Sept. 2000 <http://www.epnet.com/>.

Work from Scholarly Journal That Begins with Page One in Each Issue

Pivnick, Janet. "A Piece of Forgotten Song: Recalling Environmental Connections." Holistic Education Review 10.4 (1997): 58–63.

- The numbers between the periodical title and date indicate the volume (10) and issue (4).

Magazine Articles

Published Weekly (Paper Copy)

Woodard, Colin. "The Great Melt: Is It Normal, or the Result of Global Warming?" Chronicle of Higher Education 14 July 2000: A20-21.

- The letter "A" is included with the page number because this publication, like many newspapers, has more than one section, each with separate page numbers.

Published Monthly (Full Text Accessed Through Library Database)

Tyler, Varro E. "Medicinal Teas: What Works, What Doesn't." Prevention Apr. 2000: 127+. Proquest Research Library. Bell & Howell. Memorial Lib., Marquette Univ. 10 Sept. 2000 <http://proquest.umi.com/>.

Published Monthly (Full Text Accessed Through Magazine or Journal Website)

Barcott, Bruce. "Blow-Up." Outside Online Feb. 1999: 70+. 16 Sept. 2000 <http://www.outsidemag.com/magazine/0299/9902dam.html>.

Published Quarterly (Paper Copy)

Stephenson, Sam. "Nights of Incandescence." Doubletake Fall 1999: 46-51.

Newspaper Articles

Special Considerations When Citing Newspaper Articles

- Give the paper's name as it appears in the masthead, but omit introductory *the.*

- If the city is not included in the name, add it in square brackets after the name: e.g., *Times-Picayune* [New Orleans].
- Note the format for dates: day Month year.
- If an edition is listed, include it after the date because different editions of the same issue include different material and pagination.
- If sections of the paper are paginated separately, include identifying letters or labels (e.g., Sun. Mag.).

Article Accessed from Paper Copy of Newspaper

Claiborne, William. "Iowa Looks Abroad for Workers." <u>Washington Post</u> 16 Sept. 2000, final ed.: A3.

Article Accessed via Library Database

Claiborne, William. "Iowa Looks Abroad for Workers." <u>Washington Post</u> 16 Sept. 2000, final ed.: A3. <u>Lexis-Nexis Academic Universe</u>. Reed Elsevier. Memorial Lib., Marquette Univ. 13 Oct. 2000 <http://web.lexis-nexis.com/universe>.

Article Accessed Through Newspaper or Wire Service Website

Claiborne, William. "Iowa Looks Abroad for Workers." <u>Washington Post</u> 16 Sept. 2000, final ed.: A3. 13 Oct. 2000 <http://www.newslibrary.com/nlsearch.asp>.

Goldberg, Randi. "Man Gets 2-15 Years for Letting Gun Fall into Boy's Hands." <u>Associated Press Archive</u> 11 Sept. 2000. 19 Sept. 2000 <http://wire.ap.org/>.

Pitts, Leonard, Jr. "It's Worth Sharing Pain of Our Heroes in Raw Films." <u>Miami Herald</u> 3 July 1999, final ed.: 1E. 8 July 1999 <http://www.herald.com/newslibrary/>.

Work Without a Listed Author

Begin with the title. Do not use the word "anonymous" that appears in some databases.

"Can Antioxidants Save Your Life?" <u>UC Berkeley Wellness Letter</u> July 1998: 4-5.

Editorial or Opinion Piece

"Soft Money Travesties." Editorial. <u>New York Times</u> 16 Sept. 2000, natl. ed.: A26.

Letter to the Editor

Use the label "letter" after the title, if a title is given. Otherwise, the word "letter" follows the author's name.

Clark, Diana Shaw. "Money and Horses." Letter. <u>New Yorker</u> 18 Sept. 2000: 18.

Review

Include title of the work reviewed (film, book, play, etc.) with the label, "Rev. of," then the author of the reviewed work, as relevant.

Denby, David. "Four Kings." Rev. of <u>The Original Kings of Comedy</u>. <u>New Yorker</u> 4 Sept. 2000: 88-89. [film review]

If the review is untitled, reviewer's name is followed directly by the "Rev. of" label. Note the comma between the title of the reviewed work and "by + author."

Grimm, Nancy Maloney. Rev. of <u>Between Talk and Teaching: Reconsidering the Writing Conference</u>, by Laurel Johnson Black. <u>College Composition and Communication</u> 52 (2000): 156-59. [book review]

If the review is untitled and unsigned, begin with "Rev. of" and alphabetize the entry under the work's title. The following citation would be alphabetized under "J."

Rev. of <u>The Jerusalem Syndrome</u>. <u>New Yorker</u> 4 Sept. 2000: 8+. [theater review]

Citation Formats for World Wide Web Sources

INFORMATION TO INCLUDE

The citation models listed here will help you construct citations for materials you access directly through a Website. Unlike the citations for periodicals accessed through a database, these citations must present the specific URL for the material used. Copy and paste this information from your browser window. Each information element in the citation should be followed by a period *except* the date of access. In that case, linking the date with the URL indicates "found on this date at this address."

1. **Author,** last name first or organization name for corporate authors
   - If no author's name appears, begin with the title.
   - Your decision about whether to list a corporate author as "author" or "sponsor" will depend upon the situation, other details available for the citation, and the point you are making in your text since the word that begins the entry for the full citation is what you put in parentheses for your in-text citation. As illustration of different possibilities, contrast the three citations listed below under "Material from an Organization Site" or the Trek Bicycle and Harley-Davidson examples under "Material from a Commercial Site."

2. **Title of the page or document used**
   - Use quotation marks with titles of a distinct shorter work (e.g., a press release, article, policy document, story, poem) within a larger site; use underlining for titles of books or periodicals.
   - For a posting to an online discussion, use the subject line as a title (enclosed in quotation marks) and add the phrase "Online posting."

3. **Name of an editor, translator, or compiler if not already listed**

4. **Information about print publication of the material, if relevant**
   - Follow the guidelines for books and periodicals in the previous section; no punctuation is used between the periodical title and date of publication.

5. **Title of the overall site, underlined**
   - If no title is available—frequently the case at personal and corporate sites—use the phrase "Home page" without underlining.

6. **Name of the editor of the site or project, if available and not already listed**

7. **An electronic journal's volume and issue numbers or any identifying numbers regarding version or edition**

8. **Date of publication online, last update, or individual posting**
   - This is often available via the "page information" button on your browser even when it is not given on the page.

9. **For an individual online posting, the name of the discussion list**

10. **For material with numbered pages or paragraphs, the inclusive numbers (for material within a larger source) or total number (if you are citing the entire source)**
    - If your source does not number pages or paragraphs, do not include any numbers because browsers, monitors, and printers vary in how they present text breaks.

11. **Name of site sponsor if not already listed**

12. **Date when you accessed the source**
    - This information is crucial because Web postings change rapidly and sites may no longer be accessible.

13. **URL for the specific page(s) you refer to, enclosed in angle brackets, followed by a final period**
    - When you need to "wrap" a Web address to a second line, break it only after a slash mark.
    - You may need to adjust the "auto correct" commands on your word processor so that it doesn't turn the address into a hyperlink.
      Note: These format guidelines for Web sources were developed by the MLA primarily for scholarly research and may not always fit the material you need to cite. Our examples demonstrate how the guidelines can be used to provide the range of information elements that will best identify sites sponsored by corporations, nonprofits, government organizations, broadcast entities, periodicals with their own Website, and so forth. The various information elements listed will not all be relevant (or available) for every Website. The first model citation below, for example, provides information about items 2, 5, 12, and 13 only, but that is sufficient for a reader to understand the source's authority and to locate it if necessary. Include as much information as you can, remembering that names of site sponsors and dates of posting and access will

provide readers with crucial information about a source's reliability. If you need help, consult a librarian or your campus writing center.

MODEL CITATIONS

Online Reference Database

"Kempe, Margery." Encyclopaedia Britannica Online. 13 Oct. 2000 <http://www.eb.com:180/bol/topic?eu=46106&sctn=1>.

Online Scholarly Project

"Yoknapatawpha County." William Faulkner on the Web. John B. Padgett. 31 May 2000. University of Mississippi. 13 Oct. 2000 <http://www.mcsr.olemiss.edu/ ~egjbp/faulkner/glossaryy.html#Yoknapatawpha>.

E-Book

Bok, Edward William. The Americanization of Edward Bok. New York: Scribner's, 1921. Bartleby.Com. 5 Oct. 2000. 13 Oct. 2000 <http://www.bartleby.com/ 197/>.

Article from a Scholarly E-Journal

Mazer, Emmanuel, Juan Manuel Ahuactzin, and Pierre Bessière. "The Ariadne's Clew Algorithm." Journal of Artificial Intelligence Research 9 (1998): 295-316. 10 Nov. 1998. 13 Oct. 2000 <http://www.cs.cmu.edu/afs/cs/ project/jair/pub/volume9/mazer98a-html/ariane.html>.

Periodical or Newspaper Article Published Online

Appelbaum, Richard, and Peter Dreier. "The Campus Anti-Sweatshop Movement." American Prospect Online 46, Sept.-Oct. 1999. 7 June 2000 <http://www.prospect.org/archives/46/46appelbaum.html>.

Scodel, Harvey. "Illiteracy Test." Email to the Editors. Slate 24 Apr. 1997. Microsoft. 23 May 2000 <http://slate.msn.com/Email/97-04-24/Email.asp>.

Stolba, Christine, and Sally Satel. Rev. of Genes, Women, Equality, by Mary Briody Mahowald. New England Journal of Medicine 8 June 2000. Massachusetts Medical Society. 19 Sept. 2000 <http://www.nejm.org/content/ 2000/0342/0023/1761.asp>.

Streitfeld, David. "Court Says Napster Must Stop." washingtonpost.com 12 Feb. 2001. 12 Feb. 2001 <http://www.washingtonpost.com/wp-dyn/articles/ A59310-2001Feb12.html>.

Article Posted on a Web Site

Cohn, Ed. "The Civil Society Debate." Electronic Policy Network. 13 Oct. 2000 <http://tap.epn.org/issues/civilsociety.html>.

Puentes, Robert. "Flexible Funding for Transit: Who Uses It?" Center on Urban and Metropolitan Policy. 17 May 2000. 11 pp. Brookings Institution. 13 Oct. 2000 <http://www.brookings.org/es/urban/flexfunding.pdf>.

Material from an Organization Site

Office for Information Technology Policy. "Frequently Asked Questions on the
    Children's Online Privacy Protection Act." <u>American Library Association</u>. 13
    Oct. 2000 <http://www.ala.org/oitp/privacy.html>.
National Sleep Foundation. <u>Adolescent Sleep Needs and Patterns: Research Report</u>
    <u>and Resource Guide</u>. Home page. 30 June 2000. 26 pp. 13 Oct. 2000 <http://
    www.sleepfoundation.org/publications/sleep_and_teens_report1.pdf>.
"Oh, Why Bother?" <u>Power Smart: Easy Tips to Save Money and the Planet</u>. 22
    Sept. 1999. Alliance to Save Energy. 13 Oct. 2000 <http://www.ase.org/
    powersmart/bother.html>.

Material from an Online Information Service

"Guillain-Barré Syndrome." <u>OnHealth.Com</u>. OnHealth Network Company. 15
    Feb. 2000 <http://onhealth.webmd.com/conditions/resource/conditions/
    item,41282.asp>.

Online Transcript from Television or Radio Program

Havel, Vaclav. "Newsmaker Interview." With Margaret Warner. <u>Online News-</u>
    <u>Hour</u>. PBS. 16 May 1997. Transcript. 21 May 1997 <http://www.pbs.org/
    newshour/bb/europe/jan-june97/havel_5-16.html>.

Television or Radio Broadcast Available Online

Sound Portraits Productions. "Witness to an Execution." <u>All Things Considered</u>. 12
    Oct. 2000. NPR. 12 Oct. 2000 <http://www.npr.org/programs/atc/witness/>.

Material from a Commercial Site

"Harley-Davidson History." <u>Harley-Davidson Motor Company</u>. 17 June 2000
    <http://www.harley-davidson.com/company/history/history.asp>.
Trek Bicycle Corporation. "Mission Statement." Home page. 18 July 2000. 15 Oct.
    2000 <http://www.trekbikes.com/abouttrek/index.html>.

Posting to a Discussion List

Carbone, Nick. "Does this count?" Online posting. 9 June 1995. Rhetnet_promo.
    Daedalus. 13 Oct. 2000 <http://www.daedalus.com/promo/rhetnet_promo/
    rhetnet_promo28.html>.

Citation Formats for Other Materials
and Media

Government Publications

The information and formats required for citing government documents varies
considerably, so it is advisable to consult a specialized handbook such as the *Com-*
plete Guide to Citing Government Information Resources. The following citation,

which identifies the government "author" first by country, then by three increasingly smaller bodies, provides a basic model.

United States. Cong. Senate. Committee on Energy and Natural Resources. Global Climate Change: Hearing. 104th Cong., 2nd sess. Washington, D.C.: GPO, 1997.

If you want to cite the text of a federal bill or law directly, you can retrieve it from *Thomas*, the Library of Congress's data bank of legislative information. Use the citation model that follows below. The first date is the date of enactment (usually different from the day it was approved by Congress). The last is the date of retrieval; if a date of posting were available, it would be placed between the site title and sponsor (as in other citations for Web material).

Children's Internet Protection Act. Pub. L. 106-554. 21 Dec. 2000. Thomas: Legislative Information on the Internet. Lib. of Congress, Washington, DC. 18 Jan. 2001 <http://thomas.loc.gov/cgi-bin/cpquery/ R?cp106:FLD010:@1(hr1033):URL>.

If you are working on something that requires numerous legal citations, refer to the current edition of *The Blue Book: A Uniform System of Citation*, the standard editorial reference for attorneys. Always check with your professor about the citation systems preferred for a given course.

Biblical Citations

Material from the Judeo-Christian Bible as well as from sacred writings in other traditions is typically cited in the text by an abbreviation for the name of the book, then chapter and verse numbers. Page numbers are not used because the citation already permits the reader to find the passage in any version of the Bible. Note that in these parenthetical citations for passages from Psalm 19 no title punctuation is used on the book, a colon separates the chapter and verse, and a hyphen links opening and closing verses from a longer passage, for example, (Ps. 19:7) or (Ps. 19:7-10).

Include the version of the Bible in your first reference. For example, (New Oxford Annotated Bible, Ps. 19:7) refers to this full citation:

The New Oxford Annotated Bible. New Revised Standard Version. Ed. Bruce M. Metzger and Roland E. Murphy. New York: Oxford, 1991.

In MLA format, a particular published edition of the Bible is underlined, but the version is not. In some classes, especially in religious studies or theology courses, you may be expected to note only the version, thus eliminating the need for a citation on your works cited list. You would then use in-text citations such as these: (New Revised Standard Version Bible, Ps. 19:7) or (New English Bible, Col. 3:12-17). On later references, the version may be omitted or abbreviated, in these cases to "NRSV" and "NEB."

Whenever you plan to discuss any kind of sacred texts in a paper, be sure to ask your instructor what kind of citation information you need to provide and what format to use.

Lecture, Speech, or Conference Paper

Jamieson, Kathleen Hall. "Deliberation, Democratic Politics, and Journalism." James A. Moffett '29 Lecture in Ethics. Princeton University. 17 Feb. 2000.

Material in Varying Media from an Information Service

Follow guidelines for the original media (print publication, lecture, or paper presentation, etc.), adding the information service identification code at the end. The example is for a document available through ERIC (Educational Resources Information Center) in both paper and microfiche as well as online full text.

Citation for Print or Microfiche

Barrow, Lloyd H. "Preservice Methods Students' Response to a Performance Portfolio Assignment." Paper presented at the Annual Meeting of the American Educational Research Association. New Orleans. April 24-28, 2000. ED 442 826.

Citation for Online Text

Follow the model for periodicals accessed through a database. First provide information for paper copy, then add the database information:

Barrow, Lloyd H. "Preservice Methods Students' Response to a Performance Portfolio Assignment." Paper presented at the Annual Meeting of the American Educational Research Association. New Orleans. April 24-28, 2000. ED 442 826. ERIC Document Reproduction Service. Ovid. Memorial Lib., Marquette Univ. 10 Sept. 2000 <http://gateway2.ovid.com/>.

CD-ROM

Follow guidelines for print publications, but specify the publication medium, any vendor (e.g., SilverPlatter, Microsoft, etc.), and dates for both print and electronic publication/update, as available.

"Haiti." Concise Columbia Encyclopedia. 1995. CD-ROM. Microsoft Bookshelf, 1995.

Video Recording

Unless your discussion focuses on the contributions of a particular person (performer, director, narrator, etc.), begin with the title, underlined, and include the director, distributor, and year of release. Add other pertinent material between title and distributor.

Australia's Twilight of the Dreamtime. Writ/Photog. Stanley Breeden. National Geographic Society and WQED, Pittsburgh, 1988.

Sound Recording

Your decision about whom to cite first, the performer, composer, or conductor, depends upon the point you are making. The following citation, for example, emphasizes the performers and notes the composer.

Ma, Yo-Yo, and Bobby McFerrin. "Grace." By Bobby McFerrin. <u>Hush</u>. Sony, 1992.

If you cite liner notes or a libretto, provide that label before the title. If the original recording date is important, provide it after the title; then indicate any medium other than a CD followed by the manufacturer and production date.

Coltrane, John. Liner notes. <u>A Love Supreme</u>. Rec. 9 Dec. 1964. LP. Impulse, 1964.

TV or Radio Program

"Take This Sabbath Day." <u>The West Wing</u>. Writ. Aaron Sorkin. Dir. Thomas Schlamme. NBC. WTMJ, Milwaukee. 9 Feb. 2000.

Credits

———— • ————

Chapter 1

9 Gloria Naylor excerpt from *Three Minutes or Less*. Reprinted by permission of Sterling Lord Literistic, Inc. Copyright © 2000 by Gloria Naylor.

12 Melissa Martinie, "A Lawyer and His Reading," student essay. Reprinted by permission of the author.

Chapter 2

16 Kenneth Burke, *The Philosophy of Literary Form: Studies in Symbolic Action,* 3rd ed. (Berkeley: U of California P, 1973) 110–11.

Chapter 3

28 Alberto Manguel, *A History of Reading* (New York: Penguin, 1997) 170–71.

28 Kathleen McCormick, *The Culture of Reading and the Teaching of English* (Manchester, England: Manchester UP, 1994) 20–21.

29 "The Voice You Hear When You Read Silently" from *New and Selected Poems* by Thomas Lux. Copyright © 1997 by Thomas Lux. Reprinted by permission of Houghton Mifflin Company. All rights reserved. Previously published in the *New Yorker*.

33 Usha Lee McFarling, "Kids Clobbered by Sleeplessness: Schools Try Starting Later." Reprinted with permission of Knight Ridder/Tribune Information Services.

33 Lynne Lamberg, "Some Schools Agree to Let Sleeping Teens Lie," *Journal of American Medical Association* 276 (18 Sept. 1996): 859. Copyright © 1996 by American Medical Association. Reprinted by permission.

35 Ann Feldman, *Writing and Learning in the Disciplines* (New York: Harper, 1996) 16–17, 25–29.

36 Excerpted and reprinted from Anthony Weston, *Toward Better Problems: New Perspectives on Abortion, Animal Rights, the Environment, and Justice,* by permission of Temple University Press. © 1992 by Temple University. All rights reserved.

37 Research reported by Cheryl Geisler, *Academic Literacy and the Nature of Expertise* (Hillsdale, NJ: Erlbaum, 1994) 20–21.

38 Sheri's description of her reading process is quoted in Paula Gillespie and Neal Lerner, *The Allyn and Bacon Guide to Peer Tutoring* (Boston: Allyn & Bacon, 2000) 105.

Chapter 11

Chapter 12

338 Kenneth Burke, *Language as Symbolic Action* (Berkeley: U of California P, 1966) 45.

340 Kirk Savage, "The Past in the Present: The Life of Memorials," *Harvard Design Magazine*, Fall 1999. Reprinted by permission of the author.

349 Sarah Boxer, "I Shop, Ergo I Am: The Mall as Society's Mirror," *New York Times* 28 Mar. 1998: A13, A15. Copyright © 1998 by New York Times, Inc.

354 "Toys" from *Mythologies* by Roland Barthes, translated by Annette Lavers. Translation copyright © 1972 by Jonathan Cape Ltd. Reprinted by permission of Hill and Wang, a division of Farrar, Straus and Giroux, LLC.

357 "The Lesson" from *Gorilla, My Love* by Toni Cade Bambara. Copyright © 1971 by Toni Cade Bambara. Reprinted by permission of Random House, Inc.

364 Geoffrey Miller, "Waste Is Good," *Prospect Magazine* Feb. 1999. First published in *Prospect Magazine*, Britain's intelligent monthly, www.prospect-magazine.co.uk. Used with permission.

375 Natalie Angier, "Men, Women, Sex, and Darwin," *New York Times Magazine*, 21 Feb. 1999: 48–53. Copyright © 1999 by New York Times, Inc.

385 Heather Wendtland, "Rebellion Through Music," student essay. Reprinted by permission of the author.

Chapter 13

Fig. 13.1 Excerpt from www.millionmommarch.com reprinted by permission of Million Mom March, Inc.

Fig. 13.2 Excerpt from www.sas-aim.org reprinted by permission of Second Amendment Sisters.

405 Kathleen Parker, "For Starters, We Can Require Trigger Locks," *Milwaukee Journal Sentinel*, 5 Mar. 2000: 4J. Reprinted by permission of the author.

406 Kathleen Parker, "Revisiting the Issue of Trigger Locks," *Milwaukee Journal Sentinel*, 8 Mar. 2000: 10A. Reprinted by permission of the author.

409 Arnold Wolfendale and Seth Shostak, "Is There Other Intelligent Life in the Universe?" June 2000. First published in *Prospect Magazine*, Britain's intelligent monthly, www.prospect-magazine.co.uk. Used with permission.

416 "Statement by Alabama Clergymen," *Birmingham News*, 12 Apr. 1963.

418 Martin Luther King Jr., "Letter from Birmingham Jail." Reprinted by arrangement with the Heirs to the Estate of Martin Luther King Jr., c/o Writers House, Inc., as agent for the proprietor. Copyright © 1968 by Martin Luther King Jr., renewed 1991 by Coretta Scott King.

431 Andrew Sullivan, "Let Gays Marry," *Newsweek* 3 June 1996: 26. Copyright © 1996 by Newsweek, Inc. All rights reserved. Reprinted by permission.

434 Sallie Tisdale, "Should a Boy Be Expelled for Thought Crimes?" Reprinted by permission of the author. First appeared on salon.com.

438 "A Hanging" from *Shooting an Elephant and Other Essays* by George Orwell. Copyright © 1950 by Sonia Brownell Orwell and renewed 1978 by Sonia Pitt-Rivers. Reprinted by permission of Harcourt, Inc.

225 Robert McGuire, "Witness to Rage," *Milwaukee Magazine*, July 1999, pp. 50–55. Copyright © 1999 by Robert McGuire. Reprinted by permission of the author.

236 Beverly Gross, "Bitch," *Salmagundi*, Summer 1994. Copyright © 1994 by *Salmagundi*. Reprinted by permission.

245 Gloria Naylor, "Mommy, What Does 'Nigger' Mean?" Reprinted by permission of Sterling Lord Literistic, Inc. Copyright © 1986 by Gloria Naylor.

249 Joshua D. McColough, "Seeking Answers to the Question of Divorce," student essay. Reprinted by permission of the author.

Chapter 11

259 Kathy Wollard, "Mirage Isn't a Figment of Your Imagination," *Los Angeles Times* 23 Aug. 1999. Copyright © 1999 by Los Angeles Times. Reprinted by permission.

260 Kathy Wollard, "That Funny and Embarrassing Hiccup May Actually Be Helpful for Your Body," *Los Angeles Times* 1 Nov. 1999. Copyright © 1999 by Los Angeles Times. Reprinted by permission.

263 Marcy Gordon, "Once a Novelty, Now-Essential Credit Card Turns 50." Copyright © 2000 by Associated Press. Reprinted by permission.

267 "Credit Cards: 50 Years And Going Strong." Reprinted by permission of the *St. Louis Post-Dispatch*. Copyright © 2000.

267 "Diner's Club Card Idea Spawned a Plastic Explosion," *Milwaukee Journal Sentinel* 12 Mar. 2000. Copyright © 2000 Milwaukee Journal Sentinel. Reprinted by permission.

267 "A Humble Start for Today's Necessity," *Los Angeles Times*, 12 Mar. 2000. Copyright © 2000 Los Angeles Times Co.

267 "Novelty of Affluent Revolves into Daily Phrase: Charge It!" Reprinted by permission from the *Detroit News*.

268 "Why Do Those #&*?@! 'Experts' Keep Changing Their Minds?" Reprinted by permission of the University of California at Berkeley Wellness Letter. Copyright © 1996 Health Letter Associates. For subscription information, call (904) 445–6414.

275 Amy Wolfson and Mary Carskadon, "Sleep Schedules and Daytime Functioning in Adolescents," *Child Development* 69 (Aug. 1998): 865–87. Copyright © 1998 by Society for Research in Child Development. Reprinted by permission.

299 Paul Irgang, "When a Wet Vac Counts More than a Ph.D.," *Chronicle of Higher Education* 21 Jan. 2000. Reprinted by permission of the author.

302 Nancy Mairs, "Body in Trouble," from *Waist-High in the World*, 56–63. Copyright © 1996 by Nancy Mairs. Reprinted by permission of Beacon Press, Boston.

308 Peter Marin, "Helping and Hating the Homeless." Copyright © 1986 by *Harper's Magazine*. All rights reserved. Reproduced from the January 1987 issue by special permission.

322 Thomas Roepsch, "America's Love Affair with Pizza, A Guilty Pleasure No More," student essay. Reprinted by permission of the author.

326 C. J. Hribal, "Consent," from *The Clouds in Memphis*. Copyright © 2000 by the University of Massachusetts Press. Reprinted by permission.

Chapter 16

Index

—————— • ——————

Page references followed by the letter 'n' refer to footnotes.